P9-ECO-170

HOW TO ACHIEVE PERSONAL AND FINANCIAL PRIVACY IN A PUBLIC AGE

Fifth Edition

by Mark Nestmann

Copyright LPP, Ltd., 1989 Fifth edition, Copyright 1993
First printing, April 1993

ISBN 0-9627953-1-3 (previously published by American Bureau of Economic Research, ISBN 1-55926-135-8)

All rights reserved. Written permission must be secured from the publisher to use or reproduce any part of this special report in any form, except for brief quotations in critical reviews or articles, and then only where the name of the report and the publisher's address are listed in the review or article.

LPP, Ltd., and/or its principals, and/or its affiliates, may, from time to time, have positions in the investments, products, and/or services discussed herein.

LPP, Ltd.
1280 Terminal Way, Suite 15
Department P5
Reno, Nev. 89502
Phone: 800/528-0559 or 702/885-2509

Printed in the United States of America

This publication is designed to provide accurate and authoritative information in regard to the subject matter covered. It is sold with the understanding that neither the author nor the publisher is engaged in rendering legal, accounting, or other professional services. If legal advice or other expert assistance is required, the services of a competent professional should be sought.

Your questions, comments, corrections, and suggestions regarding this work are welcomed. Please end your comments to the above address.

For a free catalog of LPP, Ltd. publications and services, please contact the above address.

Additional copies of this publication are available.

Pages 190-192. In May 1993, the General Accounting Office released an audit for fiscal years 1990 and 1991 of the U.S. Customs Department's asset forfeiture fund. It revealed that the agency had misplaced $269 million in cash and $398 million of other seized property from this fund.

Page 196. Brenda Grantland's new address is 265 Miller Ave., Mill Valley, Calif. 94941; phone: 415/380-9108; fax: 415/380-9208

Page 197. In footnote 129, it was the owner of the boat, not the Coast Guard search team, who attempted to use a video camera to record the search.

Pages 224-226. In May 1993, Switzerland ratified the Council of Europe's "Draft Convention on Laundering, Search, Seizure, and Confiscation of the Proceeds from Crime." This is the most comprehensive anti-laundering agreement Switzerland has ratified. The agreement permits signatory nations to criminalize money laundering for any "organized criminal activity," terrorism and for "negligent" laundering.

Pages 227-229. Austrian bank accounts in any currency are insured by the Austrian government against losses up to AS 200,000 (about US $17,000).

Page 229-230. Liechtenstein has only signed a single tax treaty (with Austria). However, Liechtenstein law allows the government to ban any company or other entity formed there if it is operating contrary to the Principality's interests. In addition, any Liechtenstein entity must have a Liechtenstein resident director appointed. Finally, Liechtenstein imposes a capital tax (stamp duty) on any entity formed there that issues shares. Per the Swiss-Liechtenstein tax administration agreement, records of such payments are transferred to and maintained in Bern (the capital of Switzerland.)

Strictly speaking, the Liechtenstein "anstalt" is not a trust in the common-law sense. Several European countries prohibit their citizens from forming anstalts.

Page 231. The origins of the story of King George granting the Cayman Islands permanent exemption from taxation is murky. It is a story that "ought to be true," but may only be a legend.

The Cayman's Confidential Relationships Law covers not only banks, but trust companies, attorneys, accountants, etc. All are prohibited from discussing any aspect of a client's relationship. The law applies not only in the Caymans, but anywhere in the world. For instance, it would apply to a Cayman banker called upon to testify against a client in another country.

Pages 235-236. The foreign bank accounting reporting form (Treasury Form TD F 90-22.1) is more widely circulated than tax return information. Since it is not an IRS form, laws prohibiting disclosure of tax return data to other government agencies don't apply. The form is therefore circulated routinely to the Customs Department, FBI, BATF, and many other law enforcement agencies. Whether a relationship with a foreign entity must be reported to the IRS hinges on the definition of a "foreign financial account." For instance, a relationship with a portfolio manager in another country that does not provide banking services is perhaps not reportable. Of course, you should check with your tax advisor before not reporting a relationship that is, in fact, reportable.

Page 241. The most private way to wire transfer funds abroad is to send the funds to your foreign bank's New York correspondent bank for further credit to your account number. The originating bank has no way of knowing the ultimate destination of the funds. However, regulations issued to interpret the 1992 anti-laundering bill may require originating banks to obtain this data.

Page 243-244. In March 1993, Mocatta Metals Corp. (MMC) became a division of Standard Chartered Bank. All rights and obligations of MMC to holders of Mocatta Delivery Orders (MDOs) have been assigned to the bank, which became the contractual party for MDOs. Since all MDOs are listed in the owner's name, metals held in this form can't be commingled with the bank's assets in the event of its insolvency.

Pages 246-247. An offshore mutual fund that does not pay dividends can be used for income tax deferral by a U.S. investor who is willing to face the build-up of potential tax liability for an interest charge on his eventual capital gains. Under the "Passive Foreign Investment Company" (PFIC) rules initiated by the Tax Reform Act of 1986, this charge cannot be avoided by holding the PFIC shares until death, since the Internal Revenue Code denies the heirs a step-up in basis on inherited PFIC shares. When the heirs sell the shares, they will recognize all the deferred gain and are subject to the interest charge. The Internal Revenue Code also allows the Treasury to issue regulations that would require recognition of capital gains on any transfer of PFIC stock--which would include transfer by means of death. Thus the estate of a PFIC shareholder could incur a tax bill, including interest, for income deferred by a PFIC. No such regulations have yet been issued, but in several private rulings the IRS has taken the position that taxpayers must recognize the capital gain on any transfer of PFIC stock.

Many foreign mutual funds provide a "contract note" to verify ownership, rather than issuing the shares directly. The shares themselves are issued only in book entry form. Generally, you will find it easier to purchase shares in an offshore mutual fund using a U.S. address if you qualify as a "sophisticated" or "accredited" investor under SEC rules.

Page 248. The Anti-Drug Abuse Act of 1988 requires all passport applicants to submit their Social Security numbers to the State Department, which provides them to the IRS for a computerized taxpayer audit. But the State Department doesn't confirm the SSNs, and the only penalty for not submitting the number is a $500 fine. Many applicants leave the entry blank, according to the report, or submit a fake SSN (not a good idea).

Page 264. In Jan. 1993, a Labor Department task force recommended that pension managers no longer be required to make investment decisions for the "exclusive benefit" of retirees. This conclusion, taken together with the infrastructure development suggestions from *Putting People First* (a position paper circulated by Bill Clinton during the 1992 campaign) raises the possibility that the government could force pension funds to invest in politically-correct, but unprofitable, infrastructure projects, or in government bonds. Assistant Treasury Secretary Alicia Munnell suggests a new 15% annual tax on pension fund contributions and on the annual earnings of pension plans. She also proposes a one-time, 15% tax on all of the trillions of dollars in pension fund assets. This tax would be accompanied by a legally-mandated 15% reduction in the obligations of pension funds to retirees.

In addition, the IRS now claims that it can place a lien on a pension account that survives bankruptcy. This contradicts a Supreme Court decision last year stating that a pension is not part of a "bankruptcy estate" and is thus not accessible to creditors. But several courts have upheld the IRS position.

Pages 266-267. *Putting People First* proposes a national medical ID card. Such a universal card is indeed part of Clinton's health care "reform" plan. One Clinton staff member suggests that the Social Security number be used as the "identifier," although this suggestion has been met by brisk resistance from privacy advocates. No U.S. citizen would be able to receive medical care within the "system" without carrying such a card.

Page 268-269. As few as 10 of the new $100 bills carried together may set off metal detectors at some airports.

Page 279. The vans FEMA sent out for hurricane relief in Homestead, Florida were capable of making ordinary phone calls, but the situation was still a case of massive bureaucratic overkill.

Page 297. See new address for Ross Engineering, p. 45.

Page 300. Peter Double's address is now 322 Vista Del Mar, Redondo Beach, Calif. 90277; phone: 310/791-5811; fax: 310/373-3495

Page 302. We have removed Ankerbank from our list of recommended Swiss banks. Cambio & Valorenbank has been acquired by Union Bank Privee. In addition, we have added Bank Union de Credit (Geneva), the former Overland Bank (Geneva) to our list. Its address is: BUC (Geneva), Rue de Mont Blanc 3, P. O. Box 1816, CH-1211, Geneva 1, Switzerland.

Page 303. Royal Trust Bank (Austria) has been purchased by Royal Bank of Canada, but the deal has yet to be finalized.

Page 305. BEFI is now known as BFI. It's new address is Leibachstrasse 5, P.O. Box 101, 8123 Ebmatingen, Switzerland. Other companies offering information on Swiss annuities include: Jurg M. Lattman, AG, Germanistrasse 55, 8033 Zurich, Switzerland and Volcon, SA, P. O. Box 949, 1211 Geneva 3, Switzerland.

QUESTIONS, COMMENTS, CORRECTIONS?: If you have questions, comments, or corrections to this edition of *How to Achieve Personal and Financial Privacy in a Public Age,* please contact the author c/o LPP, Ltd., 1280 Terminal Way, Suite 15, Reno, Nev. 89502.

Current through mid-Sept. 1993. Future corrections will be published in *Low Profile*, "your monthly guide to privacy and asset protection." To obtain a free sample issue, write Low Profile, Dept. P5, P.O. Box 84910, Phoenix, Ariz. 85071 or call 800/528-0559.

Copyright page. Copyright Lonesome Pine Associates, Limited Partnership. Author and publisher warrant that to the best of their knowledge, the information contained herein is accurate and timely, and contains no errors, other than those noted herein. However, accuracy and timeliness cannot be guaranteed. Purchaser agrees not to hold author or publisher responsible for any lack of accuracy or timeliness, or errors contained herein. Purchaser's sole remedy against author and/or publisher will be to obtain a full refund of the price paid for this report.

LPP, Ltd., and/or its principals, and/or its affiliates, may, from time to time, have positions in and/or receive compensation for the sale of products and/or services discussed herein.

Page 37-38. In April 1993, President Clinton announced a plan to plant new "Clipper Chips" in all government telephones and computers to "prevent eavesdropping." Eventually, the chips would be released to private users, and the use of more effective encryption techniques banned. The Attorney General would hold the "keys" that could decipher encrypted conversations, and would release them to the FBI with a court order.

Page 42. Private Lines, Inc. has reduced the price of its domestic system to defeat caller ID and automatic number identification from $2/minute to $0.75/minute.

Page 45. The new address for Ross Engineering is 504 Shaw Road #222, Sterling, Va. 20166.

Page 46. Wiretapping your own telephone appears to be legal, but any property "facilitating" an "illegal wiretap" may be forfeited to the federal government (18 USC Sec. 2513).

Pages 63-65. In 1991, the IRS estimated nearly 4 million Americans used fake Social Security numbers.

Pages 87. I don't advise using some of the more specialized services foreign mail drops offer, such as precious metals brokering or storage, nominee checking accounts, etc. A good way to find a mail drop in Canada is to look through the yellow pages of "Mail Receiving Services" in major Canadian cities. Many U.S. libraries have the yellow pages of such cities on microfiche.

Page 109. A May 1993 report from the General Accounting Office slashed the IRS' estimate of uncollected accounts receivables 83%. GAO says the real balance should be $19 billion, not the $111 billion estimated by the IRS.

There is no evidence that the IRS is actually a private corporation or was founded as a private entity. The "Internal Revenue and Audit Service" was incorporated in Delaware in 1933, but existed only to assist individuals prepare their tax returns. It was not a precursor of the current IRS, and was dissolved in 1936--for non-payment of taxes.

Page 119. The proposed 1993 tax bill would eliminate the ability of a taxpayer to eliminate penalties for taking a controversial position on a tax return unless that position is "reasonable."

Page 122. The General Accounting Office has persuaded the IRS to renew its TCMP audits. GAO says the audits were useful in measuring taxpayer behavior, and that the IRS had not found an acceptable alternative.

Page 129. Tax protest and "untax" groups claim as many as 30 million adult Americans do not file income tax returns.

Pages 129-130. To protect their assets, many "untax" advocates hold them in a fake name. However, the courts have upheld penalties for fraud and failure to pay estimated taxes against individuals who use fake names and/or Social Security numbers when they opened bank accounts.

Page 159. The third sentence of the fourth full paragraph on this page should read: "Aversa's 'crime' was "conspiring" with a friend to hide income from a real estate partnership from Aversa's wife. The scheme triggered reports of suspicious transactions in Aversa and his friend's bank accounts." The District Court decision in *U.S. vs. Aversa* was subsequently reversed by the 1st U.S. Circuit Court of Appeals. In April 1993, the Supreme Court agreed to decide if a person who doesn't realize that "structuring" transactions in cash or monetary instruments is illegal can be guilty of "willfully" violating the criminal structuring statute, regardless of their motives. Most federal appeals courts have ruled that anyone who avoids the reporting requirement can be convicted, regardless of motive.

Page 159. New sentencing guidelines for criminal structuring convictions mean that individuals convicted of illegally structure transactions where all funds are lawfully derived and all taxes paid would be eligible for probation.

Page 175. The new address of the Cato Institute is 1000 Massachusetts Ave., N.W., Washington, D.C. 20001-5403.

Page 177. Footnote 116 should begin: "The IRS' 1992 instructions for Form 1099 provide an exemption for reporting informant commissions..."

Page 181. The Supreme Court is taking a comprehensive look at civil forfeiture in its 1993 term. It has already decided the two cases discussed in this chapter; *Republic National Bank* and the "Buena Vista" case. (In the *Republic* case, the bank lost in lower court because it had failed to request that a forfeiture be halted pending its appeal.) In two other cases, *U.S. vs. Austin* and *U.S. vs. Alexander*, the court ruled that civil forfeiture is punishment, and that a claimant may maintain that the forfeiture violates the Eighth Amendment's "excessive fines" clause. (*Low Profile* reviewed these cases in the 12/92 and 7-8/93 issues.)

In July 1993, the 11th Circuit, on remand from the Supreme Court, held that a lienholder was an "innocent owner" as defined by the civil drug forfeiture statute, 21 U.S.C. 881(a). In *U.S. vs. One Single-Family Residence Located at 6960 Miraflores Ave.*, the court rejected the government's argument that a mortgage can be forfeited based on a lender's failure to have *suspected* wrongdoing on the part of a borrower. Instead, the lienholder merely must demonstrate that it adhered to generally-accepted sound banking and prudent lending practices. It also rejected the government's claim that to prevail as an innocent owner, a lienholder must prove that it made inquiries concerning the borrower's source of funds. (*Low Profile* reviewed this case in the 9/93 issue.)

Bills that would reform civil forfeiture procedures have been introduced in the current Congress by Reps. Conyers (D-Mich.) and Hyde (R-Ill.).

Page 183. The defendant in *U.S. vs. Porcelli* was convicted of failing to pay sales taxes for several gas stations, not just one.

Pages 183-184. Federal law clearly gives the government power to seize untainted assets to satisfy a forfeiture order after a criminal drug or racketeering (RICO) conviction. But federal appeals court decisions are at odds as to whether the government may freeze substitute assets prior to conviction or even trial. This question may be submitted to the Supreme Court.

Page 186. In May 1993, the U.S. District Court in Nashville ordered the government to return $9,000 seized from Willie Jones. The court ruled that the seizure lacked probable cause, and that Jones was targeted because of his race (*Jones vs. DEA*).

Pages 186-187. Some U.S. courts are questioning the value of drug residues on cash as "probable cause" for its seizure. In *U.S. vs. $53,082*, the 6th Circuit invalidated a cash seizure, declaring that "a court should seriously question the value of a dog's alert [indicating the presence of drugs] without other persuasive evidence." And the Washington, D.C. Appeals Court declared in *U.S. vs. $639,558* that the government had improperly seized cash from a traveler on a train. In state courts, the Florida 3rd District Court of Appeals struck down a six-year prison sentence of a man convicted on drug charges based on his possession of a cocaine-contaminated dollar bill (*Leroy Lord vs. Florida*).

Page 189. In April 1993, the Ventura County (California) District Attorney's office released a report concluding that the raid on Donald Scott's ranch was motivated by the government's desire to seize the property. Although police should not have been on the property, the office ruled that Scott's shooting by a Los Angeles County sheriff's deputy was justifiable self-defense. No criminal charges were filed against the deputy or any of the other members of the forfeiture squad.

TABLE OF CONTENTS

To M.A., with all my love

PREFACE

Please answer "yes" or "no" to the following questions. Score "1" for a yes answer; "0" for a no. If you're not sure, give yourself 1/2 point:

1. Do you pay for most purchases by personal check or credit card? ___ Yes ___ No.

2. Do you use your home or office telephone to make all telephone calls, no matter how private or sensitive the matter being discussed? ___ Yes ___ No.

3. Do you receive all mail at your home or office address -- even mail you'd rather not have other people know about? ___ Yes ___ No.

4. Would people consider you wealthy if they saw where you live or the car you drive? ___ Yes ___ No.

5. Have you ever been audited by the IRS? ___ Yes ___ No.

6. If a casual acquaintance asked you your income, would you disclose it? ___ Yes ___ No.

7. Have you ever been involved in a divorce or a lawsuit, or received money through a probate court? ___ Yes ___ No.

8. Do you belong to any organizations or share a religious affiliation that are politically unpopular? ___ Yes ___ No.

9. Do you receive junk mail or unsolicited telephone sales calls from companies you never gave your name to? ___ Yes ___ No.

10. Have you ever disclosed sensitive personal information in a job application? ___ Yes ___ No ___

Your score: ____

0-2 points: Virtually unexposed. You have successfully shut off privacy invaders from your life by maintaining a low profile.

3-5 points: Somewhat exposed. You have shut down several pathways that privacy invaders could use to find out more about your life, but you can do more to lower your profile.

6-8 points: Exposed. Your life is more open that you might wish. You should take steps to lower your profile.

9-10 points: Highly exposed. You need to take immediate steps to lower your personal and financial profile. Otherwise, you could soon be a target of government and commercial surveillance.

PREFACE TO FIFTH EDITION

In the four years since the first edition of *How to Achieve Personal and Financial Privacy in a Public Age* was published, events have moved quickly in the privacy arena. Most of the news is not good.

Privacy is under assault on every front.

Congress has decreed that:

✓ You are responsible for following each law and regulation it passes, to the letter. In 1992 alone, Congress passed 2,500 new laws. In addition, there were 65,715 pages of new regulations published, in fine print, in the *Federal Register*. Millions of bureaucrats are employed by the federal government to enforce these laws and regulations. And for most statutes, "ignorance of the law is no excuse."

✓ Children one year old or older must be identified on tax returns by their Social Security number.

✓ You have no right to bail in a federal trial if the judge believes you might be a "future danger" to society. There are no exceptions, even for politically-motivated cases.

✓ Banks must spy on their own customers, and secretly report any "suspicious transactions" to the IRS.

✓ Efforts to protect your financial privacy such as taking deliberate steps to avoid completing federal currency reporting forms are now considered money laundering. You may be fined or imprisoned even if the entire sum you seek to hide, disguise, or transport privately has been legitimately earned, and all taxes paid on it.

✓ A passport application must contain your Social Security number. All passport applications be forwarded to the IRS. There are no exceptions.

✓ The government may seize your home, your bank account, your retirement account--every asset you own--with a lower standard of proof than used to apply to an ordinary search warrant. Once the government confiscates your property, it is up to you to prove that it was not involved in or facilitated any crime. *Your property is guilty until you prove it innocent.* More than 100 federal laws, and thousands of state statutes, now mandate forfeiture for crimes as trivial as minor traffic violations.

Each year, Congress introduces bills that would further restrict our liberties. One proposal re-introduced every year would curtail habeas corpus--the right of a defendant to challenge the legality of his conviction--as well as permit illegally-seized evidence to be introduced in court. Already, the United States boasts the highest per-capita prison population in the world--higher than Communist China, the former Soviet Union, South Africa, or Cuba.

The Supreme Court has ruled that:

✓ Only a "harmless error" occurs when police lose or destroy evidence that might prove a person's innocence. The act does not void a criminal conviction.

✔ Motorists can be stopped at random and forced to take sobriety tests. While stopped, police may inspect any article in the vehicle that is in "plain view."

✔ Citizens crossing U.S. borders may be searched at random

✔ Both U.S. citizens and foreign nationals may be kidnapped by U.S. police agencies operating across international borders. U.S. agents are under no obligation to obtain warrants before searching the overseas homes of non-U.S. citizens.

✔ Passengers on buses, trains, and airplanes may be asked to submit to "voluntary" searches without being informed that they have a right to refuse.

✔ Cordless telephones have no protection under federal anti-wiretapping statutes.

✔ Trash set out for collection may be inspected by government authorities.

✔ Police may search a home without a warrant when let in by someone they mistakenly believe is authorized to give such consent.

✔ Judges may not dismiss indictments returned by a grand jury simply because prosecutors failed to disclose evidence suggesting that criminal defendants are innocent.

To be sure, there are a few rays of hope:

✔ A U.S. Circuit Court of Appeals has ruled that the IRS must prove a tax deficiency actually exists before it seizes money from a taxpayer. However, the IRS has largely ignored the ruling, and is trying to overturn it through legislation.

✔ The Supreme Court has ruled that law enforcement agencies may not entrap a person into committing acts he would not otherwise be inclined to commit.

✔ The Supreme Court let stand a ruling that police officers given permission to search a home must obtain a search warrant before opening belongings left there by a visitor.

✔ The Supreme Court let stand a decision that police are not allowed to routinely search a person given a misdemeanor citation who they expect to release on the spot. Similarly, it declined to review a case where a lower court invalidated a search of a dwelling whose occupants had been removed and detained until police could obtain a warrant to search it.

✔ The Supreme Court also let stand a lower court ruling protecting the rights of innocent owners who are assigned or who purchase a property that would otherwise be forfeitable under the civil forfeiture statutes.

✔ Congress is considering legislation that would crack down on some of the worst abuses by credit bureaus and other third-party providers of personal financial information.

✔ Congress is holding hearings on expanding the Freedom of Information Act and Privacy Act to cover not just paper records, but those in electronic form as well.

Privacy is not just a concern of the left, the right, or the libertarian. It is a concern for all of us, because we all are affected by the erosion in our personal and property rights. A 1992 Harris poll found that 80 percent of Americans are concerned or very concerned about the amount of computerized information that businesses and the government collect and store about them.[1]

This fifth edition would not be possible without the assistance of many people. I would like to thank each one of them personally, but by not listing them individually, I can help them maintain their own "low profile."

I also extend my appreciation to all those who have expressed their encouragement, gratitude, and/or constructive criticism about this report, or have spoken to me personally. And finally, to all others who have helped--and I am certain I have left out many, although not deliberately--I say "thank you." You know who you are.

A stylistic note: Throughout this edition, the pronoun "he" and the possessive "his" are used in lieu of "he or she" and "his or her." The examples and suggestions I have provided are applicable regardless of gender.

---

[1] I have started a newsletter that focuses on the increasing threats to our privacy and wealth from these sources, and how to fight back legally and ethically against these incursions. It is called *Low Profile* (P.O. Box 84910, Phoenix, Ariz. 85071; phone 800/528-0559; $149/year)

FOREWORD

Gary North, Ph.D

The modern bureaucrat says, implicitly or explicitly, to a citizen under suspicion, "An honest man has nothing to hide."

The proper response to such an accusation is this: "An honest public servant who is honoring the common-law rights of all citizens has no reason to seek out private information that is protected by common law."

The modern State is messianic. It seeks to make men good. The genius of the American Revolution and the U.S. Constitution was that the civil government was seen as protective, not messianic. The State was not understood by the founding fathers to be a device to make men good; it was seen only as a means of prohibiting judicially specified public evils.

The Napoleonic Code, the legacy of the French Revolution and the guillotine, declares that the accused is guilty until proven innocent. So does the IRS tax code. So does the infamous federal RICO (racketeering) statute and the money laundering and civil forfeiture statutes. Common law says that a person is innocent until proven guilty. The former tradition expands the State and shrinks individual liberties; the latter tradition does the opposite.

The modern socialist State is premised on this presupposition: that all things belong to the State, but a portion of this State-owned capital is temporarily leased to private individuals and organizations. This view of the State has influenced much of modern democratic theory.

The free market-constitutional view of the State is that it is under legal restraints, that the citizen is the sovereign of the legal order, and that whatever authority which citizens have not formally delegated to the State belongs to them.

The battle over the rights of privacy should be seen in light of these two incompatible views of man and the State. It is a battle over the definition of what constitutes criminal behavior. The founding fathers of the United States were far more concerned about the growth of a criminal State than the growth of a criminal class. They recognized that a large and growing State would inevitably be captured and put to evil uses.

Atheist novelist Ayn Rand and Christian social philosopher R. J. Rushdoony agreed on a crucial point: The modern State seeks to create so many laws that every citizen is forced sometime in his life to become a law-breaker. The bureaucrats recognize that a guilt-ridden citizen is easier to control, they both observed.

Only God has omniscience. The State which attempts to mimic God's comprehensive knowledge has made itself into an idol. The warning of the Second Commandment regarding idols should be sufficient. "Thou shalt not bow down thyself to them, nor serve them: for I the LORD thy God am a jealous God, visiting the iniquity of the fathers upon the children unto the third and fourth generation of them that hate me" (Exodus 20:5).

INTRODUCTION

We are rapidly entering the age of no privacy, where everyone is open to surveillance at all times. Secret observation booths in government offices and closed circuit television circuits in industry, extending even to restrooms, are common. Personality tests seek to ferret out a man's innermost thoughts. Federal agents are often "wired" so that their conversations are either recorded on their persons or transmitted to tape recorders some blocks away.

The dossiers on all citizens mount in number and increase in size. Now they are being put on computers so that by pressing one button all the miserable, the sick, the suspect, the unpopular, the off-beat people of the nation can be instantly identified. Taken individually, each step may be of little consequence. But when viewed as a whole, there begins to emerge a society quite unlike any we have seen--a society in which government may intrude into the secret regions of a man's life at will.

--Former Supreme Court Justice William O. Douglas

If you are like most Americans, you have at some point in your life been the victim of a erroneous credit report or received unsolicited phone calls from telemarketers. You may have experienced apprehension from an IRS audit or the indignity of a lawsuit.

One of your first thoughts when you faced these situations may have been to prevent them from recurring. If the events passed without too much pain, you may never have acted on this impulse.

You may not only suffer from inertia, but from helplessness. After all, the accepted wisdom is that "you can't fight city hall" (or "the IRS," or "telemarketing," etc.).

The news on the privacy front is not encouraging. Marketing specialists have perfected new classification techniques that categorize audiences in the most minute detail imaginable. New legislation forces families to identify newborn children with Social Security numbers. Laws to counter money laundering threaten to convert otherwise law-abiding citizens into felons. Forfeiture laws are increasingly used to seize property from the unsuspecting. Lawsuits against businesses and professionals are at an all-time high. Violent crime rates continue to rise. Electronic eavesdropping technology has become ever more sophisticated. Indeed, it is tempting to resign to the seemingly inevitable and not even pretend to be concerned about privacy invasion.

Fortunately, there is no need to take a defeatist attitude. You are not helpless against the privacy invaders. You can secure your home against crime. You can take steps to lower your profile to the marketing mavens and government bureaucrats who would track your every footstep. You can be taken off mailing lists and refuse to listen to the telemarketer's pitch. You can pay cash or even do business outside the United States to maintain your financial privacy. Finally, you can use technology to fight technology; for nearly every technical advance that invades privacy, a corresponding advance has been developed to protect it.

If you're ready to throw in the towel and become a victim, don't bother reading on. This report isn't for you. But if you are prepared to fight back against the privacy invaders, I urge you to continue.

I encourage you to pay particular attention to Chapter 2, "Privacy in Your Home"; the information it contains could literally save your life. If you are tired of the massive invasions of privacy from telemarketers, credit bureaus and the like, review Chapters 3 and 4. And Chapter 7, "Financial Privacy, Money Laundering, and the "War on Drugs'" could save you much embarrassment (and possible arrest for money laundering).

Occasionally, my writing may appear to contradict itself. In Chapter 5, I criticize some of the new techniques employers are using to spy on their employees, even off-the-job. Yet in Chapter 8, I advise employers that they need to carefully monitor their employee's activities. The reason for this divided allegiance is simple. Employees do have legitimate privacy rights that employers should respect. But new laws and regulations force employers to take strong steps to monitor their employee's activities to prevent illegal use of the business property that could conceivably lead to forfeiture of that business-- and the loss of every employee's job.

After you finish reading this special report, and begin to adopt the strategies it suggests, you'll find it second nature not to reveal your Social Security number, to decline to participate in "marketing surveys" or "opinion polls" and to pay cash when making a purchase you'd rather keep to yourself. You will have developed that most important defense against privacy invasion: a private attitude.

Your attitude, more than any other single factor, is the key to successfully maintaining privacy in a public age. After all, as a U.S. citizen, you have a *right* to privacy. If you learn nothing else from this report, it should be not to give up that right voluntarily.

Privacy for Sale

Privacy is a market phenomenon. As William Petrocelli points out in his classic book, *Low Profile,* the very rich can afford to place legal and financial obstacles in the path of any would-be privacy invader. By placing their money in an offshore trust, living as an expatriate outside their own country and leaving bookkeeping details to a trusted attorney, a rich person can live a practically anonymous life.[2]

The very poor who refuse government assistance also lead private lives. The illegal alien or the homeless street person is likely not to file income tax, be assigned a Social Security number or apply for a driver's license. His life may be a desperate battle against hunger and despair. But it is a more private existence than most Americans live.

Millions of middle-class Americans, however, lead lives that are anything but private. Their public image resides in hundreds of government and corporate databases. Credit bureaus, banks, the IRS, the Social Security Administration, educational institutions, and perhaps the military and criminal justice system all contain snapshots of their lives, from the day they were born to the day they die.

Keeping a Low Profile

The most obvious way to react to increasing violations of your privacy is to fight back in any manner possible. But such a strategy is almost always counterproductive. By taking a militant pro-privacy stance, you are calling attention to yourself and inviting even greater intrusions.

---

[2]William Petrocelli, *Low Profile* (New York: McGraw Hill, 1981)

I have deliberately taken such a stance in order to call attention to what I believe is a problem of enormous seriousness. But for most people, it is far better to live a life that on the surface is completely ordinary, selectively protecting privacy by avoiding compromising situations and events that would decrease anonymity. The essential strategy is to live such a "low profile" existence that a potential snooper won't see anything unusual on the surface--and will never bother to look any deeper.

Keeping a low profile doesn't mean discarding all ties to society. It simply means reducing your voluntary exposure of sensitive information to the lowest reasonable level. For instance, most people own credit cards; a person living a low-profile existence will own them as well, but use them only for purchases that reveal little about his lifestyle, political or religious beliefs.

If you maintain too low a profile, you will stand out. Always keep this paradox in mind as you seek to reduce your exposure to the privacy invaders.

Your Circle of Friends

Every friendship is a sort of secession, even a rebellion. It may be a rebellion of serious thinkers against accepted claptrap or of faddists against accepted good sense; of real artists against popular ugliness or of charlatans against civilized taste; of good men against the badness of society or of bad men against its goodness.

Whatever it is, it will be unwelcome to Top People. In each knot of friends, there is a section which fortifies its members against the public opinion of the community in general. Each is therefore a pocket of potential resistance. Men who have real friends are less easy to manage or "get at;" harder for bad authorities to corrupt. Hence, if our masters, by force or by propaganda about "togetherness" or by unobtrusively making privacy impossible, ever succeed in producing a world in which all are companions and none are friends, they will have removed certain dangers, and will also have taken from us what is almost our strongest safeguard against complete servitude.

--C. S. Lewis, The Four Loves

Maintaining a low profile means reducing the information that you might otherwise voluntarily give to casual acquaintances, salespeople, employers, etc.

Still, every person needs a trusted circle of friends in which to confide. In today's mobile society, many people are placed in the difficult position of establishing new relationships and making new friends. How do you go about this process without endangering your privacy?

In our forefathers' time, the answer would be simple: Join the local church. And today, you can still use this oldest and most familiar method to become acquainted with people who not only share your religious beliefs, but perhaps also your political and financial philosophy.

In the twentieth century, religion plays a diminished role in the lives of many Americans. Not everyone is familiar or comfortable in a religious environment. Fortunately, there are alternatives to a church to which you can turn in order to build a trusted circle of friends.

One alternative is volunteer community groups. By becoming involved in efforts such as neighborhood watch groups, volunteer fire-fighting departments, community food cooperatives, etc., you are likely to encounter people who share your outlook and attitudes. If you have children, groups such as Parent-Teacher Associations, Boy Scouts and Girl Scouts, etc., are excellent places to meet other parents. Eventually, a few of these casual acquaintances may become friends.

As your friendships evolve, you will begin sharing more information about yourself and turning to these friends for guidance in meeting the challenges that you face in your life. Eventually, you will build that most valuable of assets: trust.

But one thing is for certain: You should guard your privacy as if it were an irreplaceable resource. It is.

Chapter One

PRIVACY:
THE END AND THE BEGINNING

The right of the people to be secure in their persons, houses, papers and effects, against unreasonable searches and seizures shall not be violated.

-- Amendment 4 to the U.S. Constitution

Why Worry About Privacy?

What do you have to hide? More than you might think! Mark Skousen outlines six reasons to preserve privacy in *The Complete Guide to Financial Privacy*.[3]

1. *Political, religious and racial persecution.* Over the centuries, hundreds of groups have found themselves out of favor with those in power and have suffered financially as a result. Jews, blacks, Protestants and many other groups have borne the brunt of persecution--which extended from confiscation of property to execution.

2. *Oppressive government, confiscatory taxes and war.* This second reason is closely related the first. The government has often had a direct hand in the persecution of political, religious or racial groups. Jews, Pilgrims, mystics, lepers and numerous other groups have suffered persecution, isolation and even death, often by government edict. War or the threat of war brings on a litany of government regulations, including restrictions on the movement of money and people.

Price controls, rationing, foreign-exchange controls, blocking of foreign accounts held by banks and brokers, confiscation of property and high taxes are typical ploys by the government to control people's lives in time of war, often with the support of the majority. During wartime, public outcries are made against those who consume too much gasoline or food or other essentials. In other words, the government persecutes not only minorities, but also the financially independent.

3. *Gossip and false information.* Have you ever been the subject of unkind gossip because someone else didn't like your lifestyle, your personality, your children or how much money you make? You must be careful what you say and do in front of neighbors, friends and business acquaintances. Even your doctor, sworn to protect patient privacy, can divulge confidential medical information at an inopportune time.

---

[3]Mark Skousen, *The Complete Guide to Financial Privacy* (New York: Simon & Schuster, [1979] 1983)

4. *Divorce, family disputes, and lawsuits.* Innumerable battles have been waged in the courtrooms of the world over divorces, wills and other money matters, and this information is almost always a matter of public record. Lawsuits involving large amounts of money are frequent among relatives. Medical doctors are besieged with expensive malpractice lawsuits. Similarly, high-income people who display their wealth openly are often subject to unwanted litigation.

5. *The increasing threat of burglary.* People who exhibit their wealth by driving around in big, flashy automobiles and living in mansions run a high risk of being burglarized. Crime is increasing rapidly, and the rewards are high in expensive residential areas.

Thieves are becoming more sophisticated and even expensive alarm equipment is not always a deterrent. Professional burglars often check the obituaries and society pages to learn when people will be away at a funeral or on a long trip. Some thieves even rent mailing lists of high-income investors, and then find out when they are not at home.

6. *High-pressure salesmen and "legal fraud."* Have you ever lost money investing in a managed commodity fund or in some unknown stocks pushed by your stockbroker? Have you ever fallen for the high-pressure telephone salesman who convinces you to buy gold, gemstones or strategic metals on margin, only to lose half your hard-earned money practically overnight?

By stressing private investments, managing your own money and refusing to give brokers or salesmen your real name and address, you will be amazed at the variety of intelligent investment decisions you can make.

Your Right To Privacy

Two hundred years ago, privacy was a non-issue. A person was known by his name and his occupation. He had no Social Security number, no driver's license number.

What records existed of his existence were limited to birth records, baptismal records, death records, the purchase of a home and the payment of property tax. Even this information was generally filed and forgotten, because of the considerable expense involved in paying clerks to organize it.

In the United States, the dominant political philosophy was one of limited government. This philosophy was expressed most eloquently in the Bill of Rights, which was added to the Constitution to prevent the creation of an overly powerful central government.

Unlike freedom of speech or religion, the right to privacy is not guaranteed explicitly in the Constitution or the Bill of Rights. Nonetheless, this document provides several implied privacy protections, including the right to free association (First Amendment); the prohibition against illegal searches and seizures (Fourth Amendment); and the Fifth Amendment, which protects individuals from being forced to testify against themselves and guarantees that they will not be deprived of their property without "just compensation."

An 1886 decision by the Supreme Court, *Boyd vs. United States,* held that the Fourth and Fifth Amendments create a "zone of privacy" which protects an individual and his personal records from compelled production. In other words, the government could not force a person to produce his personal books and records any more than they could force him to testify against himself. Justice Bradley delivered the opinion for the court, writing that:

> The search for and seizure of stolen or forfeited goods, or goods liable to duties and concealed to avoid the payment thereof, are totally different things from a search for and seizure of a man's private books and papers for the purpose of obtaining information therein contained, or of using them as evidence against him...In order to ascertain the nature of the proceedings intended by the Fourth Amendment to the Constitution under the terms "unreasonable searches and seizures," it is only necessary to recall the contemporary history of the controversies on this subject.

> The practice in the colonies of issuing writs of assistance to the revenue officers, empowering them, in their discretion, to search suspected places for smuggled goods, which James Otis pronounced "the worst instrument of arbitrary power, the most destructive of English liberty, and the fundamental principles of law, that was ever found in an English law book;" since they placed "the liberty of every man in the hands of every petty officer."[4]

But in 1984, the Supreme Court overturned the *Boyd* decision. In *U.S. vs. Doe,* Justice Lewis Powell delivered the majority opinion, writing that, "The Fifth Amendment provides absolutely no protection for the contents of private papers of any kind." As the law now stands, a government agency can force you or an organization holding records about you--a credit bureau, a bank, etc.--to deliver your private papers and records to it, and subsequently use them in any manner it chooses against you.

Two hundred years after the Bill of Rights was adopted, most Americans are not aware of the historical events that led to its inclusion in the Constitution. In fact, many Americans are not even aware of the protections that the Bill of Rights provides! A 1991 poll by the American Bar Association found that only one-third of adult Americans could correctly identify the Bill of Rights. More than half couldn't distinguish it from a list of choices that included "a list of rebellion from the founding fathers to the British king."

Fewer than one in 10 knew it was adopted to protect them against abuses by the federal government. In another poll by the California State Bar Association, nearly half the adults surveyed believed that individuals accused of a crime under our legal system are guilty until proven innocent. Perhaps this ignorance is why we are so passive when our rights are chipped away.

Under the English common law on which the Constitution was based, the individual's fundamental rights to life, liberty and property were held to be gifts granted by a Supreme Being, not by government. They were "natural rights" that could not be erased by the King, or by the Congress. Or so the founding fathers believed.[5],[6]

---

[4]Writs of assistance were sweeping "John Doe" type warrants that the British colonial authorities issued to Customs officials and the military. They entitled the bearer to search any property at any time, without probable cause.

[5]An excellent discussion of common law vs. laws enacted by governments is provided in "How We Lost Our Common-Law Heritage," in the March 1987 *World Market Perspective.*

It was on this basis that the Bill of Rights was created. To make certain that these rights were not later abridged by government, the Bill of Rights contains two amendments strictly limiting the power of the federal government.

The Ninth Amendment states that the enumeration of certain rights in the Constitution, "shall not be construed to deny or disparage others retained by the people." And to make certain that future generations would get the point, the 10th Amendment was added. It states that, "All powers not delegated to the United States by the Constitution are reserved to the States, or to the people." Today, even constitutional scholars have all but forgotten the original intent of these amendments.

The only discussion inside the legal mainstream of natural rights in recent years came from Clarence Thomas, who was confirmed as an associate justice of the Supreme Court in 1991. During Thomas' confirmation hearings, the Anita Hill controversy received center stage. But what riveted my attention was the spectacle of senators rising to vent their outrage over the "outmoded" doctrine of natural rights that Thomas was said to follow.

I would maintain that one of these unexpounded natural rights is the right to privacy--the right to be left alone and to seek in your own way the ideal embodied in the Declaration of Independence: "life, liberty and the pursuit of happiness."

A legal theory of privacy was first outlined in an 1890 article published in the *Harvard Law Review*. Disturbed by the relentless pursuit of "news" by society columnists covering the Boston social scene, Samuel Warren and Louis Brandeis argued that, "Gossip is no longer the resource of the idle and the vicious, but has become a trade, which is pursued with industry as well as effrontery." The Warren-Brandeis theory has been cited ever since as a legal justification for the right to privacy.

Later, as a Supreme Court Justice, Brandeis wrote that the right to be left alone is "the most comprehensive of rights and the right most valued by civilized men."

Technology Reduces the Cost of Privacy Invasion

As technology progressed, the economic disincentive for governments and corporations to use the information gathered on private citizens rapidly decreased. The invention of the typewriter and devices capable of reading punched cards in the nineteenth century reduced the costs of compiling and organizing information. But it was the development of the digital computer that made it practical to collect, store, collate and distribute data on a truly massive scale.

Until the end of World War II, most personal information on Americans physically resided in their homes. Bank records, educational records, investment records and insurance records remained at home. If government authorities wished to search a citizen's home, the Fourth Amendment required law enforcement officials to produce a search warrant.

A judge could issue a search warrant only if he found "probable cause" that a crime had been or was about to be committed. As a result, search warrants were rarely granted. Personal information remained almost totally in private hands.

But as computers became an integral part of American society, entrepreneurs quickly discovered profits could be made in compiling information on individual Americans in electronic form and making

---

[6]One of the best discussions of natural rights that I have seen is Robert F. Davilow, editor, *Natural Rights and Natural Law: The Legacy of George Mason* (Fairfax, Va.: George Mason University Press, 1986)

it available for a fee. There was nothing conspiratorial about this process. Market forces, combined with the availability of new technology, made this development inevitable.

Some of the first large-scale users of computer technology were credit bureaus. By contracting with financial institutions, department stores, local governments, etc., credit bureaus were able to create vast libraries of personal information on individual Americans--information that previously had resided at home, or did not exist in any form.

Here was a development that the founding fathers clearly had not anticipated: the growth of an industry that would hold personal records outside the home. No Fourth Amendment protection had been provided such information. The technology to store data in large quantities, and retrieve it instantaneously, did not exist in the 18th century.

The growth of credit bureaus gave both private companies and government officials access to a great deal of data on individual citizens. Such data could be retrieved quickly and efficiently with computer terminals, manufactured by the millions after World War II.

It is hard to overemphasize the importance of these developments, particularly to those readers who did not grow up with computers. Every 18-24 months, the amount of information that can be packed into a single computer chip doubles. Today, you can purchase for $2,000 the equivalent of an IBM mainframe computer that cost more than $1 million just 10 years ago.

In 1981, I helped a friend build a personal computer. We purchased the kit for $750 and built it in his electronics shop. It had 64 kilobytes (64K) of memory; a 90K floppy disk drive; and a "clock speed" of about one megahertz (MHz). We spent another $1,200 on software, a printer, a video display, etc. Our total investment came to $2,000.

Just before this book went to press, I priced computers again. For $2,000, you can buy a computer with four megabytes of memory, 62 times more than my 1981 system. Instead of a 90K floppy disk, the computer now comes a 120 megabyte model--with 1,300 times its capacity. It runs at 33 MHz; more than 30 times as fast as my first one.

Public Images: Are You Being Watched?

The information exodus from the home to the data bank has blurred the boundary between public and private information. Computers excel at analyzing information that individuals willingly share in order to obtain credit, go to work, receive welfare benefits, or purchase insurance coverage. At one time, most of this information was considered private, as were the conclusions banks, insurance companies, etc. reached after analyzing it.

This information is private no longer, a result not only of technological innovation, but aggressive use of loopholes in laws designed to protect privacy. As you'll learn in Chapter 4, both direct marketing companies and the government can cross-reference data residing in computers in the next room, the next county or on the other side of the world to create an amazingly detailed portrait of your wealth, your religious beliefs and your lifestyle.

The digital computer was not the only development the electronic revolution of the mid-20th century permitted. Other, more direct forms of surveillance were perfected.

Direct surveillance of personal, business or political rivals has a history that dates back many centuries. But it was not until the early 1900s that the first technological advance was developed that made *remote* surveillance possible: *the wiretap.* Wiretaps were used against organized crime in the 1920s and suspected spies and saboteurs before and during World War II.

Remote listening devices that could be planted anywhere were also perfected, and by the early 1950s, the development of the transistor accelerated miniaturization in this field. "Bugs" were invented that could planted in cuff-links, tie clasps and, as every James Bond fan realizes, even martini olives.

Today, electronic surveillance has matured to the point where a camera the size of a pinhead can provide both a visual record of a person's activities. Sophisticated two-way cable television hookups can even be programmed to spy on their unsuspecting owners. Annual conventions are held on this subject (many closed to the public) that display an incredible array of technological wizardry devoted to the latest developments in electronic surveillance.

If privacy is not altogether extinct, electronic technology has made it an endangered species.

Government Invasions of Privacy

The enormous advances in the speed and sophistication of computer and electronic surveillance technology were not lost upon the U.S. government.

Like their counterparts in private industry, government bureaucrats sought to use computers to increase efficiency and productivity. It only seemed rational to place computers where they could be used to relieve clerks of dull, repetitive jobs. By the 1950s, officials at the Internal Revenue Service and Social Security Administration pointed to computerization of these agencies as models for other government agencies to follow.

These computer systems were frequently upgraded, and adapted to keep pace with the increasing obligations the government assumed. From a privacy standpoint, some of the most important new responsibilities were laws relating to money, and in particular, to cash. Beginning with the Bank Secrecy Act of 1970, Congress passed an increasingly complex series of laws intended to make it more difficult to evade taxes, and later, to prevent the "laundering" of illicit income.

To keep up with the increasing flow of paper from the nation's banks to government agencies, the IRS and other agencies required almost continuous computer upgrades. These occurred in rapid succession, and are still taking place. In addition, a unique "personal identifier" was needed to track individual financial transactions. The most logical choice was the Social Security number, once assigned to virtually every American upon his entry to the workplace, and now assigned at birth.

The Social Security number thus evolved into a universal identifying code for U.S. citizens. Knowing your Social Security number, a bureaucrat can examine your tax returns on a computer screen. He can then call up records of property purchases, legal disputes, and other sensitive information on his terminal. Recent innovations make even the knowledge of a Social Security number unnecessary. The bureaucrat can obtain your file from your name, your address, or your license tag number.

I believe that the most threatening aspect of the computer revolution is the prospect of increased government scrutiny, and indeed, control, over our day-to-day lives. A new generation of government computers now communicate with one another; i.e., they compare notes and cross-reference files.

The information to which these computers have access permits the government to construct personal and financial dossiers on every American. The head of a Treasury Department intelligence unit, which has installed advanced "artificial intelligence" software to track financial transactions, boasts that the capabilities of his division are, "a lot like Big Brother."

What Records Do They Keep on You?

Federal, state, and local government agencies maintain a variety of records on virtually every U.S. citizen.[7]

✓ Motor vehicle license and registrations

✓ Professional licenses

✓ Social Security (taxes paid and benefits received)

✓ Welfare payments

✓ Federal, state and local tax returns

✓ Medical histories (public hospitals)

✓ School records

✓ Unemployment compensation

✓ Birth, marriage and death certificates

✓ Military and veterans benefits

✓ FBI and police records

✓ Court records

✓ Deeds

✓ Passports

✓ Census records

Private firms maintain computerized files that, in many cases, are freely accessible by federal agencies.

✓ Insurance companies

✓ Employment agencies

✓ Doctors (including psychiatrists)

✓ Credit bureaus

---

[7]An excellent way to find out what federal records are maintained in your name is to use the Freedom of Information Act. A guide to this act is *A Citizen's Guide on Using the Freedom of Information Act and the Privacy Act of 1974 to Request Government Records* (Washington, D.C.: Superintendent of Documents; House Report 101-193)

- ✓ Banks and financial institutions

- ✓ Brokerage houses and investment funds

- ✓ Car dealers, mail-order firms and mortgage companies

- ✓ Clubs and organizations

- ✓ Genealogical bureaus

- ✓ Churches

One study indicated that the source for 72 percent of these records is the individual in the file. *You* are the source for most invasions of your privacy. It is in your best interest not to voluntarily provide personal information unless there is a compelling need on your part to do so.

Money Laundering and Forfeiture

In the early days of the American Republic, property rights were absolute. No governmental authority could seize your property, unless it could demonstrate that it was stolen.

Today, this common-law protection has been eliminated. The federal government may seize your assets for suspected violations of more than 100 crimes. State and local laws and regulations add thousands more forfeitable offenses. In some states, your property may be seized if it is connected with "any indictable offense." All that is necessary for the seizure to proceed is for an informant--even a convicted felon paid out of the proceeds of the seizure--to allege that a forfeitable offense has occurred on your property. Chapter 8 describes the chilling implications of these laws.

Similarly, the money laundering statutes criminalize many efforts to protect your financial privacy. It does not matter if every dime has been earned legitimately, and taxes paid. Even efforts to keep the location of lawfully-earned funds a secret, or to move such funds privately, are now often illegal.

You need not know that taking such steps to protect your privacy violates the law. Since money laundering is a *strict liability* statute, the government can seize the "tainted" assets if it believes that you concealed them illegally, and even criminally prosecute you for doing so. Chapter 7 explains how this insidious process operates.

Privacy And Public Attitudes

As corporate and government access to personal information has increased, our attitudes toward privacy have changed. Our expectations of privacy have waned, and our tolerance for the privacy needs of others has also declined.

The evolution in attitudes towards privacy have made it possible for information that only a few decades ago was considered intensely personal to be released today for public consumption. Intimate details of a presidential candidate's alleged sexual behavior are routinely published for public view. In earlier years, the press would have voluntarily kept this information to itself. Today, it is front page news. A popular celebrity dies, and the division of the estate is publicized in detail. A sports figure dies of a drug overdose, and the information is quickly beamed around the world.

When Judge Robert Bork was being considered by the Senate for the Supreme Court position he was ultimately denied, one of the Senate researchers brought in a list of the movies he had rented. Apparently, the researcher was looking for R-rated or X-rated movies. The movie rental stores had all this information on computer. Some senators later stated that they were shocked by this invasion of privacy. Subsequent legislation prohibited this practice. If nothing else, at least records of the videos you purchase or rent are now protected by law!

This lack of respect for individual privacy takes other forms as well, most of them destructive. Lack of respect for information often leads to a lack of respect for tangible property. The computer hacker who, for a thrill, would scramble your credit record, shares the attitude of the vandal who would trash your home. The thief who steals your credit card number is a comrade-in-arms to the one who would rob you to obtain cash.

Fortunately, whether you are prominent or totally inconspicuous, there are decisions you can make on sharing (or not sharing) information about yourself. You can limit your exposure to credit bureaus, government agencies and marketing organizations. And you can make your home and workplace less vulnerable to thieves and vandals.

How To Achieve Ultimate Privacy

Are there ways to achieve complete privacy? Yes, but they may be extremely costly--not to mention illegal. The February 19, 1988 issue of *Remnant Review* contained 17 suggestions from editor Dr. Gary North. (These suggestions should in no way be considered an endorsement by Dr. North or the author of the techniques described.)[8]

1. Break the law and establish false identities for yourself, including fake driver's license, fake birth certificate and a fake Social Security card.

2. Sell services that are ordinarily not tax-deductible, such as home repairs or auto repairs, and insist on payment in cash.

3. Don't report your income to any government agency.

4. Never open a bank account.

5. Sell your house.

6. When you get phone service or other utilities in your apartment or rental, use a fake name.

7. Be prepared to make large cash deposits to utility companies, since you will have no credit record. Be prepared to move without getting a refund, since they will refund your money by check.

8. Cancel all subscriptions are in your name.

9. Leave no forwarding address with the post office.

---

[8]*Remnant Review* (P.O. Box 84906, Phoenix, Ariz. 85701)

10. Use mail drops for your mail.

11. Get a passport.

12. Convert all your liquid assets to cash, slowly, then go on a Caribbean cruise.

13. Get off the boat in a tax haven filled with banks, take your cash in a sack, and open an account at a bank that has no U.S. branches.

14. Set up a foreign corporation or trust and tell your banker (face to face) to transfer your money into it. This is illegal if you don't report it to the IRS.

15. Have the trust buy property in a country that has no extradition treaty with the United States. Brazil is one.

16. Be prepared to live as a visible foreigner for the rest of your life, if you have to flee the United States.

17. Be prepared to cut off all future contact with your relatives.

Are you willing to pay the price to achieve ultimate privacy? I'm not. I pay my tribute to the authorities, and thereby carve out an area of service for myself. I work to erode people's faith in the all-powerful State. I give away money to organizations that are offering private alternatives to government welfare programs. I work for a transition through the system to a constitutional society of free markets and free men.

To do this, I "compromise" with the State in that I pay my taxes and advocate *legal* strategies to protect privacy. This makes me a "collaborator" in the view of some tax protestors, but they rarely buy my books or subscribe to my newsletter, since they are too far underground to receive regular mailings.

Some people have sought ultimate privacy by creating new identities. Since the whole system rests on paper and electronic data based on paper, privacy seekers have created fake paper. These techniques are described in publications such as *The Paper Trip* and *The Paper Trip II.*[9]

Many of the recommendations these books make are illegal. I mention them here only to show the price that some people pay to achieve privacy. In 1991, a New York jury convicted a Colombian hit man--not for murder, but for using a false identity and lying about it. The two charges each carry prison terms of five years. This section is about establishing ultimate privacy. For everyone else, these publications are recommended for their entertainment value, and perhaps more important, for establishing the outer limits in the search for privacy.

I fully realize that some privacy seekers have ulterior motives in mind. This should not discourage those of you who are trying to protect your privacy for legitimate reasons. Those who seek

---

[9]Barry Reid, *The Paper Trip* and *The Paper Trip II*, available from Eden Press (address in "List of Suppliers.") I recommend ordering these books from a out-of-town bookstore; do not get on this company's mailing list. Pay cash in advance. Leave a false name; there is nothing illegal about doing so in this situation. Call in every couple of weeks from a pay phone until they arrive. Then go in, unannounced, and pick them up. (If you want a catalog from this company, which is fascinating to read, write for it only after reading "Protecting Your Correspondence" in Chapter 4, and request that all records of your correspondence be destroyed.)

privacy in order to conceal the proceeds of illegal activities demean similar efforts by everyone else. Such incidents are used by the government to justify further attacks on privacy.

The former owner of a bankrupt Orange County, California S&L for instance, used almost every "deep-cover" technique in existence to hide the funds he allegedly siphoned off from the institution. He obtained a birth certificate for an individual who had died 30 years previously, then obtained a driver's license in that name. He then applied for a passport.

The passport clerk, noting that the applicant had just received his driver's license at the age of 32, checked with California's vital records office and discovered that the driver's license had been granted to a person who had died at the age of two. The S&L owner was arrested, and in his briefcase were found records of several offshore bank accounts and tickets to a well-known bank secrecy haven.

We all pay for such misdeeds. To deal with the problem of S&L fraud, Congress in 1990 passed legislation that permits the Federal Deposit Insurance Corp. to examine the tax returns of every American--not just S&L bigwigs.

The problem with seeking privacy to hide ill-gotten gains (other than the fact that doing so is illegal) is that it creates a sense of paranoia that interferes with normal daily living. Even in our legitimate efforts to seek privacy, we should avoid paranoia. We should always strive to be productive people, leaving this world a little better than we found it. Paranoia can lead to paralysis, which is hardly constructive. What we should do is follow the biblical injunction to "count the cost" (Luke 14:28-32). We need to know what we *aren't* willing to pay, and then make rational decisions within these parameters.

Most people aren't willing to take extreme, and possibly illegal, measures to protect their privacy. Fortunately, doing so isn't usually necessary. You can dramatically lower your profile to theft, lawsuits, loudmouth salesmen, and government bureaucrats by using a combination of common-sense, remarkably simple, inexpensive and perfectly legal techniques.

It isn't always easy to find privacy in a public world. But with diligence and forethought, it is possible.

Chapter Two

PRIVACY IN YOUR HOME

There are few feelings more threatening than that of *invasion*. The prospect of someone breaking into your home represents the ultimate threat to privacy.

The most elementary level of privacy in the home is to employ tactics to keep unwanted visitors out of it. Here are a few suggestions that you should consider, none of which involve "high technology."

1. *Keep the area around your home free of obstructions that an intruder could hide behind.* Cut down shrubs to a level where you can see through to the street. In addition, shrubs surrounding a house should be trimmed back so that they offer minimal concealment.

2. *Improve the quality of your exterior lighting.* Illuminate your yard and driveway at night, or at least the areas in the immediate vicinity of your house. The easiest way to control exterior lighting is to use a photocell-controlled switch which automatically goes on at dusk and off at dawn.

High-pressure sodium lights are most economical, but give off an orange glow that you may find unpleasant. Metal halide lamps (which have a color very similar to household incandescent bulbs) are generally easier to live with than high-pressure sodium lights, and are considerably more energy efficient than ordinary floodlights. However, their use by marijuana cultivators has led to a crackdown by the government on their sale. You may find it difficult to locate these lights, and even arouse suspicion if you ask for them by name.

Many electrical utilities will install photocell-controlled exterior high-pressure sodium lights on your property and then bill you a set fee each month--usually no more than $10-$15 per month. This is an extremely economical solution if it is available in your locality.

3. *Secure all doors to make uninvited access more difficult.* Exterior doors should be solid wood; steel is even better. Cheap plywood doors can be "opened" simply by kicking them in. Buy doors with peepholes, not windows. A window can be smashed to evade the locked door. Finally, place door hinges on the inside, so that the door can't be opened by removing them. Replace the short screws that secure door hinges with longer screws that penetrate into the framing of the house. That will make the hinge side of the door much more resistant to forced entry.

Next, install high-quality deadbolt locks on all exterior doors. Cheap locks can be pried off with a large set of channel lock pliers. If you're not sure how to choose a high-quality deadbolt, ask a locksmith. Medeco, Abloy, and Fichet all produce superior locks. They are considerably more expensive than the locks ordinarily available at hardware stores, but the extra expense is well worth it.

Have a locksmith install the new locks, which should be keyed on both sides. A double-keyed lock will have to be unlocked from the inside every time you wish to exit from your home. Keep a key handy, but don't keep it in the interior door lock or other location where an intruder can simply reach in through a window that he has smashed to pick it up and unlock the door.

Many homes have sliding glass doors, which are very simple to penetrate. A skilled intruder can break into a home through a sliding glass door in a matter of seconds by lifting it off its track or by forcing its almost-always inadequate lock open. To protect a sliding glass door from being lifted off its track, drill a series of holes at eight-inch intervals on the inside of the door frame about 1/4 inch below the top of the frame. Then insert screws in these holes that are large enough so they must be twisted in and out.

To guard against locks being forced, drill a hole in the metal area where one sliding door overlaps the other when the unit is completely shut. Then place a large nail in the hole. You can also insert a metal bar or stout wooden rod in the path where the door would be forced open, bracing it against the door frame.

4. *Secure all windows.* The best window protection is replacing glass windows with Lexan (a hard, shatterproof plastic) or installing locking shutters over glass windows. Few homeowners are willing to go to this expense. In some areas of the country, locking shutters are installed primarily for hurricane protection, not burglary--but they are equally effective against both threats. An alternative is to install sensors that detect the sound of breaking glass as part of an overall security system (see "Designing A Security System," this chapter), but these are also expensive, and may be prone to false alarms.

Single-hung windows can be protected using the same method described for sliding glass doors; i.e., drill holes and insert nails in the overlapping area. You can also buy locks that fit in the window frames to prevent the window from being opened. Buy the type that is opened and closed with an allen-head (hexagonal) wrench. These are more difficult to force open than types that operate with a thumbscrew.

The jalousie windows found in Florida and other areas with mild climates are completely unsuited to security and should be replaced with crank-operated or double-hung windows. One south Florida television station once filmed an ex-con breaking into a home in less than 30 seconds by removing jalousie panes and penetrating the window screen with his fist.

5. *Get a dog.* A female is best. One technique used by serious thieves to silence or distract a male dog is to bring along a female in heat. A barking dog, no matter its size, will discourage intruders. When you're training the dog, make sure that you don't make it afraid to bark, since that's exactly what you want it to do if it hears an intruder. You can even devise your own "phantom dog" system. Install a fence around your yard and on it place "Beware of Dog" signs. Buy a doghouse and place it in plain view of the street. The finishing touch: Purchase a device (available at many home security specialty shops) that will reproduce a dog's bark if it senses the presence of an intruder.

6. *Install a floor safe.* If you keep valuables at home, this is the best way to protect them. Encase the safe in concrete to prevent it from being removed except with an extensive and time-consuming effort requiring special equipment. Make certain the safe is also fire-rated. (But be certain to read Chapter 8 to determine if you might be vulnerable to an asset forfeiture action before you follow this strategy.)

If Your Home Is Invaded

If your home is broken into, your first instinct may be to confront the intruder. I don't recommend doing so, since you have no idea how many adversaries you will be facing or how they are armed. Any confrontation with an intruder is potentially a life-and-death situation.

A better strategy is to retreat into a "citadel room" that you have prepared in advance with exterior-quality doors and deadbolts and that has no window access. If this room is equipped with a telephone, you can go to it at the first sign of trouble and call for help, knowing that you are relatively safe. If you keep firearms in your home, this is the room where they should be stored.

Never use a firearm against an intruder unless it is literally a case of life or death. Laws in most states impose a burden of self-defense on a private citizen using a firearm; you can discharge a gun only if your life is in imminent danger. Of course, if an intruder manages to penetrate into your citadel room and confronts you, your use of a firearm to stop him would almost certainly be justified.

Designing A Security System

Once you have completed these simple steps, you might wish to consider installing electronic security hardware to detect and/or deter home intrusion. An enormous variety of equipment is available to homeowners for this purpose, including closed-circuit television, motion sensors, noise detectors, etc. For best effect, this equipment should be incorporated into an integrated system.

I also recommend that you buy a system that is continuously "polled" by a central monitoring computer over a telephone line. If the phone line is cut, the computer will alert a human monitor. An intruder cannot defeat the system with a pair of wire cutters.

The following comments from Paul Nelson, author of *Designing an Alarm System,* should be helpful in designing an electronic security system for your home or business.[10]

In order to design a security system for your home or business, you must understand why they are needed. You must also think in terms of how a burglar attacks a home or business. And you must understand the reasons why different situations require different types of protection.

The best place to start is with the method of operation of the thief. (As they say on television, the "M.O.")

To design a security system, you must think like a thief. You should first ask yourself: How would I enter the building with the least risk to myself?

Doors? Windows? Roof? Wall?

FBI statistics tell us that most surreptitious entries--a full 90 percent--are made through doors; 6 percent through windows, 3 percent through the roof and 1 percent through the walls.

We must also determine the value of the commodity we want to protect. What is the thief after?

High-risk items include expensive consumer products with instant cash value; jewelry, gold, silver, furs, appliances and of course, cash itself.

Medium-risk items include expensive consumer products with instant, but lower, cash value; electric typewriters, calculators, computers, musical instruments, power tools.

Low-risk items are not easily liquidated for cash and probably will not be stolen by an experienced thief; they include books, furniture, etc.

---

[10]Paul Nelson, *Designing an Alarm System* (Nelson Associates, 9850 Sandalfoot Blvd., Suite 114, Boca Raton, Fla. 33428; 1989)

Next, we must consider when the burglary will occur. Commercial burglaries usually occur when the business is not open, primarily at night or on weekends. Occasionally, a business will be burglarized in the early morning hours. Residential burglaries usually occur during the daylight hours. Eighty-five percent of the time, the home is unoccupied at the time of the burglary.

Next, we examine different classifications of burglars.

Professional burglars can be classified according to their breaking and entering skills. A Class 1 burglar can evade most alarm systems as well as pick locks. These individuals usually go after only the high-risk items we have already described.

A Class II professional usually won't attack an alarm system. Instead, he will evade it by avoiding the points of a building that are usually alarmed (windows and doors) and entering the building through the roof or walls. He steals primarily high-risk items.

A Class III professional won't attack alarm systems at all, and will go after either high-risk or medium-risk items.

A properly designed alarm system will protect you against all except Class I burglars. And even a Class I burglar won't usually attack a home armed with an alarm. There are too many homes without alarms to attack with less risk of being caught.

A robber uses different tactics from a burglar. He places an individual in fear of his life in order to remove valuables from his person or his property. Many businesses are vulnerable to robberies or "hold-ups," particularly if they maintain large amounts of cash or other high-risk items. Banks, grocery stores, liquor stores and convenience stores are some of the most frequently robbed businesses.

In alarm security, a hold-up or robbery signal must be separate and distinct from the burglar alarm. It is usually a silent alarm. In a residence, it would be called a "panic button."

There are various types of alarm equipment used in an electronic security system.

A local alarm is a bell or siren to notify neighbors or passers-by of unauthorized entry and to frighten a burglar into leaving.

A central station alarm notifies a 24-hour alarm monitoring station of an emergency at a subscriber's home or business.

Dialer alarms use pre-recorded messages to notify someone at another location or central station of an intrusion. When the dialer is "tripped," it will call pre-programmed telephone numbers and repeat the message.

A digital dialer (communicator) uses solid state electronics to transmit data to a central station receiving unit over a regular telephone line.

Perimeter burglary protection involves connecting small-gauge wires to each door or window with a magnetic switch to form a circuit. A low-voltage current is applied continuously. Any break in the circuit activates the alarm.

Space protection devices monitor open spaces within a defined area. Devices currently in use include passive infra-red, photo-electric, ultrasonic and microwave. These are commonly called motion sensors.

The central control panel is the brain of an alarm system. There are hundreds on the market, ranging from devices that protect only against a simple burglary to micro-processor controls that have a built-in power supply, back-up battery and provide a variety of other functions and options.

The hold-up alarm (or panic button) is a silent alarm signal activated when a robbery takes place. It may be initiated by the opening of a cash drawer, a foot switch or a radio transmitter.

The practical application of an alarm system is dependent on the physical configuration of the property to be protected. A good rule of thumb is to use perimeter protection as the basic part of the system. Interior protection can be added in rooms for which you wish to provide special protection.

The main door should always be protected, as well as any sliding glass doors.

If you install a security system yourself, you should always buy good equipment, apply it properly and install it right. Read the instructions FIRST and make all connections (and double check them) before applying power to the system. Also make sure the power to the control panel is on a 24-hour circuit.

There are also some inexpensive adjuncts to a security system that you might wish to consider. Timers can make your home or business look occupied, even if it is not, by controlling lights, televisions and other appliances. They come in many different models, from one time per day on-and-off devices to remote controlled digital devices with separate modules that operate through the house wiring. Some timers are also wireless.

Strobe lights are good attention-getters and may be mounted outside to flash when the alarm system activates.

A good source for the do-it-yourself person or the technician who needs to install equipment in a hurry is Radio Shack. They carry a good variety of equipment and tools. No matter where you move, they will probably have a store.

REMEMBER: The best deterrent after installing a security system is letting the world know that you have it. PUT STICKERS ON ALL

WINDOWS AND DOORS. THIS IS SOMETHING YOU **WANT** TO ADVERTISE!

How to Purchase Firearms Privately

No free man shall ever be de-barred the use of arms. The strongest reason for the people to retain their right to keep and bear arms is as a last resort to protect themselves against tyranny in government.

> *--Thomas Jefferson*

The United States should move expeditiously to disarm the civilian population. No one should have a right to anonymous ownership or use of a gun. There can be no right of privacy in regard to armament.

> *--Dean Morris, Former Director of the Law Enforcement Assistance Administration (LEAA)*

No subject is more imbued with threatening connotations than the subject of firearms. Thousands of Americans die annually from firearms-related injuries. As a result, many politicians advocate strict firearms control, and many communities have already imposed such controls on their own. A few cities have banned private ownership of all firearms.

Advocates of gun control have hardly been able to regulate firearms with impunity. Many people support unrestricted ownership of firearms, and point to the Second Amendment to the Constitution as providing clear authority for private citizens to own them. Here is how the Amendment reads:

> A well-regulated militia, being necessary to the security of a free State, the right of the people to keep and bear arms, shall not be infringed.

To proponents of firearms control, restrictions on firearms ownership are the only possible way to reduce the carnage from their use. Their interpretation of the Second Amendment is that the justification for "the people" keeping and bearing arms has now been removed, since the National Guard has replaced citizen's militias. At the dawn of the 21st century, the average citizen is unlikely to be asked to grab his musket and fire at invaders marching over the crest of the nearest hill.

Advocates of unrestricted firearms ownership dismiss this claim. They argue that even if the constitutional justification for bearing arms may seem weaker since citizen's militias are almost non-existent, the right to bear arms is still constitutionally guaranteed. Moreover, they point to various court decisions declaring that police are not obligated to protect citizens from criminal assault. In 1856, the Supreme Court ruled that the police have "no duty to protect a particular person." In 1982, a U.S. Circuit Court of Appeals ruled that, "There is no constitutional right to be protected by the state." And in 1983, the District of Columbia Appeals Court declared that, "The police may not be held liable for failure to protect a particular individual."

One thing is certain: Regardless of how the Second Amendment is interpreted, it seems inevitable that firearms ownership and use will become increasingly restricted in the future. If you buy firearms, you may be required to register them with government authorities. While I don't advocate violating such laws, many firearms owners do.

For instance, a law which recently went into effect in California requires the state's estimated 1.8 million firearms owners to register their weapons. However, only about 10 percent of the state's firearms owners have done so, making the remainder lawbreakers. A proposal before Congress would go even further. It would repeal the Second Amendment, and ban private ownership of firearms altogether, with almost no exceptions. Such laws, incidentally, were put in place by Hitler just before the German government began its reign of terror.[11]

Should authorities in the future restrict or confiscate firearms, registration will provide a "red flag" to the identities of individuals to be targeted for searches and/or seizures. No wonder 1.5 million Californians have elected to violate the law! Purchasing a firearm privately may be the only way to insure that you will be permitted to keep it as their ownership is further restricted.

Depending on where you live, purchasing a firearm privately may no longer be possible. A handful of local governments have banned firearms altogether. Some state and local governments require that any firearm, no matter how it is purchased, be registered. Other states require that firearm owners purchase a "Firearms Owner Identification Card," but do not require registration of individual weapons. In any case, before you buy firearms, learn the federal and state laws, or local ordinances, governing their purchase.

Gun shows have for many years been touted by survivalists as the best place to purchase firearms and related items (knives, ammunition, etc.) in total privacy. While gun shows provide an excellent choice of weapons, and in many cases at a very competitive price, they are no longer the best choice to purchase firearms privately.

Many tables at gun shows are manned by federally licensed gun dealers. These dealers are subject to increasingly stringent requirements to identify both their customers and the firearms they have purchased. Such regulations apply not only to sales they make at their shops or out of their homes, but also at shows. If you want to purchase a firearm in complete privacy, you should avoid purchasing it from a federally licensed firearms dealer.

A better way to purchase a firearm privately is through a classified advertisement in a newspaper or magazine. Watch for someone to sell the weapon you want. Price the weapon new at a gun store so you know how much you can expect to pay. Visit the seller personally to inspect it carefully for proper operation. If you don't know how, take a course in firearms safety and ask the instructor for assistance. Police organizations, the National Rifle Association, and other groups sponsor firearms safety clinics in almost every U.S. city.

If you purchase a firearm from a private individual, rather than a dealer, it may not be necessary to register it with local or state authorities. But check the applicable laws where you live.

What you want is at least a .38 caliber handgun, but preferably a .357 revolver or a .45 automatic. A revolver is less likely to jam in a crisis, but an automatic holds several more rounds and is easier to reload if you purchase extra ammunition clips. If you buy a revolver, spend a few extra dollars for a speed loader so you don't have to reload one round at a time. A 12-gauge shotgun also gives pause to those facing one.

Just make sure the advertiser isn't a firearms dealer. Before you buy, ask if the seller has a federal firearms license. If he does, he is required to complete a federal form when ownership of the firearm is transferred.

---

[11]For more information on the Nazi gun control laws, and their remarkable similarities with the 1968 U.S. gun control law, see *Gun Control: Gateway to Tyranny* (Jews for the Preservation of Firearms Ownership, 2872 S. Wentworth Ave., Milwaukee, Wis. 53207).

Don't ask the seller to mail the firearm to you. Shipping or receiving unregistered firearms through the mail is a crime unless you possess a federal firearms license.

There is also a middle ground to follow in the firearms controversy. Gun control advocates point to the enormous technological advances in firearms since the enactment of the Second Amendment. Would the founding fathers really have wanted ordinary citizens to possess semi-automatic assault weapons, some of which with a simple (although illegal) modification can spew out hundreds of rounds of ammunition each minute?

Trying to assess "original intent" is a matter of great debate. No one knows for certain what the founding fathers might have thought about automatic weapons, since such weapons did not exist in their day. What the Second Amendment guaranteed was the right of citizens to own weapons typical of the late 18th century; muskets, flintlocks and other black-powder weapons. Statements such as that made by Thomas Jefferson (quoted at the beginning of this section) make this original intent unmistakable.

Coincidentally, black powder weapons have almost completely escaped the network of government regulation and registration of more modern firearms. It is still possible to purchase such weapons in complete anonymity. Ownership of black powder weapons is totally unrestricted. They are considered collector's items, not weapons, by government regulators.

Moreover, black powder weapons have recently undergone significant technological advances that overcome many of their drawbacks vs. conventional firearms. One company that makes modern black powder weapons, Connecticut Valley Arms of Norcross, Georgia, claims that a competent shooter should be able to produce a one-inch target group at 100 yards--more than adequate for self-defense purposes.[12]

Another problem with firearms is that in order to become competent at using them, you must practice. This can be expensive, and even sales of *ammunition* are coming under attack in some localities. It may also be difficult to find a location where you can legally discharge a firearm.

An ideal solution to both problems is the *airgun*. Once dismissed as toys, modern airguns shoot pellets at sufficient velocities to kill small animals and incapacitate larger ones. They are far more accurate than the "BB guns" many of us used as children. Airguns are virtually silent, extremely accurate, and their ammunition is very inexpensive. In addition, discharging an airgun is in most areas not illegal. Nor is their purchase ordinarily subject to recordkeeping requirements or a cooling-off period. Some of the highest-quality airguns are manufactured by Beeman. You can pick up their catalog at many gun stores.

Choosing to own a firearm is a serious responsibility. You should insure that access to it is limited to yourself and responsible adult members of your family. Make certain you train yourself in its proper operation and maintenance, and, as I have already mentioned, discharge it at another person only if your life or a family member's life is in imminent danger. Also familiarize yourself with local and state ordinances concerning firearms. You may (or may not) be permitted to carry a firearm in your automobile, for instance. It is illegal in almost every state to carry a concealed weapon without a permit.

Another consideration is a fire in your home, if you keep ammunition there. Don't keep very much inside your home.

---

[12]Firearms manufactured before 1898 are likewise exempt from registration. They are considered collector's items, not weapons.

Chapter Three

TELEPHONE PRIVACY, WIRETAPS, AND BUGS

Any information transmitted over wire or through the air can be intercepted. Voice, data, teletype, facsimile transmissions, and telephone beeper signals are all susceptible to bugs and wiretaps. So are mobile radio systems, local area network communications, and radio PBXs.

Most of us assume that we are not being watched, analyzed or recorded. The majority of the time, we are not. But technological development has blossomed in privacy invasion business. Victims of electronic eavesdropping are acutely aware of how vulnerable they are. You should cultivate such awareness to reduce the possibility that you might become a victim.[13]

Electronic Surveillance Law

Interception of telephone calls is the oldest technique of electronic surveillance. "Wiretapping" began before World War I, and was widely used against German interests during that conflict. In the prohibition era, federal authorities widely used wiretaps to obtain evidence with which to convict bootleggers.

The earliest U.S. example of an individual being convicted of a crime on the basis of a wiretap occurred in the 1928 case of *Olmstead vs. U.S.* In Olmstead, the Court ruled that police wiretapping without court authorization was not a violation of the Fourth Amendment's ban or unreasonable search and seizure.

Nearly 40 years later, in 1967, the Supreme Court appeared to reverse itself in *Katz vs. U.S.* The court held that police could not eavesdrop without a warrant on even one side of a telephone conversation. Indeed, the language employed in declaring this practice to be a violation of the Fourth Amendment was unusually sweeping:

> The Fourth Amendment protects people, not places...What a person
> seeks to preserve as private even in an area accessible to the public may
> be constitutionally protected.

A year later, Congress adopted the Omnibus Crime Control Act of 1968, which set up a legal procedure under which law enforcement officials could obtain a court order for wiretapping. The combination of the *Katz* decision banning wiretaps without a warrant and the careful procedural requirements of the Omnibus Crime Control Act appeared to strike a compromise acceptable both to law enforcement authorities and the public.

When it came time for the court to determine whether the government could gain access to telephone *records*, however, the Supreme Court was much less accommodating to privacy-seekers. In the 1979 case of *Smith vs. Maryland*, the court declared that telephone company customer records could not be considered private.

---

[13]I have recently completed a special report that deals with wiretaps and electronic surveillance in considerably greater detail than in this chapter. It is entitled *Counter-Surveillance: Who's Watching You, and What to Do About It*, and is available for $49 from LPP's Nevada office.

It was "too much to believe that telephone company subscribers...harbor any expectation that the numbers they dial will remain secret," the court ruled. Any subscriber thus "assumed the risk that the information would be divulged" to law enforcement authorities without a warrant.

In most European countries, disclosing the numbers a telephone subscriber dials is punishable by stiff penalties. The Nazis obtained details about phone usage from the telephone companies, and targeted for harassment people calling places the Nazis frowned upon. Europeans realize that government telephone surveillance is an important ingredient of government tyranny. Americans don't

In 1986, Congress amended the 1968 bill to supposedly close the open door that had developed due *Smith vs. Maryland*. But the Electronic Communications Privacy Act of 1986 opened the door even wider. Under the act, telephone records may be conveyed to law enforcement officials if, "There is reason to believe the contents of a wire or electronic communication, or the records or other information sought, are relevant to a legitimate law enforcement inquiry." No warrant is needed.

A law enforcement agency can also request that the subject of the investigation not be notified of the surveillance--and such requests can extend permanently. In July 1992, Bell Atlantic, the parent company of C&P Telephone, revealed that it had received 22,000 requests from government agencies for phone records in 1991 alone. It complied with more than 90 percent of these requests on a "routine basis," in many cases without notifying the customer.

Moreover, if a request is made by a "private person," not a governmental entity, even these restrictions don't apply. The bill states that, "A provider of electronic communications service may disclose a record or other information pertaining to a subscriber" to any private person.

In legal disputes, the right of litigants to gain access to telephone records is rooted more in state, than federal law, although the First Amendment may apply if the news media is involved. For instance, in 1991, Proctor & Gamble asked police in Cincinnati to investigate news leaks to a financial newspaper, citing an Ohio criminal statute that makes it illegal for "an employee to disclose business secrets to anyone outside his or her company."

The complaint was triggered by articles appearing in *The Wall Street Journal* regarding personnel changes that the company considered confidential. Police in turn obtained subpoenas ordering the local telephone company to search hundreds of thousands of phone records in an effort to trace the leak.

But a few months later, a Texas judge refused to turn over the telephone records of the *Dallas Times Herald* reporter to defendants in a lawsuit filed by a former *Herald* reporter against a former Oklahoma football coach and others.

Cordless and Cellular Phones

The Electronic Communications Privacy Act outlaws the monitoring of cellular phone calls, except by a law-enforcement agency. However, it exempts cordless phones from statutory protection by excluding "the radio portion of a cordless telephone conversation that is transmitted between the cordless telephone handset and the base unit" from any expectation of privacy.

Most cordless phones broadcast unprotected radio signals over narrow frequencies. This makes detecting the signals easy, sometimes by using nothing more sophisticated than an FM radio.[14]

The act's language is quite plain, but it was still challenged by those who believed that cordless telephone conversations should be protected by law. In 1990, the Supreme Court upheld the law and let stand an 8th Circuit Court ruling that there is no "reasonable expectation of privacy" in cordless telephone conversations.

After this ruling, government agencies began listening in on cordless telephone conversations with virtually free reign. The IRS, for instance, now instructs agents in the use of portable "scanners" that seek out conversations on various radio frequencies employed by cordless phone users.[15]

In fact, a burgeoning industry has sprung up to satisfy the requirements of one of America's newest hobbies: listening in to cordless telephone conversations. For instance, a reporter for *The Wall Street Journal* described how by using a scanner, he overheard drug deals, lovers preparing to cheat on their spouses and other choice tidbits.[16]

However, in November 1992, the 5th U.S. Circuit Court of Appeals ruled that the government can't listen in without a warrant to cordless-telephone users who exercise reasonable precautions to keep their conversations private--such as using a scrambling device (*U.S. vs. David Lee Smith*, 91-5077). The decision is binding only in Texas, Louisiana, and Mississippi, but is likely to be cited in many other cases now before other courts. A few states also extend cordless telephones statutory privacy protection.

That same month, George Bush signed HR-6191, a bill intended to crack down on 900-number abuse. Lobbyists for the cellular telephone industry persuaded Congress to include in the bill a provision banning the manufacture or sale of any "scanning receiver" that is capable of receiving cellular frequencies; can be readily altered to do so; or can descramble digital cellular calls.

But since a cellular phone is a "scanning receiver" that can receive cellular frequencies, the lobbyists inadvertently convinced Congress to shut down their industry! (Thankfully, Congress didn't make possession of now-contraband cellular phones a crime; only their replacement.) And cellular eavesdropping is so easy, and scanning equipment already so pervasive, this bill is unlikely to have much impact on illegal eavesdropping. Laws forbidding cellular or cordless monitoring equipment can be no more effective than laws forbidding people from watching television.[17]

Any call you make from an ordinary phone may be answered on a cordless or cellular phone, potentially opening the call to eavesdropping. You can buy "secured" cordless telephone units at a modest premium over ordinary units. These units allow you to change frequencies so that a eavesdropper can listen in on the entire conversation only if he succeeds in matching frequencies every time they change.

---

[14]The "baby monitor," or "wireless babysitter," operates in a manner similar to a cordless phone in that it transmits radio signals to a waiting receiver. As a result, baby monitor transmissions in your home can easily be overheard by your neighbors. If you're interested in purchasing a baby monitor, but don't want to broadcast from your home, you might consider a system that uses the wiring in your home to conduct the signals. Such a system makes casual eavesdropping very difficult. The Midland Model 72-021/022 is such a unit.

[15]Several companies have now introduced cordless telephone *headsets* into the marketplace. These devices, while unquestionably providing convenience to their users, suffer from the same privacy drawbacks as cordless telephones.

[16]"If You Don't Like Hearing All the Dirt, Don't Get a Scanner, *The Wall Street Journal*, October 9, 1990

[17]Of course, the law banning new sales of cellular phones is not being enforced. Add this legislation to the list of idiotic, unenforceable bills passed by our "public servants."

The most secure multi-frequency cordless phone units change frequencies automatically every few seconds to make it all but impossible to eavesdrop except with extremely sophisticated equipment. Even more sophisticated models use a "spread spectrum" transmission technique that makes conversations almost impossible for an eavesdropper to reconstruct. But these phones are very expensive.

Such devices may legally protect the privacy of a cordless telephone conversation, according to the *Smith* decision I previously discussed. But many secured cordless or cellular telephones, or scrambling devices that attach to them, are not particularly effective. For instance, the Tandy company recently introduced a secured cordless telephone with a "frequency inverter" feature that makes overheard conversation unintelligible.

However, it's relatively easy for an electronic hobbyist to construct a unit to unscramble calls transmitted through such a device. *Monitoring Times* magazine recently described where to purchase a unit designed specifically to unscramble conversations from this Tandy model for less than $30.[18]

Monitoring cellular is as easy as monitoring cordless, but the equipment is slightly more expensive. A 1988 program produced by Home Box Office, "No Place to Hide," presented evidence that radio hobbyists listened in to President Reagan's unscrambled cellular telephone conversations as he travelled in limousines around Washington, D.C. More recently, the cellular phone conversations of Virginia Governor Douglas Wilder were recorded and subsequently delivered to a political rival whose career he had been discussing.

Several companies are now introducing secure cellular phone services. Cycomm Corp. of Portland, Oregon provides a scrambling unit that is fully-compatible with those used by many cellular providers. In areas served by Cycomm-compatible cellular companies, you can talk in scrambled mode to another phone not equipped with a Cycomm-compatible descrambling device. This makes the scrambling device more useful. Bell Cellular of Toronto, Ontario, offers a privacy service for cellular phones. Florida's McCaw Cellular offers a similar service. GTE MobilNet is testing a cellular privacy service is southern California. Many other companies are expected to make similar services available in the near future.

Digital transmission of cellular phone calls also lends itself easily to sophisticated encryption technologies that provide even greater protection. This will dramatically upgrade the security of cellular networks in the future.

Caller ID and Automatic Number Identification (ANI)

Of all the new telephone technologies, the one that has generated the most controversy is caller ID. Local phone companies market caller ID as a means to deter bothersome or obscene phone calls, and to make it easier for police, fire, and ambulance crews to pinpoint the location of a person calling for emergency assistance.

Caller ID service requires a display unit that displays the originating number of calls within your area code. It does not display originating numbers from outside your area code.

No one relishes the thought that a call they believed to be private can instantly be traced to their phone number. As a result, some privacy advocates are pressing for caller ID technology to be banned or restricted. Telephone companies in several states offer a unit that blocks your number from being

---

[18]"Cordless Month: Tandy Introduces Cordless Phone With Frequency Inverter 'Scrambling' Feature," *Monitoring Times*, December, 1992

displayed when you dial a caller ID equipped line. The blocking unit re-establishes the privacy of your outgoing calls, but should it be activated when you call for emergency assistance, the operator would be unable to automatically pinpoint your location.

A congressional proposal would require all telephone companies offering caller ID to offer blocking on a per-call basis. Some states have already adopted such legislation. State courts also seem eager to turn back caller ID. In March 1992, the Supreme Court of Pennsylvania declared that caller ID violates state law. Courts in other states are examining the issue as well. Extended litigation has prevented some telephone companies from offering caller ID. Pacific Bell recently dropped a proposed caller ID service in California because regulatory requirements made it too costly.

Caller ID blocking sounds as if it ought to be completely effective, but it is not. It may be bypassed through subterfuge. For instance, a person who wished to learn your blocked number might purchase call screening service from the local phone company. This service permits him to screen out calls from certain originating numbers. It may also allow him to identify blocked originating numbers. He can tell the telephone company that he wants to block a number he can't identify. The company will review its records of your calls to his number at the time he specifies. It programs its computer to block calls from that number in the future.

A few days later, he can dial an automated service and request that the numbers programmed in be read to him. The computer, speaking in an electronically-synthesized voice, does so. In some parts of the country, he may hear all the programmed numbers, including those that have been blocked. In others, he may hear the word "private" instead of the blocked numbers.

Automatic number identification (ANI) is even more powerful than caller ID. Since it permits an originating number to be displayed on calls to 800 (WATS) and 900 exchanges, its reach is nationwide, not limited to a single area code.

A person calling an ANI-equipped WATS line or 900 service will have his area code and phone number displayed thousands of miles away on a computer console. In turn, the number can be instantaneously linked with data from other sources that provide a record of credit history, marital status, automobile purchases, etc. The ANI profile can be used internally or sold to other marketing companies. (Similar capabilities are now being offered to companies utilizing caller ID.) And of course, bureaucrats can use ANI; a new $1.2 billion government phone system provides many federal agencies equipped with WATS lines this capability.

ANI is used by a wide variety of companies, and much of the time, the information gathered is relatively harmless. The *Atlanta Constitution* helped Pizza Hut sponsor a contest to predict winners of football bowl games. Every person that called in had their phone number recorded and matched against a consumer database. Now the paper has a valuable list of mostly young, mostly male readers who watch TV sports, presumably like pizza, and enjoy reading about sports. Such a list could perhaps be attractive to magazines such as *Sports Illustrated* or The *Sporting News*.

But the information obtained may also be embarrassing. Jami Marketing Services, for instance, sells a mailing list for 150,000 callers to a "Love Lines Dating and Fantasy" 900 phone number, as well as lists for 12 other 900 numbers.

Legislation before Congress would prohibit data of the type gathered by Pizza Hut or distributed by Jami from being sold or rented to other companies. But ANI is unlikely to be banned, for it provides an important customer service edge to companies equipped with it. Several software programs now permit an incoming call be instantaneously linked to a customer screen, saving valuable time when taking an order or tracing its location.

Even if Congress restricts ANI use in the private sector, no proposals have been made to restrict its use by the government. Remember this the next time you call the IRS' toll-free line to complain about your late refund check.

Wiretaps

The Omnibus Crime Control Act of 1968 makes wiretapping illegal without a warrant, unless at least one party to the conversation consents to it. Moreover, the act sets up strict procedural guidelines law enforcement agencies must follow to tap a person's phone. As a result, only a few hundred wiretaps are authorized each year.

However, this number does not include wiretaps installed for "national security" purposes, which are cleared through the top-secret Foreign Intelligence Court. Hundreds, perhaps thousands, of such "black bag" jobs are conducted annually, with virtually no oversight. And don't forget that a conversation which at least one person knows is being recorded is not legally considered to be wiretapped.

Millions more wiretaps are established illegally. By far their most common use is by disgruntled spouses wishing to listen in on the activities of their wife or husband. Police may illegally listen in on the phone calls of prisoners in their custody, and police supervisors have illegally listened in on conversations of their officers. This criminal pattern has in the past extended to the highest echelons of the government: President Nixon's White House "plumbers," for instance, illegally tapped the phones of journalists, war protestors, civil rights activists and just about anyone else whose actions were deemed subversive.

A wiretapper need not gain access to your phone itself, but only to the pair of wires leading to and from it. A tap may be located anywhere in the circuit between two telephones, at the jack to which one phone is connected, at a junction box where hundreds or thousands of phone lines meet, or even miles away in a central phone switching facility. A tap can be connected to a voice-activated tape recorder (available at electronic hobby stores such as Radio Shack for less than $100) or even to another telephone line that rings in when the target line is picked up.

A "hard-wired" wiretap is the most effective, and most commonly installed variety. Such a tap may be connected in-line with the telephone circuit, in *series,* or across the target wire pair, in *parallel.* The telephone signal is diverted to a waiting tape recorder, extension telephone, or telephone line.

Wiretaps can also broadcast over radio frequencies, thereby avoiding the telltale pair of wires left by a hard-wired tap. The "series parasite radio frequency tap," for instance, consists of a radio transmitter that is installed in series with one of the two conductors comprising the target pair. It broadcasts only when the phone is off-hook, and transmits both sides of a conversation from 50 feet to a mile or more away from where it is planted. The signal is picked up by an antenna, and in turn is relayed to a waiting tape recorder.

The further away from your telephone a tap is planted, the more difficult it is to detect. Most illegal taps are installed in the same building as the target telephone, frequently in an unlocked telephone closet. Such taps can usually be found by careful visual inspection. But if the tap is planted outside the building, and is properly installed, it will be more difficult, if not impossible, to detect visually. And electronic detection of most wiretaps is extremely difficult, wherever they are installed.

One of the most ingenious wiretaps is an extension telephone line. When you pick up the phone, the tape begins rolling. The giveaway to this technique occurs if the target analyzes his phone bill and sees the charge for the new extension.

Any long-distance telephone conversation relayed by a microwave tower can be intercepted and reconstructed by relatively unsophisticated electronic equipment. The National Security Agency, for instance, has for at least 25 years routinely intercepted and analyzed virtually all telephone conversations beamed by microwave or satellite. The intelligence services of other nations have access to similar technology, and industrial spies have also employed microwave interception to great advantage. Since it is impossible to detect this type of interception, you should never assume your long-distance conversations are private.[19]

The most advanced wiretaps need not be physically connected to a phone line in order to function. They operate by identifying a "voiceprint" out of the thousands of telephone conversations taking place simultaneously in a given telephone exchange. Once again, such taps are impossible to detect. They can only be defeated by changing the sound of your voice (whispering, for instance) or using a digital scrambler. This technology is already sufficiently reliable that the IRS has suggested setting up a pilot program for taxpayers to file taxes over the telephone. A voiceprint would act as a "signature" on the tax form. No paper forms would need to be filed.

Incidentally, telephone companies have unlimited authority to listen in on conversations for the ostensible purpose of preventing "telephone fraud." However, this power is often abused. In one case, telephone employees kept a list of "hot" lines to listen in on for their late-night entertainment. Like all wiretapping, such monitoring is almost impossible to detect electronically.

Digital technology poses a new threat. If an eavesdropper can record your voice, he can digitally modify the sequence of words you are speaking. The modified recording can then be re-recorded onto the original wiretap tape. Strict chain-of-custody rules to which government agencies conducting wiretaps must adhere mean the threat from this source is lower than from a would-be blackmailer.

To illustrate the potential for embarrassment that the new technology permits, an audience at the 1992 annual meeting of the Computer Professionals for Social Responsibility heard a tape of a digitally modified segment of the testimony of Supreme Court Justice Clarence Thomas, taken from his confirmation hearings. The tape, which was manipulated on a Macintosh computer with sound editing software, featured Thomas confessing to all the sexual harassment charges leveled by Anita Hill.

Privacy and the Telemarketer

In the past two decades, the number of companies selling products and services by telephone has soared. Organizations ranging from AT&T to local civic associations regularly call prospective clients or contributors on private phone lines, at any time of day, thinking nothing of the intrusion. The newest trend is to have a computer, rather than a human sales representative, make the call. In many cases, your phone line is tied up until the computer finishes its pitch, even if you hang up. (A 1991 bill adopted by Congress made this practice illegal without the permission of the person being called.)

A recent survey conducted by a New York advertising agency indicates that 75 percent of Americans think telemarketing is an invasion of privacy, and 72 percent consider the telephone sales pitches distasteful. If you detest telemarketing, you're in good company.

---

[19]An excellent discussion of the National Security Agency, the nation's most secretive and intrusive government agency, is provided in James Bamford's *The Puzzle Palace* (New York: Penguin Books, 1982)

Sometimes the tactics of telemarketers border on outright harassment. One morning, I was sitting at my desk when my phone rang. The caller asked for me by my fake name that I list in the phone book (see "16 Tips to Maintain Telephone Privacy," this chapter). I immediately knew I was talking with a salesperson. Would I be interested in MCI long-distance telephone service, she inquired? I told her that I already had MCI service under another name, and for the company to get its records straight.

As the day progressed, I received three additional calls from MCI telemarketing representatives. Each found it impossible to believe that I had already had MCI service. None of them knew that other MCI representatives had already contacted me. That afternoon, I drove to the post office to pick up mail at my post office box. In my mail was--you guessed it--an invitation from MCI, addressed to my real name this time, to subscribe to their long-distance phone service.

Telemarketing is most often a nuisance, but it can also involve outright fraud. In the early 1980s, telemarketers operating out of "boiler rooms" hyped precious metals, penny stocks, and rare coins. Today, a favored scam is oil and gas limited partnerships. There are, of course, legitimate versions of all these investments--but they are generally not sold by telemarketers.

You might wonder where telemarketers obtain your phone number. In the case of MCI, the answer was obvious: my number is listed in the white pages, but under a fake name. But even if your phone number is unlisted, there are a number of ways telemarketers can obtain it.

The crudest way is through "sequential dialing." A sales representative begins with the lowest phone exchange in a particular area (221, for instance) and begins working his way up (221-0000, 221-0001, etc.) A call from someone who asks "for the person making purchasing decisions at this location" or simply starts a sales pitch without mentioning your name may have been sequentially dialed.

Magazines, newsletters, brokerage houses and other organizations also sell phone numbers to telemarketers. After speaking at a recent financial seminar, I was approached by an attendee. He had an unlisted phone number, he said, but had received at least two dozen unsolicited phone calls from brokers in the preceding month. I asked if he had recently subscribed to any financial newsletters. He told me he had done so several weeks previously, and had listed his phone number on the order form. Not surprisingly, he was outraged when I told him that this was the most likely way telemarketers had obtained his phone number.

Reverse directories are another rich source of telemarketing "leads." Since listings in a reverse directory are keyed to addresses, a telemarketer can target individuals in particular neighborhoods. Wealthy neighborhoods are frequent targets. So are neighborhoods with known demographic characteristics; a high proportion of ethnic residents, college-educated residents, etc.

Nationally published and computerized listings of telephone numbers are also available. Compuserve, a popular database and electronic mail company, has a national telephone look-up service. Other companies compile lists of numbers and sell them to direct marketing companies. In 1991, Nynex Corp. and Metromail, one of the largest direct mail companies in the United States, joined forces to market a national listing of more than 77 million telephone listings on CD-ROM.

Telemarketers also may obtain your name illegally. This is particularly popular among companies specializing in boiler room operations that sell whatever is "hot" at the moment. Your name might be taken off the desk of a legitimate broker, for instance, and sold to another one. Or an entire name and address list may be purloined and sold to the highest bidder.

Another method that telemarketers have to obtain your phone number is by using automatic number identification (ANI), discussed in the "Caller ID and Automatic Number Identification" section of this chapter.

In the future, it will even be easier for telemarketers to obtain your phone number. Emerging technology will enable telephone companies to assign every American a telephone number at birth, in much the same manner as a Social Security number.

The new technology, which through a global satellite network will also make it possible for you to be reached (or traced) anywhere on earth you carry your phone, is now under study by the Federal Communications Commission. The FCC anticipates the transition to this new system will be complete by the early 21st century.

The FBI and "Digital Telephony"

In April 1992, FBI Director William Sessions proposed legislation that would shift the burden of making wiretaps feasible from the government to telephone companies (telcos) and other providers of telecommunications services.

This "Digital Telephony" initiative is breathtakingly broad. It would require "providers of electronic communications services and private branch exchanges (PBXs) to ensure that the government's ability to lawfully intercept communications is unimpeded by the introduction of advanced...telecommunications technology."

What types of electronic communications does the FBI want to wiretap? *All of them*, according to a recent report from the General Accounting Office.[20]

This report claims the FBI "needs" the capability of monitoring all phone and data communications, all local area networks (LANs), all private branch exchanges (PBXs), and all "special features" offered by communication providers. This last category would include call forwarding and electronic mail. Finally, it calls for new international agreements so that the FBI can eavesdrop on Americans communicating outside U.S. borders.

Sessions admits that there have been no cases in which the FBI was unable to implement a court-ordered wiretap. Then why the Digital Telephony initiative? One possible explanation was the Department of Justice's unsuccessful effort to enact S. 266, the "Comprehensive Counter-Terrorism Act of 1991."

This bill would compel telephone companies to "ensure that communications systems permit the government to obtain the plain text contents of voice, data, and other communications when appropriately authorized by law." In other words, telephone companies would be prohibited from transmitting information encoded in any form if the government could not obtain their "plain text contents."

The FBI's new proposals don't talk about encryption. They only talk about the "threat" to wiretapping by law enforcement agencies that digital technology poses. However, encryption would have to be restricted if their objective is to listen in on digitally encrypted wire or radio communication. This, of course, is what S. 266 called for.

The effect of such an initiative, if adopted, raises a number of questions. Would it be retroactive to already-installed equipment? If it was, how would this requirement be enforced? Who would pay for the "upgrades" necessary to make the equipment compatible with the FBI's capabilities? Could a knowledgeable engineer disable the "key?" And what customer would pay for a retrofit of his digitally

---

[20]*FBI: Advanced Communications Technologies Pose Wiretapping Challenges* (Washington, D.C.: General Accounting Office, GAO/IMTEC-92-68BR, 1992)

encrypted phones, fax machines, PBXs, LANs, etc. that would render them less effective? Finally, how would the FBI prevent companies from purchasing more effective units outside the United States?

I find it hard to believe that Congress would knowingly enact legislation that calls for the U.S. government to spy over the entire world's telecommunications network. But one never knows--the digital telephony initiative is now part of the 1993 crime bill. Perhaps it will be adopted as a necessary escalation of the War on Drugs.

16 Tips to Maintain Telephone Privacy

Maintaining telephone privacy requires forethought and discretion. The following are a few suggestions to consider.

1. *Think before you speak.* Unless you have total confidence that your phone line is not tapped, don't say anything that you would rather not have overheard. Even if your phone isn't tapped, the phone at the other end may be.

2. *Use public phones.* Some public phones are tapped, but their sheer number assures that most aren't. Pay for the call with coins, not a credit card that can be traced back to your name or telephone number. The public phones that are most likely to be tapped are located in bus terminals, train stations, and airports. Public telephones at New York's Grand Central Station, for instance, have for many years tapped by the DEA. Public phones in neighborhoods with a reputation for drug dealing, prostitution, or other illegal activity are also likely to be tapped.

3. *Boil down your conversation to as few words as possible and make it on a cellular phone.* The chances are that your competitor is listening in on the right frequency (out of hundreds available) at the exact time of your transmission is almost nil. If your conversation is overheard by a hobbyist, there's almost no chance that he would recognize the value of the information obtained or how to use it. (See "Cordless and Cellular Phones," this chapter, for more information.)

4. *Disappear from the phone directory.* The best way to get a private number is at the very beginning. When you set up new phone service, do so using an assumed name. A hard-to-pronounce name is best. Look for long names in your local telephone directory for ideas. You might also consider using your mother's maiden name, or, if you are married, your wife's (or your own) maiden name.[21]

There is nothing illegal about this technique. You will probably have to pay several hundred dollars up front as a deposit to disappear, but this is the best way to buy phone service privately. There is no red flag of an "unlisted number." You disappear from all phone records and are replaced with your pseudonym.

No one who looks for your number in the phone company records can find you. Pay your phone bills on time, and put some extra cash in the account in case you forget to pay a bill one month. After a few months, the phone company will credit your account back part of your deposit.

---

[21]This strategy has been made more difficult in recent years due to telephone companies (and other utilities) requiring Social Security numbers from prospective customers prior to setting up service. Utilities that subscribe to the Equifax Utility Identification Service can obtain an instant match of the Social Security number provided with the name and credit history associated with that number. If no match is found, the utility company may require a photo ID to obtain service. Should you face this system When you apply for phone service, I don't advise giving a fake number. Simply state you'd prefer not to disclose your Social Security number and that you would be willing to pay a larger deposit in order to protect your privacy.

A variation on this is to "move out." Have the phone company cancel all service. Then call up a few days later and notify the phone company that you are the new renter. You pay your deposit and have phone service hooked up again. Do this during your normal summer vacation so that you receive uninterrupted service.

Why don't you have any past phone history? You have been outside the country. (You need not say precisely when.) You have been recently divorced or widowed, and the phone number was listed in your spouse's name. You have been living with your parents under their name. You have been living with roommates and now want to obtain phone service under your own name.

5. *Request an unlisted telephone number.* Unlisted numbers are increasingly popular solution to unwanted phone calls. A recent survey showed more than 20 percent of U.S. phone numbers are unlisted. More than 50 percent of Southern California residents have unlisted numbers.

However, telephone company repair personnel have access to all unlisted numbers. Most are honest, but a few have been bribed or otherwise persuaded to relinquish this information. Another threat comes from reverse telephone directories. Reverse directories may include your unlisted phone number if you have provided it to the company compiling the directory or to one of its suppliers.

An unlisted number is useless against the increasingly common practice of sequential dialing. Moreover, if an ex-spouse, ex-business associate, etc. is determined to contact you by phone, they will probably be able to obtain your unlisted phone number by hiring a private investigator.

6. *List your phone number, but leave out your address.* This approach at least eliminates the threat of uninvited visitors to your home who see your address in the phone book. It permits you to maintain contact with friends or relatives who might be deterred by your not being listed at all under your real name or by an unlisted phone number.

Make this arrangement with the telephone company when you have your phone hooked up. If the telephone company insists on publishing an address, ask them to list it as "General Delivery" or to use your post office box number. You should make these arrangements with a supervisor at your local phone company. Your instructions may not always be carried out by customer service personnel.

7. *Use an answering machine.* Answering machines are ideal for screening telephone calls. When you tape the message your answering machine will give to a caller, you are under no obligation to identify yourself on it. Simply repeat your number and ask the caller to leave a message. Answering machines with a remote access feature, which permit you to listen to messages left on your answering machine from another phone, are increasingly popular. While the arrangement is convenient, an enterprising privacy intruder can in many cases use *his* remote access device to listen to *your* messages.

If you purchase an answering machine with this feature, look for a model that responds only to a series of at least three true touch-tone signals.

8. *Hang up.* If you are contacted by a phone sales representative, and don't wish to listen to a "pitch," inform the caller you are hanging up. Then hang up. If you are interested, but don't wish to make a commitment over the phone, you might say something like:

I'm sorry, but I never buy anything over the telephone. Would you be willing to send me some information on your product or service? I'll call you back if it is something I could use. Please don't call me back. Also, please delete my phone number from your records.

This deters all but the most determined sales representatives. If "stronger medicine" is needed, you can make the statement similar to the following:

> I have to hang up now. If you'd like to continue, I'll have to charge you $250 per hour for my time. I'm a marketing consultant, and this is my fee to evaluate telemarketing representatives. May I have your credit card number and expiration date?

Or you could take the approach of Robert Bulmash, founder of "Private Citizen, Inc." Bulmash advises the members of his group to find out all they can about those who are calling them; their name, address, telephone numbers, name of supervisor, etc. Then twice a year, he sends out a notice to telemarketers who have contacted his members with a note that reads, in part:

> I am unwilling to allow your free use of my time and my telephone. I will accept junk calls for a $100 fee, due within 30 days of such use. Your junk call will constitute your agreement to the reasonableness of my fee.

Bulmash claims that his members experience a decline in junk calls of at least 75 percent. He has also persuaded several courts to enforce judgements against telemarketers. (See the "List of Suppliers" for his company's address.)

If you use my hard-core approach, you can always identify cold-calling salesmen from the beginning: They ask for your fake name. In previous editions of this report, I wrote that if the caller asks for you by your fake name, you can even have a little fun. For instance, you could say that you are his relative, and that he has just died. Or that he has a terminal disease, has just declared bankruptcy or just lost his job.

This is no longer a good idea. Since phone numbers are increasingly tied to credit records, Social Security records, etc., false information could get back to a credit bureau or insurance company, with potentially disastrous consequences. (See "Privacy and Your Credit Records," Chapter 4.)

You might also remind telemarketers that call late at night or early in the morning of new FCC rules that permit sales calls to residences only between 8 A.M. and 9 P.M., local time. In addition, telemarketers are banned from making automated calls on emergency lines, to health care facilities, and on common carrier lines (such as cellular) where the called party will be charged for the call. However, telemarketing firms are challenging these rules as unreasonably restricting their rights.

9. *Screen your calls.* Various screening devices are integrated into several high-end answering machines. One AT&T answering machine can be bypassed if the owner gives the caller an access code to punch in while the recorded message runs.

A device sold by a New Jersey firm, Lifestyle Fascination Inc., allows users to pre-program up to 100 phone numbers of parties whose calls are welcome. When one of these individuals calls in, the system displays the number on a small viewer. Other calls may either be automatically disconnected or shunted to an answering machine.

Several other companies take the opposite approach and allow you to program in phone numbers from which calls are *not* to be accepted. For instance, you could program the phone not to accept calls from a collection agency that has been haranguing you, or from your ex-spouse. This service may also be available from your local telephone company.

10. *Get your name off telephone solicitation lists.* You can write to reverse directory and direct marketing companies to get your name off their lists. Addresses for several such companies are in the "List of Suppliers."

11. *Discourage the release of your telephone records to third parties.* The 1986 Electronic Communications Privacy Act permits "private parties" to obtain telephone records from telephone companies. Telephone companies may sell your telephone records to private companies who reconstruct the calls you have made and sell the resulting data to direct marketing firms. Or they may use the data internally.

Several years ago, MCI used such information to promote its "Friends and Family" program. Without notifying its customers, MCI sifted through their telephone bills for the numbers of individuals who subscribed to competitive long-distance services. Then it mailed promotional literature to these non-MCI subscribers implying that a friend or relative had recommended that they should switch to MCI.

Notify both your local and long-distance telephone companies in writing that you want this information to remain confidential.

12. *Use a beeper.* Another way to protect your privacy is to rent a beeper and use the number assigned to it as your listed number. When you receive calls from numbers that you don't recognize, you can safely ignore them.

13. *Use a voice mailbox.* Phone companies and other providers now offer voice mail service. (Look under "voice mail" in the Yellow Pages.) The major privacy advantage of a voice mailbox is that the number cannot be associated with your physical address. A voice mail firm will assign you a telephone number and/or personal code, and you can customize the greeting callers receive as you can on an answering machine. Callers will usually believe that they have reached an answering machine. You can retrieve these messages, or change your outgoing message, from any touch-tone phone.

However, you need to take precautions when you use voice mail. Snoops who can obtain your access code may be able to penetrate the system and listen to your messages. For this reason, you should not pick a simple access code. In addition, voice mailboxes are a prime target of computer hackers. They crack the computer system controlling the voice mail system, change the access codes to the mailboxes, and then use them as a method of distributing stolen credit card numbers and other illicit data. Any long-distance calls billed to your voice mailbox are your responsibility to pay. The best way to prevent such access is for the computer controlling access to the system to hang up after two or three incorrect password attempts. Look for this feature when you rent a voice mailbox.

14. *Defeat caller ID.* The most basic step you can take to defeat caller ID is to make calls you wish to keep private from a pay phone, or with operator assistance. Calls made from behind a PBX may display only the main PBX number, not your extension.

Another option is to purchase caller ID blocking from your telephone company. However, not all telephone companies that offer caller ID provide a blocking service. And since blocking can sometimes be circumvented, don't think of it as a panacea.

You can also purchase a call diverter. One popular model is the LOGOS-DX, from All-American Associates. You to call in on one number and call out on another. Caller ID displays the line the call diverter is connected to, not the line from which the call originates. The system also works in reverse. People can call in and have the call forwarded to you, on a number the caller does not know. However, the outgoing line the call diverter uses may be traced.

Private Lines, Inc., a 900 number service, offers a redialing service that defeats caller ID. To use it, dial 1-900-STOPPER. When you hear a second dial tone, dial the number you wish to call privately. A caller ID display unit or ANI console will display Private Lines' number, not your own. The service costs $2/minute.

An even more secure service from Private Lines is its "Anonymous Voice Mailbox" program. For a monthly fee of $100, you can make send and retrieve voice messages without the possibility of the voice mail box phone number being traced back to you. You retrieve messages from your voice mailbox by first dialing 1-900-STOPPER, then redialing the voice mailbox, to prevent any toll records of the call being present. The service is currently available only in California.

Private Lines can record the originating numbers to its service, as any 900 service can. The telephone company can produce these records as well, with no court order necessary. But to protect your privacy for any legitimate purpose, the Private Lines approach, used in conjunction with digital encryption (see "How to Achieve Electronic Privacy," this chapter) appears to offer the closest thing to ultimate telephone privacy that now exists.

Computer hackers (and increasingly, drug dealers) use a variety of legal call forwarding arrangements and illegal pirating techniques (such as surreptitiously taking over one or more voice mailboxes) that make it difficult or impossible to trace their calls. I can't endorse their techniques, even though they are extremely effective.

15. *Beware of the voice stress analyzer.* Even if your conversations aren't surreptitiously recorded, they may be analyzed with a "voice stress analyzer." This device, which can be used with either live or taped conversation, is designed to detect vocal "microtremors." Companies selling voice stress analyzers claim that a person with microtremors in his voice may be lying.

Insurance companies, government agencies and private investigators all use voice stress analyzers. Using one is not illegal, although the conclusions of its operator are not admissible in court. If you believe that your conversation may be analyzed by a voice stress analyzer, lower your voice and whisper. The incidence of microtremors is reduced considerably in whispered or hissed speech.

Incidentally, voice stress analyzers are even less reliable than lie detectors (see "Privacy and the Lie Detector," Chapter 5). In fact, at least one test of voice stress analyzers showed them to have an accuracy of less than 50 percent--a rate that could be achieved simply by guessing whether the test subject was telling the truth.

16. *Investigate local and state telephone privacy initiatives.* Your state may have enacted laws that provide protection against objectionable telephone practices. For instance, Florida runs a statewide "don't call" system. You pay $10 to put your name off-limits to telemarketers. More than 25,000 Florida residents already have their name on the list. And in 1993, a Texas assemblywoman introduced legislation that would instruct the Departments of Public Safety and Transportation, and public utilities, to keep unlisted telephone numbers and addresses confidential.

Other Types of Surveillance

The wiretap is only one of many potential methods to eavesdrop on your conversations or monitor your movements. A wide variety of equipment is available to a determined spy.

Enter the "bug." A bug is nothing more than an device or configuration that is capable of detecting spoken conversation and relaying it to another location. The most common bugs, which broadcast over radio frequencies and are therefore designated "RF bugs," consist only of a microphone and a transmitter hard-wired into an electrical grid. Add a battery and the bug doesn't need an external source of power.

While RF bugs are now illegal to sell fully-assembled, you can construct one in a few minutes with components purchased over-the-counter at an electronic hobby store, using only a soldering gun.

The heart of one popular RF bug is a microphone sold by Radio Shack that is considerably smaller than a dime. Add a transmitter and a battery, and for less than $25, you have a device that can be hidden almost anywhere and is virtually invisible. The resulting battery-powered bug can operate from 48 hours to 10 days, or, with an advanced lithium battery, several weeks or months.

A bug tied into an outside source of power can operate indefinitely. Until the bug is detected or loses power, it will transmit any conversation in a room as far as several hundred feet to a waiting receiver. The receiver may be nothing more sophisticated than a FM radio or scanner.

An individual planting a bug is limited only by his imagination as to where he might place it. Battery-powered bugs are the most portable. They have been found on the underside of ashtrays, in wastebaskets, underneath desks, inside telephones and in light fixtures.

Other RF bugs have microphones specially-designed to fit into unusual locations. One type is a flexible "tube mike" that can be placed in electrical outlets, keyholes, air ducts, etc. A "spike mike" is more rigid and can penetrate relatively hard surfaces such as walls. A "contact mike" can be attached to any interior surface.

The basic features of a bug are simple in concept. But the actual designs can be quite complex with integrated circuits giving the device the ability to "compress" sound (making soft noises louder and loud noises softer), filtering and other special effects to enhance the signal being transmitted.

A receiver and switch may be added so that an eavesdropper may toggle the unit on and off remotely. This enables the listener to shut down the device to conserve its batteries (if not hard-wired into the building's electrical grid) and to avoid detection during a search. However, even if the transmitter is turned off, the receiver that listens for the activation signal must remain on. This receiver may emit an electronic signature that can be detected with the proper countermeasures equipment.

The newest generation of bugs record and store information digitally. They are designed to send a high-speed burst of information rather than broadcasting continuously. These designs don't contain a receiver, making them much more difficult to detect than devices that are sending out a continuous radio signal or are "listening" for activation instructions.

Other recently developed bugs provide both an audio and a visual record of their target's movement and conversation. One model is smaller than a cigarette pack and can be disguised as a book, a computer modem, a tie, a beeper, a sprinkler head or a car antenna!

But perhaps the most common bug of all is the "telephone bug." The telephone is an excellent bug for many reasons. It's a trusted tool, sits nearby the subject, contains its own microphones, and has wiring already in place to carry the signals out of the room. Converting a telephone into a bug is simple. In fact, many modern telephones are room bugs as built. Two examples are the Northern Telecom 2018 and the Comdial Executech II.

It's also easy to transform an office intercom into a bug. The intercom speakers convert the physical energy of sound (your voice) into electrical energy. All an eavesdropper must do to listen in on your conversations is attach an amplifier across the wires (about $12 at Radio Shack) and connect the amplifier to speakers or a voice-activated tape recorder.

Any office with an intercom speaker can be wired in a matter of minutes. Since there is no transmitter, this bug is practically undetectable. Every inch of the intercom wiring must be inspected to find the bug since the connection can be made anywhere along it. The best idea: Disconnect the intercom speakers![22]

You can even construct a bug from drum sets, speaker cones, even water in a toilet bowl! If power is not available to transmit the signal back to a waiting tape recorder, a device known as a "rifle mike" can be used to amplify the sound. The eavesdropper simply aims the microphone at his target, puts on a headset and begins recording.

Such devices can be effective from several hundred yards away. You've no doubt seen similar equipment in use by the media on the sidelines of football games to pick up conversation between officials or coaches. They are easy to construct; one simple model is illustrated in one of the earliest guidebooks to surveillance, entitled *The Big Brother Game*.[23]

You might also consider the "Super Electronic Sound Detector," sold by the Chemical Light and Electronics Company of Sarasota, Florida. This inexpensive system is designed to hear conversations through solid walls. It comes with headphones, a contact microphone--and instructions that warn against snooping on your neighbors. Because it does not contain a transmitter, its sale and use is completely legal. Many mail order companies offer similar equipment under the heading of "listening aids."

Other listening devices are activated by laser beams or microwave beams. The most famous case of this type was uncovered in 1952 in the Moscow office of the U.S. ambassador. A resonant cavity containing a diaphragm and an antenna was found embedded in a wall hanging of the Great Seal of the United States. The wall hanging had been presented to the ambassador as a "gift" by his Soviet hosts. Soviet technicians aimed a microwave beam at the device, enabling them to hear top-secret conversations taking place in the office.

In recent years, no listening device has received more attention than the so-called "laser window vibration reader." This device, which uses a reflected laser beam fed into a computer to reconstruct window vibrations, was featured on the cover of *Radio Electronics* magazine. Inside were step-by-step instructions on how to build the device for less than $1,000. Fortunately, it works only under ideal conditions--where nothing other than a voice is vibrating the targeted window.

Your voice is not the only "vibration" that can be detected with eavesdropping equipment. For instance, a computer emits an "electronic signature" that can be intercepted and decoded with the appropriate equipment. This is termed the Van Eck phenomenon, after the Dutch scientist who first publicized it. The U.S. government has moved aggressively to prevent electronic signatures from computers and other equipment from being detected. Military computers are often enclosed in lead sheathing and are equipped with other so-called "Tempest" features to trap these emissions.

Tuning in and making sense out of the compromising emanations from computers requires sophisticated monitoring equipment, although "home brew" gear that can supposedly decipher these emissions is becoming more common. I've seen contradictory evidence about the threat posed by this kind of surveillance. In August 1992, I attended the Surveillance Expo '92, at which one speaker claimed that not a single documented incident of espionage or theft had ever occurred using this technique.

---

[22]The "intercom bug" and other common methods of electronic surveillance are illustrated by James A. Ross in a video, "Introduction to Bugs and Taps," available from Ross Engineering, Inc. (44880 Falcon Place #198, Sterling, Va. 22170.)

[23]Scott French, *The Big Brother Game* (Secaucus, N.J.: Lyle-Stuart, Inc., 1975)

Yet Van Eck enthusiasts postulate disaster based on its widespread application in industrial espionage. Winn Schwartau, author of the novel *Terminal Compromise*, is perhaps the most articulate spokesman in this group.[24]

As those who have followed the construction of the U.S. embassy in Moscow realize, an entire building can be bugged. During assembly of the embassy's walls, thousands of bugs were implanted, each of them drawing power from the electrical grid. Cheap "diodes" were planted by the thousands as well, decoys that would respond to an electronic sweep for bugs in the same way as a bug itself. Recently, the KGB provided the U.S. State Department a comprehensive list of the listening devices installed in the new embassy. The estimated value of the list, according to the former Soviet newspaper *Pravda* was $300 million; the cost of building a new embassy.

How to Maintain Electronic Privacy

If someone who would eavesdrop on you cannot enter your living or working space, his efforts will be made much more difficult. Therein lies the secret of defeating electronic surveillance.

Place yourself in the shoes of someone who might wish to bug your home or office, or tap your telephone. Who would he hire to do the work? Your secretary? Your custodian? Your auto mechanic? Would he pose as a tradesman, an electrician, a plumber, a telephone repairman?

Restrict access to your office or your home only to those individuals who you trust implicitly. Insist on positive identification for tradesmen you admit. Don't let them work unattended.

If you feel that you may be the victim of electronic surveillance, your first instinct may be to contact your local police or phone company. Unfortunately, most police departments do not have the equipment or training to detect electronic surveillance devices. And telephone companies will seldom admit that their lines are tapped. Even if they do agree to a search, it will almost certainly result in nothing being discovered.

Also consider that if a bug or a tap is authorized by a law-enforcement agency, neither the police or the telephone company will be permitted to render assistance or even to discuss the matter with you.

A better idea is to ask trusted friends and colleagues who they would recommend for a sweep of your home or office. If they are unable or unwilling to make a recommendation, look in the local Yellow Pages for firms advertising under "Security Services" or similar headings. Many electronic surveillance professionals refuse to name references out of a desire to protect their client's privacy. But a background in military or commercial electronics is a common denominator for most, and you should check these qualifications.

James A. Ross, President of Ross Engineering, recommends the following procedure to evaluate a countermeasures service firm:

> Ask them if they will demonstrate their RF bug detector on a bugging system that you set up in plain sight. Then set up a bugging system consisting of a $20 Radio Shack wireless microphone and a $50 Radio Shack (or any other) FM receiver. In order to be a fair test, the system should be capable of transmitting audio out of the room. Ask them to

---

[24]Winn Schwartau, *Terminal Compromise* (Seminole, Fla.: Interpact Press, 1991)

demonstrate how their equipment detects that bug. Amazingly, most "experts" will not be able to pass this test!

Also according to Ross, the two dead giveaways of fraud in an electronic countermeasures company are:

1. If they say they will guarantee to detect any bug or tap.

2. If they claim that they have an electronic device that will detect a tap on your phone line. No such device is available that provides effective protection against a variety of wiretaps.

What about do-it-yourself efforts? I don't recommend them, because they are almost always ineffective. A sweep must be very thorough and performed over a wide range of electronic frequencies to have a significant chance of success. And even if you find a bug, there may be more than one planted.

In addition, much of the equipment sold or rented is practically worthless. For instance, I recently attended a seminar where the failure of a $6,000 "RF Bug Detector" to detect the presence of a $25 bug was graphically illustrated. Even worse are the "magic wands" sold at electronics hobby stores. According to the seminar leader, "a magic wand bug detector has about as much of a chance of finding a bug as a rain dance has in producing rain." If you're in doubt about how to use countermeasures equipment or what equipment to employ, hire a professional.

However, in the interest of providing accurate information to my readers, I have inserted the following section that, carefully followed, may assist *some* of you in finding *some* bugs and/or taps--particularly those placed illegally.

Wiretaps:

Contrary to popular belief, wiretaps seldom cause any change in sound quality or service. Deteriorating service almost always means a poor connection, almost never an improperly-installed wiretap. However, it certainly doesn't hurt to wiretap your own telephone to see how much (or how little) additional noise is on the line. Some other techniques that might aid you in finding some types of telephone bugs and taps include:

✓ *Take your phone apart.* You are looking for additional parts, extra wires and especially anything encased in black epoxy. If you find anything suspicious, replace the telephone and restrict access to your office to only the most trusted personnel. This search is much more likely to unearth a telephone bug--a device that transmits spoken conversation from the room in which the telephone is located--than an actual tap. Of course, most of the time you'll find nothing at all suspicious.

✓ *Take the telephone jack apart.* Check the terminal jack for the same components; extra parts, extra wires or anything encased in black epoxy.

✓ *Keep telephone closets locked and check them periodically.* Go into the telephone closet itself and check the "block" in which your telephone lines are installed for any extra wires. "Alligator clips" on the block are a dead giveaway.

Many devices are sold to electronically analyze phone lines to detect taps or to defeat them once they are installed. Unfortunately, most of this equipment is worthless.

✓ *Inexpensive tap detectors.* You should avoid these devices, which generally cost $50-$200. Not only are they generally unreliable, but they could show that your line is clean when it is actually tapped, giving you a false sense of security. Others will provide positive signals in response to a call-waiting signal or the presence of another extension on the line, even if it is not picked up.

✓ *Phone analyzers*. These devices can run a number of checks, including inspecting the line for hot (actively transmitting) microphones and voltage-activated recording devices, among other tests. However, they will not pick up voice-activated recorders, nor can they be used to test electronic phones for the presence of simple bugs. In fact, it's possible to destroy a modern electronic phone system--one with features such as call waiting, paging, and voice mailbox capability--by improper use of a telephone analyzer.

✓ *Secure phones*. Prices for these phones range from $500 to $4,000. Two kinds are widely sold; both can be easily defeated.

One type uses a "voltage adjustment system" to prevent the line voltage from changing when a phone is removed from its cradle. This in turn prevents voltage-activated tape recorders from activating. However, since taps can also be triggered by *sound*, a voice-activated tape recorder can easily defeat a secure phone that relies on a voltage adjustment system. Remember that you can purchase such a recorder for less than $100 from an electronics hobby shop.

The other type of secure phone, the so-called "white noise" phone, is even less effective. Phone lines themselves eliminate white noise from the line over a distance. Your secure phone could be defeated before the signal even reaches the tap, and certainly by the time it travels more than a few hundred yards.

✓ *Scramblers*. Scrambling converts ordinary speech into unintelligible speech by dividing the speech spectrum into chunks, and then inverting frequencies, or rearranging the speech fragments in time. Signals produced by simpler scramblers can be reconstructed into recognizable speech by someone with enough time and patience to analyze what process was used and to reverse it. You can even build a device with $5 or $10 worth of parts that would do it automatically. Some of the better systems provide a reasonable degree of security to casual eavesdropping.

The primary disadvantage of scramblers is that both parties to a conversation must have one, and the two systems must be compatible. (The Cycomm cellular security system I've already described is one of the few exceptions to this rule, at least with cellular systems that are Cycomm-compatible.) This makes using a scrambler impractical unless the scrambled phone is used to call only a few numbers, although they can be deactivated to communicate with an ordinary phone. Also consider that use of a scrambler is hardly a low-profile strategy. You are announcing to anyone that might be listening in that you have something to hide.

✓ *Digital encryption devices*. Encryption requires ordinary speech to be converted into digital signals. You add or subtract electrical information to this signal to encrypt it. The resulting signal defies breaking by anyone except by those with unbelievably powerful computers and almost unlimited amounts of time. It should also defeat any form of voice recognition, which is being used increasingly for wiretaps.

The only way a digitally encrypted signal could potentially be deciphered is by the National Security Agency. It owns billions of dollars worth of state-of-the-art computer equipment, and its assignment is to intercept and decode electronic communications. Many counter-surveillance experts believe that NSA has a "back door" into almost every domestic commercial encryption system, and most others as well. In order to get the government's authorization to sell encryption equipment, a company must first give the technology away to the government. The NSA suppresses the technologies it can't penetrate, as books such as *The Puzzle Palace* document.

Digital encryption devices suffer from the same drawbacks as scramblers in that both sides of the conversation must use one. They are available for prices starting around $1,000.

✓ *Telephone voice changers.* Both digital and analog models are available. I have no data on the effectiveness of either type, but I would presume the more expensive digital models would once again be more effective in defeating voiceprint wiretaps. Digital voice changers are considerably less expensive than digital voice scramblers. One company offering such a device is Executive Protection Products of Napa, California. The company claims that "voice prints and voice stress analyzers generally aren't effective against it."

Room Bugs:

Before you start looking for room bugs on your own, familiarize yourself with the appearance of the most common bugs. Visit a local electronics hobby store and ask to look at their wireless microphones. Look these items over carefully to become familiar with their appearance. Ask the sales representative to show you what would be required in order to transmit radio signals from the microphone to a tape recorder. (If the salesperson asks why you're interested in such components, you can always say that you're a musician interested in recording his work.)

Now that you know what you're looking for, begin with a thorough visual search in each room you suspect to be bugged. The most important item to check is the telephone. A bugged telephone (one that transmits conversation in a room, not telephone conversations) is by far the most common communications compromise. So begin your search here. Unplug the phone every time you have a sensitive conversation. Replace it if you can.

Check any recent additions to the room; a potted plant, a new picture on the wall, etc. Also examine draperies, books, lamp bases, wastebaskets, the undersides of desks and chairs, etc. With electrical power off, disassemble light fixtures, light switches and electrical outlets. Look for mismatched paint on walls, ceilings and floors that might disguise a tube microphone. A spike mike embedded in a wall often can be detected by small cracks in the wall.

The best defense against bugs is to avoid sensitive conversation in locations where they might be located, or to disassemble or disable any components that might form a bugging system. The most common: a speakerphone that can be remotely activated, or an office intercom.

Another countermeasure is to add irrelevant information to the vocal spectrum that is being recorded directly or reconstructed from vibration analysis. A "white noise" generator (often used by individuals who have difficulty sleeping in a noisy environment) is somewhat effective in masking conversation, although the interference may be filtered out by the appropriate equipment. The only type of noise generator that is really effective is one that produces sound in the human voice spectrum. These are quite expensive.

Unfortunately, the equipment sold to detect room bugs isn't much more reliable than that used to detect telephone taps. Most of it is totally worthless.

✓ *Audio feedback devices* ("squealers"). The squealer puts out an audio tone which is heard as feedback in the presence of a bug. Unfortunately, these devices are not effective; they cannot detect a simple Radio Shack wireless transmitter.

✓ *Desktop bug detectors.* These are often packaged in a box that resembles a pen and pencil desk set. As with audio feedback devices, desk-top bug detectors cannot detect simple wireless transmitters.

✓ *Spectrum analyzers.* These devices, which cost several thousand dollars, are quite useful in detecting actively-transmitting RF bugs. They may even detect the electronic signature of a bug awaiting a signal to begin transmitting. However, they require extensive training to use competently. You may find a shop willing to rent one to you, but it is highly unlikely you will be able to learn to use it in a 10-minute "get-acquainted" session. The spectrum analyzer is the least expensive device that can reliably detect a low-power wireless transmitter.

✓ *Non-linear junction detectors (NLJDs).* These are the most expensive bug detectors of all. NLJDs cost $10,000 and up, and generate a microwave signal that is said to indicate the presence of bugs and their location--even those that are turned off. Unfortunately, non-linear junctions are a common feature of many types of electronic and non-electronic equipment--not just bugs. For instance, both nails and cardiac pacemakers contain non-linear junctions. However, NLJDs are occasionally useful for detecting bugs that aren't actively transmitting. Otherwise, they are extremely effective at generating false alarms.

Should you be concerned about being targeted by a laser window vibration reader, a device costing more than $1,000 is available to sit in the vicinity of the window you suspect to be targeted and emit tones in ultrasonic frequencies. This machine is designed to make the windows vibrate continuously at a rapid rate, confusing the laser device.

I don't recommend the device, because laser vibration analysis is a very remote threat. But if you want to make certain your conversations are safe, a "low-tech" substitute for the $1,000 machine is also available: a $2 dog whistle which is equally effective at vibrating windows. Of course, to provide protection during the course of a conversation, one person must whistle while the other talks.

Even if your home, vehicle and office are fully secure, other locations you visit may not be. Bugs have been found in hotel rooms, rental cars and even in returned dry cleaning! There's also always a chance that the office or home of a person with whom you are conversing is bugged. You might want to avoid staying in the same room of a hotel every time you visit it. If security at an office you are visiting is obviously lax, you might ask that your meeting be held at another location.

Chapter Four

THE PRIVATE CONSUMER

As every man goes through life he fills in a number of forms for the record, each containing a number of questions. There are thus hundreds of little threads radiating from every man, millions of threads in all. If these threads were suddenly to become visible, the whole sky would look like a spider's web, and if the threads materialized as rubber bands--buses, trams and even people would all lose the ability to move, and the wind would be unable to carry torn-up newspapers or autumn leaves along the streets of the city.

They are not visible, they are not material, but every man is constantly aware of their existence. Every man, permanently aware of his own invisible threads, naturally develops a respect for the people who manipulate the threads.

-- Alexander Solzhenitsyn, Cancer Ward

In everyday life, you not only leave paper threads in the forms you fill out, but electronic ones in your patterns of consumption. These threads may be woven into a rich mosaic that reveals a great deal more than mere consumer preferences.

Bloc Modeling

Information for this mosaic comes from many sources. For instance, purchases made on a credit card are classified in enormous detail to make available computerized "profiles" for sale to marketing organizations. The *New York Times* of March 18, 1984 reports:

> Shoppers who think they are only vague entries in some company's list might lose that anonymity if they hold MasterCard or Visa credit cards. A new service from Citicorp Credit Services will provide businesses that accept MasterCard and Visa credit cards with a detailed profile of their customers. The data will come close to pinpointing the bank card shopper's income, education, family, housing type and value, age, vocation, even "lifestyle."
>
> Alan Newman, vice president and marketing director for Citicorp Credit Services, said that up until now, businesses that subscribed to bank cards have only been able to get generalized demographic profiles of those who use the cards. But an arrangement with Donnelley Marketing Information Services will allow Citicorp to combine Donnelley demographic data with Citicorp's own cardholder data, he says, "even to the very block of a community."

The activity the *Times* described is known today as "bloc modeling." Such analysis is designed to determine how an individual fits into an organization or group. Bloc modeling is used by private companies, employers and government agencies to classify individuals, groups or entire organizations into categories useful for marketing or other analysis.

Private companies use bloc modeling to pinpoint consumer tastes. They call it "target marketing," and employ it to remain profitable in the face of rapidly-increasing advertising costs and to better understand the buying preferences of their customers. The government uses bloc modeling for many purposes; from cracking down on welfare fraud to determining if your lifestyle fits your declared income. In the workplace, bloc modeling can construct a public image from information you disclose on your employment application, your remarks at meetings, the memos you prepare, even who you take out for dinner after work.

If you're wondering how Citicorp gets its data, the answer is simple. You provide it every time you use your credit card. Buying with a credit card is a public, not a private, act. Each purchase leaves a thread. With enough purchases, a remarkably accurate portrait of your lifestyle, income, education, home and family can be constructed.

For instance, I recently received an unsolicited invitation to apply for a "MBNA America" gold card. One of the selling features was MBNA's "gold card year-end summary of charges." This summary would list every single purchase charged to my account, and also divide each purchase into one of ten categories--dining, hotel expenses, car rental, airfare, medical, automotive, retail shopping, specialty stores, cash advances, and miscellaneous.

If you don't believe similar information is already being transmitted to direct marketing companies about *your* credit card use, you're dreaming! For instance, the American Express company for more than a decade has sold information on the purchasing patterns of its 20 million credit-card customers to direct marketing agencies. It recently spent more than $10 million to upgrade its tracking capability. Citicorp has announced plans to market similar information on its 21 million credit-card holders, although it claims only limited data will be released, and only under heavy restrictions. However, there are no laws prohibiting broader disclosures.[25]

If you own credit cards, you've probably given the issuers unlimited discretion to distribute information about your purchases to any third party. The agreement for a VISA card I use states: "We can furnish information concerning your account or credit file to consumer reporting agencies, our affiliates, and others who may properly receive that information."

Other valuable data for the bloc modeler include supermarket receipts, if you pay for your purchases with a personal check or a credit card. A scanner automatically reads and files each purchase into a central computer for later, more leisurely analysis. So-called "shopper's cards" are now offered by some supermarkets that provide an electronic rebate on your purchases.

Records of your purchases are then released to manufacturers who can then overwhelm you with sales pitches. (There is evidence, however, that shoppers are resisting these cards. The largest effort to date to promote shopper's cards, Citicorp's "Reward America" program, was canceled in 1990 after losing nearly $180 million.)

Your reading habits can also be analyzed. Waldenbooks, one of the largest discount bookstore chains, offers regular customers a "preferred reader" card. For a $5 annual fee, card-carrying readers obtain a 10 percent discount on all their purchases. The brochure extolling the benefits of obtaining the

---

[25]One of the earliest discussions of bloc modeling in a consumer publication was "Public Images," published in the January, 1985 *Whole Earth Review*. (27 Gate Five Road, Sausalito, Calif. 94965)

card, however, doesn't describe what Waldenbooks does with the data it obtains from its customers who use the card.

Do you like mysteries? History? Business? Or are your reading tastes more esoteric? Direct marketing companies would be very interested in knowing! A clerk at the Waldenbooks store where I picked up the application insisted the data would *never* be sold to a third party. But since this data is extremely valuable to direct marketing companies, Waldenbooks would be forgoing potential profits if it were not sell the information it collects, or at least use it for internal marketing purposes.

Who else manipulates the threads about which Solzhenitsyn writes so eloquently?

Dataman Information Services compiles real estate and mortgage information in 48 states and sells it to companies ranging from Neiman-Marcus to Citicorp. For an additional fee, Dataman will make your phone number available. And since Dataman is a subsidiary of Metromail, a direct-marketing company, a customer can evaluate the type of direct marketing offers to which you respond or even pre-qualify you for specific offers.

Zip-code-based marketing services, such as PRIZM, combine census data with state and local government records to divide the country into 250,000 neighborhoods of about 250 households each. Each neighborhood is analyzed according to its income, consumption patterns, etc. and broken into 40 or so socioeconomic groups. PRIZM then combines this data with information from other databases to pinpoint your tastes.

If PRIZM identifies you as a "high-tech frontier" personality, it can demonstrate to prospective clients that, based on its profile, you are five times more likely to purchase a Japanese-made car as someone outside that group. The nine-digit zip code location of your home may mean you are included in another marketing bloc. If that location is in an affluent neighborhood, it may mean you are deluged with offers for credit. If it indicates a poor neighborhood, you may be denied credit, no matter what your payment record shows. Such "red-lining" practices are illegal, but still widespread.

If you have a published phone number, the Reuben H. Donnelley Company knows it. Each year, Donnelley matches every published phone number in the United States with names and addresses. Combining this data with information from motor-vehicle registration files, census data and credit bureau records, Donnelley can guess your income, your political affiliation and your "special interests." The company is also the leading publisher of reverse telephone directories, through its Hill-Donnelley affiliate.

Almost any bona-fide marketing organization can rent the profiles compiled by Dataman, Donnelley, and similar organizations. For instance, the World Jewish Congress recently wanted to learn more about the 100,000 people on its donor list. It hired an Atlanta consulting firm to match its names against a list of wealthy people culled from credit and other records. It found 250 "multi-millionaires" and another 2,500 "millionaires." The WJC then concentrated its marketing efforts on this most affluent portion of its list.

The government can gain access to this information as well. Federal agencies use such information to update more than 85 national databases that contain some 300 million records on 120 million people. Agencies use this information for a variety of purposes: from cracking down on welfare fraud to determining if a taxpayer's lifestyle fits his declared income.

In 1992, Metromail, R.L. Polk, and Donnelley Marketing, three of the largest mailing list brokers in the country, refused to rent compiled mailing lists (lists assembled from public records) to the FBI. The FBI threatened to subpoena the lists if the brokers don't comply. However, several of these company's competitors expressed their willingness to provide this information voluntarily.

To make this information even more accessible, it is now available to anyone equipped with a personal computer and a "modem." A modem is a device that permits the user to communicate with another computer over a phone line. This setup allows you to "log on" to services such as Compuserve, and gain inexpensive access to census data.

For $10 per search, Compuserve's "Neighborhood Reports" service can give you a detailed demographic report for any zip code in the United States. The "demographic report" categorizes zip code inhabitants by age groups, racial characteristics, household income, home values, etc. The "civic/public activity" report shows how likely a person in the neighborhood is to participate in political, religious, or fraternal groups. And the "gift idea report" describes how inhabitants might react to any of 24 household gifts.

While Compuserve's demographic services do not identify individual consumers, a plan announced by Lotus Development Corp. in 1990, called "Marketplace," would have. The database would have contained shopping habits and personal data on 120 million Americans. Its most basic version was to be priced at $495 and could be used on personal computers. Within weeks of announcing the product's release, Lotus received over 30,000 requests from individuals asking that their names be deleted from the database. Astonished by this firestorm of protest, Lotus canceled the project.

While Marketplace was canceled, several alternatives are available. Some are accessible to anyone. For instance, Compuserve's "Phone File" is advertised as "a fast, efficient and convenient national phone directory that includes name, home address, telephone number and length of residence for nearly 80 million U.S. households." And of course, once you've got the zip code, all you need to do is go to "Neighborhood Reports" for more information.

An emerging source of information for Donnelley and other information providers may be the burgeoning "videotext" services, such as Compuserve and the Prodigy joint venture between IBM and Sears. With a videotext service, personal computer users can order airline tickets, buy groceries, even invest in stocks--all electronically.

Videotext service providers are not prohibited from reselling information about their subscribers or compiling data on the types of services they use. Prodigy obviously tracks this data, because after you use particular services, the system offers special promotions for the same or similar services. While Prodigy claims it does not sell the data, the company is not prohibited by law from doing so.

Another source of information are mail order purchases. Most mail order companies carefully analyze the type and frequency of customer orders. Some even prepare customized mailings reflecting their customer's interests. American Express is a leader in this technique. It can break down a customer's spending down by time, place and type, designing almost individually-tailored offerings to which its data show particular customers will be receptive.

The future of bloc modeling promises even greater scrutiny over our purchasing habits and consumer preferences. Some of the latest bloc modeling techniques use one of the oldest consumer research techniques of all: the customer survey. When you complete a customer survey, you should realize how the data will be used.

Your answers on a warranty card questionnaire or offer for discounted merchandise or service will be used to update the company's customer database. And like other information, it may be sold to direct marketers. Generally, I complete only customer surveys that offer me some tangible benefit--and then only with my name and post office box number. I mark any questions relating to age, income, etc. "N/A."

For pure intrusiveness, there are few customer surveys to equal that which came with the "Dick Tracy Radio Watch" marketed through Cap'n Crunch cereal in 1990. Buyers were asked their opinion of the following statements:

✓ Mandatory drug testing violates civil rights

✓ Citizens should have the right to own a firearm

✓ School prayer should be permitted

Along with these questions were the usual requests for income level, number of credit cards used, etc.--presumably to help Quaker Oats market Cap'n Crunch and other products more effectively.

Investment companies use similar techniques. The Investment Company Institute recently sent me a nine-page questionnaire that asked me to disclose my age, income, investments, and a great deal of other information. It requested the information so "it could help identify the range of services provided by fund companies and indicate how well services are performed." A cover letter stated that the survey was completely anonymous, and that my name would not be associated with the resulting statistical data in any way.

I have no evidence that the Investment Company Institute was misrepresenting how it planned to use the information. Only that the *potential* for abuse exists when you disclose a large volume of personal financial information and send it on its way for computerized analysis.

One of the latest applications of what direct marketing companies call "database marketing" is a combination strategy of providing low-cost or no-cost products or services to consumers in exchange for information. A typical application of advanced database marketing is the S.A.V.E. program conducted by Chicago's GRI Corp. Here's how the July 1991 issue of *Direct Marketing* describes the effort:[26]

> S.A.V.E. is a membership organization that sends its members sample packages of products at a low cost. The packages are designed to cater to the needs of individual families. Consumer profiles are developed by questionnaire for individual households.
>
> For every household that responds, S.A.V.E. will know which charge cards the household has, whether it has purchased items by mail in the past six months or a year, whether the respondent is married, the age group of the respondent, the number of children in the household, their ages and the sex of the children between 12 and 19 (very useful for targeting cosmetic, personal hygiene and audio/visual promotions).
>
> S.A.V.E. will also know what pets you have, whether you own a drip coffeemaker, garbage disposal, microwave oven, clothes dryer or VCR, if you have a telephone and your number, whether you drink Kool-Aid, whether you are likely to use famous name cosmetics, your preferences, by brand, of paper towels, coffee and type of cereal, which dishwashing products you use, and more.

---

[26]*Direct Marketing* (Hoke Communications, 224 Seventh St., Garden City, N.Y. 11530-5771)

In short, S.A.V.E. knows more about the consumer habits of respondents than do many of the spouses, children and parents of those respondents.

Another direct marketing innovation comes from utility companies. "Intelligent" electric and gas meters now being tested send information on energy use back to the utility automatically, eliminating a major expense--the meter reader. One utility, California's Pacific Gas & Electric Co., has a pilot program that links individual appliances to the electric meter. Eventually, the meter could monitor conservation efforts or even switch off appliances at times of peak demand. Carl Weinburg, a research analyst at the utility, appreciates the implications of the new technology. "We're going to know every time someone in the house turns on a toaster or an egg beater. Market-research guys would love that information. We have to be very careful or we'll look like Big Brother."

Law enforcement agencies also want access to this information, and efforts such as PG&E's could give it too them instantly. Several court decisions have upheld the right of police to scan utility bills for higher-than-normal use. Then the police obtain search warrants based on this "evidence." For instance, many indoor marijuana growers use large amounts of electricity.

The best way to avoid leaving more "threads" than you'd really like is to pay cash for any purchases you'd prefer to keep private, avoiding customer surveys, and minimizing credit card use. If you don't want your energy use monitored, you could always produce your own power, but this entails more sacrifice than most Americans are willing to take. Going off utility-produced power may also make authorities believe that you have something to hide, thus raising your profile.

Another way to lower your consumer profile is to write to the companies or banks that have issued you credit cards and request that information about your purchases not be released. Finally, you can contact national credit bureaus (addresses are listed in the "List of Suppliers" section) and ask that your name be taken off the lists they screen for offers submitted by direct marketing companies.

The only real losers are those who would manipulate the threads.

Privacy and Your Credit Records

Deprivacy

Although we feel unknown, ignored
As unrecorded blanks,
Take heart! Our vital selves are stored
In giant data banks,
Our childhoods and maturities
Efficiently compiled
Our stocks and insecurities
All permanently filed.
Our tastes and our proclivities
In gross and in particular
Our incomes, our activities
Both extra- and curricular
And such will be our happy state
Until the day we die
When we'll be snatched up by the great
Computer in the sky

-- Felicia Lamport (Look Magazine)

In 1985, a Newsweek reporter, who had written an article about teen-age computer "hackers" suddenly found himself with six-digit charge card bills. The young geniuses cracked the TRW credit bureau's security system, brought up the reporter's file and posted his card numbers on electronic bulletin boards around the country. Your numbers are there for the taking, too.

Today's credit system is a natural outgrowth of our increased mobility and the growth of computerization. In most communities, the credit bureau was started by local merchants so that individual stores would not be forced to independently evaluate applicants for charge cards. As Americans became more mobile, credit bureaus began to affiliate and exchange information with each other.

Credit bureau files list your name and address, your age, your Social Security number, your employer and the length of time you have worked in your position, your salary, the name of your spouse and your children, and information about your mortgage, outstanding loans and credit card balance.

In addition, credit bureaus may maintain records of judgments against you (taken from court records), state and federal tax liens, information on repossessions, bankruptcies, and lawsuits. All this data is available at the touch of a button and is keyed to your name and/or your Social Security number. Dennis Benner, a vice-president of TRW, boasts: "We buy all the data we can legally buy."

Today, three credit bureaus dominate nationally: TRW, CBI/Equifax, and Trans Union Credit Information Co. These companies and hundreds of smaller credit bureaus operating locally or regionally exchange information with one another and provide an instant and continuously updated record on the credit records of more than 160 million Americans.

At one time, the information in credit files was considered confidential. TRW, for instance, for decades acknowledged this in a code of ethics that was quietly discontinued a few years ago. "Credit information," the now-discarded code mandated, "shall be treated by TRW Credit Services and its subscribers as confidential. Names shall not be compiled for sale."

This philosophy ended once it became apparent that there were immense profits to be made in credit reporting. The Fair Credit Reporting Act of 1970 (15 USC 1681) was the key legislation permitting credit bureaus to aggressively market their services. The act permits anyone with a "legitimate business purpose" to purchase credit records. This language presents an extraordinarily broad authorization for disclosure of personal information.

Credit bureaus sell many types of data. For instance, they combine the information in their credit report with the bloc modeling profiles developed by companies such as Citicorp. This data can be invaluable to direct marketers in deciding whether or not you will be offered a particular product or service, sent an unsolicited offer of credit, etc.

In addition, credit bureau "consumer profiles," are marketed as credit risk evaluation services--once again, without your knowledge or consent. A typical offering is TRW's "Gold Report," a mathematical model that calculates the probability of an applicant for credit falling behind on payments or declaring bankruptcy. Employers, banks, landlords and many other creditors routinely use these services to investigate prospective employees, customers, or tenants.

However, these practices are coming under concerted attack from government regulators. In February 1992, the Federal Trade Commission ruled that such "risk profiles" must be released to consumers who request information from their credit files. In December 1992, the FTC ordered TRW to stop using credit information to develop target marketing mailing lists. (However, the company may continue to extract other personal information, including your Social Security number, in assembling such lists. It just can't use credit data.)

Equifax voluntarily took this step in 1991. The third major credit bureau, Trans Union, is challenging the FTC's target marketing decision.

Other companies don't just manipulate the Fair Credit Reporting Act for their own use, but violate it with virtual impunity. In 1991, the Office of the Inspector General, the investigative arm of the U.S. Department of Health and Human Services, began an investigation of unauthorized access to the Social Security Administration's (SSA) payroll records. What appeared at first to be the activities of a single law-breaking employee turned into a nationwide network for purloined data--not just from SSA but from the FBI's National Crime Information Center's (NCIC) computers.

Social Security payroll records are obtainable for as little as $20, according to the indictment, and sell for as much as $350. Criminal records from NCIC cost even less--about $10 each. According to a regional inspector general for the Social Security Administration, drug dealers were using the service to determine if their customers could pay for the narcotics they had ordered--and to verify their source of income. (Incredibly, the official who was allegedly bribed was not indicted.)

To date, more than 20 individuals in 12 states, including three current or former employees of the Social Security Administration, have been indicted for allegedly participating in this or similar schemes. The government is seeking racketeering convictions against these companies for trafficking in stolen data.

New York Senator Daniel Patrick Moynihan said that the "investigation appears to involve the largest theft ever from government computer files and may very involve the single largest threat to privacy in modern times."[27]

In the wake of this incident, SSA beefed up its security to create an audit trail for each computer access. However, the FBI made no major changes in NCIC. The agency justified its position by reasoning that NCIC existed to exchange data between the FBI and state and local police agencies. Beefing up security too greatly would defeat the original purpose for the system's creation, it concluded.

Authorities in the "information underground" say that the indictments reveal only the tip of the iceberg in illegal credit reporting. Profit margins are too great, and security too lax, for it not to continue. According to "John Branch," a composite character created by author Jeffrey Rothfedder in his book *Privacy for Sale*:[28]

> The biggest surprise is that this so-called private data is available through
> dozens of arteries, not just one. So you can never block access to it.
> Shut one channel down, ten others open up.

Branch is right. In February 1993 I received a mailing from "Intelligence, Inc.," an information reseller (and vendor of electronic surveillance equipment) in California. While this company claims that its search requests "must comply with credit search laws," it also says that it searches "special databases the others don't." The menu of applications for data search is staggeringly large. *Anyone* can run searches in the following categories, although not all search categories are available in every state:

---

[27]The most complete account of the investigation leading to these arrests that I've yet found is, "Data Bank Cowboys: We Told You So," a presentation by a regional inspector general for the Department of Health and Human Services. For more information, contact the American Society for Industrial Security, 1655 N. Fort Myers Drive, Arlington, Va. 22209.

[28]Jeffrey Rothfedder, *Privacy for Sale* (New York: Simon & Schuster, 1992)

1. I²'s FIRSTSEARCH will find *ANYONE* who can be found--fax (or mail) us the full name and last know address of the SOB (or maybe ex-girl friend) and we will run through **1 BILLION** records to return the latest address and usually a SSN. (Search fees are non-refundable but we hit 90%). We route this search through U.S. Datalink or CDB and Metronet. **FIRSTSEARCH** uses credit header information, postal forwarding data, phone books, criss-cross directories, and magazine subscription/warranty cards for the best "find" rate available ($35).

2. **Background Search**. Same as above but includes a list of neighbors, DOB, other household members, AKA's, usually a phone number, past addresses, other data. This search works best if we have a valid SSN. If you need the SSN run **FIRSTSEARCH** first ($45). For a small additional charge we will run the subject through several hundred newspapers and magazines. **MEDIA FIRSTSEARCH** is great if he has done anything newsworthy, made a police blotter, gotten married, taking out a business license, etc ($75).

3. **Surname by State**. Provide a last name (first if you have one) and we'll run out every person with that name in any state ($25).

4. **National Surname** for entire U.S. both searches sometimes produce phone numbers ($75).

5. **Phone Numbers to Address**. Listed numbers only ($25).

6. **Address to Phone Number**. Usually only listed but sometimes we get lucky ($25).

7. **Address Verifier**. Current resident and change of address if on file. Verifies if the subject is still there ($25).

8. **Neighbor Search**. Give us a name and address, we'll get you 10 nearbys, sometimes length of residence. Excellent for "social engineering" whereabouts and phone numbers ($25).

9. **P.O. Box Owner**. Need name and P.O. box number, get back home address on file with Post Office ($75).

10. **Public Filings**. Need a name and state, will show municipal, civil, and small claims court, bankruptcy, defaults, foreclosures, and liens ($35).

11. **Property Search**. Real property by name and state ($85).

12. **Real Property**. By county ($99).

13. **Marriage by State**. ($25)

14. **Divorce by County**. ($25)

15. **Consumer Credit Report U.S.** MUST comply with credit search laws! ($30)

16. **Bank Asset.** Need name and SSN ($150).

17. **Death Records U.S.** ($25).

18. **Criminal Court Filings** by state ($35).

19. **Criminal Convictions** by county.

20. **Employment Search U.S.** ($120)

21. **Federal Tax Liens** (varies).

22. **Federal Court Records--Criminal** ($35)

23. **Federal Court Records Civil** ($35)

24. **Driver's License** in all available states. Need name address, DOB, you get driver's license number, address, and in some states a SSN ($35).

25. **National Driver's License search** (varies).

26. **DMV Records.** Driving record from name.

27. **Driving record by state** from name and driver ID number ($35).

28. **Autos Owned** (alpha search). You must provide name and address where vehicle is registered, get back other vehicles owned, legal owner, makes, models, and serial numbers ($35).

29. **Tag Search.** License plate or VIN number to owner ($30).

30. **College Degree** and attendance and verification ($35).

31. **Business Credit** report on most businesses, public or private ($75).

32. **Business Intelligence Report.** Lists owners, media reports, insider information ($75-$100).

To put it mildly, the average American has no idea that his public image casts such a large shadow!

Moreover, the best-connected information brokers are protected from prosecution, and actually receive protection from the government for their activities. You'll no doubt find the following excerpt from *Privacy for Sale* highly enlightening:

> According to very deep sources and internal court documents, in 1988 a veteran high-level secret-information seller--a consummate pro so mysterious that most other information resellers don't even know him; they just call him Jim--created an uncharacteristic blunder. He approached a clerk working for the IRS and offered to pay him top dollar for someone's tax records. The clerk took the money from Jim, and

immediately informed his superiors of the dirty dealings. Jim was arrested for attempting to blackmail a federal employee and conspiring to traffic in illegal information.

But Jim had a trump card up his sleeve. It turned out he had a roster of clients that included some of the mightiest in Hollywood and the intelligence establishment. Jim threatened to use the trial as a showcase to disabuse the public of the naive notion that the authorities are vigilantly guarding our privacy.

By early 1989, federal prosecutors were anxiously pushing for a deal with Jim. And what was eventually agreed upon was remarkably cushy. For 12 months Jim could not violate any law. Secondly, according to settlement papers, "For a period of six months, Jim had to provide full and complete cooperation with the IRS and the FBI with respect to any unauthorized disclosure of, and/or access to, taxpayer information or confidential investigative files of those or other federal agencies." Meaning, in simpler terms, that Jim had to rat on others.

To Jim, it was a deal made in heaven. The feds were not shutting down his business. At the same time, he was given carte blanche to put his competitors effectively out of commission by notifying the authorities of their underhanded hawking of contraband information.

Given the type of information your credit files contain, and the wide access information resellers have to it, it behooves you to make certain this data is accurate. Unfortunately, credit bureau files often contain outdated information. In fact, a recent survey by Consumers Union found that 48 percent of credit bureau files were inaccurate, with one in five containing serious errors or omissions.

I do not know of a single person (including myself) who has found 100 percent-accurate information in their credit files. Your file may show you as having been fired from a position when you actually resigned or as owning credit cards for which you never applied. It might say that you were once jailed when you were never were. The credit bureau may confuse you with someone with a similar name or Social Security number. If that person has a bad credit rating, your chances of obtaining credit--not to mention gainful employment--will suffer.

Credit bureau files are skewed to record negative information. For instance, TRW permits only large (over 4,000 accounts) businesses to report individuals paying their accounts on time. Smaller businesses are permitted only to report negative information about their customers. Your good credit and business relationships with local merchants is deemed meaningless.

Moreover, the more negative information a credit report has, the more valuable it becomes. According to Ralph Spargin, the top credit executive at The Limited clothing store chain, "A credit bureau that invests in keeping errors down only makes its reports skimpier and thus less attractive to credit report buyers."

In a worst-case scenario, you may become the victim of deliberate fraud at the hands of a "credit-repair" scam. Legitimate credit repair businesses help their clients learn to budget their money and begin paying back creditors to improve their credit ratings. They also will challenge erroneous disclosures on credit reports. You can take these steps on your own to improve a poor credit rating.

Credit repair scams, on the other hand, create an entirely new identity for their clients by assigning them a fake Social Security number paired with a clean credit record. Since Social Security numbers and credit files are easily accessible, obtaining the information is simple. This fake number is used to receive fresh credit, loans, etc.

While this practice is illegal, it is far from uncommon. If you are turned down unexpectedly for credit, and your credit record contains information about loans you have never taken out, credit cards you have never owned, etc., you may be the victim of such a scam.[29]

It is difficult to recover from such victimization unless you obtain a new Social Security number. Unfortunately, these are not easy to obtain; you may have to go to court to convince the Social Security Administration to issue a new number.

You have the right to inspect your credit records, according to the Fair Credit Reporting Act of 1970. If you have been turned down for credit in the last 30 days, the credit bureau that issued the report on which the negative decision was based must show you your credit report at no charge. Otherwise, you will be asked to pay a nominal fee (usually $5-$15) to obtain a copy of it. TRW has agreed to give consumers one copy of their credit report free each year.

If the information contained in your credit file is incorrect, you have the right to contest it. The credit bureau must investigate your claims promptly. If it cannot verify information which you contest, the data must be eliminated. However, you need to re-check your file a few months later to make certain the erroneous data hasn't been re-inserted. Companies providing data to credit bureaus may not always update their files, even if the credit bureau has done so.

If the credit bureau refuses to correct its records, you have the right to insert a statement into your file explaining your side of the issue. The statement can be up to 100 words in length for each item with which you disagree. At least this is how the system works in theory. In practice, it is not always easy to obtain a copy of your credit report. I recently applied for a credit card, but was turned down. When I called the credit analyst for the company, she told me that credit had been denied on the basis of a five-year old delinquency that showed I owed $38.

I telephoned Equifax, the credit bureau that had issued the negative report, to request a copy of my credit report. After holding the line for nearly 30 minutes, I was given an opportunity to leave a recorded message describing my problem. The recording giving me instructions assured me that I would have a copy of my credit report within a week.

A month later, I still had not received the credit report. Rather than go through the same system again, I contacted the main switchboard and requested that a supervisor call me back. I was placed into the same queue in which I had waited 30 minutes the previous month.

Next, I contacted the credit card company analyst who had turned me down in the first place. Yes, she had my credit report in front of her. Yes, she could see it was who I owed the money to. But "for my protection," she was not permitted to tell me who it was. I would have to obtain that information from the credit bureau. However, she also informed me that she no longer believed the $38 was a significant enough factor to deny credit to me on that basis alone. Three days later, I received my credit card. But I still had not received my credit report.

---

[29]One guide to *legitimately* repairing a damaged credit record is my special report *The Credit Con Game*, available for $29 from LPP's Nevada office.

I still wanted the report, so I could find out to whom I owed $38. After calling Equifax a third time, the receptionist promised to have a supervisor contact me. She did, and I finally received the credit report. Examining it, the $38 delinquency was nowhere to be seen. However, the report showed me working for a company that had declared bankruptcy nearly a decade earlier, and also listed me as owning several credit cards that I had canceled.

Two years later, when I applied for credit again, the $38 delinquency was back on the report. This time, however, I finally learned who had placed it on my record. It turned out the entire problem was caused by a single bill not being forwarded by the Post Office to a new address.

One program worth investigating if you need to obtain your credit file frequently is TRW's "Credentials Service." It permits you to ask for your credit report as many times as you need it. The company will also send a revised credit report at your request to any merchant you specify. It will also inform you when it issues a credit report. TRW will give you the opportunity to update your credit report when you apply and anytime thereafter simply by filling out a form.

A word of caution: The 24-page survey that TRW requests you to complete before sending your credit report asks for a great deal of information that you may wish to keep confidential. You are not required to complete the entire form in order to receive your credit report, despite instructions to the contrary. It's a good idea to list only your name, address and Social Security number on this application. Once you receive your report, you can ask TRW to add additional information that is beneficial to your credit standing.

Nor should you give TRW any of your credit card numbers (although this information would presumably be in your credit files). When I did so, TRW used one of the card numbers I had submitted to automatically renew my Credentials subscription when it expired, without my permission.

Other companies may examine your credit records if you have assigned them that right. American Express, for instance, routinely reviews its customers' credit files (and even their bank account balances!) to determine if they have enough money to pay their credit card bills. This is part of the cardholder agreement the customer signs, which authorizes the company to conduct "additional credit checks" any time it wishes.

My VISA card agreement authorizes the bank to at any time "make credit, employment, and investigative inquiries as we deem appropriate for the extension of credit or collection of amounts owing on the account."

For years, credit bureaus have come under concerted attack from consumer groups, and more recently, from state attorneys general. After a Wyoming court awarded $290,000 in 1991 to a consumer who claimed that TRW deliberately posted erroneous data to his credit report, 19 states sued the company over its credit practices.

The problem affecting the largest number of consumers occurred in the summer of 1991, when TRW's computers identified 1,400 residents of Norwich, Connecticut as not having paid their property taxes. It turned out a company compiling local tax records for TRW had confused the list of *taxpayers* with *tax delinquents*. Many residents were shocked to discover that as a result, their credit cards had been canceled, mortgage applications disapproved, or employment denied.

TRW called the Norwich episode "an isolated incident," but settled the lawsuits a few months later by making it easier for consumers to view and correct errors in their own credit files. The company agreed to:

✓ Pay a fine of $125,000 to the state of Vermont

✓ Pay up to $1,000 to each Vermont resident it incorrectly identified as being delinquent

✓ Provide toll-free access to its credit reporting center

✓ Make its reports easier for its consumers to read

✓ Expedite consumer complaints

✓ Offer one free credit report annually to consumers

✓ Install upgraded computer software to prevent individuals being re-classified as poor credit risks due to inaccurate information provided by TRW's suppliers.

Even though Equifax and Trans Union have not been targeted by state attorney generals as was TRW, these companies are now under pressure by Congress to initiate similar improvements.

Legislation before Congress would amend the Fair Credit Reporting Act by requiring credit bureaus to update information more frequently, prohibit data "screening" without permission from the person whose files are being matched, and permit individuals whose credit is damaged because of erroneous information contained in credit bureau files to sue for damages.

In 1992, this legislation bogged down after disagreements on whether a state could enact more stringent restrictions than Congress. However, a similar bill was introduced in 1993.

Privacy and Your Social Security Number

If I have your name and your Social Security number, I own you.

--18-year old computer hacker speaking to author

The original Social Security card had written on it "not for purposes of identification." The nine-digit code that was originally created in 1935 for efficient administration of a retirement program has come a long way. Congress has decreed that everyone, even babies, must be assigned a Social Security number.

A five-minute examination of my files shows that I have disclosed my Social Security number on tax returns, mortgage applications, credit card applications, life insurance and medical insurance applications, employment applications, to my bank and to companies with whom I invest. Your files would probably show a similar pattern. Even if the Social Security number is "not for identification," it has evolved into a de facto national identification card.

Does a computer hacker who has your name and Social Security number really "own" you? Well, not exactly. But armed only with this number, he can find out a great deal about you and even impersonate you. He can probably acquire information about your bank account over the phone. If he can obtain the appropriate password into a credit bureau network, he can look up your credit records--including credit card numbers, bank account numbers, and of course, your home address.

He may even be able to redeem money from investment accounts you have set up, if he knows which companies to call. (For this reason, if you set up a "telephone switch" or "telephone redemption" privilege in any investment account, make certain you require the company maintaining it to ask for a back-up authorization code before making a transaction; not merely your Social Security number.)

Other problems can arise as well. A Chicago resident has in the past seven years been arrested twice for desertion from the U.S. Navy--even though he never enlisted. Someone used his Social Security number to enlist, and then deserted.

In another case not involving fraud, two women shared the same name and birthdate--and, because of a clerical error, the same Social Security number. After 17 years of struggling to convince disbelieving bureaucrats that a problem existed, and appearing on a national television show to discuss it, the two women finally were assigned separate numbers. According to a 1991 study by the IRS, as many as four million U.S. residents use fake Social Security numbers--many of them illegal immigrants who can't get one legally.

Your legal obligation to disclose a Social Security number is limited. You must give it to your employer so that he can withhold income tax from your paycheck. The IRS requires a Social Security number on your tax return. It also prints your Social Security number on the tax forms it mails to you each year. In 1992, the IRS beat back a challenge from a taxpayer who claimed this practice violated the Privacy Act. You must also provide it to be eligible for government benefits, and in some states, to register to vote.

To obtain a driver's license in most states, you must disclose the number. Many states even publish Social Security numbers on driver's licenses. Other states permit the use of an alternative number. Ask for the alternative number to be imprinted on your license, if this option is available.

The Privacy Act of 1974 (5 USC Sec. 552a (d) and (e)) limits government use of your Social Security number. The agency requesting your Social Security number must tell you for what purpose it is being used and whether or not its use is mandatory. However, there are numerous exemptions. For "routine" use or if "national security" is at stake, notification is not required. Subsequent laws have broadened the exemptions. (See "The Privacy Act of 1974," this chapter, for additional information.)

There is no legal limitation on the private use of Social Security numbers. You'll find that everyone wants your number, all for what they consider legitimate reasons. Even your grocery store will ask for your Social Security number when you sign up for a check cashing card. If you refuse to give out the number, it may be obtained from a credit bureau.

The following are a few suggestions to protect your Social Security number:

✓ *Try to obtain an alternative number on your driver's license.* Laws in some states require it be imprinted on the license, but most states permit you to ask for a substitute number.

✓ *If you work for yourself, you can be assigned a "Federal Employer Identification Number."* This number will identify you for tax withholding purposes. If someone insists on obtaining your Social Security number, ask if the FEIN would be an acceptable substitute.

✓ *Ask for alternative ID numbers for your brokerage accounts.* If you invest in mutual funds or brokerages that permit "telephone switching," request a personal identification number different from your Social Security number. This makes it more difficult for a person imitating you to obtain information about your account or redeem investments.

✓ *Don't disclose your Social Security number to anyone that doesn't have a legal responsibility to obtain it.* The Social Security Administration, the IRS brokerages, and a handful of other government agencies are the only ones legally required to obtain it. Credit card companies, banks, brokerages, and landlords will ask you for the number when you apply for their services, but you are under no legal obligation to provide it. (On the other hand, your application may be turned down if you don't.)

However, banks and brokerages interpret a 1982 law as requiring them to deduct 20 percent of the interest or dividends earned if you refuse to provide your Social Security number. They send the funds deducted directly to the IRS. In addition, they must maintain a list of individuals refusing to disclose their Social Security number. The list must be made available for inspection by the IRS.

✓ *Check your Social Security records at least every three years.* If a person is fraudulently collecting benefits on your number, or if payments to Social Security haven't been recorded at all, you have only three years, three months, and three days to make a legal challenge.

✓ *Don't give out your Social Security number over the phone.* A number of telephone scams involve calling a supposedly lucky "winner" of a contest. The telephone salesperson insists that no prize money can be paid unless the winner discloses his Social Security number. The prize, of course, is completely fictitious--and armed with your Social Security number, a fraudster can impersonate you in many ways, as you've already learned.

Some people make up a Social Security number in situations where they don't wish to disclose it. This may be illegal, particularly if the request is made to comply with a law or regulation. It is also illegal in a commercial transaction if fraud is at issue. A better strategy is to write "N/A" on the form you're presented with. When I've done so, I've rarely been challenged.

To learn how to "opt out" of the Social Security system, see Chapter 9, "Social Security's Last Gasp."

Privacy and Your Insurance

The following account is a true story. It could happen to you.[30]

> When I was a younger man, I made an application for life insurance, and it was rejected. I could not understand why because I felt pretty healthy, and the company did not give me the reason why. Because I pressed and pressed, I was finally able to secure an off-the-record statement from the individual who had solicited the account. He said, "Well, we have information in our records that 10 years ago you had cancer."
>
> I asked what the nature of this cancer was. The records showed it was leukemia. I asked, "Where did you get this information?" The company indicated they had obtained it from a neighbor. The truth is I did not have cancer. Had I not pressed on that matter, I would not have known, and I would not have been given an insurance policy. I brought this matter to the company's attention and demanded that they analyze their file again, and finally they agreed that the information that had been provided them had been given maliciously.

Who was the victim? It was Ed Koch, the former mayor of New York City.

The "trade in gossip" that so worried Supreme Court Justice Brandeis 100 years ago has now evolved into a sophisticated industry. Huge companies working at the behest of the insurance industry

---

[30]*Congressional Record* (October 17, 1974)

send out representatives to neighborhoods across the United States inquiring about the health, personal habits, even the "moral fitness" of individuals applying for insurance coverage.

Insurance companies will tell you that you have authorized them to obtain this information. And by signing the application form when you requested coverage, you have.

A typical form might have the following release on it:

> I hereby authorize any physician, medical practitioner, hospital, clinic or other medical or medically-related facility, insurance company or other organization, institution or person that has records or knowledge of the health, observation, diagnosis or treatment of either myself or any member of my family, to give to _____ Insurance Company any and all such information it requests with respect to such records or knowledge. A photocopy of this authorization shall be as valid as the original.

When you sign such a form, you are endorsing a blank check for a "fishing expedition" of unlimited duration. But like other contracts, this one can be modified. For instance, you might wish to delete the references to "other organizations, institutions or persons" in order to protect yourself from an investigative inquisition such as the one Ed Koch suffered through. You might also wish to insert a clause stating a time limit for information to be disclosed. Ninety days should certainly be adequate.

Do not lie on insurance application forms. The agent will sell you the policy, and the company will accept your premium payments. But if any discrepancy is found after you or your heirs apply to receive payment, the company can nullify your policy retroactively.

The largest investigative service firm is Equifax Investigative Services. Equifax offices are located in most major cities, and the company has been implicated in numerous abusive information-gathering procedures.

One South Dakota Equifax report stated that its subject practiced "moral standards and habits which may not be accepted standards of society." Another one described its subject as "extremely 'claim-conscious'... has submitted several minor claims... known to be the type person that will submit any claim and usually has a full knowledge of what is covered and what is not."[31]

Many field employees of investigative service firms are young and inexperienced. Their compensation may be based on the number of investigations they complete, not by how thorough or accurate the investigation is. Investigations typically consist of a representative phoning your employer, your neighbors and any references you might list on your application, or less often, paying them a personal visit. These representatives will try to verify the information you have provided on your application for credit, insurance or employment. Respondents are guaranteed anonymity, but anything they tell the representative is noted in your file.

In August 1992, Equifax admitted that for many years it had simply ignored laws restricting these practices. While acknowledging no wrongdoing, in a settlement with the New York Attorney General,

---

[31]Under the Fair Credit Reporting Act, you have a right to examine the records that investigative bureaus such as Equifax may have gathered on you. In practice, this is easier said than done. For instance, when I applied for disability insurance several years ago, the insurance company called in Equifax to investigate. When I asked for a copy of the investigative file, the company shunted me to five different departments--none of which had the information I was requesting. Finally, an investigator gave me a number to call to get the file--a number that never was answered.

Equifax pledged to discontinue asking questions about physical and psychological disabilities, arrest records, and drug and alcohol abuse.

When you apply for insurance, ask your agent if the company underwriting the policy employs independent firms to make background checks on prospective clients. If you are to be investigated by such a firm, tell your employer, your neighbors and your friends that they are under no obligation to cooperate. You should also let your agent know that you consider such investigations to be a violation of your right to privacy, in addition to not being particularly accurate.

You might even ask them to speak with Ed Koch and find out *his* opinion.

Privacy and Your Medical Records

Whatever, in connection with my professional practice or not in connection with it, I see or hear, in the life of men, which ought not to be spoken of abroad, I will not divulge, as reckoning that all such should be kept secret.

-- a portion of the oath of Hippocrates, the "father of medicine," that U.S. physicians are sworn to uphold

In Hippocrates' day, in ancient Greece, medical technology was non-existent. An extract of willow bark might be given to relieve pain and swelling. The foxglove plant might be administered to relieve chest pains of a person suffering from heart disease. A patient would pay the physician a modest fee out of his own pocket, or perform some services on his behalf.

Similar arrangements were often routine, until very recently. I have childhood memories of my physician father, who practiced medicine for nearly 50 years, accepting many services in lieu of payment. One time a patient brought him a bushel of tomatoes. Another patient gave him several large sacks of candy, which I eagerly consumed.

In today's modern medical system with multi-million dollar "CAT scanners," "NMR imagers," and the like, few individuals can afford to pay for treatment out of their own savings. And the informal barter arrangements physicians have used for thousands of years are today considered tax evasion by the IRS. As a result, third-party billing for medical services is a fact of life. Private insurance companies and government agencies that pay for medical care want to know what services their funds are buying. If the physician doesn't provide enough detail, you may not be reimbursed.

Neither the federal government nor most states protect the confidentiality of medical records. In fact, most states require your physician to reveal his diagnoses of certain conditions, including tuberculosis, polio and venereal diseases (but in many states, not AIDS). The traditional "doctor-patient privilege of confidentiality" is the only privacy protection available. For the physician, this is normally a professional, not a legal, obligation.

This privilege is gradually eroding as result of the 1974 *Tarasoff* decision. In that case, a judge ruled that psychotherapists who believe their patients to be a risk to specific individuals must warn these potential victims that they are at risk. In turn, this decision has been used to erode the doctor-patient privilege further.

For instance, in 1990, a California judge ruled that audio tapes of psychotherapy sessions could be admitted as evidence in a murder trial. And in September 1992, the 5th U.S. Circuit Court of Appeals ordered a psychiatrist to release patient data to the IRS, ruling that no doctor-patient confidentiality privilege applies under federal law.

Most physicians take the doctor-patient privilege of confidentiality seriously. And in fact, it is patients who take the first step authorizing disclosure by signing forms authorizing "any licensed physician, medical practitioner or other person to disclose information relating to my condition or treatment."

"Other persons" include both private investigators and a number of organizations under contract to insurance companies which specialize in collecting medical records. By far the largest of these companies is the Medical Information Bureau. If you are unexpectedly denied insurance, the reason may be out-of-date or erroneous information in MIB's files.

Information submitted to MIB stays on file for at least two years, often longer. For instance, if your blood pressure is tested regularly and on one occasion it is elevated, your physician will report that fact to MIB. Even if subsequent tests show normal blood pressure, the report of elevated blood pressure is the one that will show up in MIB's records. Write to them for a copy of your file. (See the "List of Suppliers" for MIB's address.)

Incredibly, when updated or corrected information is submitted to MIB, the company does not delete the old or erroneous entry. It simply adds the new information to what's already there. So if, for instance, your physician were to erroneously inform MIB that you suffer from AIDS--and then attempt to correct the entry--the original entry would not be deleted. Instead, a second entry, saying that you really *didn't* have AIDS would be inserted.

A newer trend is to sell the records to third parties. In Taylors, South Carolina, a physician in 1991 auctioned his medical records to the highest bidder. A junkyard owner paid $4,000 for the records, and promptly resold them. There are many willing buyers, particularly when such data is gathered systematically.

The Physician Computer Network, Inc. will lease a doctor's office or clinic a complete personal computer system at a below-market rate in exchange for the company having access to patient records. The data is sold to pharmaceutical companies eager to learn how their products are selling--and how physicians are using them.

Nearly half the prescriptions written each year in the United States are similarly tracked. While physicians and pharmacies promise this practice doesn't compromise privacy, the information sold may include a patient's age, sex, and an "identification number"--in many cases the patient's Social Security number. Many smaller medical practices and independent pharmacies don't participate in these marketing schemes, but most larger clinics, hospitals, and pharmacies do.

Some of the fastest growth in this new industry comes from dispensers of mail-order pharmaceuticals. The largest such company in the United States is Medco Containment Services, Inc., which recently created a subsidiary to sell patient records, along with prescription data it buys from the American Association of Retired Persons.

Hospitals also use patient records for marketing purposes. For instance, computer programs sold to hospitals track potential customers who respond to free outpatient "health screening" services in affluent neighborhoods. Once the screening is complete, the hospital has a database of potential customers. It can then tailor its most profitable services to individuals it knows are predisposed to purchase them.

Government regulation is also shredding medical privacy. In July 1992, for instance, the Ohio Supreme Court upheld a local ordinance requiring pharmacists to disclose certain prescription records to police. In Congress, legislation introduced by California Congressman Pete Stark would require pharmacies to transmit all prescriptions for painkillers and other commonly-abused drugs into a national database.

Already, doctors who accept payment from Medicare patients risk being disbarred if the don't file the appropriate forms. If you're covered by Medicare, your doctor risks losing his license if he treats you privately! Finally, the Department of Health and Human Services is moving forward with a plan to link computers in 52,000 pharmacies nationwide to centralize, exchange, and audit information on Medicare beneficiaries.

Another trend that may affect medical records' confidentiality is the rationing of government-funded treatment programs. In several states, administrators of underfunded Medicaid programs have proposed that medical services be allocated so that the diseases and conditions that are the most cost-effective to treat are covered, but other conditions (including some chronic, incurable illnesses) are not. Oregon proposed such a system in 1990, but the Bush administration recently rejected it due to its potential conflict with the Americans With Disabilities Act.

Some opponents of rationing have suggested a substitute system in which individuals who use private insurance or their own savings to pay for their medical treatment be taxed on "luxury" health care services; baldness treatment, cosmetic surgery, etc. The proceeds would be used to finance the public aid system. Presumably, if the anti-rationing forces prevail in the future, a recordkeeping system would be set up to monitor these procedures and insure that the beneficiaries have been taxed upon their completion.

The following suggestions may be helpful in protecting your medical records from unauthorized or unwanted access.

1. *Discuss your concern for privacy with your physician.* Ask your physician to inform you if he plans to test for a condition that must be reported to MIB or to a government agency. Ask him not to report any condition he is not required by law to disclose. Remind him that you expect your medical records to be held in strictest confidence, and not sold or otherwise conveyed to third parties for any purpose other than insurance reimbursement. Request that he complete insurance forms only to the extent required to satisfy any claim.

2. *If your condition requires a prescription, ask your physician for "professional samples."* Many pharmaceutical companies distribute drugs for use by medical professionals. If your doctor has the medication you need in stock, he may be able to give it to you privately, rather than send you to a pharmacist. An added bonus: You will ordinarily not be charged for such medication.

3. *Before signing any admission or treatment forms, examine the admission documents carefully.* Most forms request your permission to distribute your medical file to virtually any medical professional, professional standards review organization, insurance company or government agency.

When you face such a form, you might consider adding the following clause:

> I authorize Dr. _____, _____ Hospital and members of its medical staff who attended to me to furnish to the ____ Insurance Company or its representative(s) information concerning my current treatment for purposes of verifying my claim for insurance reimbursement. I do not authorize the copying of and taking of medical records from the hospital without my further consent. This authorization expires in 90 days.

This language is suggested by Robert E. Smith, editor of *Privacy Journal*, who further suggests that you make the changes to the contract and then return it along with other papers in such a way that the admissions clerk may overlook the modifications.

4. *Consider obtaining medical treatment under an assumed name.* If you need treatment for a condition you'd rather not have revealed to your insurance company or MIB, you can always go to another doctor and use a pseudonym. Of course, you'll need to pay cash for the visit.

5. *Minimize routine visits to the doctor or hospital, even if they are covered by insurance.* Or pay for routine visits out of your own pocket. Insurance companies are known to cancel the coverage of individuals who make what they feel are "excessive" claims, or hike their rates dramatically.

6. *Carefully consider medical treatment alternatives.* As the son of a physician, I am acutely sensitive to the discomfort many medical professionals feel when their patients seek treatment from practitioners they perceive as unqualified, unethical, or both. Yet if you're not benefiting from, or can't afford, traditional medical treatment, you may have no choice but to seek alternative therapies. Many alternative practitioners don't accept third-party reimbursement and aren't government-sanctioned. But they may offer you more private treatment than you can receive from many physicians.

The government is cracking down hard on alternative practitioners. In May 1992, a Washington state physician was met at his office by Food & Drug Administration auditors accompanied by armed federal marshals. The marshals confiscated all equipment and medical records, temporarily shutting down the office. His "crime": administering preservative-free vitamins that were not FDA-approved.

In the future, we can expect that the trend toward less medical privacy will continue. For instance, Arizona Congressman Jim Kolbe and Delaware Senator Joseph Biden introduced in 1992 legislation (HR-4930) that would set up a sharing mechanism to encourage states to seize the assets of physicians suspected of committing "federal health care offenses."

Already-forfeitable offenses for which sharing would be mandated under HR-4930 include: (1) fraudulent or false billing for a medical product, service, or test and (2) inflated cost of a service or procedure performed by a health care provider. Given the "creative" use of existing forfeiture statutes by prosecuting attorneys (see "Asset Forfeiture and the Death of Property Rights," Chapter 8), I believe that physicians who seek to protect their patient's privacy could forfeit their assets.

They would be at particularly high risk if they accepted payment from the patient instead of filing the forms and waiting for government reimbursement. As the U.S. Attorney prosecuting a case in Ohio remarked: "The seizure of assets is a common tactic in the war on drugs. It will now become one of our major weapons in the war on health care fraud."[32]

If you've wondered what life might be like in the United States once Congress establishes a national health insurance plan, this proposal provides an important clue.

---

[32]In 1991, the Department of Health and Human Services filed a claim that the desire for privacy between Medicare beneficiaries and their physicians "cannot excuse [the physician] from compliance with the claim-submission requirements of the Medicare Act under any circumstances" (*Stewart vs. Sullivan*). However, a New Jersey U.S. District Court recently ruled against the government in this case. It declared that there is no law, no regulation, and no "clearly articulated policy" against private contracting between patients and their physicians. This is a critical victory in the battle for medical privacy, and yet another case of bureaucrats trying to enforce laws and regulations that don't exist. For more information, see the December 1992 *AAPS News* (1601 N. Tucson Blvd., Suite 9, Tucson, Ariz. 85716).

Privacy and the Grand Jury

A skilled prosecutor could indict a ham sandwich.

--Thomas W. Brothers, Davidson County, Tenn. Judge

Historically, the role of the grand jury is to insure that there is "probable cause" to indict a person for a crime. Prosecutors claim that the "proof" that the grand jury system is not abused is that the overwhelming majority of indictments end in convictions.

Grand juries have an important constitutional role. The Fifth Amendment states that, "No person shall be held to answer for a capital, or otherwise infamous crime, unless on a presentment or indictment of a grand jury." Supreme Court Justice Potter Stewart wrote that the proper function of a grand jury is to "clear the innocent, no less than to bring those to trial who are guilty."

However, the modern grand jury has few oversights to protect the innocent. Part of the problem is that the grand jury hears only one side of the story--the prosecutor's. Grand juries must determine, without hearing evidence from the defense, whether a person should be charged with a serious crime.

Another problem is that grand jury proceedings ordinarily are secret. If you are the subject of a grand jury probe, you need not be informed. Chances are, you will learn of the proceedings only after you receive official notification of an indictment. If you are called to testify before a grand jury, many constitutional provisions don't apply. You're not entitled to have an attorney appointed for you if you can't afford one. No judge is present to rule a prosecutor's questions out of order.[33]

These shortcomings of the grand jury system can lead to serious prosecutorial abuse. For instance, a Texas prosecutor on three different occasions sought a murder indictment against a Vietnamese man accused of shooting a black man. In theory, a prosecutor has no limit to the number of times he may present a case to a grand jury as long as the statute of limitations has not expired. In cases with no statute of limitations, you could subjected to grand jury harassment the rest of your life.

In a recent federal case, a grand jury returned an indictment against a Mexican physician, Humberto Alvarez Machain, accused of involvement in the torture-murder of a DEA agent. According to the indictment, the physician injected the DEA agent with medication to keep him awake while he was tortured.

One of the witnesses who testified before the grand jury was a paid DEA informant suspected of involvement in the murder of four missionaries. After the judge dismissed the case, prosecutors admitted they possessed information from a FBI informant naming another physician as the one who had injected drugs into the agent. However, this information was not disclosed to the grand jury.[34]

By the way, if you're ever called to testify before a grand jury, or to give a deposition that will be presented to one, the best procedure is to answer the questions as literally as possible. If you don't recall the answer to a question, don't guess at it. Simply state, "I don't know." If the prosecutor asks you to interpret a proceeding or event, decline the invitation. Just say: "I don't have any opinion."

---

[33]At least, the proceedings are usually secret. In November 1992, two computer hackers were arrested in Seattle for allegedly using their personal computers to gain unrestricted access to federal grand jury files.

[34]In this case, the doctor was kidnapped from his Mexican office by individuals working under contract to the DEA. In June, 1992, the Supreme Court upheld the practice of kidnapping foreign nationals and bringing them to the United States to stand trial.

Privacy and Your Legal Records

Over the last few decades, an explosion in new legal "rights" has led to a corresponding explosion in litigation. While litigants who recover damages for "lost zest for life" or "mental cruelty" have gained monetarily, both sides in a dispute brought before any court always lose from the perspective of privacy.

The reason is that court records are almost always *public* records. Consider the following item from the San Rafael, California *County Seat Digest:*

> DOROTHY and HAROLD ALLEN: husband pays $3,000 a month spousal and child support for five months; then for the next seven months to 25 November, 1980, $2,500 a month, then $2,300 a month thereafter; wife to get all net proceeds from sale of 133 Santa Maria, Tiburon, California.

Had the Allens known that their divorce settlement was a matter of public record, they might have made some effort to protect their mutual interest in privacy. (I've left out the grounds for divorce, which are also made public in many states).

Publications such as the *County Seat Digest* are distributed in nearly every county in the United States. Litigants may sue to keep the information out of the public's eye, but they almost invariably lose. Town gossips, government agents and the merely curious can catch up on local events simply by subscribing. Non-subscribers need only visit their county courthouse to do the same.

Protecting your privacy from the legal system requires determination and forethought. The following suggestions may prove useful.

Divorces. Uncontested divorces usually require much less disclosure than contested ones. If possible, try to arrange distribution of assets, child support arrangements, etc. out of court. Some states treat every divorce as contested. This may require the partners in even a friendly parting to supply financial statements, reports from marriage counselors, etc. into the public record. The final terms of contested divorces are almost always published, including the grounds for divorce, details of child support arrangements, custody, visitation rights, etc.

If an uncontested divorce is impossible, or you live in a state that requires total disclosure in all divorces, consider a settlement in another state. An attorney specializing in divorces may be helpful in this regard. (Divorces outside the United States aren't recognized in most states, but check your state statutes.)

You might think that avoiding marriage to be the ideal answer to sidestep a nasty divorce. This method is hardly foolproof. Common-law marriages, for instance, are still recognized in a number of states. In addition, many states also treat separations of unwed couples as divorces, particularly if children are involved.

Lawsuits. If you've ever been involved in a lawsuit, you already know that they are among the least private of legal proceedings. If you haven't been, you should do everything in your power to avoid them. In a lawsuit, the opposing attorney will challenge every statement you make, cast doubt upon your good character and try to make your claims appear inconsequential. Your attorney will do the same to your opponent.

These challenges may open doors that you might prefer remain closed. A good example is a lawsuit in which you claim to have experienced emotional suffering. Once you make this claim, your opponent's attorney will do everything in his power to disprove it. In fact, he is likely to ask you to describe every potential emotional trauma you have ever suffered. He even has the right to subpoena records relating to these experiences.

Even a simple lawsuit will result in a transcript hundreds or even thousands of pages long. Only a small portion of the transcript relates to courtroom proceedings. The remainder consists of records, testimony or other information disclosed out-of-court in the pre-trial "discovery" process. Much of this information may have only a remote bearing on the trial, or no bearing at all. But it all remains in the final, public record, even if it is shown to be false, hearsay or otherwise inadmissible in court.

Attorneys are famous for their zeal in uncovering information you'd rather keep confidential. Have you ever had a drinking problem? Engaged in extra-marital affairs? Earned income you didn't report on your income tax return? This is exactly the type of information an opposing attorney will go to almost any length to obtain, via private investigation, surveillance, interviews, etc. Not surprisingly, court records relating to lawsuits brought by (or against) prominent or wealthy people are fertile sources of information for IRS audits.

What about "sealing" the records after a lawsuit is settled? Many states at one time had fairly liberal policies for sealing litigation records. Judges would also grant secrecy orders on almost any reasonable grounds. However, attorneys involved in personal injury litigation have fought for many years to loosen these laws, and have met with success in a number of states, including Florida, New Jersey, New York, and Texas. These states now apply a "presumption of public access" to discovery and settlement information. An "Open Records Act" has been introduced in Congress that would apply similar standards to federal litigation.

The result of this new attitude is demonstrated in recent decisions such as *In the Matter of Grand Jury Proceedings: Krynicki*. In this case, an Illinois federal judge denied the motion to seal legal records of a family involved in a financial dispute. Protection from the prying eyes of reporters, ruled the judge, is insufficient reason to seal public records.

The best way to avoid being sued to is not appear as a tempting target. If you live in a mansion in the best part of town, send your children to the best private schools, make large contributions to charities in your own name and drive an expensive, imported European sedan, your financial success is obvious. Your high profile makes it much more likely that a potential litigant will consider you as lawsuit target, even with only the flimsiest of cases--hoping you will offer a generous settlement out-of-court.

On the other hand, you can live in a nice, upper-middle-class neighborhood in a home that is modest on the outside, but impeccably furnished inside. If you wish to send your children to private schools, you can have them attend locally rather than at a nationally-recognized academy. You can drive a mid-priced automobile, but have it customized. You can give to your local church or charity anonymously. Finally, you can use family limited partnerships and asset protection trusts to make it more difficult for a litigant to seize your assets (see "Asset Protection Techniques," Chapter 8.) All these steps lower your profile to a potential litigant, and lessen the probability you will be sued.

To avoid contractual disputes from ending up in court, have contracts drawn up to state that any disagreements will be handled through impartial, expert arbitration.   The American Arbitration Association is one of the largest provider of such services in the United States (address in "List of Suppliers.")

The attorney-client privilege of confidentiality. The notes and records your attorney keeps in connection with matters you discuss with him are generally treated as confidential, but there are important exceptions. For instance, these records can be subpoenaed by another attorney in a lawsuit. Indirectly, they can even be examined by the IRS.

In 1989, the Supreme Court in *U.S. vs. Zolin* ruled that judges may examine privately communications between attorneys and their clients to determine whether or not such information should be handed over to the IRS. In 1991, a U.S. Circuit Court of Appeals ruled that a law firm suspected of involvement in a money laundering conspiracy must comply with a grand jury's subpoenas for its financial records. Another appeals court ruled that an attorney must disclose client billing data to bank regulators. The attorney's firm was a client at a bank under investigation for violations of banking regulations.

Also in 1989, the IRS began enforcing provisions of a five-year-old law that requires recipients of cash payments over $10,000 to identify the source of those payments. The agency wrote to nearly 1,000 attorneys and gave them 30 days to identify their clients who had paid them cash in excess of this amount. Not only were cash records subpoenaed, but all financial records, including bank statements and payment records.

Several law firms refused to comply, and sued the IRS on the basis that providing this information would be tantamount to testifying against their own clients. However, in 1991, a U.S. Circuit Court of Appeals ruled that the government's need for the information outweighs the sacrifice of attorney-client confidentiality. (See Chapter 7, "The Deficit Reduction Act of 1984," for more information on how legal privacy is threatened by federal legislation.)

Law office searches for records of cash payments are becoming increasingly common. In 1992, a federal judge in Iowa upheld a search of an attorney's office because of evidence showing that cash payments were not being deposited into ordinary business accounts (*U.S. vs. Humphreys,* N.D.Ia., 91-3812).

Nor are telephone conversations with your attorney always privileged. The Supreme Court in 1989 upheld a lower court ruling that a government agency can wiretap your attorney without a court order. Attorney Arthur Kinoy's phone was wiretapped for more than 20 years by the FBI. Bringing a lawsuit against the agency, he claimed the wiretap violated his clients' rights to a confidential relationship with their attorney.

The lower court opinion upheld by the Supreme Court read in part: "Kinoy, as an attorney, possessed no constitutional right, independent of his client's rights, to communicate with his clients without government intrusion."

One of the newest threats to attorney-client confidentiality originates in California. Legislators have introduced a state Freedom of Information Act far more sweeping than the federal statute that would invalidate the confidentiality provisions in virtually all legal documents--both public and private! The proposed new law reads, in part, that, "No confidentiality agreement, settlement agreement, stipulated agreement or protective order which bars public disclosure shall be valid except with respect to trade secrets."

The proposed law is designed to make it more difficult for large companies to seal records that might make them vulnerable to product-liability lawsuits. However, its impact will go far beyond its intended target. *All types* of documents, contracts and professional agreements would be open to public inspection.

Because the attorney-client privilege of confidentiality is not absolute, ask your attorney to destroy all notes and records pertaining to your case (or return them to you) once it has concluded. In particularly sensitive matters, you might even ask your attorney not to take notes. In addition, you may wish to simply show your attorney confidential documents, rather than turning them over to him. Finally, try to avoid discussing confidential matters with your attorney over the telephone.

Outside the courtroom, attorneys spend much of their time conducting legal research. This is something you can learn to do yourself. If you can't find a friendly librarian at a law library, a good written introduction to this topic is *Using the Law Library: A Nonlawyer's Guide*.[35]

An excellent legal survival guide for non-lawyers is Michael Louis Minns' *The Underground Lawyer*. It's a real eye-opener on how the legal system *really* works, and what you can do to protect yourself from it. I recommend it highly.[36]

The Private Estate

When you die, your property will be distributed to your heirs. Most people assume that the only way to insure that their property will be divided as they wish is with a will. While a will does insure that property is distributed to your designated heirs, it does not protect them from a system known as "probate." You should shield as much of your estate from probate as possible.

Probate almost always involves large attorney fees and delays in your beneficiaries receiving the property they are due. It also involves legal advertisements and publicity. For prominent families, probate can be a nightmare of competing claims, shouting reporters and expensive attorneys. It can be an expensive and a high-profile system to distribute your assets.

You should always prepare a will. But you should also arrange your estate so that you avoid the public distribution of assets that a will requires.

After your death, your executor presents your will to the probate court with an inventory of your estate's assets and liabilities. After examining your will to insure that it is legally binding, the court places a legal advertisement in your town's newspaper.

This advertisement invites creditors to submit claims against your estate that are to be passed down through probate. The notice also alerts anyone else who wishes to make a claim, such as an ex-spouse, a disinherited child, etc.

While the probate procedure is relatively straightforward, more abuse occurs in probate than perhaps all other legal procedures combined. Even moderately-sized estates can be ravaged by the probate system.

One of the more insidious ways that estates are ravaged is if a probate attorney's fees are based on the estate's *total market value* and not its *equity value*. For example, your estate may be worth $300,000, including a $250,000 home on which you carry a $200,000 mortgage. The total equity value of the estate would therefore be $100,000.

If an attorney's 5 percent fee is based on the equity value, it would be $5,000. On the other hand, if it is based on total market value, it would be $25,000. The insertion of a single phrase in the agreement your executor signs with a probate attorney could wipe out $20,000 of your estate.

---

[35]*Using the Law Library: A Nonlawyer's Guide* (Washington, D.C.: Halt Publications, 1982, 1988)

[36]Michael Louis Minns, *The Underground Lawyer* (Katy, Tex.: Gopher Publications, 1989)

No one wants probate fees to eat up 20 percent or more of his estate in before the rightful heirs obtain their property. No one wishes to open the private affairs of their family to the scrutiny of gossip columnists. Most importantly, no one wants to see their heirs deprived of their property. The moral is simple. *Take whatever steps you can to reduce the size of your probatable estate.*

Property that passes to your heirs outside the probate system includes:

1. *Any property with a named beneficiary or beneficiaries.* Assets such as a life insurance policy, an IRA, Keogh, profit-sharing plan, etc., usually have a named beneficiary. When you die, the proceeds are automatically passed on to that individual or individuals.

2. *Property owned jointly with someone else.* If you own property jointly, the surviving co-owner may be eligible to inherit your portion of the property outside of probate through a *right of survivorship.* The form of ownership required for this to take place is called "joint tenancy."

However, there are risks to this form of ownership that you should discuss with an estate planning professional or an attorney. For instance, if you are not married to the person with whom you jointly own property, the right of survivorship may result in a gift tax liability at your death, or the death of the other joint owner. It is also easy to disinherit children from a previous marriage through joint ownership.

3. *Property transferred into living trusts.* A popular legal structure that is very effective in avoiding probate is the *living* or *inter-vivos* trust.

Any trust relationship requires three participants: the *settlor* or *trustor* who forms the trust and contributes assets to it; the *trustee* who accepts and manages these assets; and the *beneficiary* who receives the assets after the settlor dies. In the simplest trusts, the settlor and the trustee are the same individual--you--and the beneficiary will be your spouse.

The living trust permits you as trustee to maintain full control over your property, yet insure that it is passed on to the named beneficiary upon your death, without probate. You may change beneficiaries any time you like, or even revoke the trust completely. For the living trust to be effective, you must formally transfer title to your property into it.

Don't let an attorney convince you to set up a death or testamentary trust to transfer your property into trust after your death, unless you have no objection to the property going through probate. (In some states, probate is relatively painless. It may also be desirable to send a small portion of an estate through probate to eliminate the possibility of a creditor's future challenge to the estate settlement.)

Setting up a living trust typically costs $1,000 to $1,500. While this fee is much higher than the cost of a simple will, the benefits at death--both in terms of privacy and probate cost--can be considerable.

Other types of trusts may provide both asset protection and estate planning advantages. "Asset Protection Techniques," Chapter 8, provides a brief overview of how trusts may be used to protect your assets. For more information on the estate planning advantages of trusts, I recommend two highly readable books by attorneys Robert A. Esperti and Renno L. Peterson: *Loving Trust* and *The Handbook of Estate Planning.*[37]

---

[37]Robert A. Esperti and Renno L. Peterson, *Loving Trust* (New York: Viking-Penguin, 1988, 1991); *The Handbook of Estate Planning* (New York: McGraw Hill, 1991)

Privacy and Your Financial Records

What do your canceled checks indicate?

I recently reviewed an old check register to see if it revealed anything embarrassing. While I already try to keep a low profile, I was surprised at some of the conclusions an investigator might be able to make about my life, simply by examining my canceled checks.

For instance, the register recorded many relatively large checks to grocery stores, which might indicate to an investigator an "abnormally large appetite." In truth, I often write a check larger than my actual purchase and get the difference back in cash. It also recorded large payments for phone service. As a journalist, I use the phone extensively. But a routine search through my checkbook might lead to the conclusion that I (or my spouse) were simply gossips.

A good summary of the information revealed in your canceled checks comes from Robert Ellis Smith, publisher of *Privacy Journal*.

> Your canceled checks record the names of your doctors and hospitals, the publications you read, the relatives you help, the religious and charitable activities you support, the volume of business you give your liquor store and the amount you spend on transportation (including whether or not you consume more than your share of gasoline.) The information in canceled checks can be a mirror of your life, a reflection that you do not want seen by the wrong set of eyes.

Your canceled checks are your property, and until 1970, no government official could inspect them without your consent or a search warrant. However, the Bank Secrecy Act of 1970 requires your bank to photocopy both sides of canceled checks over $100 before returning them to you. These records must be made available to the IRS under conditions I'll describe in a moment.

Most banks copy *all* checks, to avoid having to segregate the smaller ones that don't require duplication. The act also requires banks to record any extension of credit over $5,000 and any cash transaction of $10,000 or more. Records of these cash transactions must be forwarded directly to the IRS. (For more information on this act, see Chapter 7, "The Bank Secrecy Act of 1970.")

Banks may request information prior to opening an account that is not required by law. A bank must obtain your Social Security number when you open an interest bearing account, or withhold 20 percent of the interest.

But other information the bank may request, such as your occupation, your income, length of time at your job, etc., will be used to determine your creditworthiness. There's no legal obligation to answer the questions, but if you refuse to do so, the bank may not accept you as a depositor. If you answer the questions, the bank may be compelled to disclose the information to the IRS.

Banks may also use information about your account activity for marketing purposes. Fleet/Norstar Financial Group, for instance, recently examined customer checks written for more than $1,000 to see how depositors were investing their money. Employees looked at both the payee and memo lines on the check to obtain the information, which a bank spokesman said was used "to help the bank provide better service to its customers."

And according to William McGeevy, vice-president of Chase U.S. Consumer Services, his company spies on home-equity loan credit line checks. "We spot-check the drafts to see if the customer is using the money to pay for college tuition, hire a contractor, consolidate his debts, or buy a car," McGeevy says. "So far, we're not doing anything with this information. It's just sitting in a database somewhere."

Your bank need not notify you when a private company (credit bureau, insurance agency, etc.) asks for information on your account if the firm can demonstrate that you have authorized the inquiry. Forms you sign when you apply for insurance or credit authorizing "all institutions and individuals having relevant information concerning me to release such information" are ordinarily sufficient authorization to the bank for the account information to be disclosed.

Your bank may even release confidential information to private parties with no authorization whatsoever! A study commissioned by University of Illinois Professor David Linowes, former Chairman of the Privacy Commission, concluded that almost all banks give out information about your account balance, if your account has ever been overdrawn, etc. to credit bureaus, other banks and even individuals who casually inquire over the phone! About 75 percent of the time, according to Linowes, the customer is not informed.[38]

In addition, account information is often available informally. It's easy if you know how, according to *Privacy for Sale*:

> The instructions on the screen asked Van Winkle [a corporate security consultant] to input the network node he wanted to access and the password. He did and the system welcomed him to the First Citizens Bank network.
>
> Van Winkle typed in my Social Security number. Seconds later my account balance, last few checks, and other extraneous items were displayed. Total elapsed time: five minutes.
>
> Van Winkle said getting the password for First Citizens network--or any other bank's, for that matter--isn't very difficult. Heads of security at banks and stores know each other pretty well; many of them worked together in law enforcement. And they're feverish information junkies, even to the point of sharing intimacies about each other's computer systems. And when that doesn't happen, as most private investigators know, bank-system passwords are for sale, compiled by information resellers who purchase the codes from bank employees.
>
> But even if he didn't have the password, there are other ways to get the data, Van Winkle explained. "Most likely you have a MAC-system ATM (automatic teller machine) card in conjunction with your account. I have access to the MAC network through my bank's ATM network. So all I need to do is dial into the MAC computer through my bank, and through the MAC system access First Citizens' computer, where I can call up your account."

Other banks provide 24-hour information lines that let consumers use touch-tone phones to inquire about their account balances and whether or not checks have cleared. However, a recent survey by a

---

[38]The Privacy Commission report, *Personal Privacy in an Information Age*, now nearly two decades old, remains fascinating reading (Washington D.C.: U.S. Government Printing Office, Stock No. 052-003-00395-3.)

consumer group indicates that 11 of 24 banks surveyed in California don't require any password beyond an account number and a Social Security number. Given the ease with which a hacker or a thief can obtain this data, this finding is extremely troubling. My own bank offers this service, but it may be blocked at a customer's request.

Additional invasions of privacy occur when you write a check. You are likely to be asked to provide positive identification, such as a driver's license, and the driver's license number will be noted on the check. If this number matches your Social Security number, anyone handling your check from that point forward will have all the information required to impersonate you in a variety of ways. (See "Privacy and Your Social Security Number," this chapter.)

10 Tips to Protect Banking Privacy

To lower the profile of your bank account, and reduce the information that an investigator could glean by inspecting your canceled checks, consider the following techniques.

1. *Write personal checks only for ordinary, everyday expenses.* Don't write a personal check for any purchase that you'd rather keep private. Pay for such purchases with cash or a money order.

2. *Carry a minimal account balance.* Larger accounts merit investigation much more often than smaller ones.

3. *Open an account that does not pay interest, and maintain only a minimal balance.* There are no withholding requirements in non-interest-bearing accounts, but you will still be asked to provide your Social Security number. You're not required to disclose it, but if you don't, the bank may refuse to open the account. In addition, the bank must keep names of customers who refuse to disclose their Social Security numbers on file, and provide this list to the IRS on demand.

In 1990, the Treasury Department ordered banks to report "suspicious activity" by their depositors to the IRS Criminal Investigation Division. As a result, if you refuse to provide your Social Security number to a bank, the bank may report you to the IRS as a suspected money launderer.

Be particularly wary of this requirement if you want to open a substantial (over $1,000) account with cash, cashier's checks, money orders, bank drafts, or traveler's checks, since use of such "monetary instruments" is now under intense IRS scrutiny. The best strategy may be to disclose the number, to avoid being targeted as a potential criminal. (See Chapter 7, "How to Avoid Being Arrested for Money Laundering," for details.)

4. *Consider the private and secure use of your safety deposit box.* You are not required to disclose your Social Security number when you rent a safety deposit box, although all U.S. banks will ordinarily request this information. However, you should use your real name. If you use an assumed name, your heirs may not be able to gain access to the papers and valuables in the box when you die.

Many banks will not permit you to rent a safety deposit box unless you open an account there. To preserve your privacy, open a small (under $1,000) non-interest-bearing account. Several weeks later, go back and rent a safety deposit box. Since the account is non-interest-bearing, no annual earnings record need be sent to the IRS. In effect, your account is hidden from view--even if you disclose your Social Security number when you open it. So is the fact that you have rented a safety deposit box.

Or rent the box in the name of a trust or corporation. Since neither a trust nor a corporation can die, this is an excellent way to insure that your valuables are accessible to your loved ones after your death. Your attorney can even prepare a "safety deposit box trust" for this explicit purpose.

Another consideration is theft. It's surprisingly easy for a thief to break into bank vault, and several hundred safety deposit box lease-holders lose their possessions to theft each year. When a theft occurs, they are often shocked to learn that the agreement they have signed specifically excludes the bank from any liability except in the case of "gross negligence."

For this reason, you will want to obtain your own insurance for your safety deposit box holdings. Unfortunately, materials held in a safety deposit box or private vault are not ordinarily insured against theft or other loss, even with a "valuable items" rider to your homeowners insurance. Safety deposit box coverage up to $50,000 is available from Investment Rarities, Inc. You are not required to declare what specific items you keep in the box, unless you make a claim.

Most safety-deposit box thefts follow a pattern. The thief penetrates the vault and then targets large boxes located at eye-level. To discourage theft, rent the smallest-size safety deposit available, and obtain two or more boxes if a single box will not hold your valuables. Try to obtain a box at the top or bottom of the vault, not at eye-level. It's also a good idea to keep valuables in more than one bank. If one bank is broken into, you will at least have access to some of your assets elsewhere.

5. *Consider non-bank safety deposit box services.* Many private vaults are more secure than banks, making your holdings less expensive to insure. In addition, most private vault services do not monitor obituary listings, so it is unlikely the box would be sealed upon your death. Private vaults are more expensive than safety deposit boxes, but lower insurance costs may make up for the additional fees.

The most secure private vault I know of is Arlington Security Vault, Inc., located outside Washington, D.C. This facility features a state-of-the-art security system and a vault rated "9R," the highest insurance rating (7-inch thick steel doors and 18-inch reinforced concrete walls, floors and ceilings). Most bank vaults are rated only 5R; 3 1/2-inch thick steel doors and surrounded by only 12 inches of concrete.

The boxes can be rented individually, jointly, by a corporation, etc. You need not disclose your Social Security number to open an account. Secret numbered accounts are also available, although they must be opened in person. The company also offers "long-distance accounts" that permit you to do business by mail. When Arlington receives your valuables, two officers of the company, supervised by a public notary witness, will place your valuables in your box and send you the key. An affiliate company buys and sells precious metals, numismatic coins, and foreign currencies.

Still, keeping a portion of your wealth in a private vault service raises potentially troubling issues. What would happen, for instance, if Arlington, in business since 1983 (although now under new ownership), declared bankruptcy?

The rental agreement is explicit in its provisions that the relationship between Arlington and a box-holder is that of landlord and tenant; the company has no claim whatsoever over the contents of your box. Still, this provision hardly guarantees that you would be able to get to your assets easily if the firm were to shut down.

In the end, each depositor must decide if the additional security and privacy of any private vault facility, including Arlington, adequately offsets the risks. And losses of this type are ordinarily *not* covered by insurance. (The address for this company is provided in the "List of Suppliers" section.)

6. *Ask your bank if it has an official written policy on financial privacy.* When I made this inquiry at my local bank, the vice-president and chief counsel for the bank explained to me that such a policy existed, but was circulated only to employees. Allowing depositors to see the policy, he said, would open the bank to a potential liability if it were not followed to the letter. However, my account

balance is small, and you may well be more successful than I was if you make an inquiry at a bank where you have substantial funds on deposit.

7. *Ask your bank to provide a written guarantee that it will not release information regarding your account without either your written permission or a legal summons.* Such an agreement merely restates the legal protections you already have, although it does not consider the legal impact of the Anti-Drug Abuse Act of 1988 or the *Raikos* decision. As such, it may be difficult to persuade your bank to sign the document.

The following is a model for such a document:

A. The bank recognizes that its position permits it access to confidential information relating to the financial transactions of its customers, and has therefore adopted a general policy not to make such information available to third parties.

B. The bank further pledges that without specific written authorization from its customers or a written legal order from a government agency, it will not provide such information to a third party. It further pledges to not disclose information based on a mere demand unsupported by legal process from a government agency.

C. The bank understands that pursuant to the Right to Financial Privacy Act of 1978, depositors have a statutory right to challenge the disclosure of financial information to a government agency. The bank therefore pledges that before complying with any order to disclose such information, whether in the form of a formal subpoena, court order, or other form, it shall make a reasonable effort to communicate the existence of this order to the customer within two days of its receipt by the bank.

D. The bank shall not comply with such a demand until the customer involved has had an opportunity to respond, within 14 days of receiving notice, unless such action is specifically prohibited by statute. The mailing of a copy of the subpoena, court order or statute mandating release of such records to depositor's address of record shall constitute a reasonable effort to communicate the demand to the customer.

E. The customer recognizes that in the course of routine examination and audit of a banking institution, access to confidential financial records may be required. The customer therefore agrees that the bank's non-disclosure of such information shall not extend to the examination and audit of the operation of the bank in accordance with applicable state and federal banking laws, provided that no auditing or examining agency shall use the information in any manner other than for regulatory or statistical purposes.

F. The bank will not charge fees, deduct interest or in any other manner treat the account or accounts of the customer differently from customers who have not requested the bank's adherence with this agreement.

Unfortunately, most bankers will respond negatively to any agreement that restricts their right to distribute information about your account to anyone they choose. The same officer of my local bank to whom I previously referred told me that neither he nor any other officer of the bank would sign the preceding agreement.

While he told me he found "most of its provisions" reasonable, he refused to specify which ones made him feel uncomfortable. He also told me that signing such an agreement, or any agreement at all, for that matter, would unnecessarily increase the bank's liability. When I pressed him for more information, he told me that I was taking an "extreme position." Finally, he said that complying could get the bank's charter revoked for money laundering.

Even if your bank also refuses to adopt this agreement, you may be able to persuade it to sign an acceptable substitute. Once again, the size of your account will be a major factor in determining whether you receive cooperation. If you sensitize your bank to the fact that you value your privacy, its officers may think twice the next time they are asked to release information informally about your account.

On the other hand, the bank may decide your "militant" pro-privacy stance is unreasonable, and sever the relationship. This is a perfect example of where the desire to stand up for your rights conflicts with the need to maintain a low profile. Only you can draw the line.

8. *Don't release more information than is absolutely required when you write a check.* For instance, if a merchant wants to record your driver's license number, ask him to write it in on a separate sheet of paper, not on the check itself. (And again: Make certain your driver's license number is *not* the same as your Social Security number!)

If the merchant asks for a credit card number, remind him that this practice is prohibited by most credit card companies and illegal in some states. You might even want to begin carrying a credit card with a zero line of credit (expired or canceled, for instance) to show merchants that insist on writing a credit card number on my checks.

9. *If you need to borrow money, consider a private loan.* Almost everyone needs to borrow money at some time in his life. However, you may not wish to publicize the fact that you are doing so. The simplest and most private of loans is provided by a cash advance on a credit card. The bank issuing the credit card has no idea what use you are making of the cash. Almost as private is an overdraft checking account. While the bank routinely photocopies all checks, there is no reason you could not use such an account to write a check to "cash" and use the proceeds for any purpose you choose.

Then there's the neighborhood pawnbroker. While interest rates may be exorbitant, to redeem your property, all that is needed is the pawn ticket, along with cash to repay the loan. At least this used to be the case.

Today, law enforcement agencies have enlisted pawnbrokers into the War on Drugs. In April 1992 police seized one of the largest pawnshops in Atlanta--along with property its customers had pawned! Authorities accused the owners of participating in a money laundering scheme. To redeem property, depositors had to bring their pawn tickets to a local FBI office. And of course, present *positive identification*--preferably a driver's license with a Social Security number.

Finally, home equity loans are relatively private, with the added bonus that the interest is tax-deductible. For utmost flexibility, you can obtain a home equity loan as a line of credit with a checkbook. However, the IRS has been aggressive in its efforts to discourage home-equity loans. If you take out such a loan, you must prove that the loan was not taken out to pay off other loans where the interest paid would not have been tax-deductible.

10. *Keep your money in a strong bank.* A stark example of what happens to depositors in weak financial institutions occurred in 1991, when Rhode Island closed 14 state-chartered savings and loan institutions. Shortly thereafter, the names of 972 depositors who each had deposits of $100,000 or more in the failed institutions were published in local newspapers.

Even if you keep your money in a federally-insured bank, you may not recover your funds quickly if the bank should fail. The IRS already has a congressional mandate to withhold refunds to individuals who owe the federal government money.

Some in Congress have suggested that the agency apply the same requirements to refunds due depositors of failed banks or thrifts. One proposal would require the IRS to examine the financial affairs of large depositors in failed banks or S&Ls before refund checks are issued. And don't forget that the Federal Deposit Insurance Corp. has now won the right to examine income tax returns--a policy that could delay return of your money for an even longer time.

Your bank failing could also lead to your account being frozen and any outstanding checks bouncing. In that event, you or your business might have to apply for bankruptcy. If you want your funds released for emergency use, you must plead your case to a FDIC bureaucrat.

The 10 strongest U.S. banks, along with the addresses of rating services for U.S. banks, are provided in the "List of Suppliers."

Protecting Your Correspondence

It is a felony for you to open another person's mail, but not for the U.S. government to do so. Each year, the U.S. Customs Service opens more than 300,000 packages leaving or entering the United States. No warrant is required. And, in a program beginning in the 1950s, the CIA and FBI, with the cooperation of the Postal Service, opened and subsequently copied millions of overseas letters. All the agencies concerned claim the program has now been discontinued.

The Postal Service responded to these abuses by prohibiting other agencies from opening mail in its custody. But it is not against Postal Service policy for a government agency to open mail when that mail is not in the hands of the Postal Service. Mail can still be turned over to the CIA, FBI or IRS, opened, resealed, and then returned to the Postal Service. To intimidate tax protestors, for instance, the IRS often stamps mail it opens, "Misdirected by Post Office; Opened in Error by Internal Revenue Service." In addition, Postal Service inspectors can open mail at any time.

Historically, international correspondence has been the most likely target of surveillance. For instance, the IRS in the 1960s routinely photocopied all correspondence between Switzerland and the United States, and later matched the postal codes stamped on the envelopes with the names and addresses of particular Swiss banks. Then agency then audited anyone who had received correspondence from a Swiss bank. Dozens of depositors were prosecuted for income tax evasion.

The IRS also opens mail illegally, and in many cases obtains convictions against taxpayers, even if it is caught. One recent example took place in New York. An IRS agent illegally monitored the correspondence of a neighbor with whom he was having a dispute. Based on the information obtained in this manner, the neighbor was convicted of conspiring to hide the existence of foreign bank accounts. When the illegal monitoring was discovered, the judge ordered a new trial. But he did not throw out the IRS' case.

Even international correspondence having nothing to do with investing can arouse intense government scrutiny, as a New Jersey elementary school student discovered. In 1983, 11-year old Todd Patterson, began preparing a "personal world encyclopedia," compiled by writing to representatives of nearly 170 nations and asking each one for information about their peoples and governments.

The FBI, alerted to the large amount of international mail being generated, began an investigation. It was discontinued only after agents visited Patterson and his parents personally and determined that he posed no national security threat. However, the FBI refused to release Patterson's file, even after a Freedom of Information Act request in 1987 and a lawsuit in 1990.

The monitoring of mail by a government agency is known as a "mail cover." The agency obtains permission from a postal inspector to obtain a copy of the address, sender, return address, place and date of postmark and class of mail for all mail delivered to a particular address. Since the mail isn't opened, the government doesn't consider a mail cover to be an infringement of the Fourth Amendment's prohibition of unreasonable searches and seizures. For this reason, neither a warrant nor notification of the targeted individual is required.

The Postal Service is deeply concerned that details of its mail cover operations will become public knowledge. It discourages law enforcement agencies from using the information they obtain in this manner in anything except an *investigation*. Normally, the information will not be used in an actual prosecution.

However, there are important exceptions to this policy that relate to narcotics offenses. According to a recent article in *Full Disclosure* newsletter, the Postal Service regularly opens Express Mail packages that originate in certain zip codes. Here's how the program works in Chicago, as taken directly from documents filed in federal court.[39]

> The Chicago Division of the U.S. Postal Inspection Service has implemented an Express Mail Profile program at the Air Mail Facility at Chicago O'Hare International Airport. This program consists of a physical profile of Express Mail parcels which have been mailed to or from locations within the Northern District of Illinois. Targets were cities and/or areas of the United States which have been identified by law enforcement personnel as being source areas for the distribution of narcotics and/or controlled substances.
>
> After the packages are identified, they are placed in front of Drug Enforcement Agency dogs trained to sniff for the smell of drugs. If the dogs "alert" to the presence of drugs, the packages are then opened for inspection. Should drugs be found, the package is delivered to the address, and the recipient arrested.

This program is enormously threatening to anyone who values privacy in their correspondence. To begin with, virtually every mid-size or larger city in the United States could certainly be considered as a "source area for the distribution of narcotics and/or controlled substances." In addition, I have been informed by Atlanta attorney Bruce Harvey that the DEA's dogs are also trained to sniff not only for the presence of drugs, but also for the scent of *cash*.

The Postal Inspection Service is therefore not only serving as a drug police force, but also as a *cash police force*. Under current law, cash thought to be the "probable proceeds of a drug transaction" or contaminated with drug residues may be confiscated by the government. (For details, see "Attack of the Cash Police," Chapter 8.)

Full Disclosure found that many packages that were opened contained no cash or drugs. The official procedure for the Postal Service to follow under such circumstances is to enclose a copy of the warrant in the package and to deliver it. In addition, an acknowledgement that nothing illegal was discovered is to be included. However, in many cases, the packages were simply resealed and delivered to the addressee with no indication that a search had taken place.

---

[39]*Full Disclosure* (P.O. Box 903, Libertyville, Ill. 60048)

Even if your mail is not opened or monitored, the Postal Service invades your privacy in several other ways. The agency is still losing hundreds of millions of dollars each year, even after the latest rate hike. So it has come up with a new revenue-raising idea; to compile the first-ever nationwide electronic address list, and to sell it to direct-mail companies or whoever else might be interested.

Unlike other types of mailing lists, you would only be able to get off this one if you don't receive mail. Since the Postal Service is a legal monopoly, you don't really have a choice. If you want to receive mail, you'll be on the list. The real problem isn't with the list itself, but how it will presumably used in conjunction with data from credit bureaus, insurance companies, and government agencies. The plan has met with stiff opposition from privacy advocates, and may yet be terminated. But even if it is, you may be interested in other violations of your privacy rights by the Postal Service, which include:

✓ *Offering a free service to direct mail companies permitting them to convert five-digit zip codes to nine-digit codes.* The last four digits of the nine digits give federal authorities and direct marketers the *exact location* where mail is delivered, down to the block. Together with your Social Security number, the nine-digit zip code gives privacy invaders the ability to pinpoint your precise whereabouts, personal habits, investment portfolio and financial status.

✓ *Providing change-of-address information to direct marketing companies, credit bureaus, and government agencies.* When you complete a "change-of-address" form at the U.S. Post Office, this information is automatically forwarded to more than 70 direct marketing companies. Government agencies, including the IRS, also have access to this information as well. Instead of completing this form, consider contacting all correspondents personally to let them know of your address change. Or list your post office box number or mail receiving service address on the form, not your home address.

In December 1992, the House Committee on Government Operations issued a report saying that consumers should be able to opt out of having their names forwarding to direct marketing companies. But the practice continues.

✓ *Creating a "holiday card file" for individuals and businesses.* The Postal Service says this practice helps it handle the enormous volume of mail it must handle during the Christmas and Hanukkah seasons. The FBI, IRS, and other agencies have access to the lists, and might be interested, for instance, in identifying with whom someone they suspect of a crime is corresponding during the holidays.

✓ *Creating a secret intelligence unit to analyze the mailing patterns of "suspicious mailers".* This information is used to determine if a Postal Service customer might be involved in drug trafficking or other illicit activity. Mail covers directed against such suspects may last for months or even years.

It's not easy to protect your privacy from a government monopoly, but there are a few steps you can take to minimize the privacy intrusion:

1. *Don't count on the mails to communicate sensitive information.* One alternative to the post office are private carrier services, such as Federal Express or UPS. Packages sent via private carrier can still be intercepted and opened, but probable cause must be established beforehand (although this requirement is increasingly ignored). If you'd rather not have your home or office address known to a private carrier, take your packages to one of their offices or to a mail forwarding facility. You can place any return address you'd like on the package, and your home or office address won't show up on the company's computers.

Another alternative to the mails are fax machines. Although the federal government has purchased several *thousand* pieces of equipment that intercept fax transmissions in recent years, at about $20,000 per system, several fax machines are available with "secure" features that scramble the signal and decode it at the other end. The Omnifax brand is the least expensive one I know of. Two machines that use the same scrambling technique must be used.

2. *Leave your return address off mail.* Leaving your return address off correspondence that you deliver to a public mailbox almost guarantees anonymity.

3. *Obtain a post office box.* For only a few dollars a year, you can remain accessible to those wishing to contact you by mail without giving out your home address. If you must provide a return address, why not use your post office box number? When you complete the paperwork at the post office, be certain to indicate that the box will *not* be used for business or commercial purposes. This will prevent the Postal Service from releasing your street address in a casual inquiry.

There are several disadvantages of post office boxes. The most serious is that as a government-supported entity, the Postal Service is obliged to cooperate with other government agencies in any investigation of mail delivered to it, without your knowledge or consent. (Of course, this is also true of mail delivered to a street address. Increasingly, it is also true of private carriers.)

Another disadvantage is that UPS, Federal Express and other private carriers discourage parcels being sent to post office boxes. Some private carriers will mail a post card to your post office box, or contact you by phone, to inform you that they require a street address before they can deliver your parcel. If you'd rather not disclose your address, pick the parcel up personally.

This will delay your receiving parcels by a few days, but will maintain your privacy from the sender. You can also use your post office box as a return address on a parcel you send by private courier. Just make certain that you also leave a phone number so that the courier can contact you if there is a delivery problem.

4. *Ask for sensitive information to be directed to "Occupant" or "Current Resident" care of your post office box number.* The Postal Service may or may not deliver correspondence to a name or company not explicitly listed on your application. But it will almost always deliver mail addressed to "Occupant" or "Current Resident."

5. *Use an assumed name or company name in your correspondence.* Using an assumed name in this context is legal in most states as long as you have no intent to defraud. Your mail will almost certainly be delivered, especially if you add "or current resident" to your fake name.

6. *Rent a private mail box.* Almost every city has companies listed under "Mail Receiving Services" or similar headings in the Yellow Pages. Such "mail drops" charge higher fees than the Postal Service for receiving mail. But they are more discreet and may provide better service. For instance, you can direct that correspondence in any name be directed to your private mail box.

Another advantage of a private mail box is that it provides you with a street address and suite number, not a post office box. You can use this street address as an alternative to your home address for many situations; obtaining a driver's license (in some states, the home address is required); having your checks imprinted; for Federal Express and UPS delivery and pick-up, etc. Moreover, if you change your local address, this forwarding address can remain the same. This avoids the inconvenience of notifying each of your correspondents of your new address.

When you rent a private mail box, you will likely be required to show a photo ID that positively identifies you as the owner. In the past, this was not always necessary, but mail receiving services have come under government pressure to require positive identification of their customers. In addition, the manager will ask you to complete Postal Service Form 1583, "Application for Delivery of Mail Through Agent."

Form 1583 lists your name, address, the address of the mail receiving service and also authorizes information about your correspondence "to be disclosed to an appropriate law enforcement agency for investigative or prosecution proceedings." However, *completion of Form 1583 is voluntary, as the form itself states*. But if you do not complete the form, the Postal Service may return correspondence sent to your mail receiving service address to the sender. However, in most cases, your mail will be delivered.

Some mail receiving services will not provide you with a private mail box if you refuse to fill out the form, particularly if the company has recently been visited by a Postal Service inspector. You may also receive periodic requests to complete the form, but you are under no obligation to do so--unless the operator changes his mind and refuses to deliver your mail without the form. Under this circumstance, your only choice is to complete the form or find another mail forwarding service.

One way to complete this form without revealing more than you might want to is to simply leave the "home address" section (line 4a) blank. Some people insert their business address or post office box number on this line. However, I can't endorse any effort to provide inaccurate information on this form; it is considered perjury to do so. (Form 1583 is reproduced in Appendix A.)

A practical tip: If a private mail facility insists on the completion of Form 1583, and you'd rather not, don't argue. Arguing only raises your profile and makes it more likely the agent might wonder what you are trying to hide. The manager might even contact a Postal Service inspector to report your "suspicious activities."

Some states are cracking down on mail receiving services because unscrupulous marketing companies use the "suite" addresses to defraud customers. The Pennsylvania attorney general announced in 1991 that Mail Boxes, Etc., one of the biggest firms in the private mailbox business, had agreed to stop calling its boxes "suites." The company didn't admit wrongdoing but paid $12,500 in penalties and costs to settle a state civil suit alleging illegal marketing practices.

7. *Use a foreign mail receiving service.* If you receive mail from outside the United States, you might arrange for service at a mail receiving service outside the United States. This foreign service could then direct correspondence to your domestic mail receiving service. This delays correspondence considerably, but may be worthwhile if you really value your privacy.

A Canadian mail facility is ideal for this purpose; the address of one is listed in the "List of Suppliers" section. There is little stigma attached to receiving mail from Canada (unlike Switzerland or other foreign tax havens). Moreover, the sheer volume of mail, hundreds or thousands of times that between the United States and tax haven nations, insures that most correspondence to and from Canada remains private.

If you're interested in a foreign mail drop, I recommend that you obtain a copy of *Budd's Official Remailing Guide*. Published by one of the most experienced mail forwarding services in Canada, this guide is useful in learning how these services can be used.[40]

8. *Make your correspondence tamper-resistant.* Corporate spies and U.S. intelligence agencies have perfected many techniques to open mail. An expert can surreptitiously open even the best-protected mail, but you can discourage casual examination by carefully taping the flaps and sides of your envelopes. Use foil lined envelopes to prevent someone from reading the contents of letters by applying oil to the envelope or holding it up to a light. You can also wrap your correspondence in aluminum foil or carbon paper.

---

[40]Wayne and Lois Budd, *Budd's Official Remailing Guide* (R.R. #1, Box 63, Eldorado, Ontario, Canada; 1988)

9. *Use codes and ciphers, and change them frequently.* This may sound like a cloak-and-dagger strategy, but it's one of the oldest ways to protect correspondence. You can make up your own code, using indirect language and code words--but natural sounding ones, so your correspondence doesn't sound contrived. The ultimate guide to using codes is *The Code Book,* which describes techniques to create codes using a microcomputer, a calculator or even by hand.[41]

10. *Communicate via computers using data encryption.* There now exist mathematical techniques to create unbreakable codes that may even outwit the National Security Agency's supercomputers. NSA is seeking to have Congress pass legislation that would ban such codes from being offered to the public, but they remain legal as we go to press, although are difficult to sell commercially. As a result, several such programs have been introduced into the public domain.

To protect your correspondence using these codes, simply communicate materials you need to keep confidential using encrypted electronic mail. Unbreakable codes use two keys. Either key can be used to encode a message, but the corresponding key must be used to decode it. AT&T, MCI, and Compuserve all offer electronic mail services. Or you can mail encoded floppy disks. Even if your mail is opened, and the disk intercepted, your message remains secure.

One of the best programs of this type is "Pretty Good Privacy," or PGP. You need to use a modem to "download" the program into your computer from an electronic bulletin board. Hundreds of local electronic bulletin boards have this program in their files.

11. *Get off mail lists.* You may not mind remaining on some lists, but it's in neither your interest nor that of marketers to send you offers you either dislike or ignore. At least two organizations have mail preference services which will take your name off (or place it on) various mailing lists. The oldest program is run by the Direct Marketing Association, and is free. Other programs that involve annual fees are run by Equifax and a company called "Junk Mail Busters." (Addresses for these companies are in the "List of Suppliers.")

12. *Be wary of sending cash through the mail.* The government already seizes millions of dollars in cash each year from mailed envelopes and packages. Dishonest postal employees target greeting cards, in particular, because they realize they often contain cash. (So don't use the envelope supplied when you send a greeting card. Use a plain white one instead.)

Several bills before Congress would permit the Postal Service to seize any "suspicious" cash it finds, without a trial. Since the new $10s, $20s, $50s, and $100s introduced in 1991 and 1992 contain magnetized ink and other metallic components (see "The New Money," Chapter 10), the Postal Service can now screen "suspicious packages" simply by running them through a metal detector. A "hit" would mean your package could be opened--and any cash it contains confiscated.

13. *If you do not wish to receive sexually-oriented direct mail advertising, ask your local post office for Form 2150.* Material marked "sexually-oriented" will be withheld from both your residence and your post office box.

14. *Be alert to unusual patterns or delays in how you receive your correspondence.* If you notice a sudden delay in your correspondence, or notice that receive no mail on Saturday, but a large batch the following Monday, that may be a tip-off to a mail cover. Government employees outside the Postal Service rarely work on Saturday, so correspondence they are examining is delayed until Monday for delivery to the recipient.

---

[41]Michael Moretta, *The Code Book: All About Unbreakable Codes and How to Use Them* (Port Townsend, Wash.: Loompanics Unlimited, 1987). Take the same precautions in ordering materials from this company as you would for orders from Eden Press. (See "List of Suppliers" for this company's address.)

The Privacy Act of 1974

The Privacy Act, it turns out, is no protection at all. You can drive a truck through the Privacy Act.

-- Robert R. Bellair, counsel to the National Commission on the Confidentiality of Health Records

By the early 1970s, the proliferation of personal data in government databases had reached an all-time and uncontrolled high. The IRS, FBI, CIA, Department of Defense, National Security Agency and dozens of other federal agencies kept files on U.S. citizens. These agencies had no legal obligation to verify that the data that they maintained was accurate. Nor were they required to disclose to citizens what records were being kept.

The Privacy Act was intended to bring this propagation of data, and its sharing, under control. Under its provisions, a government agency gathering data on an individual is required to keep a list of disclosures of personal information to other agencies. It gives citizens the authority to examine their files and challenge information they felt to be inaccurate.

Opposed by virtually all government agencies, the act was adopted only after Congress inserted large loopholes. The most significant loophole is that "routine use" of information or transfers of information require no notification or consent.

Another loophole is that information with potential national security and law enforcement uses is exempt from the act's provisions. In practice, this has meant that many agencies encourage bureaucrats to co-mingle ordinary records with those having national security applications, thus exempting all such records from reporting requirements. (Could we call this practice "data laundering?") Finally, many agencies interpret the act as covering only *paper* records; the much-more-extensive computerized records maintained on Americans don't count.

The Privacy Act also prohibits a state, local, or federal agency from requiring an individual's Social Security number as a condition of receiving services or benefits, unless this is authorized by law. Yet since its passage, Congress has since not only authorized the use of the number, but mandated it. The most striking example is the Tax Reform Act of 1986, which requires children over the age of five (since reduced to one) claimed as dependents on tax returns to have a Social Security number listed.

In the two decades since the Privacy Act was enacted, it has had little effect in government efforts to gather information on individual citizens. In practice, just about any use of personal data by a government agency is considered routine. Test yourself: When was the last time you received a letter from a government agency informing you that information about you had been distributed to another agency? I have *never received* such a letter. Have you?

The Privacy Act also requires the government to publish an annual census of files containing personal information. However, many files are excluded because they contain information relating to national security. Other files aren't counted because of sloppy bookkeeping. Still, the 1977 census reported that more than four *billion* files were being kept on U.S. citizens--more than 16 files for every American. Later census figures showed lower numbers of files, but only because of a progressively longer list of agencies claiming exemptions under the act.

Nor are restrictions placed on government agencies sharing data with state and local jurisdictions. Criminal records, tax records and other sensitive information continue to freely change hands without the knowledge or consent of the individuals the records concern.

The act also prohibited federal, state, or local government agencies from denying a benefit to anyone who refuses to provide a Social Security number. But two years later, Congress created another loophole in the Tax Reform Act of 1976. With this legislation, Congress expressly exempted state welfare, tax, and motor vehicle agencies from this restriction.

Finally, no agency was put in charge of enforcing the Privacy Act. As a result, government agencies have been loosely policed in acting on its provisions.

Chapter Five

PRIVACY AT WORK

Have you ever consulted, been counseled or treated by a psychiatric social worker, psychologist, psychiatrist, therapist or mental health specialist of any kind?

Are you now an officer of, employed in any capacity, or do you work for a political organization?

Do you have any foreign connections, such as academic affiliations, business or financial interests, or personal associates?

What was the annual income of your spouse during each of the preceding five years?

> *-- excerpts from a proposed questionnaire for the U.S. Customs Service to administer to current employees for "re-investigation" of their right to security clearances*

"If you don't answer, you could lose your job, and if you do answer, you could lose your job and be prosecuted as well." Minnesota Congressman Gerry Sikorski was speaking of a 18-page Customs Service questionnaire, excerpts from which are listed above. The questionnaire was designed to re-certify security clearances for existing employees--but Sikorski's words could refer to virtually any job application form.[42]

There are few privacy rights in the workplace. Before you are hired, your employer may ask you to answer questions that invade not only your privacy, but that of your family. Once you are working, he may deny you the right to speak freely, search you or your office or force you to undergo drug testing. He may even hire informers to spy on you (as the Customs Service has admitted it does). If your work involves the national security or handling large amounts of money, your employer may require you to submit to a polygraph, or "lie detector" test to qualify (or re-qualify) for your job.

Once you are hired, there is virtually no limit to the information your employer can gather. He may listen to your telephone conversations, monitor your keystrokes on a computer terminal, and even ask your neighbors to describe your habits at home. If you make a worker's compensation claim, he may place your name in a computerized database that other employers may consult when they are making hiring decisions. He may even hire informants to spy on you. The Customs Service, for instance, now has in place a network of undercover employees to watch other employees and report any suspicious activities to supervisors.

You have a right to inspect files government agencies and credit bureaus keep on you. But you have no such right to inspect your own employment records (except in a few states). Your only recourse is to negotiate with your employer to regain some of the rights you have lost as an employee.

---

[42]A public employees' union filed a lawsuit in May 1992 to force the government to reduce the intrusiveness of the questionnaires it requires existing Customs employees to complete.

Privacy in Your Job Application

Your first line of defense in maintaining on-the-job privacy is your application. Obviously, the more important a position for which you are applying, the stronger your bargaining stance--and the more discretion you have in completing (or not completing) the most objectionable portions of the application form.

Employers clearly have an interest in learning about disabilities or other factors that might affect your on-the-job performance. On the other hand, you may choose to ignore questions that are clearly irrelevant.

If you are being hired for an office position that involves little or no physical activity, there may be no reason to answer a question that inquires about physical limitations. Should your prospective employer insist that you complete the entire application, simply mark the sections that don't apply "N/A" (not applicable).

Most employers are reluctant to release information in personnel files for fear of lawsuits. But to guard against this practice, you might ask that your employer sign an agreement not to release the information in your personnel file without notifying you and receiving your written consent. Depending on your importance to the organization, your employer may or may not be willing to sign such an agreement.

Many employment applications ask you to give approval to a personal investigation of virtually unlimited scope. You should insist that the investigation be limited to issues that clearly relate to your work. At the least, ask your prospective employer if he would be willing not to maintain the files from the investigation in the company's permanent records.

Questions about past employment usually provide the most anxiety to job applicants. Many employers ask for details of every job you have held since you entered the work force. If you have changed jobs frequently, or have been discharged from a job, you may feel compelled to "fudge" and lengthen the time you spent at one employer or another, or not list jobs that didn't work out.

Most employers do not want to hire individuals that tend to "hop" from one job to the next--but providing false information on an employment application is *always* grounds for dismissal. One possible solution: Inform your prospective employer that, in your opinion, jobs you held five or more years ago have little relevance to the position for which you are applying, especially if they were in another line of work.

You might also do a little investigation. If companies you have worked for in the past are no longer in business, or a former supervisor has retired, you can mention to your prospective employer that there is no one at a company at which you were once employed that could possibly provide a reference.

Many job applications will ask you if you have ever been *arrested* for a crime. (This question is illegal to ask in some states.) Only *convictions* should be of interest to your employer, not arrests. One way to deal with this issue (without admitting to any arrests) is to explain to your prospective employer that you would be willing to answer a question relating to convictions--but not arrests.

Once you complete your job application, you may be asked to sign a form authorizing a background investigation. Depending on the importance of the job for which you're being considered, this investigation may take a variety of forms. It will often involve your name being submitted to Employer's Information Service (EIS), a company that maintains files on individuals who have filed workman's compensation claims. Many companies automatically reject job-seekers who have filed such claims, no matter what the circumstances. This is illegal in most states, but is a widespread practice.

A more thorough investigation may involve hiring a company such as Equifax to conduct a complete pre-employment screening. The firm will gather together information from various databases to obtain a summary of an applicant's employment history, financial condition, criminal background, driving record, etc.

If you've made a workman's compensation claim, or have suffered financial or other reversals in life, it's very difficult to get a "fresh start." You no longer get a second chance.

Drug Tests

The collection site person shall ask the individual to remove any unnecessary outer garments that could be used to tamper with or adulterate his/her urine specimen. Also, all personal belongings must remain with the outer garment; the individual may, however, retain his/her wallet.

The collection site person shall note any unusual behavior or appearance. After washing his/her hands, the individual shall remain in the presence of the collection site person and not have access to water fountains, faucets, soap dispensers or cleaning agents.

The individual may provide his/her specimen in the privacy of a stall or otherwise partitioned area that allows for individual privacy. The collection site person shall note any unusual behavior. If an individual fails for any reason to provide the necessary specimen, collection site personnel shall contact the appropriate authority.

Immediately after collection, collection site personnel shall measure the temperature and conduct an inspection to determine the specimen's color and any signs of contaminants. Any unusual findings resulting from inspection must be included on the chain-of-custody form.

-- excerpt from "U.S. Scientific and Technical Guidelines for Drug Testing Programs," U.S. Health and Human Services regulations pursuant to Executive Order #12564

A Navy lieutenant was court-martialed in 1989 for her unwillingness to submit a urine sample while being observed by a "collection site person." For her refusal, she lost seniority, $500/month pay and undoubtedly incurred a permanent record as a troublemaker. (In a later, private test, the lieutenant tested negative for drugs.)

Drug testing has exploded into national prominence in the non-military sector as well. More than 60 percent of large companies already test their applicants for drug use, according to a recent survey, and the percentage is rapidly increasing.

Some industries are mandated to test for drugs by federal statutes. The most important such statute is the Anti-Drug Abuse Act of 1988. This act requires companies that under contract to any federal agency to certify that their workforce is drug-free and to institute drug-testing programs. In addition, federal law requires drug testing in the aviation, railroad, marine, trucking, mass transit and pipeline industries.

In 1989, the Supreme Court upheld the mandatory testing of certain railroad and Customs Service employees for drug and alcohol use, ruling that the government's compelling interests in safety and halting illegal drug trafficking outweigh traditional privacy concerns.

This decision makes it difficult to challenge drug testing in federal courts, but employees are having greater success in state courts. In at least a dozen states, drug testing is restricted by statute. For instance, in 1990, the California Supreme Court virtually halted random drug testing by private employers. In Massachusetts, a Superior Court judge ruled in 1992 that Motorola's drug screening program violated workers' privacy because it required testing regardless of duties performed.

Employers have legitimate concerns regarding drug use. If you arrive at work in an impaired state from the use of any drug--including legal drugs such as alcohol or prescription medicines, or are discovered using drugs on the job--your employer clearly has reasonable cause to take disciplinary action. A drug testing program in an occupation where an employee is operating dangerous machinery or is responsible for the safety of others may be justified, but only under narrowly defined circumstances.

If you don't use illicit drugs, why might you want to think twice before taking a drug test (assuming that you don't find being forced to urinate in a jar an infringement of your privacy rights?)

There are several reasons. To begin with, "random" drug testing is seldom random. Low-level employees are much more likely to be asked to submit to a drug test than highly-paid executives. I don't know of any congressmen or senior military officers who have been asked to take a drug test.

Nor are all drugs alike. To place a casual user of marijuana in the same category as someone addicted to crack cocaine is ludicrous. Yet most company's drug policies provide for outright dismissal if either drug is detected in a urine test--while providing exemptions for users of other potentially harmful, but legal drugs, including alcohol and prescription medicines. Furthermore, the illicit drug that is widely considered the least harmful--marijuana--shows up in tests for as long as 30 days, vs. three to five days for more dangerous drugs such as cocaine and heroin.

Drug tests also aren't particularly accurate. The most common drug screening programs routinely confuse licit and illicit drugs. The over-the-counter medication Advil, for instance, may trigger a positive response for marijuana use. So will certain drugs that contain chemicals derived from marijuana, used to reduce the severity of side-effects from other drugs given to fight cancer and AIDS. Some antihistamine medications will make urine test positive for the presence of amphetamines. And even if you are "clean," sloppy testing could get you fired. According to a survey conducted by the Forensic Science Foundation, 35 percent of urine and blood samples subjected to drug testing analysis are analyzed improperly.[43]

An even bigger problem with drug tests is that once you submit a urine sample, you don't know what other tests might be performed on it. One police department that administered drug tests to job applicants also analyzed urine samples to determine if applicants had a higher-than-average risk of developing diabetes and heart disease. Applicants that tested negative for drug use, but were shown to be at relatively high risk for these conditions were eliminated from consideration. (See "Biological Privacy" in Chapter 10 for more information on the proliferation of these tests.)

If you are asked to take a drug test, and would rather not, you may be protected by state laws. While drug testing for government employees has been cleared in most cases by Supreme Court decisions, private companies must test in accordance with state laws, as long as these statutes are not in conflict with federally mandated testing programs.

---

[43]This survey was conducted in 1978. Drug testing advocates claim today's tests are far more accurate.

Should you be concerned about the possibility that a random drug test might indicate a "false positive" drug use profile or reveal a health condition you'd rather not have publicized, discuss your concern with your employer. If testing is non-negotiable, ask your employer to sign a statement guaranteeing that the test will not be used for any purpose except to detect the presence of illicit drugs.

You might even want to point out to your employer the results of a study of drug testing conducted by the Department of Labor in 1991. It found that most companies with fewer than 50 employees were abandoning drug testing as uneconomical. Overall, one out of three companies that conducted drug tests in 1988 had discontinued them by 1990. On the other hand, your employer may quote the results of a 1990 Postal Service study suggesting that those who tested positive in a pre-employment screening were at least 50 percent more likely to be fired, injured, disciplined, or absent than those who did not.[44]

Should you try to "beat" a urine test? Adding bleach to a urine specimen, for instance, will cause most samples to test negative. I don't condone taking this or similar steps outlined in books such as *Steal This Urine Test*. Such measures are illegal in some states. Being caught could get you fired or even prosecuted.[45]

Recently, alternatives to urine tests have been developed for detecting the presence of illicit drugs. The best-known alternative is "immunoassay," a technique where shreds of a person's hair are analyzed for the presence of illicit drugs.

Former Washington, D.C. mayor Marion Barry was found to have cocaine residues in his hair after submitting to this type of test. More recently, such a test was administered to a Miami city commissioner to determine if he used cocaine. The California company that developed the hair testing method claims that its analysis is more accurate than urine testing, since hair samples hold drug residues for a longer period of time than urine.

However, the Food and Drug Administration concluded in 1990 that this technique "is an unproven procedure unsupported by the scientific literature or well-controlled studies and clinical trials...the consensus of scientific opinion is that hair analysis by [immunoassay] to detect the presence of drugs of abuse is unreliable and is not generally recognized by qualified experts as effective."[46]

This has not stopped employers from conducting such tests, even though they cannot be sold commercially. In one of the few court challenges to this practice, a Nevada state judge upheld an employee drug testing program at Harrah's Lake Tahoe casino that includes both hair analysis and urinalysis.

Other new methods to detect drug use are also being introduced. The FBI has introduced an experimental drug testing kit that merely involves wiping your hands on a specially-treated towellette. The towellette is then placed in a fluid that changes color in the presence of residues from illicit drugs or explosives. According to the agency, the test is calibrated so that positive tests won't result from handling currency, which the FBI admits is almost always contaminated with cocaine residues.

Even less intrusive is a performance test. Tests developed by companies such as California-based Performance Factors, Inc., are less expensive than urine tests and produce results immediately. The

---

[44]"Costs and Benefits of Pre-Employment Drug Screening," *Journal of the American Medical Association*, January 1, 1992

[45]Abbie Hoffman with Jonathan Silver, *Steal This Urine Test* (E. Rutherford, NJ: Viking-Penguin, 1988.)

[46]*Federal Register*, June 13, 1990.

system, which is similar to a computer game, generally links a control knob to a personal computer to evaluate a worker's responsiveness. It takes less than a minute to administer.

"Honesty Tests"

Another screening technique used by many employers is the written test, often known as "honesty tests." These tests aim to predict whether you might steal, lie or become involved with illegal drugs on the job. An estimated 3 million such tests are administered each year in the United Tests. Their use has soared as a result of a 1988 law that bars most employers from using polygraph tests.

Many employees feel that honesty tests are inaccurate and that they brand anyone with unorthodox beliefs or ideas as a potential thief. Several lawsuits are proceeding against companies who employed written tests as part of their pre-employment screening.

Most of these lawsuits target tests that ask embarrassing questions about sexual preferences or bodily functions (examples: "I am strongly attracted to members of my own sex" or "I have never had any black, tarry-looking bowel movements.") Employees have a right to ask what such questions have to do with anticipated job performance. In 1991, a California Court of Appeals refused to dismiss a lawsuit against a department store that contained such questions, along with inquiries about religious and political affiliation.[47]

The Office of Technology Assessment, which conducts research for Congress, in 1990 questioned the credibility of research evaluating these tests--but did not dismiss it. While employers have a legitimate reason to avoid hiring thieves, users of illicit drugs and other equally undesirable employees, the study may lead Congress to order that further research be conducted. However, it appears unlikely that Congress will ban or restrict these tests in the near future.

Surveillance on the Job

More than six million American clerical workers work under continuous electronic surveillance. These individuals, many working in data entry or customer service positions, have their typing speed, input accuracy, length of time at their work station, etc. automatically monitored. For instance, IRS phone representatives are electronically monitored 13 different ways, according to *USA Today*. Not measuring up to the standards electronically monitored by your employer could result in your dismissal.

Telephone use may also be closely monitored on the job. One device, a "station message detail recorder," provides employers with a printout of every call made from every extension in an office. Your employer may also monitor or record your phone calls without your consent or knowledge.

New technology makes it possible to monitor workers in vehicles as well. The Safeway grocery chain recently initiated a program where it installed computers in its fleet of nearly 800 trucks. The computers monitor driving speed, oil pressure, idling time, and several other factors. If anything is abnormal--for instance, if the computer discloses that the engine was idling longer than normal--the driver may be questioned. Without a satisfactory answer for the unusual reading, he may be suspended or fired.

Not only is such surveillance bothersome, it may also entail health risks. Researchers from the University of Wisconsin found in a nationwide survey that electronically monitored workers suffered

---

[47]Additional information on written tests, their use (and abuse) is contained in "Should You Tell All?," *Parade*, May 27, 1990.

significantly more headaches and wrist, arm, shoulder and neck pains than workers who were not monitored. In addition, these workers were more likely to be troubled by depression, tension, extreme anxiety and severe fatigue.

Other measures companies have initiated in the name of efficiency also may sacrifice privacy. One example is "electronic mail," a method of communicating using computer terminals, rather than with a written memo. Electronic mail, or e-mail, has in many organizations been effective at reducing paper clutter and is popular among employees. At many companies, workers are told that their e-mail messages are confidential--a statement that may or may not be true depending on how the e-mail system is set up. However, most employees believe that a message sent by e-mail is more private than a paper one. This is part of the attraction of e-mail; to attract honest, give-and-take discussion.

However, e-mail messages can often be collected by a system administrator and categorized according to subject, author, addressee, etc. In extreme cases, workers have even been dismissed as a result of e-mail messages they originated. In one incident, an employee of the Defense Department was fired after he complained via a Pentagon e-mail system about cost overruns in a weapons research project. In another incident, Epson America fired an employee who complained that her boss was reading her e-mail messages.

Another new trend is to use e-mail archives in litigation. Attorneys conducting discovery proceedings now dig up old, lost, and even "deleted" e-mail messages. Since many e-mail systems create permanent "archives" of e-mail messages--even those deleted from the primary system--old messages can be highly incriminating. Since e-mail promises anonymity, such messages can be far more damaging that a written memo. E-mail records are most often requested in cases relating to trade secret, patent, and copyright cases.

Nor are files you store on a personal computer necessarily private, especially if the computer operates as part of a local area network. Network-management programs now allow administrators to read, rewrite, and delete files from personal computer hard disks. Some of the programs even allow the administrator to monitor what's being typed by an operator. A spokesman for *XTree,* a software developer that introduced such a program in 1990 is uneasy about the privacy implications of this program. He admits that having the program look at the files in your computer is a little like "someone was rummaging through your desk drawers while you were working on the desk top."

Congress seems likely to restrict work-place monitoring. In 1992, the House Education and Labor Subcommittee approved HR 1218, the Privacy for Consumers and Workers Act. This act would require employers who monitor workers electronically to provide notice of such monitoring. Employees would be notified of the hours and days that monitoring would occur and the uses to be made of the data collected. Random monitoring--the practice many workplace privacy advocates say is most stressful-- would be sharply restricted, and banned entirely for employees who have worked at a company for at least five years. The bill has an incredibly sweeping range--time clocks, for instance, are considered "electronic monitoring devices."

Even without such limitations, the courts are slowly recognizing the right of employees to be free of the most exaggerated surveillance. An Arkansas District Court ruled in 1992 that a business owner may not wiretap an employee's phone call without informing the employee of the activity. Snooping in this case went far beyond mere listening to determine if the phone was being used for business purposes (*Deal vs. Spears*, W.D.Ark., 92-1143).

On the other hand, surveillance of a person receiving disability benefits, conducted by an insurer, does not stand as the basis of a claim for intentional infliction of emotional distress. In *Thorpe vs. Mutual of Omaha Insurance Co.* (91-2306), Frank Thorpe was a police officer who sustained serious injuries in an employment-related automobile accident. Thorpe then retired and began receiving disability benefits. Mutual of Omaha began a program of systematic surveillance, including on one occasion following him in his car with the insurer's agent allegedly trying to ram him. The 1st District Court of Appeals rejected the claim.

As health insurance rates skyrocket, employers are now finding it attractive to restrict their employee's off-the-job activities. Many companies have banned smoking on--and off--the job, and obtain a break on their health insurance premiums as a result. A study by Atlanta-based Health Associates, Inc., found that 35 percent of a company's health insurance bill is dictated by employee's with lifestyle-related risks, such as smoking, overeating, or drinking alcohol. Are we coming to a time when employers ban all these activities, on or off the job? The trend appears to be moving in that direction.

Short of finding a new job, it is not easy to reclaim on-the-job privacy if your employer is determined to invade it. But you can minimize the privacy invasion by avoiding the use of your employer's e-mail and telephone systems to send messages or make calls that you'd rather not be a matter of record.

Or you could take collective bargaining or legal action. Under an agreement in April 1992 with the Communications Workers union, Centel (a telecommunications company) ended undisclosed eavesdropping. And the employee fired by Epson, for instance, sued the company for wrongful discharge. However, the case was brought under California statutes, not federal law. California is one of only 10 states that provides an explicit right to privacy in its constitution.

Privacy and the Lie Detector

In 1988, the Employee Polygraph Protection Act took effect, barring most private employers from using polygraph tests to screen job applicants. The law also greatly restricts use of lie detectors to test present employees.

Lie detector tests can only be used for the following types of personnel or circumstances, according to the act:

✓ Employees of federal contractors engaged in national security, intelligence or counterintelligence operations

✓ Federal, state and local government employees

✓ Employees who are reasonably suspected of involvement in theft or other loss

✓ A workplace incident that results in economic loss or injury to an employer's business

✓ Prospective employees of private armored car, security alarm and security guard firms

✓ Current and prospective employees of firms engaged in the manufacture, distribution, or dispensing of controlled substances

Lie detectors are more than an invasion of privacy. They are frequently inaccurate. Even the industry council promoting lie detector tests, the American Polygraph Association, claims an accuracy rate of only 90 percent. Indeed, even if these figures do not exaggerate the polygraph's accuracy, they imply that one out of ten individuals who take polygraph tests could be falsely implicated for actions they did not take or crimes they did not commit.

You should resist any efforts your employer makes to force you to take a lie detector test. Should you try to defeat the test? As in the case of drug tests, doing so may be illegal, and I cannot endorse such efforts. Still, since lie detector tests are wrong at least 10 percent of the time, and since flunking the test can get you fired, you might be interested in the following thoughts from the February 15, 1987 *The Royal Society of Liechtenstein* communique.[48]

A polygraph measures bodily functions in the form of electrical impulses. These impulses are converted to mechanical signals which in turn move a series of pens over graph paper.

Polygraph theory says that when one lies, these measurements will fluctuate more widely from a normal, "control" baseline than when one is telling the truth. This baseline is established at the beginning of the polygraph session by plotting the body's response when the subject answers questions to which the examiner already knows the truthful answers.

For instance, the subject may be asked to confirm that he has the same name as that identified on his birth certificate. A trickier baseline question is "Have you ever stolen anything?" The examiner realizes that virtually everyone has stolen something in their lifetime. A "yes" answer is the proper response. Such questions establish a baseline against which the examiner can ask increasingly incriminating questions later in the session.

To defeat the polygraph, all one must do is insure that the control baseline is unrealistically high. When incriminating questions are asked later in the session, the examiner will be comparing the body's response against an already-high baseline. No matter how the subject responds to the incriminating questions, the examiner will be unable to conclude that he is guilty.

Therefore, when the examiner asks a control question, one must make certain his body reacts as if he were under tension. For instance, one could flex his toes or press his foot against the floor as he answered. Another technique would be to clench one's teeth or bite one's tongue as he answers. Or muscles could be tightened in the arms, shoulders or legs.

Most polygraph examiners are trained to intimidate their subjects, and will express doubt about one's willingness to cooperate when it becomes clear that they cannot construct an accurate baseline. At this point, one should simply tell the examiner that he is doing the best he can. One should emphasize his willingness to cooperate, all the while keeping up the same procedure each time the examiner asks a control question.

The examiner will not wish to let the subject or the organization sponsoring the tests know that anyone can "beat" the machine. There-

---

[48]*The Royal Society of Liechtenstein* is now known as *The Oxford Club;* c/o Agora, Inc., 824 E. Baltimore St., Baltimore, Md. 21202

fore, the odds are excellent that the examiner's failure to establish an accurate baseline on his subject will not be publicized outside the examination room.

Privacy and Working For Yourself

If you are weary of on-the-job privacy invasion, you might consider working for yourself.

Self-employment, by its very nature, is more private than working for someone else. You are responsible only to yourself. No background investigation is necessary in order to go into business. If your business prospers, you reap the rewards of an owner, not an employee.

Depending on the type of work you do, you may find it necessary to register your business with the appropriate governmental authorities. But as long as you don't hire employees, allow public access to your business or pollute the environment, the government shouldn't be very interested.

Of course, you'll still have to pay taxes on your income. And you raise the possibility of a tax audit working for yourself, since the IRS believes that many self-employed individuals do most of their business "off the books." So you'll want to take the steps to "audit-proof" your tax return outlined in Chapter 6, along with following the recommendations in this section.

What type of business should you form? It should involve work you enjoy doing, that you are good at and that you are convinced can supplement (or replace) your existing income.

For instance, a friend in Fort Lauderdale worked as lead mechanic at an automobile repair shop specializing in luxury vehicles--Mercedes, Porsches, Corvettes, etc. After 10 years, he opened his own shop in a rented garage. Loyal customers sought him out, and today his business is thriving, and the profits are his to keep.

A Chicago man I know working for a large manufacturing firm felt his job threatened in a leveraged buyout. A skilled draftsman, he purchased a personal computer and learned how to operate computer-aided-design software. While he is still working in his full-time job, he constantly upgrades his skills and equipment at home. And he is now making money doing small drafting jobs for his friends and associates.

Other people turn hobbies into profitable businesses. One associate of mine--a rare coin dealer--started his business at the youthful age of 45 after he discovered the joys of coin collecting.

While the classic dream of the entrepreneur is to turn a small company into another Ford Motor Co. or Apple Computer, there are advantages in staying small, even if your business becomes a roaring success. Small businesses maintain a much lower profile than large ones. In this age of frivolous litigation and constantly expanding government, staying small helps avoid the limelight.

Of course, you can't avoid interaction with the government altogether. For instance, many local governments will require purchase of a license if you are self-employed. There may be an exemption if you work out of your home or don't deal with the public. The license will cost you anywhere from $10 to hundreds of dollars for every community in which your business operates. Most must be renewed annually.

You should avoid purchasing a business license unless it is illegal not to do so. The reason: Businesses are one of the first sources of revenue bureaucrats turn to when governments need income, via "business and occupation" taxes. A business license also makes you vulnerable to surprise inspections by bureaucrats administering programs ranging from zoning laws to building codes.

Using a fictitious name has its advantages from a privacy standpoint. For instance, if you have correspondence you'd rather keep private sent to "ABC Corp." rather than "John Smith," only the most ambitious telemarketer will be able to determine your true identity. However, using a fictitious name may require that you register it with local government authorities by filing a "Fictitious Name Statement," negating part of this advantage. In most counties, this information is published in local newspapers and the applications are available for public inspection.

Dealings with the federal government usually aren't a major ordeal as long as you don't hire employees. You must file quarterly reports and tax payments with the IRS, but this is the only federal agency with which most one-person or two-person businesses must deal.

Interestingly, the rate that small businesses are audited is considerably lower than the individual audit rate. However, the IRS announced in 1991 that tax compliance by small businesses eroded dramatically in the 1980s, and that it planned new enforcement measures. For instance, IRS audit results suggest that small corporations pay only about 61 percent of the tax they actually owe.

To increase compliance, the U.S. General Accounting Office suggests that the IRS initiate an income document matching program for corporations--similar to the one already in effect for individuals. Whether or not this proposal is implemented, expect a steady rise in audit rates for small businesses and corporations in the next few years.[49]

If your self-employment venture is successful, you may eventually find that you cannot handle all the work yourself. Instead of hiring employees, turn first to members of your family for help. Keeping a business in the family lowers your profile and the risk of lawsuits, theft, etc. In addition, there may be significant tax advantages to such an arrangement.

If your business grows beyond the ability of you and your family to run, consider temporary help. This is particularly appropriate if you need the extra help only on a seasonal basis. Unskilled workers can often be hired out at minimum wage from local labor pools. Skilled workers can be found through temporary help agencies such as "Manpower," etc. Due to the greatly increased volume of federal regulations affecting small business, a large number of temporary help companies are available from which to choose.

Don't become an employer except as a last resort. Employers are obliged to comply with thousands of federal, state and local laws, regulations and ordinances which do not apply to a sole proprietor or a family business. If you fire an employee, you may have to pay unemployment benefits or even face a lawsuit for "wrongful discharge" or discrimination. Employers must also make payroll deductions to the IRS, the state and possibly local tax authorities.

New regulations are constantly coming on line; a recent "pay or play" congressional proposal would require all employers to either buy private health insurance for their employees, or pay into a national health insurance fund. Similar legislation is already in effect in Massachusetts and has been proposed in several other states.

Congress takes the position that employers are wrongly avoiding government regulatory efforts by not hiring employees. The Clinton administration may take the approach favored in many European

---

[49]*IRS' Efforts to Ensure Corporate Tax Compliance* (Washington, D.C.: General Accounting Office; GAO/T-GGD-91-21, April 17, 1991)

nations, where in Greece, Italy, and Sweden, temporary employees have been banned. A move in this direction came in the 1990 Omnibus Budget Reconciliation Act, which required that all public employees, working for any length of time, be covered by a pension plan. This act virtually wiped out the temporary market for the public sector. Unfortunately, the alternative to hiring temporary employees for many firms is going of business.

Even if the government bans temporary employment, there is still an alternative to becoming an employer. That is to *lease* your employees. A growing number of companies are turning responsibility for their company's employees over to an employee leasing company. Such companies take care of much of the paperwork that small businesses dread; tax forms, worker's compensation payments, withholding, insurance, etc. The fee for these services range from 12 percent to 20 percent of payroll.

Independent Contractors

Another alternative to employees is to hire independent contractors. This provides three major benefits:

✓ *Unlike an employee, an independent contractor exists as a business associate of the employer, not as an employee.* This relationship can be broken at any time by the employer at its sole discretion, without due process or right of appeal.

✓ *There is no need for an employer to withhold income taxes, Social Security payments, unemployment tax, or union dues.* This is the responsibility of the independent contractor. Nor is the employer responsible for an independent contractor's health insurance. The independent contractor is responsible for these payments.

✓ *Since an independent contractor is not under the direct supervision of an employer, he is more accountable for his own actions than he would be as an employee.* If the contractor commits an act that causes harm, even while performing work for the company that has temporarily retained him, the company may be less liable for his actions than they would be if he were an employee.

Unfortunately, the IRS considers independent contractors to be a threat to the tax withholding system. Since independent contractors don't have taxes withheld from a regular wage, the IRS wishes to narrow the definition of work that qualifies for independent contractor status in any manner possible.

In short, the IRS has made it very difficult for businesses to engage in long-term employer-independent contractor arrangements. If someone works for you for at least 30 days, in your location, under your direction, that individual is considered by the IRS to be an employee. (Some IRS agents would argue the employer-employee relationship begins the day a worker sets foot in your office.)

Unless those working for you meet the following criteria, they are considered employees, not independent contractors:

✓ They must have a regular place of business outside your office

✓ They must work on their own time

✓ In general, they must bill by the job, not by the hour, week or month

✓ They must not be working under your direct supervision or the supervision of another employee

For these reasons, most businesses do not qualify for having their workers considered as independent contractors. Many firms have paid huge tax penalties to the IRS for mistakenly classifying their employees as independent contractors.

Even cases that do not appear abusive have been targeted. For instance, one firm that appeared to be ideal for independent contractor arrangements--a maid service that treated individual maids working for it as independent contractors--was declared by the IRS to be employing them.

The government's attitude toward independent contractors is contradictory. A congressional report released in 1991 criticized the IRS for using a "nonsystematic and subjective approach for selecting misclassification cases." The report found many cases where one business was forced to reclassify its workers, but another business engaged in a similar line of work was not. It also pointed out that many businesses shut down because they had been unable to pay back taxes and penalties applied by the IRS were no longer paying taxes at all. As a result of this practice, concluded the report, "Future income tax loss to the Treasury could be considerable."

After this stinging rebuke, you might have expected the IRS to ease its enforcement of borderline misclassification cases. But instead, the agency intensified audits of businesses that use independent contractors, focusing most closely on small firms. In several cases, the agency has disallowed claims it had approved in previous audits.

A 1992 report from the General Accounting Office lent credence to the IRS crackdown. It stated that there was widespread "non-compliance" among independent contractors in reporting income, despite the 1099 reporting requirements. It suggested that Congress require employers to withhold taxes for independent contractors, and fine them much more heavily for not reporting payments subject to reporting.[50]

If you declare independent contractor status for your employees, you need to be vigilant to avoid fines, penalties, and of course, back taxes. The most frequent targets of the IRS have been trucking and construction companies, courier and delivery services, and travel agencies. Nurses and consultants have also been targeted by the IRS. Talk the decision over with your accountant or tax attorney. Be ready in advance for a challenge from the IRS.

If you pay an independent contractor more than $600 in any one year, you must file a Form 1099 with the IRS. You will need the independent contractor's Social Security number in order to do so.

Should You Incorporate?

With the passage of the Tax Reform Act of 1986, many tax advantages associated with incorporation disappeared. Yet for certain income levels, incorporation retains significant tax advantages, the scope of which is beyond this report.

In addition, there are privacy and asset protection advantages to incorporation. Small corporations are audited by the IRS at a far lower rate than sole proprietors at the same income level, although as I've already mentioned, this status is beginning to change. Corporations also generally have limited liability in that they can only be held responsible for their debts and obligations only to the limit of their financial resources. Corporate officers and directors are generally not responsible for corporate

---

[50]*Tax Administration: Approaches for Improving Independent Contractor Compliance* (Washington, D.C.: General Accounting Office; GAO/GGD-92-108, July 1992)

debts, unless they have personally guaranteed such obligations. However, this is *not* the case with tax obligations.

Forming two corporations can make it extremely expensive for a would-be litigant to recover assets from you. One corporation holds the money, the other does business by borrowing the money from the first. If the court enacts a judgment against the first, it then has to collect from the second. The more complex the spider web, the more expensive the lawsuit.[51]

Incorporating in a state like Nevada has many advantages. Nevada is one of the few states that do not have an automatic exchange of tax data with the federal government. In 1991, the governor of Nevada reaffirmed this status after he accused the IRS of planning a "reign of terror" in the state. In addition, there is no corporate income tax in either Nevada.

It is no more expensive to incorporate in Nevada than in other states. Nevada is particularly popular as a location for entertainers to incorporate in, primarily because disclosure requirements are minimal. Madonna, Michael Jackson, and Diane Keaton are among the many celebrities who have formed Nevada corporations.

In 1990, Wyoming passed a statute that was modeled after the Nevada corporate enabling legislation. Wyoming has similar advantages to Nevada, in that there is no corporate income tax and the state does not exchange tax data with the IRS. Companies that can form Nevada or Wyoming corporations are included in the "List of Suppliers."

However, incorporating outside your own state may raise difficulties. Many California businesses that have incorporated in Nevada, for instance, have been taken to court by California tax authorities. Without an actual business presence in Nevada, they are usually forced to pay state taxes on their Nevada corporate income. Several companies listed in the "List of Suppliers" section will provide a staffed Nevada office for out-of-state owners or operators of Nevada corporations.

In addition, you may find it difficult to engage in normal banking relationships with a bank outside your state. The out-of-state bank may refuse to consider lending your corporation money, even with a personal signature guarantee. If you accept credit cards as payment for your product or service, the out-of-state bank may refuse to process these transactions. Before you incorporate, do your homework!

Forming a corporation also raises your profile in some ways. You must register in a state of your choice and file both state and federal corporate tax returns. You become subject to even more government red tape. Finally, despite the privacy advantages I have pointed out, courts have ruled that corporations have no right to privacy. Only individuals have that right.

Barter

Capitalism, it has been said, is what people do when the government leaves them alone. No doubt. But bartering is what they do when things get desperate.

Barter is perhaps the least-understood $600 billion business in the United States. You almost certainly barter already, whether you realize it or not. Are you a member of an airline Frequent Flyer

---

[51]An excellent guide to the use of multiple corporations for tax avoidance and asset protection is *The Nevada Corporation Handbook*, available for $69.95 from LPP's Nevada office.

club? When you exchange the points you earn in it for a free flight or first-class upgrade, you are bartering. If you use coupons to save money at the grocery, you are bartering. When you offer your neighbor use of your lawnmower in exchange for his power saw, you are bartering.

Bartering is pervasive because above all, it makes economic sense. If you have goods or services to exchange for something you need, you conserve cash. Barter can also reduce excess inventories that would otherwise deteriorate to the point of uselessness.

Barter is a necessity when cash is short. In the frontier days of our nation, little money changed hands. Until the mid-1800s, government currency was almost unknown. Most people bartered goods and services.

Barter always flourishes amidst financial catastrophe. In the Great Depression, my grandfather (a musician) played organ at weddings and funerals in exchange for goods or services. Barter works because it is based on the relative values of goods, rather than their absolute value as defined by money. This makes bartered goods much more resistant to deflation, as defined by the dollar price of an item. Bartered goods also maintain their value in inflation. When paper currencies depreciate, the goods that change hands in lieu of cash maintain their values. Barter is therefore the backbone of a hard-times economy.

Today, barter is becoming less a disaster hedge and more a mainstream business. Companies as large as Amoco and USX are involved in barter arrangements--often as an alternative to repatriating profits from nations where doing so is restricted or prohibited outright.

Barter is often promoted as a crafty way to avoid taxes, but most exchanges are taxable. According to the Internal Revenue Code, you must include in your income the fair market value of property or services you receive in barter. If you exchange services with someone else and you both have agreed ahead of time as to their value, that amount will be accepted as fair market value unless you can show that it is different. IRS Form 1099-B is used to report barter income.

One significant exception to this rule is barter of real estate, in certain cases. For instance, if you buy and renovate a house, you may be able to trade it instead of selling it! Many successful real estate entrepreneurs have built up their holdings, tax-free, using such techniques.

Becoming involved in a barter club is an excellent way to meet like-minded traders. But it is not a particularly private way of doing so. A 1982 law requires trade exchanges and barter clubs to report the bartering activities of individual clients and corporations to the IRS. Another IRS ruling states that barter *credits* received through such organizations must be reported as taxable income they year they are received, not when they are spent.

If you exchange property or services through a barter exchange, you will receive an annual statement from the exchange listing the credits you earned during the year. The IRS even has won the right to seize barter club membership lists and transaction records.

If you're just starting to barter, you might want to contact the organizations mentioned in the "List of Suppliers" for up-to-date information on ideas and also IRS rulings on this topic. But I don't suggest that you get on the mailing lists of these organizations. You also might want to purchase a copy of *The Complete Barter Home Study Guide*, by Gary North.[52]

---

[52]Gary North, *The Complete Barter Home Study Course* (c/o Low Profile, Ltd., P.O. Box 84910, Phoenix, Ariz. 85071; $69)

Moonlighting in the Underground Economy

No one can escape totally from increasingly oppressive government tax policies and regulations without becoming an outlaw, or leaving the United States. But there are ways to minimize their impact, stay in the United States, and not become a lawbreaker.

The cardinal rule that I've already described is to *lower your profile*. If your wealth is not noticed, less of it is accessible to lawsuits and governmental "due process."

We can all lower our investment profile by following the steps that you'll learn about in Chapters 7-9. And by participating in businesses and transactions that bypass the ordinary, heavily-regulated economy, we can protect our livelihood and our wealth.

This is *my* definition of the "underground economy." My definition does not agree with the U.S. government characterization of the underground economy as an illegal network of drug dealing, money laundering, loan sharking, prostitution and the like.

The underground economy I endorse is a legal one. Its participants don't engage in illegal activities. They pay taxes on their income. They simply seek to avoid government regulation wherever possible. This economy is "underground" because most people don't realize it exists and so decentralized that the goods and services it provides are difficult or impossible for government to totally control.

The underground economy is the businessman who barters excess inventory for raw materials he cannot do without. It is the factory worker who purchases a duplex with his savings and rents out the second apartment while living in the first, thereby *legally* opting out of the Social Security system. (No Social Security taxes are due on rent or royalty income). It is the businessman who turns a furniture-making hobby into a profitable sideline.

More than anything else, the underground economy is a legal and profitable way to become financially independent--and avoid giving up more of your wealth than is absolutely necessary to the government.

The underground economy is the sworn enemy of messianic government. And the government will go (and is going) to great lengths to wipe it out. But the government will never be successful: Underground economies flourish in even the most regimented societies. In some cases, the authorities finally give up and legalize the underground economy. China and most of Eastern Europe are recent examples.

One way the government fights back against entrepreneurs is to try to entrap them into tax evasion, or even money laundering (see Chapters 6 and 7). Sooner or later, an individual operating his own business is likely to be invited to sell his products or services "off the books." One example in "Adam Cash's" *Guerilla Capitalism* is "Sam," the appliance repairman.[53]

> When Sam makes a house call to fix a furnace or repair a refrigerator, he will tell the homeowner, "Look, I have a lot of expenses if I have to run this job through the books. If you just pay me cash, I can do it for

---

[53]Adam Cash, *Guerilla Capitalism* (Port Townsend, Wash.: Loompanics Unlimited, 1984)

35 percent less." Usually, people will jump at the chance to save that much, and Sam is glad to get the untraceable cash. Sam reports none of this income, although the expenses for parts, etc. are buried among his on-the-books business.

People such as Sam give self-employment a bad name, and invite further incursions by the IRS against legitimate entrepreneurs. Sam has crossed the line from legitimate tax *avoidance* to illegal tax *evasion*. Crossing the line is tempting, particularly if you're sure you "can't get caught." Just remember that tax evasion is a federal felony, punishable by up to five years in prison and a $50,000 fine.

Moreover, spending the proceeds of any transaction you know to be derived from any of more than 100 "specified unlawful activities" (such as tax evasion) is now considered to be *money laundering*. To enforce a judgment against you, the IRS can confiscate your home, your vehicle, even your entire business, without even accusing you of a crime.

Adam Cash doesn't mention Sam's cash-paying customer might obtain a reward for turning Sam in to the IRS, or even be an undercover IRS agent himself. In the year ending September 1992, 10,966 tattletales claimed rewards. The maximum reward is $100,000.

There are still plenty of opportunities for tax avoidance through legitimate deductions, barter, etc. Take full advantage of these opportunities, as well as reducing your profile from the IRS and other government agencies and private concerns through the *legal* techniques I describe elsewhere in this manual.

But don't resort to tax evasion to reduce your taxes. To do so only places you in the company of the drug dealers, the money launderers and the other unsavory individuals who make up the criminal segment of the underground economy.

Chapter Six

PRIVACY AND THE IRS

It is with considerable pride that I approve the Strategic Plan to carry out the mission of the Service.

The Plan consists of the Statement of Strategic Direction and the 55 initiatives to translate them into action. It provides a strong foundation for directing tax administration efforts well into the 1990s and lays the groundwork for the Service's entry into the 21st century.

Within the next five to 10 years, paper returns will be a thing of the past. And tax processing procedures that now take weeks and months will be reduced dramatically. Early indications are that the automated system enables us not only to collect more efficiently but to collect more dollars in less time.

-- Roscoe Eggar, Jr., former IRS Commissioner, "Internal Revenue Service Strategic Plan," document #6941, May 9, 1984

Former commissioner Eggar's "strategic plan," with its automated return system and reduced processing time, is unquestionably raising IRS efficiency. But in the process, the already enormous potential for abuse of innocent taxpayers by this powerful bureaucracy may become even greater.

Congress has assigned the IRS enormous power and authority. Without a court order or jury trial, the IRS can:

✔ Sell your home at auction and use the proceeds to pay off taxes that it claims you owe

✔ Gain access to and seize the assets in your bank account and safety deposit box

✔ Compel you to turn over personal records and give testimony against yourself

✔ Seize your paycheck and force you to support yourself and your family on no more than the standard deduction for you and your dependents. For tax year 1993, this amount is $6,000 for a married couple. The IRS may increase this amount if you are undergoing "significant hardship," which according to the IRS means "privation"--not necessarily financial. Mere "economic or personal inconvenience" doesn't count.

✔ Confiscate your Social Security check or pension check, even if that is your only source of income[54]

---

[54]Section 207 of the Social Security Act states that "the right of any person to any future payment under this title shall not be transferrable or assignable....and none of the moneys paid or payable or rights existing under this title shall be subject to execution, levy attachment or any other legal process, or to any bankruptcy or insolvency law." This statement would appear to make efforts by the IRS to seize Social Security benefits outside its authority. However, Section 6334(c) of the Internal Revenue Code reads: "Notwithstanding any other law of the United States (including Section 207 of the Social Security Act), no property shall be exempt from levy other than the property specifically made exempt by subsection (a)."

If your Social Security checks are electronically deposited into your bank account, it is obviously simpler for the IRS to seize the funds than if you cash your check over-the-counter each month.

The IRS and the Abuse of Power

A hand from Washington will be stretched out and placed upon every man's business; the eye of the federal inspector will be in every man's counting house. The [income tax] law will of necessity have inquisitorial features, and it will provide penalties. It will create a complicated machinery. Under it businessmen will be hauled into courts distant from their homes. Heavy fines imposed by distant and unfamiliar tribunals will constantly menace the taxpayer. An army of federal inspectors, spies, and detectives will descend upon the state. They will compel men of business to show their books and disclose the secrets of their affairs. They will dictate forms of bookkeeping. They will require statements and affidavits. On the one hand the inspector can blackmail the taxpayer and on the other, he can profit by selling his secret to his competitor.

--Richard E. Byrd, Speaker of the Virginia House of Delegates, speaking in opposition to the income tax, in March 1910

Congress has granted the IRS immense powers because it is the agency's responsibility to keep the federal government's $1.5 trillion budget on track, or as close to on-track as 1993's estimated $400 billion deficit permits.[55],[56]

Congressional pressure on the IRS to intensify demands for constantly increasing revenues is immense. In fact, Congress has authorized the IRS to set up its own court system, the Tax Court. In a juxtaposition of traditional American justice that is becoming all too common, defendants in Tax Court are guilty until proven innocent. Before challenging a tax assessment in Tax Court, a taxpayer must pay the tax imposed by the IRS.

If it loses in court, the IRS may ignore the decision. For instance, in 1991, a U.S. Circuit Court of Appeals ruled that the IRS must prove that a taxpayer under-reported income before seizing his assets. However, the IRS has ignored the decision--and Congress has introduced legislation that would override it. Otherwise, says former IRS Commissioner Shirley Peterson, "the entire tax system will eventually crumble."

Given the power of the IRS, it is remarkable that U.S. taxpayers owe it nearly $100 billion, according to the General Accounting Office. This sum represent "accounts receivable;" taxes assessed or otherwise calculated, but not paid. In addition, the IRS itself postulates the existence of an *annual* tax gap that will exceed $114 billion in 1992; the difference between what it believes Americans owe and what they actually admit to owing. According to the GAO, the largest and most rapidly-growing component of the tax gap is unreported income from self-employed individuals and small corporations.[57]

---

[55]For the sake of convenience and continuity, I refer to the IRS throughout this report as a "government agency." In reality, its status is somewhat more muddled. In the 1930s, the IRS was incorporated in Delaware under contract to the Federal Reserve System (another private corporation) to collect taxes. It may sound incredible to believe that the IRS is actually a private entity, but I have seen no evidence that contradicts this status.

[56]This $400 billion figure includes all off-budget items and does not add the Social Security surplus into the overall deficit figure to reduce it. It is the most realistic figure of government indebtedness, but is very seldom cited by the media.

[57]For more information on the government's analysis of the tax gap, see *Tax Administration: Profiles of Major Components of the Tax Gap* (Washington, D.C.: General Accounting Office; GAO/GGD-90-53BR; April 1990)

Such enormous numbers seem to justify in the minds of Congress virtually any action by the IRS to collect the money that is supposedly due, no matter how extreme. Typical is the comment of Ohio Senator John Glenn, who remarked, "The rapid, out-of-control growth in unpaid taxes threatens to overwhelm the IRS and is absolutely unacceptable." The GAO suggests that the agency hire private debt collectors to persuade delinquent taxpayers to pay up, as is the practice in many states.

While the "tax gap" is large, *overpayments* to the IRS are not uncommon. According to *Money* magazine, about 50 percent of the 36 million collection notices mailed in 1989 by the IRS were mailed in error, collecting $7.1 billion in taxes that were not owed. (The IRS disputes the figure, claiming that "only" 38 percent of collection notices were mailed in error. Currently, the agency says only 14 percent of collection letters are sent erroneously.)

Until 1989, the IRS had a policy of not informing taxpayers when their tax payments were too large. While this policy has been discontinued, the size of the tax gap must be kept in perspective given the reality of current and continuing overpayments.

Even if the IRS is correct in claiming that you owe it money, it routinely adds interest and penalties to its assessment. A recent GAO survey found errors in one-third of the cases it reviewed-- *nearly all of which were in the taxpayer's favor!*

The IRS claims that the tax gap would be substantially narrowed, and accounts receivable sharply reduced, if it only could receive additional funding to increase salaries, hire new agents and upgrade its computer system. But to do so, one study concluded, the IRS would need to triple its $5 billion annual budget and increase employment from 120,000 to nearly 300,000.

Clearly, IRS efficiency is not as great as it might be. Testimony from the GAO in September 1992 claims that IRS mismanagement of seized assets has led to huge losses, not the least to taxpayers whose confiscated assets are misplaced and therefore *never credited against their alleged tax deficiencies.* Moreover, assets often deteriorate in IRS possession and are sold for pennies on the dollar, GAO concluded. In 1991 alone, the IRS seized more than $128 million to satisfy alleged income tax deficiencies.

In 1989, the IRS admitted it lost about 2 million tax returns or related documents from its files, primarily because of inexperienced clerical workers. And in 1987, the agency spent a great deal of time and effort locating a taxpayer whose permanent address was a federal penitentiary!

Still, the IRS has hardly been starved for money in the last decade. From 1981 to 1991 IRS outlays soared 50 percent. In the same time frame, IRS employment increased nearly 40 percent. For fiscal 1993, former President Bush approved outlays totalling $7.1 billion for the IRS. The agency plans to spend another $6.5 billion on new computer capability in the 1990s. President Clinton suggests adding $148 million to the $563 million already appropriated for this task in 1993. How much stronger or more efficient do we want the IRS to become?

The additional funding has permitted former Commissioner Eggar's strategic plan to be rapidly implemented. One key facet is a transition from paper filing to electronic filing. In 1992, more than 10 million Americans filed their taxes electronically. The IRS expects 14 million electronic filings in 1993.

The IRS favors electronic returns because processing tax data by computer is far more efficient than organizing the same quantity of data manually. For instance, a 1979 study by the IRS concluded that it cost the agency $400 to process 100,000 documents submitted on magnetic media, compared to $20,000 to process the same number of documents on paper.

This gives computer processing a 50:1 cost advantage over manual processing; I would guess the advantage would be 200:1 or more today, given the huge advances in computer technology over the past decade. Seen in this light, another IRS objective, to "audit every taxpayer, every year" does not appear to be all that unrealistic.

But this is only the first step. Nearly 40 years ago, the IRS secretly studied a system to "eliminate the need for filing tax returns by wage earners when tax is withheld by employers." The technology for a return-free system was not available then, but the idea remains under consideration. Ultimately the IRS will develop computer systems capable of calculating the taxes each American owes. The agency calls this the "return-free system."

Once this project is completed, the IRS will simply send you a bill for the sum it has determined that you owe. If you don't pay up, the agency plans to seek authority to electronically transfer funds out of your bank account to make up the difference.

In May 1992, the GAO released its latest research on this topic in a report entitled *Opportunities to Reduce Taxpayer Burden Through Return-Free Filing*. The report concludes that a true return-free system is still not practical. However, it suggests an alternative: the "final withholding" system in use by more than 30 countries. Employees would supply employers with withholding information and the funds transferred to the IRS would be the final tax liability. No returns or refunds would be necessary for more than 40 million Americans.

For those of you who even after reading Chapter 3 still believe your telephone conversations are private, the report contains this nugget: Under the new program, the IRS would not require a *written* affirmation from taxpayers that enough money had been withheld, but an *oral* one. The IRS believes that voice recognition technology is sufficiently advanced that a "voice signature" could take the place of a written one.

In the interim, the IRS plans to initiate a system that will overhaul the federal tax deposit program used to collect more than $700 billion annually from U.S. employees through employer withholding. The employer's account will be debited directly through a central clearing agency set up by the IRS. This system will make it far easier for the IRS to levy employee wages. It will simply increase the amount electronically deducted each paycheck from the employer's account.

The IRS must walk a tightrope between Congress (demanding more money, and constantly changing the rules) and those who it collects from, who are understandably outraged at some of the tactics the agency has adopted. The overwhelming majority of IRS agents are dedicated and honest. But not all employees, as the following examples illustrate:

✔ IRS agents detained seven children at a Detroit area day care center, changed the locks on the doors, then called the children's parents. The children were released only after their parents paid fees due the school that the IRS applied to a tax levy.

✔ An Alaska couple, disputing a tax assessment, had it tripled. To enforce the assessment, IRS agents seized the couple's car while they were in it. Smashing the windows, the agents dragged the couple from the vehicle, leaving them bleeding on the pavement as a tow truck hauled their vehicle away.

✔ The home of an Amish farmer was raided by IRS agents and armed federal marshals in an effort to collect several thousand dollars in back taxes. The marshals brandished loaded machine guns at the unarmed farmer, his wife, and five-year old daughter.

✔ IRS employees destroyed or diverted thousands of tax returns in an effort to meet quotas and deadlines set by supervisors. In California, IRS employees hid 39 bags of mail. In Austin, 27,000 tax returns were hidden. In Philadelphia and California, thousands more were simply tossed in the trash. The result: late fines, liens, and harassment for thousands of innocent taxpayers.

✓ The IRS has won the right to seize bail money to satisfy a tax lien. A man charged with tax fraud in 1985 persuaded his friends and fellow investors to put up $100,000 to get him out of jail. A jury found him guilty, and he reported to prison. The judge ordered the bail money released, but the IRS appealed, arguing that a federal court must honor an IRS levy and cannot inquire into its validity. The judge found for the defendant, but the 9th U.S. Circuit Court of Appeals ruled that the tax law gives the IRS the power to impose a tax lien on "all property and rights to property" of a taxpayer.

✓ An IRS agent in Philadelphia boasted that he told a mother behind in her tax payments who had no income, "If you don't pay your taxes, then bring in your kids and we'll sell them for you."

✓ IRS tactics have on many occasions led to suicide. One woman who testified in favor of the Taxpayer Bill of Rights II in 1991 described how continuous IRS harassment of her husband for nearly a decade finally led him to commit suicide so she could use money from his insurance policy to continue to fight the agency. Homeless advocate Mitch Snyder faced IRS assessments of $90,000 before his suicide in 1990.

An ex-IRS agent, Paul J. DesFosses, has formed an organization known as the National Coalition of IRS Whistleblowers, and have compiled many such incidents in a special report, *The Internal Revenue Service: An Agency Out of Control.* (The Whistleblowers are partially funded by the Church of Scientology, which has more than 80 lawsuits pending against the IRS.)[58],[59]

With all the unfavorable publicity generated over these and similar incidents, you might think the IRS would tone down its most abusive behavior. After all, it was the agency's outrageous conduct that led to the adoption of the Taxpayer Bill of Rights (discussed later in this chapter), which the IRS vehemently opposed. But consider the following cases, all of which occurred after this law passed:

✓ Six IRS agents raided a Georgia convenience store and seized not only the store's assets, but property owned by its customers. A U.S. District Judge later ruled that the owners were victims of "bureaucratic incompetence, aggravated by hostility and arrogance."

✓ The IRS sought to exhume the body of a taxpayer who died in the course of an audit in order to verify the victim's identity. Said the executor of the estate, "They're just mad because he had the audacity to die without settling his account."

✓ Several tons of food and a dozen vehicles donated to an El Paso, Texas relief group were confiscated by the IRS based on allegations that the group owed $22,000 in back taxes, interest and penalties. Confronted with bad publicity, the IRS gave back the food, which was designated to feed the hungry and the homeless, but kept the trucks that were being used to distribute it.

✓ After spending more than two years scraping together $1.5 million to repay investors defrauded in a Ponzi scheme, Florida securities regulators had the entire amount impounded by the IRS to satisfy federal tax claims.

---

[58]*The Internal Revenue Service: An Agency Out of Control* (Los Angeles: Freedom News Journal, 1986). The address of the National Coalition of IRS Whistleblowers is P.O. Box 65471, Washington, D.C. 20035.

[59]Other excellent sources of information on abuses of IRS power include *To Harass Our People,* by former Congressman George Hansen (Washington, D.C.: Positive Publications, 1984) and *A Law Unto Itself: Power, Politics and the IRS,* by David Burnham (New York: Random House, 1989).

✓ A woman objected to the confiscation of vehicles on her property by armed men who refused to identify themselves, but turned out to be IRS agents accompanied by armed U.S. marshals. Seven months pregnant with twins, she resisted, and was beaten to the ground with the butt of an automatic weapon. One twin was born dead, the other brain-damaged. Several weeks later, the agent in charge of this operation received a commendation. (This incident was recounted in 1990 on the Larry King television show.)

✓ The IRS has randomly selected several thousand *children* for tax audits. Parents receive letters that say: "Your child has been selected for an interview... we encourage you to be present."

✓ In 1990, a taxpayer in San Jose, California was billed for $68,000 in back taxes--plus a penalty of $647 *million*. When she called the IRS for assistance, she was told she had to pay the assessment before she could challenge it in Tax Court.

✓ In 1991, the Executive Life Insurance Co. was shut down by state regulators in California. Three days after the shutdown, the IRS presented Executive Life with a bill for $643 million in taxes--which could have prevented the company from paying off its obligations to the owners of its 170,000 life policies, 70,000 annuity policies, and more than 3,000 guaranteed investment contracts. Fortunately for policyholders, the IRS eventually settled for a much smaller amount.

✓ The IRS vigorously enforces laws prohibiting companies from contributing too much money to their pension plans--even when these plans, according to the Pension Benefit Guaranty Corp. (PBGC), are grossly underfunded. One company, Loews Corp., would like to get off the PBGC's list of employers that owe the most to their pension plans--but the IRS won't let them make extra contributions without being subject to heavy penalties.

Sometimes, IRS actions are so outrageous, they are almost comical--until you consider the consequences to the victims:

✓ The IRS fined a Virginia businessman $400 for failing to pay two cents of his $22,894 payroll withholding tax bill

✓ The IRS ordered a police commission in a small town in Pennsylvania to pay $700 on a one cent underpayment in its deductions from employee paychecks

✓ The IRS confiscated the bank account of a nine-year old girl to pay part of a tax claim against her grandmother and the $10.25 life savings of a 12-year old boy because of his parent's tax debt

✓ A man purchased what he believed to be a 14-karat gold chain at an IRS auction for $815. The IRS stated the chain had a retail value of $1,920. When the man discovered that the chain was a worthless imitation containing no gold, he asked for his money back. The agency refused, saying "all sales are final."

Nor is the IRS bound by the conclusions of other government agencies. In 1988, a company gave the Library of Congress films that experts hired by the library appraised as being worth $16 million. Based on this appraisal, the company claimed a $16 million deduction on its federal tax return. The IRS made its own appraisal of $1.26 million and took the company to Tax Court, which ruled that the IRS was free to make its own, binding appraisal.

Even if you win against the IRS, you sometimes still lose. That's what happened to a man fired from a manufacturing firm who sued for age discrimination, and won a $180,000 judgment. Most legal experts agree such payments are not subject to income tax, but the IRS disagreed, and sought $68,000 in taxes. The man took the agency to court, and won--but only after ringing up $88,000 in legal fees.

However, the U.S. District Court denied his request for the IRS to pay his legal fees, which were $20,000 more than the original tax claim.

A taxpayer can recoup attorney fees and court costs from the IRS only if a judge concludes that the IRS was wrong *and* that the agency has taken an "unreasonable" position.

In practice, this means that almost the only way you can recover legal fees from the agency is if IRS agents engage in outright criminal activities. In one case, Daniel Neil Heller, an attorney and reporter for *The Miami News,* wrote a series of articles criticizing an IRS investigation of prominent Miami citizens.

Heller was promptly indicted for tax evasion, and convicted based on testimony from his accountant. He appealed, contending that an IRS agent had intimidated his accountant into lying at his trial. Heller won the appeal, but the IRS fought a $20,000 settlement that he had obtained against the agency for the agent's misdeeds. After a long court battle, a U.S. District Judge ruled that Heller was entitled to recover these costs as well.

Other IRS misdeeds are even more serious. Between April and September 1990, investigators from the Treasury Department investigated 1,700 cases of bribery, smuggling, embezzlement and theft, the vast majority of which were allegedly committed by IRS agents.

IRS agents in North Carolina and California have been accused of laundering drug money and using a government computer to help a drug dealer avoid prosecution. Another agent was convicted on charges that he accepted more than $400,000 in bribes to help a wealthy California lettuce grower avoid tax payments. In New York City, a former IRS agent was charged with giving the home addresses of jurors to a man accused of attempted murder. Two clerical IRS employees were indicted on charges that they embezzled more than $39,000 worth of money orders while working for the agency. Another agent in Florida was accused of soliciting a $1 million bribe.

Congressional investigators have also discovered that the IRS has routinely ignored reports of wrongdoing among high-ranking employees of the agency's elite Criminal Investigation Division (CID), which investigates criminal violations of the tax laws, and the Office of Inspection, which polices employee conduct. After reporting misconduct by a CID supervisor, three IRS agents were demoted and allegedly told by their superiors that "the organization will get you, you whores."

The former branch chief of an IRS compliance center was indicted in January 1992 for filing false income tax returns using the names and Social Security numbers of individuals he knew would not file. The returns all showed large refunds due, which he pocketed. If this scam hadn't been uncovered, the individuals named on the returns could have been responsible for paying back the government nearly $500,000, plus penalties and interest. In a separate incident, a retired CID chief was indicted for selling non-public marital records to a California private investigator while still employed by the IRS.

A 1990 investigation by the House Commerce, Consumer and Monetary Affairs Subcommittee focused on eight cases involving 25 senior officials in 10 cities. The offenses ranged from minor (personal trips on the agency's tab) to major (the head of the Los Angeles CID allegedly arranging a system under which clients of his personal lawyer could obtain immunity from prosecution for tax evasion if they anonymously paid their taxes into a lockbox.)

The IRS consequently embarked upon a campaign to root out wrongdoing among all its employees and established an independent office to investigate misconduct. It is being assisted (involuntarily) by the National Association of IRS Whistleblowers, which has launched a campaign to entice rank-and-file IRS employees to report wrongdoing by supervisors. The Whistleblowers are offering a reward of up to $10,000 to employees who provide information leading to the conviction of a top IRS official.

However, the coverup of misconduct continues, according to William C. Duncan, a former IRS criminal investigator, who said he was encouraged by agency attorneys to lie to a congressional subcommittee investigating it.

> To my knowledge, not one of the IRS attorneys has been punished, additional IRS executives have provided false, misleading or incomplete testimony to investigators, and the conspiracy to cover up the illegal acts continues.

Moreover, IRS abuse of its employees who report abuses continues, despite the best efforts of Congress and organizations such as the Whistleblowers coalition. In the summer of 1992, an employee at the IRS national computer center in West Virginia when he discovered that his supervisor was improperly operating government computers and other equipment for personal benefit. He reported the activity, and was then pulled off the project he was working on and transferred to a dead-end job.

Most victims of unwarranted or even illegal IRS abuse are those least able to defend themselves: lower-income and middle-class taxpayers, as opposed to the wealthy and large corporations. One reason is that lower-income taxpayers tend not to challenge IRS assessments, while individuals and corporations with larger resources can afford to take the agency to court--and often win. In addition, the IRS has the resources to track every penny of income earned by the average wage-earner through W-2s, 1099s, and similar reports that must be submitted by employers, banks, brokerages, etc. It has no comparable system to track the earnings of the wealthy or of corporations.

However, it is not just middle-class and lower-income Americans whose records reside on IRS computers. The IRS has compiled an "Individual Master File" on every U.S. taxpayer. These files were once unavailable to taxpayer scrutiny. But in a 1989 decision, a U.S. Circuit Court of Appeals ruled that the IRS had to open its files in a case where a father and son were accused of helping to prepare false tax returns and defraud the government.

The IRS has therefore been put on notice that taxpayers may obtain information from their master files. But you may need to conduct a Freedom of Information Act (FOIA) inquiry in order to obtain yours. Dan Pilla's *Taxpayer's Ultimate Defense Manual* contains a model letter for a FOIA inquiry to obtain your file.[60]

The "Outrageous Code"

> *The greatest challenge to our tax system is to ease the burden of complexity on taxpayers. Once people conclude that it is too difficult, too time-consuming, or too expensive to comply, many will stop complying."*
>
> *--Fred Goldberg, former IRS Commissioner*

You might think that the easiest way to avoid IRS scrutiny would be to pay your fair share of taxes. Unfortunately, determining what that share is may not be easy, even with professional assistance.

---

[60] Dan Pilla, *Taxpayer's Ultimate Defense Manual* (St. Paul, Minn.: Winning Publications, 1989)

No one, including anyone at the IRS, has a precise knowledge of our nation's complex tax laws. The text of these laws fills several thousand pages and has sections numbered up to 9,602. Regulations published to interpret the code occupy several thousand more pages. And to really understand the tax laws, you must be familiar with the IRS Manual, which fills an entire bookshelf. Yet "ignorance of the law is no excuse."

Nowhere does the complexity of these laws become more apparent than when you call the IRS for assistance. A 1988 survey by the Government Accounting Office revealed that IRS agents responding to phoned-in questions from taxpayers provided the correct answer only 61 percent of the time. By 1991, the figure had improved to 81 percent, and by 1992, to 84 percent.

However, the accuracy rate varies inversely with the complexity of the questions asked. For instance, the IRS answers questions regarding capital gains taxes correctly less than half the time. Unfortunately, unless the advice provided is in writing, the IRS is free to impose penalties based on taxpayers following erroneous information given by its employees.

Poor as tax advice from the IRS may be, it's far better than the average American fares on his own. A 1988 study conducted by the Akron University School of Law found that only 11 percent of taxpayers with less than a high school education understand the instructions to complete their tax forms.

Even honest taxpayers face excruciating dilemmas in determining what they owe. The owner of a Louisiana company, William Boettcher, wondered if his firm could deduct the cost of insuring three employees who were family members. Here's what he was told, according to *The Wall Street Journal*.[61]

No, said Mr. Boettcher's accountant.

Outraged, Mr. Boettcher called the toll-free taxpayer hotline. An IRS employee said the firm could, in fact, deduct costs for all three.

Both were wrong, an IRS specialist ultimately told Boettcher's befuddled accountant, Thomas Brock. The son's health insurance could be deducted, but not Mr. Boettcher's.

Mr. Brock, the accountant, turned to yet another accountant, who sided with the second IRS employee. Yet Mr. Brock still tells his client he shouldn't take a chance by taking the deduction.

Mr. Boettcher himself says he only wants to pay his taxes -- "every penny I owe." But in this case, he adds, "it's so totally unfair and so totally confusing that nobody knows."

Not even tax preparation professionals are much help. A survey by *Money* magazine in 1991 asked 50 tax preparation specialists to calculate and prepare a family's 1990 tax return. The specialists--most of them certified public accountants--came up with 50 different answers, with only *one accountant* providing the correct answer. Their top estimate of tax liability in this study was more than *ten times higher* than the lowest estimate. -

---

[61]"Tax Law is Growing Ever More Complex, Outcry Ever Louder," *The Wall Street Journal*, April 12, 1990

It's no surprise that even accountants are confused by the IRS code. Consider the following regulation regarding passive income losses, which in 1989 the officials of an Illinois tax service gave their "Most Incomprehensible Government Regulation Award."

> If the taxpayer's passive activity gross income from significant passive activities (within the meaning of section 1.4692T(f)(2) through (4)) exceeds the taxpayer's passive activity deductions from such activities for the taxable year, such activities shall be treated, solely for purposes of applying this paragraph (f)(2)(i) for the taxable year, as a single activity that does not have a loss for the taxable year.

Given regulations that read like this one, it's mind-boggling that legislation adopted in 1989 imposes penalties on tax preparation professionals who suggest deductions or strategies that are later rejected by the IRS. Until then, a professional preparer could approve any tax return position so long as he had a "reasonable basis" for his decision.

Today, the "reasonable basis" rule has been replaced by a much more stringent "realistic probability of success" standard. Tax preparers whose positions in the opinion of the IRS don't adhere to this standard can be fined $250 for each violation. The preparer also may also lose his right to practice before the IRS.

Except for the simplest of returns, neither the IRS nor tax professionals agree on what your "fair share" of taxes is. Under these circumstances, it falls to individual IRS agents to interpret the tax code as best they can. Some agents will take a liberal interpretation and enforce the law with some discretion. Others will insist on the strictest interpretation possible. Obviously, with even the IRS confused as to what the tax law really is, it's in your best interest to avoid a run-in with the agency.

Fortunately, there are indications that the IRS is seeking to make its regulations somewhat more understandable. In 1992, the IRS announced that it would no longer write detailed regulations for every possible tax scenario. It has already replaced hundreds of pages of regulations of passive loss regulations--including the one I just described--with a few pages of simple principles. Hopefully, this initiative will be the first of many to reduce the complexity of the "outrageous code."

The IRS took some other positive steps in 1992. Examiners are now authorized to accept "offers-in-compromise" to satisfy tax debts for pennies on the dollar if complete repayment is clearly unrealistic. Country music singer Willie Nelson, the first major beneficiary of the new policy, had his tax assessment cut by nearly 50 percent.

One reason the IRS' acted so decisively in this area, according to Dan Pilla, editor of *Pilla Talks Taxes* newsletter, was that too many taxpayers were taking the IRS to court--and winning. The agency is also seeking to persuade Congress not to pass the "Taxpayer Bill of Rights II," discussed later in this chapter. Pilla feels the new attitude from the IRS is nothing less than a "tax amnesty"--something the agency said it would never grant.[62]

The IRS has also revised penalty assessment procedures, in compliance with the Improved Penalty and Compliance Act of 1989. It has prepared a manual to insure that frivolous penalties are not tacked on as a "bargaining chip" against taxpayers and that they are applied uniformly and consistently. Taxpayers who show "reasonable cause" for not complying with tax laws may have penalties eliminated

---

[62]For an excellent summary of these changes, see the Sept.-Oct. 1992 issue of *Pilla Talks Taxes*, c/o Winning Publications, 450 Oak Grove Pkwy #107-C, St. Paul, Minn. 55217.

altogether. The new policy replaces the hodge-podge of more than 150 different IRS penalty assessments, which were routinely added on to virtually every tax deficiency.

16 Steps to Protect Yourself From IRS Scrutiny

1. *Maintain a low profile.* Don't flaunt your wealth; doing so raises the envy of all, and IRS agents are not immune from this human frailty. If you crave luxury, purchase it where it is not necessarily visible "from the outside."

2. *File a tax return, and pay whatever taxes you have calculated that you owe.* The IRS' rapidly-expanding computerized auditing capability makes it increasingly likely that individuals who don't file tax returns will be caught. Filing a return and not paying what you owe is even worse. This is an open invitation for the IRS to seize whatever assets are available to satisfy the liability you have brought to their attention. Even taxpayers who have taxes withheld by their employer, and whose taxes are *overpaid,* are being fined for not filing returns!

This recommendation has become all the more important in light of the IRS's August 1992 announcement that it has initiated an all-out assault on the estimated 10 million Americans who do not file income tax returns. The agency has reassigned 2,000 agents full-time to this task. The IRS' policy manual now states that it will not criminally prosecute those who "voluntarily" come forward to comply with filing--but that they will still be responsible for past due taxes, interest and penalties. Those that don't come forward face criminal penalties.

3. *Keep records substantiating the income and deductions you claim on your tax returns--and proof that you filed.* Thorough records are essential in proving that you are entitled to the deductions you claim and that your income is no greater than you have declared. You can safely discard records of income, deductions, etc. after three years--the statute of limitation for an audit. Keep them for seven years if you believe you might be accused of tax evasion or tax fraud.

Particularly important are records of large deductions. If you make large contributions to church or a charity, maintain meticulous records of them. If you take a large deduction for business use of a vehicle, keep a log of this use. In many cases, if the records for large deductions are in order, an auditor may assume other records are equally well-maintained.

Organize the records, and attach all the bills together that you are claiming for a particular deduction, along with an adding machine tape matching the number on your tax return. Also make certain that you have an explanation for any large deposits in bank or brokerage accounts that you have not declared as income.

If you think you might be under IRS surveillance, you might want to shred these records before you dispose of them. A 1988 Supreme Court decision gives police agencies the authority to search trash placed out for collection (*California vs. Greenwood*, 108 S.Ct. 1625). However, a U.S. District Court ruled in 1991 that the IRS violated the privacy of a taxpayer by seizing shredded papers from his garbage and piecing them together to support a tax fraud charge.

But don't discard the returns themselves! The IRS can claim decades after a filing deadline that you never submitted a return for one or more years--and collect penalties and interest for the entire interval. So keep copies your returns forever, along with the certified mail receipt proving you filed.

4. *Avoid "red-flag" items on your tax returns.* Questionable deductions almost always bring at least a cursory examination from the IRS. Favorite targets include moving expenses, medical expenses,

entertainment expenses and home office expenses. (This last expense will be a big favorite of IRS auditors now that the Supreme Court has made it much more difficult to qualify for the exemption.) In addition, expenses that don't match the profession you list on your return may draw IRS scrutiny.

Certain occupations also may bring unwelcome attention from the IRS, including those in which a substantial portion of income is derived from tips and sole proprietors of unincorporated businesses. Auditors also focus on returns that show invalid retirement account deductions or premature withdrawals from them and also those that hint at international financial transactions.

Another way to protect yourself if you're taking a controversial position on a tax issue is to disclose that fact by filing Form 8275 with your return. This form red-flags your return to the IRS, which may then examine it more closely. But disclosing your position in advance means that IRS may not penalize you for taking it. More often than not, your stance will not be challenged.

5. *Make certain your tax return is neat and contains no mathematical errors.* Type your return, or even better, prepare it with a computerized program. A very good one is the Mac-In-Tax for Macintosh computers. Two good ones for IBM personal computers are Turbo-Tax and TaxCut 1040. All three programs are widely available at computer stores.

6. *Have a professional prepare your return.* According to an ex-IRS regional commissioner, signing your own return as the preparer increases your chance of being audited. If your return is at all complex, professional preparation is essential.

Use a certified public accountant or tax attorney to prepare your taxes. Don't make the mistake of having your taxes prepared by someone who doesn't know what they're doing. One inept preparer tried to pass off a pet cat as a client's dependent, thus supposedly entitling the taxpayer to a deduction. (The "client" in this case was an undercover IRS special agent.)

7. *Know the odds.* The odds of an audit in any one year are not high; less than eight in 1,000 (0.8 percent). But if you have an annual income exceeding $100,000, the odds rise to about one in 15. As your income rises further, your chances of being audited increase correspondingly.

Prime IRS targets include independent contractors, small business, professional pension plans, and anyone doing a substantial cash business--restaurants, movie theaters, etc. If you earn more than $100,000 annually, and are in one of these categories, your audit potential increases dramatically.

However, the IRS' information return and document-matching programs provide a rough audit of anyone whose primary sources of income are disclosed to the IRS. This means the *effective* audit rate of the IRS is far higher than 0.8 percent. A more realistic figure would be 70 percent or higher, since most Americans' earnings are now reported to the IRS.

The IRS might even ask you to audit yourself! In an effort to increase the numbers of taxpayers it audits, the IRS has instituted an effort to encourage taxpayers to audit their own returns. In an experimental program, the agency will send letters to 2,000 taxpayers in New England with income between $50,000 and $100,000 asking them to correct suspected errors on their 1989 returns.

8. *Make certain your return is internally consistent.* IRS auditors will examine different portions of your tax return for internal consistency prior to deciding whether or not a full-scale audit might be worthwhile. For instance, if you make large deductions for medical insurance premiums, the IRS may look twice at deductions for medical expenses as well. The IRS also expects you to take certain deductions. If you are a self-employed salesperson, the IRS expects you to declare at least some travel and entertainment expenses. Here's a situation where not claiming a high enough deductions might raise a red flag!

9. *Take the standard deduction unless itemizing your deductions will save you a significant amount of money.* Itemized returns are audited much more frequently than non-itemized returns, and itemizing may result in your disclosing information that you might prefer remain private.

10. *Be respectful of the IRS at all times.* If you are audited, act in a professional, low-key and helpful manner, but at the same time, insist that the auditor respect your rights. Have the records requested available in an organized form. Even if you're not audited, don't make the same mistake as the Montana grandmother who was fined $500 for writing an obscene comment on her tax return. Or of the Massachusetts family who refused to file a return on moral grounds and had their home seized. "Tax protestors" are given special scrutiny by the IRS.

If you assault, threaten, or harass an IRS agent, he may file a Form 4652 on you, which goes into a computer database of "potentially dangerous taxpayers." Then the next time an agent visits, he may be accompanied by armed federal marshals.

11. *Keep meticulous records of all contacts with the IRS.* Send all correspondence by certified mail, return receipt requested. Also notify the IRS of a change of address in this manner, especially if you are involved in any dispute with the agency. Courts have ruled that delivery receipts from UPS and Federal Express are not acceptable substitutes for a post office return receipt. And tape all conversations with IRS agents, both over the telephone and face-to-face.

The IRS frequently takes the position that the contents of certified letters it receives did not match what you claim to have sent. Courts almost never uphold this claim, but to avoid it, you might have a notary sign a letter verifying the contents of the package you are sending, and enclose a copy of the letter in the envelope. If you have the time to spare, it's even better to hand-deliver documents to an IRS office. Hand-delivering a document and obtaining a signed receipt prevents the agency from making this claim in the first place.

12. *Try to deal with the same IRS representative each time you contact the agency.* IRS agents may discourage you from asking their name, but it is to your advantage to find out who you are speaking with, requesting the number of their direct line (or extension), and obtaining their assistance every time you call. You will then have the name of a single employee that you can hold responsible for the agency's actions. Doing so now should be easier than it has been in the past due to a new policy initiated in 1991 by former IRS Commissioner Fred Goldberg.

All letters from the IRS requesting information or demanding payment from a taxpayer are now supposed to contain the name of an IRS employee who originated the letter, Goldberg promised a congressional committee. The employee initiating the contact, said Goldberg, will be given "ownership" of the case until it is finally resolved. But in 1992, unionized IRS employees won the right to use their last names only in dealing with the public, or even aliases if their last name is an unusual one. Obviously, Mr. Goldberg's initiative is being resisted by rank-and-file IRS employees.

13. *Ask for advice in writing.* To protect yourself from being penalized for erroneous advice provided by the IRS, ask for opinions from the agency in writing. You even have the right to request that an entire audit be conducted in writing, although the IRS will usually strenuously object. On complex matters where the Internal Revenue Code is open to a variety of interpretations, an agent may understandably be reluctant to go "on record."

However, on simple procedures, such as abatement of penalties, investigations, etc., try to obtain a commitment in writing that a given procedure has been undertaken. Such letters aren't necessarily legally binding, but they greatly increase the probability that the promised action will occur.

Asking for advice in writing is not the same as requesting a "private letter" ruling. Such rulings, which provide the agency's official opinion in regard to questions submitted on behalf of a single taxpayer, are expensive to obtain and rarely granted.[63]

14. *Don't participate in state tax amnesties.* In recent years, several states have recovered millions of dollars from taxpayers whose accounts were delinquent, and were allowed to pay what they owed without additional penalties. However, states offering such programs don't generally disclose that all records relating to these amnesties are exchanged with the IRS, which has never declared a tax amnesty for federal taxes. Nor does it plan to. Michael J. Graetz, former deputy assistant Secretary of the Treasury for tax policy, stated that:

> A federal amnesty program is a gamble with our tax system's most important asset--the general willingness of taxpayers to obey the law. The vast majority of taxpayers who already comply with tax laws might feel cheated if they see that those who knowingly broke the rules are allowed to escape punishment.

15. *Don't sign your name on a company's tax forms unless you are prepared to personally pay any deficiencies the IRS later determines are present.* When you do so, you are as responsible as you would be for your own tax return. The former controller of a computer company who informed the IRS that his firm wasn't paying all its taxes was stuck with the $69,000 tab since he had signed tax forms submitted to the agency. Subsequently, a lien was placed on his home. Similar incidents occur thousands of times every year. Ask to IRS to send you Notice #784 if you have questions about the agency's official policy on this matter.

16. *If you receive a check from the IRS that's clearly in error, don't cash it.* In 1992, the IRS mistakenly sent refund checks by mistake to thousands of low-income taxpayers, most of whom eagerly cashed them. Now the agency is seeking to get the money back from the recipients. When you return the check, get a receipt, preferably by hand-delivering it to an IRS office.

But if you're due a refund check, don't assume the IRS will send it. The IRS takes only the most basic steps to find people to whom it owes money. After three years, the government gets to keep it. In a recent case, the IRS issued a news release listing 1,068 residents in one city to whom it owed refunds, but couldn't find. A newspaper reporter decided to try to find one of the recipients, and did so in less than 10 minutes.

If You are Audited...

Few events are as dreaded as much as an IRS audit.

A tax audit is a chance for the IRS to penetrate any cloak of privacy that you've tried to construct around your financial affairs. Yet by knowing your rights going into an audit, you can increase the odds significantly of emerging with your finances--and your financial privacy--relatively intact.

Not all audits are the same. Your actions in an audit should relate to the type of audit you face.

The simplest audits are conducted by letter, and indicate that an IRS computer has found a discrepancy on your tax return or that you have failed to make a payment on time. The IRS may have

---

[63]Three excellent newsletters that highlight legitimate tax avoidance strategies are *Pilla Talks Taxes* (op. cit.), *Tax Avoidance Digest* and *The Jacobs Report. Tax Avoidance Digest*, 824 E. Baltimore St., Baltimore, Md. 21202-4799; *The Jacobs Report*, c/o Research Press, Inc., Box 8136, Shawnee Mission, Kan. 66208)

discovered that the income you reported on your tax return is less than that reported by an employer, brokerage firm, etc. Similar letters are generated when you fail to sign your return or make a mathematical error.

A "letter audit" is not an indication that you are being investigated for fraud or criminal tax evasion. It is simply a notification that an IRS employee (or computer) believes you have made an error. Since the IRS sends a substantial number of erroneous letters demanding tax payments, interest, and penalties, you should examine the IRS' claims carefully before paying up.

If you believe the IRS position is wrong, write to the address listed on the letter and carefully document your position, sending copies of receipts, check stubs, etc. Also make certain to request an *abatement* of all penalties and interest. Once again, be certain to send all correspondence certified mail, return receipt requested, or hand-carry the letter to an IRS office.

If you relied on a financial consultant, broker, accountant or attorney who provided erroneous advice, you may request that all *negligence* penalties be waived. In some cases, it's even possible to have interest charges waived as well, although this is ordinarily much more difficult.

You should take a phone call or letter from an IRS field auditor more seriously. A field auditor is trained to provide a comprehensive examination of tax returns, although not to search for tax fraud and money laundering violations. This is the province of a "special"--an IRS special agent. A visit from a special agent promises a comprehensive audit and a complete review of every aspect of your income, investments, deductions, etc. Special agents are part of the agency's elite Criminal Investigation Division, who are trained to search for *criminal* tax fraud--and in particular, for tax violations that can be prosecuted under the money laundering laws.

The most comprehensive audits are Taxpayer Compliance Measurement Program (TCMP) audits. Approximately 25,000 Americans are randomly chosen annually to undergo these audits, which are designed to provide the IRS with statistically valid information for upgrading its regular audit programs.

Data sought by the IRS include what types of deductions are most often taken with poor documentation; what types of income most often go unreported; what types of taxpayers have the largest income discrepancy, etc. Those chosen for such audits are asked to produce documentation of the source of every single bank deposit made in one or more years or to demonstrate that every deduction taken is warranted.

The only good news about a TCMP audit is that you have the right to refuse to participate. However, if you exercise this option, the IRS will make its own assessment. In most cases it will disallow itemized deductions and anything else that requires verification for the years under consideration.

In 1992, the IRS announced it would temporarily discontinue its TCMP audits. This is excellent news to anyone who has ever been subjected to one of these grueling audits. Of course, the IRS can renew this program any time.

When you are audited, the law requires the IRS to inform you of your rights. This is generally provided in writing, and I have found the IRS publication entitled "Your Rights as a Taxpayer" to be fairly comprehensive. However, the agent is not required to notify you verbally of your rights, as in a "Miranda warning" that you would receive if you were arrested; i.e., "anything you say may be used against you."

Your rights include:

✓ *The right to have the audit conducted at a convenient location.* Except in unusual circumstances, there is no reason for the IRS to ask you to travel a long distance to be audited. However, I don't recommend that you invite the IRS into your home or office. A better location might be the local IRS office or the office of your accountant or attorney.

✓ *The right to request a postponement of the audit in order to assemble your records.* The IRS audit notice will generally provide at least two or three weeks for you to prepare. If this is not sufficient time, ask for a temporary postponement.

✓ *The right to request that the IRS give you specific information about what questions the audit will address.* You can frame your request in terms of the records the IRS wishes to examine. For instance, you are entitled to ask what specific years and what specific items the agency wants justified. The auditor may respond that you should bring "all your financial records." This is clearly an unreasonable demand, and you should insist on narrowing the scope of the audit.

✓ *The right to be accompanied by an accountant or an attorney.* In fact, you can have your accountant or attorney go in your place! Professional representation is expensive, but highly recommended if your tax situation is complex. But if the scope of the audit is narrow, or if the items under consideration don't present a potentially expensive liability, you might wish to represent yourself.

If you are represented by a professional, I recommend a tax attorney. An attorney's services are likely to be more expensive than those of an accountant, but an attorney is legally entitled to refuse to divulge information that may incriminate you. (However, as I described in Chapter 4, "Privacy and Your Legal Records," this privilege is *not* absolute.)

Your accountant, on the other hand, is obliged to disclose any information you have confided in him, even if it would hurt your case. Moreover, the IRS holds accountants responsible if their clients are accused of under-reporting income. You should never disclose to your accountant information that might imply that you have income that you haven't reported or that you have any doubts about a particular deduction.

The very best (and most expensive) tax attorneys are former IRS prosecutors with courtroom experience. If you're up against the IRS for criminal tax or money laundering violations, I highly recommend you seek out and retain such a professional.

✓ *The right to record the audit proceedings.* There's nothing like a tape recorder to put an auditor on his best behavior! If you're going through an audit without professional representation, this precaution may be particularly important. The IRS requires that you notify it 10 days in advance of the audit if you intend to record the proceedings. Taping the audit may make the auditor uneasy, but with tape rolling, you can be certain he'll think twice before engaging in unprofessional or unethical behavior.

✓ *The right to bring witnesses.* You might want to bring someone with you simply to help you overcome any nervousness you may experience or to verify information that you may not be able to remember clearly. Once again, a witness lessens the probability that an auditor might try to bully or intimidate you.

✓ *The right to refuse to respond to inquiries not related to the original investigation.* This is where your earlier insistence that the scope of the audit be narrowed can pay big dividends. For instance, if you were told that the audit would relate to income for a particular year, but the auditor instead asks you to justify deductions in another year, you have no obligation to answer any questions on this unrelated topic until you have time to gather records on it.

✓ *The right to not extend the three-year statute of limitations.* Under circumstances not involving tax fraud, the IRS has only three years to find any deficiency in your tax return. After that time, it must accept your returns for previous years, unless you sign a waiver permitting the agency to review them. Never sign such a waiver unless you are advised by a professional to do so.[64]

✓ *The right to consult an IRS "consumer advocate" if you feel you are being treated unfairly.* If an IRS auditor threatens, intimidates or otherwise acts in an unprofessional manner, contact the IRS and ask to speak to the IRS ombudsman. This individual has the authority to halt property seizures, levies on wages, etc. that may be threatened if he feels they are unreasonable considering the circumstances of the case. Ask for Form 911 to stop a collection effort you feel is unreasonable, a wrongful seizure, etc.

However, a recent survey by the Administrative Conference of the United States, an independent research group, showed that the ombudsman had intervened only 13 times since the passage of the Taxpayer Bill of Rights to stop premature property seizures or other IRS abuses. Yet in fiscal 1986 alone, the agency instituted more than 12,000 erroneous levies, according to a GAO investigation.

✓ *The right to break off the audit.* If an audit is going badly, you are confused by a question, need to obtain more information to support your position, or are afraid of revealing more information than you believe is prudent, you may request that the audit be halted. You may reschedule the audit after a reasonable period of time has elapsed and arrange for your accountant or attorney to represent you once it resumes.[65]

✓ *The right to consult with the auditor's supervisor.* If you disagree with an IRS auditor's position, you have the right to go to his supervisor and ask for a second opinion. The supervisor has the authority to overrule the auditor's decision. If he doesn't, you can still go to the IRS Appeals Office, which will often overrule line auditor decisions unless it feels the agency can prevail in Tax Court.

✓ *The right to request an "audit reconsideration."* If the IRS is adamant that you owe it money, and begins collection proceedings, you may be able to stop them dead in their tracks by requesting an audit reconsideration. All collection efforts will be halted while your case is referred to the Examination Division. You qualify for an audit reconsideration if you changed your address after a return was filed and did not take steps to directly inform the IRS; you did not receive a notice of deficiency from the IRS or received it too late to file a petition with the Tax Court; or you located documentation that proves your position that was not available during the audit.

✓ *The right to conduct the audit in writing.* If you truly dread meeting with the IRS face-to-face, you may request a written audit--and the IRS must comply with your request!

One thing you should probably *not* do is to purchase "audit insurance" from a firm promising to defend you against the IRS. One firm offering such services in the 1980s to subscribers of various financial newsletters later went out of business after accepting hundreds thousands of dollars in premiums. At the least, check out the financial standing of such a firm carefully before you send it any money.

---

[64]According to *Pilla Talks Taxes* newsletter (op. cit.), one method the IRS has to bypass the statute of limitations is to intercept refunds for current-year taxes and then apply those refunds to taxes that are "allegedly delinquent" for previous years-- and not provide any details.

[65]Several books dealing exclusively with audit-preparation strategies are available. These include Jack Warren Wade, Jr., *Audit-Proofing Your Return* (San Francisco: Laissez-Faire Books) and Daniel J. Pilla, *The Naked Truth: Everything You've Always Wanted to Know About the IRS But Couldn't Afford to Ask* (St. Paul: Winning Publications, 1986.) For fighting back in an IRS "take no prisoners" audit, I recommend Pilla's *Taxpayer's Ultimate Defense Manual*

What if you or your representative before the IRS believe the agency's position is justified? The IRS is obligated to negotiate with you to arrive at a "reasonable" repayment plan, which can include installment payments over a number of months or even years. Of course, the definition of "reasonable" may be the focus of intense debate between you and the IRS. Once this repayment plan has been signed by both parties, the IRS may not challenge its validity. If the agency does challenge its validity (and this occurs often), you are under no obligation to agree to stricter terms that might be imposed retroactively.

If the agency takes an unreasonable position, one way to discharge your tax liability is to *declare bankruptcy*. Most tax professionals claim that bankruptcy cannot discharge tax debts, but in 1966, Congress revised the bankruptcy code to permit this practice. A congressional research report relating to this legislation states:

> Frequently, the non-dischargeability of taxes prevents an honest but unfortunate debtor from making a fresh start unburdened by what may be an overwhelming liability for accumulated taxes. Consistency with the rehabilitative purpose of the Bankruptcy Act, as well as fairness to individuals, demands some time limit upon the extent of taxes exempt from discharge.

According to Dan Pilla, editor of *Pilla Talks Taxes*, taxes are dischargeable in a Chapter 7 bankruptcy proceeding under the following circumstances:[66],[67]

✓ They are for a tax year which precedes the filing of bankruptcy by at least three years. The three-year rule is determined by reference to the due date of the tax return, including extensions of time to file.

✓ The tax was assessed for at least 240 days prior to filing in bankruptcy. The date of assessment is critical. The assessment date is the date the assessment officer signs an assessment certificate. The date is noted on the face of federal tax liens and is noted in your Individual Master File.

✓ The return must have been filed in a timely manner. if it were filed late, it must have been filed at least two years prior to filing in bankruptcy. The timely filing rule takes into account extension of time to file.

✓ The tax may not be the result of fraud. Fraud exists if the IRS can prove with "clear and convincing evidence" that you committed an affirmative act calculated to deceive or mislead the IRS, with the goal of evading payment of all or part of your income tax liability. However, the so-called fraud penalty is subject to discharge.

Could Your Accountant Be an IRS Informant?

Each year just prior to tax season, "scare stories" regarding the IRS seem to proliferate. While I have no proof of such a policy existing, I would not be surprised to learn that the IRS deliberately leaks these stories to selected members of the press.

The one that aroused my own "fear quotient" the most was the well-publicized incident in which the chief witness against a taxpayer was his own accountant, who turned out to be an IRS informant. In

---

[66]*Pilla Talks Taxes*, June 1992

[67]Under certain circumstances, you may also discharge taxes under Chapters 11, 12, or 13 of the U.S. Bankruptcy Code.

1990, the Missouri Board of Accountancy revoked the certification of the accountant who provided the information to the IRS. His victim faced 24 years in prison and nearly $1 million in fines. However, in 1991, the Justice Department dropped tax evasion charges against the victim in response to a rebuke from a federal judge for the agency's tactics.

A little arithmetic, however, is all that is needed to discover that the chances of becoming the victim of an IRS "mole" are slim indeed. The IRS admits to having 750 to 900 "controlled informants." But the number of *accountants* serving as informants, as of October 1989, was only 40. The American Institute of Public Accountants has approximately 290,000 members. In other words, only about one in every 7,250 CPAs could potentially be an IRS informant.

It is appalling for the IRS to utilize informants against taxpayers, and equally so for members of the accounting profession to participate in the practice. Still, *the odds are decidedly against your being a victim of an IRS "sting"* conducted through your accountant.

The Taxpayer Bill of Rights

In 1988, Congress enacted the "Taxpayer Bill of Rights" as part of an overall revenue package. This important bill incorporated several important reforms. The key provisions of the final package:

✔ Require the IRS to waive any penalty imposed because of underpayment of tax if the underpayment was caused by erroneous written IRS advice

✔ Increase from 10 days to 30 days the advance written notice the IRS must give a taxpayer before seizing property, except for "jeopardy assessments" in an emergency as defined by the agency

✔ Prohibit the IRS from evaluating employees on the basis of how much tax they collect

✔ Require the IRS to explain in detail how any interest or penalties attached to a notice of tax deficiency were calculated

✔ Bar the IRS from backing out of an agreement to settle a tax obligation on an installment plan

✔ Increase the value of income and property that are exempt from IRS seizure

The Taxpayer Bill of Rights is a step forward in dealing with the abuses I have briefly described and that books such as *To Harass Our People* discuss in detail. But some of its strongest provisions were dropped. One was a requirement that would have required the IRS to demonstrate that its tax assessments were correct before seizing taxpayer property. (As I mentioned earlier in this chapter, a 1991 U.S. Circuit Court of Appeals decision concluded the IRS must do so, but the agency has ignored the ruling and is seeking to have it overturned in separate legislation.)

Moreover, Congress did not authorize any money for the IRS to implement the provisions of the Taxpayer Bill of Rights that will cost money. Until the IRS is given money to administer this new legislation, don't count on the agency enforcing it very enthusiastically.

Finally, the Taxpayer Bill of Rights ignored one of the biggest sources of taxpayer discontent, and one totally unrelated to IRS policy: retroactive changes of the tax laws by Congress. A taxpayer arranges his affairs based on one set of laws, then Congress changes the law and makes the changes retroactive prior to the date the law is enacted.

For instance, the Tax Reform Act of 1986 retroactively disqualified tax shelters used by hundreds of thousands of taxpayers. The Constitution explicitly prohibits retroactive, or "ex post facto" laws, but a 1990 Tax Court decision declared that such laws are unconstitutional only when criminal activities are involved. If only your money is at risk, the Constitution doesn't apply.

What took Congress so long to react to the long pattern of IRS abuses? In part, it is because the IRS has for many years engaged in a program of "dirty tricks" aimed at its Congressional opponents. According to Paul DesFosses, President of the National Coalition of IRS Whistleblowers, at least three Congressional representatives have been defeated due to illegal IRS activities.

In the 1970s, New Mexico Senator Joseph Montoya exposed some of the IRS abuses of various religious groups. In retaliation, the IRS targeted him for defeat, and the leaked doctored income tax records that made it appear he was engaged in unethical behavior to the press. He was defeated.

The next target of the IRS was Idaho Representative George Hansen, the original proponent of the Taxpayer Bill of Rights. The IRS assigned top IRS personnel to leak his tax return information in an effort to bring about his defeat at the polls. It took them six years, but they finally defeated him, according to DesFosses, by outright vote fraud.

Finally, former Senator Paul Laxalt was targeted. The IRS was afraid that he might be nominated for President, so top IRS officials were assigned the task of destroying him politically. They created false documents intended to discredit him and leaked that information to a California newspaper. This caused major problems for Laxalt, and he decided to retire from politics.

Not surprisingly, this pattern of retribution has made many in Congress reluctant to take on the IRS. But Congress finally seems determined to reform the agency--and as I've already mentioned in this chapter, the IRS has already taken some steps to reform itself.

In December 1991 and February 1992, hearings on the Taxpayer Bill of Rights II (TBOR-II) were by held the Senate Subcommittee on Private Retirement Plans and Oversight of the IRS (Senate Hearing 102-616). In response to the outrageous IRS misconduct this hearing highlighted, Congress passed TBOR-II. However, President Bush vetoed the bill. Congress then placed TBOR-II into its 1992 tax reform measure, which Bush also vetoed. It has already been re-introduced in the 1993 Congressional session.[68]

One of the bill's most far-reaching provisions would be to establish an independent taxpayer advocate office, to serve on the side of taxpayers in disputes with the IRS. This office would have the power to review IRS collection actions before the agency seizes assets. The bill would also require the IRS to notify credit agencies when the agency mistakenly applies a lien against a taxpayer. It would also have to publicly report the results of its own investigations of employee misconduct. But it would not require the IRS to demonstrate that its tax assessments are correct before seizing property.

Even if Congress does not pass TBOR-II, the courts are cracking down on some IRS abuses. In 1992, a U.S. District Court ruled (again) that IRS claims do not have priority under bankruptcy law. The Supreme Court declined to review a federal appeals court decision ruling that the IRS must make an honest effort to find someone who's moved before assessing more tax. IRS challenges to small business pension plans have been rebuffed in two Tax Court decisions. And a federal appeals court upheld a taxpayer claim that the IRS had to pay court costs where the IRS position was "indefensible."

---

[68]For more information on some of the specific abuses that has led to the introduction of Taxpayer Bill of Rights 2, see Senate Hearings 102-616, December 10, 1991 and February 21, 1992. Transcripts are available from the U.S. Government Printing Office.

But the IRS is hardly retreating on other fronts. A federal appeals court ruled that the IRS can keep overpayments of taxes other than income tax payments. And a minister was jailed for three years because a court concluded that a trust sold to an IRS undercover agent *could have been used* to defraud the government, even though there was no evidence of such use.

In addition, the IRS continues to use the money laundering statutes as a "bargaining chip" in tax fraud and tax evasion cases. In a recent case, a physician pleaded guilty to not declaring "foreign financial accounts" exceeding $10,000 on his tax return and a separate disclosure form. He was fined $50,000 and jailed for nine months. In another case, a man was sentenced to four years in jail for opening a bank account in a fake name, among other crimes.

There are also those who believe that not only is TBOR-II not needed, but that the original Taxpayer Bill of Rights goes too far. That was the focus of testimony from a GAO tax specialist before a House Appropriations subcommittee in February 1993. The specialist told the subcommittee that the original Taxpayer Bill of Rights had "the unintended effect of hampering revenue collection" and criticized the bill for prohibiting IRS employees from being compensated on the basis of the amount of property they seize. Permitting IRS agents to be paid as bounty-hunters, in other words, is not only effective, but good public policy.

For a detailed explanation of the original Taxpayer Bill of Rights, please see Appendix B.

Protecting the Privacy of Your Tax Return

A growing trend by retailers, employers, mortgage brokers, etc. is to demand access to your tax return as a condition for credit or employment.

Your tax return contains a complete record of your income and your investments and may contain details of medical expenses and a host of other information you'd rather keep private. If a bank or an employer asks for a copy of it, you should express your concern to them about your financial privacy.

One possibility is to show the return to the bank or employer, but not permit it to be copied. If a permanent record is required, you might permit your W-2 or 1099 records to be copied, but nothing more. Or provide a copy of your Form 1040, but none of the accompanying schedules.

You might also request that the bank provide you with a written guarantee that information in the tax return will not be disclosed except in the course of a bank examination by auditors or by subpoena. Another "solution" (which I cannot endorse) is to provide a copy of your tax return on poor quality fax paper. Over time, the image on the paper will fade until it becomes illegible.

The IRS will ordinarily protect the privacy of your tax return, but recent legislation has eroded this protection. For instance, the Resolution Trust Corp., established to sell properties owned by bankrupt savings and loan institutions, was authorized in 1990 to examine tax returns in order to fight fraud. In addition, the IRS may release returns to FinCEN, the Financial Crimes Enforcement Network, a Treasury Department intelligence agency authorized by the Anti-Drug Abuse Act of 1988. (See Chapter 7, "The Bush Administration's War on Privacy.")

The IRS also may be asked to share data on your tax return in other circumstances, as described in Chapter 7, "The Annunzio-Wylie Anti-Money Laundering Act of 1992." And as I've already mentioned, there are several documented cases of the IRS releasing tax return data in closely-contested Congressional races.

Should You "Untax" Yourself?

Some people believe that they are under no legal obligation to file a tax return. They may claim that the income tax, as levied, is unconstitutional. Or that even if it is constitutional, there is no requirement for a person whose primary income consists of salary or wages to file. "Patriot" and other untax groups say that if you reside in one of the 50 states--as opposed to the District of Columbia--you are not a U.S. citizen for tax purposes. These groups also claim the Internal Revenue Code applies only to individuals employed by the federal government, and that compliance with its provisions is *strictly voluntary* for anyone else.

Other tax protestors raise religious issues. They point out that when Jesus instructed his followers to, "Render therefore unto Caesar the things that are Caesar's" (Matthew 22:21), he was telling them that there was no religious reason not to pay the tax of a single denarius that was assessed each year by the Romans. At that time, the average wage for a day's work was one denarius. If a man were to work six days a week, the tax was equivalent to 1/313 of his annual income. Even a tax of 20 percent to 25 percent is eight times the Islamic zakat, the alms-giving required by the Koran; double the tithe of the Christian church and twice the royal tribute that the prophet Samuel warned the Israelites against when they wanted him to appoint a ruler.

Unfortunately, virtually all these claims have been rejected by the courts. Tax protest organizations may ignore these decisions, say that the court was wrong, or even misquote the decision as supporting their claims. Today, individuals who raise such issues risk not only losing their case, but having the courts tack on penalties for "frivolous arguments."

The only court case supporting any of these claims was the 1991 Supreme Court decision in *U.S. vs. Cheek* (111 S.Ct. 604). In *Cheek,* the court ruled that if a person sincerely believes the income tax law doesn't apply to him, he can't be charged with "willful," or *criminal* tax evasion. Perhaps inevitably, the implications of *Cheek* have been misinterpreted. The court held, for instance, that a person's view about the constitutionality or validity of the tax laws are irrelevant to the issue of willfulness. Moreover, the decision doesn't apply to civil litigation; the IRS can still seek to seize property of those who seek to untax themselves to satisfy their alleged tax obligations. There is no statute of limitations for a "failure to file" civil charge.

To protect their assets, many untax advocates have formed various trust arrangements. Most of these have not been upheld by the courts, as you'll learn in Chapter 8, "Defective Asset Protection Structures." To avoid visible assets, untax advocates participate in the underground economy. They deal strictly in cash. Unfortunately, participation in the underground (cash) economy is considered a "badge of fraud" by the IRS, and may result in a tax fraud (criminal) charge.

Moreover, dealing in cash to disguise the proceeds of a crime (such as tax evasion) now constitutes *money laundering* (see Chapter 7, "The Money Laundering Control Act of 1986"). In addition, some forms of tax evasion can now be prosecuted under the racketeering (RICO) statutes, which like the money laundering laws, authorize pre-trial asset freezes. Not only untax advocates themselves, but those who accept their funds, can have their assets frozen under these statutes. It's relatively easy for the IRS to win convictions in money laundering cases, because of the alleged tie-in between laundering offenses and drug trafficking.[69]

---

[69]In February 1993, the IRS began a concerted campaign to destroy the untax movement in a series of raids against publishers of tax protest literature and promoters of asset-protection schemes designed for tax protestors.

In summary, while I sympathize with the motives of untax advocates, I cannot endorse their efforts. As the disclaimer for one of the most complete guide to the untax process I have seen, *Goodbye April 15*, states:[70]

> There is an element of risk in standing up for one's constitutional rights in the face of an oppressive taxing agency backed by a biased federal judiciary and an ignorant, intimidated jury. Therefore, the author and publisher disclaim any responsibility for any liability or loss incurred as a consequence of the use and application, directly or indirectly, of the information presented herein.

Tax Avoidance is Legal

Death and Taxes

Tax his cow, tax his goat
Tax his pants, tax his coat
Tax his crops, tax his work
Tax his tie, tax his shirt
Tax his chew, tax his smoke
Teach him taxes are no joke
Tax his tractor, tax his mule
Teach him taxes are a rule
Tax his notes, tax his cash
Tax him good and let him know--
After taxes he has no dough
If he hollers tax him more
Tax him 'til he's good and sore
Tax his coffin, tax his grave
Tax the sod in which he lays
Put these words upon his tomb:
"Taxes drove me to my doom"
And after he's gone he can't relax
They'll still be after inheritance tax!

--Anonymous

While the IRS aggressively targets those who wish to "untax" themselves, there is no doubt that you have the right to arrange your affairs in a manner so that you are liable for the lowest possible tax liability.

For instance, former President Bush has skillfully--and legally--reduced his state income taxes by maintaining his official residence in a rented hotel suite in Texas, which levies no personal income tax. If a former President of the United States has the right to avoid taxes, don't you? The answer is an unambiguous *yes*.

---

[70]"Boston T. Party," *Goodbye, April 15th* (Austin, "Texas Republic:" Javelin Press, 1992)

Here's how offshore trust promoter Robert Chappell described tax avoidance in *Secrets of Offshore Tax Havens*.[71]

There is a simple truth at the heart of the tax battle--and it is just that, a battle for survival by the American taxpayer--which cannot be repeated too often or too strongly: *Tax avoidance is legal...tax evasion is illegal.*

The more you learn about the two subjects, the clearer the line becomes between tax evasion and tax avoidance. The internationally known Paris lawyer Edouard Chambost, an authority on the legal use of tax haven jurisdictions, put the issue into perspective when he said:

"Avoiding unnecessarily high taxes is like looking for the best bargain-- buying in the cheapest store. Evasion, by contrast, means that you are walking away without paying your bill."

The reason so many Americans are unaware that such an important distinction even exists is because the IRS has worked very hard to keep them unaware, even to the point of twisting the truth. The IRS, through intimidation, inflammatory news releases, and other means of propaganda, wants you to believe that tax avoidance is illegal, if not un-American.

However, nothing could be more clear than the fact that tax avoidance is legal and a legitimate right to be fully exercised by every American.

The dividing line between legal tax avoidance and illegal tax evasion was drawn many years ago and the validity of it repeatedly enforced by rulings from the highest courts in the land. For instance, Supreme Court Justice Felix Frankfurter could not have been more clear on this point when he wrote:

"As to the astuteness of taxpayers in ordering their affairs as to minimize taxes, we have said that 'The very meaning of a line in the law is that you intentionally may go as close to it as you can if you do not pass it.' This is so because nobody owes any public duty to pay more than the law demands. Taxes are enforced extractions, not voluntary contributions."

How much clearer can it be? Read what another Supreme Court Justice, Learned Hand, said about your patriotic duty to pay taxes:

"Anyone may so arrange his affairs that his taxes shall be as low as possible; he is not bound to choose that pattern which will best pay the Treasury. There is not even a patriotic duty to increase one's taxes."

Not that Justice Hand said "anyone." He does not say Rockefellers, Kennedys, Hunts, or the super-rich. Tax avoidance, while it is also available to and is more commonly utilized by the super-rich, is not

---

[71]Robert Chappell, *Secrets of Offshore Tax Havens* (ABM Publishing, 1985). I do *not* recommend the "contractual company" or other offshore trusts that Chappell describes in this book. Several such trusts have been disallowed in federal court, and Chappell was recently jailed in Indiana and convicted of 96 counts of fraud in New Mexico on unrelated matters.

strictly their right. The right belongs to anyone who is willing to exercise it. In fact, the system rewards those who exercise this right, and punishes those who don't. On this you have the word of a federal judge, who wrote in a tax ruling:

"The average citizen believes that the government prosecutes only the recalcitrant, uncooperative individual who is unwilling to pay what he owes. Who would believe the ironic truth that the cooperative taxpayer fares much worse than the individual who relies upon his constitutional rights?"

What is logical or equitable about the fact that the average hard-working American, struggling just to stay even, pays a third or more of his income in taxes while some of the richest individuals and largest, most profitable corporations in the United States pay no taxes at all? The average American has to work 121 days to earn enough money to pay his federal, state, and local taxes each year. In 1929, the average person worked just 40 days to satisfy his total yearly tax levies. Yet a small group of super-wealthy Americans--299 couples and individuals with incomes totalling $149 million--paid no income tax to the government.

I am not singling out these super-rich for criticism. *They have made full use of the tax avoidance laws and that is their constitutional right.*

Chapter Seven

FINANCIAL PRIVACY, MONEY LAUNDERING, AND THE "WAR ON DRUGS"

Financial transactions can reveal much about a person's activities, associations and beliefs. At some point, government intrusion upon these areas would implicate legitimate expectations of privacy.

--Supreme Court Justice Lewis Powell

In this country, under drug siege, we have the strongest motivation for sacrificing a certain measure of bank privacy--and risking some loss of more legitimate depositors--to bring international money launderers to justice.

--Former Attorney General Richard Thornburgh

The right of U.S. citizens to spend or invest their own money as they see fit, in any manner they choose, and to do so in a privately, has been greatly restricted in the years since World War II. Much of the erosion in financial privacy has taken place as a result of the government's continuing vendetta against the underground economy, and more recently, in the "War on Drugs."

The Historical Erosion of Financial Privacy

For the first 150 years of U.S. history, the entire American economy was "above ground." With very few exceptions, virtually every enterprise from which a person could generate a profit was legal.

The federal government collected tariffs and a few miscellaneous taxes, but workers were free to keep all of their wages for their own needs and those of their families. In fact, the writings of the founding fathers clearly indicate they intended for the taxes necessary to support the federal government to come primarily from foreigners, not from U.S. citizens!

With few enterprises illegal, and with no income tax, there was no economic incentive for an underground economy to develop and no demand for money laundering services. All this began to change in 1913, when the United States instituted a permanent income tax. (In 1894, the Supreme Court ruled an income tax unconstitutional, so a change in the Constitution--the 16th amendment--was necessary in order to implement one.) The top rate at the time was 6 percent, paid only by those earning $500,000 per year or more, a princely sum even today, after 75 years of inflation.

As time passed, tax rates gradually increased. By the 1930s, top income tax rates were approaching 70 percent. As tax rates increased, efforts of individuals to minimize their tax liability gradually increased as well. Most people seeking relief from increasingly heavy tax burdens chose to engage in legal tax avoidance. But a few crossed the line into tax evasion.

Government policy began shifting to discourage "defections" from the tax system. World War II brought a perfect opportunity, in an emergency program that was soon made permanent: tax withholding.

This was probably the most important invention ever to destroy financial privacy. Even today, the government withholds (and over-withholds) income from our paychecks. Then we are required to file a return in order to get our zero-interest refund. If we under-withhold, on the other hand, the government makes us pay usurious interest rates and penalties.

World War II also brought rationing and strict economic controls. A thriving black market developed in ration coupons, gasoline, tires, etc. Economists began to speak of black markets and the underground economy as a measurable proportion of the Gross National Product.

The hundreds of billions of dollars of debt the United States incurred in World War II led to intensified government efforts to stamp out tax evasion and the underground economy. One of the most popular methods for wealthy individuals to evade taxes was by establishing bank accounts outside the United States. Switzerland, with its strict bank secrecy laws, was particularly favored for this purpose. (See "Switzerland, the Quintessential Haven," Chapter 9.)

The Bank Secrecy Act of 1970

Experience should teach us to be most on our guard to protect liberty when the Government's purposes are beneficent. Men born to freedom are naturally alert to repel invasion of their liberty by evil-minded rulers. The greatest dangers to our liberties lurk in insidious encroachments by men of zeal, well-meaning but without understanding.

--Former Supreme Court Justice Louis Brandeis

As the 1960s ended, the underground economy was booming. Illegal trafficking in narcotics was at record levels. Organized crime figures, testifying before Congress, repeatedly invoked the Fifth Amendment when asked about their income and investments.

Reports from Switzerland showed deposits in secret Swiss bank accounts were at an all-time high, and the U.S. government had no way of obtaining these records. Repeated Treasury inquiries to Swiss banks regarding the accounts of suspected tax evaders almost always went unanswered.

The Nixon Administration lobbied Congress to pass a law that would prohibit U.S. citizens from taking cash out of the United States and outlaw foreign bank accounts. In addition, the administration requested that Congress require all cash transactions of $1,000 or greater be reported to the IRS.

In 1970, Congress responded with the "Financial Recordkeeping, Currency and Foreign Transactions Reporting Act" (P.L. 91-508; codified as amended at U.S.C Sections 5311-5322). President Nixon got much, but not all, of what he wanted.

Today, this law is known as Bank Secrecy Act, a grossly misleading designation given its provisions. This act represented the first federal effort to register foreign bank accounts and impose currency and foreign exchange controls on individual Americans. As such, it was an enormous reversal in our rights to both personal and financial privacy.

Today, the Bank Secrecy Act, as amended, requires U.S. citizens to report:

✓ Any transporting of more than $10,000 in cash, negotiable securities, or certain monetary instruments across a U.S. border. The applicable reporting form is Customs Form 4790.

✓ Any cash transaction or series of transactions with a bank or other financial institution exceeding $10,000. The applicable reporting form is IRS Form 4789.[72]

✓ The presence of foreign bank or financial accounts totalling more than $10,000. You must acknowledge such accounts on Schedule B of your tax return, and complete each year a separate reporting form, Treasury Form TD F 90-22.1 (reproduced in Appendix A).

Violations of the act are considered money laundering offenses. "Willful" violations may be punished by fines as high as $250,000 and/or prison terms as long as five years.

No industry has been affected more by the Bank Secrecy Act than U.S. banks. The paperwork burden is enormous, and as years have passed, the penalties for non-compliance are draconian.

Banks are required to maintain copies of deposit slips and both sides of checks drawn for more than $100. In addition, they must keep permanent records of any loan over $5,000. If a depositor makes a deposit or withdrawal of more than $10,000, the bank is required to notify the Treasury Department via a "Currency Transaction Report," or CTR (Form 4789).

The act also requires banks to request the Social Security number of all account holders, and to maintain a file of those individuals who refuse to provide these numbers for Treasury Department inspection.

But banks are hardly the only "financial institutions" affected by the law. The act also defines "financial institutions" as:

✓ All securities brokers and dealers

✓ All investment companies and currency exchange houses

✓ All "issuers, redeemers or cashiers" of traveler's checks, money orders, or similar instruments

✓ All operators of credit card systems

✓ All insurance companies, dealers in precious metals, stones, or jewels, pawn brokers, loan or finance companies, travel agencies, money transmitters, casinos, and telegraph companies

✓ All automobile, aircraft, and boat dealers, real estate brokers and settlement agents

✓ All accountants and attorneys

✓ The U.S. Postal Service

✓ Any business or agency which engages in any activity which the Secretary of the Treasury determines by regulation to be similar to, related to, or a substitute for any business otherwise defined as a financial institution

✓ All other businesses in which the Secretary of the Treasury determines such reports would provide "a high degree of usefulness in criminal, tax, or regulatory matters"

---

[72]In 1991, the IRS criminally prosecuted an individual for money laundering for keeping more than $10,000 in a bank safety deposit box without filing a Currency Transaction Report with the bank. A U.S. District Court ruled in favor of the IRS, but the decision was overturned by a federal appeals court (*U.S. vs. Bell*, 936 F.2nd 337, 1991).

Amendments added in 1984 to the act encourage individuals to spy on one another in order to collect rewards. Up to $150,000 may be awarded to anyone who provides information leading to a criminal fine, civil penalty, or forfeiture, or up to 25 percent of forfeited property. Thousands of Americans claim rewards each year.

The Bank Secrecy Act also authorized the U.S. Customs Service to set up a system to enforce the legislation's foreign exchange control provisions. The Customs Service responded with a computer system known as "TECS"--the Treasury Enforcement Communications System. TECS terminals are now in place at every major port of entry to the United States. When your name is entered into the system, TECS will report:

✓ If you are a suspected or a convicted tax evader

✓ Whether you have arrest records or convictions listed in the FBI's National Crime Information Center (NCIC) database

✓ If you have been suspected, arrested or convicted for possession or sale of illegal drugs

✓ If you have been suspected, arrested or convicted of smuggling or a similar offense

✓ If you are currently sought by any law enforcement agency for any criminal or civil offense

TECS provides the Customs Service with a nationwide computer network that tracks not only criminal convictions, but arrests and even *suspicion* of criminal activity. In 1987, when the FBI requested authority to set up such a system, "NCIC 2000," civil libertarians reacted with horror. Little did they realize that the Treasury Department had operated a similar system for more than a decade.

An "expert system" enhancement of TECS in 1987 gives it the ability to construct computerized profiles of individuals suspected of money laundering, drug smuggling, etc. By answering a few questions at a computer terminal, a customs agent can make an almost instantaneous decision whether to detain someone who appears to fit a criminal profile as defined by TECS.

Apparently, such individuals have little to fear from TECS in its current configuration. A 1990 report from the General Accounting Office concluded that TECS contains incomplete and highly inaccurate information and that major drug traffickers and other criminals may be able to enter the country without detection.

But if TECS identifies you as a potential criminal, you could be targeted for seizure of whatever cash or other valuables you are carrying on your person or in your luggage. The exact profile is secret, but some of the signs the Customs Department looks for, according to testimony in a 1988 case, include:

✓ Paying for airline tickets in cash

✓ Travelling under a name that does not match your telephone listing

✓ Having a "known illicit drug center" or "money laundering center" as your point of departure or destination (in practice, any large city in the world)

✓ Appearing nervous

✓ Not checking any luggage

Almost immediately after the Bank Secrecy Act was adopted, its constitutionality was challenged. But in case after case, the courts have ruled that the act does not violate our constitutional rights. The best-known challenge, *California Bankers Association vs. Shultz* (416 U.S. 21), came before the Supreme Court in 1974.

The court dismissed the argument that reporting provisions of the act violated constitutional privileges against compulsory self-incrimination (Fifth Amendment) or unreasonable search (Fourth Amendment). Essentially, the court ruled that bank records of a customer's transactions belong to the bank, rather than the customer. Under this logic, the bank has no standing to invoke the rights of the customer to dispute turning over such records to the government, since it can assert neither ownership nor possession of these documents.

But some serious constitutional issues were raised in dissent. Justice William O. Douglas made the following observations in his dissent regarding the recordkeeping provisions required of U.S. banks:

> It would [likewise] be highly useful to have reports from all our bookstores, all our hardware and retail stores, all our drugstores. These records too might be "useful" in criminal investigations.

> One's reading habits furnish telltale clues to those who are bent on bending us to one point of view. What one buys at the hardware and retail stores may furnish clues to potential uses of wires, soap powders, and the like used by criminals. A mandatory recording of all telephone conversations would be better than the recording of checks under the Bank Secrecy Act, if Big Brother is to have his way.

> It is, I submit, sheer nonsense to agree with the Secretary [of the Treasury] that *all bank records of every citizen* "have a high degree of usefulness in criminal, tax, or regulatory investigations or proceedings." That is unadulterated nonsense unless we are to assume that every citizen is a crook, an assumption I cannot make.

> Since the banking transactions of an individual give a fairly accurate account of his religion, ideology, opinions, and interests, a regulation impounding them and making them automatically available to all federal investigative agencies is a sledge-hammer approach to a problem that only a delicate scalpel can manage.

> Bank accounts at times harbor criminal plans. But we only rush with the crowd when we vent on our banks and their customers the devastating and leveling requirements of the current act. I am not yet ready to agree that America is so possessed with evil that we must level all constitutional barriers to give our civil authorities the tools to catch criminals.

> Suppose Congress passed a law requiring telephone companies to record and retain all telephone calls and make them available to any federal agency on request. Would we hesitate even a moment before striking it down? I think not, yet a checking account, as I have said, may well record a citizen's activities, opinion, and beliefs as fully as a transcript of his telephone conversations.

In 1976, the Supreme Court gave the Bank Secrecy Act practically limitless application in the *U.S. vs. Miller* decision (425 U.S. 435). Miller was accused of selling unlicensed whiskey, and his bank was served with secret subpoenas requiring it to turn over records of his checks and deposits to the government. The bank complied without notifying Miller or contesting the subpoena in any manner.

Miller's attorney argued that the seizure of his client's bank records represented a violation of the Fourth Amendment, which prohibits unreasonable searches and seizures of "private papers." But the court's majority opinion, written by Lewis Powell, stated in part: "The depositor takes the risk, in revealing his affairs to another, that the information will be conveyed by the person to the government."[73]

Powell and his fellow justices also determined that Miller, or for that matter, *any depositor,* lacked "standing" to object to the release of records by a third party. If anyone were to complain about the forced release of records, it should have been Miller's bank, not Miller himself, they concluded. Yet in *Shultz*, the court dismissed just such a complaint.[74]

The Supreme Court, in effect, ruled that a citizen lacks any protection whatsoever from the government seizing financial records held by a third party. Furthermore, the court ignored the fact that it was the government itself that had forced the bank to maintain these records in the first place!

Paul B. Rasor, Professor of Law at the Washburn University School of Law, described the legal implications in the law school's legal journal:[75]

> Under the court's view, the mere existence of third-party recordkeepers deprives personal information of all constitutional protection. That bank customers expect their financial institutions to keep their records confidential requires no authority. For the court to suggest otherwise is absurd.

Perhaps the ultimate example of the lack of any limit in the power of the government to seize financial records came in *Payner vs. U.S.* Payner was a depositor in a Bahamian bank being investigated by the IRS. In 1977, when a representative from the bank visited the United States, the IRS introduced the banker to a female undercover operative, who persuaded him to accompany her to dinner.

When they departed, IRS agents illegally broke into the banker's hotel room and took his briefcase. In it they found approximately 400 pages of documents, which were photocopied and then returned. Records on Payner's account were among those found, and he was subsequently convicted of tax evasion based on this evidence. Payner appealed the conviction, and his case was overturned by an appellate court. But the Supreme Court reinstated the conviction when the IRS appealed.

Taken together, the *Shultz, Miller,* and *Payner* cases demonstrate that government seizure of confidential financial records from third parties, even when conducted illegally, are not "unreasonable"

---

[73]The *Miller* case also relied heavily on the logic developed in the 1976 case of *Fisher vs. U.S.* (425 U.S. 391), in which the court ruled that, "A subpoena to a third party to obtain the records of the party does not violate the rights of a defendant, even in the midst of a criminal prosecution."

[74]These records are not available only to the IRS, but to any other federal agency if the agency states that the information is sought for "criminal, tax, or regulatory purposes." The agency is supposed to keep the released data confidential, with one "small" loophole: if the information will be used for "official" purposes, there are no restraints.

[75]Paul Rasor, "Controlling Government Access to Personal Financial Records" (*Washburn Law Journal,* Washburn University School of Law, vol. 25, 1986)

under the Fourth Amendment. In ruling out Fifth Amendment challenges to the Bank Secrecy Act, the Supreme Court has concluded that individuals may not claim involuntary self-incrimination when the government subpoenas (or simply steals) financial records from third parties.

Governmental Abuses of the Bank Secrecy Act

1:14 PM URGENT 5-11-72
TO: ACTING DIRECTOR
ATTENTION: DOMESTIC INTELLIGENCE DIVISION

THESE ACCOUNTS ARE MONITORED BY [NEW YORK OFFICE] FBI THROUGH MR. [name deleted] ASSISTANT VICE PRESIDENT, MORGAN GUARANTEE TRUST CO. FONDA'S ACCOUNTS ARE MADE AVAILABLE MONTHLY ON CONFIDENTIAL BASIS WITHOUT SUBPOENA TO AGENT OF [NEW YORK OFFICE] WHO REVIEWS ACCOUNTS AND SENDS PERTINENT DATA TO LOS ANGELES FOR INCLUSION IN SUBSEQUENT REPORTS.

CHECK#	DATE	PAYEE	AMOUNT
2039	11/27/70	BREMER PHOTO	$837.32
2044	12/9/70	CHELSEA HOTEL	241.57
2048	12/14/70	CAPEZIO	32.71
2047	12/12/70	MAYFAIR MARKET	15.83
2074	12/22/70	CREATIVE PLAYTHINGS	61.19

-- excerpts from FBI memos regarding Jane Fonda's bank account

Only a few months after the enactment of the Bank Secrecy Act, the Nixon administration put it to work investigating individuals it considered "enemies." One was Jane Fonda, an actress active in supporting peace initiatives to end the Vietnam war. The FBI found nothing to incriminate Fonda in her account. But it did find the names of firms whom she patronized and organizations to which she contributed.

All this information was used to open up new avenues of inquiry. Government investigators also routinely investigated the bank accounts of dozens of left-wing and right-wing organizations, people who advocated revolutionary social or political changes--and just about anyone who opposed Richard Nixon.

Another war protestor targeted by the Bank Secrecy Act was Daniel Ellsburg, who in June 1971 passed a copy of the *Pentagon Papers* to The *New York Times*. The *Pentagon Papers* were top-secret documents containing embarrassing details of the Vietnam conflict. After a consultation with the National Security Agency, the *Times* deleted passages that could have compromised national security and began publishing excerpts.[76]

President Nixon was furious over the disclosures. Under the authority of the Bank Secrecy Act, he ordered the FBI to investigate Ellsburg's bank account. After canceled checks made payable to a psychiatrist were discovered, Nixon ordered an illegal break-in into the psychiatrist's office in search of

---

[76]A fascinating account of how the National Security Agency sought to seize the *Pentagon Papers* and quash the entire *New York Times* inquiry into the conduct of the Vietnam war is contained in James Bamford's book, *The Puzzle Palace*, chapter 7 (New York: Penguin Books, 1982)

Ellsburg's records. Then the administration leaked to the press the information that Ellsburg was under the care of a psychiatrist.

Investigations by the *Washington Post* in 1972 and 1973 led to disclosure of repeated government abuses of the Bank Secrecy Act. In response to these reports, Congress in 1974 enacted the Privacy Act, which requires the consent of individuals before a government agency collects and uses information relating to them for a different purpose than the information was intended. (But as described in Chapter 4, this protection has now been nullified by subsequent legislation.)

But it was not only war protestors who had previously confidential financial records examined surreptitiously by the IRS. The IRS now had the power to conduct "fishing expeditions" on the filmiest imaginable pretense. The following excerpt from *The April Game,* a book written by an experienced IRS agent, indicates how this power was used.[77]

> Four times out of five, when I walk into a bank and flash my credentials, I get to see anything I want to see. When they don't want to cooperate, it is seldom difficult to change their minds.
>
> "You won't show me the records?" I asked the plump little banker. He had pale-blue eyes, and he had a habit of blinking them rapidly. He looked almost as though he were about to burst into tears. "I'd really rather not," he said. "I'd like to check with some other people around here first. I don't quite know what our position would be in a situation like this."
>
> I nodded, then made a production of pulling a small black notebook and pen out of my inside breast pocket. "May I have your full name, sir?"
>
> That got him. It almost always does. There is hardly an American citizen above the poverty level whose tax conscience is so completely clear that he isn't afraid of being audited.
>
> He mumbled, "Well, maybe we can." He scurried out of the room. A few moments later he was back, brimming over with cooperation. "My secretary will show you any records you want to see," he said. "But just to protect myself--in case my customers get mad, you know, may I ask you to serve me with an official summons?"
>
> It was a common request, quickly arranged.[78]

The Match Game

Soon it will be possible to assert almost continuous surveillance over every citizen and maintain up-to-date complete files containing even the

---

[77]"Diogenes," *The April Game,* (Chicago: Playboy Press, 1979)

[78]A "summons" differs in important respects from a search warrant or a subpoena. A *search warrant* is a court order to seize materials or documents. A *subpoena* is also a legal order, but is signed by a court clerk, not a judge. A *summons* is simply an order signed by an IRS administrator.

most personal information about the citizen. These files will be subject to instantaneous retrieval by the authorities.

--Zbigniew Brezhinsky, Between Two Ages

In 1977, Secretary of Health, Education and Welfare (HEW) Joseph Califano announced "Project Match," which would compare the data in the individual personnel files of federal employees with information collected about welfare recipients. The key to the matches were to be Social Security numbers. My special report *Counter-Surveillance* describes what occurred next.

> HEW's legal counsel advised Califano that Project Match was illegal. For instance, the Privacy Act of 1974 requires that "each federal agency that maintains a system of records not to disclose any record from that system to any person or to other agencies without prior written consent of the individual."
>
> The attorneys also pointed out that the Privacy Act further stated that a federal record could only be utilized "for a purpose that is compatible with the purposes for which it was collected." While this requirement could be circumvented in "routine use," Califano's novel manipulation of this data could hardly be considered routine. HEW's legal counsel further stated that the routine use provision implied that "information will not be disclosed without some indication that a specific violation has occurred or might have occurred."
>
> Even though Project Match apparently violated at least three provisions of the Privacy Act, it was allowed to proceed. Two years later, in order to apply a veneer of legality to the proceedings, the Carter administration issued guidelines for computer matching. These guidelines permitted matches to occur after the agency making them had cleared the activity with the Office of Management and Budget. In the five years OMB received requests from agencies for matches, it never turned one down.
>
> Later, President Reagan created an interagency committee to work on new guidelines. One of its members, Hugh O'Neill, one of the government's Privacy Act experts, said that one of the goals of the new committee was to make rules "consistent with our technology." He said nothing about making the rules consistent with the law.

Califano now acknowledges that the reason that he proposed Project Match was purely political. He knew that the Great Society programs developed by the Johnson administration (with Califano playing a major role) were in trouble with voters outraged over their soaring costs. The programs couldn't survive politically unless the Carter administration came up with a way to make it appear that fraud and mismanagement in the programs were being addressed. Project Match was the answer.

But Project Match was only the beginning of the government's flouting of the Privacy Act. In 1982, as you'll soon learn, it began a program of computer matching based on pulling together information in federal databases to reduce fraud in entitlement programs. All the data was keyed to Social Security numbers.

The Right to Financial Privacy Act of 1978

The Right to Financial Privacy Act (codified at 12 U.S.C. 3401, et. seq.) was an effort by Congress to overcome some of the abuses of due process conducted under the authority of the Bank Secrecy Act. Its premise was that financial records maintained by banks and other financial institutions should remain confidential. It also was designed to give citizens the right to challenge disclosures of such information to government authorities.

However, government agencies fought successfully to riddle the law with loopholes. The largest loophole permits disclosure of records in "law enforcement proceedings," which exempts the IRS, the FBI, and any other government agency from challenge if the agency claims it is investigating a crime or possible crime. Nor are there any restrictions on the ability of state and local police agencies to conduct such searches.

Another loophole is that a "customer" of a financial institution is defined only as an individual or a partnership of not more than five partners. Corporations, trusts, and other entities are completely unprotected by the act's provisions.

In fact, the act dramatically widens the scope of government financial surveillance in a provision that permits any government agency access to financial records upon the submission of a formal written request. This provision provides a grant of administrative subpoena power to government agencies not explicitly granted such authority in other legislation. (As you'll soon learn, the Tax Equity and Reform Act of 1982 broadened this authority even further.)

Originally, the act required that government agencies go to court to obtain depositor records, and gave the depositor the right to contest such access--with the usual exemptions for "legitimate law enforcement inquiries, etc." But the IRS cherished the power to snoop informally in bank accounts. In 1979, it regained this ability. In *U.S. vs. McKay* (608 F.2nd 830), the 10th Circuit Court of Appeals ruled that the IRS could issue an *unwritten* (i.e., verbal) summons to a bank to obtain the records of a depositor, and that the bank had to comply. Neither the agency nor the bank are legally required to notify the depositor.[79]

Over the next decade, the right of the IRS to informally inspect bank account records was repeatedly affirmed. In the 1989 case of *Raikos vs. Bloomfield State Bank,* a U.S. District Court found that the IRS has a legal right to examine bank records without a summons, search warrant or court order. The court ruled that the Internal Revenue Code gives the IRS the power to "examine any books, papers, records or other data."

Confirming that the Right to Financial Privacy Act contains exemptions for law enforcement proceedings, and that the IRS is a law enforcement agency, the court concluded that the Internal Revenue Code provides sufficient authority for an informal request to be binding on a bank official. A logical extension of this decision would also permit informal searches of credit records or any other personal financial records kept by a third party.

A decade after the Right to Financial Privacy Act passed, Congress came full-circle by enacting the Anti-Drug Abuse Act of 1988. This law permits a bank to disclose information on any customer's account to the government if the bank believes the customer may be violating drug, money laundering, or other laws. It specifically indemnifies banks from prosecution by customers who are harmed by such disclosure. (For more information on this act, see "The Anti-Drug Abuse Act of 1988" this chapter.)

---

[79]The right to contest an IRS summons was nebulous to begin with since the Supreme Court had already ruled in the *Miller* and *Fisher* cases that once a depositor has no Fourth or Fifth Amendment right to contest the release of such records to the government.

It's no wonder that John Byrne, the federal legislative counsel for the American Bankers Association says, "There's not a lot to this act anymore."

However, banks do not have unlimited freedom in this regard. In 1990, the 10th Circuit Court of Appeals held in *Neece vs. IRS* that a bank is not exempt from the requirements of the Right to Financial Privacy Act when the bank voluntarily allows the IRS to examine a taxpayer's records. In this case, an Oklahoma banker became suspicious of a Tulsa couple who applied for a loan. The bank president voluntarily turned over copies of the couple's mortgage, loan application, etc. to the IRS.

The court rejected the IRS's right to this "informal access" to bank records in this particular case, because the bank had no specific evidence of wrongdoing. The IRS was outraged, and promised at a 1992 banking seminar that a customer would never again prevail in a lawsuit brought against a bank making a Neece-type disclosure.

The Reagan Administration's War on Hidden Wealth

When Ronald Reagan was elected to the presidency in 1980, he promised to "get the government off the back of Americans." Yet the actions his administration took in regard to personal and financial privacy had the opposite effect.

Why did the Reagan Administration, pledged to streamline government operations, greatly expand them, at least in terms of financial controls over ordinary Americans?

The problem for Reagan and every president that follows him is simple: The federal government is broke. It has guaranteed virtually every special interest group in existence easy access to federal dollars, but has no money appropriated to pay for these commitments. Extrapolating from government statistics analyzed by the National Taxpayer's Union, these future obligations to Medicaid, Social Security, savings and loans, federal pensions, etc. will cost at least *$15 trillion* to pay off--nearly four times the current national debt and nearly 40 times the $400 billion annual deficit.[80]

There are only four ways these obligations will ever be paid. The first way would be for Congress and the President to bite the bullet, cut spending, and balance the budget. But this option has no constituency in Washington, or anywhere else. Congress is addicted to deficit spending. So is the U.S. population. This option is very unlikely to be adopted.

The second way would be for the Treasury Department and Federal Reserve to issue more debt--lots of it. However, the Fed faces a dilemma--issue too much debt, and no one will buy it! Eventually, investors will begin to associate "Treasury securities" and "junk bonds" in the same breath.

There are several reasons why this process hasn't already started. One reason is that foreign investors, reacting to crises in other parts of the world, have been heavily adding to their inventory of U.S. government securities in recent years. At the end of 1992, foreigners held nearly $500 billion in U.S. government debt. In addition, battle-scarred investors are increasingly unloading their holdings of speculative bonds and investing the proceeds in "ultra-safe" U.S. Treasury bills.

Finally, U.S. banks have come to the rescue of the Federal Reserve and U.S. Treasury. Over 80 percent of available credit in the United States is now extended to the federal government. In the midst of recession (and stricter regulation), U.S. banks are reluctant to lend money to private businesses.

---

[80]*Entitlements and the Aging of America* (National Taxpayers Union, 325 Pennsylvania Ave. SE, Washington, D.C. 20003)

But loans to the government are guaranteed. Essentially, U.S. banks can borrow from the Fed at 3 percent and lend back to the government at 7 percent--a guaranteed profit of 4 percent.

With interest rates slashed by two-thirds in recent years and the U.S. dollar down 70 percent from its value in 1970, one wonders how long foreign and domestic investors will be willing to buy and/or hold U.S. debt. If their losses continue, there will eventually be a backlash against U.S. government securities. Moreover, the recession will eventually end. Eventually, banks will conclude they can make better profits lending to rebounding businesses than to the federal government. At that point, banks will drastically reduce their current *weekly* $20 billion investment in Treasury securities.

Allen Greenspan, the Fed Chairman, realizes this. That's why he never misses an opportunity to advise Congress to cut the deficit. Congress, of course, ignores him. So does the President. Greenspan also realizes that the more debt the Fed brings to market, the higher interest rates will rise-- thus choking off any chance for meaningful economic recovery.

Thus this second choice is really a non-choice. But it is the choice the Fed has been forced to make. Eventually, the Fed and Treasury will not be able to sell all the debt the government needs. At that point, the government will be forced to take measures to "enhance revenues." You'll read more about them in "Government by Emergency," Chapter 9, and in the remainder of this chapter.

The third choice would be for the President to instruct the Treasury to declare a "debt holiday" and divest itself of its debt. I don't think the President will pressure the Treasury to take this step, at least not voluntarily. Not only would it be illegal, but would result in no one ever voluntarily purchasing Treasury debt again. And a significant side-effect would be the total destruction of the U.S. dollar.

A variant of this choice is more conceivable. It is outlined in Alfred Malabre's *Beyond Our Means*. Malabre, a former senior editor of *The Wall Street Journal*, predicts that the Treasury might convert short-term Treasury bills into long-term Treasury bonds. The Treasury would still pay interest, but not permit investors to redeem the principal for an extended period. An extension of maturity on a bond lowers its value, and is in itself a form of default. But Malabre feels most people would go along. I agree, particularly if default is justified on the basis of dealing with some threat--for instance, a "just war" similar to that carried out against Iraq in 1991, or to escalate the War on Drugs.[81]

I describe another variation of this choice in "The New Money," Chapter 10. It is for the Treasury to issue a two-tiered currency, one to circulate in the United States, one internationally. The government would default only on its domestic debt obligations, not on its foreign ones, which would be denominated in an "international" dollar.

The fourth choice has already been taken. It is to expose all the money Americans have hidden away or circulating in the underground economy, thereby making it more accessible for progressively higher taxes or for use as "loans" to Social Security, Medicare, etc.

Until the Reagan Administration took office, there was no practical way for this fourth option to be implemented. Once taxes were paid on income, there was no other obligation for a U.S. citizen to tell the government what the money was used for or how it was invested. Other than a foreign bank account, there was no "paper trail." U.S. citizens had stashed away trillions of dollars in private investments that didn't need to be reported to anyone. Reagan's task, and that of his successors, was to find ways to track, and ultimately gain access, to these funds without alienating voters who would never voluntarily consent to a $15 trillion bailout.

---

[81]Alfred Malabre, *Beyond Our Means* (New York: Random House, 1987)

One way the government insures that this wealth remains accessible is to do persuade people to keep their assets visible. Congress gives tax deferrals for IRAs and Keogh plans. It gives tax deductions to parents who identify their children to the Social Security Administration. Another way it is kept accessible is with the enormous expansion in reporting requirements that began with the Bank Secrecy Act, and with the creation of financial dossiers on every U.S. citizen. These regulations, and these dossiers, are justified as the price of fighting the government's War on Drugs.

While drugs are nothing less than a scourge, the last way I would fight the drug war is ask ordinary citizens to sacrifice their few remaining personal and financial privacy rights, and indeed, the Constitution itself. But that is the sacrifice the government has asked you to make.

The Tax Equity and Fiscal Responsibility Act of 1982

One of the Reagan Administration's first initiatives in the War on Privacy was to hire 5,000 new IRS agents, and to accelerate the agency's program of "cross-matching" tax returns against other databases which might indicate a taxpayer was "living beyond his means." The Social Security number was used as the common denominator for all these efforts.

Next, the administration began pressuring Congress to adopt legislation giving the government vast new powers to gather, cross-reference and distribute personal data, and to continue dismantling the Privacy Act of 1974 and the Right to Financial Privacy Act of 1978.

The administration's first major victory in this effort was the Tax Equity and Fiscal Responsibility Act of 1982 (TEFRA). TEFRA was a significant expansion of the financial and foreign exchange controls first adopted in the Bank Secrecy Act. The act dramatically boosts the power of the IRS and imposes additional reporting requirements on financial institutions.

TEFRA requires banks and brokerage firms to report most types of investor income to the IRS, including interest, dividends and the gross proceeds from sales, redemptions and exchanges. It requires that any company doing business as a "broker" maintain a list of the names and addresses of all its customers, available for IRS inspection at any time. It also requires barter organizations to report credits earned by their subscribers to the agency. And it forces banks, brokerages, etc. to deduct 20 percent of the earnings of anyone who does not report their "taxpayer identification number;" for almost everyone, their Social Security number.

TEFRA also requires that anyone who pays an "unincorporated entity" more than $600 in the course of a year submit a form to the IRS to insure that the income is declared on the recipient's income tax return.

In addition, TEFRA made certain that several private refuges for wealth were hidden from the government no longer. It banned new publicly-traded issues of bearer (anonymously-owned) stocks and bonds in the United States, and mandates that anyone turning in a bearer instrument for redemption identify himself with a Social Security number. Otherwise, the holder forfeits 20 percent of his interest. Finally, Congress declared that the refusal of an individual to comply with an order to produce personal records in relation to overseas transaction eliminates that person's right to use such records in his defense.

To enforce these new provisions, Congress granted the IRS vast new information-gathering powers. The IRS could now gain access to third-party records by issuing a simple "administrative summons," rather than go through the procedure to obtain a subpoena mandated in the Right to Financial Privacy Act of 1978. Moreover, the administrative subpoena could now be used not just to determine tax liabilities, but for any criminal investigation.

The granting of this sweeping administrative subpoena power flew in the face of the Fourth Amendment. But the courts dismissed this claim repeatedly, culminating in *Matter vs. Newton*, when the court held that absent a specific grant of privilege by Congress, third party recordkeepers could not hold back information in violation of Congressional intent.

From the administration's viewpoint, TEFRA had the desired effect. IRS levies jumped from 740,103 to more than 1.6 million from 1981 to 1986.

The Deficit Reduction Act of 1984

By 1984, computer matching was thriving in the federal government. In that year government agencies computer matched more than 2 billion records from 110 databases. A typical match: The Selective Service Administration compared its files with birthday party lists subpoenaed from ice cream parlors, looking for 18-year old men who hadn't registered for the draft.

The Deficit Reduction Act in 1984 authorized the first full-scale effort to link data in various federal government and private databases. The stated intention was to weed out cheating by beneficiaries of federal programs. It linked databases containing information on wage, pension, unemployment insurance, and other income data, including unearned income from IRS files. Keep in mind that many of the activities this legislation authorized had been taking place *illegally* since 1977, as I described in "The Match Game," this chapter.

The Social Security Administration used cross-matching to insure that individuals who receive disability benefits were actually disabled. The Customs Service used it to upgrade TECS into a more advanced system, TECS-II. An expert system program that constructs "computer profiles" to identify individuals who might be likely presidential assassins was constructed by the Secret Service. The Department of Transportation set up a computer listing every driver's license from every state. Its announced purpose was to end the practice of people who lose their driving privileges in one state from simply applying for a license in another state.

However, the biggest beneficiary of cross-matching is the IRS. The Deficit Reduction Act gives the IRS a mandate to crack down on individuals who fail to repay money borrowed from the federal government. Today, the IRS has a list of nearly 1,000,000 people who owe money to the government.

One of its first uses of this list was in 1987, when it was employed to deny refunds to individuals who had defaulted on loans from the federal government. In 1991, the IRS withheld $370 million in tax refunds that would have otherwise been distributed to nearly 600,000 taxpayers. It withheld an additional $600 million from individuals behind in child support payments.[82],[83]

In addition, using the bloc modeling techniques I described in Chapter 4, the agency created an "Individual Master File" for every U.S. taxpayer. Data are gathered from government files, banks, insurance companies and direct marketing companies that construct computerized profiles of consumer spending. Today, the IRS possesses a financial dossier on every U.S. taxpayer.

---

[82] The Cash Management Improvement Act of 1992 permits the IRS to withhold refunds and apply the money toward any debt owed *any federal agency*. This initiative effectively eliminates all constitutional restraint on the federal government's debt collection practices.

[83] Legislation introduced in 1993 by Illinois Representative Henry Hyde would have the IRS take over all collection of child support payments and authorize withholding from worker paychecks in the same manner as income taxes are now withheld.

The act also authorizes states to "compare notes" by computer and thereby identify individuals who fail to pay state income taxes. In exchange for IRS access to state computer records, state tax authorities have been given direct access to IRS computers. The IRS has also signed information-sharing agreements with at least 35 states to coordinate filing of IRS forms with both federal and state governments.

This access, in turn, has led several states to form "compacts" to exchange tax-related information. For instance, the Great Lakes Interstate Sales Compact signatory states have agreed to "vigorously pursue by audit the discovery of untaxed sales made by in-state vendors to individual or business consumers in other Great Lakes States."

To make information exchange even easier, in 1991 the Federation of Tax Administrators and the Multistate Tax Commission opened "TaxExchange," a computer network open to all state tax authorities. The network promises to widen and speed up exchanges of taxpayer files among states and with the IRS for compliance projects concerning income, sales, and other taxes.

But perhaps the ultimate invasion of privacy spawned by computer matching came in Oklahoma. In 1991, a law went into effect which requires residents to declare everything they own to the tax collector: guns, coins, art, business equipment, etc. Anyone who refuses to disclose this information will be visited by a tax assessor. If permission to enter the home is denied, a search warrant will be issued. *All* the data gathered is presumably accessible to both IRS computers and tax authorities in other states.

The wholesale use of computers to conduct general searches of both public and private databases by the IRS, other federal agencies, and the states is not only a gross violation of our common-law rights, but of the Fourth Amendment. As Robert Messick of the University of Santa Clara states:[84]

> Computer matching of data banks by the IRS exhibit many [indications] of a general exploratory search typical of general writs of assistance prohibited by the Fourth Amendment. Full-blown searches, dragnets, wholesale rummaging through possessions, or "fishing expeditions" in search of potential evidence are prohibited by the Fourth Amendment; such exploratory searches cannot be taken by the government with or without a warrant. Likewise, it arguable that a generalized search through a computer data bank constitutes a massive dragnet into the private affairs of substantial numbers of persons.

Finally, the act intensified the "War on Cash," extending cash reporting provisions that had previously applied only to financial institutions to many other businesses. A business receiving more than $10,000 in cash or monetary instruments in one or more related "designated reporting transactions" must now complete a Form 8300 similar to the Currency Transaction Report used by banks. The form asks for the client's name, address, Social Security number, passport number and details about the services provided for the payment.[85],[86]

---

[84]"IRS Computer Data Bank Searches: An Infringement of the Fourth Amendment Search and Seizure Clause" (*Santa Clara Law Review*, University of Santa Clara, Santa Clara, Calif., vol. 25, 1985)

[85]"Designated reporting transactions" include the sale of "consumer durable" (products that have a useful life exceeding one year); "collectibles" (art, antiques, rugs, gems, medals, stamps, and coins); "travel or entertainment activities"--and today, legal representation as well.

[86]The maximum punishment for failure to file the form is five years imprisonment and/or a fine of $25,000 ($100,000 for corporations). Willfully filing a false Form 8300 may be punished by three years imprisonment and/or a $100,000 fine ($500,000 for corporations). Section 6050I of the Internal Revenue Code provides the authority for the collection of this information.

For nearly five years, this provision went virtually unenforced. However, in 1989, the IRS threatened criminal sanctions against attorneys who did not report cash payments from their clients. The warnings, issued to more than 1,000 attorneys nationwide, sparked an outcry over the erosion of the attorney-client privilege. According to Neal R. Sonnett, president of the National Association of Criminal Defense Lawyers, "The IRS is asking lawyers to red-flag a criminal problem in front of the government, forcing the lawyer to be a witness against his client."[87]

But not *all* lawyers. If you turn in your own client, you're exempt from the law. That's what attorney Ronald Fink allegedly did, in a scheme where he convinced a series of clients to testify against other clients in cases dating back to the early 1980s.

For arranging the deals, Fink's clients paid him nearly $1 million in cash. However, a U.S. Attorney ruled that Fink was not required to report the cash transactions. Nor has the IRS challenged Mr. Fink's account of the cash-reporting arrangement or penalized him for reporting violations. The judge presiding in this case eventually threw out the indictment, but sweetheart deals between the attorneys and prosecutor don't appear to be against Justice Department policy.

New Form 8300s introduced in February 1992 contain a section for a merchant to report "suspicious transactions" by his customers that would otherwise be not be reportable. The National Automobile Dealers Association immediately requested that this box be eliminated, so that dealers wouldn't be forced to draw conclusions about their customers and thereby subjected to civil liability.

The IRS didn't delete the box, but the instructions for Form 8300 now say that completion of the "suspicious transactions" box is voluntarily. (See Appendix A for a copy of this new form and the flyer the IRS published to explain how to complete it.)

Merchants also must report "related transactions" that exceed $10,000 in cash or monetary instruments in any 12-month period. IRS Publication 1544 states that transactions are related if they occur within 24 hours of one another. They're also related even "if they are more than 24 hours apart if you know, or if you have reason to know, that each one is a series of connected transactions."

"Willful ignorance" of the transactions being related is specifically a crime. (To me, this means that any series of transactions the IRS deems related, is in fact related.) In addition, retailers with knowledge that they are being given a monetary instrument in an effort to avoid the reporting of a transaction, regardless of its amount, must report it.

According to the Industry Council for Tangible Assets (ICTA), IRS districts in some states are applying even stricter standards. IRS agents in Colorado and Louisiana have requested that coin dealers report any series of transactions by a single customer over $10,000, even if otherwise unrelated, in any 30-day period. In Texas, merchants are instructed to combine all transactions in any 12-month period and report them if they exceed $10,000. Merchants who violate the interpretations of agents in their respective districts risk forfeiture of the "tainted" assets, arrest, and a potential prison sentence.[88],[89]

---

[87]In 1991, the 2nd Circuit Appeals Court ruled that the cash-reporting requirements as applied to attorneys are constitutional and do not violate the attorney-client privilege (*U.S. vs. Goldberger & Dubin, P.C.*, 935 F.2nd 501).

[88]ICTA, a non-profit lobbying group for rare coin and precious metals dealers, is one of the few, if not the only, entity pressing for the clarification of IRS cash reporting and broker reporting requirements. You may contribute to these efforts by sending your donation to ICTA's "Cash Reporting Fund" and or "Broker Reporting Fund" c/o ICTA, 6728 Old McLean Village Drive, McLean, Va. 22101.

[89]Civil sanctions for failure to file Form 8300 when it would otherwise be required are $50 per return, not to exceed $250,000 for a calendar year for simple failure to file or for filing an incomplete or incorrect version of the form. The civil penalty for an "intentional" failure to file is the greater of $25,000 or the amount received in the cash transaction(s), not to exceed $100,000 per incident. The cash is also subject to forfeiture. "Willful" violations may be punished by criminal penalties

To insure compliance, the IRS has embarked upon a vigorous campaign of stings using a small army of undercover agents. An agent from the IRS Criminal Investigation Division approaches a merchant and tries to convince him to accept more than $10,000 in cash without reporting it on Form 8300. If the merchant agrees, he may be arrested on the spot for money laundering, or the IRS may arrange other transactions to provide an even more convincing case. The IRS issues then a press release announcing the arrest to provide the strongest-possible deterrent to other merchants. Prime targets include any "big ticket," cash businesses--car dealerships, precious metals dealers, jewelry dealers, etc.

In 1991, the IRS announced it had visited more than 5,000 retail stores in undercover and compliance operations to determine if the required records were being maintained and turned over to the government.

Compliance is still lacking, says the IRS; only 66,000 of the forms were filed in 1991. However, this figure is more than double the number filed in 1990.

Who Is Watching You?

"Coming under surveillance is a privilege"

--anonymous employee of the Swedish tax board

The following fictional scenario, set out in the August 1987 issue of *The Gary Allen Report*, was made possible by the linking of computerized government databases authorized during the Reagan years in the Deficit Reduction Act of 1984, the Anti-Drug Abuse Act of 1986 and other legislation:

> George was attracted to her the moment he saw here while he was driving to work. She was in her mid-thirties, elegantly dressed, with long blonde hair that fluttered in the breeze as she drove her red Porsche convertible in the adjacent lane of the crowded California freeway. Letting her get a little ahead of him, George was able to read her vanity license plate: MINE.
>
> When he arrived at his office in the local government building that housed the Department of Health and Human Services, where he worked in the social welfare division, George quickly brought up his file of codes on his computer terminal; tracking down that beauty would be a snap, he mused to himself. After all, he had access to numerous government records and private data banks. Checking people out was part of his job to distinguish valid welfare applicants from chiselers and illegal aliens. It was all part of the administration's drive to reduce waste, fraud and abuse in federal welfare programs.
>
> At the computer prompt, George entered his authorization code on the keyboard, hit the "execute" button and accessed the Department of Motor Vehicles database. He typed in the license plate letters "MINE" and ordered a search of the DMV files. After less than a minute's wait, the monitor screen displayed the information he wanted: License   tag:

---

that start with a prison term of four years or more, and a fine of $25,000 per transaction. Criminal penalties for participating in an illegal cash transaction are $250,000-$500,000, or twice the amount of the transaction(s), plus 10 years or more in prison.

MINE.   Vehicle: 1983 Porsche 944.   Owner: Julie Jameson, 1509 Appleton Drive, Laguna Heights, CA.   Driver's license: U0834725. Date of Birth: 5/14/52.   Sex: Female.   Height: 5'6".   Weight: 105 lbs. Social Security number: 552-58-2436.

Entering another data bank, George used the SSN as the key data element to search wage records that employers are required to file with state unemployment compensation and tax offices.   Julie's record came up with more information: SSN #552-58-2436.   JULIE JAMESON. Employer: Toltech Manufacturing, Inc., 921 Wilshire Blvd., Los Angeles, CA.   Employed from 1/10/77--current.   Position: National Director of Sales and Marketing.   Gross pay for 1986: $63,124. Earnings for First Quarter, 1987: $16,542.

"Not bad," thought George.   Next, he typed Julie's address into the computer and told it to search the records of the Laguna Heights deed registration office.   Soon the screen filled with a new data record: 1509 Appleton Drive.   Block 351, Lot 3.   Land Assessment: $35,685.   Total Assessment: $114,006.   Built: 1978.   Use: Residential.   Deed of trust recorded: October 11, 1978.   Loan Instrument: 23997.   Amount: $75,000, between Joseph James and Julie Jameson Nelson and First National Savings & Loan.   Other personal assets listed as collateral: 25-foot sailboat, assessed at $16,000.

Julie Jameson had once been Julie Nelson.   George decided to check county divorce records to see what was on file.   He found the record: Divorce awarded 7/18/85.   Julie Jameson Nelson vs. Joseph James Nelson.   Married: 6/12/76.   Children: Anthony Michael, born 4/3/78; Carolyn Marie, born 12/24/80.   Grounds for divorce: Infidelity. Divorce sought by: wife.   Race: husband, Caucasian; wife, Caucasian. Number of previous marriages: husband, none; wife, one.   Date first marriage was terminated: 9/24/74 in Reno, Nevada.

Being a curious fellow, George then decided to check local school enrollment records.   He found that "Tony" went to Ben Franklin Elementary School.   Carolyn Marie was enrolled at Montgomery Special Education Institute, a school for children with learning disabilities.

Next, George decided to look into IRS files.   But such records are confidential, so George's office computer terminal could not access the IRS data in Washington by an on-line connection.   Instead, he put Julie's name and SSN on a request list that was mailed by his welfare office to the IRS the next day.   In less than a week, George received a magnetic storage tape from the IRS that contained tax information on Julie Jameson's other sources of income.

Data from Form 1090 (Unearned Income) revealed that her interest income included $2,100 from a $23,000 Certificate of Deposit from First National Bank, $4,200 from a $48,000 CD at the same bank and another $1,600 from a $28,000 passbook savings account.   Dividend income was also listed--including $9,754 from 4,000 shares of Toltech Manufacturing stock.   Capital gains income of $5,600 came in from the sale of IBM stock. Even $3,235 in winnings from betting on the horses at Los Alamitos Race Track was listed.

Chuckling to himself, George mentally reviewed what he had learned about his mark. Julie Jameson was recently divorced after a nine-year marriage; it had been her second marriage and she had ended it with a divorce by charging her husband with adultery--and had apparently wound up with a hefty settlement as well as custody of the kids; she lived in an expensive home in a nice neighborhood (George had driven by to check it out); she worked at a secure high-paying job; she had additional income from interest and dividends; she enjoyed sailing and betting on the ponies; her six-year-old daughter had a learning disability; and she owned a status-symbol car. He decided he had enough information to make a phone call and strike up an acquaintance!

The Money Laundering Control Act of 1986

"The only way for businesses to protect themselves is to steer clear of cash completely"

--Charles Intriago, Money Laundering Alert

By 1986, it became clear to both Congress and the Reagan Administration that the cash reporting measures that had implemented since 1970 had not had the intended effect of wiping out the underground economy. It was time for stronger measures. The Money Laundering Control Act of 1986 (part of the larger Anti-Drug Abuse Act of the same year) was the centerpiece of the Reagan administration's latest escalation in the War On Drugs.

In 1985, an international anti-laundering task force estimated a $50 billion turnover in laundered drug money each year. At a 1992 meeting of the European Community's Financial Action Task Force, set up to fight money laundering, one speaker estimated that the problem was six times larger--more than $300 billion per year. But the latter estimate included proceeds laundered from "other serious crimes."

Perhaps no phrase conjures up a more vivid picture of illegal activity than money laundering. It evokes images of jewel-bedecked foreign nationals carrying briefcases of cash onto private airplanes bound for secret European and Caribbean tax havens, shadowy businessmen opening crates full of automatic weapons for distribution in our central cities and numbered bank accounts in foreign countries.

But money laundering is a much more mundane activity than these popular images convey. According to the November 1990 *Money Laundering Law Report,* money laundering refers to any violations of:

✓ Federal or state financial reporting and recordkeeping laws and regulations, and/or

✓ Making any effort to evade such reporting and recordkeeping provisions.[90]

---

[90]*Money Laundering Law Report* (Leader Publications, 111 Eighth Ave., New York, NY 10011). Subsequent court decisions made conscious *avoidance* of such laws or regulations subject to the same penalties, at least as far as the anti-structuring statutes were concerned. Tax avoidance is legal, but not avoidance of a reporting requirement.

Under this definition, failing to file your income tax might be considered money laundering. Certainly failing to disclose a reportable foreign bank account would be considered a money laundering offense. In fact, *you* may be a money launderer, and not even know it![91]

The scope of the Money Laundering Control Act is breathtaking, and as you'll soon discover, it overturned the following common-law and constitutional precedents:

✓ Greatly expanded the definition of a "criminal conspiracy"

✓ Greatly restricted the Sixth Amendment right of a defendant to seek legal counsel

✓ Greatly expanded the ability of the government to seize property without due process

Other parts of the act further narrows the scope of the Right to Financial Privacy Act of 1978. It makes clear that financial institutions must report suspected violations of money laundering laws, and lists the types of information that may be freely released without fear of suits from depositors. In addition, it greatly broadens the circumstances under which depositors need not be informed that an investigation is taking place. Finally, it extends the bounty-hunter provisions of the Bank Secrecy Act to all types of money laundering. Turn someone in and you'll receive up to $150,000, or 25 percent of the assets the government can seize.[92]

The heart of the Money Laundering Control Act is Section 1956, which makes unlawful any transaction involving the proceeds of "specified unlawful activity:"

A. with the intent to promote that activity; or

B. knowing that the transaction is designed in whole or in part --

(i) to conceal or disguise the nature, the location, the source, the ownership, or the control of the proceeds of specified unlawful activity; or

(ii) to avoid a transaction reporting requirement under state or federal law.

The prescribed punishment borrows from the racketeering (RICO) statutes and is almost unbelievably harsh: fines up to $500,000, or twice the value of the transaction, pre-trial restraint or seizure of any property involved in or traceable to an illegal transaction, and imprisonment for up to 20 years. Forfeitures may take place in advance of any trial or even arrest. As you'll learn in Chapter 8, the government has moved aggressively to use its expanded pre-trial forfeiture powers, in many cases leaving accused defendants unable to procure competent legal representation.

For money laundering "conspiracies," fines can reach $25 million. Criminal forfeiture provisions also borrow from RICO and potentially reach all assets, not just those that are criminally-derived.

---

[91]An excellent legal reference for coverage of the money laundering laws is *Money Laundering and Forfeiture* (New York: New York Law Publishing Co., 1992).

[92]The scope of the Money Laundering Control Act is so vast that it has spawned a minor publishing boom. Banks and other financial institutions are scrambling to avoid prosecution, and several newsletters have started circulation to keep them appraised of the laws, regulations, and court cases. Two of the most-widely circulated are *Money Laundering Law Report* (Leader Publications, 111 Eighth Ave., New York, N.Y. 10111) and *Money Laundering Alert* (12515 N. Kendall Drive, Suite 302, Miami, Fla. 33186).

Given such awe-inspiring deterrents to criminal behavior, law-abiding citizens might want to know exactly what the money laundering statutes prohibit. Section 1956 lists some fairly obvious "specified unlawful activities:" drug trafficking, murder, kidnapping, tax evasion, embezzlement, fraud involving a federal program, etc. But it includes some not-so-obvious crimes, such as violations of the Emergency Economic Powers Act of 1977 and the Trading With the Enemy Act of 1917.

Subsequent amendments add bankruptcy fraud, bank fraud, government procurement fraud, real estate fraud, wire fraud, mail fraud, political corruption, and theft from governmental assistance programs to the list of specified unlawful activities. Even proceeds a company earns while in violation of environmental laws are now (since 1990 amendments were passed) considered to be "laundered." Such monies, and even the proceeds with which a company pays back a loan, are now subject to forfeiture, and the bank that receives them liable for criminal prosecution.

Regulations issued to interpret the act have made clear that any crimes which generate money and involve the conversion of such funds into other forms, are *all* specified unlawful activities that can be prosecuted as money laundering offenses. In most cases, the government can obtain punishment that far exceeds the penalties associated to underlying criminal conduct by adding one or more money laundering counts to an indictment. The government can freeze, seize, and forfeit otherwise untouchable assets using this tactic.[93]

Furthermore, the courts have ruled if the proceeds from criminally-derived property are mingled with other, legitimate funds, the entire commingled sum is liable for seizure! If you deposited $10 of "criminally derived proceeds" into a $100,000 bank account, the government may seize the entire account. For instance, in *U.S. vs. All Monies ($477,048.62)*, the Hawaii U.S. District Court found that all the proceeds of a bank account containing both allegedly illegally-derived and legitimate funds could be forfeited to the government because the legitimate money facilitated the laundering of illegal proceeds through the account.

Amy Rudnick, former director of the Treasury Department's Office of Financial Enforcement, explains the implications of the commingling doctrine in a recent issue of *Criminal Justice*:[94]

> Assume that a public official accepts a $20,000 check from a constituent at the officials $350,000 home in exchange for voting against a particular bill, in violation of 18 U.S.C. Section 201. The public official endorses the check to her husband at her home. The next day she puts the case in a $300 leather briefcase, puts the briefcase in here $25,000 car, and deposits the check in her and her husband's joint account at a bank where they maintain a balance of $50,000. The public official then has the

---

[93]The July 1992 *ABA Banking Journal* describes how the Environmental Protection Agency (EPA) can use money laundering laws against lenders that provide money to corporate polluters.

The Crime Control Act of 1990 permits the EPA to apply money laundering laws in criminal violations of most federal air and water pollution legislation. A lender may be convicted of money laundering if it advances more than $10,000 to a company that it knows *or has reason to believe* has violated environmental laws. Violators may be fined $500,000 or twice the value of the property involved, whichever is greater.

The article suggests that lenders should adopt "due diligence" measures to avoid lending to companies in violation of environmental laws; make personnel aware of environmental and money laundering laws; require payment in "clean" funds and provide that payment in "dirty" funds shall be deemed to have not been received; and avoid actions that might be seen as promoting or concealing activities made illegal under federal environmental legislation.

[94]"Cleaning Up Money Laundering Prosecutions; Guidelines for Prosecution and Asset Forfeiture," *Criminal Justice*, Spring 1992

bank wire-transfer $20,000 from the joint account to an account of a college in New Haven to pay for her son's law school tuition.

None of this property could be forfeited if the public official were convicted of accepting a bribe. However, if she were convicted of money laundering, the government could forfeit not only the $20,000 that she accepted from her constituent but also all of the property that was used in the money laundering scheme and is traceable to it--the briefcase, the car, her personal residence, and possibly even all other monies in the joint bank account. Furthermore, the government could seize and restrain all of this property, including the residence and other bank accounts, prior to the return of any indictment.

Rudnick goes on to suggest the need for tighter guidelines to avoid abuses in money laundering and asset forfeiture cases. These would be welcome, but the incredibly broad sweep of this law is an open invitation to prosecutorial misconduct.

Placed in charge of enforcing the money laundering laws is the IRS Criminal Investigation Division. By definition, tax evasion is a crime that involves money. Using this logic, money laundering prosecutions in tax evasion cases should be soaring. And they are.[95]

The new pattern of prosecution is clear: Depositing and/or using cash on which taxes have not been paid is money laundering, and will be prosecuted as such. The maximum 20-year prison sentence and $500,000 fine for money laundering is far harsher than the maximum penalties for ordinary tax evasion. Moreover, convictions are far easier to obtain, since "money laundering" and "drug crimes" are inexorably linked in the minds of juries.

Even everyday IRS tax inquiries can lead to a money laundering prosecution. During routine audits, where a taxpayer's income and expenses are verified, IRS employees are now trained to check the agency's computerized data banks. These data banks contain information from the agency's currency and banking reporting system, its information return master files, and also from a newly-established Treasury intelligence unit, the Financial Crimes Enforcement System (FinCEN). (For more information on FinCEN, see "The Bush Administration's War on Privacy," this chapter.)

Here's how the investigative procedure is described in the November 1990 *Money Laundering Law Report:*

> The Currency and Banking Report handbook reveals how a routine tax examination can result in a [money laundering] compliance examination or review of a taxpayer or unsuspecting third party who conducted a transaction with such taxpayer.
>
> [Attorneys] may wish to approach every IRS inquiry as one that could result in compliance review or money laundering investigation of the client or its customers. What may appear or actually be a simple tax inquiry may become a money laundering case.

---

[95]See, for instance, "IRS Likely to Increase Use of Money Laundering and Related Statutes" (*Journal of Taxation,* November 1990)

Spy on Your Customers, or Go to Jail

The first impression that you might gather after reading Section 1956 of the Money Laundering Control Act is that you are immune from prosection for money laundering if you avoid any of the specified unlawful activities the law lists, or avoid illegally concealing your own lawful earnings.

But you're not, if you do business with the public in cash or other "monetary instruments," according to Section 1957. This section makes it illegal for a merchant to receive funds that have been derived from *suspected* specified unlawful activities. Violators may be fined as much as double the value of the criminally-derived property changing hands, sentenced to 10 years in jail, or both.

As the House of Representatives debated how to best react to the money laundering "crisis," Florida Congressman Bill McCollum remarked:

> The corner grocer in a community is aware of the reputation of the local drug trafficker. That person comes to the store and buys five pounds of hamburger. The grocer has to know what he is coming in to buy groceries with is indeed the money derived from a particular designated crime. I don't have any problem whatsoever holding the grocer accountable for money laundering.

Could you be thrown in jail for selling hamburger to a person with a "reputation" as a drug dealer? Congressman McCollum thinks you should be. Your ignorance of the hamburger buyer's criminal activity is no excuse. Section 1957 of the act reads in part:

> The government is not required to prove the defendant knew that the offense from which the criminally derived property was derived was a specified unlawful activity.

Of course, the hamburger buyer would not have to be a suspected drug dealer for you to land in jail. He could have allegedly committed any one of the dozens of specified unlawful activities listed in the act. Why not imprison merchants who sell hamburger to people he suspects of violating the Emergency Economic Powers Act of 1977? Surely not one in a thousand merchants have heard of this law, but they now risk losing their business and their freedom for merely doing business with someone they should suspect of violating it.

There is no minimum dollar limit under which Section 1956 money laundering prosecutions may proceed. For Section 1957, transactions under $10,000 are exempt. However, any pattern of "related transactions" totalling $10,000 or more in any 12 month period are enforceable. So, if over a period of several months, a person violating some emergency regulation you didn't even know about (but supposedly should have) were to buy groceries totalling $10,000 or more, and pay with cash or other negotiable instruments, you could still be found guilty under Section 1957. Proposed revisions to the act would reduce this threshold from $10,000 to $3,000.

A even more insidious result of Section 1957 is its revolutionary impact on the common-law definition of a *conspiracy*. The common law requires a person to have both *knowledge* of an illegal action and an *intent* to encourage it in order to enter into a criminal conspiracy. But Section 1957 eliminates those requirements. You can now engage in a criminal conspiracy if you do not take someone's *reputation* into account before doing business with him. You need not know what law your customer might be breaking, or indeed even realize he is breaking a law at all, to become part of the conspiracy.[96],[97],[98]

How can a businessman protect himself from entering into an unknowing criminal conspiracy with his customers? Should he ask each and every one of his customers to sign a statement certifying that the funds being paid for his product or service have not been gained through "specified unlawful activities as defined by Section 1957 of the Money Laundering Control Act of 1986?"

In many U.S. cities, violent gangs rule the streets, yet police provide little protection to merchants operating there. Many of these gang members regularly commit crimes that are specified unlawful activities under the act. When a merchant accepts business from a gang member, he risks prosecution for violating Section 1957. Yet if he refuses to do business, he risks the "Sicilian solution" of extortion, kidnapping, and even execution by the gangs. Is it any wonder that we find it difficult to attract businesses to our central cities?

An equally-threatening result of Section 1957 is its erosion of the Sixth Amendment right to legal representation. Criminal defense attorneys who accept money that they suspect may be derived from specified unlawful activities may be punished in the same manner as Congressman McCollum's grocer. In the words of Jeffrey G. Huron:

> The threat of a felony conviction [under Section 1957] may cause defense attorneys to be reluctant to take certain cases. To convict a defense attorney, the government must show that the attorney was engaged in some form of monetary transaction, that the attorney knew the property was in fact derived from an unlawful activity, and that the property involved had a value of more than $10,000.
>
> By accepting payment for services, a defense attorney meets the first element of engaging in a monetary transaction. In addition, defense lawyers will seldom be completely without knowledge of the guilt of innocence of a client. In addition, fees for complex cases frequently run over the $10,000 statutory limit.
>
> The threat of criminal sanctions seriously implicates the constitutional rights of the defendant. A criminal defense attorney may be unwilling to represent certain criminal defendants because of the criminal penalties. This chills the Sixth Amendment right of the defendant to retain counsel of choice.[99]

I believe the situation to be even more serious than Huron describes, since the actual statute reads: "The government is not required to prove the defendant knew that the offense from which the

---

[96]However, in *U.S. vs. Campbell*, a U.S. District Court rejected this reasoning. It ruled that a real estate agent could not be found guilty of money laundering for selling property to a drug dealer merely because he failed to take the dealer's reputation and flamboyant lifestyle into account.

[97]A discussion of the evolution of conspiracy law through the enactment of the Money Laundering Control Act is contained in "Money Laundering: The Crime of the Nineties" (*American Criminal Law Review*, vol. 27, 1989)

[98]In December 1991, in *Griffin vs. United States*, the Supreme Court ruled that an individual may be convicted of being involved in a criminal conspiracy relating to money laundering even if their participation in the conspiracy was not proven.

[99]Jeffrey G. Huron, "The Money Laundering Control Act of 1986: Tainted Money and the Criminal Defense Lawyer" (*Pacific Law Journal*, vol. 19, 1987)

criminally derived property was derived was a specified unlawful activity." Once again, the attorney need not realize his client is guilty to enter his conspiracy; he need only *suspect* that he *might* be guilty.

Another threat to legal representation, you'll recall, was the Deficit Reduction Act of 1984, which in effect, forces attorneys to testify against their clients by completing currency transaction forms that identify the source of the funds with which their clients are paying. Section 1957 adds the distinction of having the forms potentially serve as the "smoking gun" for prosecution of the defendant's attorney.

Prosecutors know that Section 1957, if vigorously enforced, would spell the end of the free-enterprise system in America. It would break down any semblance of trust that might exist between a businessman and his customers, or an attorney and his client. So it has not been vigorously enforced--at least not yet. The Justice Department's prosecutorial guidelines state that no Section 1957 prosecutions are to be made against anyone who doesn't reasonably suspect, or is not "willfully blind," of his customer's illegal income.

Through the end of 1991, the Treasury Department conducted only seven Section 1957 prosecutions. However, I've been told by several attorneys that Section 1957 prosecutions in 1992 were up sharply.

The "Crime" of Structuring

A new crime defined under the Money Laundering Control Act is "structuring;" any act an individual takes in order to evade (or more recently, avoid) filling out a Currency Transaction Report. This might seem a fairly trivial offense, but criminal violators face a mandatory prison term and $250,000 fine, in addition to forfeiture of the funds involved.[100]

What exactly is "structuring?" Section 5324 of the act reads, in part:

> No person shall for the purpose of evading the reporting requirements of Section 5313(a) [i.e., the requirements of the Bank Secrecy Act] with respect to such transaction--
>
> (1) cause or attempt to cause a domestic financial institution to fail to file a report required under Section 5313(a);
>
> (2) cause or attempt to cause a domestic financial institution to file a report required under Section 5313(a) that contains a material omission or misstatement of fact; or
>
> (3) structure or assist in structuring, or attempt to structure or assist in structuring, any transaction with one or more domestic financial institutions.[101]

---

[100]The anti-structuring statute is outlined in 31 U.S.C. Section 5324. Sections 5321-22 sets the civil and criminal penalties for violations of the structuring law.

[101]Section 5313(a), you might recall, is the original Bank Secrecy Act, which requires banks to report any transactions in cash or monetary instruments which exceed $10,000.

This incredibly vague statute potentially makes any attempt you make to protect your financial privacy from government financial inquisitors unlawful! Because of the law's wording, not even IRS agents are sure what structuring is, and what it is not.

But the penalties leave no room for uncertainty: Criminal violations may be punished by a five-year prison term and a fine up to $250,000. The civil penalty for a "willful" violation is a fine of $25,000, or forfeiture of the amount involved in the "crime," whichever is greater. The maximum civil penalty is $100,000. If you willfully violate this law while breaking any other law, you can be fined up to $500,000 and imprisoned for 10 years. And the courts have ruled that you can willfully violate the law even if you don't realize that the anti-structuring statute exists.

It is clear from the regulations issued to guide banks in interpreting Section 5324 that a person who deposits $9,000 in cash into an account on two consecutive days is structuring. But twelve consecutive $900 deposits may also be structuring as well. The regulations don't address this possibility, or any of an infinite number of other possibilities. No one knows for certain.

Given the heavy penalties that individuals who structure transactions face, along with the common-sense reluctance of any depositor to face IRS surveillance when a currency transaction form is filed, you would think the Treasury would have gone to great lengths to inform depositors that structuring is unlawful.

In fact, many pages in the *Federal Register* were devoted to this topic. For instance, the March 11, 1988 issue included the following suggestions to help notify people who deal in cash that they needed to be aware of the new law:

> 1. Require that a short notice of the provisions of Section 5324 be posted at every location where customers may conduct cash transactions; e.g., bank teller's windows, casino gaming tables and cages.
>
> 2. Require that a short Treasury form notice of the provisions of Section 5324 be handed to any person conducting currency transactions over a certain amount; e.g., $1,000 or $3,000. Currency transactions would include deposits to accounts and purchases of monetary instruments such as cashier's checks, official bank checks, money orders or traveler's checks.
>
> 3. Require that all deposit tickets be imprinted with a short Treasury form notice of the provisions of Section 5324 that a person making a currency deposit over a certain amount; i.e., $1,000 or $3,000, sign the back of the deposit slip as an acknowledgement of reading such notice.
>
> 4. Require that a short Treasury form notice of the provisions of Section 5324 be sent to all customers by a certain date and to all new customers upon the opening of an account.
>
> 5. Require that a short Treasury form notice of the provisions of Section 5324 be included periodically, e.g., quarterly, in all customers' monthly statements of accounts, and upon opening a new account.
>
> In the event that financial institutions receive inquiries from customers as the result of any of the above proposals, Treasury could make available a form to give to customers giving a more detailed explanation

of the provisions of Section 5324 and a toll-free number for the customer to call for further information.

Unfortunately for those individuals who might have wanted to comply with the law, *none of the preceding suggestions were implemented.* Structuring remains a federal crime punishable by a mandatory prison sentence, yet the government has taken no action to inform bank customers that any effort they make to avoid reporting to the government deposits or withdrawals of cash from their own bank accounts is illegal.

Federal courts have repeatedly upheld criminal structuring convictions for violations that concealed no criminal activity. These frivolous prosecutions make it vital for you to carefully examine any large cash transaction in which you are involved to determine if it might be reportable.

One of the first individuals prosecuted for the crime of structuring was Charles Scanio, who in 1988 was prosecuted for attempting to pay off a $13,000 loan in cash without filing a currency transaction report. The government made no claim that Scanio had any criminal intent, but eventually obtained a conviction. Scanio's attorney's argued that the structuring statute was unconstitutionally vague and that there was no statute of limitations or specific cash limit stated in it, but the court rejected these claims (*U.S. vs. Scanio*, 705 F.Supp 768).

Structuring prosecutions today may be based on even more tenuous circumstances. In *U.S. vs. Aversa* (762 F.Supp. 441), a federal judge delivered a scathing critique of the government's use of the criminal structuring statute. Aversa's "crime" was initiating a scheme to help keep information about his wife's infertility private. The scheme included a secret loan, which triggered reports of "suspicious transactions" in Aversa's bank account.

Aversa Judge Loughlin was particularly critical of the circus atmosphere surrounding the U.S. District Attorney's office when the indictments were announced, and wrote:

> Defendants should never have been prosecuted for structuring currency transactions...where evidence showed that defendants were not attempting to avoid paying tax on money or disguise where it came from...The evidence shows that [Aversa] did not believe that [he] was breaking any law...
>
> This is a case that was never contemplated by the drafters of the statute and that never should have been brought by the U.S. Attorney. There is only one explanation for the bringing of these charges--it was easy.[102]

This is not an extreme case. Structuring is a "pure liability" statute, with no underlying criminal intent required for conviction. If the IRS wins a conviction, the judge must sentence the "criminal" to a mandatory prison sentence. A Treasury Department analysis in 1991 concluded that over 75 percent of the property seized under the structuring law belonged to persons *not involved* in any illegal activity.

---

[102]In January 1993, the 1st U.S. Circuit Court of Appeals vacated the criminal structuring conviction in *Aversa* because he had not "willfully" violated the statute. The court ruled that a willful act is "one committed in violation of a known legal standard or in consequence of a defendant's reckless disregard of such a duty." Since Aversa (and another defendant) had no knowledge of the structuring statute, they could not be held criminally responsible for violating it.

But in another case, the 3rd Circuit ruled that despite a defendant's acquittal for criminal tax evasion, he was not entitled to a lesser prison sentence for his criminal structuring conviction (*U.S. vs. Shirk*, 92-7123). These apparently contradictory decisions make an appeal of the criminal structuring statute to the Supreme Court likely.

This fact makes it vital for you to carefully examine any large cash transactions to determine if they might be reportable.

In a 1989 decision, *U.S. vs. Kimball,* a judge decided that the word *evade* in the structuring statute could also be considered synonymous with the word *avoid.* Am I splitting legal hairs? Not at all. Tax *avoidance* and tax *evasion,* as I explained in Chapter 6, are vastly different. An extension of the court's logic would have us believe that these activities are one in the same. Such a conclusion clearly violates decades of judicial doctrine, but neither the Constitution or judicial doctrine are to stand in the way of enforcing the money laundering statutes.

The IRS Criminal Investigation Division recognizes that the structuring statute can be abused by prosecutors. In a 1991 article in the *Akron Tax Journal,* the CID's Peter J. Kacarab wrote the following:[103]

> A good example of the power, and the almost draconian effect, these forfeiture statutes have can be illustrated by the following hypothetical situation.
>
> Let's say Mary Doe is an elderly woman whose husband has died and left her with a substantial amount of cash at the bank. Mary Doe has heard about the requirements which require a Currency Transaction Report to be filed for cash transactions of amounts greater than $10,000 which involved financial institutions. Mary Doe is along in years, and she wants to give some cash gifts to her three grandchildren of $7,000 each. However, Mary, like many law-abiding citizens, is wary of having the bank fill out a form and send it to the government to report her banking activities. Mary decides to break up her $21,000 cash withdrawal into three transactions of $7,000 each. So Mary goes to the bank three days in a row, each day to a different branch, and withdrawals $7,000 each day. She then goes to the financial institution of each of her grandchildren and deposits the cash in an account in each of their names.
>
> The bank, seeing that Mary has "structured" such transactions, files a CTR for the transactions and notifies the local IRS Criminal Investigation Division office of the suspicious transaction.
>
> Based on this information, these monies deposited by Mary Doe into her grandchildren's account are technically subject to civil forfeiture. All the government must do to effect a forfeiture is to prepare a forfeiture affidavit and present it to the magistrate showing him a probable cause basis of a violation of Section 5324, which in this situation should be no problem, since we have a prima facie violation. Once the forfeiture warrant is signed, the government then descends on the three bank accounts of Mary Doe's grandchildren containing $7,000 each. The gifts [are] seized and Mary Doe faces a possible [criminal] indictment for violation of Section 5324. Note that this example encompasses forfeiture of Mary Doe's taxed income, and the money has no taint of illegal activity.

---

[103]"An In-Depth Analysis of the New Money Laundering Statutes," *Akron Tax Journal*, Spring, 1991

Kacarab goes on to recommend strict guidelines be developed to guard against abusive forfeitures and prosecutions for violations of the structuring laws. But as you have already learned, the laws have given the IRS and the Justice Department "open season" on technical violations that can lead to both forfeiture and criminal indictment.

Even transactions that look completely harmless on the surface may be attacked as structuring. In 1992, I learned of a particularly abusive structuring prosecution in Alaska. A woman's daughter had asked her to withdraw funds from the mother's bank account to help pay for the daughter's criminal defense in a money laundering case.

The IRS discovered that the mother and two friends had purchased cashier's checks made payable to her daughter's attorney with cash from the daughter. The attorney would not accept cash. However, the attorney didn't need the money and the mother cashed in the checks, returning the cash to her daughter. Here's what happened next, as I described in the July 1992 *Low Profile*:

> Several weeks later, investigators from the Drug Enforcement Administration arrived at the mother's home with a search warrant. Her husband (a retired policeman) answered the door and ushered in the armed agents. They stormed upstairs, meeting the mother as she emerged nude from the shower. She and her husband were separated and interrogated for three hours. The agents accused her of money laundering and told her that if she "didn't come clean," she would go to jail. They would not permit her to speak with her husband or contact an attorney. The agents later testified that they had a "cordial" conversation and had neither forcibly separated the couple nor prohibited them from using the phone.
>
> During a closed pre-trial hearing, the federal prosecutor objected to the judge appointing an attorney for the mother's defense. The prosecutor's reasoning: She had sufficient assets to pay for her own defense. (Later, the mother learned an asset listing she had submitted to determine her eligibility had been altered by multiplying each figure by 10!) A private attorney wanted $40,000 up-front, which she could not afford, so she was forced to defend herself. When the woman's daughter learned that her mother could not obtain an attorney, she pleaded guilty to two money laundering charges, each carrying a five-year prison sentence. The daughter is now in a federal prison. Charges against her mother were dropped.
>
> There are important lessons to learn from this incident. Don't conduct cash transactions that might appear suspicious to a third party, even with family members. You should also tape record (or even better, videotape) all interactions with police agencies. Finally, make certain to have notarized any materials you submit to a court, and keep a notarized copy in your possession.

If the IRS believes it has a weak case, it will drop the criminal charges if you allow your assets without going to trial or pay a stiff fine. This is very common in drug kingpin cases. The drug dealer goes free, and the police keep his assets.[104]

---

[104]For a critique of this practice, see Martin L. Haines, "Prosecutors and Criminals Sharing Wages of Crime," *The New Jersey Law Journal*, October 19, 1992

The definition of structuring was greatly expanded in the 1990 Omnibus Budget Reconciliation Act to include not just cash, but other "monetary instruments" as well. For details on this provision, see "The Bush Administration's War on Privacy," this chapter.

The structuring law is an absurdly vague, all-inclusive statute. How do you prevent yourself from being tripped up by it? The solution, many drug dealers have found, is to simply "file and forget" Currency Transaction Forms.

That was the conclusion of Texas Congressman J. J. Pickle's Ways and Means Oversight Committee, which in June 1992 held hearings on enforcement of the money laundering laws. Representatives from the Treasury Department's Office of Financial Enforcement (OFE) testified that delays of *four years* are not uncommon before it examines the more than 38 million Currency Transaction Reports (CTRs) that have been filed with it.

Former federal prosecutor Charles Intriago, publisher of *Money Laundering Alert*, described how one New York City money launderer filed nearly 1,700 CTRs over a four-year period. The filings went uninvestigated until a zip code analysis by the Customs Service revealed a large number originating from a single bank. He told the subcommittee that professional money launderers now realize that properly completed CTRs are generally ignored, and therefore routinely file them.

If professional money launderers who file hundreds or thousands of CTRs are ignored, then it's likely law-abiding Americans who merely file an occasional CTR will be ignored as well. For this reason, it's far better to file a CTR for occasional lawful cash transactions than to engage in a series of "structured" (and illegal) transactions that will be reported as "suspicious" by a bank. Tell the bank teller you would be thrilled to complete the form, and that you just want to help out in the War on Drugs. The IRS investigates suspected structured transactions much more diligently than the 8 million or so CTRs filed with OFE each year.[105]

The Anti-Drug Abuse Act of 1988

In the 1988 presidential campaign, both candidates Dukakis and Bush made dramatic promises as to how they would intensify the War on Drugs. Dukakis promised to hire 6,000 new IRS agents. Bush, focused on international cooperation to eliminate money laundering.

In Congress, pressure was building to pursue big-time money launderers who dealt in cash and didn't file tax returns or currency transaction reports. David Pryor, an Arkansas senator chairing the committee that oversees the IRS, cited a 1986 audit concluding that the agency should be doing a better job enforcing the currency transaction laws. The audit had found that in many cases, banks had filed the reports as filed, only to have the IRS ignore them.

In an election year, Congress was anxious to crack down on drug abuse and money laundering. The Anti-Drug Abuse Act of 1988, was the result.

Some of the act's provisions include:

✓ A requirement that federal agencies feed data into the Custom Service's TECS computer at least monthly

---

[105]According to the 1992 American Bankers Association/American Bar Association Money Laundering Enforcement Seminar *Workbook*, a banker was informed by a senior IRS official that in the past five years, only one criminal prosecution has been initiated from the entire Northwestern District as a result of Currency Transaction Report filings.

✓ A requirement that the Customs Service begin issuing machine-readable passports

✓ Authorization for the Treasury Secretary to negotiate with finance ministers of foreign countries to establish an "international currency control agency"

✓ Authorization for the Secretary to encourage foreign countries to adopt uniform cash reporting transaction forms and anti-money-laundering statutes. (The "progress" that has been made in this regard is described in "The International War Against Banking Secrecy and Money Laundering," Chapter 9.)

✓ Authorization for the Secretary to lower the cash transaction reporting requirements set forth in the Bank Secrecy Act at any time, and to "target" individual banks or banks in certain areas, forcing them to report *all* cash transactions, even as small as $1

✓ Expansion of the structuring law to make illegal any effort to avoid completing Form 8300 for any "designated reporting transactions."

✓ A requirement that all financial institutions maintain comprehensive logs of the cash sale of all monetary instruments larger than $3,000, including bank checks, cashier's checks, traveler's checks, and money orders

✓ Authorization for the Secretary to create a national intelligence network to track financial crimes. (This network, the "Financial Crimes Enforcement Network," or FinCEN, is now in place.)

✓ Authorization for the U.S. government to impose sanctions against the banks of nations that refuse to adopt uniform cash reporting and anti-money-laundering statutes. (Most nations are coming into line with the U.S. government; see "The International War Against Banking Secrecy and Money Laundering," Chapter 9.)

Perhaps the most frightening provision of the act is its requirement for machine-readable passports. What would happen if as you were preparing to leave the United States, your machine-readable passport indicated that you were suspected of a crime? Or that you owed the IRS money? Would the Customs Service permit you to leave, or would you be detained? Laws like this have no place in a nation that values its freedoms so greatly that it adopted a Bill of Rights to protect them.

Finally, the act calls for the federal government to encourage states to adopt uniform asset forfeiture and money laundering laws. To measure the "progress" states were making in this area, the General Accounting Office in October 1992 issued a report entitled, *Money Laundering: State Efforts to Fight it Are Increasing But More Federal Help is Needed*.

The report concluded that the biggest obstacle to enhanced state co-operation with federal law enforcement efforts are states laws that require that a person be found guilty of a crime before his assets are seized. It recommends that Congress encourage states to change their laws in return offering them increased access to federal financial data. This recommendation was adopted in the Annunzio-Wylie Anti-Money Laundering Act of 1992.

Most legal challenges to the Anti-Drug Abuse Act of 1988 have been rejected by the courts. For instance, in 1991, the Supreme Court ruled that a section of the act which permits random, warrantless searches of suspects at airports, bus stations, train stations, and border crossings is not unconstitutional. Similar challenges are in process for other provisions of the act. However, lower courts are generally upholding the laws and regulations as written.

Even more "interesting" were some of the provisions that were deleted at the last moment (but have been re-introduced in other forms):

✓ A proposal requiring the president to bar foreign banks from access to Federal Reserve check clearing and wire transfer systems if they fail to comply with the U.S. Treasury requests for information on U.S. depositors

✓ A proposal requiring all *foreign* banks wishing to do business in the United States to keep records of any U.S. currency transaction in excess of $10,000 at their non-U.S. branches--and to make such records available to the U.S. law enforcement agencies.

✓ A proposal to permit illegally-gathered evidence to be used against someone accused of *any suspected crime* (not just drug related) if the authorities gathering it have a "good faith belief" they did not violate the Fourth Amendment

✓ A proposal to permit the Secretary of State to revoke passports of those convicted of a "drug or money laundering offense"

✓ A proposal that financial institutions be required to maintain records of all international wire transfers and forward them to the IRS on request. (This provision became law in 1992 as part of the Annunzio-Wylie Anti-Money Laundering Act.)

✓ A proposal to permit the military to shoot down unidentified planes flying over U.S. borders suspected of carrying drugs

Even without these provisions, the Anti-Drug Abuse Act of 1988 immediately became a powerful weapon, not just against money launderers, but honest citizens seeking to protect their privacy. The Secretary of the Treasury, as authorized by the act, has already declared lower cash transaction limits than those mandated by the Bank Secrecy Act at certain banks in Florida, Texas and southern California. In these banks, customers depositing or withdrawing more than a nominal sum--as little as $100--are asked to "voluntarily" comply by completing a CTR.

In 1990, regulations issued under the act's authority went into effect that compel financial institutions to record any cash transactions that a broad reading of the Bank Secrecy Act would require. If the transaction is "suspicious," the institution must immediately inform the IRS Criminal Investigation Division and complete a Criminal Referral Report. In certain cases, even a CTR isn't enough; banks must ask their customers where the money came from! Regulations outlined in the *Federal Register* provide five hypothetical examples for banks to follow when asking customers for this additional information.

> 1. Linda Scott has had an account with the bank for 15 years and tries to deposit $15,000 in cash. The bank knows that she is an artist who exhibits and sells her art work, and her art is currently on exhibit at the local gallery. The bank also knows that her paintings are worth $15,000. The bank can accept the money as long as she fills out a CTR. There is no need to inquire further about the source of the funds.

> 2. Dick Wallace recently opened a personal account and wants to transfer $18,000 in currency to a foreign bank. His identity was verified when he opened it, but not since. The bank cannot accept the money without inquiring about the source of the money, recording it on a CTR, and reporting it to the IRS.

> 3. Dorothy Green, a partner at a law firm, wants to make a $50,000 cash deposit into the firm's trust account. The money came from three

clients. The bank must know the names of the clients, their Social Security numbers, and that information must be sent to the IRS.

4. Carlos Gomez enters a currency dealer's office and asks to buy $12,000 in traveler's checks with cash. The dealer must know the source of the money, and whether he is acting on the behalf of another party, and that information must be sent to the IRS.

5. Gail Julian, a trusted employee of a large retail chain, makes three large cash deposits during one day totalling $48,000. The bank knows that Julian normally makes the store's deposit, but the store's exemption limit is only $45,000. The bank must have strong "know your customer" policies, but doesn't have to ask and record further information than the normal CTR requirement.

How to Avoid Being Arrested for Money Laundering

In the last decade, the federal government has thrown a wide net in its effort to thwart money laundering. Getting caught in this net can be catastrophic. Since most of the laws aimed at money laundering rely upon financial institutions to serve as agents of the federal government, it behooves you to avoid activities that might lead them to suspect you of trying to illegally protect your financial privacy. One good place to start is by knowing how banks have been instructed to look for prospective money launderers.

The Treasury Department has distributed to all U.S. banks a booklet entitled *Money Laundering: A Banker's Guide to Avoiding Problems*. This booklet identifies numerous "behavioral patterns" that may indicate a customer is laundering money or structuring his transactions to avoid currency reporting. Activities considered suspicious include:

✓ Opening accounts in several different names, none larger than $10,000

✓ Paying down a delinquent loan all at once

✓ Objecting to completing federal CTRs

✓ Changing currency from small to large denominations

✓ Buying cashier's checks, money orders or traveler's checks for less than the reporting limit

✓ Opening an account and use it as collateral for a loan

✓ Coming to the bank with another customer, and each making a cash transaction under the $10,000 ceiling

✓ Making deposits in cash, then having the money wired somewhere else

✓ Ordering internal transfers between accounts, followed by large outlays

✓ Making an international wire transfer

✓ Making a wire transfer of any kind without a past record of such transactions

✓ Appearing to use an account as a temporary repository for funds transferred overseas

Other experts have added additional transactions that might be suspicious, and that banks should therefore be on the alert to detect. These include:

✓ Presenting a transaction that involves a large number of $50 and $100 bills

✓ Presenting a transaction without counting the cash first

Other suspicious transactions, according to the Treasury Department include small businesses depositing sums of money not commensurate with their normal activities, or two or more businesses depositing cash into commonly-owned multiple accounts. The suspicious pattern involves alternating deposits between two accounts.

And according to the *ABA Banking Journal,* the following situation is a suspicious transaction that should be immediately reported to the IRS:[106]

> You are the personal banker for a successful local businessman in your small town. Three months ago, he opened a checking account for his 12-year-old son. You have noticed that about one month ago, the businessman began depositing a significant amount of business receipts into his son's account. The account balance has grown from $150 to $36,000.
>
> You have just received a call from the businessman. He has asked you to wire transfer $35,000 from the account to a major New York bank to the account of Spring Trust. You have never hear of Spring Trust.
>
> Is this a suspicious transaction? Yes, definitely, according to Charles Morley, head of the consulting firm The Morley Group and a former IRS agent and Senate investigator. "We're not just talking drugs and drug cash," said Morley. "The businessman may be trying to evade taxes. Or he may wish to hide money from his spouse."

Some of these "behavioral patterns" could implicate anyone. For instance, I've long been an advocate of reducing personal debt. But paying off a loan now marks you as a money launderer! And if you want to build up your credit with a secured loan (where you must deposit collateral in an account first), that action now brands you as a criminal as well.

And what if you're going on a vacation and want to purchase a small quantity of traveler's checks? Or want to set up a trust for your children's college education? Or have transferred some money from one account to another to make a large purchase? Every one of these activities now marks you as a suspected criminal!

The only saving grace is that banks have been instructed to pay more attention to *patterns* of transactions than to a single transaction. Most of us don't buy traveler's checks frequently, but if you do, even for legitimate reasons (you travel widely, for instance), be prepared to answer to the IRS.

---

[106]*ABA Banking Journal,* January 1991 (345 Hudson St., New York, N.Y. 10014)

Some banks have reacted to the new regulations by restricting sales of products and services they view as high-risk. Many banks have stopped selling money orders larger than $3,000. Other banks require depositors to purchase negotiable monetary instruments only in conjunction with a checking account. You must first deposit cash into your account, then write a check to purchase the money order, thereby creating a paper trail. And a few, mostly smaller, banks have stopped wiring money overseas, or have centralized their wire operations.

Other banks now file CTRs for every large cash transaction, even if there is no requirement to do so. Their reasoning is similar to the judgment of banks who photocopy all checks, not just those larger than $100. The *ABA Banking Journal* recently recounted how the president of one bank undergoing a Bank Secrecy Act compliance examination was presented with 14 pages of cash transaction records for which the examiner claimed CTRs should have been submitted.

This discovery, warned the examiner, might warrant a full-scale money laundering enforcement action against the bank and its officers. The bank was able to prove the transactions represented nothing more than customers depositing loan proceeds into their own accounts, but only after spending many hours reconstructing each one of them. Well-publicized incidents such as this one insure that most banks will find it easier to file a CTR for every large cash transaction, rather than risk later investigation.[107]

How might you determine if your bank has been targeted for a Treasury Department money laundering crackdown? Targeted areas include southern border areas, particularly in Florida, California, and Texas. If you live in one of these areas, be alert to a surly attitude among employees. (The cost and time required for banks to comply with money laundering laws is huge, and bank employees do not enjoy spying on legitimate customers.) You might also be alert to sudden personnel changes. In a handful of banks, I'm told, the regular tellers have actually been replaced by IRS agents!

The IRS and Drug Enforcement Administration also target banks that take in a great deal more cash than they distribute. Targeted banks may be required to complete a CTR for customers depositing or withdrawing any amount of cash (not just $10,000 or more), which greatly adds to paperwork. Don't inform the customer, says the IRS: Just spy.

Gentle reader, *you* could be the next target. Remember the words of the American Bankers Association training film, "Dirty Money," another effort to train banks to thwart money laundering: "The only people concerned about Currency Transaction Reports are drug traffickers."[108]

Sting operations are a major part of the IRS crackdown against money laundering. Royal Lamarr Hardy, a tax protestor, was a recent target of such an unsuccessful sting operation--but his ordeal illustrates the lengths to which the IRS will go to "get" someone it sees as a threat. The IRS failed on numerous occasions to persuade a grand jury to indict Hardy for criminal tax evasion, so it set up a money laundering sting.

After rejecting repeated offers from an undercover IRS agent to participate in a money laundering conspiracy, Hardy was then approached by a second undercover agent from the DEA who had set up a phony check-cashing service. The undercover DEA agent asked Hardy if he knew anyone who had extra cash available to launder through his check-cashing business. Only then did Hardy mention that he knew

---

[107]"You Can Survive a Compliance Exam," *ABA Banking Journal*, October 1991

[108]A handful of financial institutions have challenged the targeting provisions of the Anti-Drug Abuse Act of 1988 in federal court. In a preliminary ruling in May 1991, District Judge John Rainey refused to issue an injunction barring implementation of the law, but ordered the Treasury Department to get court approval if they want to extend targeting provisions for more than 60 days. (The ruling applies only to the federal district encompassing Houston.)

of a pawnshop (the IRS operation) that had repeatedly asked him to exchange cash for traveler's checks. Hardy put the two informants together, and was then indicted for money laundering.

The government thus created the crime, supplied the means to commit it, laundered more than $300,000 in cash, and repeatedly tried to involve Hardy in the illegal activity. Realizing that Hardy would accuse the government of entrapment, federal prosecutors stated on the indictment that any tax protester, such as Hardy, was *already guilty of money laundering*. From this perspective, there was no need for a trial. Hardy (and for that matter, any tax protester) should have simply gone directly to jail for the maximum 20-year term!

Hardy's attorney repeatedly tried to get the case dismissed on entrapment grounds, but the judge denied each motion. However, testimony from the IRS and DEA informants destroyed the government's case. The informants admitted they had no evidence that Hardy was predisposed to launder money, and that they had created the entire operation to entice him into committing criminal acts.

This testimony led Hardy's attorney to remind the jury that a 1992 Supreme Court decision, *Jacobson vs. U.S.*, had invalidated an abusive government sting. In *Jacobson,* Justice White wrote that, "Government agents may not originate a criminal design, implant in an innocent person's mind the disposition to commit a criminal act, and then induce commission of the crime so that the government may prosecute."

The jury found Hardy innocent on all laundering charges.[109]

Given the tone of the regulations issued by the Treasury Department and the constant call for more restrictive laws, you might believe that a vigorous enforcement effort against the biggest money launderers would have been launched immediately. But most prosecutions involve a bank customer depositing or withdrawing slightly more than the reportable limit to or from his bank account, and clumsily trying to disguise the attempt. The biggest money launderers have scarcely been affected, as demonstrated in Congressional hearings in June 1992. (See "The 'Crime' of Structuring," this chapter.)

The best-known example is the case of Bank of Credit and Commerce International (BCCI). Reading the headlines about the BCCI scandal, you might believe that U.S. regulatory agencies were genuinely surprised by the news that the bank had engaged in massive fraud and money-laundering. But the truth is that U.S. regulators had known for years about BCCI's misdeeds.

In 1978, documents submitted to a federal court described a scheme by BCCI to illegally take control of a Washington, D.C. bank. Nothing was done to investigate the charges, perhaps because the documents alleged that a former CIA director was behind the successful takeover effort. Nor was BCCI required to sell the interest in the bank that it had illegally acquired.

In 1984, the IRS identified BCCI to the Federal Reserve as a money laundering center, and informed the Fed that the bank was not completing CTRs. Once again, the allegations were not followed up. When money laundering violations were brought to the attention of the Treasury and Justice Departments in 1987, both declined to investigate, although a small sting operation in Florida was allowed to proceed. In 1988, this operation resulted in the conviction of several bank officials for money laundering.

When a unit of the Justice Department pressed ahead with an investigation in 1989, senior officials quashed it. When Customs Commissioner William von Raab insisted on a full nationwide

---

[109]For more information on *Hardy vs. U.S.*, see the Sept.-Oct. 1992 *Freeman Letter*; Freeman Educational Assoc., 8141 E. 31st St., Tulsa, Okla. 74145

investigation of BCCI, Treasury Secretary Nicholas Brady fired him. It was only when the Bank of England announced its own investigation of BCCI in May 1991 that the cover-up finally unraveled.

Government officials are now using BCCI's illegal activities as a justification to call for even stricter anti-laundering regulations. Influential journalists are pushing hard for this agenda. Columnist William Safire, for example, called on the President to establish a global "Untouchables" unit--a network of law enforcement officers, global bankers, securities experts and customs enforcers--to enforce U.S. money laundering laws worldwide.

A Dartmouth University professor, Anant K. Sundaram, has proposed a global regulatory commission that would abolish banking secrecy and enforce draconian money laundering laws worldwide. Sundaram evidently does not care that many of BCCI's clients live under totalitarian governments which have made violations of foreign exchange laws punishable by fines, imprisonment, or in at least one country (Iran), death. Perhaps Professor Sundaram would prefer that the Iranian laws be applied worldwide.

Why did the government try to hide the truth about BCCI, known as far back as 1984 by the Central Intelligence Agency as the "Bank of Cocaine and Criminals?" We may never know the full story, but apparently the CIA and other intelligence agencies found the bank a convenient conduit to support covert military operations in Nicaragua, Afghanistan, and elsewhere. In other words, the bank was so useful (and so successful in cultivating contacts with the "right" people in Washington, D.C. and elsewhere) that it was allowed to operate above the law.

Even more secretive operations are carried out by the Federal Reserve, our nation's privately-owned central bank--operations that could be construed as money laundering, but cannot be verified as such because of the Fed's legislatively-mandated secrecy in carrying out its open-market operations. For instance, in November 1989, the central bank of Panama wire transferred $2.7 billion to the Federal Reserve Bank of Miami. Where did the money come from? Why wasn't anyone arrested--or at least *investigated*--for money laundering?

Also consider this exchange, which took place before a Senate subcommittee in 1988, with convicted money launderer Ramon Milan Rodriguez describing how he laundered billions of dollars annually on behalf of the Columbian drug cartel.

> Q. Who have you dealt with? Let's lay it on the table. Give me the name of an American bank that "courted" you.
>
> Rodriguez: Virtually all of them. I've dealt with Citicorp, Bank of America, First National Bank of Boston, and others, which are the real money center banks. They're the kind of banks that can take a $200 million CD easily. You just can't place that kind of money with some ma and pa bank in Des Moines, Iowa. Basically, I handled most of my U.S. banking business in New York, out of their headquarters.

No bank executive was ever indicted for dealing with Rodriguez.

The Bush Administration's War on Privacy

The more corrupt the state, the more numerous the laws.

--Tacitus

169

When George Bush was elected president in 1988, he claimed that his legacy would be a continuation of the initiatives that Ronald Reagan had started. His words were prophetic in terms of the rapid and continuing erosion of privacy rights that took place during his administration.

Declaring that he would show no mercy to drug pushers, money launderers, and the like, Bush appointed a Secretary of the Treasury, Nicholas Brady, who rapidly began implementing the powers granted the Treasury in the Anti-Drug Abuse Act of 1988. Brady restricted cash transactions even further, expanded financial reporting requirements, stepped up seizures of properties owned by suspected drug dealers and/or money launderers and pressured foreign governments into compliance with the administration's anti-laundering initiatives.

In addition, Brady created a national intelligence network for financial crimes, as authorized by the Anti-Drug Abuse Act of 1988: the Financial Crimes Enforcement Network (FinCEN). This network uses an advanced analysis method called artificial intelligence to investigate complex financial dealings among disparate individuals and institutions.

The Drug Enforcement Administration, the IRS and the Customs Service make their databases available to FinCEN. Your file can be accessed through a variety of means: name, Social Security number, by nine-digit zip code, and demographically. The whole program, brags the head of FinCEN, "is a lot like big brother."

Almost immediately, the IRS declared that FinCEN was paying big dividends. In early 1991, for instance, the agency claimed that more than 400 investigations were initiated on the basis of FinCEN's analysis of 17 million currency transaction reports filed between 1987 and 1989.

The truth is that the FinCEN program was far more successful at gathering information on ordinary Americans than it was in ferreting out crime. In fact, the head of the Drug Enforcement Administration's financial investigations division, David Wilson, admits as much. Analyzing millions of random banking transactions without some prior indication of wrongdoing, says Wilson, "rarely produces fresh leads."

What, then, is FinCEN's real purpose? Read what former Congressman Ron Paul had to say about FinCEN in the August 15, 1990 *Ron Paul Investment Letter*:[110]

> The feds admit that FinCEN is a trial run for a world system, and they also admit that they want all bank employees to function as virtual spies for the government. If they refuse to treat their customers like criminals, they will be punished.
>
> One of the rules that used to apply to government collection of financial data was that it could not be shared among agencies. For example, the IRS is supposedly banned from giving information to Customs. FinCEN is designed in part to circumvent that.
>
> FinCEN accumulates specific information about individuals and businesses, including bank records, census data, and driving records. To make sense of it, FinCEN relies on "artificial intelligence," a computer system that learns from its mistakes and successes. "We will search the

---

[110]The *Ron Paul Investment Letter* is now known as the *Ron Paul Survival Report* (18333 Egret Bay Blvd. #265, Houston, Tex. 77058)

database using any combinations you can think of, and any patterns that we can think of," says the acting director.

FinCEN has 200 employees from the IRS, the FBI, the Secret Service, and the FDIC, and works closely with the Bureau of Alcohol, Tobacco, and Firearms, the CIA, and the Defense Intelligence Agency.

FinCEN currently has access to over 35 financial databases, and they will acquire another 100, including computerized land records, real estate records, and credit reports. FinCEN doesn't have access to tax returns-- only currency transaction reports, 8300s [the retail equivalent of a currency transaction report], bank reports, etc.--but I predict it won't be long before they do, despite what the federal law says. The only output for FinCEN data is the IRS and its Criminal Investigative Division.

The IRS connection shows that the purpose of FinCEN is not to catch drug-related money laundering operations. That is only an incidental function of the wider goal of centralizing financial information on every honest American.

The models, data, financial patterns, and individual names generated by FinCEN will be shared with state and local governments. Before a recent amendment to the Right to Financial Privacy Act, this too used to be illegal.

The development of the FinCEN database is one of the most frightening aspects of the War on Drugs. The agency represents nothing less than a federal secret police, with the IRS at the helm. Its sole purpose is to spy on us.

To provide a veneer of law over the unconstitutional invasions of our privacy taking place through FinCEN and similar data-gathering efforts, Congress in 1988 adopted the Computer Matching and Privacy Protection Act. This misnamed act protects no one's privacy. It simply opens the doors for government agencies to conduct computerized matches under the flimsiest of pretenses. All that is necessary is for a "matching agreement" to be signed between the agencies that wish to exchange data. The 1992 anti-laundering bill, as you'll soon learn, opened the doors even wider.

The Treasury Department has big plans for FinCEN, according to its in-house newsletter, *FinCEN Trends*:[111]

In view of the tremendous effort involved in completing and filing criminal referral forms, the U.S. government is taking every step to maximize the utility and usage of the forms. A uniform criminal referral form has been prepared for use by the six regulatory agencies, and a project to create a database at FinCEN for information from those forms is underway. When the database is completed, it will serve as a central repository for all the Criminal Referral Forms filed by financial institutions, and database information will be shared by the six agencies. The database will use state of the art scanning technology, and its information

---

[111]*FinCEN Trends*, Financial Crimes Enforcement Network, U.S. Department of the Treasury, 3833 N. Fairfax Drive, Arlington, Va. 22203

retrieval system will provide query capability for the information contained on the forms, permitting investigations and prosecutions to be more effectively traced and analyzed.

The Annunzio-Wylie Anti-Money Laundering Act of 1992

Murderers can go to the electric chair, but until now, no one has found a way to execute a bank.

--Illinois Congressman Frank Annunzio

In 1989 and 1990, the Bush administration pushed hard for legislation that would crack down even harder on money launderers. Its resurrected many of the proposals rejected in the Anti-Drug Abuse Act of 1988. These included forcing foreign branches of U.S. banks to apply the U.S. law to their operations overseas, even if it conflicted with legislation in other nations.

The 1990 anti-laundering bill bogged down in the Senate, but one of its provisions was inserted into the Omnibus Budget Reconciliation Act of 1990. This provision instructed the IRS to issue regulations that would force merchants and banks to treat cash *equivalents* the same as cash for IRS reporting purposes. The act also requires that banks and merchants report any series of related cash transactions that total more than $10,000 over a 12-month period.

As Congress intended, the final regulations issued by the IRS in February 1992 define monetary instruments as cash, money orders, cashier's checks, and traveler's checks. Financial institutions must now maintain meticulous records of all related transactions paid for with such monetary instruments. So do merchants who sell merchandise considered by the IRS to be subject to its "designated reporting transactions" requirements.

Once the IRS issued final regulations, the agency began a vigorous enforcement program. As I described in "The Deficit Reduction Act of 1984," this chapter, undercover IRS agents are targeting car dealers, coin shops, and other businesses to try to entrap merchants into accepting cash without filling out the necessary forms. They are now expanding their efforts to entrap merchants who accept monetary instruments without maintaining the required records.

In the spring of 1991, as the scope of the BCCI scandal became apparent, sentiment mounted in Congress to severely punish banks that participated in or consented to money laundering. And on June 11, 1991, the House of Representatives approved the "Money Laundering Enforcement Amendments of 1991" by a unanimous, 406-0 vote.

Fifteen months later, in October 1992, President Bush signed a slightly modified version of this bill, the "Annunzio-Wylie Anti-Money Laundering Act."

Among other provisions, this bill:

✔ Authorizes the "appropriate federal banking agency" to remove the officers and/or directors of a financial institution accused of any money laundering offense, and prohibit them from ever working for any other financial institution, *even if they are acquitted of all wrongdoing.*

✔ Prohibits financial institutions from disclosing to a depositor the fact that their account is the subject of a money laundering investigation

✓ Requires financial institutions or others who sell or redeem monetary instruments (cash, cashier's checks, money orders, or traveler's checks) or transmit funds by wire, to maintain records of any international transactions, and make them available for warrantless inspection. The American Banker's Association estimated in 1991 that this provision would cost banks alone at least $160 million in additional compliance costs.

✓ Permits the Treasury Secretary to issue regulations that require financial institutions to report "suspicious transactions" that could involve a violation of any law or regulation, not just money laundering laws. The institution is not allowed to notify the suspect of the report. Nor may the suspect sue for damages, even if the resulting investigation uncovers no wrongdoing.

✓ Permits the government to seize monetary instruments or financial accounts even if it cannot specifically identify the property allegedly subject to forfeiture. Thankfully, this authority expires one year from the date of the alleged offense.

✓ Prohibits any action to structure or assist in structuring the transfer of monetary instruments across U.S. borders in any effort to avoid reporting the transfer. Any property involved in any structured transaction is subject to forfeiture.

✓ Applies the full weight of the anti-laundering laws to those who "conspire" to violate them, even if no violations take place.

✓ Permits any federal agency to share any data it holds with any other federal agency. This sharing is to occur "without waiving any privilege of confidentiality," which according to Congress makes it legal.

✓ Permits the Treasury Secretary to issue regulations requiring depository institutions to identify their customers, "in such manner as the Secretary shall prescribe." Depending on the wording of final regulations, this could force banks to obtain copies of currency transaction reports (CTRs) filed by trade and business customers.

✓ Gives the Justice Department national jurisdiction to file civil forfeitures. In a worst-case scenario, that means DOJ could file a forfeiture proceeding in Hawaii for property located in Maine. The Maine property owner would be responsible for assembling a defense in the Hawaii U.S. District Court. The bill also authorizes forfeitures across U.S. borders.

✓ Extends the definition of a "financial transaction" to include transferring title to vehicles, boats, and real estate. Lawyers and others who accept title to tangible property instead of payment in monetary instruments must now complete CTRs for one or more such "related" transactions if they exceed $10,000.

Dropped from the original Money Laundering Enforcement Amendments of 1991 were its provisions for the Treasury to study a two-tiered currency. According to the September 15, 1992 *Ron Paul Investment Newsletter*, the reason may have been pressure from the Mafia. Paul writes that New York Senator Alfonse D'Amato, who had pushed hard for the two-tiered currency, mysteriously backed off after complaints from "big-money" interests. Also dropped was a proposal that would require churches to report to the IRS the names of donors who give more than $500 annually.

Still, this bill strengthens the government's hand immensely in money laundering and forfeiture cases. The vague "international structuring" ban is particularly frightening. In theory, anyone transferring more than $10,000 in installments below that amount across a U.S. border without notifying the Customs Service could be illegally structuring their transactions. They would then be subject to criminal penalties and forfeiture. Even a person transferring funds over $10,000 that aren't otherwise reportable might be committing a crime! I'll talk more about these provisions in Chapter 9.

But even this isn't enough for some anti-laundering enthusiasts. In a 1991 interview in *Bank Management* magazine, Michael Zeldin, the acting director of the Justice Department's Money Laundering Office, and his wife, Amy G. Rudnick, former director of the Office of Financial Enforcement at the Treasury Department, made the following suggestions for improving anti-laundering laws:

✔ Outright prohibitions on wire transfers to bank secrecy havens unless such transfers can be shown to have a "legitimate business purpose"

✔ Lowering bank recordkeeping requirements for cash reporting transactions below the current $3,000 limit

✔ Requiring bankers to regularly review the account activity of their customers to insure that the customers are not involved in suspicious financial activity

✔ Requiring mandatory money laundering compliance programs initiated for financial institutions that are not banks. (In case you've forgotten, "non-bank financial institutions," according to the Bank Secrecy Act, include accountants, attorneys, car dealers, etc.)

✔ Increasing sting operations against merchants suspected of accepting cash for merchandise over the $10,000 reporting limit

Zeldin and Rudnick's parting shot to those of you who might have constitutional qualms about the growth of a financial police state is as follows:

> The more assets you can identify and seize, the more money you've got, either going into the general treasury or into asset forfeiture funds. That money can be used to help law enforcement in criminal prosecutions. I see this as a money-making enterprise for the government, and anything that's going to make money is not going to die too quickly.

Now, isn't that reassuring?

Chapter Eight

ASSET FORFEITURE, ASSET PROTECTION AND PRIVATE INVESTING

How is legal plunder to be identified? Quite simply. If the law takes from some persons what belongs to them, and gives it to other persons to whom it does not belong. See if the law benefits one citizen at the expense of another by doing what the citizen cannot do without committing a crime.

When a portion of wealth is transferred from the person who owns it--without his consent and without compensation, and whether by force or by fraud--to anyone who does not own it, then I say property is violated; that an act of plunder is committed.

When the law itself commits this act that it is supposed to suppress, I say that plunder is still committed, and I add that from the point of view of society and welfare, this aggression against rights is even worse. In this case of legal plunder, however, the person who receives the benefits is not responsible for the act of plundering. The responsibility for this legal plunder rests with the law, the legislator, and society itself. Therein lies the political danger.

--Frederick Bastiat, The Law

Asset Forfeiture and the Death of Property Rights[112]

In 1988, George Bush pushed asset forfeiture to the forefront of his administration's anti-drug strategy. Drug czar William Bennett announced the details: Henceforth, there would be "zero tolerance" for drug abuse. In this new war, the government may seize your property if it contains even the slightest trace of drugs, or if the government can demonstrate probable cause that it has been acquired or used illegally.

Bennett kept his promise, and so have his successors. In 1985, seizures by the federal government totalled less than $30 million annually. But in 1991, seizures of what the government calls "illegal assets" deposited into the Justice Department's asset forfeiture fund soared to $644 million--an increase of more than 2,000 percent in six years. In 1992, seizures by the Customs Department alone exceeded $1 billion.

Vehicles, boats, and even cash in which traces of illicit drugs are found, or in which illegal activity is alleged to have occurred, may be seized as well. Even a single marijuana seed is sufficient cause to seize your vehicle or your boat, and in some states, your home as well.

---

[112]This section relies heavily on a CATO Institute policy analysis entitled "American Forfeiture Law: Property Owners Meet the Prosecutor" (CATO Institute, 224 Second St., S.E., Washington, D.C. 20003). An excellent discussion of U.S. forfeiture laws since the time of British colonial rule, is "Seizures of Houses and Real Property Under Marijuana Forfeiture Laws," in the May 1987 *Search and Seizure Law Report* (Clark-Boardman Co., Ltd., 375 Hudson St., New York, N.Y. 10014)

Nor do the laws apply merely to drugs, either on the state or federal level. Federal laws permit forfeiture for any of more than 100 crimes, including money laundering offenses, drug offenses, environmental offenses, and any "predicate offense" under the racketeering statutes. The SEC now has the power to seize assets in advance of any trial. So do *administrators* in the Office of Thrift Supervision, who used this authority in April 1992 to freeze $275 million in assets from New York law firm. The law firm's "crime?" It objected to the virtually unrestricted use OTS's discovery authority against its client.

The Department of Justice, which says forfeiture laws have "unlimited potential," is seeking sweeping new forfeiture powers. As Cary Copeland, head of DOJ's asset forfeiture division testified before Congress in September 1992:

> On the legislative front, we have proposed that the scope of asset
> forfeiture be expanded to include white-collar crimes, particularly the 14
> most commonly used federal fraud statutes. We also support expansion
> of forfeiture to embrace proceeds derived from counterfeiting, explo-
> sives, and firearms offenses, and smuggling of illegal aliens.

The Justice Department also suggests that the time limit for returning "wrongfully seized" property be extended from six months to six years. The Crime Control Act of 1993 would authorize forfeiture for *political dissent*, if "violence" or "coercion" occurs during a political activity that would otherwise be permissible under the First Amendment.

The federal government has encouraged state, local and county governments to ratify their own forfeiture statutes, some of which are even more sweeping than federal laws. The Justice Department spends more than $60 million annually funding the "Bureau of Justice Assistance." BJA has published a 14-volume set of publications intended to train state, local, and county prosecutors how to seize property without due process.

Titles from this series include: *Disclosing Hidden Assets: Plea Bargains and the Use of the Polygraph* and *Tracing Money Flows Through Financial Institutions.* The effect of such massive federal assistance, combined with the information-sharing efforts I described in earlier chapters, is nothing less than the "federalization" of law enforcement agencies nationwide.[113],[114]

The states are learning quickly. A growing number of states require that property owners police their property against criminal activity, or it will be forfeited. California and New York are leaders in this area. New Jersey law now permits forfeiture for "any indictable offense" that occurs in connection with any property. Arizona permits forfeiture of any property owned by a criminal, whether associated with the crime or not. The Arizona Attorney General's office recently stated that the mission of that state's forfeiture law was "social engineering" to be accomplished through government intercession in commercial activity. Forfeiture, according to this office, represents "the leading edge of civil remedies for economic injustices." The National Association of State Attorneys General is seeking to have states adopt model asset forfeiture legislation based on the Arizona statute.

A massive increase in forfeitures on the state and local level demonstrate the "success" of these efforts. One New Jersey medical school graduate set up a counseling office in his parents' home in

---

[113]BJA is the successor to the 1970s-era Law Enforcement Assistance Administration, which as I described in Chapter 2, sought to disarm law-abiding Americans. (Bureau of Justice Assistance, 633 Indiana Ave. N.W., Washington, D.C. 20531).

[114]I do not mean to imply that ordinary, on-the-beat law enforcement officers are being trained to seize property, using any method at their disposal. The emphasis has been to train elite police units, or "forfeiture squads," at the state, local, or county level. They go by names such as the "Drug Interdiction Unit," and generally are equipped with weaponry and equipment far superior to that available to regular police officers.

Monmouth County. Before doing so, he was assured by the local Mental Health Director that this was legal. But a few weeks later, police arrested him for "practicing psychiatry without a license," and seized the contents of the home. Under New Jersey law, his challenge of the seizure will be heard by a single judge. No jury trial is permitted.

In another case, New Jersey officials seized an entire business because it submitted a defective bid for a state purchasing contract. Officials of Burlington County, New Jersey sought to seize the home of a gynecologist after he allegedly performed an illegal pelvic examination. (The forfeiture complaint was later dropped.)

Other forfeitures have occurred with police officials supplying their own "probable cause." In Maryland, a member of the Carroll County Narcotics Task force disguised as a UPS driver delivered a parcel containing a small quantity of marijuana to the owner of a 54-acre estate. The county is now seeking to seize the entire estate. One task force member commented during the bust that the property "would make a great police retreat."

In co-operation with the DEA, some cities have set up spy networks to maximize forfeiture revenues. In Nashville, the DEA visits with managers of local hotels and motels to encourages them to spy on their guests. They are asked to tip off the local drug interdiction unit when guests engage in "large" cash transactions, make more than the "ordinary" number of phone calls, or host "excessive" numbers of visitors. Managers who inform on their guests under these vague guidelines are eligible for rewards if their tips lead to forfeitures--and presumably avoid seizure of their facilities if illegal activities are uncovered.

With budget cutbacks, shrinking tax bases, and soaring crime, forfeited assets are a valuable supplement to law enforcement budgets. This is particularly true since the agency making the seizure keeps up to 80 percent of the proceeds (up to 100 percent if the seizure occurs under state or local jurisdiction). This provision makes forfeiture laws particularly popular, since it allows politicians to hold the line on tax increases, while increasing funding for law enforcement. Since law enforcement agencies keep the fruits of their seizures, with virtually no oversight, forfeiture laws provide an almost irresistible temptation to go after the richest and least well-defended targets.

Such funding provisions are more serious even than the "legal plunder" of socialism criticized by Bastiat. Since the seizing agencies keep all or most of the fruits of their forfeitures, the only possible result is the development of a most insidious bounty-hunter mentality in law enforcement efforts.

Informants under forfeiture laws are abundantly rewarded. Turn in your friends, neighbors, business competitors, and/or family members, and you're eligible for a commission as high as 25 percent for any property police seize as a result of your tip. At airports, railroad stations, bus stations, and hotels, ticket agents, security personnel, and desk clerks supplement their income by tipping off drug interdiction units to anyone acting suspiciously or carrying large quantities of cash.[115]

In 1991, 65 informants made over $100,000 in forfeitures from just one agency--the DEA, according to data provided by the House Operations Committee. According to the committee report, informants may smuggle drugs on the side while acting as DEA informants.[116]

---

[115]Even children are eligible for rewards for informing on their parents, as in Nazi Germany and the Soviet Union, although I am not aware of any examples. However, in the federally-funded "Drug Abuse Resistance Education," or D.A.R.E. program, children are encouraged to let law enforcement officials know about illegal activity that might be taking place at home. In theory, if the tip leads to a forfeiture, the children would be eligible for a commission.

[116]The IRS' 1992 instructions for Form 1040 provide an exemption for reporting informant commissions via Form 1099. Essentially, the IRS is telling informants that their commissions are tax-free.

The huge increase in property forfeitures has been made possible by the government using the most sweeping legal theories possible. The most popular rationale is to confiscate property that somehow "facilitates" criminal conduct, as I explained in "The Money Laundering Control Act of 1986," Chapter 7.

The oldest and most frequently used form of forfeiture is civil forfeiture. These statutes apply indiscriminately to property, regardless of the guilt or innocence of the owner. Under civil forfeiture statutes, which are modeled under admiralty law, property is assigned a "personality" and held accountable for its violation of law. Thus, the government may seize your property if "probable cause" suggests that it has been "tainted" by illegal activity.

For instance, if your child uses the family home for an illegal purpose, the home may be forfeited, even if you knew nothing of the unlawful act. You can contest the seizure under the "innocent owner" exemption in federal and some state forfeitures, but as you'll soon learn, the standard applied to qualify is very strict.

In some cases, the courts have ruled, the government need not even show probable cause to seize your property; circumstantial evidence is sufficient. This was the reasoning for the 8th U.S. Circuit Court of Appeals in *U.S. vs. U.S. Currency in the Amount of $150,660*. Drug residues on the cash, its odor, and the fact that it was wrapped in rubber bands made it possible for the government to seize it without further justification.

Your property may even be seized in a drug-related forfeiture even if no drugs are found. One federal prosecutor who seized a Connecticut home in a drug forfeiture was asked by a reporter for CBS' *Street Stories:* "Is it true that not a seed of marijuana was ever found in the [forfeiture victim's] house?" The prosecutor's answer: "How could it be found? The house was never searched."

Forfeiture laws provide the government with unique advantages that it does not enjoy in any other area of law. The government authorizes a seizure in an "ex parte" (secret) hearing before a judge, magistrate, or even a mere administrator. You are not informed of this hearing, and thus may not attend it, much less contest the seizure.

At this hearing, prosecutors may introduce hearsay and other evidence inadmissible in criminal court to establish probable cause. Once the government does so, the seizure may proceed. There is no need for a grand jury proceeding to indict your property; forfeitures are ordinarily authorized by a single judge. The government need not post a bond covering possible damage to your property.

The burden then shifts to you to prove by a "preponderance of the evidence" that the property was seized in error. This power of immediate possession provides the government with immediate bargaining advantages. Possession, after all, is nine-tenths of the law. If you cannot, forfeiture occurs, and your property now belongs to the government.

Other constitutional protections also tumble, including the presumption of innocence, the right not to be punished prior to being found guilty, the right to be represented by counsel, the right to confront your accuser (if an informant was involved) and the right not to suffer disproportionate punishment.

Conversely, the government's rights are dramatically expanded if a forfeiture is litigated. It enjoys virtually unlimited discovery privileges (see "Privacy and Your Legal Records," Chapter 4). In addition, Justice Department policy states that the "probable cause" necessary for a seizure to occur provides "reasonable cause" for each side to pay their own legal costs, even if the forfeiture is subsequently reversed. This implies that even for the most unjust forfeitures, the defendant cannot recover legal costs from the government. Finally, the government is ordinarily immune from paying for any damage it causes to the property while in its possession.[117]

Generally, you cannot challenge a seizure until the government files a civil forfeiture complaint. Yet there is no requirement that the government do so in a timely fashion. In fact, the government may delay filing a forfeiture complaint 18 months or more after it seizes property. The courts have ruled repeatedly that such delays are not a violation of the due process clause of the Constitution. For instance, in *U.S. vs. Ivers,* a federal judge wrote in 1978 that:

> Ordinarily, Constitution demands that a person not be deprived of his property without previously having been afforded notice of proposed action and opportunity to be heard, but extraordinary situations may justify departure from such mandates and permit postponement of notice and opportunity for hearing, *and seizure of property for forfeiture to government is such a situation* [emphasis added].

Even if a court orders that your forfeited property be returned to you, it may not be. For instance, in 1991, a Florida court ordered that a county sheriff return $358,000 in cash seized from a Louisiana motorist. The order was ignored, according to the sheriff, because the money had already been spent! "Things happen," said Sheriff's Commander Jack Pate, explaining that the money went toward the construction of a new courthouse. The irony of a courthouse built with the fruits of an seizure a court invalidated was apparently lost on Commander Pate.

Civil forfeiture laws date back to common law, and thus to the Bible. Exodus 21:28 states that: "If an ox gore a man or woman and they die, then the ox shall be stoned and his flesh not eaten; but the owner of the ox shall be quit (free of further obligation)." The ox violated the law, but the owner's culpability is questionable. Therefore, the owner's property is taken from him.

It is not difficult to establish the ox's "guilt" in this biblical example. Yet civil forfeiture laws stretch this logic beyond its limit by establishing a legal fiction that not just animals, but totally inanimate objects are somehow imbued with personality and can thus be held accountable. As a result of this legal fiction, the courts have historically disregarded the owner's guilt or innocence.

Again, forfeiture is deemed an action against a piece of property, not its owner. This makes it difficult if not impossible to raise due process arguments against the government, such as that the owner has not been charged with a crime, that he is presumed innocent of any wrongdoing, or that the government has taken his property without affording them notice of a hearing.

The Constitution (Article 3, Section 3) implies that the government may not seize property unless that owner is convicted of treason. Even then, the forfeited lands are to be returned to the heirs upon the owner's death. In addition, the Fifth Amendment states that no person shall have his property "taken for public use without just compensation."

However, the same Congress that enacted the Bill of Rights in 1789 authorized civil forfeiture for failure to pay duties on imported goods. The only justification needed was a finding of probable cause that the duties had not been paid. Forfeiture could occur without trial, indictment, or arrest of the owner.

---

[117]In October 1992, a U.S. District Judge in San Francisco ruled that homeless people whose belongings were destroyed by police can sue the state for damages to their property. Asset forfeiture laws, however, deny the same rights to anyone other than the homeless.

The "taint" doctrine of civil forfeiture also has a long history. In 1921, the Supreme Court upheld it in refusing to overturn the forfeiture of a vehicle used to transport alcoholic beverages in violation of prohibition laws *(Goldsmith-Grant vs. U.S.*, 254 U.S. 505). In this case, a car dealer forfeited his secured interest in the vehicle, even though he had sold it to a bona-fide purchaser for value. The court, while sympathetic to the dealer's plight, relied on common-law precedents for its decision, including Justice Story's opinion in the 1827 *Palmyra* case, which upheld seizures against innocent owners because, "The thing is primarily considered the offender" (25 U.S. (12 Wheat) 1).

As recently as 1974, in *Calero-Toledo vs. Pearson Yacht Leasing Company*, the Supreme Court reaffirmed the right of the government to seize property from an innocent owner (416 U.S. 663).

Another significant legal fiction in forfeiture cases is the "relation-back" doctrine. Under this doctrine, the title to illegally used property transfers to the government the moment the offense is allegedly committed, not when the forfeiture judgment is entered, which could be months or years later. Thus, if a tenant was to use his landlord's house illegally in 1988, the title to the house transfers to the government at that time, even if the forfeiture complaint wasn't filed until 1992.

Again, this doctrine dates back to the common law. In 1814, Supreme Court Justice Story, writing a dissenting opinion in *U.S. vs. 1960 Bags of Coffee*, criticized this doctrine as "monstrous," writing that, "No man, whatever may be his caution or diligence, can guard himself from injury and perhaps ruin" (12 U.S. 398, 415). This may be true, but the relation-back doctrine is enmeshed in both federal and state forfeiture statutes.

A corollary to the relation-back doctrine is the theory of "conversion." Returning to our example of a tenant using his landlord's house illegally, the landlord will be held personally liable, under the conversion theory, for profits derived from the house beginning the moment the state took title to it in 1988. If the owner can't pay up, the state may seize any other assets he owns to make up the difference. New Jersey authorities recently published an article encouraging prosecutors to use this theory to maximize forfeiture revenues in a newsletter circulated to state Attorneys General nationwide.[118]

For more than 180 years, the government used its forfeiture power sparingly. But in 1970, Congress adopted the Racketeering and Corrupt Organizations (RICO) statute (codified as amended as 18 U.S.C. Sections 1961-68). This law for the first time sanctioned forfeiture as a punishment after a criminal conviction. Unlike civil forfeiture, criminal forfeiture was justified as a punishment for the guilty, and imposed through a criminal proceeding. It also permitted pre-trial restraint of potentially forfeitable property through asset freezes and seizures.

Fourteen years later, in 1984, Congress enacted the Comprehensive Crime Control Act, which authorized both criminal and civil forfeitures for a variety of drug offenses. In 1986, with the passage of the Money Laundering Control Act, Congress extended both types of forfeiture to violations of the Bank Secrecy Act and other violations of the cash reporting laws, along with a number of other federal offenses. (See "The Money Laundering Control Act of 1986," Chapter 7.) In 1990, Congress extended forfeiture remedies to environmental crimes. The 1984 law alone has led to nearly 200,000 seizures.

Recognizing the potential for abuse in civil forfeiture law, Congress and a number of states have enacted forfeiture exemptions for "innocent owners." The intent is to protect innocent owners from loss of their property under the forfeiture statutes.

---

[118]For details of this policy, see "Supplementing the In Rem Arsenal: Using Common-Law Conversion to Reach Unavailable But Once Forfeitable Assets," (*Civil Remedies in Drug Enforcement Report*, National Association of Attorneys General, 444 N. Capitol St., Washington, D.C. 20001, April/May 1992).

However, "proof of innocence" is not easy to establish. It means a great deal more than mere proof that you are not a criminal. For instance, Department of Justice guidelines require that to establish an innocent owner defense, a defendant must demonstrate that he had no knowledge of the illegal use of his property (and was not "willfully blind" to it), did not consent to the illicit activity, and took all reasonable steps available to prevent it. The Justice Department argues that it should prevail if it can demonstrate probable cause that one or more of these factors were present.

Moreover, until 1993, the Justice Department argued consistently (and for the most part successfully) that the innocent owner defense cannot overrule the relation-back doctrine. For instance, a July 1992 internal Justice Department memorandum sent to the head of every government agency and all Assistant U.S. Attorneys stated that, "The innocent owner defense is not available, as a matter of law, to one who has acquired an interest in the forfeited property after the illegal acts which resulted in the forfeiture."

In other words, an innocent owner is not entitled to having his property returned if the forfeiture is due to an unlawful act by someone else before he acquired the property, or a lienholder interest in it. The "taint" caused by the illegal activity is not erased when the property is sold or transferred, even to a bona-fide purchaser for value. *The alleged illegal act eliminates forever any subsequent rights to the property by any party other than the government.* Not surprisingly, most title insurance polices now exclude from coverage any pre-existing "taint" that could lead to forfeiture.

However, in February 1993, the Supreme Court overruled the Justice Department's position in *U.S. vs. A Parcel of Land, Buildings and Appurtenances, and Improvements Known as 92 Buena Vista Avenue* (91-781; the *"Buena Vista" case*). This is an extremely important decision, because it permits subsequent owners and lienholders to assert the innocent owner defense. It explicitly rejects the reasoning upheld in forfeiture cases dating back to the 1827 *Palmyra* decision. In spite of this striking affirmation of the rights of innocent lienholders and bona-fide purchasers for value, prevailing in an innocent owner defense is hardly automatic, as I've already mentioned.

Because of the obvious difficulties in establishing this defense, the principal way for property owners to have their forfeited property returned is through an administrative hearing. The owner applies for a mitigation or remission of forfeiture. However, such pleas are granted only at the unreviewable discretion of the Attorney General or other seizing agency.

Moreover, taking this route precludes any right to challenge the forfeiture in court. In practice, the Justice Department has required granted administrative forfeiture relief only to petitioners who meet all the criteria that would be required to prevail in an innocent owner defense.

The following letter published in the December 1992 *Low Profile* illustrates the mitigation of forfeiture procedure in a money laundering case:

> In 1991, I refinanced my home in New Jersey to raise money to help provide for a son's education and to pay some overdue bills. I received a $38,000 cashier's check which I deposited into my checking account.
>
> I withdrew $15,000 in cash from this account and purchased with these funds several money orders from post offices in my area. I deposited the funds in a custodial account set up in Maryland to pay for my son's education.
>
> Three weeks later, the Postal Inspection Service (PIS) seized this account on probable cause that a violation of USC 31 Sections 5313(a) and 5324

had occurred. These regulations require customers to report same day money order transactions between $3,000 and $10,000, and prohibit structuring transactions to avoid any reporting requirements, respectively.

I was unaware of such requirements, nor did any of the post offices where I purchased the money orders have signs advising customers of them. No Postal Service employee notified me of the regulations.

In February 1992, my attorney filed a Petition for Remission or Mitigation of Forfeiture with the Postal Service. To receive remission, the petitioner must establish that he: (1) Has valid interest in the property; (2) Had no knowledge that the property was or would be involved in any violation of law; and (3) Had no knowledge of the violation which subjected the property to forfeiture. I established all three elements for remission of forfeiture. However, in April 1992, the PIS denied the petition, stating that I failed to provide sufficient evidence to support my claim.

Under this law, you are guilty until proven innocent. The appeal is decided by the same agency that seized your money. This is unjust, unfair, and unreasonable--they still have my son's money.

--Name withheld by request

My response was as follows:

This letter underscores the fact that ignorance of the money laundering statutes is no excuse for their violation. Personnel at banks, post offices, etc. are instructed not to let customers know that they might be violating the law. Indeed, a person making such notification is now considered to be a co-conspirator in any crime the customer might be engaged in!

Instead, personnel are instructed to report to a compliance officer that a "suspicious transaction" has occurred. Certainly, the transactions described in this letter (repeated purchases of "monetary instruments" in denominations under $3,000 at several different locations) fit the suspicious transaction profile.

This case also highlights the "Mitigation of Forfeiture" procedure. This system is set up to provide an administrative remedy for forfeiture victims short of going to court. Unfortunately, in choosing this route a forfeiture victim gives up his right to a trial and has no further legal recourse to recover the money.

An experienced forfeiture attorney could perhaps have recovered a portion of this victim's money. On the other hand, under the "taint" theory of forfeiture, the PIS could have seized the remaining $25,000 in the victim's New Jersey account, and perhaps the house itself. He could even have been charged criminally, since structuring is a "pure liability" statute.

Are forfeiture laws really worth the abolition of our common-law rights as Americans? Isn't the anti-drug campaign being used as an excuse to annul these rights? Isn't the federal government likely to use such legal precedents to expand its anti-privacy campaign into other areas of life? The side-effects of zero-tolerance laws are a lot higher than simply salaries and equipment costs.

Forfeiture Victims: The New Outcasts

Criminal forfeitures under the racketeering statutes are even more sweeping than civil ones. Civil forfeiture requires that property at least "facilitate" criminal conduct. But under RICO, a convicted defendant must forfeit any property interest, however legitimately acquired, if that interest affords the defendant a "source of influence" over the alleged racketeering "enterprise."[119]

In *U.S. vs. Porcelli*, for instance, a RICO defendant convicted of failing to pay New York sales taxes from his gas station franchise was ordered to forfeit not only an amount equal to the delinquent tax obligation, but also 29 separate corporations through which he owned and operated the chain of gas stations (865 F.2d 1352, 2d Cir. 1989).

Pretrial restraining orders in criminal forfeiture cases can deny a defendant the use of his assets to pay living expenses or even the costs of hiring defense counsel. In 1989, the Supreme Court ruled in *Caplan & Drysdale, Chartered vs. U.S.* that RICO authorizes pre-trial freezing of assets even where a defendant seeks to use those assets to pay his attorney (491 U.S. 617). Today, the Justice Department interprets this decision so literally that it claims that even funds contributed by friends, family, or business associates to a RICO defendant are forfeitable.[120]

The relation-back doctrine compounds the defendant's problems by sending a clarion call to friends, neighbors, family members, and business associates that they deal with him at their peril. The defendant may not be able to perform his contractual obligations. Any property transferred from him may be tainted and thus subject to forfeiture. Family members may have assets acquired from the defendant prior to the indictment frozen, dating back to the time they were allegedly "tainted." Even charitable contributions aren't exempt; a federal judge in February 1993, permitted prosecutors to seize a loan made by a Maine accountant suspected of bank fraud to a New Hampshire college.

Forfeiture, combined with the negative publicity accompanying a RICO prosecution, can quickly destroy a once-thriving business. In February 1992, police broke into the apartment of Harry Davis of Washington, D.C. as part of a crackdown on the "P Street Crew," an alleged cocaine distribution ring. Police charged that Davis used his car-leasing business to launder $100 million in drug money. Inside his apartment, they found $8,000 in deposits from customers who had leased cars from him. There were no drugs, no guns or any evidence of the dirty millions that he was supposed to have washed.

Nevertheless, then-Attorney General William Barr held a spectacular news conference and announced that 450 law enforcement officials had smashed the notorious P Street Crew. Davis was implicated as the mastermind and portrayed on television every night for nearly a week as a cocaine kingpin.

One year later, a U.S. District Court dismissed the case against him--although prosecutors reserved the right to re-file charges. This lingering taint, along with the adverse publicity that had

---

[119]An excellent guide to RICO is Rakoff & Goldstein's *RICO Civil and Criminal Law and Strategy* (New York: New York Law Publishing Co., 1992)

[120]The majority opinion in *Caplan & Drysdale* also states that the government has a legitimate financial interest in maximizing forfeiture solely for the purpose of raising revenue. At the very least, this is not a traditional goal of the criminal justice system. At worst, it implies that there are few, if any, limits on government bounty-hunting. The Pittsburgh U.S. Attorney's office, for instance, boasted in a recent press release that the assets it had seized through forfeiture more than paid for the operations of the entire office.

already occurred, destroyed Davis' business, which he had painstakingly built up over several years. No one in their right mind, he told the court, would ever conduct business with a suspected drug kingpin. And of course, Davis has no recourse against the government's actions unless he can prove they were malicious or totally unfounded.

"What about my reputation? I have done nothing wrong," Davis said to the judge. "You break into my home, destroy my business and after investigating me for a year, just drop the charges. What can you say to me?" "You're free," the judge told him. "Next case."

Forfeiture creates a class of financial untouchables. Not only are their assets seized or frozen, their employers and business associates are afraid to have anything to do with them. Not surprisingly, many forfeiture victims end up on public assistance, or homeless.

Forfeiture Laws: Targeting the Innocent

The most comprehensive analysis compiled of forfeitures that I've seen was completed in 1991 by *The Pittsburgh Press*. Reporters reviewed records from 25,000 seizures by the Drug Enforcement Administration. In *80 percent* of these seizures, the victims were never *charged with any crime*.[121]

Does this mean that 80 percent of forfeitures occur in error? Again, since property is "strictly liable" for crimes that occur on it, guilt or innocence is of no consequence, at least in a civil forfeiture.

However, some major forfeiture campaigns have clearly targeted innocent owners. For instance, in a 1989 report to Congress, the Customs Service admitted that 42 percent of its seizures were made in error. Yet if the search is "reasonable," it cannot be held liable for any damages, even if it destroys the property!

In 1990, the IRS seized 700 bank accounts containing nearly $350 million. In conducting "Operation Polar Cap," the agency claimed that contents of these accounts were derived from drug trafficking or other illegal activity. But within a few months, it released all but 100 accounts, conceding that they belonged to legitimate businesses or investors. Most of the accounts belonged to Latin Americans who kept money in U.S. banks to escape hyperinflation and government corruption in Brazil, Argentina and elsewhere.

A 1990 decision in U.S. District Court denied a motion to release 88 Florida accounts containing $11 million seized as part of Operation Polar Cap. The judge ruled that the account owners had to prove that their funds were not derived from drug trafficking or other unlawful activities to have them released. Some of the accounts are still frozen, since their mainly foreign owners are unable to afford a trip to the United States to get their funds released, or are unfamiliar with the U.S. justice system.

The devastating impact of forfeiture affects victims far removed from any wrongdoing. *Presumed Guilty* describes several women whose husbands were imprisoned for drug crimes who lost their home to forfeiture. In a number of cases, mother and children are now facing life on the streets.

In Texas, a drug trafficker purchased a mall and leased individual stores to legitimate businesses. Then the DEA seized the mall. Tainted by allegations that the legitimate businesses might be fronts for illegal activity, several stores lost most of their customers and declared bankruptcy.

---

[121]"Presumed Guilty: The Law's Victims in the War on Drugs" (*The Pittsburgh Press*, August 11-16, 1991)

It is not just *individuals* who are at risk from government property seizures. Any third party connected in even the most remote manner may be affected. Banks are particularly susceptible to having deposits or collateral owned by accused racketeers, drug traffickers, or money launderers forfeited to the government.

✓ In 1988, a Miami bank loaned $1.1 million to a Panamanian company to purchase a luxury home in south Florida. The home was seized by the government, which refused to pay off the mortgage. The reason: The bank "should have known" that drug money was being used to purchase it.

In December 1992, the Supreme Court unanimously reinstated the efforts of the bank to collect on its mortgage. The Justice Department argued that since it had already transferred the funds from Florida to Washington, D.C., federal courts had no jurisdiction over the matter. *It claimed that only an act of Congress could reverse the forfeiture.* Thankfully, the Supreme Court rejected this claim (*Republic National Bank of Miami vs. U.S.*, 91-767).

✓ In 1990, a depositor opened a $50,000 account at a Virginia bank. Several months later, the depositor was found guilty of drug trafficking. The bank was ordered to forfeit the deposit, even though, according to a bank spokesman, "There were no telltale signs of anything illegal."

However, if the Virginia bank had taken steps to separate itself from its depositor, it could have been sued. That's what occurred in 1982 to the banking subsidiary of Key Bancshares of Maine, Inc. The bank cut off a credit line to two customers after agents from the FBI erroneously informed the bank that one of the two had links to organized crime. Outraged at what was later proven to be a false accusation, the men sued the bank, and in 1987 were awarded $15 million in damages.

Other third parties are held responsible for the misdeeds of their customers as well. In 1989, hundreds of garden shops were raided by the DEA on the suspicion that they might be selling "grow lights" to indoor marijuana cultivators. In "Operation Green Merchant," the DEA seized millions of dollars worth of equipment. It was up to garden shops to prove that the lights they had sold were not used for illicit purposes. Much of the equipment seized was never returned, and compensation for the seizures is only now being negotiated.

In 1991, the DEA was back, and tried to subpoena customer records from roughly 60 garden shops. But in a rare example of judicial restraint, the judge approached by the DEA to grant the subpoena to obtain the customer lists refused to issue it. In 1992, the U.S. Attorney in San Francisco once again demanded that three garden shops provide customer lists, sales receipts, and shipping records.

A roughly equivalent activity might involve the Justice Department trying to obtain the names of subscribers to *Playboy* magazine, because a few subscribers might possess child pornography. Would this be considered an invasion of privacy by the courts?

Increasingly, businesses are seized based on information supplied by competitors. From the competitor's standpoint, this has three major benefits. First, it puts you (his competition) out of business. Secondly, it makes him eligible for a generous portion of whatever assets the government can seize from your business. Third, it may allow him to purchase the assets of your business for pennies on the dollar at government auction. (Your competitor might even offer to "help you out of a jam" you by purchasing your business from you, at a substantial discount to its actual value.)

The pattern is frighteningly similar to that which developed in Nazi Germany after Hitler suspended the seven sections of the German Constitution which guaranteed civil liberties. Realizing that he could not attack rich Germans directly, Hitler devised a brilliant plan to seize their assets. Approaching rich competitors, a Hitler lieutenant would tell one that he could use the S.S. (the Nazi secret police) to arrest and seize the assets of the other. All that was needed was some allegation of illegal activity. Naturally, the remaining competitor would benefit financially by the elimination of the other.

Most businesses to which the Nazis presented this option were eager to oblige. Surely they knew of some illegal statement or activity by their rival, or were willing to make one up. Perhaps the competitor was Jewish, or a Jewish "sympathizer." In many cases, businesses would implicate each other. The S.S. forfeiture squads would confiscate the business, then tell the forfeiture victim that the only way he could recover his property was to inform on his competitor. The S.S. would then use this evidence to seize the other business, or at least extort protection money from its owner.

Such forfeitures are becoming increasingly common in the United States. The owner of a New Mexico chemical business lost his company due to a false tip from a competitor. It turned out the competitor was operating under the control of the DEA. A thorough search of the company premises turned up nothing illegal. Neither did warrantless (and therefore illegal) searches of UPS deliveries to the company.

The DEA kept the business anyway, along with the owner's personal belongings, including two vehicles. The owner was never charged with any crime. When he told the DEA he would appeal, he was told that it would "bankrupt" him to fight the government. He decided not to fight. In February 1993, he signed his chemical business over to the DEA.

Attack of the Cash Police

Of all the assets subject to forfeiture, cash is the most-frequently seized. In many cases, forfeiture squads seize cash without due process, once again from individuals far removed from any wrongdoing.

The best-known case is that of Willie Jones. Jones, whose story was featured on *60 Minutes*, paid for an airline ticket in cash at the Nashville airport. The ticket agent informed the airport drug interdiction unit of the cash purchase. While Jones was waiting in line to board his flight, two representatives from this unit asked him to step aside. Jones did so and consented to a search. The officers discovered $9,600 Jones was carrying and asked him why he was carrying such a large quantity of cash.

Jones told the officers that he was on his way to Houston to purchase plants for his nursery business. Most of the smaller suppliers Jones dealt with, he added, preferred cash--although he also carried his checkbook. But the officers confiscated the money as "the probable proceeds of drug transactions," even though Jones had earned every dollar legitimately, and could prove it. It made no difference. In the War on Drugs, anyone carrying large quantities of cash, for any reason, is presumed guilty. Jones was unable to meet the cash bond requirement to contest the forfeiture--and thus could not contest it judicially.

Some local police districts specialize in cash seizures. In June 1992, *The Orlando Sentinel* ran a series of articles describing how sheriff's deputies in Valusia County, Florida seized more than $8 million in cash from motorists on I-95 in the last two years. Typically, the deputies stop vehicles that meet a secret "drug courier" profile. If the driver refuses permission to search the car, the sheriff brings out a drug sniffing dog to inspect it. Based on the 1983 Supreme Court decision in *U.S. vs. Place*, police claim that the dog "alerting" (barking or wagging his tail) constitutes probable cause to search the vehicle.[122]

Any cash found is assumed to be the "probable proceeds of drug transactions," and seized. As usual, police rarely file charges. To recover their cash, the victims must prove in court that they earned it legitimately. Except for the largest seizures, the cost of a court fight exceeds the value of the seized cash. In practice, most cases are settled out of court, with fines and attorney's fees deducted from the amount returned.

Is a dog "alerting" to the presence of drugs on cash sufficient probable cause to seize it? Both federal and state law enforcement officials say it is. But over a seven-year period, scientists at Miami-based Toxicology Consultants, Inc. tested currency from major U.S. cities--and found that 96 percent of it contained cocaine residues. Does this mean that carrying cash is now illegal? You be the judge!

But the most conclusive evidence comes from the DEA itself. In 1985, a DEA laboratory issued a classified report concluding that, "The Federal Reserve may be contaminating the currency through normal procedures." This report was only made public in the summer of 1992 through discovery to the attorney now representing Willie Jones. The report found that belts from the Fed's high-speed sorting machines are themselves contaminated with cocaine, thereby contaminating vast amounts of currency with drug residues. The study recommended that the DEA discontinue seizing cash contaminated with trace amounts of drug residues, concluding that, "Forensic usefulness of trace analysis is at best limited."[123]

Yet eight years later, cash seizures based on trace analysis, and other equally questionable logic, continue. For instance, in March 1992, a U.S. District Judge in Michigan ruled that DEA agents could seize $26,000 in cash from a defendant at an airport because of four prevailing factors:

1) The DEA received a confidential tip that the defendant was carrying a large sum of cash (perhaps from an airline ticket agent who stands to profit from the seizure);

2) The fact that the cash was concealed

3) The fact that drug residues were detected on the money

4) The fact that the defendant was traveling under an assumed name

Without dramatic policy changes, cash seizures should increase greatly in years to come. In 1991, Thermedics, Inc. introduced equipment to screen for possible drug use in the workplace without the knowledge of employees. The equipment is so sensitive, says the company's president, that it can easily detect traces of narcotics on cash.

He adds that, "It isn't uncommon to find traces of cocaine on $100 bills even after it has changed hands several times." If this technology is released to law-enforcement agencies, super-accurate field tests for narcotics on currency at airports and other locations may become widespread, and seizures even more common.

---

[122]In April 1992, the Supreme Court let stand a ruling that police are not allowed to routinely search a person given a misdemeanor citation who they expect to release on the spot. This decision would appear to provide a sound legal footing for a person to refuse a voluntary search of his vehicle (*State of Arizona vs. David Lesley Taylor*, 91-1351). However, under the earlier *Place* ruling, he has no right to do so if a dog alerts to the presence of suspected illegal substances or cash.

[123]According to statements from 21 separate agencies that seize cash, drug-contaminated currency is not destroyed. It's deposited in banks and re-enters circulation, perhaps to be seized once again,

Real Estate Forfeitures

Despite the popularity of cash seizures, it is real estate owners who are most seriously affected by forfeiture laws. Take the case of Gussie Mae Gantt. Gantt, an elderly widow, discovered her children might be selling drugs out of her home in Montgomery, Alabama. She evicted the children, then erected "no trespassing" signs on the property when it appeared crack dealers were continuing to use the area around it as an open-air drug market.

Gantt called police repeatedly and urged them to arrest the pushers. Police made no arrests, and the dealers didn't leave. After six months of surveillance, city police obtained a warrant to search Gantt's home. They found no drugs or any sign of drug activity, but a federal magistrate ordered the home seized based on affidavits provided by law enforcement officers. No charges were filed against Gantt. U.S. Attorney Jim Wilson accused Gantt of complicity in the crimes allegedly committed on her property. "Anybody that owns property can do more than [she did] to keep crack dealers from selling drugs," said Wilson.

Gantt's attorney appealed the seizure order in U.S. District Court. During the hearing, the judge stated, "We have the wrong defendant on trial here." In July 1992, he ordered the Justice Department to give Gantt back her home. In his decision, he wrote that, "Gantt wanted the drug activity in front of her house stopped" and that she "took all reasonable steps that a person of her abilities could be expected to take." He ordered the Justice Department to return her property and to pay her legal bills and the costs of the government's forfeiture action.

But a few days later, the judge issued a "certificate of reasonable cause" reversing part of his original order. It stated that the "probable cause" necessary for the forfeiture to take place provided "reasonable cause" for each side to pay their own costs (28 USCA 2465). This statute implies that even for the most unjust forfeitures, if probable cause exists, *the defendant cannot recover legal and other costs from the government.* It is bolstered by the Supreme Court decision of *Kosak vs. U.S.*, in which the court ruled that the Federal Tort Claims Act prevents the government from being sued as a result of damages to property seized in a forfeiture action (465 US 848).

In 1990, a U.S. Circuit Court of Appeals decision ruled that even if you are innocent of any wrongdoing in a real estate seizure, you must meet a very stiff standard to recover your property. If you are a landlord, lack of knowledge of illegal activity on your property is no excuse. You must also demonstrate that you took "strong steps" to prevent such illicit use.

Several months later, I sold a house I owned that I had rented out to a group of young people. Did they use drugs on the property? I had no way of knowing, although after I sold it, I was told by a neighbor that one of the tenants had allegedly used crack cocaine in the house.

The lease my tenants signed prohibited "any unlawful activity." Would this phrase have been sufficient to avoid seizure if police had entered and found cocaine on the premises? Should I have required my tenants to take periodic drug tests? Surely any court would have considered this an unreasonable invasion of privacy. Should I have installed a closed-circuit television system to monitor their activities? Again, I find it hard to believe that any court would have permitted such surveillance.

Still, every property owner in the United States is potentially liable to having his property seized unless he initiates such "strong steps" against drug use on it. And if he does so, he risks being sued for invasion of privacy by his tenants! Moreover, according to civil forfeiture's "relation-back" doctrine, the government's title to forfeitable property begins the instant the property is used unlawfully.

This title is superior to that of any subsequent purchaser, although by virtue of the *Buena Vista* case, recipients of gifts of tainted property, bona-fide lienholders or purchasers for value can at least now argue the innocent owner defense. The government's hidden lien on property expires only when the statute of limitations for the forfeiture ends, although the government has recently asserted that the hidden lien is permanent.

Owners of rental and timeshare properties are at particularly high risk. If a tenant commits a forfeitable offense on the property, the property is potentially tainted forever. Five, ten, or even 50 years later the government can seize the property from the new owner, unless he can prevail in an innocent owner defense. Moreover, under the conversion doctrine, all profits from the property since the forfeitable offense allegedly took place are due the government. (It's true that the DOJ's guidelines discourage seizing property from bona-fide purchasers and lienholders--but as the *Republic National Bank* case demonstrated, guidelines can be and are ignored.)

Potentially, not only real property, but all property, could be affected. It means, for instance, that the government potentially has a permanent and hidden lien on every estate settlement. If you inherit $100,000, the government could several years later claim that the funds are subject to forfeiture and seize them from you, their new owner. You could retrieve your lawful inheritance only by prevailing in an innocent owner defense. To protect themselves, executors of estates will be forced to maintain a large portion of every estate in an escrow account, permanently, in order to avoid government forfeitures.

In a few cases, forfeiture victims have died trying to defend their property from seizure. One morning in October 1992, Mrs. Donald Scott was awakened by a commotion outside her home in Ventura County, California. Mrs. Scott looked out the window and saw a large group of armed men milling around outside the house. She went downstairs to investigate. Moments later, Mr. Scott, 62, heard a cry for help from his wife. He rushed downstairs with a handgun held over his head. He was ordered to drop it, and was shot twice in the chest while lowering it. He died instantly.

Scott's killers were members of a task force consisting of officers and agents from the Los Angeles County sheriff's department, Drug Enforcement Agency, National Park Service, California Bureau of Narcotics, and California National Guard. The task force claimed that the search resulted from a tip they had received that Scott was growing marijuana on his 200-acre estate. No drugs were found, and none of his killers were indicted, demoted, or disciplined in any way.

The real motivation for the search, according to the Ventura County District Attorney, was so that it could be seized by the government. Scott's estate, which lies adjacent to land owned by the National Park Service, has long been coveted by the government.

There is no theoretical limit to the size of a civil forfeiture. A person could walk into Rockefeller Center, commit an illegal act in the lobby or a restroom, and thereby taint the entire complex. Should the government bring forfeiture proceedings, the owner, or future owners, could recover the property only by prevailing in an innocent owner defense.

However, from a political standpoint, such a seizure would be unlikely to be sought by a U.S. District Attorney. One DEA official recently admitted as much when he remarked that if the government ever began seizing the properties of politically-connected owners, the entire civil forfeiture campaign would be jeopardized.

You'll be glad to know that government officials are essentially immune from forfeiture of their homes, no matter what offenses allegedly occur there. In 1992, the Connecticut U.S. District Attorney declined to pursue forfeiture proceedings against an Assistant U.S. Attorney, Leslie Ohta, whose 18-year old son was accused of selling narcotics out of the family home. Ohta has seized dozens of homes where drug dealing allegedly took place, even when their owners were not aware of the activity.

Noriega and International Forfeiture

The U.S. government has in some cases succeeded in using forfeiture laws to seize assets (or at least freeze them) across international borders. One recent case involves former Panamanian dictator Manuel Noriega. I have little sympathy for Noriega, but his plight is symbolic of our possible fate at the hands of an all-powerful government.

After a U.S. invasion drove Noriega from power, kidnapped him, and expatriated him to the United States, the U.S. government arm-twisted governments worldwide into freezing his assets. Total frozen assets in these accounts came to more than $20 million.

Prosecutors claimed that all of these funds, along with Noriega's cars, real estate, and other personal effects, had been generated through illicit activities--although Noriega was on the CIA payroll for nearly 20 years. Unfortunately for Noriega's attorneys, these seizures left nothing with which a defense could be mounted. After a dispute lasting nearly a year, the judge convinced prosecutors to release $1.8 million for Noriega's defense.

Now that a Miami jury has found Noriega guilty, U.S. officials are now seeking to seize the accounts outright. It is proceeding even without proof that all or even most of the money in these accounts derived from any illegal activity. Similarly, in 1992, the U.S. government succeeded in persuading the United Nations to freeze Iraqi assets worldwide.[124]

The Annunzio-Wylie Anti-Money Laundering Act of 1992 should make this process easier. It calls for any U.S. District Court to be able to issue an order for international forfeiture, and for Congress to prepare regular reports on the progress of other nations implementing the provisions of various international treaties encouraging cross-border asset forfeiture. (See "The International War Against Banking Secrecy and Money Laundering," Chapter 9.)

Forfeiture and Government Corruption[125]

As federal and state forfeiture programs are brought under increased scrutiny by the news media, reporters have discovered that police and prosecutors who managed the forfeited assets are profiteering off them. No wonder the forfeiture program is so popular with law enforcement! It's not just the boon to their department's budgets, but the ability to line their own pockets, that makes them strenuously resist any talk of legislative oversight.

The problem of seized property disappearing from inventory, being used by a cop or purchased by a relative or friend of someone connected with the forfeiture program, is coming out around the country. Judging from the frequency with which such reports are popping up, it seems that the foxes guarding the henhouse have been eating chicken all along. Here are some examples:

---

[124]As the Noriega trial progressed, it was revealed that while Noriega was forced to forfeit millions of dollars of his ill-gotten gains, witnesses against him were permitted to keep their tainted earnings. The DEA called one of them, Max Mermelstein, the "Godfather of Cocaine." Mermelstein stood accused of importing cocaine worth $12 billion and arranging four murders. But once he struck a deal, the government released him from prison, granted him immunity from prosecution, and handed him nearly $700,000 in cash.

[125]This section is taken from the December 1992 *F.E.A.R. Chronicles* (1735 N. Broadway, Walnut Creek, Calif. 94596)

Washington, D.C. This spring, *The Washington Post* reported 40 guns missing from the D.C. Police Property Clerk's office. That discovery was made after two guns used as murder weapons showed up as having been previously impounded by police. The report made heads roll at the Property Clerk's office. The Property Clerk conducted an internal audit. The results were shocking.

In September [1992], WRC-TV obtained a copy of the confidential audit and discovered that as many as 2,864 confiscated guns were missing from the D.C. Property Clerk's Office. The guns "were often left in unsealed boxes for extended periods," the audit said. "Employees who have access to guns also control the inventory records," and "the gun room doubled as a lunchroom."

Theft and mismanagement of forfeited assets has been rampant in D.C. since the forfeiture boom began. In 1989, several Fourth District police were charged with money-skimming from suspects, after numerous complaints that certain cops would regularly shake down suspects and take their money, reporting only a portion of it as seized. At least one officer pleaded guilty to skimming.

This type of profiteering is not limited to officers on the street. In 1987 *The Washington Post* reported that Effie Barry, wife of then Mayor Marion Barry, was driving a forfeited Lincoln Town Car. The government argued that this was within the definition of taking the forfeited property "into government service"--but the Mayor's wife was not a city employee, so why should she have the use of her own vehicle?

Somerset County, New Jersey. On August 2, 1992, *The New York Times* reported how Somerset County prosecutor Nicholas Bissell, Jr.'s office made a deal with a newly- arrested suspect, James Guiffre. They threatened him with felony charges carrying 10 year prison terms, and forfeiture of his residence, unless he agreed to sign over the deeds to two vacant lots that he had bought in 1988 for $174,000. Guiffre did so within 26 hours of his arrest without being allowed to consult counsel. The lots were sold several months later, with Bissell's approval, for $20,000 to a buyer who conveyed them to "two men with at least a nodding acquaintance" to Bissell's chief detective, Richard Thornburg, the *Times* reported. Thornburg was the officer who had made the deal with Guiffre in the first place.

Somerset County, though 13th in the state of New Jersey in population, ranks number one in the state for assets seized in 1991, with $1,029,341 in seized cash alone, not to mention vehicles, real estate, and other property seized. Three hundred thousand dollars from the forfeiture fund controlled by Bissell was placed in a small bank (total deposits $1.3 million) belonging to Bissell's "longtime business associate," according to the *Times*.

Suffolk County, New York. On October 2, 1992, *The New York Times* reported that Suffolk County District Attorney James M. Catterson exercised complete control over the assets his office confiscates through its forfeiture program. Until Long Island's *Newsday* brought it to their attention, Suffolk County officials knew nothing about Catterson's handling of the forfeited assets. Catterson drives a BMW 735i seized from a drug dealer. He spent $3,412 from the forfeiture fund for mechanical and body work on the BMW, including $75 for pin striping. Also from the fund, he purchased a $300 watch for a retiring secretary, and $3,999 for chairs, among other things.

Catterson told the *Times*: "By my view, I really don't have to ask anyone else's permission to spend monies that come to me."

Pine Lawn, Missouri: The May 1, 1991 *St. Louis Post-Dispatch* reported that in the tiny community of Pine Lawn, one detective, Marvin Shannon, was charged with stealing money from the police. Another officer kept a television set seized in a raid. Detective Shannon also wound up with a Camaro Z28-IROC sports car which he seized from a drug suspect who didn't own it. At the forfeiture auction, the detective bought it for far less than it was worth. In another case seized cash and jewelry valued at $13,000 was missing.

Pine Lawn's mayor, Pelton Jackson, called in the FBI to investigate the missing property, as well as reports that police were allowing drug dealers to go free in exchange for money.

Los Angeles, California: On January 31, 1992, six L.A. narcotics officers were tried on charges of stealing hundreds of thousands of dollars in cash and property during drug raids, beating suspects, planting narcotics and falsifying police reports, according to *The Los Angeles Times*. On March 19, 1992, the *Times*, reporting on another trial involving two L.A. narcs charged with money-skimming, described the testimony of former L.A. county sheriff's deputy Eufrasio G. Cortez:

"Cortez...said that a money-skimming scandal that has shaken the Sheriff's Department began with narcotics officers taking 'a few dollars off the top' to buy law enforcement equipment or dinner after a successful drug raid--but quickly spiraled out of control.

Narcotics officers also began stealing seized property, including television sets, stereos, and jewelry that had been confiscated during raids, he said. Before long, officers were skimming hundreds of dollars, then thousands, in cash."

How to Prevent (or Reverse) Forfeiture

The government's asset forfeiture program, the centerpiece of the Reagan/Bush War on Drugs, has been an unqualified success. Just ask the Justice Department, whose Asset Forfeiture office claims that forfeiture has "unlimited potential." But forfeiture has already caught hundreds of thousands of property owners and investors in the crossfire. How do you protect yourself from becoming the next statistic in the War on Drugs?

The following are some suggestions on how to protect yourself and your property. It is illegal under both state and federal law to hide or otherwise make unreachable forfeitable assets. However, if you take such actions before you become the victim of a seizure, you would presumably not be violating any law.

✔ *Cash.* Most forfeitures involve the seizure of cash. Since cash can be seized if it contains any trace of drug residues, you need to make certain you carry "clean" cash if you're transporting a large quantity of it.

When you withdraw cash from your bank account, ask the teller to provide you with new and uncirculated bills, which should be free of drug residues. Have the teller put the bills into a bank envelope with the withdrawal slip. Then have the teller seal the envelope and stamp over the seal with the bank's date stamp. This may not prevent a cash seizure from occurring, but certainly demonstrates that you took affirmative steps to establish a paper trail, and to obtain uncontaminated funds.

In addition, *never* "flash" a large quantity of cash in a public place, such as an airport, railway depot, or bus station. Use traveler's checks as a cash substitute whenever possible. (However, purchases with traveler's checks can in many cases be traced, particularly checks issued by large companies such as American Express.)

✔ *Your home.* Rent or lease your home--don't own it outright. Or hold it in a name other than your own--your spouse, for instance. If you have children living at home, let them know that the consequences of their drug use or drug cultivation could result in your home being seized.

The easiest way to protect the equity in your home is to sell it. You may find an investor who is willing to buy your home and permit you to continue living in it as a renter. If the property is seized, it's the buyer's problem, not yours. The new owner may sue you for damages, but his rights as a litigant are far more limited than those of the government. Obviously, you have a legal and ethical responsibility not to knowingly commit or allow to be committed acts on the property that might result in its forfeiture.

However, you should never take back a second mortgage. If the new owner commits a forfeitable offense, you might lose your lienholder interest. That's what happened to Carl and Mary Shelden. In 1979, the Sheldens sold their home in California for $289,000 to a man later convicted of racketeering. They agreed to carry a $160,000 second mortgage. The government seized the property, and refused to pay the Shelden's mortgage. After a 13-year court battled, they are bankrupt. They got back the house, but it is now so badly damaged that is virtually uninhabitable.

If you can't sell your home, you can still remove most of the equity by borrowing against its value. It's easy and lucrative for a forfeiture squad to seize a home from an owner that has few if any assets left to fight back. But a bank or mortgage company with experienced attorneys can wage a much more effective battle. By contesting a forfeiture, the lien-holder (bank or mortgage company) is simply exercising its interest in the property on which it has loaned you money. By borrowing money, you shift your exposure to a third party.

This strategy is not risk-free. You will be responsible for making up the bank's loss if the house is seized, and to pay the bank's legal expenses, even if the bank prevails as an innocent lien-holder.

You should invest the proceeds of your mortgage in a manner that permits you to pay back the loan. One option is an account in a foreign currency that pays higher interest rates than the rate on your loan. Better yet, invest the money in an annuity with a guaranteed payout sufficient to make all or most of the mortgage payments. Annuities generally contain an "anti-alienation" clause that prohibits the funds from being seized by creditors.

A more sophisticated version of this strategy involves forming a foreign trust or other international structure, then borrowing money from this structure and pledging the equity in the home as collateral. Then default on the loan. The trustee places a non-recourse foreclosure on the home, and records the foreclosure in official records. Official notice of the foreclosure makes it very unattractive to any prospective creditor, but due to its non-recourse nature, it is not enforced. You continue to live in the home. Of course, such action would also make it difficult or impossible for you to obtain credit. (See "Asset Protection Techniques," this chapter, for additional thoughts on this topic.)

Don't keep too much cash, precious metals, or other valuables at home. If you have a safe, for instance, and your home is searched, the police will simply break into it and take whatever it contains. There are numerous examples of police raiding homes, breaking into and seizing the contents of safes, and leaving without charging the occupants with any crime. Instead, keep these valuables in a safety deposit box or private vault--preferably one 100 miles or farther from your home.

Finally, follow the suggestions in Chapter 2 to improve the security in your home, particularly if you leave for extended periods. If you don't, and someone breaks in and commits a forfeitable offense there, such as selling drugs from it, it could be seized.

✓ *Rental property.* If you own rental property, I suggest selling it. If you'd rather not, or can't, then place language in the lease agreement setting up your innocent owner defense in advance. For instance, the lease should state that the tenant takes full financial responsibility for any forfeitable offense that takes place on or in the property during the lease period. It should also state that any illegal activity, contemplation of illegal activity, or activity that disturbs neighbors may result in the lease's termination. (In some states, these provisions may not be legally enforceable.) Finally, conduct a thorough background check of all applicants to make certain that they have not been convicted of a forfeitable offense in the past. This last practice may violate state or federal civil rights or disability statutes; consult with your attorney.[126]

What should you do if you have someone renting from you that you believe is dealing drugs or committing other crimes that could result in the forfeiture of your property?

● *Discuss the problem with the tenant.* It's best not to accuse the tenant of illegal activity. Instead, tell him that you've received complaints about noise, excessive traffic in and out of the house or apartment, etc. If the problem continues, you'll be forced to terminate the lease. Follow up with a certified letter, and keep a copy (and the return receipt) for your records.

● *Ask around.* If you talk to other tenants or neighbors, you may find them willing to discuss the activities on your property. This shields you from the government's claim that you were "willfully blind" to the activity taking place. Ask neighbors to keep records of people coming and going into the building, and if they would be willing to testify in court. (In some states, this practice could lead to an invasion of privacy lawsuit.) Keep notes of your conversations with neighbors, and have them notarized. Doing so makes your notes admissible in court.

● *Contact the local police or sheriff's department.* This might appear counter-productive at first glance, but most police agencies will at least try to help. You'll probably be told, however, that there's nothing they can do until they uncover evidence of a crime. If you have such evidence, submit it. In doing so, you'll establish another pillar of the innocent owner defense: that you did not consent to the illicit activity, and took all reasonable steps available to prevent it.

If the evidence against your tenant is strong, the police may ask you to testify. Refusing to do so may be grounds for forfeiture. In the Gantt case I described in "Real Estate Forfeitures," this chapter,

---

[126]Landlords, of course, face many other regulatory burdens. For instance, recent court decisions have affirmed that a landlord is personally responsible for sexual harassment, and/or discrimination suffered by a tenant, even if landlord's employee or agent was the guilty party.

a drug enforcement unit seized a house from an elderly widow who repeatedly called for police to disperse drug-dealing gangs in her yard, but refused to testify against them.

 ● *If problems continue, terminate the tenant's lease.* Don't accuse the tenant of illegal activities that you can't prove. Doing so only invites a lawsuit. Rather, stick to issues that clearly violate the lease, such as engaging in activities that disturb other tenants.

Taking such steps only lowers the odds of forfeiture; it does not eliminate the possibility. The trend is clearly toward holding landlords responsible to police their property, with or without the aid of police. But in some parts of the country, you're not allowed to hire a private security service to do so. For instance, the Los Angeles Police Commission recently announced a crackdown on private security squads landlords have hired to control criminals when police failed to respond to their complaints.

A protective ownership strategy is to hold each piece of rental property you own in a separate legal structure, such a family limited partnership. If you structure the arrangement properly, authorities will not be able to connect one piece of property with another. A forfeitable offense on one property won't necessarily lead to the loss of another (although in a RICO criminal forfeiture, it might). You might also consider this strategy if you own large tracts of unoccupied land. Drug cultivation on private land is a major problem, and your entire plot may be seized if a single marijuana plant is found growing on it. (In many parts of the country, marijuana grows wild, and indeed, during World War II, millions of acres of hemp--marijuana--were planted to be woven into rope.)

 √ *Automobiles.* If you drive an expensive vehicle, lease it, don't own it. Lease agreements generally state that the renter is responsible for any forfeiture by police. But again, the owner has far fewer rights in a lawsuit against you than does the government. There is also a privacy advantage to leasing. In many states, license tag records are open to the public. If you lease your car, your home address won't ordinarily be associated with the license plate number. Ordinarily, the leasing company's address will be listed.

If you buy a used car, have it professionally cleaned before you drive it to eliminate any drug residues in the carpets, upholstery, and ashtrays. Never allow someone you even remotely suspect might be involved in illegal activity to drive or ride in your car. Doing so is grounds for its forfeiture. You could even be imprisoned. In one case, a man who accepted $5 from a friend for a ride was sentenced to a 10-year prison term. It turned out he was driving his passenger to a drug deal. By accepting money for the ride, the driver became a co-conspirator, and thus subject to a mandatory prison term.

If your car is stolen, it has by definition been used for an illegal purpose. Under forfeiture laws in a number of states, this makes it forfeitable. I'm not aware of any forfeitures from car theft victims under this theory, but it's something to keep in mind, particularly if you live in a state such as New Jersey which permits forfeiture for "any indictable offense" connected with property.

 √ *Businesses.* Corporate America is becoming an increasingly frequent forfeiture target. Most business exposure is brought about by actions of employees. For this reason, I recommend hiring as few employees as possible. Use subcontractors, independent contractors, or lease your employees as I described in Chapter 5.

The most frequent offenses that may lead to forfeiture that are committed on business property are violations of federal mail fraud and wire fraud statutes. These are not yet in themselves forfeitable offenses, but are "predicate offenses" to the RICO statute, which permits pre-trial asset freezes. Surprisingly innocent activities may constitute a pattern of racketeering. An employee using a fax machine more than one time to place an illegal bet on a football game may be violating wire fraud statutes. An offense as simple as exaggerating the benefits of your product in an advertising campaign may constitute "mail fraud." Either offense could ultimately result in the forfeiture of your business.

You should conduct a thorough investigation of a prospective employee. Make certain that he does not have a history of committing forfeitable offenses. Insist on a written employment contract that forbids any illegal activity, or contemplation of illegal activity, on the business property. Violations should subject the employee to termination--and you should enforce these provisions. Have the signed contract notarized, which makes the document admissible in court. Of course, you should explain to your employees your reason for taking these precautions. You're not being nosy, but protecting their job. If you lose your business, your employees lose their livelihood.

The anti-laundering laws I discussed in Chapter 7 heavily penalize business engaging any of the "specified unlawful activities" prohibited in the Money Laundering Control Act of 1986 and subsequent legislation. This means you need to be extremely careful of the business conduct you condone by word, deed, or implication.

For instance, if you let a business partner know that you are willing to look the other way while he conducts an illegal act, from that point forward, the government has a lien on your business. Anyone who discovers the illegal act is eligible for the generous informant awards forfeiture actions offer. Even the business partner whose illegal activity to which you consent could eventually turn you in, and obtain a generous informant commission for his information, along with immunity from prosecution.

Finally, don't keep large quantities of cash on your business premises. Any property located in a safe, particularly cash, is a magnet for seizures.

✓ *Other assets*. Bank and brokerage accounts are also frequent forfeiture targets. Follow the suggestions in "Privacy and Your Financial Records," Chapter 4, to set up more discreet banking relationships. If you don't need funds instantly available, consider investing them into an annuity. Foreign investments are also difficult to seize, as you'll learn in Chapter 9.

What should you do if despite your precautions, a government agency seizes your property? Under the admiralty laws under which forfeitures take place, you must within 10 days of receiving notice of the action file a statement asserting your claim to the property and disputing the government's seizure. You must also post a bond (ordinarily about 10 percent the value of the property seized) or file a sworn affidavit of indigence. Otherwise, the government will assume you have conceded your ownership to the government. The courts have repeatedly ruled that strict adherence to these regulations is necessary to reverse a forfeiture.[127]

Your only other option is to pursue the administrative "Remission of Forfeiture" procedure I described earlier in this chapter. However, since you can't appeal if the remission is dismissed, I don't recommend this procedure.

I highly recommend that you hire an attorney experienced in forfeiture law if you experience this type of seizure. One that I recommend is Brenda Grantland. Grantland is the author of *Asset Forfeiture, Motions for Return of Property, and Other Procedures Governing Recovery of Property Seized by Police.* You might also consider joining an advocacy group formed to contest civil forfeiture for which she serves as legal counsel: F.E.A.R. (Forfeiture Endangers American Rights.)[128]

---

[127]The cost bond provisions are strictly enforced. While you may file a petition that you do not have sufficient funds to post the bond, in most cases, these are almost never accepted by seizing agencies. In federal cases, and in many states as well, failure to pay the cost bond deprives the property owner of any judicial hearing. No judge ever reviews the government's probable cause to seize if you fail to post the bond. The DEA is now seeking authority to prohibit judicial review of any denial of an application to waive the cost bond.

[128]Brenda Grantland, 1735 N. Broadway, Walnut Creek, Calif. 95496. This is also the address for F.E.A.R.

Asset Forfeiture and "Voluntary" Searches

If police ask you to submit to a "voluntary" search of your person or your luggage at an airport, bus terminal, train station, etc., you may refuse. You may also refuse to submit to a search of your vehicle. Police aren't permitted to detain you while they obtain a search warrant of your luggage or your vehicle, unless they have probable cause to do so. You are also entitled to see a search warrant before police search your home.

If you refuse permission for the police to search, and they do anyway, you may be able to force a probable cause hearing over the seizure. If a judge agrees with you, your seized property may be returned. (Of course, the government can always--and often does--appeal if it loses in court.)

The following comments from my special report, *Counter-Surveillance,* should be helpful in avoiding seizures when they are preceded by a search of your person, your vehicle, or your home. Please note: These suggestions do not apply to searches by Customs officials. A Customs official does not need probable cause to conduct a search of you or your property when you cross a U.S. border.

When you voluntarily consent to a search, you are *voluntarily giving up your rights*. With unconstitutional laws that make it your responsibility to prove your property's innocence after it has been seized, any other strategy is foolhardy.

Let's say you are walking through an airport with cash that you have withdrawn from your safety deposit box. A dog approaches you, with a man in a suit holding it on a leash. Another man is walking beside him taking notes. The dog sniffs the bag in which you are carrying the cash. The man taking notes identifies himself as an agent for the airport's Drug Interdiction Unit. He tells you that there have been problems with drugs in the airport. Would you mind answering a few questions?

The correct answer is to say "no," and to keep on walking. You will not talk with the agents. You will not answer any questions. Politely inform the agents that you are under no obligation to discuss anything. If you have a tape recorder with you, turn it on. A video recorder is even better. You want an exact record of the events that are about to occur.[129]

If the agents persist, ask them in a respectful tone of voice if you are under arrest. The agents cannot detain you or search you without probable cause. They can, however, search your bag based on the dog alerting to it. If the agents proceed with a body search without your consent, you may be to prevail in a probable cause hearing, particularly if you have a visual record.

---

[129]This may not be a good strategy to follow if you are confronted by law enforcement authorities in a non-public location. A boat owner recently confronted a Coast Guard search crew with a video camera. The crew leader smashed the camera, removed the phone, and his crew subsequently wrecked the boat in its search for illegal drugs. They found none, but caused more than $35,000 damage. The owner says that if he had not insisted on videotaping the search, the crew would probably have not been as destructive.

If you agree to talk with the agents, they'll generally ask where you are going and why you are travelling there. The agents will ask for identification, and ask to see your ticket. Then comes the kicker: "Are you carrying any large sums of cash or monetary instruments?"

No matter how you answer this question, the next request will be for you to submit to a voluntary search. The correct answer, of course, is "no," but forfeiture squad members are well trained in psychological intimidation. At this point, it's hard to refuse. And even if you do, unless you have a visual (best) or audio (better than nothing) record of the proceedings, it your word against theirs whether you consented to the search.

Once the search begins, the agents will of course find the cash. Then they'll place in a bag alongside two other bags filled with paper towels. The dog, visibly excited, will paw at the paper bag filled with cash. The agents will then inform you that the dog has identified your cash as containing drug residues. They are confiscating the cash subject to Title 21, United States Code Section 881 as suspected proceeds of a narcotics transaction. Then you'll receive a receipt for the cash. You're free to go, but without your money.

The Future of Asset Forfeiture

Our aim is nothing less than to create a world system of financial control in private hands able to dominate the political system of each country and the world economy as a whole. Freedom and choice will be controlled within very narrow alternatives by the fact that [every man] will be numbered from birth, and followed, as a number, through his educational training, his required military or other public service, his tax contributions, his health and medical requirements, and his final retirement and death benefits.

--Tragedy and Hope, by Carroll Quigley

As a teenager, I heard John Kennedy's summons to citizenship. And then, as a student at Georgetown, I heard that call clarified by a professor I had named Carroll Quigley.

--Bill Clinton, July 16, 1992

On July 16, 1992, Bill Clinton accepted the Democratic party's nomination for the Presidency. Four months later, he was elected to the office. What will the next four years bring in terms of new encroachments on our right to privacy?

One clue came during a televised debate with George Bush and Ross Perot, when Clinton outlined his plans to fight crime. Clinton called for a "national police force" of 100,000 men and women. He also told an audience of prosecutors during the campaign that the federal government needs to dramatically expand money laundering prosecutions of "illegal financial transactions that cross state lines." That is "what the federal government ought to focus on: Go after the money." It's hard to imagine a more blatant endorsement of the terror tactics used to enforce the money laundering and forfeiture laws.

It is disconcerting at the least to have a President who openly admires a man that called for "freedom and choice to be limited among very narrow alternatives" and for "every man to be numbered from birth." Freedom and choice, of course, are most effectively limited when a sense of crisis is created. And Clinton's campaign revolved around the need to end the "economic crisis," the "health crisis," the "environmental crisis," and (of course) the need to win the War on Drugs.

To fight these crises, I believe Clinton will call for (and receive) new legislation that allows him to "fight" these evils more effectively. The Clinton Justice Department, as the Bush Justice Department, will rely on "creative" uses of money laundering and forfeiture laws to achieve its goals. Here are a few trends that I believe we'll see:

✓ *Vigorous enforcement of the Annunzio-Wylie Anti-Money Laundering Act of 1992.* Among the many new crimes this act creates, perhaps the most insidious is "international structuring." Any effort you make to avoid reporting movements of "monetary instruments" across a U.S. border is now considered money laundering. If the international structuring provisions are enforced in the same manner as the domestic structuring ones are, it means that even individuals who inadvertently violate the law will face fines, forfeiture, even imprisonment. (You'll learn more about the implications of this law in Chapter 9, "Moving Your Money Privately.")

As I described earlier in Chapter 7, Section 1957 of the Money Laundering Control Act makes lawyers criminals if they accept money from clients they suspect of "specified unlawful activities," including any forfeitable offense. They can be stripped of their fees, and even jailed if they assist in their client in structuring payments to avoid reporting them, even if the funds have been earned legitimately. Section 1957 was not vigorously enforced in the Bush administration; the Clinton years may give it a new lease on life.

✓ *Expansion of forfeiture laws against white-collar criminals.* Count on the Clinton Justice Department to vigorously pursue forfeiture against those allegedly violating more than 100 different federal statutes. Existing law already permits forfeiture for bankers making bad lending decisions. U.S. District Attorneys in New York have applied forfeiture law for the first time to bankers allegedly engaged in a "lending conspiracy."

Other professionals face equal if not greater risks of having their assets seized without due process. A U.S. District judge ruled in January 1993 that an auditor could face a RICO claim due to his alleged role in a conspiracy to defraud investors in a publicly-traded company. Physicians already face a variety of threats, including the threat of the government seizing their bank accounts if authorities believe that the physician inflated a Medicare or Medicaid claim.

If you run a mail order business, you'll be glad to know that if you do business through the mail, and don't give someone back a prompt refund if they request one, you face a potential mail fraud charge-- a predicate offense under the RICO statutes. One former prosecuting attorney told me that mail fraud is included in almost every RICO prosecution. Any business that uses the Postal Service or any private carrier is potentially at risk for an asset seizure. Even if it somehow avoids using the mails or private carriers, but uses the telephone, it is open to a wire fraud charge--another RICO predicate offense.

Forfeitures will proliferate in all these areas, but in none of them as much as in the "environmental crime." The Superfund law states that anyone that even remotely contributed to pollution at a contaminated site is responsible for cleaning up the entire site. I believe this will be the single biggest growth area for forfeiture in the entire Clinton administration.

✓ *Forfeitures against those holding politically incorrect views will escalate.* Because the forfeiture and money laundering laws are so vague and all-encompassing, it is inevitable that they be placed to political purposes. All over the United States, politicians are learning that an efficient way to put opponents in their place is to seize their property.

In Colorado, state officials seized a church savings account because the church actively supported a successful ballot initiative that barred any local government from giving homosexuals a privileged minority status. A Missouri politician saw his campaign funds frozen after he made statements indicating his opposition to abortion. A newspaper publisher in Connecticut who called police in New Haven "northern rednecks" was threatened with a RICO suit. As politicians become more accustomed to forfeiture laws, they will put them to new and ever-more-inventive uses.

Such abuses will continue on the federal level as well. *The National Law Journal* recently asked former Bush Administration Solicitor General Kenneth Starr for his thoughts about what legal issues would be the most likely to be resolved in the future by the Supreme Court. (The solicitor general is responsible for arguing the government's case before the Supreme Court.) Starr predicted that First Amendment (free speech) issues would be a "major frontier" before the court, including racketeering and forfeiture cases relating to free speech.[130]

√ *Fast-track development of a "national public network" to be subjected to continuous surveillance by government computers.* This may sound far-fetched, but Clinton's own *Putting People First* campaign document claims the nation needs to "create a national information network to link every home, business, lab, classroom, and library by the year 2015. The person who told me about this planned network asked me, "Why does this remind me of Big Brother's 'telescreen' in Orwell's *1984*?"

A "national public network" is particularly unnecessary given the huge investments private companies are prepared to make in virtually identical (but not government-controlled) technologies. Time-Warner, for instance, announced plans in early 1993 to spend billions of dollars developing an "electronic superhighway" into more than seven million homes to deliver cable subscribers "unlimited" choices in video, shopping, and telecommunications services.

In a society where property rights mean little or nothing, your only alternative (other than leaving that society) is to move your assets into forms that attract less attention, and into structures that offer protection from seizures devoid of due process. That is the subject of the remainder of this chapter, and all of Chapter 9.

A Survey of Private Investments

When you help out, you're helping out in the War on Drugs

--radio advertisement urging bank depositors to cooperate with banks administering the targeting provisions of the Anti-Drug Abuse Act of 1988

The government's messianic quest for more information about its citizens is insatiable. The "Wise Men" know their plans will not work if the public transfers its wealth into hidden places.

Is there any way out of this tightening noose? Yes, but it is becoming more and more difficult. Even after the enactment of the Bank Secrecy Act, and additional legislation from the Reagan-Bush era, there are still private refuges for your investments. This section outlines a few of them.

---

[130]"Solicitor General May Seek Balance," *The National Law Journal*, February 22, 1993

Some of the techniques illustrated in this section may well be used for fraudulent purposes. I want to make it clear that I am not advocating tax evasion, fraud, money laundering, or other illegal actions. After all, why should you take *illegal* steps to conceal assets, evade taxes, or launder money when there are many *legal* techniques you can use to protect your privacy, move money outside the reach of litigants and/or the government, and at least defer (if not avoid completely) taxation?

A reminder: The IRS considers income from any source in the world to a U.S. citizen or corporation to be taxable. (The United States is one of the few nations in the world with such a policy.) You have a legal obligation to declare such income on your tax return, even if it is not reported to the IRS.

1. *Non-bank financial institutions.* Financial institutions that are not federally-chartered banks operate under a slightly lower burden of compliance with federal money laundering statutes. This does not mean that the laws are ignored. It does mean that these institutions have not yet been forced by law and regulation to spy on their customers.

The most common non-bank financial institutions are storefront investment companies and brokerages offering money market accounts. In many cases, these accounts offer check-writing privileges. Storefront investment companies are typically located in the poorer sections of our central cities. They may have the word "bank" in their name, but they are not federally chartered, and do not carry federal deposit insurance.

These companies are patronized primarily by immigrants, some of them who have arrived illegally, and by the poor who cannot afford to open bank accounts. Such individuals may not have a Social Security number, which banks are required to ask for prior to opening an account. Or they may not have a credit record, which most banks now require, or have sufficient funds to meet the bank's minimum balance requirements.

Storefront investment companies offer fewer services than banks, and because they are largely unregulated, some are thinly-disguised scams. For instance, the 1990 failure of the Latin Investment Corp. storefront investment company in Washington, DC, led to losses of $13 million from thousands of Hispanics who had placed their life savings in the institution.[131]

On the other hand, because storefront investment companies may not require a Social Security number to open an account, they represent a step away from the constant surveillance of the U.S. banking system. If you open an interest-bearing account, you will be asked to submit your Social Security number. But many accounts in such companies are non-interest-bearing.

The Annunzio-Wylie Anti-Money Laundering Act of 1992 calls for a major crackdown on non-bank financial institutions. If this law is vigorously enforced, storefront financial institutions will no doubt lose much of their appeal to privacy seekers. Many will close rather than comply with onerous regulation.

2. *Stocks.* While most stocks pay dividends, not all do. Only dividends must be reported to the IRS, not the purchase of the stock itself. However, any profits you generate when you sell must be reported by both you and your U.S. broker. Low-priced stocks seldom pay dividends. Nor do precious metals mining stocks.

---

[131]In April 1992, trustees appointed for this firm offered to begin paying back depositors some of their lost funds. However, the IRS attached a $857,000 lien against these funds, preventing the trustees from distributing the money.

Non-dividend-paying stocks are popular outside the United States. In many funds, dividends are merely reinvested. However, the Tax Reform Act of 1986 has imposed complex requirements for translating deferred dividend payments into theoretical capital gains for such investments. Tax must be paid on these paper profits. (For information on how to legally defer these dividends, so they remain non-reportable until you sell, see "Advanced Offshore Investment Strategies," Chapter 9.)

For greater privacy, and to guard against the possibility of some future catastrophe, have your stock certificates sent to you, and keep them in a safe place. This is getting more difficult as time goes by. Big brokerages (and Big Brother) are encouraging "book entry" recording of all securities ownership. In a book entry holding, your ownership of a security is recorded only on a computer. You have no proof of ownership other than your monthly or quarterly statement.

Brokers like book entry because they get the interest and dividend payments first and have use of that money until the checks they send to customers are cashed and cleared. Because the book entry system is also less expensive, states, cities, and other issuers of municipal bonds are also increasingly turning to it. But if possible, try to get the certificate itself. You never know when computer failure or banking collapse might separate you from your assets.

To discourage individuals from holding stock certificates, some companies are beginning to charge customers who request them. Merrill-Lynch, for instance, recently began imposing a fee for this service. On the other hand, most companies impose an annual fee for book entry maintenance of securities for an account without recent trading activity. So you may actually save money if you hold your own stock certificates.

3. *Bearer securities.* "Bearer" stocks and bonds are not registered in any form and provide a completely anonymous form of ownership. TEFRA made it illegal for publicly-traded U.S. companies to issue bearer stocks or bonds, but those issued prior to 1982 are still available. However, you are required to disclose your Social Security number and provide positive identification when you turn in a bearer certificate for redemption in the United States. Otherwise, 20 percent of the proceeds must be deducted and forwarded to the IRS. Bank tellers are also not as familiar with bearer stocks and bonds as they once were, and may hesitate to pay cash until their authenticity is verified.

Bearer stocks and bonds are still widely available outside the United States. For more information on other types of bearer instruments, see Chapter 9, "Advanced Offshore Investment Strategies." Bearer shares may also be issued for privately-held corporations unless their issuance is prohibited by the laws of the state in which the company is incorporated. Nevada is one state with no law prohibiting the issuance of bearer shares.

4. *Municipal bonds.* Municipal bonds are exempt from federal taxation. However, the Tax Reform Act of 1986 requires you to list all municipal bond holdings on your tax return. In 1988, the Supreme Court dismissed a challenge to this requirement. Bonds issued before 1982 in the United States may be available in bearer form, but the same restrictions on redeeming them in the United States apply as with other bearer instruments. That is, paying agents may be obligated to withhold 20 percent of the redemption price from any bondholder who has failed to furnish the agent with a valid taxpayer identification (i.e., Social Security) number. According to the Public Securities Commission, an industry trade group, between 20 percent and 25 percent of the $784 billion in municipal bonds outstanding are in bearer form.

5. *Treasury securities.* Until recent years, purchases of Treasury bills, notes, or bonds were relatively private. You would purchase them at a bank and would be mailed the actual certificate. When the bill or bond matured, you would present it at the bank and instantly obtain your money, with no questions asked. Some Treasury securities were also issued in bearer form, without your name appearing on the certificate.

In 1986, allegedly to safeguard certificates against accidental loss and to save money, the U.S. Treasury introduced "Treasury Direct," a program converting all government securities to book entry form. In this program, you no longer receive a Treasury security, only an acknowledgement that you own it. When the security matures, your funds are wired to a bank. There is no way to bypass the bank; you must designate a bank in order to receive the proceeds of your investment. Both security--and privacy--suffer as a result.

Older Treasury bonds issued in bearer form prior to 1982 are still available from bond dealers. The certificates will go from the seller to the seller's broker to your broker. However, a U.S. broker is not permitted to deliver the certificate to you; it will be held in book entry form on your behalf. There is no need to cancel old certificates or issue new ones.

U.S. savings bonds are still relatively private. While your name and Social Security number is imprinted on each bond, they are the only type of Treasury security that you can still hold in your personal possession (other than older T-bond and T-note issues). You can purchase them at any bank.

6. *Precious metals. Purchases* of gold, silver, platinum or palladium coins don't have to be reported to anyone. But in 1982, the IRS adopted regulations which dictated that all sales of certain "commodities" by an "unincorporated individual" to a "broker" be reported to the IRS.

For nearly a decade, the IRS did not issue final regulations on this matter. In the interim, it was up to each individual IRS agent to interpret the preliminary rules. As a result, enforcement was wildly inconsistent and has led to considerable abuses by individual agents. In one case a precious metals dealer who laboriously completed hundreds of reporting forms by hand was fined $50,000 for not submitting them on magnetic tape. In another case, a dealer was fined for not reporting the purchase of a single silver dime from a small child.

But in December 1992, the IRS declared a truce in part of its 10-year campaign against precious metals investors and dealers. It issued new rules which establish an "excepted sales" category, retroactive to July 1, 1983. Dealers must report only those purchases that equal or exceed minimum Commodity Futures Trading Commission approved contract sizes, as follows:

✔ *Gold bars.* 1 kilogram (32.15 troy oz.), .995 fine or higher.

✔ *Silver bars.* 1,000 oz., .999 fine or higher

✔ *Platinum bars.* 25 troy oz., .9995 fine or higher

✔ *Palladium bars.* 100 troy oz., .9995 fine or higher

✔ *1-oz. gold coins: Maple Leafs, Krugerrands, and Mexican Onzas.* 25 coins

✔ *Pre-1965 silver U.S. dimes, quarters, and half dollars.* $1,000 face value (full bag)

Many transactions are exempt from reporting, no matter how large, including sales of fractional (smaller than one ounce) gold coins, formerly circulating gold coins, and silver dollars. In addition, the reporting regulations also apply only to "unincorporated individuals." So if you sell your precious metals through your corporation, no report need be filed with the IRS. You can also buy and sell coins through your retirement plan without triggering the reporting requirements, although profits from all sales (other than for U.S. gold and silver eagles) are taxed as ordinary income. Finally, you can sell to a fellow collector or investor, either at a coin show or in a classified ad in a publications such as *Coin World* or *Numismatic News,* which are available at any newsstand.

A dealer must notify the IRS if a customer appears to be deliberately "structuring" multiple sales under the reporting thresholds to avoid dealer filing. Dealers must also combine multiple sales by a customer within a 24-hour period for reporting purposes. The dealer faces a civil penalty of $50 for each failure to file when a customer makes a reportable sale. Criminal penalties may apply if the dealer "willfully" fails to file the form for a reportable transaction.[132]

I'm not aware of any additional penalties applicable to a *customer* for structuring sales to avoid the broker reporting requirements. It seems unlikely that the IRS could prosecute you for structuring commodity sales under the much harsher statutes that relate to *currency structuring*. However, I'm not advocating that you violate the law.

If the IRS determines that this exemption is being "abused," it can go back to its stricter regulations that require any sale of be reported. Should that occur, you might be interested in knowing that in 1984, the IRS issued preliminary regulations which provided for an exemption to 1099 reporting for precious metals sold to a dealer for more than a 15 percent premium over their bullion value.

In light of the IRS' relaxed interpretation of the commodity reporting law, this "numismatic reporting exemption" may not appear particularly relevant. But if the stricter rules are reimposed, this exemption could provide a valuable aid to private investing. As long as your coins are clearly worth 15 percent or more than their equivalent bullion value, their sale to a dealer need not be reported.

Many foreign banks offer precious metals accumulation and safekeeping accounts. Sales of precious metals outside the United States are not reportable, although you are required to pay tax on any profits you make. For more information, see "Advanced Offshore Investment Strategies," Chapter 9.

7. *Collectibles.* Art, diamonds, antiques, stamps, rare coins, etc. are among the most private of investments. No government reporting applies to either purchases or sales of collectibles. While such investments may be relatively difficult to sell and are often subject to high dealer buy/sell spreads, they are usually not purchased purely as an investment.

One reason collectibles are valuable as private investments is that they do not generate current income. This means that no annual reports need be made to the IRS regarding interest or dividends. Nor are any reports generated when you purchase or sell collectibles, unless the transaction (or a series of related transactions) involves more than $10,000 in cash or other monetary instruments.

Among collectibles, rare coins are probably the most liquid and subject to the smallest dealer mark-ups. However, prices are quite volatile. In recent years, prices have fallen 50 percent or more, after a spectacular run-up in the 1980s. Part of the fall-off is the result of much stricter enforcement of the cash reporting laws.

Rare *gold* coins are favored by many investors because they represent a form of tangible money directly backed by gold. For larger gold coins in lower grades, a significant percentage of the value of the coin comes from the gold they contain.

When President Roosevelt issued an emergency order in 1933 forcing owners of privately-owned gold to sell, the directive specifically exempted "gold coins having recognized special value to *collectors* of rare and unusual coins." This wording is of utmost importance. *Collectors* were exempt from turning in their numismatic gold coins. *Investors* were not.

---

[132]The IRS published the new regulations December 28, 1992 as Revenue Ruling 92-103. They apply to Section 6045 of the Internal Revenue Code.

Could the President once again order Americans to turn in their gold? He could, because the laws authorizing him to do so are still on the books. Confiscation would be unlikely unless the dollar collapses, which could be several years away, but it's something to keep in mind.

Why did the government exempt numismatic coins? Primarily because it was difficult then, as it is now, to determine a precise value of all but the most common numismatic coins except by selling them. In addition, numismatic coins are not particularly liquid items; the government could not hope to sell them for a quick profit, as it could with bullion. Finally, the value of all numismatic coins owned by U.S. was (and still is) negligible in comparison to the value of privately-held bullion.

If the government imposes another emergency order to sell gold, numismatic coins may enjoy a similar exemption. Therefore, even if your primary motive for purchasing rare gold coins is investing, try to obtain as many different dates and issues as possible. For instance, you might wish to collect $20 Liberty gold coins minted prior to 1907. Start your collection by purchasing folders designed to hold these coins from a coin shop. Try to fill in as many dates as possible. Many dates in lower grades command only slight premiums over the equivalent amount of bullion gold. Hopefully, your accumulation would count as a collection in the event of another forced gold sale.

For the sake of privacy, it might be preferable to purchase uncertified coins (not pre-graded in plastic "slabs"). However, if you're new to coin collecting, you'll probably want to purchase certified coins to help guard against overgrading--although even some certified coins are overgraded. The Professional Coin Grading Service and the Numismatic Guaranty Corporation are the best-known certification services. The most private way to buy numismatic coins or any other collectible (other than firearms) is at a show or over-the-counter at a shop. Pay cash, and don't leave your name or address.

However, the structuring laws for cash and other monetary instruments make anonymous transactions in coins or precious metals with local dealers problematic. In addition, local dealers may not have an extensive inventory or the ability to pay full market value for your holdings. For relatively small transactions, however, local dealers remain a good source for coins or precious metals.

Unfortunately for investors seeking privacy, dealers in collectibles are one of the prime targets of the IRS in its continuing money laundering crackdown. Purchases of collectibles are "designated reporting transactions" under the cash reporting laws. As a result, many dealers no longer accept payment in cash or other monetary instruments. The most visible targets of these investigations to date have been dealers in coins and jewelry, but antique dealers have also been targeted as well.

8. *Cash* is obviously private. The only way the government would ever know you're holding cash is to "call in" old bills and issue new ones. Legislation that would mandate such a recall has already been introduced, provisions of which are described in Chapter 9, "The New Money." For this reason, I don't recommend holding large sums of money in the form of cash. In fact, you shouldn't hold more than $1,000 in cash unless you can prove beyond a shadow of a doubt where it came from and that all taxes due have been paid. Otherwise, it could presumably be confiscated once a currency recall begins.

One way to provide a paper trail that might protect you from this possibility is to withdraw funds you want to hold in cash form from your bank in the manner I described in "How to Prevent (or Reverse) Forfeiture," this chapter. In addition, try to hold mainly $10s and $20s. Recall of $50s and $100s is much more likely than recall of smaller denominations. Ex-Treasury Secretary Donald Regan made such a proposal in 1989, shortly after he left office.

If you try to spend large bills in certain parts of the country, be careful. During a recent trip to south Florida, my wife gave a $100 bill to a post office clerk to buy some stamps. She was asked to submit a driver's license in order to have it honored. Counterfeiting was a big problem, the clerk said, even though she admitted the bill looked genuine.

Asset Protection Techniques

You should also be aware of some of the ways you can protect your assets from being seized by creditors or by the government. My philosophy is to try and structure assets so that they are protected from a government seizure. In so doing, they become virtually invulnerable to almost any private lawsuit, since private litigants don't have anywhere near the power of the government.

Remember: In a government seizure, the burden of proof is on you to demonstrate by the preponderance of the evidence that your assets have been seized in error. On the other hand, if your assets are in a form that the government (or any other litigant) cannot attach prior to trial, you will be in a much stronger legal position.

It's also important to take these steps before you are subject to litigation. Any effort you make to protect your assets after litigation begins may be illegal under the fraudulent conveyance statutes. Conceivably, they could even constitute criminal offenses under the racketeering or money laundering statutes.

There are a variety of domestic legal structures that provide varying degrees of protection. They include:

1. *Corporations.* This is the most basic type of protection, and I described its key elements in Chapter 5. A domestic corporation, however, may not protect your assets adequately unless it is used in combination with other measures. Multiple corporations will generally provide more protection, for the reasons I described in Chapter 5. Foreign corporations offer somewhat greater liability and asset-seizure protection, but can be expensive to set up and maintain. In some situations, however, they can be highly effective. For more information, see "Advanced Offshore Investment Strategies," Chapter 9.

2. *Trusts.* The revocable trusts I discussed in Chapter 4 are flexible, because you can cause the existence of the trust to cease at any time, change the beneficiaries of the trust, etc. However, they provide very little asset protection in the event of a judgement or asset seizure. Since you maintain control over the trust assets, these assets are not legally separated from you.

Irrevocable trusts, on the other hand, have been recognized by virtually every U.S. court to be separate from the estate of the individual who established the trust. Assets in a properly-structured irrevocable trust cannot be seized to satisfy a judgement or seizure order.

However, there are situations in which an irrevocable trust may be invalidated by creditors or (particularly) the IRS, which may be able to invade the trust when no other creditor can. The most common attacks include:

✓ *Claims that the trust assets were conveyed in a manner violating federal and/or state "fraudulent conveyance" statutes.* If the IRS is seeking to collect a past tax liability, it will claim that the liability occurred before the trust's creation, even if has not yet assessed any tax. The IRS can make such a claim as long as three years after the tax returns were filed (or due, if none were filed)--six years if it is alleging a 25 percent or greater understatement of income or seven years if it is alleging fraud. In addition, it can claim that any tax liability incurred as long as one year after the trust's creation is collectible.

✓ *Claims that the trust was created only to avoid existing or future creditors and is a sham.* This attack is most frequent if you incur a liability, particularly if the transfer leaves you insolvent, or if you declare bankruptcy one year or less after creating the trust.

✓ *Claims that the trust is a sham because there is no true separation between trust and the person who created it.* If you live in a house transferred to an irrevocable trust, but fail to pay fair market rent for its use, or if trust income is used to pay personal expenses, etc., the trust can be attacked as a sham, or alter ego.

✓ *Claims that because of improper wording of the trust instrument, creditors are entitled to claim all or part of the trust assets.* The trust may state that the beneficiary will receive *mandatory* payouts of income (as well as trust principal) if needed for support, illness, emergency, etc. This can make it possible for creditors, particularly government agencies, to attach trust assets for a *beneficiary's* liabilities.

For instance, the trust instrument may state that the "trustee *shall* distribute trust income (or principal) to the beneficiary" at the trustee's sole discretion if any of these situations develop. Unfortunately, courts have ruled that creditors (and government agencies in particular) are entitled to receive the *maximum amount* that could be received by the beneficiary. Government agencies employ similar attacks in seeking to attach trust assets after the trust creator has applied for Medicaid or other governmental assistance, or is alleged to have incurred a tax liability.

A better word to use is "may" instead of "shall" or "will." Other protective language is also required for successful asset protection.

An irrevocable trust carefully drafted to avoid these challenges should survive an IRS attack. For instance, a Tennessee man recently prevailed against the IRS and two other creditors that sought to attach his trust assets. He transferred assets to the trust two or three years before unexpected liabilities occurred. The assets included a personal residence, other real estate holdings, and investments valued at $700,000. Under a written lease agreement, he paid fair market rental for the use of the house. There was thus no doubt that the arrangement was an "arm's length" one.

While the liabilities had rendered him practically penniless, the trust assets were secure. After six months, the IRS and creditors conceded there was no way to pierce the trust. Of further interest is the fact that his attorneys strongly opposed creating the trust.

One hybrid asset protection technique consists of forming a corporation and placing the corporate stock into an irrevocable trust. To provide even greater protection, you could form several trusts. For instance, you could place corporate stock into a trust set up for your spouse, and other assets into a trust set up for your children. A third trust might be set up to hold a portion of your assets jointly for you and your spouse. If one trust is seized, others would continue to protect at least a portion of your assets.

Some attorneys structure irrevocable trusts that permit you to maintain some degree of control over how the assets in the trust are invested. But be careful! If you have access to the trust assets, or benefit from them outside a true arm's-length arrangement, a litigant will be able connect you to those assets, and persuade a judge to seize them. For instance, if you transfer your home to an irrevocable trust, but fail to pay fair-market rent to the trust for the use of the home, the arrangement might be dismissed as a sham.

A trust set up in a foreign country offers even more protection, but can be expensive to create and to maintain. For more information, see "Advanced Offshore Investment Strategies," Chapter 9.

3. *Family limited partnerships.* These structures can be very effective in protecting assets from both litigation and seizures. They can be used either by themselves or in combination with other structures. For instance, you can form a corporation and transfer the stock into one or more family limited partnerships.

The ideal arrangement is for the corporation itself to serve as the general partner. An even more effective strategy is to appoint a corporate general partner not connected to you in any manner. You, your spouse, and your children then become the limited partners and hold the remainder of the partnership's assets in this form.

The asset-protection features of a limited partnership derive from partnership laws that date back more than 75 years. While a creditor can seize the partnership interest of a general partner, it can obtain only what is known as a "charging order" against the limited partners in a limited partnership. This order represents only a right to assets when and if they are actually distributed.

The charging order does not give the creditor the right to dissolve the partnership or to force the general partners to make a distribution. With a creditor waiting, the partners need not be in any hurry to make distributions. Moreover, if the creditor isn't the government, the creditor actually has to pay income taxes on the distributions it hasn't yet received, according to IRS Revenue Ruling 77-137.

You can still receive monies from the limited partnership in the form of advances, loans, or any other benefit from the limited partnership which is not classified as a distribution which a creditor may be allowed to seize. In the meantime, the limited partnership can continue to carry on its business and enter into new ventures and business activities without being hindered by the creditor or its charging order.

A limited partnership is tax neutral, so it can't be considered a "sham" for tax purposes. Income or losses of the partnership is distributed to the limited partners in proportion to their limited partnership interests. However, your limited partnership interest (like other assets) can be gifted in portions, over time to your intended heirs. This has the advantage of not requiring any gift in cash, but only of a part of your limited partnership interest. This form of gifting has been confirmed by the IRS as an acceptable form of gifting for tax purposes.

Retirement plans are also subject to seizure by creditors and the government. A "pension limited partnership" (PLP) can be a useful way to hold such assets to make them difficult or impossible to attach. Your pension plan, IRA custodian or Keogh becomes a limited partner in a limited partnership that has a totally independent (i.e., not a relative or employee) person or corporation acting as sole general partner.

This independent general partner of the PLP can then invest your pension assets anywhere in the world. The documents of title evidencing the overseas investments; i.e., the share certificates, must be kept in the United States. Ordinarily, the plan custodian will hold them, but the general partner could maintain them as well.

If a creditor sues you, your IRA custodian, or pension plan trustee, each of you can legitimately state that the only asset held by the plan is limited partnership interest in the PLP. Once again, the only remedy for the creditor is to obtain a "charging order" against the PLP.

Obviously, this type of plan is best-suited for those who have control over their own pension plans. One attorney experience at setting up this type of plan is Peter Double. His address is in the "List of Suppliers" section of Appendix A.

There are two potential disadvantages to placing property in a limited partnership. The first is that a creditor (in particular the IRS) can challenge the transfer for up to seven years (if it is alleging tax fraud) after it takes place. The government has a number of legal options. Some of the most frequent challenges are based on state or federal "fraudulent conveyance" statutes. But after the statute of limitations expires, even the government's sole remedy is to obtain a charging order.

Furthermore, as in an irrevocable trust, for the transfer not to be dismissed in court as a sham, you may need to pay rent to the partnership for the continued use of the home. This rental payment is not tax-deductible, and the income to the partnership will flow through to you personally. On the other hand, the partnership can deduct repair expenses, depreciation, etc.

4. *Charitable trusts.* If your estate is a large one, you might consider forming a *charitable remainder trust*--another form of an irrevocable trust. While you must make a charity the ultimate beneficiary when both you and your spouse die, you can structure the trust so that you and your family are beneficiaries of the income the trust generates. This gives you the right to receive income from the trust as long as you live.

To provide your children with an inheritance, you can purchase a life insurance policy with a portion of this income. After both you and your spouse have died, the life insurance monies are paid out to your named beneficiaries free of estate taxes. The premiums can be part of your annual $10,000 "free of gift tax" allowance.

If the life insurance policy permits "pour in premiums", you can make a capital contribution to the policy. This will not affect your $10,000 gift allowance, or your $600,000 lifetime exemption. If you paid all the premiums by the capital contribution, the premiums are discounted. The monies for such capital contribution could be borrowed against your other life policies.[133]

A creditor seeking to attach the underlying assets will be faced with the unpleasant publicity of fighting a charity for control of the assets you have pledged to it, not to mention taking on a trust. Most creditors will not persevere in such efforts.

The reporting requirements for a charitable trust are quite complex. It should be set up only by a experienced professional.

5. *Business trusts.* One of the "hottest" asset protection techniques promoted in recent years is the business trust. This is a hybrid instrument that has elements common to both trusts and corporations. It is also known as the "Massachusetts trust," "common-law trust," "contractual company," "unincorporated business organization (UBO)," "constitutional trust," "business trust organization," and by many other names as well.

Business trusts can be useful, but their benefits are often overstated by their promoters. Several promoters are currently engaged in publicizing the benefits of and selling so-called business trusts that have been dismissed as outright shams by the IRS, with heavy fines accruing to their founders (grantors). See "Defective Asset Protection Techniques," this chapter, for details.

It is critical that you obtain the advice of a qualified attorney when transferring personally-owned assets into a corporation, trust, or limited partnership. It is best to consult with a specialist in such structures, since the laws in this area are exceedingly complex. In particular, you should avoid any asset transfer which could be construed as a "fraudulent conveyance," thereby nullifying the asset protection features that you seek. Generally, if you transfer assets *prior* to any judgement, bankruptcy, or attempted seizure, or before such actions are pending, the conveyance will not be considered fraudulent.

My newsletter, *Low Profile*, focuses on these topics. For a list of companies that specialize in setting up asset protection plans, please see the "List of Suppliers" section.

---

[133]Legislation introduced in 1992 would reduce the amount of money that can be transferred free of estate taxes from $600,000 to $200,000.

Defective Asset Protection Structures[134]

Recently, "xerox-copy" promoters claiming to be experts on trust law have sprung up throughout the United States like mushrooms from a well-stocked compost pile. Some cite a multitude of state and occasionally, federal court decisions as "proof" of the "legality" of such trusts, which, to the amateur, is impressive.

To the professional, however, most such legal references are irrelevant to the validity of such so-called trusts and whether they comply with U.S. tax laws. While a trust agreement may be considered legal under state law, the instrument and trust's operations may contain defects, thus failing to comply with federal income, gift, and estate (i.e., transfer) tax laws or provide any form of liability protection.

In most cases, these defective trusts are promoted under such high-sounding names as "pure," "equity," "constitutional," "family estate," "common law," "liberty," "apocalypse," "Massachusetts business trust," "business trust organization," "contractual company," "family preservation trust," and "unincorporated business company."

Promoters of such trusts misrepresent the law and conceal that courts have consistently ruled that such trusts were "shams," "lacking in economic substance," and "invalid" for tax purposes.

Most of these trust promotions evolved from the 1930-1960 schemes of disbarred Illinois attorney Harry Morgan Phipps. Several of these arrangements were struck down in the courts for failure to comply with various aspects of the 1954 Internal Revenue Code.

Of those claiming to have derived their trust "expertise" from Phipps, the best known is James Robert Walsh. In 1966, Walsh formed Americans Building Constitutionally (ABC) in 1966 to "Henry Fordize" the "tax-dodging specialties that were once associated only with millionaires." Subsequently, Walsh formed Trust, Inc. and Educational Scientific Publishers to escape the heat put on ABC by the government. Walsh also assisted John Bridston in the establishment of the Institute of Individual Religious Studies. In 1981, Walsh received a five-year prison sentence after pleading guilty to conspiracy to defraud the government.

Around the same time, other promoters appeared claiming to have derived their expertise from Phipps. These included Peter Taylor, Sr., of Apocalypse, Ltd., Karl L. Dahlstrom of the American Law Association, and Robert L. Preston of the Institute to Perpetuate the American Family. These individuals were followed by John Matonis with his Estate Guardian Trust and Gordon S. Buttorff of Constitutional Trust Associates.

---

[134]This section is adapted from William Comer's, *Freedom, Asset Protection and You*. This book is available through LPP's Nevada office for $69.95.

In 1978, Martin A. Larson published his manual on *How to Establish a Trust and Reduce Taxation* involving the Family Preservation Trust (FPT) and making claims nearly identical to the preceding groups. The Tax Court ruled that the Courtney Smith FPT was a "sham" and "not a separate taxable entity." In addition, the U.S. District Court ruled that the trust transactions were a "sham" and that the "trust is defective for violations of the grantor-trust provisions and for lack of substance." The District Court also issued a permanent injunction against such FPT promotions by Smith and his associates. Its decision and injunction were both upheld by the Fifth Circuit Court of Appeals.

Other self-proclaimed experts, some promoting similar domestic and offshore trusts, include: Lowell G. Anderson and Arthur P. Tranakos; Gerald J. Landsberger; Frank Forrester; Robert S. Chappell of Scientific Asset Management and Nassau Life Insurance Company; and Michael Jaworski and Paul Davis. Smith, Buttorff, and Landsberger were prohibited from making any further such promotions. Others, like Walsh, James Russell, Earl Schoof, Jaworski and Davis, were convicted of various criminal activities. Chappell was imprisoned for an unrelated criminal conviction in Indiana, and recently convicted of 96 counts of fraud involving other matters in New Mexico.

Despite this appalling record, dozens of new "experts" constantly appear promoting similar defective trusts. One is Leroy ("Roy") E. Fritts of National Trust Service from Sunnyvale, California. Fritts is marketing virtually identical trust documents to those he purchased from ESP in 1975, and making the same misrepresentations long ago shot down by all courts. After issuing their negative position in Revenue Rulings 75-257 through 75-260, the IRS has maintained a 100 percent "batting" record in taking more than 100 such trusts to court.

Taxpayers who claim Fifth Amendment privileges for their trusts quickly discover there is "no such privilege for an artificial entity, such as a trust." Those taxpayers who have transferred pre-tax personal service income to such trusts by various "contractual" devices, even when self-employed, have met with no success in the courts since 1977.

The major problem with these trusts is that the trust instruments are poorly drafted, contain language prohibited under established tax/trust law, and lack certain provisions required under these laws. They thus violate the grantor trust provisions of IRC Sections 674-677 and the estate tax provisions of IRC 2036 and 2038. However, the IRS's most successful attack has been to argue that such trusts are "shams" and/or "devoid of economic reality," starting with the *Markosian* case in 1980.

Claims that taxpayers can establish such trusts, transfer to the trust their personal residence and live in it rent-free are consistently denied by the courts. So are claims that the trust can pay transportation, medical, insurance, vacation and other expenses, tax-free. Taxpayers making such claims have been subject to negligence penalties and other sanctions.

Nor do such defective trusts provide estate tax savings. In one case, the value of assets transferred to such a trust were included in the estate at death under IRC Section 2036. In another instance, the court ruled that such a trust constituted a taxable gift under Treasury Regulations Section 25.2511-2(a).

Such trusts may not even avoid probate. Numerous state and federal courts have ruled they are invalid under state law. This means that the assets will be treated as if the trusts never existed.

In addition, the courts have repeatedly ruled that these trusts provide absolutely no liability protection against the claims of personal creditors or the IRS. Thus, the courts have allowed creditors, including the IRS, to seize the trust's assets for the individual settlor's personal liabilities.

Properly drafted and operated revocable, irrevocable, charitable, and on rare occasion, even business trust arrangements can be extremely beneficial. They will provide substantial gift and estate tax savings, and probate avoidance. In some cases, an irrevocable trust may provide minimal income tax savings, maximize privacy, provide substantial incapacitation protection, and maximize asset protection and estate preservation while maintaining control within the immediate family. But such benefits cannot be obtained through the foregoing grossly defective trusts.

When it comes to the promotions of combination domestic and foreign trust arrangements, the "compost pile" is even larger. Promoters claim to be experts on this unknown "secret" area of trust law used only by the "Super-Rich." Alleged benefits include: avoidance of income taxes, gift taxes, excise taxes on the transferred assets; avoidance of probate on trust-owned assets; and isolation of such assets from seizure by creditors, provided no violations of fraudulent conveyance statutes had occurred.

These arrangements go by such names as the contractual company, business trust organization (BTO), unincorporated business organization (UBO), common law trust organization (COLATO), pure trust, and many others. While several promoters claim "their" structure has been upheld by the courts, I have yet to find a single case supporting this assertion. Promoter after promoter is shot down by the government, along with their taxpaying victims.

Some of these promoters include: Karl Loren of the Bigelow Charter Society and Karl Loren Publications; Howard Pohrman, joined by Marsha Morris, of The Marketing Group; Association of Independent Business Managers (AIBM); Dave Hall, Hall-Hamill trust, re the American Institute for the Republic; Robert L. Strong, of System Two, Ltd; Robert Pine, of International Financial Estate Planning Trust; Larry Turpen of LAD Financial Services; Don Turner of First America Research; and Louis Mayer of Florida.

Promoters often point to the tax and trust laws of the foreign domicile as justifying their claims. However, these laws are basically irrelevant if the individual instituting a foreign trust arrangement is a U.S. citizen. Generally, any foreign trust arrangement established by a U.S. citizen

212

MUST be tax-neutral to pass muster by U.S. courts. The single major exception is a testamentary trust established at death.

While the instruments of defective foreign trusts vary, all are similar in basic format to the defective domestic trusts described previously. Typically, the promoters claim that if they establish enough "layers," they will eventually circumvent U.S. tax laws. The basic arrangements are as follows:

(1) The U.S. settlor (the individual funding the trust) establishes one or more domestic business trusts using a U.S. corporation or U.S. persons as trustees; (2) Net profits of Trust(s) #1 are distributed, allegedly tax-free, to Trust #2, which is a foreign trust created by a foreign person and which holds all units or shares in Trust #1; (3) Distributions received by Trust #2 are then distributed, also allegedly tax-free, to Trust #3, which is also a foreign trust created by a foreign person, and holds all units or shares in Trust #2; (4) Trust #4 (or a foreign corporation) is created to add another layer of "privacy." The claimed result of these arrangements is that the foreign trusts have no U.S. grantors, no U.S. trustees, and no U.S. beneficiaries, therefore allowing them to operate tax-free.

Trust(s) #1 files a Form 1041 (Fiduciary income tax return) reporting that all net income was distributed to Trust #2. Trust #2 files a 1041NR (non-resident) income tax return. While the return constitutes an acknowledgment that some, or all, of its income may have been "effectively connected to the operation of a U.S. business," Trust #2 allegedly owes no tax because of its distributions to Trust #3. Because Trust #3 received its income from Trust #2, which is not connected with the U.S. such income is allegedly "not subject to U.S. income taxes." Therefore, Trust #3 allegedly need not file a tax return.

The IRS has developed sophisticated guidelines for detecting foreign trusts and transactions related to them. IRS examiners are instructed to attack on the basis of substance vs. form; sham theory; assignment of income; disallowance of deductions under IRC 162; associations taxable as corporations; excise taxes on transfers of property; grantor trusts; gift taxes; and several others. Examiners are encouraged to raise other issues depending on the individual situation.

The sham and grantor trust challenges are perhaps the easiest to prove. Both state and federal courts have disallowed various "common law" or "business trust" arrangements as being nothing more than "legal nullities." If the trust is a sham, the IRS will contend that assets transferred to it are subject to ordinary income tax, estate tax, etc. Or if not a sham, that it violates the grantor-trust provisions of IRC 671-679 and/or that the transfer of funds to the trust is subject to excise tax and gift tax.

According to documents provided by Loren, and others, trustees are given absolute and unconditional discretion concerning property transferred to the trust, and have no enforceable obligations to the beneficiaries. However, the courts have found such arrangements invalid due to these extraordinary powers. Moreover, in *Zmuda*, the court held

213

that such "foreign" BTOs had "no economic substance and were nullities for tax purposes," and that they were mere "paper entities created solely to avoid taxes."

In determining the true status of a foreign trust for U.S. tax purposes, the IRS carefully scrutinizes how it is created. According to promoters of defective foreign trusts, a third party "settlor" creates (for instance) a BTO by transferring a certain amount of assets (usually $100) to the trust in "exchange" for all 100 capital units (e.g., trust certificate units, etc.), at which time, "the business trust is already in existence." Furthermore, in attempts to circumvent the grantor-trust provisions of IRC Sec. 671-679, promoters use third parties as so-called "creators" and "exchangers."

However, U.S. courts have not accepted such arrangements for 20 years, beginning with the *Bixby* case. More recently, courts have looked unfavorably at efforts by Americans to designate third parties in foreign countries as the settlors of foreign trusts. In *Zmuda,* followed by many others, the court held that, "We look beyond the name grantors to the economic realities to determine the true grantor." In addition, despite the claim that a third party is actually the settlor because of the transfer of $100, the courts have ruled that any person who transfers assets to a trust is a grantor (settlor) for tax purposes.

If the trust is not a sham, any arrangement by the true settlor to transfer assets to the BTO in exchange for the 100 capital units constitutes a gift (subject to gift tax) at full value of all assets valued in excess of $100. Furthermore, there is no statute of limitations when either a false gift tax return, or no return, is filed. If the value of the assets exceeds $600,000, a gift tax commencing at 34 percent is imposed on the fair market value that exceeds this exemption. In addition, this sets up the settlor for the imposition of the 35 percent excise tax, imposed on the difference between the cost and the fair-market value of the fixed assets (as represented by the trust certificates).

For instance, if an individual transfers $1 million in appreciated assets with a cost basis of $200,000 to the domestic BTO, then transfers the trust certificates to the foreign BTO, he is subject to the 35 percent excise tax on the $800,000 difference. His immediate excise tax liability is $280,000. In addition, he is subject to a 35% gift tax liability on a gift of $400,000, after subtracting the $600,000 exemption, leaving him with a gift tax of $153,000. The total excise tax/gift tax liability is a whopping $433,000.

Another claim made by promoters is that while the settlor should not be a trustee or beneficiary of the trusts he has created, he can be appointed by the so-called trustees as a "manager" entitled to a salary. Unfortunately, such arrangements are in violation of IRC Sec. 2036, applied whenever the settlor retains "the possession or enjoyment of, or the right to the income from, the property." If the settlor has retained too many "strings" attached to trust property, the value of these assets are included in his or her gross estate. Claims that settlors can maintain their lifestyles by receiving "intangible gifts tax free" and "tax free loans" have fallen upon equally deaf ears.

In addition, asset transfers to foreign trusts are reportable to the IRS under IRC Sec. 6048--a fact usually ignored by promoters. Furthermore, transfers in monetary instruments which exceed $10,000 must be reported on a separate form to the Customs Service. Failure to immediately report such transfers on the appropriate form(s) subjects the transferor to civil, and possibly criminal, penalties, and in the case of monetary instruments, forfeiture.

Fortunately, there are means to provide limited tax savings, and substantial liability protection, using safer alternatives such as tax-neutral foreign situs trusts. The courts have upheld their status repeatedly. So long as these structures are carefully constructed to avoid the foregoing traps, they are unquestionably effective. Readers with assets exceeding $1 million may want to seriously consider such trusts.

Chapter Nine

PRIVATE INVESTING
OUTSIDE THE UNITED STATES

If it weren't for the lies, distortions, and self-serving propaganda distributed by the government, the IRS, and the bankers, you wouldn't cringe every time you hear the term "offshore banking."

Most people don't have the foggiest idea of what offshore banking is. They accept the distortions they read in the controlled media and assume that offshore banking is some sort of criminal activity. Or they ask their lawyer, accountant or financial planner, and he, being as uninformed as they are, advises that it is too risky, illegal, immoral, or unethical.

The truth is that you as a resident of the United States, may legally move your money anywhere in the world that you want it. There is no restriction on the amount you move, where you move it, or how you move it. The only requirement imposed upon you by the U.S. government is that you must report any movement of cash or certain monetary instruments out of this country.

> *--Offshore Banking is Not Evil, by Jim Straw and Bob Riemke[135]*

Why invest outside the United States? Among the most important reasons are protecting your investments against the declining international value of the dollar and the opportunity to participate in markets not ordinarily accessible to U.S. citizens. In addition, many tax haven nations have low or non-existent taxes on many different types of income, even though taxes on such income must be paid by U.S. residents.

But an equally compelling reason is *financial privacy.* A handful of nations have policies or explicit legislation embracing financial secrecy for non-resident (but less often for resident) investors.

The oldest of such banking secrecy laws date back to the 1930s, when the government of Switzerland enacted a law prohibiting the nation's banks from releasing information on depositors. Many other nations enacted similar legislation after World War II. Today, 20 or 30 "tax havens" exist worldwide that cater to private investors.

Some of these havens, such as Panama, have less than savory reputations. Others, such as Vanuatu (the former Dutch New Hebrides) are politically unstable. And a number of other nations-- Egypt, Hungary, and Malaysia, for instance--are too new in the "tax haven business" to be seriously considered for private investing.

---

[135]Jim Straw and Bob Riemke, *Offshore Banking is Not Evil* (Dalton, Ga.: Worldwide Investment News, 1986)

Switzerland remains the largest tax haven in terms of foreign funds invested there. Other significant havens include Liechtenstein, Austria, Luxembourg, the Cayman Islands, the Channel Islands, Bermuda, the Turks and Caicos Islands, and the Bahamas.

How to Choose A Foreign Haven

Once you've decided to diversify your holdings overseas, the next step is to choose an appropriate place. Here are the questions to ask, according to the *Ron Paul Investment Letter*.

1. *How strict are the secrecy laws?* Surprisingly, few havens have unambiguous secrecy laws. Some countries only have a non-legal tradition of secrecy; others have "confidentiality" laws where the local government has access to records but is itself sworn to secrecy--a promise that may or may not be kept. Some have laws that are not always enforced; others have laws with loopholes. And not a few are tax havens without pretense to secrecy. Even if the haven has secrecy laws, banks may ask U.S. residents to waive secrecy protection, in response to pressure from the U.S. government.

2. *How long a tradition has the haven had?* The longer the tradition, the safer the haven. A country with several centuries experience, like Switzerland, or even several decades, like Luxembourg, won't be in as much of a hurry to change as havens like Vanuatu in the Pacific, which only recently proclaimed itself a tax haven.

3. *Does the haven status have local support? Do the haven's citizens also use the facilities?* There's a world of difference in this regard between the Bahamas, where locals seem resentful of the haven provisions, and Austria, where average citizens regularly use the completely anonymous "password account," and thus have a vested interest in its continued existence.

4. *Is the haven stable?* Any financial haven must also be a haven in non-financial ways. It must have a high degree of personal freedom. Of course, even free-market havens are not always stable. For example, Margaret Thatcher gave in to Red China's demands on Hong Kong, abandoning it to the 1997 deadline.

5. *Is it important to Washington?* Costa Rica, because it is a "friendly" nation in an unstable region, enjoys the favor of the U.S. government. Haven income is important to it and Washington won't want to lean too hard on it over a "non-strategic" issue. And, since the CIA uses Liechtenstein for its financial transactions, the U.S. won't seek to wipe out its haven status. The Cayman Islands, on the other hand, have no strategic value to Washington.

6. *Does it wave a "red flag"?* Public dealings with high-profile havens can raise a red flag in tax collectors' offices around the world. The Caymans, Panama and Liechtenstein are examples. Switzerland is in the second tier, and Austria and Luxembourg are another step below that

level. Bermuda is lower still, though it doesn't offer the secrecy the others do.

7. *Does it protect its sovereignty?* Has the haven caved in to the demands of the great powers, even in non-financial matters? The Dominican Republic has bank secrecy laws, but when ex-CIA agent Edwin Wilson travelled there incognito in 1983, U.S. agents were waiting for him, ready to hustle him back to the United States. There were no legal extradition formalities. U.S. agents operated in the Dominican Republic as they would in Kansas City. More recently, with the Marcos, Duvalier and Dennis Levine insider trading cases, Switzerland has shown that it is not quite as safe as was previously thought.

8. *How efficient and convenient are the services?* Are competent staffs available to serve the customer? How well do they speak English? Finally, how convenient is the haven to deal with? It's best to visit one's money periodically, and so much the better if it's in a place that one enjoys visiting.

9. *What taxes are levied on the haven's users?* The first requirement of a haven is that it offer capital preservation. Nonetheless, to include a haven country which scores heavily in capital preservation but which also has high withholding, corporate, estate or other taxes, is to ignore an important consideration.

Types of Offshore Investments

Before you open an offshore bank account, you need to choose the type of account and currency in which you wish to invest. My special report, *How to Open a Foreign Bank Account Close to Home*, describes some of your options:[136]

✓ *Checking accounts.*

Advantages:

- Low minimum deposits

- Possibility of capital gains from currency appreciation

Disadvantages:

- Generally pay no interest

- Possibility of capital loss from currency depreciation

✓ *Savings accounts.*

---

[136]Mark Nestmann, *How to Open a Foreign Bank Account Close to Home (3rd ed.)*. This report is available from LPP's Nevada office for $29.

Advantages:

- Some interest income, although less than you would earn with a CD

- Possibility of capital gains from currency appreciation

Disadvantages:

- Taxable income to declare on your tax return

- Possibility of capital loss from currency depreciation

- Some governments impose a withholding tax on the earnings from this type of account.

✓ *CDs.* These are generally written in the Eurocurrency market, where your funds are loaned to companies or governments at the current market rate prevailing in a particular currency. These CDs generally have terms from 90 days to one year.

Advantages:

- Much higher interest rates

- In most cases, no withholding tax

- Possibility of capital gains from currency appreciation

Disadvantages:

- Little or no recourse if the loan is not repaid; banks generally do not back Eurocurrency CDs. While most of these loans are safe, you should discuss with your banker your concerns for safety.

- You lose part of the interest if you cash in the CD before its maturity date

- Possibility of capital loss from currency depreciation

✓ *Eurobonds.* These instruments may be denominated in any currency. Their quality varies widely, and you should insist on an investment-grade rating to protect yourself. Maturities range from two years to 15 years or more.

Advantages:

- Can sell without sacrificing interest

- Many Eurobonds are rated by credit rating agencies. It is therefore easier to evaluate their safety than that of a CD.

- Possibility of capital gains if interest rates decline

- Possibility of capital gains from currency appreciation

Disadvantages:

- Possibility of capital losses if interest rates increase. The longer the maturity of the bond, the higher the risk.

- Possibility of capital losses from currency depreciation

- Possibility of default for lower-rated issues

✓ *Precious metal accounts.* Many foreign banks buy and sell precious metals. The bank stores the metals in its own vault or in a tax-free holding facility.

Advantages:

- No current income to declare on your tax return

- A precious metals account may not count toward the $10,000 reporting limit (ask your tax adviser)

- Very competitive prices on precious metal acquisition if your purchases are pooled with others

- Possibility of capital gains from increases in the prices of the metals

Disadvantages:

- No income, although you can usually borrow against your holdings to purchase investments that do generate income

- Storage fees (typically 0.375 percent of the value of the metals annually)

- Risk of commingling with bank's assets upon its liquidation unless the metals are held in your own name, rather than the name of the bank

- Possibility of capital losses from decreases in the prices of the metals

✓ *Investment accounts.* These usually consist of mutual funds in stocks, bonds or commodities operated and managed by the bank itself. The funds may target a single country or many different countries. Larger banks may be able to purchase individual stocks or bonds for you.

Advantages:

- No withholding tax

- Potentially better return on investment

- Potential to defer gains if no dividends or interest are credited to the account, but are reinvested

- Possibility of both capital gains and currency gains

- Purchases can often be made in street name; the bank's name (not yours) is tied to the transaction.

Disadvantages:

- High minimum investments (typically, US$20,000 or more)

- Potentially high front-end commissions (up to 8 percent or more)

- Potentially high management fees (typically 1 percent-2 percent annually)

- Possibility of both capital losses and currency losses

√ *Managed accounts.* Larger deposits may be individually tailored to your own investment objectives.

Advantages:

- Potentially higher profits from both currency gains and capital gains

- More personalized attention to your investment objectives

Disadvantages:

- High minimum investments (typically, $100,000 or more)

- Potential for both currency losses and capital losses

- High management fees (typically 2 percent-3 percent annually)

√ *Trust accounts.* In this type of account, you set up a trust on behalf of a beneficiary. This can involve complex tax planning, but for large estates, it can provide significant tax and privacy advantages.

Advantages:

- Maximum asset protection potential against litigation

- Potential estate tax and income tax reduction if structured properly

Disadvantages:

- Complicated and expensive to set up and maintain

- High minimum investments

- Potential "red flag" to the IRS

Offshore Investing: Risks and Rewards

While there are excellent opportunities in international investments, there are risks involved. You should no more suspend your judgement in evaluating an offshore investment than you would in the case of a domestic one. Skepticism is a healthy trait when it comes to any investment, particularly those that appear to be "too good to be true."

✓ *Risk #1: Changing currency values.* The success of any offshore investment depends on the relative values of the currency in which you wish to redeem your investment vs. the value of the currency in which your investment is denominated.

The "best of both worlds" offshore investment is denominated in a currency that is rising against the dollar, and is itself rapidly appreciating in value. When you redeem your investment in dollars, not only have you profited from the investment itself, but made an additional profit from the gains the foreign currency has made against the dollar.

German government bonds can serve as an example of this ideal situation. If you had purchased these bonds in 1985, their dollar value would have doubled by early 1991 due to the increasing value of the German mark vs. the U.S. dollar. Your six-year return on investment, including interest payments and the appreciation of the currency, would have been more than 140 percent! And this in an investment guaranteed by one of the world's most conservatively-managed central banks.

German government bonds can also serve as an example of the "worst of both worlds" offshore investments. If you had purchased these bonds in January 1991, you would have lost nearly 25 percent of your investment in the next four months. During that four-month period, the dollar soared against the German mark, and German interest rates rose, depressing the values of the bonds.

✓ *Risk #2: High commissions.* It is fundamentally expensive for Americans to deal overseas. Most Americans can expect to pay *double commissions* on any offshore investment if they buy through a U.S. broker. The reason is simple: To execute trades, the U.S. broker must go through a foreign intermediary, which also takes a chunk of your funds as a commission. For instance, for purchase of a mutual fund operating on the London Stock Exchange, your broker could place the order through a British broker. The British company, of course, would insist on being compensated for its time and trouble.

While the double commission problem can be sidestepped by dealing with a trusted overseas broker, most U.S. investors don't have the resources to allow them to personally interview a series of prospective investment advisors. One solution is to deal with a bank in an offshore haven that has a universal banking system; one where banks are permitted to serve as investment brokers. Most of the havens described in this report have universal banking systems.

✓ *Risk #3: Scam artists and shady or uninformed promoters.* While I can't provide a formula for avoiding all such risks, I can alert you about what to avoid. Some of the worst scams are promoted by companies promising almost-unbelievable returns on investment in "total secrecy." Costa Rica and Panama have been a favored operating locale for many of these scams, although a few have even operated out of conservative Switzerland.

I can't emphasize enough that you need to exercise at least as much (if not more) due diligence when you evaluate an offshore investment as you would a domestic one.

✓ *Risk #4: Lack of information.* How do you keep appraised of the value of your offshore investments? Most foreign banks provide (at most) quarterly statements of value; some only send you an annual summary. Or you might prefer not to receive regular correspondence from the bank to protect your privacy. To keep up with the progress of your investments, the best advice is to keep them simple, so that calculating their value involves nothing more than checking currency values, stock prices, interest rates, etc. in a newspaper or investment magazine.

✓ *Risk #5: Changing government laws and regulations.* Here at home, Congress could at any time ban offshore investing, or demand that investors with overseas interests repatriate such investments within a short period of time. I don't consider this likely, since an outright ban on overseas investing would paralyze many portions of the economy. More likely, Congress and the IRS will simply continue to make it more difficult to invest outside the United States with any degree of privacy.

But if such legislation were enacted, you would need to make a decision--whether to obey the law or to risk fines or imprisonment as a lawbreaker. (It is extremely unlikely that the IRS could force an overseas bank to send it the proceeds of your investment--at least for the time being.)

You can also count on more calls from Congress and the IRS to force U.S. residents to provide information about their offshore accounts to grand juries and other investigative bodies. In a 1988 decision, the Supreme Court ruled that prosecutors may compel the target of a grand jury investigation to provide written authorization so foreign banks will disclose records of the target's accounts there (*Doe vs. U.S.*, 86-1753).

For these reasons, you will want to construct a "cover" for your offshore investments that would legitimize them in the eyes of the government should foreign exchange controls be imposed or these investments be banned, or if you become the target of an investigation. For instance, if you decided to invest in the Bahamas, you might want to start a small business there, or purchase a condominium. My special report *How to Open A Foreign Bank Account Close to Home* contains additional ideas on constructing such a cover.

I think it would be quite unlikely for the government to ban legitimate businesses from operating overseas, or restrict the right of Americans to own property outside the United States. Too many of the richest and most powerful bureaucrats in Washington, D.C. do so. For instance, according to the *Offshore Financial Review*, published by London's *Financial Times*, Nicholas Brady, former U.S. Treasury Secretary, is a frequent traveller to the Bahamas. He even owns a home in Lyford Cay, where prices start at around $5 million.

Does Mr. Brady own property in the Bahamas simply to enjoy the warm weather? Or does he (perish the thought!) use the Bahamas as an offshore financial center, just like tens of thousands of other law-abiding U.S. citizens?[137]

The U.S. government is not the only potential source of problems. The laws in the haven you choose may change, or your funds might be frozen outright, or converted into a less attractive form. A classic example occurred in 1982, when Mexico converted U.S. dollar accounts held by foreigners to peso accounts, which rapidly depreciated against the dollar. Investors in these accounts lost almost their entire investment in U.S. dollar terms.

Switzerland: The Quintessential Haven

Middle-class taxpayers are showing increasing interest in Swiss banking accounts. Most are attracted by the Swiss government's stiff banking

---

[137]"Where Sun, Tax Freedom, and the U.S. Treasury Meet," *Offshore Financial Review*, September 1992

secrecy laws. In other words, they want to evade their federal income taxes.

--Orlando Sentinel, May 31, 1988

My personal experience with those who invest in Swiss banks is that they have no intention of evading federal income taxes. They simply wish to avail themselves of international investment opportunities, protect a portion of their assets from judgement or confiscation, or escape from the collapsing U.S. banking system. But our government seeks to discredit such depositors, and the media, as expressed by this excerpt from the *Orlando Sentinel,* routinely echo these sentiments.

This mountainous nation in the heart of Europe is synonymous with not only banking privacy and investment savvy. Voltaire is quoted as having said:

> If you see a Swiss banker jump out a window, follow him, for there is surely money to be made.

Voltaire's comment, made in the 1790s, reflected not Switzerland's reputation as a privacy haven, but the enormous knowledge and integrity of its bankers. Two hundred years later, that knowledge, and that integrity, have not changed. Today, Swiss banks manage nearly $1 trillion in private funds.

Switzerland has a centuries-long tradition of financial privacy. But formal bank secrecy laws date from only 1934. They were adopted in response to inquiries from Gestapo agents inquiring at Swiss banks into the financial affairs of German nationals. Since at the time having a foreign bank account was a capital crime in Germany, Swiss bankers who revealed such information to the Gestapo were in effect sentencing their depositors to death.

Swiss banking secrecy laws cover every conceivable person--bank employee or not--who might have access to personal information about a bank customer. Bank employees, auditors, regulators and anyone else with access to bank data are required to maintain silence regarding bank accounts. Not only are such individuals prohibited from disclosing account balances, but they may not even acknowledge that an account exists.

Penalties are strict for those violating bank secrecy laws. Each breach of secrecy is punishable by a fine of SFr 50,000 (about $32,500) or six months imprisonment.

Secrecy may be waived at the client's request, or if the Swiss government has evidence that a crime has been committed. Should the crime have taken place outside of Switzerland, the law requires that the offense also be considered a criminal offense in Switzerland. Tax evasion, for instance, is a civil, not a criminal, offense in Switzerland. Nor are violations of other nations' foreign exchange laws or laws regarding the reporting of certain investments criminal offenses in Switzerland.

If evidence exists that a depositor in a Swiss bank has committed a crime in another country that is a criminal offense under Swiss law, the government can try to get a court order forcing the bank to release information relevant to the crime under investigation. When a judge grants a court order, the government may examine only those bank records related to the crime under investigation. "Fishing expeditions" are expressly prohibited. Unlike an IRS "investigative summons," a Swiss court order requiring breach of bank secrecy is rarely granted.

In the past 20 years, Swiss banking secrecy has been relaxed considerably. In 1984, a Swiss banker, Maurice Aubert, wrote an article entitled "The Limits of Swiss Banking Secrecy Under International Law," observing that "over the past decade, the scope and practical effect of Swiss banking secrecy have been so significantly reduced that the remaining criticism [of banking secrecy] is attributable largely to misunderstandings based on inadequate information."[138]

Incidentally, the "numbered" accounts for which Swiss banks are famous do exist, but provide no additional statutory privacy protection. Their only difference from an ordinary Swiss bank account is that only a few top officials of the bank know the depositor's name. The bank's remaining employees only have access to an account number. Such accounts aid in securing the privacy of well-known depositors, but can be obtained only after convincing bank management that such an arrangement is necessary. Contrary to popular belief, Swiss "anonymous" accounts do not exist.

Because of Switzerland's relatively high profile as a secrecy haven, the United States and other nations have made relaxation of Switzerland's bank secrecy laws a top priority. Under U.S. pressure, Switzerland has adopted laws in recent years that make both money laundering and insider trading criminal offenses, thereby permitting bank records to be released to foreign authorities if evidence of such offenses having been committed by a depositor exists. In 1991 Swiss police arrested an U.S. citizen carrying more than $500,000 in cash in response to a U.S. warrant alleging money laundering and delivered that individual into U.S. custody.

Switzerland's enforcement of anti-laundering laws and international agreements has accelerated sharply since 1990. In June 1992, Switzerland's Federal Banking Commission issued guidelines requiring banks to report any *suspicion* of money laundering to Swiss law enforcement authorities. The next month, Switzerland endorsed the findings of the Basle Committee on Banking Supervision, including its recommendation that bank regulators should use their "best efforts" to share information with each other.

Then in October 1992, a new diligence code went into effect lowering the limit for anonymous cash transactions from SFr 100,000 to SFr 25,000. The diligence code also makes it a criminal offense for any person who in accepting, managing, investing, or transferring a third party's assets does not identify their beneficial owner and maintain accurate records of the transaction(s). This regulation covers not only the Swiss banking industry, but Swiss attorneys, fiduciaries, money managers, etc. It has the effect of banning "nominee" or "Form B" accounts, where funds are held in the name of a trust or an attorney, not an individual, and are known only to a Swiss accountant or attorney.

Still, the average American with a Swiss bank account, even an American deliberately evading U.S. taxes, is in little danger of being exposed by Swiss authorities. Even if he is exposed, a bank account in Switzerland is nearly impossible for the IRS or any other government agency to impound. Five years after the death of Ferdinand Marcos, the Philippine government that Marcos had once overseen as dictator has been unable to recover any of the billions of dollars he allegedly transferred illegally to Switzerland.

The best it could do was to get Marcos' widow to "voluntarily" transfer funds back to the Philippines. But the Philippine government will not have access to the funds until judicial proceedings determining the true ownership of the funds are complete. (On the other hand, the Swiss government took the unprecedented step of freezing Marcos' assets before it even received a formal request from the Philippine government.)

Moreover, there are limits to how far the Swiss will go in relaxing bank secrecy. In 1991, Swiss authorities broke off tax treaty talks with the United States because of a Swiss refusal to consider exchanges of information on taxpayers. The stated purpose of tax treaties is to assist taxpayers in avoiding duplicate tax payments, and many are already in effect between the United States and

---

[138]Maurice Albert, "The of Swiss Banking Secrecy Under International Law" (*International Tax and Business Lawyer*, vol. 2, 1984)

Switzerland. But the U.S. Treasury also finds them convenient for fishing expeditions, which Swiss law expressly prohibits.

In addition, the Financial Action Task Force, set up by the G-7 group of the world's seven leading industrial nations, wants Switzerland to ratify the United Nations Convention Against Illicit Traffic in Narcotic Drugs and Psychotropic Substances. Among other initiatives, this treaty calls for banning all efforts to disguise money movements, even if the funds are legitimately earned

Will banking secrecy continue in Switzerland indefinitely? While there is no immediate threat, in the longer term, it seems inevitable that banking secrecy laws will be eased further, despite a 1984 referendum that endorsed their continuation by a 2:1 margin. Pressure from a vocal minority of its population, from the United States, and from the European Community make it likely that over the next decade or two, Switzerland will become less attractive as a secrecy haven than it is today.

Perhaps the most significant pressure for Switzerland to relax bank secrecy is economic. Switzerland depends on free trade for its prosperity, and applied to join the European Community in May 1992. The EC has adopted uniform banking policies that restrict bank secrecy. EC membership will force Swiss banks to follow the cash-reporting and anti-laundering policies set by the EC Banking Commission. Several of these policies (including the lower anonymous cash transaction limit I just mentioned) are already in effect.

However, in December 1992, Swiss voters derailed the momentum building toward full EC membership. By a razor-thin margin of 50.3 percent-49.7 percent, they opted not to join the "European Economic Area," an organization of non-EC nations that eventually plans to merge with the EC. Under Swiss law, a referendum passes only if both a majority of voters and a majority of Swiss cantons (states) vote in its favor. (Fifteen of 24 Swiss cantons rejected the proposal.) Switzerland values its sovereignty and will not permit any governmental or non-governmental organization to dictate to it. No wonder *The Economist* magazine, claims that one of Switzerland's biggest obstacles to joining the EC is that it possesses "too much direct democracy."[139]

The obstacle will hopefully be permanent. With the EC in disarray after the currency crisis of 1992, pressures may ease for Switzerland to join. Moreover, the price for joining may simply be more than most Swiss residents wish to pay. For instance, when Sweden applied to join the EC, it was asked for "specific and binding assurances" that it would fulfill obligations on "the framing of a common defense policy" and "the possible establishment in time of a common defense." I find it highly unlikely that Swiss voters, living in a nation with a 150-year tradition of neutrality, would ever consent to a "common defense policy" under the control of EC bureaucrats.

Even if Switzerland eventually eliminates banking secrecy, it will remain a very attractive financial haven due to its uniquely stable legal, fiscal and military status. For instance, the Swiss National Bank (SNB) has authorized printing 27 billion Swiss francs (SFr) of banknotes. The bank holds approximately 83.3 million ounces of gold. At a market price of SFr 500 ($325) per ounce, SNB's gold hoard has a value of SFr 41.6 billion. In other words, every Swiss franc banknote in circulation is backed 154 percent by gold.

When added to the SNB's currency reserves of $27 billion (80 percent of which is in currencies other than the U.S. dollar), the bank's total reserve position comes to about $54 billion--$9,000 for each of Switzerland's 6 million citizens. The comparable U.S. position, including gold reserves, comes to about $530 per person; only about 1/17th as much.

---

[139]"Switzerland Joins the Queue," *The Economist*, May 23, 1992

Swiss financial institutions are managed in an equally prudent manner. Under Swiss law, the securities portfolios of banks and insurance companies must be listed at market value. In addition, many Swiss financial institutions maintain huge "hidden reserves" not listed on their balance sheets.

This is definitely not the case with U.S. banks. In fact, in April 1992, the Fed quietly squelched a proposal from the General Accounting Office that would have forced U.S. banks to list securities portfolios at market value. And any U.S. bank that claimed to maintain "hidden reserves" would undoubtedly become the subject of a fraud investigation.

Finally, the high level of Swiss savings (second highest in the world; nearly $20,000/year per capita) and Switzerland's continued reputation as a "safe haven" virtually ensures its survival in a dollar collapse. The reality is that very few Swiss banks failed in the 1930s depression. Thousands of U.S. banks did. As a result, the Swiss franc is one of the world's strongest currencies. Since 1970, the value of the franc vs. the U.S. dollar has nearly tripled.

The Swiss government goes to enormous lengths to protect the integrity of its banking system, its currency and its territory. Switzerland actively protects its neutrality with its army and local defense forces. In both World Wars I and II, Switzerland demonstrated to Germany and the Soviet Union that it could not be easily conquered, and was left alone by both sides.

Today, Swiss army strength stands at 625,000. (A recent referendum to abolish the army was voted down by a 2:1 margin.) Every soldier is obliged to keep a loaded automatic rifle in his home, ready for instant use if the nation is invaded. Switzerland is also the only nation in the world where virtually every citizen would be protected in the event of a nuclear war. Most homes have bomb shelters, and new homes must be equipped with them.

There are many different types of accounts available in Swiss banks, corresponding to the list described in "Types of Offshore Accounts," this chapter. Switzerland imposes a 35 percent withholding tax for interest earned in many types of accounts. However, you may recover 6/7 of this amount upon application to the Swiss government, if you demonstrate that you have paid U.S. income taxes on these proceeds.

Swiss banks also offer many investments exempt from the tax, including Eurocurrency CDs, which generally pay considerably higher interest rates than savings accounts or investments in Swiss federal bonds. (See "Types of Offshore Investments," this chapter, for more information.)

The names and addresses of several Swiss banks appear in the "List of Suppliers" section.

Anonymous in Austria

A relatively low profile haven located in central Europe, Austria has bank secrecy laws than Switzerland, although they have been in effect only since 1979. Bank secrecy may be lifted only in connection with criminal proceedings, probate proceedings, or penal proceedings instituted because of "deliberate offenses against tax laws." This language makes tax fraud an offense justifying the lifting of secrecy, but not tax evasion.

Austria's secrecy law in some ways is even stricter than Switzerland's, particularly in calling for heavier penalties (one year in prison vs. six months in Switzerland) for unauthorized disclosure of account information. However, disclosure due to negligence is not a crime in Austria, as it is in Switzerland. Moreover, prosecution for an alleged breach of secrecy can take place only after a depositor's bank

227

makes a complaint. The victim has only six weeks to bring suit against the bank, and unlike Switzerland, he, not the government, must pursue the complaint.

Despite these limitations, Austrian banking secrecy is under attack by both the United States and the European Community. Since Austria is a relatively small country heavily dependent on export earnings, it is vulnerable to such pressure, particularly when applied within Europe. For instance, in 1991, Austria applied for membership in the European Community--a move government officials hoped would insure that the nation's traditional European markets would remain open.

However, an August 1992 opinion poll showed that only a small majority of Austrians wanted to join the EC. And Austrian officials have made it clear that it would never give up restrictions on the swapping of information about bank clients with EC authorities, unless evidence was presented the depositor was engaged in criminal conduct.

Once the application was in place, EC bureaucrats promptly told Austria it would have to abolish banking secrecy in order to join. Austria responded to the EC's request in January 1992 by tightening bank cash reporting requirements. Under these new regulations, Austrian banks must report cash deposits larger than AS200,000 (about $17,000), down from the previous requirement of $50,000. The new rules apply to deposits in any currency; previously, they had applied only to deposits in U.S. dollars. But it does not appear to violate Austrian law to "structure" your deposits into smaller amounts in an effort to avoid this reporting requirement.

However, in August 1992, Austrian authorities banned money laundering, defined as trying to disguise illegally-obtained money by placing it in the Austrian financial system. A new Austrian law banning insider trading took effect that same month.

Austria has demonstrated its seriousness in fighting money laundering on several occasions. In 1991, it participated in an international account freeze of funds deposited by deposed Panamanian dictator Manuel Noriega. More recently, it has begun freezing accounts allegedly connected to drug money. For instance, a U.S. attorney was arrested in Austria in 1992 for allegedly trying to withdraw drug money from an account that had been frozen. (He was acquitted by an Austrian jury.)

One reason that governments worldwide have attacked Austrian bank secrecy is because of the types of accounts that Austrian banks permit. For instance, the Austrian anonymous account ("sparbuch") provides total anonymity for the depositor. Almost every citizen in Austria has such an account. The account must be opened in person. Any future transactions must be keyed to a password that you choose. Your name is not associated with the account; only your password.

It goes without saying that you should not forget your password. If you do, or if you lose the passbook, you must publish the imaginary name of the account, your real name, and your account number in an official government newspaper before you'll be granted access to your funds. As you might imagine, the tax authorities of many different nations subscribe to this publication.

Under Austrian law, only Austrian nationals can open an anonymous account. But in order to keep the account anonymous, bankers are not permitted to request any form of identification from the depositor. Not all banks offer anonymous accounts. Those that do won't set them up from anyone who does not speak German fluently. (Correction sheets for some fourth editions of this report incorrectly stated that sparbuch accounts had been abolished. They have not--although Austria is under great international pressure to do so, and a number of Austrian banks have stopped offering this service.)[140]

---

[140]A consulting firm based in the United Kingdom claims to offer a consulting service to set up a sparbuch account for non-Austrian residents. I do not know of anyone who has used this service, or if it is even legal for a U.S. resident to do so. For more information, contact Scope International, Ltd., 62 Murray Rd., Waterlooville, Hants PO8 9JL, Great Britain.

Another difficulty with the anonymous account is that taxes are deducted automatically on interest earned. In early 1993, the Austrian government raised withholding tax for this type of account from 10 percent to 22 percent.

Offering almost as much secrecy is a *numbered account,* where your identity is disclosed only for the purposes of opening the account. The government also imposes withholding tax on interest you earn, but as in Switzerland, investments are available that are exempt from the tax. Again, you must appear in person at the bank to open the account. All dealings with the bank from that point on require only that you submit your account number, not your name.

Of course, ordinary accounts where your name is known are also available at Austrian banks. You are still protected by Austria's strict secrecy laws, but you do not have to travel there in order to open the account in person.

Another potential threat to Austria stems from its location, Lying at the geographical center of Europe, Austria for centuries has served as a conduit for invaders from Asia, the Middle East, and of course, from Europe itself. Austria was occupied by German forces in 1938 and by the Soviet Union in 1945. It was not until 1954 that Austria regained independence. The breakup of the Soviet empire lessens the threat of another invasion, but if one were to occur, Austria's self-defense forces would be no match for a well-equipped invading army.

The names and addresses of several Austrian banks appear in the "List of Suppliers" section.

Other Tax Havens of the World

Many other nations have enacted laws that provide tax advantages and financial secrecy to individuals and companies doing business there. The banking systems in the havens described in this section all permit accounts in any freely-traded currency and generally provide higher interest rates than those available in the United States. And of course, *none* of these havens require banks to spy on their customers, as is now the law in the United States.

The Principality of Liechtenstein. Liechtenstein, a tiny central European haven, offers perhaps the most adaptable company law in the world. This is the likely reason, for instance, that the late billionaire financier Robert Maxwell chose Liechtenstein as the base for his holding company. The principality is an independent entity, but is largely dependent on the Swiss banking system. The Swiss franc is the official currency. Liechtenstein has strict bank secrecy laws and will not share tax information with any other nation, except in cases that involve criminal matters. It has signed only one tax treaty (with Austria).

However, as in other secrecy havens, Liechtenstein's tradition of inviolate privacy is under attack. The most recent challenges have come from unions defrauded by Maxwell, whose members now face inadequate or non-existent pensions. Liechtenstein has already relaxed its banking secrecy laws so as not to shield criminal gains, and outlawed insider trading. In addition, in December 1992, voters in Liechtenstein approved joining the European Economic Area--only days after the Swiss had turned down EEA membership.

There are several types of Liechtenstein companies; perhaps the best-known is the *anstalt* (trust), which one banking authority claims "can be adapted to be all things to all people." However, the IRS has resisted recognizing the anstalt as a legal entity, and some European courts have refused to do so as well. According to Thomas Azzara, writing in *Tax Haven Reporter,* Americans might be better served by setting up a domiciliary or holding company in Liechtenstein. There are no taxes on the dividends, capital gains or profits earned by a Liechtenstein domiciliary company, so long as the company does not develop business activities within Liechtenstein.[141]

Setting up a Liechtenstein domiciliary or holding company is not an inexpensive undertaking, but the flexibility of Liechtenstein company law, along with the privacy of its corporate structures, attracts wealthy investors (and spy agencies anxious to deal in complete secrecy) from all over the world.

Liechtenstein's association with Switzerland makes any threat to its sovereignty unlikely; the Swiss armed forces could be expected to step in to meet any anticipated threat.

The names and addresses of several Liechtenstein banks and firms capable of setting up Liechtenstein companies appear in the "List of Suppliers" section.

The Isle of Man. Located in the Irish sea between Great Britain and Ireland, and only a 90-minute flight from London, the Isle of Man boasts the world's oldest parliament, which has existed for more than 1,000 years.

While officially a possession of the English crown, the Isle of Man maintains its sovereignty with the exception of its currency, which is the British pound sterling. There are no capital gains taxes, death taxes, wealth taxes, capital transfer taxes or foreign exchange controls on the Isle of Man.

While no bank secrecy legislation is in effect in the Isle of Man, a strong custom of financial confidentiality prevails under the English common law. The parliament has scrupulously avoided signing any sort of reciprocal tax treaties with other nations. The single exception is the United Kingdom.

Among offshore investors, the Isle of Man is best known for its flexible company law. It is easy to incorporate there. There are no taxes on most types of corporate earnings, as long as the money is not earned on the Isle of Man itself.

Many insurance companies also do business on the Isle of Man. One of their most innovative products are single-premium policies which allow U.S. residents to make a one-time investment and have those funds accumulate tax-free. The investor can direct that his funds be placed into virtually any investment. One major disadvantage I've found with such arrangements is a stiff front-end load; typically 6 percent. Minimums for such policies start around $50,000.

A scandal which became public in 1990 raised questions over the commitment of the government to effectively regulate its burgeoning banking industry. The scandal involved the now-defunct Savings and Investment Bank, which offered unrealistically high interest rates in order to attract deposits. These deposits were in turn lent to high-risk borrowers. The cascade of high-risk loans eventually led to the failure of the bank. More than 3,000 depositors lost nearly $100,000,000.

The parliament has now taken strong steps to prevent a repetition of this bank's collapse. It has set up a banking commission to regulate banking activities on the island, and has also instituted an insurance scheme that protects 80 percent of deposits up to £20,000 (about $28,000).

The Isle of Man's historic association with Great Britain make a threat to its sovereignty highly unlikely; the British armed forces could be expected to step in to meet any anticipated threat.

The names and addresses of several Isle of Man banks, insurance companies, and firms capable of setting up companies there or in other jurisdictions appear in the "List of Suppliers" section.

---

[141]*Tax Haven Reporter* (P.O. Box CB-11552, Nassau, the Bahamas)

The Bahamas. The nearest haven geographically to the United States, the Bahamas' closest islands are located only 60 miles east of Miami. The Bahamas have one of the largest volumes of tax haven business in the world. The reason is easy to understand. There is no personal income tax, corporate income tax, capital gains tax, withholding tax, business tax, estate tax, gift tax, employment tax, sales tax, or probate tax in the Bahamas.

Until 1973, the Bahamas were a colony of Great Britain, but in that year, the islands became independent. The newly-independent nation soon enacted legislation establishing itself as one of the world's premier tax and secrecy havens. Strict bank secrecy laws and numbered accounts are available in Bahamian banks, but this haven has developed a relatively high profile in recent years as a result of well-publicized tie-ins with drug smuggling. Pressure on the Bahamas to relax banking secrecy has been unsuccessful, but some Bahamian banks now require U.S. depositors to waive confidentiality provisions.

One of the most attractive features of the Bahamas is the ease of incorporation there. Bahamian companies are permitted to use nominees to mask ownership, issue bearer shares, and take other steps to preserve the anonymity of the stockholders. However, the use of nominees to mask the true ownership of a corporation is not recognized by the IRS.

As with the Isle of Man, the Bahamas' historic association with Great Britain make a threat to its sovereignty in the future highly unlikely.

The names and addresses of several Bahamian banks appear in the "List of Suppliers" section.

Cayman Islands. The Caymans are the archetypical island paradise, located 500 miles from Miami, off the southwest coast of Cuba. In 1788, an English convoy foundered on the reefs off the Caymans (today world-famous as a snorkeling and scuba-diving mecca). Islanders rescued the passengers, including a relative of King George III. In gratitude, the king issued an edict giving the islands perpetual freedom from English taxation.

The tradition of no taxes has been maintained for more than two centuries. Like the Bahamas, the Caymans are a "no-tax" haven, and have no personal income tax, no corporate income tax, no estate tax, no gift tax, no inheritance tax, no sales tax, no duties, and no probate tax.

The Cayman bank secrecy act is similar to that of the Bahamas; in fact, the Cayman act was modeled after the Bahamian act. In addition, the Caymans have no tax treaties with any other nation, although in 1986, the nation did sign a "Mutual Legal Assistance Treaty" with the United States. However, the treaty specifically excludes tax offenses unless they involve the proceeds of crimes (primarily drug-related) covered by the treaty.

Because of its reputation, the Caymans have been the frequent target of the U.S. government. U.S. Customs agents routinely search baggage headed to and from the Caymans for cash. This crackdown has resulted in the arrest of thousands of Americans who face stiff penalties for failing to abide by the reporting provisions of the Bank Secrecy Act. This high profile was recently made even higher because of the Cayman's association with BCCI, which has a branch on the island. Assuming that you don't object to a haven with an extremely high profile, the Caymans have a great deal to offer.

As is the case with the Bahamas, the Cayman's historic association with Great Britain make a threat to its sovereignty highly unlikely.

The names and addresses of several Cayman banks appear in the "List of Suppliers" section.

Other European tax havens include *Luxembourg,* the *Channel Islands,* and *Campione.*

Luxembourg is located at the confluence of France, Belgium and West Germany. While bank secrecy laws date only from the early 1980s, Luxembourg has a tradition of banking confidentiality dating back to the years following World War I. Luxembourg does not withhold taxes on interest earned in bank accounts, a fact that makes it a popular destination for West Germans fleeing their nation's new withholding tax. However, Luxembourg's banking system is nowhere near as efficient or well-developed as that of Switzerland. And in response to the Bank of Credit and Commerce scandal, Luxembourg in 1990 enacted strict anti-money laundering legislation.

The Channel Islands are located in the English Channel a few miles off the coast of France. The most important of these islands are Jersey and Guernsey. The islands are close historically and geographically to Great Britain, but are not subject to British taxation. Many Swiss banks do business here in order to avoid high Swiss withholding taxes. It is also a popular jurisdiction for foreign trusts, because of relatively low administrative costs. However, no banking secrecy legislation is in effect.

Campione is a tiny Italian enclave totally surrounded by Switzerland. It owes its status to a rather unique stand-off between the two nations. Italy has never imposed taxes on Campione because Italian tax agents would have to pass through Switzerland in order to collect them. Switzerland, on the other hand, has no jurisdiction in Italy! As a result, Campione is a favored location for wealthy expatriates to live tax-free.

Other Caribbean tax havens are *Bermuda, Panama, Barbados* and the *Turks and Caicos Islands.*

Bermuda, while having no formal bank secrecy legislation, enjoys a tradition of confidentiality in financial matters, political stability and a much lower profile than most Caribbean havens. Taxes on non-residents are low or non-existent, and several Swiss banks have opened branches on the island.

Panama is one of the world's premier tax and secrecy havens. Unfortunately, the corrupt regime of Manuel Noriega openly consorted with money launderers and drug kingpins, leading to a 1989 invasion by U.S. military forces. The number one target, reliable sources tell me, were banking records. For the moment, I recommend avoiding Panama, not only because of the red flag it raises, but because it is home to some particularly vicious banking scams.

Barbados is the easternmost island in the West Indies. A large number of U.S. and multinational corporations have set up offshore subsidiaries to take advantage of its low tax rates. Company law in the Barbados is adaptable to many enterprises, and most companies owned by non-residents need not pay income tax or capital gains tax.

The *Turks and Caicos Islands* is one of the few remaining British crown colonies. It is a no-tax haven with a common-law court system and strict financial privacy laws. There is no central bank and the U.S. dollar is the official currency.

In recent years, many other nations have declared themselves tax and/or secrecy havens. They include Sri Lanka, Egypt, Mauritius, Grenada, Labuan in Malaysia, and several nations in Eastern Europe, including Hungary. U.S. authorities often tie foreign aid requests to the relaxation of secrecy laws, but, with the exception of Egypt, the amount of foreign aid flowing to these nations is negligible. However, I cannot recommend these havens until they have established a longer track record.

For additional information on offshore havens, I recommend *Tax Haven Reporter* newsletter, which cover developments in the Bahamas and other offshore havens. A good source for comprehensive background information is *The Encyclopedia of Offshore Banking*.[142]

How to Choose the Right Offshore Bank

Offshore banks come in all shapes and sizes. You may choose from a large bank, such as Swiss Bank Corporation, which has 14,000 employees and assets of $100 billion. Or you may choose a bank that exists as merely a "brass plate" in the sun on a Caribbean tax haven. Or anything in between.

Your first consideration should be the quality of service you expect. If you want to be in constant touch with the bank, and anticipate making investments in far-flung markets all over the globe, a large bank is probably most suitable. This is particularly true if you wish to target somewhat obscure or emerging markets in third-world countries. But if your only concern is maintaining a financial presence outside the United States, any offshore bank should be capable of accommodating your needs.

The next consideration is the minimum account balance. Some offshore banks (particularly private Swiss banks whose primary business is portfolio management) require opening account balances of $200,000 or more. But this is not typical. There are many offshore banks that will accept initial deposits of $10,000 or less. However, there are tradeoffs between the size of your initial deposit and the level of service you can anticipate. As is the case with U.S. banks, a $200,000 depositor can anticipate much more personal interaction and efforts on his behalf than a $10,000 depositor.

Another decision is whether or not to set up the account in person. It's always preferable to visit a bank before setting up an account relationship, but it is usually not mandatory. A personal visit provides both you and the bank a chance to get acquainted in a relaxed atmosphere. You'll also have an opportunity to educate yourself in the world of international investment by making such a visit.

If you decide to visit the bank personally, it is obviously more convenient to travel to one in relatively close proximity to your own location. For this reason, Caribbean havens are favorites of U.S. residents and corporations; European havens to European nationals.

A great deal has been written in recent years regarding the susceptibility of offshore banks with U.S. affiliates to having their records subpoenaed by U.S. government agencies. The IRS, the SEC, and federal grand juries have on many occasions sought banking records from the U.S. branches of a foreign bank. Based on the 1984 *U.S. vs. Bank of Nova Scotia* decision, the bank must comply, even if doing so violates bank secrecy provisions in its primary jurisdiction.[143]

An example of the sweeping impact of *Nova Scotia* occurred in 1986, when the Securities and Exchange Commission and the IRS forced the Bahamas Branch of Bank Leu, a large Swiss bank, to release information relating to suspected insider trader Dennis Levine. The bank originally cited Swiss banking secrecy laws as not permitting it to release the information. But after the agencies informed Bank Leu that all accounts in the bank's New York branch would be frozen if the records were not turned over, the bank capitulated.

---

[142]*Tax Haven Reporter* (op. cit.); *The Encyclopedia of Offshore Banking* (International Institute, 3601 S.E. Ocean Blvd., Suite 103, Stuart, Fla. 34996)

[143]This case and several other cases are described in Charles Thelen Plombeck, "Confidentiality and Disclosure: The Money Laundering Control Act of 1986" (*The International Lawyer*, Spring 1988, vol. 22, no. 1)

To save face, Bank Leu released the records under the pretense that the funds deposited by Levine had been obtained through insider trading, an activity that violated Switzerland's newly-enacted ban on this practice.

The *Nova Scotia* decision would appear to provide a powerful incentive to avoid foreign banks with U.S. branches. And in February 1992, the Supreme Court affirmed it by ordering Union Bank of Switzerland to hand over bank records held by its Panamanian subsidiary, denying the bank's appeal against a U.S. grand jury subpoena for the records.

Still, it seems highly unlikely that the average U.S. investor would be the object of a subpoena that would place his bank in the same situation Bank Leu found itself in 1986. Even avoiding offshore banks with a presence in the United States is not a panacea. Virtually every bank in the world invests in U.S. financial markets. Even without a U.S. presence, the government could shut down the U.S. investment accounts of an offshore bank if it desired to do so.

On the other hand, you'll almost certainly want to avoid the foreign branches of U.S. banks operating in tax haven countries. For instance, U.S. clients of the Zurich branch of Bank of America received in 1986 a letter which began:

> As an American bank operating in Switzerland, we are compelled to observe the laws and regulations as they apply to banking in the United States, as well as in Switzerland. Recently enacted IRS reporting regulations require that we report earnings on account relationships maintained for U.S. citizens or residents.

To its credit, Bank of America asked its U.S. customers to terminate their account relationships, rather than violate Swiss secrecy laws by providing the IRS with the requested information.

Keeping these factors in mind, I recommend that you write to the banks noted in the "List of Suppliers" section of this report, or to other banks that may have been recommended to you. Ask for an annual report (in English), account opening information, minimum balances, and the types of investments that are available.

You might also wish to enclose a copy of a letter from your U.S. bank addressed, "To Whom It May Concern" attesting to your good character and your account status. If your U.S. bank asks why you are requesting such a letter, simply tell them the truth--that you considering opening a new bank account. (You need not say it is outside the United States.)

You should also request that the bank disclose its equity-to-assets ratio and its liquidity. This information may be contained in the annual report, but is not always included. In the United States, the equity-to-assets ratios at even the strongest banks is seldom higher than 10 percent. Liquidity rarely rises above the 35 percent-50 percent range. But in Switzerland and some other nations that lack deposit insurance, banks are forced to compete on the basis of safety. Equity-to-assets ratios are often 15 percent or higher, and liquidity at some banks may actually exceed 100 percent.

Once you have assembled this information, you will need to make your choice. If you can, visit two or three banks personally to get a feel for their personnel and services.

Depending on the bank that you choose, you will be asked to complete a variety of account-opening forms. For a Swiss bank account, for instance, a U.S. citizen will be asked to complete and/or sign:

✓ An account application

✓ A signature card

✓ A general declaration of pledge (in the event you wish to borrow against your account or other assets placed with the bank)

✓ Mail forwarding instructions (in the event you wish to have correspondence held by the bank or sent to another address)

✓ Rules and regulations concerning deposits of precious metals and coins (in the event you wish to have the bank store precious metals on your behalf)

✓ A statement acknowledging that the bank may release information to the Securities and Exchange Commission if evidence exists that your account was involved in the misuse of inside information

✓ A declaration that you are acting on behalf of yourself, and are not an agent for another party. (If you are acting on another person's behalf, the bank is required under a new Swiss law to obtain this person's identity)

✓ A statement acknowledging the limitations of Swiss banking secrecy law, and that if the bank receives information that you have committed certain criminal acts, bank secrecy may be waived

✓ A fiduciary agreement (for use when and if you want the bank to place time deposits with foreign banks in the bank's name as your agent)

Reportable and Non-Reportable Offshore Investments

Many people become terrified when they discover that if they open one or more bank accounts outside the United States, Uncle Sam wants to know about it. The original version of the Bank Secrecy Act required U.S. citizens holding more than $1,000 in one or more "foreign financial accounts" outside the United States to report them on their federal income tax return. This reporting threshold has now been raised to $10,000.

In truth, terrifying things start to happen only if you *don't* report the presence of these accounts. Not filing can result in stiff fines, even imprisonment. At one time, the IRS did not generally criminally prosecute taxpayers who did not report the presence of such accounts when they were required to do so. This is no longer the case. For instance, in October 1992, a Michigan physician was sentenced to nine months in jail and fined $50,000 for not reporting a foreign bank account from 1986 through 1989.

The IRS does not make it easy to report foreign bank accounts. You must do so on Schedule B, not on Form 1040. Instructions for 1992's Form 1040, Schedule B, Part III, state that you must check "yes" on line 11a if either (1) or (2) applies:

1. At any time during the year you had an interest in or signature or other authority over a financial account in a foreign country (such as a bank account, securities account, or other financial account).

However, you may check "no" on line 11a if the combined accounts were $10,000 or smaller for the entire year. Other exceptions apply to officers or employees of commercial banks or large domestic corporations for accounts in which they have no personal financial interest.

2. You own more than 50 percent of the stock in any corporation that owns one or more foreign financial accounts.

If you answer yes on line 11a, you must also file Form TD F 90-22.1 by June 30 of the following year. This "Foreign Bank Account Reporting Form," or FBAR, goes directly to a Treasury Department intelligence center in Detroit. FBAR data then is transmitted to the Treasury Department's Financial Crimes Enforcement Network (FinCEN). According to *FinCEN Trends* newsletter, 116,000 Americans filed FBARs in 1991.

However, the instructions for Part III of Schedule B and Form TD F 90-22.1 are, to put it mildly, ambiguous. The definition of a "foreign bank account" or "foreign securities account" appears clear enough. But just what is an "other foreign financial account?"

And if you wouldn't otherwise be required to file Schedule B, would you need to complete it simply to check "yes" on line 11a? The instructions don't say. (You must complete Schedule B each year you earn more than $400 in interest or dividend income.)

In addition, is there a $10,000 exemption for reporting the foreign bank accounts of a domestic corporation in which you hold 50 percent or more of the stock on your personal tax return? Neither the instructions for Schedule B nor those for the FBAR say anything about an exemption for corporate accounts less than $10,000. On the other hand, instructions for Form 1120 (corporate income tax return) provide the same $10,000 exemption for corporations as for individuals.

Moreover, do both corporations and individuals enjoy a separate $10,000 exemption? In other words, if you have signature authority over both foreign personal accounts under $10,000 and corporate accounts under $10,000 (and you own 50% or more of the stock of the corporation), but the combined total of the personal and corporate accounts exceeds $10,000, do you need to check yes on line 11a and complete a FBAR for both sets of accounts? Again, neither form's instructions give any clue to the answer.

Finally, how much of a "red flag" does checking "yes" on line 11a and completing a FBAR raise to the IRS? Are you more or less likely to become the target of an IRS audit?

To learn the answers to these questions, I turned to attorney Ron Rudman, senior partner in Engel & Rudman, the firm that first introduced the tax-neutral "foreign security trust" into wide use in the United States. (The address is published in the "List of Suppliers.") Rudman told me the following:

✓ The "foreign financial account" statement on the Schedule B instructions exists because of the variety of financial institutions outside the United States. However, instructions for the FBAR state (Section F) the following:

> The term "other financial account" means any other account maintained with a financial institution or other person who accepts deposits, exchanges or transmits funds, or acts as a broker or dealer for future transactions on (or subject to the rules of) a commodity exchange or association.

This definition excludes several types of foreign investments from reporting, including real estate, insurance policies, safety deposit boxes, custodial arrangements outside a bank, and stocks, bonds, or mutual funds that you purchase without opening a brokerage account. Of course, you can also accumulate foreign currency in the United States without it being considered a "foreign financial account." This is an excellent option for those who want investment diversification outside the dollar, but who would rather not open a foreign bank account, or lack the means to do so.

✓ You must complete Schedule B to indicate the presence of a reportable foreign account, even if you would not otherwise be required to do so because of insufficient dividend and/or interest income.

✓ The instructions for Schedule B imply that if you hold 50 percent or more of the stock in a domestic corporation with a foreign bank account of any size, you must report its presence. However, this contradicts instructions for Form 1120, the corporate tax return. The $10,000 exemption exists for corporate accounts as well.

✓ Individuals and corporations enjoy a separate $10,000 exemption. For example, if you have signature authority over foreign bank accounts totalling more than $10,000, but neither corporate or personal accounts exceed this threshold by themselves, they need not be reported on either your personal or corporate return.

✓ Checking "yes" on line 11a and completing a FBAR only raises a red flag if the size of the accounts is considerably larger than your declared income might otherwise indicate. For instance, if you declare income of $50,000/year, but disclose that you have $750,000 in foreign accounts, this might raise a few red flags. On the other hand, a foreign bank account only slightly larger than the reportable maximum would not necessarily draw undue attention from the IRS.

However, the head of the IRS international compliance office stated recently that tax returns with foreign transaction forms attached would be reviewed by an IRS employee to see if they warranted further investigation.

Penalties for non-compliance with the FBAR filing requirements are defined in USC Sec. 5322 (a) and (b) and USC 31 Sec. 1001. Sec. 5322 applies to penalties for not reporting the transport of $10,000 or more of monetary instruments across a U.S. border. Willful violations may be punished by a five-year prison sentence and/or fine not to exceed $250,000. USC 31 Sec. 1001 adds the possibility of felony prosecution under the false statements statute (if, for instance, you check "no" on line 11a when you should have checked "yes").

Since a tax return isn't the same as a Currency Transaction Report, and doesn't involve either an effort to avoid currency reporting requirements at a domestic financial institution or at the U.S. border, placing your assets in non-reportable offshore investments does not appear to constitute structuring. (See "The 'Crime' of Structuring," Chapter 7.)

You can use the $10,000 exemption in a number of creative ways to control assets worth many times this sum. For instance, you could deposit $7,000 in your foreign bank account, and then pay a personal visit to your bank and use the money to buy gold coins. This need not be a major sacrifice; for instance, you could visit your Bahamian bank in January, for instance. Store the coins in your safety deposit box at the bank. Then deposit another $7,000 in the account. You now have $14,000 offshore, but only half that amount in a "foreign financial account." The entire $14,000 is therefore non-reportable.

To keep your foreign investments non-reportable, you must maintain personal control over these assets. If a bank keeps track of them on your behalf, clips coupons, or performs similar duties, the IRS could argue that an account relationship existed that you are obliged to report.

Moving Your Money Privately

I include this section only to show how preposterous the whole anti-laundering campaign really is, and to help you obey the law, instead of inadvertently falling afoul of it. Any criminal can use these methods, but these laws are not aimed at criminals. They are aimed at honest citizens who think they deserve some privacy.

Now that the Annunzio-Wylie Anti-Money Laundering Act of 1992 has been adopted (Chapter 7), some of these strategies may be illegal. But no one knows for certain. The wording of the law, as most laundering laws, is both sweeping and vague. No regulations have yet been issued to help interpret it.

The new law prohibits any action to structure or assist in structuring the transfer of monetary instruments across U.S. borders to avoid reporting the transfer. Any property involved in a structured transaction is subject to forfeiture. My intent is not to encourage you to structure your international transactions, or to assist you in doing so. Rather, it is to help you obey the law, and avoid breaking it.

Please discuss the recommendations on the following pages with a qualified attorney to make certain you are not violating U.S. laws or regulations.

For the moment, it remains legal to move as much money out of the United States into a foreign country as you'd like. However, the Bank Secrecy Act requires any person transporting, causing to transport, or mailing more than $10,000 in cash or certain cash equivalents, or an equivalent amount of foreign currency, across a U.S. border to declare that fact to U.S. Customs.

But the instructions for Form 4790, the Customs Department form you must complete in this circumstance, state that: "A transfer of funds through normal banking procedures which does not involve the physical transfer of currency or monetary instruments is not required to be reported."

I don't advise violating the reporting requirements. The penalties for doing so are extreme, and the laws are strictly enforced, even for those who are unaware of them. If you are in doubt as to whether or not funds you are transporting or mailing across a U.S. border are reportable or not, it is best to report them. Otherwise, you risk their possible confiscation and prosecution for money laundering.

For instance, a Japanese national who immigrated to the United States failed to notify Customs that she was carrying her life savings in cash, which exceeded $10,000. There was considerable doubt the woman, who spoke little English, understood the law, or could even read the reporting form. In addition, there was no question that the funds had been earned legitimately. Nevertheless, the money was confiscated and the Justice Department prosecuted the woman for violating the Bank Secrecy Act.

Customs will seize your money even if you're just carrying a *little* over the reporting limit. In a 1984 case (when the reporting limit was $5,000, not $10,000) a man carrying $5,393 had the entire amount confiscated when he failed to declare it. He sued to recover the funds, but lost the case.

You should also take scrupulous care to complete the reporting form accurately. One man who declared the funds he was transporting across a U.S. border, but trusted a Customs official to list the currency denominations properly (the agent didn't) had the entire amount seized, although he wasn't criminally prosecuted. A federal court later upheld the seizure.

Until the passage of the Annunzio-Wylie Anti-Money Laundering Act, reportable cash equivalents included bearer stocks and bonds and monetary instruments in an immediately negotiable form (endorsed or made out to "cash," for instance). They did not include monetary instruments such as cashier's checks, money orders, or traveller's checks bearing restrictive endorsements (e.g., endorsed over to a third party). Without such an endorsement, these monetary instruments are reportable if their aggregate value exceeds $10,000.

I think the regulations issued to interpret the act will continue to exempt these latter instruments from reporting. The catch is that the very act of using them could in theory expose you to the charge of "international structuring." I don't believe the law would be interpreted in this manner, but it could be. This is simply another example of how open-ended, vague, and all-encompassing the anti-laundering laws are.

Customs Circular ENF-4-R:E:P, originally issued in 1976, makes a clear distinction between those monetary instruments which bear restrictive endorsements and those that do not. So does Form 4790. At present, these requirements are not as strict as the new *domestic* cash reporting requirements that took effect in February 1992. These domestic regulations apply to all monetary instruments, with or without a restrictive endorsements.

1. *Personal checks.* If you wish to avoid any appearance of impropriety in transferring funds overseas, a personal check is ideal. Transferring any amount of money abroad with a personal check is not private, but it is perfectly and unambiguously legal. Once your money is offshore, it is, for all practical purposes, out of reach of the U.S. government. There are no laws which restrict your ability to move money from one offshore bank to another once you have taken it beyond U.S. borders, without informing the IRS.

You also may endorse a personal check written to you in any amount over to an offshore bank without reporting the transfer to Customs. Simply endorse the check, then write below it, "pay to the order of [name of bank]." When the check is returned to the person or company that wrote it, the reverse will show the endorsement, but it will not be directly traceable to you.

Don't merely endorse the check. Be sure to also make payable to a third party. Endorsing a check without making it payable to a third party converts it into a bearer instrument, thus making it subject to Customs reporting if it exceeds $10,000.

2. *Money orders.* You can also use a money order to open your foreign bank account. Money orders are not the same as cash for reporting purposes if they bear a restrictive endorsement. Transporting one or more money orders bearing restrictive endorsements across a U.S. border, even if the aggregate amount is larger than $10,000, is not a reportable event according to the instructions on the reverse of Customs Form 4790.

Purchasing the money orders privately may pose a problem if you are paying for them with cash. It is money laundering to make any effort to avoid completing a currency transaction form when making a cash transaction. So if you wished to purchase $12,000 worth of money orders with cash, and bought them $500 at a time at different locations in order to avoid completing a currency transaction form, this action would constitute structuring.

But perhaps you only have $3,000 now to open a foreign account. You purchase three $1,000 money orders to open the account, and subsequently add $500 to it each month as you save the money. Is this structuring? Probably not, since you are making no deliberate effort to evade the reporting requirements. But the structuring laws are so vague that an aggressive U.S. Attorney could conceivably prosecute you for *any* regular pattern of monetary instrument purchases that eventually exceed $10,000.

On the other hand, if you make a single money order purchase exceeding $10,000, the bank or merchant must report it. And he must maintain detailed records of any transaction over $3,000. One strategy to avoid structuring would be to combine purchases to make a single transaction greater than $10,000. The transaction is reportable, but wouldn't constitute structuring since it exceeds $10,000. You could move the funds without reporting the border crossing to Customs if you have the money order made payable to you, then endorse it over to your offshore bank.

The best place to purchase money orders is at a convenience store, a mail receiving service, or currency exchange. Simply make yourself the payee, then endorse the money order over to your foreign bank to avoid reporting it at the border. Don't make the money order payable to cash. This converts it into a bearer instrument, which you must report if you are sending more than $10,000 overseas at one time. Keep the receipt in case the money order is lost to obtain a refund.

Don't buy money orders at a U.S. bank. Most banks charge much higher fees for money orders than convenience stores or currency exchanges. In addition, U.S. banks will require you to identify both yourself and the payee, imprint both names on the money order along with your account number and/or Social Security number, and keep a copy of the transaction for their records. U.S. banks must also notify the IRS when anyone purchases a money order larger than $3,000 who is not a depositor.

3. *Cash*. Many individuals use the mail to transfer cash overseas. While relatively reliable, you have no recourse if the money is lost. In addition, many overseas banks no longer accept deposits of cash except from known customers. Furthermore, cash is a frequent target of Customs Department seizure policy. If you mail more than $10,000 in cash or other monetary instruments in one package, of course, you must notify U.S. Customs.

If you have a large quantity of cash, negotiable instruments, precious metals, or other valuables to transport overseas, make advance arrangements with the foreign bank to make certain they will accept it. Rather than transporting the funds personally, consider using a courier (such as Purolator) to do so. The courier will be responsible for complying with all reporting requirements, although it must disclose that it is acting on your behalf. On the other hand, since such currency movements are an everyday occurrence, the appearance of a courier carrying a large quantity of cash at a U.S. border is not particularly unusual.

4. *Precious metals*. In the first two editions of this report, I stated that legal tender (or formerly legal tender) gold and silver coins could be declared at their face value to U.S. Customs, rather than their market value. This is no longer the case. When I tried to re-verify this policy in 1991, a Customs representative told me that precious metals are now considered monetary instruments and are subject to the $10,000 reporting limit based on their market value. Customs Circular ENF-4-R:E:P clearly states that gold coins are not reportable. But don't argue with the Customs officer.

5. *Coins and jewelry*. Numismatic coins are likewise officially exempted from reporting, but may be treated as monetary instruments at U.S. borders. The Customs official may ask you the market value of the coins, if you declare them. If you're not sure, the official may simply confiscate the coins until the agency obtains an independent appraisal. For this reasons, I no longer recommend using numismatic coins to privately transport assets into or out of the United States.

You can cross a U.S. border wearing or carrying any amount of jewelry (diamonds, collector watches, etc.). When you get to your destination, you can sell the jewelry and use the proceeds to open or add to your foreign account. You'll want to take the receipt with you to prove that you own it. One of the most liquid jewelry investments are Rolex watches. However, counterfeit Rolexes are very common.

6. *Wire transfers*. You can transfer any amount of money overseas via a wire transfer. This is unquestionably the quickest and most convenient way to transfer money overseas. However, banks have been alerted by the IRS to closely question individuals who use wire transfers to transfer assets out of the United States if they do not have a prior history of such transactions.

The 1992 anti-laundering law sets up a recordkeeping and IRS submission procedure for all international wire transfers. However, the Federal Reserve Board, in December 1992, made a startling admission: The Fed's wire network ("Fedwire") may not permit enough information about wire transfers to include details of the identity of both sender and recipient, as the final regulations issued by Treasury Department would presumably require. Although the Fed could change Fedwire's format, it would be both expensive and time-consuming to do so.

If your bank asks you why you are transferring the funds out of the United States, you are under no legal obligation to answer. On the other hand, if you refuse to answer, or answer in an evasive manner, the bank is required to immediately inform the IRS Criminal Investigation Division of suspected money laundering. Moreover, the bank may refuse to transfer the funds.

The best reply is to tell the truth and inform the bank that your purpose is to take advantage of investment opportunities not available in the United States. Tell them you'd be glad to have them submit any paperwork necessary to the Treasury Department, and that you have nothing to hide. This should reassure them that you're not attempting to avoid any reporting requirements.

7. *Transfer pricing.* This is a technique favored by multinational companies to move funds into tax-favored jurisdictions. In its simplest form, a company imports or exports merchandise to or from a high-tax jurisdiction through an intermediary company in a low-tax jurisdiction, such as the Bahamas. The transactions are structured so that the intermediary company keeps most of the profits in the low-tax jurisdiction.

While transfer pricing is a perfectly legitimate tax avoidance technique used by multinationals ranging from Sony and Honda to Boeing, President Clinton claims that the U.S. government could collect billions of dollars in additional tax revenues by cracking down on transfer pricing abuses. Congress is now holding hearings to determine how to collect more tax from companies that use transfer pricing.

Many multinationals disagree that transfer pricing is abused. The director of international taxation at a Big 8 accounting firm, for instance, said trying to define transfer pricing "abuse" is similar to counting how many angels can fit on the head of a pin.

Transfer pricing has also been implicated as a form of money laundering. Researchers at Florida International University claim to have found evidence that a form of transfer pricing may be used to launder money. In a study concluded in 1991, researchers found some startling import/export transactions in a computerized evaluation of trade reports. These included salad dressing valued at $720 a bottle and instant cameras that cost $3,127 each. FinCEN claims the study confirms suspicions that money laundering goes far beyond the drug trade.

8. *Overbilling.* If you do business overseas, you could ask a trusted firm to overbill you for the goods or services they provide. Simply have the company divert the excess funds to your foreign account. This is illegal if done to avoid paying tax on the money diverted, or to avoid reporting the presence of the foreign account, and I cannot condone this practice. It may also be illegal under other laws. However, it would not appear to constitute "international structuring" under the 1992 anti-laundering legislation.

9. *Sell your accounts receivable.* If you have a domestic business with accounts receivable, you have a marketable asset. Many organizations will purchase this asset at a discount. If a non-U.S. company purchases them, you can request that the funds generated be transferred to an offshore account, rather than repatriated domestically. You can find the names of companies willing to purchase receivables at a discount in such publications as *The International Herald Tribune* and the London *Financial Times.*

Another technique is to use an international structure you set up yourself to purchase these assets. This is described in "Offshore Trusts and Other Foreign Asset Protection Structures," this chapter.

10. *Private exchange with foreigner*. If you know a foreigner who has assets abroad that he would be wiling to put in your name, or the name of your structure, and you trust that person to do so, you could exchange assets. Give the foreigner a personal check or other compensation, and ask him to transfer an equivalent amount of assets to your foreign account. I am not aware of any law prohibiting such a transaction or making it reportable.

11. *Walk across the border*. The easiest way to move money outside the United States is to simply carry cash across the border. There is no limit to the number of times you could cross the border carrying less than the $10,000 reportable limit. However, the international structuring provisions of the 1992 anti-laundering legislation would appear to make repeatedly crossing the border in a deliberate effort to avoid the reporting requirements illegal.

One popular way to combine opening an offshore bank account with pleasure is to put cash into your suitcase and go on a Caribbean cruise. If you're carrying more than $10,000, go ahead and declare the money to Customs, tell them that you are a heavy gambler, and that both the ship and the islands for which you are bound have *great* casinos.

When you get off the boat at a tax haven, wear a really ugly polyester shirt, a funny hat, and have an old Japanese camera around your neck. Carry the money in a paper bag or inside your camera bag, get a taxi, and go to your bank. Make an appointment in advance; very few banks are willing to accept cash from U.S. citizens without letters of reference. No customs inspectors ever greet Caribbean cruise ships.

If you think the Mafia hasn't figured out these techniques, think again. Anti-laundering laws are aimed at us, not the Mafia.

Consider in advance the private repatriation of funds you hold in an overseas account. Strict foreign exchange controls that could be imposed in the future, however, might complicate your efforts. While it would make little economic sense to prevent repatriation of funds, Congress and the president don't always act rationally. (It would be more logical to ban moving money out of the United States, in order to prevent "capital flight" and thereby support the U.S. dollar.)

You can use most of the same techniques employed to take money out of the United States to bring it back; checks, money orders, wire transfers, etc. The same reporting requirements that apply to taking monetary instruments out of the United States also apply to bringing money back in.

Many overseas banks have correspondent banks in the United States. You may be able to ask your offshore bank to transfer your funds to a U.S. correspondent bank with the transfer recorded in the bank's name, rather than your own. Then have the U.S. bank send you a check, cash, or whatever form of payment that you prefer. This avoid the stigma of having to deposit or cash a check from an offshore bank in your U.S. account. This isn't a particularly private technique, since it creates a paper trail from the U.S. bank. But it would not appear to involve "international structuring."

A credit card from a foreign bank that you can use to draw on your account is also a private repatriation technique. This is discussed in the following section.

Advanced Offshore Investment Strategies

Once you've grown accustomed to offshore investing, you can begin taking advantage of some truly unusual, completely private--and in some cases, extremely *profitable* investment opportunities. This section provides a glimpse at some of the most rewarding.

1. *Foreign real estate.* Real estate purchases outside the United States need not be reported to the IRS as long as you earn no income from the property. You can purchase a fishing cabin in Canada, a timeshare in the Cayman Islands, a villa on one of the outer islands of the Bahamas, a flat in London, or a condominium in Switzerland. *Resident Abroad* magazine is an excellent source of information for offshore real estate purchases.[144]

From many standpoints, Swiss real estate is particularly desirable. Switzerland is one of the most politically stable nations on earth. Violent crime is almost non-existent. Its banks enjoy a worldwide reputation for expertise and discretion. Switzerland also suffers from a chronic land shortage. Construction is difficult and expensive in the ecologically-sensitive mountain areas, expensive in the cities, and often prohibited in farming regions.

In most areas of Switzerland, it is difficult or impossible for foreigners to buy real estate. I have found a U.S. broker, Ted Thomas, who has a limited number of condominiums available near the town of Brig. They are small by U.S. standards, but beautifully-constructed and offer a stunning mountain view. (See "List of Suppliers" for Thomas' address.

As in many other countries, Swiss real estate has been overdeveloped and is now in a bear market. Please don't approach Swiss real estate strictly as an investment. Real estate prices in Switzerland, as elsewhere, can go down as well as up.

2. *Mocatta delivery orders.* These are documents issued by Mocatta Metals of New York City, providing legal title to a specified quantity of gold or silver stored in Switzerland. You can instruct the Swiss custodian to deliver the precious metals to you at any time, or to the custody of any offshore bank. Mocatta (U.S.) is affiliated with Mocatta and Goldsmid, a firm with more than 300 years of experience trading precious metals. (See "List of Suppliers" for Mocatta's address.)

The MDO lists a serial number for each of your gold or silver bars or coins and the location where they are stored. Your metals are not mixed with those belonging to anyone else. They belong to you until you to sell or transfer ownership. They cannot be mixed with the custodian's assets in order to satisfy claims against it by creditors. Such *non-fungible* storage is in contrast to precious metals "warehouse receipts" from other companies that usually do not provide for segregated storage.

Storage in Switzerland is overseen by MAT Securitas, one of Europe's largest precious metals distributors. All metals held as a MDO are insured by Lloyds of London against virtually all risks short of war or government confiscation. (In Switzerland, of course, both war and government confiscation are highly unlikely.)

The MDO may be purchased by an individual, husband and wife, jointly by unrelated individuals, or, for maximum privacy, through a trust. You may transfer or sell title to the precious metals at any time. However, there is no public resale market; Mocatta Metals has no repurchase obligation or guarantee. Some brokers will repurchase the certificates; ask the broker when you buy. Of course, you could arrange to have the gold delivered and sell it to a dealer after paying delivery charges.

A MDO has important privacy advantages. Since you purchase it domestically, you are subject only to domestic reporting requirements, not foreign exchange reporting. In addition, the Swiss storage of your metals is analogous to a safety deposit box, and does not appear to constitute a reportable "foreign financial account."

---

[144]*Resident Abroad* (Subscriptions Department, Central House, 27 Park St., Coydon CR0 1YD, Great Britain)

Once you receive your MDO, treat it as a bearer instrument. Keep the MDO in a safe place, as it cannot be easily replaced. MAT Securitas will issue a duplicate certificate only after you post an indemnity bond equal to twice the then-prevailing market value of the metals.

MDOs can be purchased through Mocatta Metals directly and also through many precious metals dealers. Mocatta will encourage you to buy through a broker unless your order is larger than 100 ounces of gold or a roughly equivalent amount of silver. The company will send a list of recommended brokers at your request. The minimum purchase is 10 ounces of gold or 400 ounces of silver. Storage fees are 0.5 percent annually, based on the market value of the metals.

3. *Offshore precious metals storage.* There are a huge variety of precious metals storage and accumulation accounts available through offshore banks. Such accounts often permit you to purchase gold, silver and platinum at wholesale prices. Your investment dollars are lumped together with those of other investors to make purchases at regular intervals. Since the purchases are relatively large, the fund manager can often purchase the metals at very low premiums.

4. *Foreign credit cards.* Credit cards issued by U.S. banks provide a handy record of your purchases for credit bureaus, private investigators and even the IRS to delve into. If you'd prefer not to have such purchases open to inspection, one option is to obtain a credit card from a foreign bank. The card also provides a private method to repatriate assets from your foreign bank account. When you use a credit card issued by a foreign bank, records of purchases on that card will be maintained by that bank, not by a domestic entity.

To obtain a foreign credit card, you must first open a foreign bank account. Simply arrange in advance for the bank to issue you a credit card. Most foreign banks will deduct each individual purchase from your account, rather than billing you. Such a card is technically a debit card, not a credit card.

Credit cards from foreign banks may be imprinted in any language, but English, German, and French are most common. To maintain a low profile when using the card, request that it be imprinted in English. This is less of a concern, of course, when you use the card overseas.

Foreign credit cards can be used to obtain cash ($200-$300 at a time) anonymously through an automatic teller. You need to make advance arrangements to be assigned a personal identification number that can be used in U.S. automatic teller machines. If you travel overseas frequently, you'll also want to make certain it can be used in international teller networks.

One of the best foreign credit cards is the "Eurocard;" a gold Master Card. Most Swiss banks offer this card. Another good program is offered by Trustee Savings Bank in the Channel Islands (address in "List of Suppliers.") VISA and American Express cards are also available from many foreign banks.

When you complete an application for a foreign credit card, read the "fine print" carefully for information about charges associated with its use. Some banks will debit your account several dollars (or the equivalent in foreign currency) as a transaction charge in addition to the amount of your purchase or cash advance. Other banks impose steep currency conversion fees if you use the card for U.S. dollar purchases and debit those purchases against an account in another currency. To eliminate or at least reduce these charges, you may wish to maintain a U.S. dollar account to draw against when you use your credit card in the United States. (The November and December 1992 issues of *Low Profile* have a complete discussion of credit cards from foreign banks.)

5. *Foreign annuities.* With this investment, you can invest as much money as you'd like offshore, and the entire amount is non-reportable on your tax return. However, you must pay a 1 percent

excise tax on a foreign annuity when you purchase it outside a retirement plan. Purchases inside a retirement plan are not subject to the tax.

An insurance policy constitutes a long-term contractual agreement protected by the contracts clause of the U.S. Constitution (Article I, Section 10, Paragraph 1). Many attorneys feel that insurance policies held outside the United States would not be subject to future foreign exchange controls the U.S. government might impose when the dollar collapses. Even Great Britain, which imposed draconian foreign exchange controls in the 1960s (and has no written constitution guaranteeing contractual rights) exempted foreign insurance policies from its provisions.

U.S. law gives *deferred* annuities, which pay no immediate income, an important tax advantage. You purchase a deferred annuity by paying an insurance company a lump sum or several payments over a fixed period. During the deferral period, you receive no income, but the face value of the annuity increases.

You need not pay tax on this increase in value until the funds are actually withdrawn. However, a tax bill introduced in 1992 would eliminate this tax advantage. Therefore, if you're interested in purchasing annuities of any type, you should do so in the near future in case this provision is enacted.

Annuities in which your heirs receive back the investment principal upon your death are subject to U.S. estate taxes, even if the proceeds are not taxable in the jurisdiction where you purchase them. The IRS will not be deterred by foreign law in their inclusion of the annuity in your estate. The agency is unlikely to pursue the matter in a foreign jurisdiction. It is far more likely to simply tax a larger portion of the U.S. estate in order to recover the taxable portion of the annuity.

Annuities are available in many countries outside the United States, but my favorite source for foreign annuities is *Switzerland*. In the 130-year history of the Swiss insurance industry, not a single company has failed. Contrast this with the almost-daily announcements of downgrades and outright bankruptcies in the U.S. insurance industry. Minimum investments for Swiss annuities start at $10,000.

Swiss insurance companies aren't permitted to invest in junk bonds, third-world debt or risky real estate ventures. The great majority of their assets are maintained in Switzerland, and consist primarily of Swiss government bonds, blue-chip stocks, and first mortgages on Swiss real estate (values of which are considerably more stable than in the United States, although as I've already stated, real estate prices can decline anywhere.)

Swiss annuities also have important asset-protection features. If you name your spouse or children as beneficiaries, creditors may not attach the annuity in a bankruptcy proceeding. Even if you name another beneficiary, creditors must take up their claims in *Swiss courts*--which are far less friendly to frivolous litigation than are U.S. courts.

Yields of Swiss annuities are slightly less than U.S. annuities. However, the interest yield will vary depending on the currency in which your annuity is denominated. Several companies offer single premium annuities that provide the opportunity to switch currencies between the U.S. dollar, Swiss franc, German mark, or European Currency Unit.

Yet like all annuities, these policies need not be reported to the IRS until you begin receiving income from them. Annuities denominated in the Swiss franc are perhaps the most conservative choice, but also offer lower interest rates than the German mark or the European Currency Unit (ECU).

If you place a Swiss annuity into a U.S. retirement plan, the certificate must be held by a U.S. trustee. But if you hold it outside a retirement plan, you hold the certificate yourself, anywhere you want to keep it. Obviously, the certificate is safer from seizure if it's not held by a U.S. custodian. But no matter where you hold it, a Swiss annuity is among the safest of all investments.

The "List of Suppliers" provides the address of a company you can contact for a Swiss annuity proposal.

6. *Foreign security certificates.* It is perfectly legal for a U.S. citizen to purchase stocks or bonds issued by any company or government in the world. Moreover, if you take delivery of the certificates, the IRS could hardly consider their possession to constitute a "foreign financial account."

Many financial advisors recommend purchasing bearer shares to maximize privacy. But stock and bond exchanges worldwide are gradually switching from bearer to registered shares, and you may prefer registered shares since they can be replaced if lost. If you take personal possession of registered share certificates (to avoid having a reportable "foreign financial account") and cross a U.S. border with the certificates in your possession, you are under no obligation to report them, even if their value far exceeds $10,000. Since the certificates aren't "monetary instruments," it's probably not "international structuring" to follow this strategy. Bearer shares with a market value exceeding $10,000, however, would have to be reported.

You must report any dividends your stock certificates earn, but if the company declares no dividends, or reinvests them, no reporting is required. However, if you don't pay tax on reinvested dividends each year, there is a catch. When you sell, you are assessed the normal tax you would have paid throughout the period in which you held the fund. You must also pay interest on the deferred tax. The current interest rate on this deferred tax is around 6 percent. Of course, you have the option of paying tax annually, but this requires that you disclose the investment on your tax return.

The U.S. government goes to great lengths to prevent U.S. citizens from learning about investments in bearer stocks and bonds. In March 1992, for instance, the State Bank of Pakistan published an advertisement in *The Wall Street Journal* and other major newspapers announcing the availability of "bearer certificates" in foreign currencies with "no questions asked about source of funds." Within hours, two U.S. senators requested "swift regulatory action" to cancel the sale because it appeared to violate U.S. anti-laundering laws. Pakistan canceled the sale in the United States.

Over the next two weeks, U.S. Treasury officials quietly lobbied banks worldwide to boycott the sale. One foreign banker stated that his bank had declined to participate in the offering because, "Our bank does not encourage buyers to invest in bearer certificates until clearance is received from the United States." The new rule seems to be: If the U.S. government opposes a particular investment, no bank in the world may offer it.

While it may be possible for a U.S. resident to purchase such bonds using a foreign address, inquiring about the bonds using a U.S. address could raise your profile to an unacceptable degree. The IRS has already petitioned the Pakistani government to identify respondents who requested information on the bond sale.

7. *Roll-up funds.* A roll-up fund is an offshore mutual fund that reinvests, or "rolls up" its dividends. Mutual funds might appear to be a "foreign financial account" according to IRS instructions on Schedule B, and therefore reportable. But they need not be, according to Adrian Day, editor of *Adrian Day's Investment Analyst.*

In his March 1990 issue, Day describes how you can avoid the reporting requirement by purchasing the fund directly from the sponsor without opening an account. Pay a personal visit to the sponsor and pick up the shares in bearer form. Keep the share certificates in your foreign safety deposit box. However, you will need to retrieve your certificate when you sell your mutual fund. As with a bearer stock certificate, if you bring a bearer mutual fund certificate back to the United States, and its value exceeds $10,000, you must report that fact to U.S. Customs.[145]

There are thousands of offshore mutual funds, including many of the roll-up type. One roll-up program is offered by Luxembourg's Commercial Union company. The company's "Assetmix" is an umbrella fund similar in concept to those offered in the United States by companies such as Fidelity and Vanguard. There are a total of 14 funds. Seven invest in different global stock markets, four in global bond markets, and three are cash reserve funds (similar to money market funds) in different currencies. You decide how to allocate your investment, and certificates are issued to you in that form. The minimum investment is $20,000; $2,500 for each fund you choose.

Unfortunately, Commercial Union and many other roll-up fund sponsors do not sell directly to U.S. citizens. You must purchase shares in the fund through an intermediary. Many offshore banks are willing to function as intermediaries for modest fees; one I have found useful is Royal Trust Bank (Vienna). Its address is in the "List of Suppliers."

Again, when you invest in a foreign mutual fund, you must report any dividends the company pays. However, if no dividends are declared, or if the dividends are reinvested, no reporting is required. If dividends are reinvested, you're subject to the same interest penalty on the tax that you didn't pay as you would be for shares of non-dividend paying foreign stock. And of course, any profits you make when you sell are reportable.

The most comprehensive listing of offshore mutual funds that I've seen is Gary A. Scott's *World Mutual Fund Survey*.[146]

8. *Swiss money market certificates.* Some of the safest money market instruments in the world are issued by the Swiss government. Debt securities issued by the Swiss National Bank on behalf of Swiss governmental units, and in particular the Swiss federal government, are generally far safer than their U.S. counterparts. The highest quality, shortest term, debt securities issued by the Swiss National Bank are known as "Schweizerische Eidgenossenschaft." Some Swiss banks provide private placement type services for their purchase.

Many Swiss banks refer to these debt securities as Swiss money market claims (SMMCs), although the German language labeling is far more often employed. The minimum investment is generally SFr 50,000. Interest earned can be subject to the 35 percent Swiss withholding tax. However, if disposed of 10 or more days prior to maturity, no withholding tax will apply.

My recommendation is to purchase SMMCs backed by the Swiss federal government. Whenever these investments become available, a competent Swiss bank can advise you about the issue dates. Since some Swiss municipalities and cantons (states) are experiencing huge (by Swiss standards) budget deficits, I recommend avoiding these issues. In particular, I wouldn't recommend SMMCs from the canton of Geneva.

9. *Swiss federal bonds.* Another ultra-safe Swiss investment are bonds issued by the Swiss federal government. These bonds are issued in bearer form and their ownership is not considered to be a "foreign financial account" if you hold them personally or in a safety deposit box.

---

[145]*Adrian Day's Investment Analyst* (c/o Agora, Inc., 824 E. Baltimore St., Baltimore, Md. 21202)

[146]Gary A. Scott, *World Mutual Fund Survey* (International Service Center, 3106 Tamiami Trail N., Suite 264 P, Naples, Fla. 33940; 1991)

Swiss bonds are denominated in Swiss francs and are issued for periods as long as 25 years, although 10-year issues are most common. Interest rates are comparatively low (the yields are around 5 percent), but the appreciation of the franc vs. the dollar over the last 20 years has more than made up for the difference.

Interest on Swiss bonds is paid annually. If you prefer, the bank through which you purchase these bond will clip the coupons and credit your account, although this type of custodial service will make your ownership of the bonds reportable as a "foreign financial account." Or you may make these arrangements yourself, using the techniques I described in "Reportable and Non-Reportable Offshore Investments," this chapter.

Switzerland imposes a withholding tax of 35 percent on income from these bonds. However, you may recapture 6/7 of the tax withheld by application to the Swiss government under the terms of the U.S.-Switzerland tax treaty.

10. *Alternative travel documents.* The Anti-Drug Abuse Act of 1988 instructs the State Department to issue machine-readable passports. It also requires all passport applications (including renewal applications) to include your Social Security number. Anyone who refuses, the application says, will be reported to the IRS.

Another recent innovation will require travelers to submit to a "hand scan" to verify their identity at U.S. borders. Does that mean that the IRS might be able to prevent you from leaving the United States? This new requirement, combined with the new identification technology, makes the conclusion obvious.

One way to avoid such a prohibition, should it be imposed, would be to have in your possession a travel document from another country when you cross a U.S. border.

There are many misconceptions about alternative travel documents, the most common form of which is a second passport. Many Americans believe they're illegal; they are not. It's perfectly legal for a U.S. citizen to use a document other than a U.S. passport to cross a U.S. border. If the Customs Department were to determine from its computer that you are also a U.S. citizen, you might be detained for questioning. But you could not be arrested for using the alternative documents themselves. After all, even the United States offers a program for wealthy non-residents to obtain resident status by making a substantial capital investment. The Immigration Act of 1990 provides for "job creation" visas for foreign investors who will invest $1 million or more in a U.S. business that will hire 10 new employees. They also receive visas and "green cards" for all family members.[147]

Alternative travel documents are useful only if they provide citizenship or legal residency privileges. However, residing permanently in the nation where the document is issued may make you subject to its laws. The most useful documents are therefore from countries that permit you to be classified as a foreign resident, thereby exempting you from such obligations.

Remember, a U.S. citizen is required to pay income tax on worldwide income, no matter where he resides. Even if you renounce your U.S. citizenship, the IRS may elect to subject you to income taxes for a period of ten years.

---

[147]Theoretically, the U.S. government could revoke your U.S. citizenship if you become a citizen of another nation. But this is rare except in cases of war with the nation issuing the documents. In addition, you must certify when you complete a U.S. passport application that you have not become a naturalized citizen of another nation. However, a new regulation from the State Department says that Americans can hold onto their U.S. citizenship and passport even if they take an oath of allegiance to another country--which is almost never necessary to acquire an alternative travel document.

Maintain a permanent address in the country from which you obtain the documents, and have your correspondence directed to this address. You may spend as much time as you'd like at this location, as long as your length of residence does not make you subject to taxation, service in the military, etc. You will want to obtain a driver's license and other forms of identification verifying your identity as a resident. Whenever you return to the United States, simply request that your mail be forwarded.

The easiest and cheapest way to obtain an alternative travel document is to take advantage of your nationality. If you were born in Ireland, England, Germany or Holland, you may claim citizenship in that nation. Israel offers automatic citizenship to anyone of Jewish descent, or who converts to Judaism.

In fact, almost every country has some sort of program offering citizenship or passports to individuals with a family history in that nation. Consider the following (admittedly unlikely) scenario, described in *PT: A Coherent Plan for a Stress-Free, Healthy and Prosperous Life Without Government Interference, Taxes, or Coercion*:[148]

> If you have $25,000 and were born in the United States of a Turkish speaking Jewish mother who herself was born in Canada of a Paraguayan father and a Danish mother; and if your father was a one-time Thai Buddhist monk, born in Northern Ireland with a Brazilian mother and Mexican father who lived in New Zealand for two years; further assuming that you marry the only daughter of an Andorra father and a mother with Liechtenstein nationality whose mother fled Germany where she resided during the Hitler era, then there is a good chance that could legally obtain and hold all the following passports: United States, Turkey, Israel, Canada, Ireland, Paraguay, Spain, Denmark, Sweden, Norway, Andorra, France, Liechtenstein, Austria, Australia, New Zealand, Cook Islands, Tonga, Germany, Finland, Thailand, Mexico, Brazil, Portugal, Great Britain, Belize, St. Kitts, and the Dominican Republic. Plus a few dozen others!

If you don't qualify under any of these programs, you can purchase alternative travel documents from several different nations. The contacts listed under "alternative travel documents" in the "List of Suppliers" section offer complete information. Costs for alternative travel documents start at around $25,000. Availability may be sporadic due to pressures placed by the United States and European Community on nations providing these documents.

You'll find an alternative travel document most useful to identify yourself at foreign banks and financial institutions where you plan to invest. You need not mention your U.S. citizenship when you meet with or correspond with such institutions. In fact, it's best if you don't volunteer this information. Many of Geneva's private banks, for instance, which have operated continuously for 200 years or more, no longer accept deposits from individuals who identify themselves as U.S. citizens. On the other hand, a person who *appears* to be an American, but has travel documents identifying him as a resident of another country, will be accepted as a client without question if he passes the bank's background check.

The biggest practical problem with alternative travel documents is that many of the 35 or so countries with which the United States signed Mutual Legal Assistance Treaties (MLATs) now provide the IRS with lists of Americans holding second passports and residency visas in their jurisdiction. The

---

[148]W. G. Hill: *PT: A Coherent Plan for a Stress-Free, Healthy and Prosperous Life Without Government Interference, Taxes, or Coercion* (Hampshire, England: Scope Publications, 1989).

IRS then uses this data to target these individuals for audits. Just avoid these countries for your second passport or similar document.

Another alternative travel document is the "diplomatic passport." These have several additional tax and privacy advantages. Under international law, income derived from service rendered by a diplomat in his home nation on behalf of the country he represents cannot be taxed. And depending on his position, a diplomat may also enjoy "diplomatic immunity" from crimes he commits in the host country. Finally, the luggage of a diplomat crossing national boundaries may not be searched.

The most common type of diplomatic passport is issued for an "honorary consul" of the issuing country. Unfortunately, it is difficult for a U.S. citizen to qualify for honorary consul status in the United States. To begin with, you must pass a strict background check by the U.S. government. This makes appointment as honorary consul a high-profile activity, and one certain to draw an investigation by the IRS and Customs Service. Only after this check is complete will you be issued the "exequatur"--the document acknowledging honorary consul status.

When I contacted the IRS to request an opinion on how the agency would view income earned by U.S. citizens as an honorary consul, I was told by an agent of the Criminal Investigation Division that the agency would apply a "very strict standard" in determining if such funds would in fact be free from U.S. taxation. In other words, every penny you earned tax-free as honorary consul would be subject to intense IRS scrutiny.

Sadly, scams abound in the alternative travel document business. Many wealthy Americans have been fleeced by purchasing such documents for $1 million or more for documents that can only be used in one or two countries, or worse, are bogus. This fact, along with nations such as Panama and Argentina selling citizenship and travel documents to terrorists, drug traffickers, and Nazi war criminals, has given a legitimate technique to seek privacy and freedom an undeservedly bad reputation.

Offshore Trusts and Other Foreign Asset Protection Structures[149]

One of the major methods used throughout the world to achieve asset protection and/or tax planning advantages is the international trust (sometimes referred to as a foreign trust or offshore trust). This structure can be used in various ways to effect various asset protection and tax benefits.

From a U.S. point of view, there are three types of international trust.

The first type gives you asset protection and the availability (if applicable) of income and estate tax benefits, and is known as the non-grantor trust.

The second type, designed solely for asset protection, is a tax neutral document in that there are no tax advantages or disadvantages. You continue to pay your usual U.S. taxes on its income, capital gains, and estate taxes, but you also have all the usual allowances and deductions.

---

[149]This section is adapted from Peter Double's *Outline of Domestic and International Asset Protection Coupled With Estate and Income Tax Planning* (Robertson, Double & Boase, 6917 Kings Harbor Drive, Rancho Palos Verdes, Calif. 90274).

This type of trust is known as a grantor trust, and is sometimes called a foreign security trust.

The third type of international trust is the completely foreign trust with a foreign settlor (a person who is not a U.S. citizen or resident), foreign assets, and which may have U.S. citizens or residents among its beneficiaries. This type of trust is called the foreign grantor trust.

1. *The non-grantor trust.* This trust is designed so that the trust assets upon your death (and/or your spouse) go to your intended heirs in much the same way as your domestic revocable living trust. When combined with a foreign corporation, it also offers asset protection and estate and income tax planning benefits. This is why foreign corporations are frequently used by large public corporations as part of their tax planning strategies.

To secure the advantages of a non-grantor trust, it must be irrevocable. The trustees must not be U.S. citizens or residents. Moreover, your heirs cannot receive a distribution from the trust as your heirs until at least one complete tax year after the death of you and/or your spouse. In the meantime, your heirs are entitled to receive advances or loans, but they cannot receive distributions as heirs. Finally, there must be no U.S. beneficiary of the trust for U.S. income tax purposes during any U.S. income tax year for the remainder of your, and your spouses, lifetimes.

When the assets are ultimately distributed to your U.S. citizen or resident child or other heir, there will be an annual deferred interest charge payable on the amount of the taxes that have been deferred, from the date of deferral until the date of distribution, which may be after many years have passed. The deferred interest charge is at a rate of approximately 6 percent and therefore you have to ensure that your non-grantor trust is making at least a 6 percent annual return to pay the deferred interest charge. However, you usually keep the assets of the trust at a minimum level and place your assets into a foreign corporation which is owned by the trust.

The trust income is therefore deliberately kept very small. The trust will usually own mainly non-income producing assets. The amount of the deferred interest charge is therefore very small. The cash retained by the trust is usually little more than the amount needed to pay all the usual annual expenses.

Depending on the flexibility and work required, the trustee can be as small as a one man firm, to as large as a multinational firm with offices in virtually every jurisdiction. Who to choose as the trustee is generally determined after a review of the activities that you anticipate will be handled through your international structure (which can also include one or more additional trusts, corporations, partnerships and joint ventures, which may be formed in same jurisdiction as the non-grantor trust, or in other foreign jurisdictions, depending on the tax consequences and your personal comfort level).

You will want a jurisdiction that has a lower tax base than the United States, especially if you are looking to reduce or avoid taxes without evading them. There are currently approximately 40 acceptable jurisdictions in the world that have legislation designed for international trusts and which also have a lower tax rate than the United States. The most commonly used jurisdictions by U.S. residents and citizens are Barbados, Bermuda, British Virgin Islands, Cayman Islands, Cook Islands, Cyprus, Gibraltar, Guernsey, Jersey, Isle of Man, Netherlands and Netherlands Antilles, Panama, Turks & Caicos, and Vanuatu.

The preceding nations represent the majority (approximately 65 percent) of jurisdictions used by U.S. citizens or residents. Which jurisdiction to use will again depend on many factors, such as the types of activities in which the trust will be involved and your own personal comfort level.

After the trust is established, it will then capitalize and own a foreign corporation which has been formed in a foreign jurisdiction. The foreign corporation will generally have a small amount of capital issued to the non-grantor trust; $1,000, for instance. You must determine the jurisdiction of the foreign corporation and who will serve as corporate directors. You should not serve as a director yourself. In many cases, the jurisdiction chosen for the formation of the foreign corporation will be the same as that chosen for the non-grantor trust.

Once the trust and foreign corporation are established, there are several ways in which you can use that combination for asset protection and tax planning purposes, as shown in the following example.

Utilizing this structure, you can transfer your interest in your family limited partnership to your non-grantor trust and/or foreign corporation. You can do this by a gift or by a sale, with the net result that all or a portion of your limited partnership interest is now owned by your international structure which in turn means that your creditors will be unable to seize your assets unless they are prepared to take legal action in a foreign jurisdiction. This is very costly and the laws of the foreign jurisdiction will usually tend to support your asset protection planning against creditor attack.

Even if the creditor is able to obtain a judgment against you or your international structure in that foreign jurisdiction, by proper planning you will have since moved all your assets to another favorable jurisdiction, thereby completely frustrating the efforts of your creditor to try and seize your assets.

In some cases, transferring your limited partnership interest to your international structure is more beneficial than transferring the interest directly to your children. This is because if your children have creditor problems, the creditor is again left with the same problems of trying to seize assets.

You may also borrow money from your international structure. In order to secure your promise to repay the money, you can encumber most of your remaining assets, including your limited partnership interest and

252

your general partnership interest. You can make the terms of repayment extremely unattractive so that a creditor (even if he were able to secure the attachment of an asset of yours) will not be able to do anything with it, in view of the prior lien in favor of your international structure. This method has the advantage of further encumbering any of your assets under conditions that make them very unattractive to any creditor. In this respect you can, for example, use a shared appreciation mortgage.

You can also lend money to your international structure upon terms that require repayment over a long period of time and with no prepayment being permitted except with severe penalties, and with the risk that the entity to which you have loaned the money may not be able to pay you back; i.e., it has used the money in other activities in which you wish to invest.

Because of your close connections with your international structure, you have the power to modify the terms of payment or forms of security that are in your best interest at any point of time in the future and to the detriment of your creditors.

Another option is to sell the receivables (if any) of your [domestic] business to your international structure on a discounted basis (known as factoring). This provides several advantages. First, if properly structured, the difference (gain) between the discounted purchase price and the actual total payments received from the receivables can be tax deferred until your death. Second, you can guarantee to your international structure that you will make good on any receivables that are uncollected, and that the receivables are in fact good receivables.

In order to secure the loan, you can encumber all of your future receivables and all of the assets of your business, including in particular the inventory that you probably have transferred to your family limited partnership. The final result is that you have taken advantage of long term tax deferral while creating asset protection for your future receivables which have already been encumbered prior to you receiving the same, because of your guarantee to deliver good receivables to your international structure.

You may also borrow money from your international structure on what is known as a shared appreciation mortgage. By using this type of mortgage you are able to borrow money from your international structure and promise to repay the loan at a lower-than-market interest rate in exchange for giving your international structure (usually your foreign corporation) a percentage of the appreciation in the future value of the property.

The result of this arrangement is that your promise to pay interest plus a portion of the future appreciation becomes a lien against the property, to the further detriment of any creditor. In addition, the "profits" that eventually arrive in your international structure are tax deductible, since the interest is a legitimate tax deduction. Moreover, taxes payable thereon while owned by your international structure are deferred until your death. This structure is a considerable deterrent to any creditor who wishes to attach your assets. The shared appreciation mortgage will usually remove a substantial portion (if not the whole) of an equity appreciation that the creditor thought he or she could seize.

Finally, you may sell your assets to your international structure in return for a private annuity. This is defined as an agreement by your international structure to pay you (and/or your spouse) a certain sum of money beginning at a time in the future, and continuing until the time of your death.

The private annuity has two compelling advantages. Assets that are transferred to your international structure in exchange for the private annuity are not part of your estate and so are not available for a creditor to seize. In addition, any assets transferred have the effect of reducing your estate by the value of the assets transferred. There is an excise tax of 1 percent payable on the value of the assets transferred to your international structure at the time of the creation of the private annuity.

2. *The grantor trust.* The second type of international trust, the grantor trust or foreign security trust, is a tax neutral document that has no tax advantages or disadvantages. This means that upon your death there may be capital gains taxes. They will be payable on difference between the value of the asset when you first acquired it, and its value when it was transferred to the trust, not the value of the asset at the date of your death which may be higher or lower. The transfer of money (cash) to the trust avoids this potential tax. Likewise the transfer of assets which have not increased very much in value will also reduce your estate's exposure to such tax. The foreign security trust has the same affect as the non-grantor trust in protecting your assets from creditors, but it provides no tax advantages.

This type of trust does, however, enable you to regain full control and possession of your assets that have been transferred or sold to it during your lifetime. The foreign security trust is usually irrevocable for a period of time e.g. five, ten, or 15 years, and at the end of that time the trust's assets are distributed back to yourself or as you may wish to direct. This means that if you establish this trust, you can make a creditor wait until the end of the irrevocable period before it can seize any of your assets. However, the trust usually contains provisions for extending the irrevocable period until the creditor gives up hope of ever seizing any of the assets owned by the trust.

Again, choices such as who are to be the trustees, the jurisdiction to be chosen, and what types of assets are to be put into your trust are reviewed by your attorney after a determination of your objectives, your activities, and the types of activities in which you want your trust to become involved.

3. *The foreign grantor trust.* This type of trust is especially useful if you have relatives (by blood or by marriage) who are not U.S. citizens or residents. Alternatively, if you have close business friends and associates who are not U.S. citizens or residents and who live and work overseas, this type of trust may be beneficial. By careful tax planning, it is

possible for your non-U.S. assets to be placed into the trust, and thereafter for you and your family to receive income from it, and ultimately the principal, tax free. However, this trust must be carefully established, created and managed, or you will lose all the tax advantages.

We do not recommend that you try and place your existing U.S. assets into this trust as the IRS rules are extremely complex. The IRS could treat you as the settlor of the trust even though you are not in fact the settlor. Such treatment can have severe U.S. tax consequences.

One problem which arises is how to place your own existing overseas assets into this trust. You can irrevocably transfer those assets to the trust, but this may give rise to gift tax problems, particularly if the assets are of a substantial value. You could consider selling the assets to the trust either for a long term promissory note or you could sell those assets in return for a private annuity from a corporation which is owned by the trust. You could also sell the assets to the trust in return for a self canceling promissory note payable in installments. Upon your death, the promissory note is canceled and no further payments are due, so that there are no estate taxes payable by your estate on the balance due to you under the promissory note.

Nothing prevents the foreign grantor trust from investing directly into the United States by using its foreign assets for such purposes. Such activities can have tax advantages, but many U.S. activities will give rise to local U.S. taxes upon those local U.S. activities. Such activities should not give rise to U.S. taxation upon the trust's other foreign activities.

As regards asset protection, your creditors will be forced to go overseas in order to try and secure any interest that you may have under the trust. As grantor trust is discretionary, the creditor will be unlikely to obtain any security over your interest. He will not be able to seize any of the assets of the trust. Even if he does obtain any security over your interest (which is extremely unlikely), the foreign grantor trust contains provisions for your protection.

4. *Deferred Compensation Structures.* If your annual income exceeds your annual liabilities by at least $25,000 a year, you may be interested in a deferred compensation structure. This structure takes advantage of the double taxation treaty between the Netherlands and the United States. If carefully planned and managed, the structure permits you to move some of your earnings offshore to the Netherlands for onward overseas investment, and at the same time enables you to defer the payment of U.S. taxes on those earnings until you eventually remit them back to the United States, which can be many years later, if at all. The structure involves you being employed in the United States by a domestic corporation at a reduced salary, upon which you will pay all your usual taxes and will receive all the usual allowances.

An additional advantage of the deferred compensation structure is that if a creditor wishes to attack you personally, the only salary which could be subject to seizure would be the actual salary that you receive under be subject to seizure would be the actual salary that you receive under your reduced salary employment agreement with the domestic corporation. The monies that are paid offshore as your deferred compensation should not be subject to seizure by your creditors, particularly as such monies never actually pass through your hands until after they arrive in the Netherlands and until you start to use such monies for your own personal benefit.

5. *Compliance requirements.* An important aspect of international tax planning and asset protection is to comply with any and all applicable reporting requirements of the IRS or other state and federal agencies. Your international structure is so potentially beneficial to you in giving you asset protection that it is not worth taking a chance of not reporting a transaction when reporting is required. If you have not reported such transactions when you should have done so, you must report them, and if necessary file corrected tax returns. Your failure to report or disclose the transaction can lead to both civil and criminal penalties. These can not only be financially devastating, but also have considerable long term effects upon your liberty!

However, just because you must disclose or report a transaction does not mean that you must automatically pay taxes on it. Tax deferral is a completely legitimate avoidance technique. Obviously, the longer you can defer payment of any taxes, the more advantages you have because of your use of that tax money until payment. Your funds will accumulate much more quickly when the gains are tax-deferred.

Even if you are wrong in your position that an investment is tax deferred, when it is not, the worst that can happen is that you are required to pay the proper amount of tax due, with perhaps an interest payment for the delay in payment.

You should therefore be willing to give a creditor (including the Internal Revenue Service) a copy of every document and details of every entity that you have used for asset protection and tax planning benefits. These documents should be able to tell your creditors that they simply do not have the ability to seize your assets and if the calculation of your tax payment is not accurate, then the proper amount of taxes will be paid. If you are going to do any offshore tax planning, you must do it right. *Do not take any unnecessary or unwarranted chances that create a greater tax or other creditor liability than the one you are trying to avoid.*

Offshore Investing and Tax Treaties

The United States maintains a network of bilateral tax treaties with more than 50 countries. These treaties are designed to eliminate double taxation of incomes by the two nations that are parties to the agreement.

For instance, the tax treaty between the United States and Switzerland calls for Switzerland to refund 6/7 of its withholding tax on certain interest and dividends when a taxpayer provides the Swiss government proof that the income has been declared on his U.S. income tax return. It does not require the Swiss to violate their strict bank secrecy laws by disclosing information regarding individual accounts to the IRS.

The existence of such treaties permits U.S. investors to go "treaty shopping" for the most favorable provisions possible. It may even be possible to obtain a lower overall tax rate on income earned in a particular offshore jurisdiction in this manner. For instance, investors who purchase preferred stock in a British company through an offshore broker obtain a substantial tax savings over doing so through a U.S. broker.

Here's how it works: Suppose a British corporation issues a $1,000 dividend on its preferred stock. This sum does not represent the amount you would actually receive, since Great Britain imposes a 25 percent dividend tax, withheld by the corporation. So the $1,000 gross dividend is reduced by 25 percent, or $250, to produce a $750 net dividend. But what the taxman takes away, he also gives back. The tax treaty between the United States and Great Britain allows a U.S. shareholder in a British company a tax credit equal to one-third of the net dividend. One-third of $750 is $250, which represents this credit.

However, Great Britain also imposes a 15 percent withholding tax on the sum of the net dividend and the net tax treaty credit. The withholding tax amounts to 0.15 x (750 + 250) or $150. You end up with a $750 dividend, plus the $250 tax credit less the $150 withholding tax, or $850. Back in the United States, let's presume you're in the 33 percent tax bracket. The foreign tax credit allows you to offset a foreign withholding tax against your U.S. income tax. This reduces the tax on the dividend to $180; you keep $670.

The point of this strategy is that you keep nearly 90 percent of the net dividend of $750. In the 33 percent tax bracket, your effective tax rate is only one-third the amount that you would pay had the dividend been distributed by a U.S. corporation.

Other types of bilateral treaties, known as "MLATs," or mutual legal assistance treaties, are somewhat more threatening. These are described in the following section.

The International War Against Banking Secrecy and Money Laundering

The U.S. government has for many years tried to discourage its citizens from investing overseas, particularly in tax or bank secrecy havens. I've already described some of the excesses that have resulted from these efforts in "Governmental Abuses of the Bank Secrecy Act," Chapter 7.

Behind the scenes, a much larger effort is taking place. The U.S. government has implemented a series of bilateral and multilateral agreements that permit the exchange of confidential banking and investment records. Most of these agreements relate only to insider trading, money laundering related to drug trafficking, and drug trafficking itself. However, the Treasury is pushing hard to include tax offenses in the list of crimes for which information may be exchanged. As you'll see in this section, its success has been mixed, but its record is improving.

Another clever effort to pry off the lid of offshore banking secrecy was President Reagan's Caribbean Basin Initiative. Realizing that many of the Caribbean nations are dependent on the receipt of U.S. tourist dollars, the Treasury offered these countries the following bargain: Open up your banking records to IRS inspection, and we'll allow U.S. businessmen attending conventions in your jurisdictions to continue writing off their expenses as business deductions. In effect, the Treasury was saying it would be willing to overlook a few questionable business travel deductions in exchange for an opportunity to audit offshore bank accounts.

Barbados, the Dominican Republic, and Costa Rica soon signed the agreements. However, most other Caribbean nations hesitated, because the U.S. was driving a very hard bargain. And others, such as the Cayman Islands, rejected the U.S. offer out-of-hand.

The Anti-Drug Abuse Act of 1988 requires the Treasury department to set up international efforts to discourage money laundering worldwide. The first milestone in this effort was a December 1988 conference in Basle, Switzerland. Ten nations (including the United States, Great Britain, France, West Germany, and Japan) published a set of principles that they felt bankers should adhere to in discouraging laundering activity. These principles dealt with such items as customer identification, compliance with international law, and cooperation with law enforcement authorities.

That same month, 67 members of the United Nations signed a comprehensive treaty which focused on worldwide trafficking in narcotics. Called the "Convention Against Illicit Traffic in Narcotic Drugs and Psychotropic Substances," its 34 articles are a through assault on the world's drug problems-- not to mention our freedom. The treaty has now been signed by more than 70 nations, and ratified by more than 20 countries (including the United States. The U.S. Senate ratified the treaty in 1990.[150],[151]

This treaty, which like all treaties is binding on the United States even if its language violates the U.S. Constitution, defines money laundering as "the concealment or disguise of the true nature, source, disposition, movement or ownership of proceeds and includes the movement or conversion of proceeds by electronic transmission." It does not define "proceeds" as being derived exclusively from drug sales or any other illegal activity. Hiding your own lawfully earned money, under the U.N.'s definition, constitutes money laundering.

Another U.N. treaty written in a similar vein is the "Draft Convention on Mutual Administrative Assistance in Tax Matters." This treaty, which is not yet in effect, calls for:

✓ "Automatic and spontaneous" exchanges of taxpayer data between nations, without notifying the taxpayer

✓ Cooperation between authorities to recover taxes owed in another country, including taxes on income and profits, capital gains, net wealth and compulsory social security contributions

✓ Granting tax agents in one nation access to records of corporations and individuals in another nation, even if no crime has been alleged

✓ Tax agents in one nation to be empowered to confiscate property owned by a taxpayer in another nation, even if the dispute is not with the latter nation

Nor does the treaty distinguish between tax evasion and tax avoidance. Simply to bank, invest, work or carry on a business in an area where tax treatment is more favorable than at home would expose you to investigation. Finally, it contains no language to prevent witch-hunts or fishing expeditions against taxpayers innocent of any illegal act.

---

[150]The Annunzio-Wylie Anti-Money Laundering Act of 1992 calls for annual reports to Congress regarding the "progress" other nations are making implementing the U.N. Convention Against Illicit Traffic in Narcotic Drugs and Psychotropic Substances.

[151]*The Economist* recently carried an advertisement soliciting applications for the directorship of the U.N. drug enforcement program. The post pays $100,000 annually, free of income tax from any country.

The treaty would also establish an "international currency control agency" and establishes globally standardized tax forms and tax laws. Finally, to enforce these provisions, a global tax police force would be established. Critics have dubbed it "InterFipol," the International Financial Police.

Two of the treaty's other provisions include:

✔ Article 17, paragraph 5: permits the use of mail to serve documents in another treaty country, and the documents need not be translated

✔ Article 9: permits foreign tax officials to be present during audits

Consider the likely fate of a German Jew who smuggled cash to Switzerland to escape the Nazi terror of the 1930s and 1940s, had this treaty had been in effect. Switzerland would have been required to notify German authorities of suspected "foreign exchange violations." The German government would have then seized the assets in any account he had set up in Switzerland. The Jew, seized by agents of InterFipol in Switzerland, would then be turned over to the Gestapo. Before being sent to the gas chamber for the crime of possessing a foreign bank account, he would be accused of one more crime: failing to fill out a government form to take money out of Germany--*money laundering!*

The United States, France, the United Kingdom, and the Scandinavian nations strongly supported this treaty. But it was vigorously opposed in many other countries, including Austria, Belgium, Ireland, Italy, Portugal, Liechtenstein, Switzerland, West Germany, and Luxembourg. Opposition in these and other nations accounts for the delay in its final ratification. In 1990, the U.S. Senate ratified the treaty.

Since 1988, at least 40 nations have banned money laundering, or are in the process of doing so. However, anti-laundering laws in most other countries apply penalties only for activities explicitly tied to drug trafficking, and not to tax offenses as in the United States.

The most important recent anti-laundering initiative was the 1991 adoption by the European Community of legislation criminalizing money laundering. Beginning January 1, 1993, anyone wanting to deposit more than ECU 15,000 (about US$18,000) in cash or monetary instruments in a bank in any of the EC's 12 member states will have to identify the source of the money. Banks will also be obliged to report any "suspicious transaction" to authorities.

EC banks must confiscate not only proceeds from illegal activity, but any legitimately-obtained property allegedly co-mingled with such property. No conviction is necessary. All that's needed, as under U.S. forfeiture law, is a reasonable belief that the funds are connected with criminal activity.

One of the first tests of this new framework occurred in Luxembourg. In a test case brought before a Luxembourg court, the government sought forfeiture of $36 million in suspected drug profits. But the judge ruled that since the individuals who owned the account had been convicted of no crime, the forfeiture could not proceed. She ordered that the funds be released.

The court's insistence on due process provoked outrage on both sides of the Atlantic. The DEA vowed to block release of the money. Luxembourg's Justice Minister tried to reassure the DEA and other governmental authorities that the "loophole" had been closed, and that since March 1992, Luxembourg permitted money to be forfeited regardless of whether its owners had been convicted of a crime.

Yet another initiative in this regard is the Financial Action Task Force. This entity was set up in 1989 by the Economic Summit of the Group of Seven Countries (G7), which consists of the heads of government of the seven most powerful western nations. The G7 concluded that the narcotics problem had reached "devastating proportions" and stressed the immediate need for both domestic and international remedies. One of its primary recommendations is to encourage worldwide compliance with the U.N. Convention Against Illicit Traffic in Narcotic Drugs and Psychotropic Substances.

The U.S. government has also moved aggressively to sign MLATs with nations it considers bank secrecy havens. These treaties provide for the exchange of financial records for certain types of crimes, and have been signed with the Bahamas, Bermuda, Barbados, the Cayman Islands and many other countries. The crimes with which most MLATs deal are limited to drug trafficking, money laundering strictly related to drug trafficking, and insider trading, but the Treasury is determined to expand the list.

One of the first expanded MLAT treaties was signed with Venezuela in 1990. The Venezuelan agreement has ten articles which focus primarily on the exchange of currency transaction information. Venezuela is obliged to provide this information not only in cases involving narcotics trafficking, but in any suspected "violation of currency transaction reporting and recordkeeping laws and administrative regulations." It is therefore obliged to release records on individuals whose alleged crimes have nothing to do with narcotics.

To enforce these rules, Venezuela must enact legislation requiring records of large currency transactions be maintained by its banks, which it has promised to do. Then, it must train its bankers to enforce the laws. This has already been arranged, when a team of former IRS enforcement officials travelled to Venezuela to conduct seminars on this subject.

More recently, the Treasury tried to consummate a similar agreement with Panama. Under immense pressure, and even the implied threat of a second invasion, Panama refused to permit U.S. authorities routine access to confidential bank records. The final agreement, signed in 1991, gives the U.S. government access to Panamanian bank records only when investigating murder, kidnapping, and money laundering explicitly tied to drug trafficking. Tax evasion is not included in the agreement.

In the meantime, the Treasury is not above using subterfuge to obtain information that it would otherwise not be entitled to acquire. In a recent case, Swiss banking authorities authorized the release of bank records of a man the IRS claimed was suspected of racketeering, an offense that under the U.S.-Swiss MLAT calls for the release of banking records (*U.S. vs. Sturman*, 951 F.2nd 1466, 6th Circuit, 1991).

Sturman was actually suspected of tax evasion, which under Swiss law is insufficient cause for release of these records. He was convicted of this crime based on the information released under false pretenses. This case underscores the importance of complying with IRS reporting regulations on foreign accounts, and paying any tax due.

The only good news to report is that, as yet, few of these international anti-laundering initiatives have had an impact on ordinary Americans seeking private investment alternatives. But the framework has been set up for even offshore barriers between you and your government to be eliminated. How long these barriers will remain standing remains to be seen.

Chapter Ten

PRIVACY IN THE TWENTY-FIRST CENTURY

The ability of the computer to link seemingly unrelated facts about individuals constitutes perhaps the most threatening development for the future of individual privacy. But this is hardly the only threat to privacy for the remainder of the 20th century--and beyond.

Social Security's Last Gasp

What we are looking at is a shell game. There are no trust funds--just a bunch of IOUs.

--Dorcas Hardy, former Commissioner, Social Security Administration

The Social Security system has been a part of U.S. life for nearly 60 years. To be sure, Social Security has been an enormous success for the first two generations of retirees. And its aging architects assure us that "the system is fundamentally sound."

Such statements are wonderful for public consumption. But you shouldn't believe them. Bankrolling Social Security into the 21st century will require not only much higher payroll contributions, but far greater intrusions into our private affairs.

To finance the centerpiece of the "Old Age Insurance Plan" (the original name of Social Security), Congress in 1935 imposed a tax on the wages of employees, to be matched by employers. That tax, just like the income tax of 1913, now seems incredibly low: 1 percent of wages, which was paid on the first $3,000 of income. The *maximum* annual contribution from an employee was only $30, to be matched by a $30 contribution from the employer.

As we all know, Social Security taxes are much higher today. Employees pay 7.65 percent of the first $57,600 in income into the program. Employers make an identical contribution. The maximum annual employee contribution is $4,406.40--147 times higher than the 1935 maximum. The maximum Social Security tax burden has increased by nearly 15,000 percent since it was first imposed 56 years ago. (Of course, your "contribution" now includes Medicare premiums as well.)

Unfortunately, the upward momentum in Social Security taxes is unlikely to let up anytime soon. The population distribution of the United States makes it impossible. The number of workers making contributions to the Social Security system is increasing at a much slower rate than the number of beneficiaries.

This is a direct consequence of the "baby boom" of the 1950s and 1960s and the "baby bust" of the 1970s and 1980s. By the time "boomers" are set to retire in the early 21st century, the dependency ratio--the number of workers available to support one retiree--will have shrunk from 3.2:1 in 1980 to 2:1 in 2020. When Social Security began, this ratio was 140:1.

Since Social Security operates on a "pay as you go" basis (current revenues are spent on current beneficiaries or to lower the federal deficit, and are not saved), the only possible result of these demographic realities is higher--much higher--Social Security taxes. The Social Security

Administration's own "most pessimistic" (read *most realistic*) assumptions project payroll tax rates of an incredible 37.5 percent by the year 2020.

It doesn't require a great deal of imagination to consider how workers of the 21st century will react to Social Security tax rates of 37.5 percent. Workers will "opt out" of the system any way they can to avoid being trapped by rising tax rates. Evading Social Security taxes is tax evasion. But with Social Security tax rates of 37.5 percent, combined with federal taxes of 30 percent or more, many workers will feel they have no choice.

To once again quote former Social Security Administration Commissioner Hardy:

> Until now, the public has generally been tolerant of Social Security
> taxes, but we may be reaching the point where the ability to pay may not
> match the willingness to pay.

One of Hardy's responsibilities was to prevent "desertions" from the Social Security system. And as Hardy's successors perform their duty, they will preside over a massive and further erosion of personal and financial privacy.

Hardy's new book, *Social Insecurity: The Crisis in America's Social Security System and How to Plan Now for Your Own Financial Survival*, tells a different story. Hardy now admits that the benefit checks will begin running out in less than 20 years. The trust funds now invested in government bonds will then be insufficient to meet anticipated benefit levels. Hardy's suggestion is for prospective retirees to not depend on Social Security benefits. That suggestion is a good one--but you may not have a great deal of money to save if the tax burden increases as quickly as Hardy believes it will.

To make certain that all of us pay our "fair share" into Social Security, Congress wants to prevent desertions from it at all costs. Preventing desertions is the real reason for the 1986 requirement that all children be assigned Social Security numbers at birth if their parents wish to obtain tax deductions for the new arrival. Some parents might not list their children as dependents in order to protect them from becoming part of a government data bank from infancy.

But even this strategy is obsolete. The Family Support Act of 1988 mandates that states will forfeit federal funds if they do not enact legislation requiring parents to submit *their* Social Security numbers before the state issues birth certificate for a newborn baby. Even if the parents do not apply for a Social Security number for the baby, the government will know the parents Social Security numbers, and be alerted to the fact that an infant has been born.[152]

This latest initiative by the government to obtain the names, ages, and addresses of every child in the United States will be used for many purposes. For instance, I can foresee local public school truant officers making use of such information. Of course, all this data will officially be "for internal use only."[153]

---

[152]The IRS will bend these rules if it is convinced that a person has a legitimate religious objection to assigning their children a Social Security number. For instance, in 1991, a California taxpayer successfully filed a tax return without providing Social Security numbers for her three children. She claimed doing so would have violated her Christian beliefs. (Revelation 13:16-17 warns that whoever worships a Satanic beast that issues a mark or number to all persons will incur the wrath of God.) The deductions were turned down by an IRS auditor, but later upheld by an IRS appeals officer after the woman provided other proof that the children really existed.

[153]A new proposal before Congress would require all fathers to list their Social Security numbers on the birth certificates of their children. The federal government would then promise to collect support payments from the father if he were to abandon his children.

You can also be assured that the Selective Service will know which young men are legally eligible for the draft. There is little doubt that young men are refusing to register for the draft. The Selective Service has run hokey skits on rock radio shows that tell the audience that it's illegal not to register if you're male and 18. I have heard estimates that up to 40 percent of the 18-year olds are not registering.

This IRS registration program will put an end to the low-risk status of the young man who refuses to register. All dependents will be listed on a parent's IRS form. All of them will have Social Security numbers. The computers will be able to sort through millions of names in a manner of seconds.

But the invasion of privacy to come from Social Security will be far greater than the assignment of a mere number. For instance, to keep tax rates from going higher than even 37.5 percent, you can count on more "means-testing" before you obtain Social Security benefits. The means-test concept is simple: If you aren't poor, you don't get benefits. The debate over means-testing Social Security benefits promises to be one of the hottest political issues of the 1990s. President Clinton's new tax proposal, for instance, would require high-income taxpayers to pay income taxes on their Social Security benefit.

Once means-testing is implemented, the government will demand "proof" that you are poor enough to deserve benefits. This function is likely to be turned over to the IRS. In the future, you can look forward to intrusive applications, unannounced visits by caseworkers and Social Security audits, all conducted by agents of the IRS Criminal Investigation Division. To insure compliance, the IRS will have the same power to examine bank records, listen in on telephone conversations, and seize assets in relation to Social Security benefits as it does currently in regard to income tax matters.

Social Security will evolve from its current status as primarily a pension-welfare system into a pure welfare system. The "wealthy" (read middle class) will pay increasing taxes on Social Security benefits, while their children struggle with the burdens of higher and higher tax rates.

Another way the system will be bailed out will be the elimination of the wage ceiling on which Social Security taxes must be paid. A bill to this effect was narrowly defeated in the 1988 congressional session. Another proposal came from Illinois Senator Paul Simon. In 1991, he introduced legislation to raise payroll taxes an additional half percent, and eliminate the cap on income subject to the Medicare payroll tax to fund a national health insurance scheme. Now President Clinton wants "wealthy" Social Security recipients to pay higher taxes on their benefits.

As Social Security tax rates rise relentlessly, calls will arise for *all* income--not just income from wages and salaries--to be subject to Social Security tax. Any other policy, proponents will claim, would permit the wealthy to evade their legitimate obligation to the less fortunate. Rental, royalty, interest, capital gains, and dividend income will thus become subject to Social Security tax.

The government knows that the Social Security System will cave in on the generation of workers who are now being assigned numbers at birth. These people will never, ever be paid off, and they will have to support the rest of us with up to 37.5 percent of their annual income. There will be a political revolt eventually. The kids aren't going to pay.

But before the revolt begins, there will be attempts by people to get out of the Social Security System. This is legal if you have a legitimate religious objection to the system. To qualify for the exemption, you must complete IRS Form 4209, "Application for Exemption from Social Security Taxes and Waiver of Benefits." This form calls for you to certify that you object on the basis of his religious beliefs to:

1. Accepting any benefits of any private or public insurance that makes payments in the event of death, disability, old age or retirement, or that

2. Makes payments toward the cost of or provides services for, medical care.

Once you complete this form, you cannot purchase private health insurance, private disability insurance, or private "Medigap" insurance. Your religious group must provide these benefits to its membership, and have been in existence since 1950. Modern tax protestors need not apply. The IRS knows that most people are not willing to give up private insurance benefits just to opt out of Social Security. But even this small loophole may eventually be closed as Social Security edges closer to bankruptcy.

The best way to avoid Social Security, of course, is to never apply for a card. "Just stay in the cash economy, my son, and never sign up." It's much more difficult today. Opting out requires the completion of Form 4029. And any effort you make to use the underground economy to avoid paying into Social Security is now money laundering, not tax evasion.

A more workable solution for most people is to opt out of the Social Security system by shifting income from wages to royalties, interest, dividends, rents, etc. that are not *currently* subject to Social Security tax.

In earlier versions of this report, I've recommended setting up Keoghs, IRAs, etc. to legally defer income for retirement. This is a less attractive option now that President Clinton has proposed financing "infrastructure investments" with pension fund monies. Other proposals advocate forcing retirement plans to invest some of their funds into "safe" investments such as government bonds. Still others call for "consolidating" the Social Security system with privately-held retirement funds to insure the future financial solvency of Social Security.

A consolidation would constitute a bailout of Social Security by those prudent enough to have taken their own measures to insure a safe retirement. Since a consolidation would also lower tax rates for those who have not been so prudent, it will be very difficult for Congress to defeat.

If these proposals become law, and if they require mandatory participation, they will constitute nothing less than confiscation of retirement funds. The government's $4 trillion debt will never, ever, be paid off. Neither will the funds it "borrows" from retirement plans to pay the interest. You may get interest payments on the funds the government "borrows" from you. But you will never see the principal again.

When Congress begins holding hearings on this topic--and it may as early as this year--you should liquidate your retirement plan immediately. The tax penalties for doing so are severe, but taking this step is far preferable to having your retirement assets placed into the Social Security "black hole."

The "Demand" for a National ID Card

Eventually, the Social Security card may be replaced by a national ID card. The official reason will be to prevent immigration fraud. It's remarkably easy to obtain false ID in the United States. For about $25, an illegal immigrant can purchase a fake Social Security card. Then he takes the fake card to a check-cashing company to get a check-cashing card. Then he presents the check-cashing card, together with the Social Security card, to obtain a driver's license. This gives him enough identification to open a bank account, apply for credit, file tax returns, etc.

What's the solution to immigration fraud? A good beginning would be to make Social Security cards much more difficult to counterfeit. (This would also be an important first step toward solving the problem of impersonation by Social Security number that I discussed in Chapter 4.) But that's not the answer the bureaucrats have for us, as my special report, *Counter-Surveillance,* explains:

In May 1991, rioting erupted in Washington, D.C. Miraculously, no one was killed, but dozens of injuries and arrests occurred, along with tens of millions of dollars in property damage.

After calm was restored, an exhaustive analysis into the causes of the disturbance began. Many commentators blamed the disorders on Hispanics, who were accused of first illegally entering the United States, and subsequently fomenting anarchy.

It turns out that most of the rioting Hispanics were unemployed. They couldn't find jobs because prospective employers in Washington, DC were afraid to hire them. These employers feared the sanctions that were included in the 1986 Immigration Reform and Control Act, which, for the first time, penalized employers hiring aliens who had entered the United States illegally.

No self-respecting bureaucrat would ever suggest junking the intrusive bureaucracy that's developed at the Immigration and Naturalization Service to administer employee sanctions. Instead, the agency suggests that every U.S. worker--not just immigrants--carry a national ID card in order to verify citizenship. Any employer hiring a worker possessing this card would presumably not be penalized, even if the worker later turned out to have illegally entered the country.

Indeed, this suggestion was made in 1990, when the General Accounting Office published a report which concluded that after employer sanctions began in 1987, employers became reluctant to hire individuals they suspected might be illegal aliens. This in turn, said the report, had led to increased discrimination against foreign nationals and even U.S. citizens who spoke accented English.[154]

To prevent discrimination, the GAO presented several alternatives, including "applying new documents to all members of the workforce." Continuing, the GAO claimed that its research indicated that nearly 80 percent of employers sought a "simpler" verification system. What could be simpler than a national identification card? Of course, to prevent abuse, the report continues (in a masterful example of understatement):

"Should Congress opt for a single-card system, it should assure that the system will not be administered by law enforcement agencies. There would be a temptation for misuse of information if any law enforcement agency controls the computer system and information going into it to assure the validity of the issued cards. *For the cards to be optimally effective in reducing discrimination, all members of the workforce (citizens and aliens) would have to receive the new cards."* [emphasis added]

---

[154]*Immigration Reform: Employer Sanctions and the Question of Discrimination* (Washington, D.C.: General Accounting Office; GAO/GGD-90-62, March 1990)

Of course, even under this scenario, provisions would almost certainly be made for information exchange between the administering agency and other federal agencies. Practically every other piece of personal information in government custody can be freely traded between agencies, either through loopholes in the law or by ignoring the law. Why not national identification card data as well?

The demand for a national ID card continued in testimony before Congress in 1991. Much of the testimony favored such a card. David Simcox of the Center for Immigration Studies, for instance, testified that a national ID card "can help protect our liberties, not diminish them."

Perhaps Simcox is right. However, evidence suggests that he is not. The use of Social Security numbers by government agencies as "personal identifiers" to carry out computerized matches of unrelated databases hardly "protects civil liberties." And in Australia, where a national ID card proposal was defeated in 1987, supporters claimed that opponents to the card were merely "tax evaders" afraid of being caught.

Even if a national worker's ID card is not legislated into existence, other de facto national IDs may develop in addition to the ubiquitous Social Security card. For instance, the Institute of Medicine recommends a national *medical* ID card, which would provide instant access by doctors and hospitals to medical records. In addition to basic medical information--blood type, allergies, and the like, physicians would have a complete medical history of the person carrying the card as well.

While the concept of a national medical ID card could be lifesaving, I fear that once people become accustomed to carrying one, they will be anesthetized to the abusive possibilities of a more general card that would be required for everyone.

The original Social Security card had written on it "not for purposes of identification." But that is precisely how it is used half a century later. An act authorizing a national ID card might specify that use of the card not be mandatory, that citizens could not be penalized for not carrying it, etc. But how long would such safeguards stay in place?

Several versions of a multi-purpose computerized ID card are already in use. In Singapore, every person over the age of 15 must carry such a card, which is tied in to computerized data banks, and permits access to information ranging from police records to school loans.

In the United States, the Bush administration's 1988 drug bill called for a national ID card for gun-owners, and the Justice Department, IRS, and FBI have long advocated such a card. Eventually, the card would include a holographically-produced photograph, your fingerprints, a retinal scan, a genetic scan, and (of course!), your Social Security number. The Justice Department listed several potential drawbacks to the plan. One was that creation of a massive data bank to store all this data "may be controversial." But if found "no constitutional impediments" to the plan.

Another national ID trial balloon came from the pen of former foreign service officer William Ridgeway. He suggests outlawing all cash, bills and coins. To replace cash, Ridgeway proposes a foldable card the size of a dollar bill that would contain information on your bank balance, credit limits, medical records, passport and driver's license. To guard against theft, the card would contain both a thumbprint and a photograph. These features would be verified every time you used the card.

Every individual transaction using the card would build an electronic trail leading back to the purchaser. Drug abuse and money laundering would cease to exist, says Ridgeway. The underground economy would be wiped out. Since every transaction would create its own record, no one would dare do anything illegal! One advocate of the program, Harvey Wachsman, president of the American Board of Professional Liability Attorneys, suggested an Orwellian-sounding name for the new card: the "Americard."

The new driver's licenses in California and New York are a blueprint for this new system. They contain a computer-readable magnetic strip encoded with a variety of personal data about the holder. California promotes the card as a way for citizens to obtain access to government services without bureaucratic interaction, so it is extremely popular with many of the 2.5 million drivers who have already been issued the new licenses. The data encoded in the magnetic strip cannot be read by the holder of the license.

The next step after a national ID card would be a *world* ID card. If this sounds unbelievable, you'll be interested in knowing about a 1991 conference in Barcelona, Spain that brought together members of the International Card Technology Institute. Attendees heard speakers advocating the use of a "world passport card," which would contain an identification number unique to each carrier, along with medical data useful in an emergency. It would also contain data about income, debt, criminal offenses, and other information.

At any foreign border, the card would be placed into a card reader. If "travel privileges" had been suspended, the card would be impounded and the traveller detained. All restaurants, hotels, banks, and other retail establishments would be required to use card-reading equipment to verify the identity of their patrons. If the card wasn't approved, police authorities might be summoned, or at the least, the guest wouldn't be permitted to stay. "Smart passports" that permit this type of surveillance are already in use in several European countries.

Many Americans living today, or their ancestors, fled totalitarian societies where one of the most repressive instruments of political and social control was a national ID card. How long before a world police force begins asking the 21st-century version of the question that haunted the streets of Nazi Germany and Stalinist Russia: "your national ID card, please?"

To those of you who remember those days, and believe that it couldn't happen again--it is.

The "New Money"

"If we can't eliminate cash right away," one bureaucrat might say to another, "why not manufacture it so that we always know where it is?"

"Simple," says the second bureaucrat. "We call in all the old money and issue new money with magnetic strips. Then we install metal detectors at all border crossings. Anyone crossing the border will set off an inexpensive alarm if he is carrying cash."

"Brilliant!" exclaims the first bureaucrat. "When do we start?"

267

Government bureaucrats don't like cash transactions. Cash is difficult, if not impossible to trace. Cash makes it easier to do business "off the books." Cash is a *private* way of doing business. The anti-drug initiatives of the Reagan-Bush era are nothing less than a war on cash.

If the government can't eliminate cash use through draconian anti-drug legislation, from a bureaucratic perspective, the next-best solution might be to require all citizens to use currency whose movements can be tracked. But first, it must frighten its own citizens into demanding that the old currency be withdrawn.

Fear of counterfeiting is the most widely-heard justification for a new currency. There is some justification for this fear. In July 1992, a Congressional task force announced that Middle Eastern nations are manufacturing billions of dollars of "nearly perfect" counterfeit U.S. $100 bills. According to the report, the counterfeit currency distributed by Iran, Syria, and their agents is distributed into the international marketplace though drug money-laundering by banks.

The currency is first tested locally in the Middle East and is then expanded to Europe, and ultimately, with the aid of [terrorist] networks, the United States. If the counterfeit operation is not stopped, the report claims, the continued spread of counterfeit dollars throughout the world could ultimately erode the unique position of the dollar as the world's medium of exchange.

The researchers note that the fakes are so good that they often fool the Federal Reserve's currency counting machines. They claim that Iran alone produces nearly $12 billion of fake currency each year. (The U.S. government itself counterfeits billions of dollar of foreign currency each year; its primary target is Iraq.)

Is the threat real? It really doesn't make any difference if enough people believe that it is. The Fed took the report seriously enough that one of its regional banks published an article denying that the fakes would affect its measurement of currency in the economic statistics it constantly gathered. And in November 1992, the Fed sent a letter to every U.S. bank requesting that no pre-1990 series $100s be recirculated. In effect, the Fed began a currency recall.

Ostensibly to deal with the threat of counterfeiting, the Treasury Department introduced a new generation of U.S. currency in 1991. The first issued was the $100 bill. The new $100s contain several new "security" features. The first is a security thread; a strip of polyester with "USA $100" repeated in an up-and-down pattern around the Federal Reserve seal. The strip is visible only when held up to light, and can't be duplicated in a copier.

The second improvement is microprinting: "The United States of America" is printed repeatedly around the portrait. You need a magnifying glass to read the letters, which are too small to reproduce well in a copier. In 1992, new $10s, $20s and $50s containing similar elements were introduced.

Now that the new currency has its new anti-counterfeiting elements, all is well, right? Perhaps not. According to a test conducted by a Georgia electronics laboratory (and reported by the newspaper *Coin World*), microprinting and a security thread aren't the only differences between pre-series 1990 currency and the bills printed since that time. And according to test results published in *The Lyke Report*, the ink at the bottom of the note is *magnetized* and laid out to provide a read-out in a bar code format.[155],[156]

---

[155]"Testing Detects New Magnetic Pattern on Series 1990 Notes," *Coin World*, March 23, 1992

[156]"Our Test Results of the New $20 Bills," *The Lyke Report*, February 1993 (Lyke Publications, Inc., P.O. Box 290, Glenview, Ill. 60025-0290)

The bar-coding format at least theoretically makes it possible to register each bill to an individual owner. It would be quite simple, for instance, to magnetically encode an 18-digit number into the bill-- nine digits for your Social Security number and the remainder for your nine-digit zip code.

Moreover, since the ink is magnetized, a large concentration of the new currency could conceivably be detected at border crossings and other locations by nothing more sophisticated than an airport metal detector. In the 1960s, the British government implanted metal threads in the nation's currency to help enforce that country's draconian foreign exchange laws. Could the U.S. government be considering a repetition of the British plan?

For an answer, we need look no further than the actions of our "public servants." In 1989, Massachusetts Senator John Kerry introduced an act that called for machine-readable bar codes on all U.S. currency so that all $20s, $50s, and $100s would be "more traceable." Kerry recommended that serial numbers on these bills be tracked by optical scanning devices such as those used at grocery store check-out counters. In this manner, perhaps in combination with a national ID card, you would disclose your identity every time you made a cash purchase.

In testimony before the Senate, a Treasury official said that while Kerry's suggestion would be "highly effective" in combatting money laundering and tax evasion, it would be very expensive to set up. This means we probably don't need to worry about our new magnetically-encoded currency being used to track our every cash transaction--at least not yet.

Tiny printed letters, polyester threads, magnetic ink, and bar codes certainly will be effective to reduce counterfeiting, and may even help the IRS, Customs Service and Postal Service seize more cash. But these steps won't by themselves wipe out the cash underground economy. What would be effective would be a *sudden and unannounced recall* of U.S. currency.

If you think a currency recall is a paranoid delusion of a few right-wing fanatics, think again. Several spokesmen from the highest levels of the U.S. government have made proposals suggesting that our currency be recalled all at once, and a "new money" issued. And the new money is now here.

In 1989, a suggestion for currency recall came from a very respectable source: former Treasury Secretary Donald Regan. He recommended that all $50s and $100s be recalled and replaced with a new currency. The changeover would occur in a 10-day period, Regan proposed, and the old money would no longer be legal tender after that time.

Furthermore, Regan recommended that anyone turning in more than $1,000 in old bills be forced to prove that all taxes on the cash had been paid, and that it had not been generated through illegal activity. Otherwise, the funds would be impounded by the IRS--and their former owner would face further investigation.

If a sudden currency recall were to take place, it would presumably be justified as part of the War on Drugs. And once the old money had been recalled, the Treasury could announce that money laundering, for all intents and purposes, had been eliminated.

Are there any historical precedents for such action? Most certainly. After the bombing of Pearl Harbor in 1941, Hawaiians began withdrawing currency from banks in an effort to save their assets from destruction in the event of the anticipated Japanese invasion. The invasion never came, but Hawaiian banks were threatened with collapse.

To save the banks, the U.S. military police outlawed holding of more than $200 in cash. The remaining currency, along with dollar-denominated stocks and bonds, had to be turned over to the government for "safekeeping." Anyone who violated the law was subject to fines or imprisonment.[157]

To enforce this provision, military police opened and inspected all safety deposit boxes in Hawaii for cash and securities. All that were found were confiscated. Once the money had been seized, the police mandated a currency switch, to a dollar with the words "Hawaii" imprinted on the reverse. Cash that had been turned in was exchanged for the newly-imprinted currency.

Another World War II-era recall occurred in an effort to control black market military scrip. Military authorities announced that soldiers, sailors, and airmen had five hours to turn in their scrip. A new scrip was issued and anyone left with the old issue couldn't use it.

Even if you don't think you have anything to hide, currency recall could touch your life directly. Millions of us have perfectly legitimate reasons to hold cash. These reasons do not relate to any improper or unlawful activity. For instance, many people who experienced the Great Depression firsthand recall that thousands of banks failed during those years.

The present economic situation looks frighteningly familiar to anyone who lived thorough this period. Anyone who lost money in a failed bank during the Depression, or fears that the government might possibly violate its current deposit guarantees, might prefer to keep his money in cash.

Fear of banking collapse in today's economy is hardly irrational. The agency set up during the Depression to prevent a recurrence, the Federal Deposit Insurance Corporation, is now bankrupt. In 1991, Congress lent $70 billion to the FDIC in an effort to preserve public confidence in the banking system. However, a deputy Treasury secretary admitted in 1992 that the funds could be used up in the failure of a single large bank.

He also admitted that the funds would almost certainly not be repaid, and that much larger expenditures would in all likelihood be necessary--all at taxpayer expense. (The banking bailout is of course in addition to the cost of the S&L bailout, which the government now admits could ultimately cost more than $500 billion.) In October 1992, experts interviewed on CNN predicted as many as 2,000 U.S. banks were seriously undercapitalized, and could ultimately collapse.

If you think that there would be massive opposition to a new money conversion, you're not reading the same opinion polls that I am. Market Facts, a market research company, showed enormous public support for any currency exchange that was part of a fight against counterfeiting or drug trafficking.

Columnists such as William Safire and William Raspberry have gone on record as favoring currency recall to fight drug trafficking and money laundering. And when former Treasury Secretary Regan proposed the recall of all $50 and $100 bills and their replacement with a new currency, his suggestion met no criticism that I read about outside the alternative press.

Certainly, there have been few protests in previous gold or currency recalls. Roosevelt's confiscation of privately-owned gold resulted in a few squeals from the wealthy, and a massive outflow of gold from the United States to Switzerland, but most people went along. Those that didn't were subject to a 10-year prison sentence and a $10,000 fine.

---

[157]For more information on this episode, see "The Overprinted Notes of World War II," (*The Numismatist*, December 1991)

The Coming Two-Tiered Currency

It's possible for a currency recall to have much wider implications than it might appear at first glance. This would be particularly true if the recall were combined with a suggestion that has also been made repeatedly by high-level government officials: the introduction of a "domestic" currency that would circulate in the United States and an "international currency" would circulate outside the country. The two-tiered system could be justified as providing a permanent end to the money laundering problem.

The first proposal for a two-tiered currency was made in 1989 by the Drug Enforcement Administration. It suggested that a multi-colored currency be introduced, one form of which would circulate domestically, and one internationally. The two forms of currency would be exchangeable only at selected U.S. banks.

What would be the threat of a two-tiered currency? Wouldn't such a currency eliminate money laundering? I don't believe that it would. It would simply make money laundering more inefficient, as the underground economy shifted to barter. But this is how the program would be sold to the American public. The real reason for the changeover, however, will have nothing to do with money laundering. It will be to establish a two-tiered exchange rate for the dollar.

At first, the values of the domestic and international dollars would be equal. However, having a currency that cannot leave the country except under restricted conditions would permit the Federal Reserve and the Treasury to inflate away the government's gargantuan debts and unfunded obligations, using the power of the printing press. This would rapidly depreciate the value of the domestic currency against the international currency.

Many economists say that such a step would be illegal, and could never occur. Even if it were legal, they argue, surely the Federal Reserve and Treasury would never preside over the greatest debasement of the dollar in history. However, these agencies have already presided over a 95 percent depreciation of the dollar in terms of gold since 1933--the greatest debasement of our currency since our nation was founded. Moreover, a law on the books for nearly a decade makes even greater debasement completely legal. U.S. Public Law 96-221, the Depository Institutions Deregulation and Monetary Control Act of 1980 made the following change in what constitutes *legal monetary reserve* for the U.S. money supply:

> Bills, notes, revenue bonds and warrants with a maturity date not exceeding six months and obligations of, or fully guaranteed as to principal and interest by a foreign government or agency thereof.

In other words, it is perfectly legal for the U.S. government to simply buy or borrow a few trillion dollars worth of foreign bonds denominated in the Brazilian, Nicaraguan, Soviet currencies or any other third-world currency. It could then use these "assets" as a "legal monetary reserve" in order to print as much currency as is required to meet its obligations to the welfare state.

Furthermore, as former Congressman Ron Paul discovered more than a decade ago, the Federal Reserve refuses to tell Congress when or where it buys these "assets" and how much of them it owns. In fact, Fed officials instructed their New York office to quit releasing these figures to Congressman Paul, even though he was a member of the House Banking Committee. We the people have no right to know. It's none of our business.

The Fed could allow the international dollar to float in the international currency markets. U.S. Treasury securities issued for purchase by foreigners would be denominated in this new currency, perhaps even backed by gold. This would have the effect of greatly increasing foreign purchases of U.S. Treasury debt, which have declined dramatically in recent years.

On the other hand, Treasury securities held by U.S. citizens would be denominated in the virtually worthless, non-gold-backed, domestic currency. Only selected banks would be authorized to exchange domestic dollars for international dollars, and the amount of currency that could be exchanged at one time could be made progressively smaller. The domestic dollar would thus become a "blocked" currency, no longer freely exchangeable in world markets.

The suggestion that a two-tiered currency might be introduced has been ridiculed in some quarters. For instance, one newsletter editor dismisses the idea in the following analysis, which I've substantially shortened:

> The idea is that greenbacks would be good overseas, but that U.S. chumps like you would have to use new multi-colored banknotes that had no value outside this country. It's a rumor that's been floating around for over 20 years.
>
> But the rumor runs aground on several counts. For instance, most of the dollars held by foreigners are in accounts at banks that actually hold the dollars in U.S. banks--or are hedged against accounts in U.S. banks--or are loans or deposits in which the U.S. dollar is the currency of account, but for which there are no banknotes involved.
>
> There would be little to be gained by instituting a two-tiered currency system. More likely, the government would simply impose exchange controls that prevented Americans from opening foreign bank accounts and that restricted the transfers that U.S. banks could make for overseas customers. But governments impose exchange controls only when they're desperate to rescue a nose-diving currency. And the dollar is still about where it was 15 years ago against most major currencies.
>
> The likelihood of the U.S. government imposing full-blown exchange controls is slim. The U.S. is the world's biggest exporter; millions of American jobs depend on exports. Exchange controls would be devastating to foreign trade. The restrictions and increased paperwork would slow down American's purchases of imports, which would probably provoke retaliation by foreign governments.
>
> The motive for a two-tiered currency is supposedly to permit the U.S. government to inflate away its debt. But it's far more likely that rapid inflation would inspire the politicians to run up even bigger deficits.
>
> No one ever seems to name the Machiavellians who are secretly plotting to eliminate the federal debt through inflation. Is it David Rockefeller? Dan Quayle? Jimmy Carter? Dana Carvey? What do they have to gain from doing so? Conspiracies sound good on paper, but it's pretty tough to find one that has succeeded in real life.
>
> Newsletter writers have to make a living somehow, but they aren't responsible for the losses you suffer when you respond to their alarms.

This analyst is correct about the practical difficulties of instituting a two-tiered currency. The most important impact, as he states, would be retaliation by foreign governments against U.S. exports denominated in the increasingly worthless domestic dollar. He's also correct that it would most likely be imposed in a currency collapse. (And yes, newsletter writers do need to make a living.) But I don't think the threat can be dismissed as easily as he states.

The fact is that there would be a great deal for the government to gain by instituting such a system as opposed to mere exchange controls. The major benefit to the government would be that it could continue to sell debt overseas (particularly if the international currency were gold-backed)--while simultaneously inflating the domestic currency, thus making the national debt more manageable. Yes, Congress would probably continue to increase spending--and thus make the domestic dollar depreciation even worse.

Will this scenario unfold? I hope not. Could it occur? The legislative history of this proposal gives mixed signals. For instance, as I mentioned in Chapter 7, the Money Laundering Enforcement Amendments of 1991 would have required the Treasury Department to "study proposals" for a two-tiered currency. This bill was passed *unanimously* by the House (406-0) in June 1991. It died in the Senate that year. However, the proposal for a two-tiered currency was dropped from the Annunzio-Wylie Anti-Money Laundering Act of 1992.

However, the threat of currency controls remains, despite the current strength of the dollar. The government can't continue to run deficits of $400 billion annually (the total deficit, including all off-budget items) and have the dollar remain at its current level. Once the deficit swells to the point where all tax receipts are not sufficient to even pay interest on the national debt, the dollar will fall. According to *Bankruptcy 1995*, by former Grace Commission co-chairman Henry Figgie, this could occur by 1995. The decline could be breathtakingly rapid, since trillions of dollars are held overseas, and could quickly be exchanged for other currencies and gold.[158]

At this point, I believe the Clinton Administration would be likely to impose currency controls in an effort to slow the dollar's decline. The controls would likely not cause *additional* pain to exporters--a dollar collapse, with or without exchange controls, would be perceived internationally as legitimate cause for trade retaliation.

The Cashless Society

To fool the masses into [accepting] an irredeemable paper [currency], a middle step was needed between gold and paper--the redeemable Federal Reserve Note--a hybrid gold/paper medium. Similarly, a hybrid paper/electronic medium will be necessary before our monetary system can truly become cashless. The next middle step will be the new electronically-traceable paper greenbacks replacing today's Federal Reserve Notes. Then, after a short period of time, electronic banking (already a familiar, parallel system) will replace all paper media of exchange.

--"Boston T. Party," Goodbye, April 15

---

[158]Harry A. Figgie, Jr., *Bankruptcy 1995* (Boston: Little, Brown, & Co., 1992)

The new money and two-tiered currency is only an intermediate step toward the bureaucrats' ultimate goal: the society in which "all men are numbered from birth," as envisioned by Bill Clinton's mentor, Carroll Quigley (see Chapter 8, "The Future of Asset Forfeiture").

One way for bureaucrats to make people demand controls on cash is to create crises, such as the War on Drugs. Another way is to make possible substitutes very convenient. Today, credit cards and personal checks have done away with most cash transactions. And tomorrow, electronic "debit cards" promise to do away with the remainder.

With a debit card, you pay for your purchases with a card read by a merchant's computer terminal. The terminal automatically debits your bank account for the amount of purchase. Simultaneously, the system applies a credit to the merchant's account, minus a service charge. The process is neat, simple and all the paperwork is done automatically. It creates an electronic trail on every item you purchase. But if you are making a purchase or contribution that you wish to keep private, then you have a problem.

Debit cards are popular with merchants because they permit an instant, foolproof credit to be applied to their accounts. They eliminate bouncing checks and credit card chargebacks. Debit cards also permit a merchant to categorize his customers by what they purchase and how much they spend. This analysis permits him to direct his marketing efforts appropriately.

Banks like debit cards because they can deduct a service charge for making the transaction. My bank recently began imposing a service charge for use of its automatic teller machines (ATMs), which are nothing more than debit card terminals. Yours will too, if it isn't already doing so. According to a 1991 survey by the U.S. Public Interest Research Group, approximately twice as many banks are charging customers for use of ATMs as in 1987, and fees are rising sharply. Marketing firms like debit cards as well, since the profile created from individual purchases will create a much more detailed picture of consumer spending patterns than is currently available.

Government bureaucrats like debit cards best of all, because they eliminate cash and permit much more detailed financial surveillance. One of the first nationwide uses of debit cards by Americans will be by food stamp recipients. New federal rules permit states to computerize their food stamp programs so recipients can purchase food with plastic cards. The new program is designed to reduce fraud in the program; many recipients use food stamps as substitute cash to purchase drugs or other items on the black market. One of the first efforts in this direction started nearly seven years ago in Reading, Pennsylvania.

The ultimate plan is to use a single card for all welfare "entitlements." A welfare agency sets up an account in the recipient's name and credits it every month, with cash, food stamps, and/or other benefits. The recipient gets a plastic debit card to draw against the benefits.

Debit card experiments are under way in Singapore, Germany, Taiwan, Baltimore (for welfare recipients), and the Marine Corps base at Parris Island, South Carolina. Students at the University of Florida now use the "Gator One" card for everything from opening a dorm entrance to paying for their tuition. The consulting firm of Global Concepts, Inc. hopes to implement a cashless society in Atlanta, Georgia by the mid-1990s.

Canadian banks launched a national debit card system in 1992. A recent agreement between a dozen of the largest regional ATM networks in the United States would set up a national debit card system that would allow consumers to instantly deduct purchases from their checking accounts anywhere they travel. In the near future, a debit card may be coming to your hometown--if it hasn't already.

Unfortunately for banks and bureaucrats, consumers don't like debit cards. In 1991, only about 0.4 percent of store purchases were made with them. Even optimistic visions of their future use foresee them accounting for less than 3 percent of store purchases by the end of the decade. Another barrier to their universal acceptance is that some 14 percent of the U.S. population do not have bank accounts. Perhaps the government will eventually require banks to subsidize accounts for these individuals, so everyone can carry a debit card.

If consumers can't be persuaded to use debit cards voluntarily, suggests author David Warwick in the Nov.-Dec. 1992 issue of *The Futurist*, perhaps the government should force them to do so. Warwick claims that crime and tax evasion would be eliminated by ridding society of cash. The 40 million Americans who use cash exclusively would "have to adjust." For those worried about privacy, Warwick claims the system would be "even more confidential than Social Security and Census records." If you've read the earlier chapters in this report, of course, you already know that these systems are anything but well-protected.

Are there alternatives to debit cards that might actually enhance privacy? There are, but don't expect to learn about them from advocates of big, all-seeing government. One anonymous debit card works in much the same way as a copier card. You program your card by inserting cash into a device that automatically credits the card. You then use it anonymously, and "recharge" it when the credits run out. This system is already widely used in Europe and Japan. One version of the system found at Japanese airports and other public locations even allows you to exchange one currency for another.

Another even more sophisticated experiment is underway in Denmark. It involves a cryptographic invention known as a "blind signature" that would replace debit cards with personal identifiers on them. It permits anonymous transactions, and does not permit the construction of personal or financial profiles.[159]

Big government advocates of debit cards, and of the cashless society, would have you believe that its arrival would spell the end of tax evasion, money laundering, the drug trade, and black markets. But it won't work. Instead of wiping out the underground economy and black markets, the cashless society will expand both dramatically.

Exchanges in the cashless underground economy will be made in the form of *barter* (see Chapter 5). Barter, already under attack by the IRS for over a decade, will come under renewed assault. But the sheer volume of barter exchanges will overwhelm any enforcement policy short of "stationing IRS agents in every American kitchen," as George Bush once accused Michael Dukakis of proposing.

Government by Emergency

Today, the United States faces a multitude of crises. The banking system is collapsing. So is the insurance system. Our central cities are crumbling. Local governments are declaring bankruptcies. Debt at all levels--personal, state and federal--stands at an all-time high. Approximately $15 trillion in unfunded obligations the federal government has promised to meet are coming due over the next few decades. The AIDS epidemic threatens to overrun us.

Any one of these crises could result in economic or physical devastation for the United States. And if devastation appears imminent, the president is empowered to declare a national emergency to deal with the crisis.[160]

---

[159]For more information on this experiment, see "Achieving Electronic Privacy" in the August 1992 *Scientific American*.

[160]One book dealing with this topic is Dr. Gary North's *Government by Emergency* (American Bureau of Economic Research, P.O. Box 84906, Phoenix, Ariz. 85071; 1983)

The scope of the president's powers in wartime are familiar to older Americans. For instance, during World War II, the Roosevelt administration, without consulting Congress, froze wages and prices nationwide and began a strict program of rationing many essential goods, seized industries that were vital to the war effort, and imprisoned more than 120,000 Americans of Japanese ancestry, many of whom had already been naturalized.

A half-century later, most Americans believe that the only time the president assumes such extraordinary powers is in wartime. But thousands of emergency regulations explicitly state that war is the *most likely* but not the *exclusive*, reason to force a declaration of a state of emergency.

And national emergencies are routinely declared in peacetime. President Reagan used emergency powers to impose a trade embargo against Nicaragua, declaring that its Communist government posed "an unusual and extraordinary threat to the United States." Reagan also declared a national emergency in relation to South Africa. On September 9, 1985, he issued Executive Order 12532, which stated that the "policies and actions of the government of South Africa constitute an unusual and extraordinary threat to the foreign policy and economy of the United States."

The Nicaraguan situation comprised a legitimate national security concern, even though it is difficult for me to see how it could be construed as a national emergency. But in the case of South Africa, there was no threat whatsoever. South Africa never threatened to cut off supplies of strategic metals, or take any other aggressive action against the United States. What South Africa had was a social system that many Americans found repugnant. But is a repugnant social system in a nation 8,000 miles from our borders a legitimate reason to declare a national emergency?

For a president to sign an executive order declaring a national emergency in peacetime is a bad habit. But it is a bad habit that goes back 150 years. In 1842, President John Tyler signed an executive order authorizing the army to round up Seminole Indians in Georgia and Florida and force them to march to Arkansas. Executive orders were also used by President Franklin D. Roosevelt to confiscate privately-held gold in 1933 and by President Nixon to impose wage and price controls in 1971.

According to Article II of the Constitution, the president has the responsibility to "preserve, protect, and defend the Constitution." However, nowhere in this document are executive orders authorized, and the term has never been defined by Congress. Nor has Congress ever been consulted prior to the president issuing an executive order. And there is no provision in the Constitution for executive orders to be reviewed by the judiciary. And even the rare article in the mainstream media that discusses the topic of executive orders tends to focus on non-emergency use of the presidential authority to issue them.[161]

In the words of former Senator Charles Mathias:

> Emergency regulations clothe the president with virtually unlimited powers with which he can affect the lives of American citizens in a host of all-encompassing ways. This vast range of powers confers enough authority on the president to rule the country without reference to normal constitutional processes.

---

[161]In a Sept. 29, 1992 article in *The Washington Post*, entitled "Executive Fiat: How a New President Could Make a Big Difference," *Post* writer Al Kamen focused exclusively on issues such as timber harvesting, abortion counseling, and gay rights. He, nor any other mainstream writer I've come across, said anything about a network of emergency regulations that can suspend the Constitution.

The president may seize property; organize and control the means of production; seize commodities; assign military forces abroad; institute martial law; seize and control all transportation and communication; regulate the operation of private enterprise; restrict travel; and in a plethora of particular ways, control the lives of all American citizens.

The size of this network of emergency regulations is huge--and totally undocumented. Even the Library of Congress has no centralized record of emergency regulations. According to a study by the U.S. Air Force, more than 13,000 executive orders have already been issued. To overturn an executive order requires a 2/3 majority of Congress--so they are not often reversed.[162]

One of Colonel Oliver North's assignments that was unrelated to the Iran-Contra scandal was to draft a plan in 1984 to impose martial law in case of a national emergency. When North was asked about this assignment during his testimony before Congress, the exchange went like this:

Rep. Jack Brooks (D-Tex.): "Colonel North, in your work at the National Security Council, were you not assigned at one time to work on plans for the continuity of government in the event of a major disaster?"

Brendan Sullivan, North's attorney: "Mr. Chairman!"

Sen. Daniel Inouye (D-Hawaii): "I believe that question touches on a highly-sensitive and classified area, so may I request that you not touch upon that, sir?"

Brooks: "I was particularly concerned, Mr. Chairman, because I read in the Miami papers and several others, that there had been a contingency plan in the event of an emergency that would suspend the American Constitution, and I was deeply concerned about it. I'm wondering if that was an area in which he had worked. I believe that it was...[interrupted by Chairman]."

Inouye: "May I most respectfully suggest that the matter not be touched upon at this stage? If we wish to get into this I'm certain that arrangements can be made for Executive [secret] session."

Obviously, Senator Inouye had no desire for the scope of the government's vast network of emergency regulations to be broadcast to millions of listeners. His desire for secrecy is not surprising, since many of these regulations involve, as Congressman Brooks correctly stated, literally suspending the Constitution.

With more than 13,000 executive orders on the books, a comprehensive listing is obviously beyond the scope of this report. But some of the orders that would mandate profound changes in the relationship of the government to U.S. citizens include:

✓ E.O. 11002, which authorizes the president to direct the Postal Service to register the location and identity of every U.S. citizen in preparation for other emergency procedures

---

[162]The most comprehensive summary of these powers I've seen is a collection of documents several thousand pages long assembled by a patriot group in Colorado. The *Emergency Powers Package* includes the out-of-print Senate Report 93-549 "Emergency Powers Statutes" (600+ pages) plus many other invaluable reference materials, many obtained through Freedom of Information Act inquiries. For more information, contact H. Nelson, P.O. Box 192, Evergreen, Colo. 80439.

✔ E.O. 11921, which calls for total censorship--not just press censorship, but the total control of all "devices capable of emitting electromagnetic radiation." Translated into English, this means regulation, perhaps even *confiscation,* of C.B. radios, televisions and computers.

Continuing, E.O. 11921 authorizes "utilization of excess and surplus real and personal property." My interpretation: Property owned by "hoarders" will be confiscated and sold. Who is a "hoarder?" To the bureaucrat, perhaps anyone with the foresight to prepare in advance for an extended bout of emergency controls.

✔ E.O. 10995, which takes over where E.O. 11921 leaves off, authorizes the president to take over all other "communications media"

✔ E.O. 11004, which authorizes the president to forcibly relocate individuals from their homes to new areas designated by the government

✔ E.O. 11000, which authorizes the president to forcibly enlist civilians into work brigades under the command of the military. In other words, slave labor.

✔ E.O. 10999, which authorizes the president to take over of all modes of transportation, highways, etc. President Bush invoked this executive order in the autumn of 1990 in preparation for war with Iraq.

✔ E.O. 11005 and E.O. 11003, which authorize the president to take over all other modes of transportation including airports, railroads, inland waterways, and public storage facilities

✔ E.O. 10998, which authorizes the president to commandeer the nation's food supply, and to divert it to whatever purposes he so orders

President Nixon in 1969 combined many of the powers granted above into a master plan, implemented as E.O. 11490. This executive order stated that all power may be transferred to the president under "any national emergency *type* situation that might conceivably confront the nation." One power it provides is authorizing the president to "utilize non-industrial facilities in the event of an emergency in order to reduce requirements for new construction and to provide facilities in a minimum period of time." In other words, it authorizes confiscation of commercial and residential property--a direct violation of the Fifth Amendment.

In addition, it calls for the president to "develop plans and procedures for the provision of logistical support to members of foreign forces, their employees and dependents as may be present in the United States." In other words, it authorizes the military to force private citizens to accommodate foreign soldiers on their property.

Finally, E.O. 11490 permits the president to seize all sources of public power and freeze all wages, prices, and bank accounts. In 1971, Nixon invoked this executive order to impose wage and price controls. Amazingly, almost no one complained. Even more remarkably, the controls were imposed at a time when inflation was only *4 percent.* Today, a 4 percent inflation rate is considered "normal," but a precedent has been set for emergency economic controls to be imposed if inflation rises above this level.

Until the 1970s, it was assumed that the *military* would administer the provisions of executive orders. But one of President Carter's first executive orders, E.O. 12148, created an agency known as the Federal Emergency Management Agency (FEMA), whose responsibility it was to plan continuously for the implementation of emergency powers. The order also explicitly authorizes the president to declare a state of emergency, under conditions solely defined by him.

Today, FEMA headquarters sit behind the barbed-wire fences of Fort Meade, Maryland, part of the National Security Agency's giant intelligence complex. In this top-secret location, FEMA bureaucrats labor to develop contingency plans for emergency operations of the U.S. government.

Of course, the official reason for FEMA's existence is "disaster relief." In this context, FEMA has in recent years borne responsibility for coordinating emergency services in the wake of Hurricanes Hugo (in 1989) and Andrew (in 1992). After thousands of complaints, the General Accounting Office conducted an investigation of FEMA's response, concluding that its actions had been "inefficient" and "weak."

Ten months after Hurricane Hugo hit, according to the report, most of the families left homeless "had not yet been provided with housing assistance from FEMA." On the other hand, private relief organizations such as the American Red Cross were providing such assistance to hurricane victims within hours of the storm's arrival.

FEMA's reaction after Hurricane Andrew weren't much better. In one hilarious example, the Mayor of Homestead, Florida requested that FEMA provide it with emergency telephone services. FEMA responded by sending out vans equipped with coded multi-frequency systems designed to communicate with U.S. military aircraft--but which could not make ordinary telephone calls.

FEMA admits that less than 10 percent of its employees are devoted to natural disaster relief efforts. The remainder continue to prepare for a "nuclear disaster evacuation" scenario--and their activities are still classified "top secret."

One of the top priorities for FEMA is to identify potential "troublemakers;" i.e., anyone who might object to suspending the Constitution and imposing government by emergency. To meet this objective, a top-secret database of several hundred thousand suspect U.S. citizens has been prepared to be arrested and detained in an emergency.

President Bush has secretly mobilized FEMA on at least two occasions. Prior to his 1989 trip to Colombia for a regional drug war summit meeting, FEMA prepared secret plans to round up 10,000 Americans with "known terrorist sympathies" in the event of Bush's assassination.

A year later, prior to the U.S. invasion of Iraq, FEMA alerted the U.S. army to begin activating detention camps in preparation for an anticipated wave of anti-war protests. These camps--11 huge federal detention centers--were authorized under a National Security Directive called "Rex 84" by President Reagan.

A joint task force of staff officials from six national security agencies and FEMA began meeting in August 1990 to locate Americans suspected of being potential supporters of Iraq, in preparation for their possible detention. Fortunately, the U.S. armed forces had such a decisive victory over Iraq, and with so few U.S. casualties, that widespread protests never developed.[163]

Today, the "son of Rex 84" is falling into place with the completion of the "MJTF" project--the Multi-Jurisdictional Task Force. The mission of the MJTF, according to its mission statement, is to conduct "house-to-house search and seizure, separation and categorization of men, women and children, in large numbers, categorization and transfer to detention facilities and the running of detention facilities."

---

[163]The largest of these 11 detention facilities is the Elmdorf facility in Alaska. Originally created to house Alaska's "mentally ill" population, federal authorities are now surrounding this huge enclave (more than 1600 square miles) with barbed-wire fences.

MJTF is composed of elements of the National Guard, local law enforcement, and even street gangs. National Public Radio's September 25, 1992 broadcast described a contractual agreement between the city of Los Angeles and two of the city's most violent criminal gangs, the Crips and the Bloods. The agreement calls for gang members to be trained, uniformed, equipped, and armed as part of the MJTF. The primary aim of MJTF, according to Tom Valentine's October 13, 1992 "Radio Free America" broadcast, is to confiscate firearms in any emergency situation.

Valentine's broadcast stated that MJTF operates in conjunction with the Financial Crimes Enforcement Network (FinCEN), the operations of which I described in Chapter 7. FinCEN has control of more than 300,000 military and civilian personnel, according to the broadcast. The FinCEN uniform is an all-black ninja-like outfit.

Some, but not all, FinCEN units are identified by a FinCEN emblem on the shoulder and/or helmet, and a United Nations flag crest. They operate in black helicopters and other assault aircraft that have no markings on them, in violation of FAA regulations. But since these troops operate under executive order, and no other law, they are exempt from such regulations. These troops have already been deployed in several operations, according to the Valentine broadcast, most recently in the deadly Ruby Creek, Idaho raid against alleged white supremacist Randy Weaver and his family.

Anyone who blows the whistle on FEMA or its progeny is subject to retaliation. In 1989, a federal contractor who reported problems with the "Doomsday Project," a top-secret program to keep the government running after a nuclear war, asserted in a sealed lawsuit that FEMA burglarized his office. The burglary allegedly occurred after the contractor rejected a FEMA demand that he turn over all his business records to a competitor. Shortly thereafter, FEMA obtained a secret court order which prohibits the contractor from discussing the case with anyone, or be held in contempt of court, fined, and/or imprisoned.

In addition, Congress is perfectly capable of declaring a national emergency on its own. A bill introduced in 1990 by Texas Senator Phil Gramm and Georgia Representative Newt Gingrich would have imposed "A Declaration of National Drug and Crime Emergency" in the United States. If enacted, the bill would have instituted a five-year state of emergency, authorizing the government to imprison without trial, build concentration camps, and arbitrarily seize property. While not explicitly calling for the suspension of the Constitution and Bill of Rights, the language of the bill makes it clear that its provisions could not be implemented without "drawing on the lessons of World War II," when many constitutional rights were suspended.

The Gramm-Gingrich emergency declaration didn't pass, but it really didn't matter. More than a decade earlier, President Carter had already signed an even more sweeping bill, the "International Economic Powers Act of 1977." It was this act that President Bush invoked in order to freeze Kuwaiti assets within hours after Iraq's invasion of Kuwait on August 2, 1990. The act permits the president to:

A. investigate, regulate or prohibit --

(i) any transactions in foreign exchange,

(ii) transfers of credit or payments between, by, through, or to any banking institution, to the extent that such transfers or payment involve any interest of any foreign country or a national thereof,

(iii) the importing or exporting of currency or securities.

Anyone who violates these rules is subject to a fine of $1 million per violation and a 12-year prison sentence, and forfeiture of any assets involved in or connected to the violation.

You'll be happy to know, however, that if a national emergency is declared, the IRS will be ready. A section of the *Internal Revenue Manual* provides for the agency to resume collection of taxes within 30 days of a nuclear attack (or presumably, any other type of emergency). The section reads in part:

> On the premise that the collection of delinquent accounts would be most
> adversely affected, and in many cases would be impossible, the service
> will concentrate on the collection of current taxes. However, in areas
> where the taxpaying potential is substantially unimpaired, enforced
> collection of delinquent accounts will be continued.

A full-scale nuclear war, while not an impossibility, no longer appears to be the most likely precursor for the imposition of emergency controls. Natural disasters--such as Hurricane Hugo--offer a compelling rationale to impose them. So do man-made disasters such as the 1992 Los Angeles riots.

During President Bush's May 1992 address on the Los Angeles riots, he stated he would use "whatever force is necessary" to contain them. He ordered 4,500 military troops deployed into Los Angeles, federalized the National Guard, and instructed General Colin Powell to place these troops under central command. Under the circumstances, Bush's actions were not surprising. But they set a dangerous precedent. Subsequent government investigations "proved" that the causes of the riot were the easy availability of guns and drugs.

A politically expedient way for President Clinton to condition the American people to a permanent state of emergency would be to impose emergency controls on a limited scale--perhaps in the most-blighted neighborhoods of one or two large cities, using MJTF personnel.

In the name of escalating the War on Drugs, or simply to enforce "law and order," Clinton could authorize his new 100,000-man national police force--perhaps composed of ex-members of Los Angeles street gangs--to conduct house-to-house searches for illegal guns, illegal drugs--and of course, illegal cash.

I suspect that most Americans would support such "strong action." In this manner, neighbor-hood-by-neighborhood, city-by-city, Clinton could impose his own vision of government by emergency--and gain immense media credit for his "political courage."

Toward a New Constitution

The greatest fear of Congress and the FEMA bureaucrats is that a court might conclude that there is no provision in the Constitution for emergency powers to be invoked. While the Constitution provides no such authority to the judiciary, neither does it authorize executive orders to be issued.

To deal with this problem, Congress in 1974 authorized a task force to convene a convention with the objective of creating a new Constitution. The fact that a constitutional convention has not yet been held 18 years after Congress first suggested its convening demonstrates how sensitive this subject is in the eyes of many Americans.

The most likely basis for the new Constitution is a document created by an misnamed organization known as the Center for Democratic Institutions, supported by organizations ranging from the League of Women Voters to the Rockefeller Foundation. The *40th draft* for the Constitution of the "Newstates of America" is reprinted in Rexford G. Tugwell's *The Emerging Constitution*. Here are some of the new Constitution's provisions, should it ever be adopted:[164]

✓ *Preamble.* "Justice and domestic tranquility," guaranteed in the preamble to our existing Constitution, have been replaced by "good order." No mention is made of the need to protect individual rights. Instead, the very first words are "so we may join in common endeavors." No mention is made of defense or general welfare, or of liberty itself. Instead, the preamble calls for "an adequate and self-repairing government."

Could it be that under this definition "adequate" means too powerful to be challenged, and "self-repairing" means the laws can be changed at any time to deal with whatever objections to the Constitution might arise?

✓ *Article I.* There are two parts to the article, defining "rights" and "responsibilities." All the rights granted to citizens are appropriated by the government, not by a higher authority, and may be terminated at any time. Individual responsibilities to the government--to pay taxes, serve in the armed forces, etc.--are absolute and unconditional.

✓ *Article II.* This article describes the "Newstates;" the 50 states would be eliminated, and 10 Newstates would take their place. These 10 Newstates would have no independent governing authority, and would be totally subservient to the federal government.[165]

✓ *Articles III through VIII.* These articles define the branches of the government. Instead of three independent branches--legislative, judicial, and executive--designed to prevent the abuse of power, we would have six branches, totally eliminating our existing system of checks and balances. These would include a regulatory branch, to control everyday life and commerce; a planning branch, to plan the nation's economy and industrial policy; an electoral branch to oversee and regulate all elections, etc.

✓ *The Bill of Rights.* Under the new Constitution, no Bill of Rights exists. For instance, instead of each citizen being given the right to bear arms, "the bearing of arms or the possession of lethal weapons shall be confined to the police, members of the armed forces, and those licensed under law."

Trial by jury disappears, replaced by a judge who decides whether a trial is to be "investigative" or "adversarial." Investigative trials are the kind pioneered under the Napoleonic Code, where the accused is presumed guilty and must prove his innocence. In other words, the provisions of RICO, the tax code, and the money laundering statutes would now apply to any case where the judge decides such a procedure to be appropriate. Adversarial--i.e. jury--trials are permitted, but the judge may decide how many jurors are to be appointed. A jury of one's peers is not necessary. If you request a jury trial, and the judge agrees, he could appoint a federal prosecutor as a jury of one.

Searches and seizures "shall be made only by judicial warrant," in the Newstates of America. There is no prohibition against "unreasonable" searches and seizures, as the Fourth Amendment to our current Constitution guarantees. The practice of religion is "privileged," but like other privileges in this new Constitution, the government may revoke this right at any time.

The Fifth Amendment to our current Constitution guarantees that no private property will be converted to public use without "just compensation." The new Constitution has this same provision, but

---

[164]Russell G. Tugwell, *The Emerging Constitution* (New York: Harper & Row; 1974)

[165]In 1969, Richard Nixon issued E.O. 11647, which authorized the division of the United States into 10 regions, as *The Emerging Constitution* suggests.

leaves out the word "just." In other words, the government could seize your property, give you a pittance of what it's worth, and order you off of it, without even resorting to civil forfeiture.

Other provisions of this document permit the President to issue decrees which automatically go into effect unless overruled by a majority of Congress and establishes a permanent "Office of Emergency Organization." In fact, the word *emergency* appears a total of 134 times throughout this document.

How do you prepare for a national emergency, the seizure of your property, the suspension of the Constitution, or its replacement by a document making a mockery of our common law rights? If a full-blown emergency is declared, with the military forcibly relocating innocent civilians, there is no effective defense short of leaving the United States, if travel beyond U.S. borders has not already been banned. However, there are a number of steps you can take to prepare yourself for lesser emergencies.

✓ *Keep at least a 90-day supply of food, water, and heating fuel in your home.* Begin acquiring these supplies now. If you try to purchase them after a crisis begins, you may be considered a "hoarder" and subject to arrest.

✓ *Keep a supply of currency and small-denomination gold and silver coins at hand.* A national emergency could be declared in the event of hyperinflation or depression, and gold and silver may replace currency as the most widely accepted trading medium in the underground economy. To make certain that currency you hold is not tainted with drug residues, follow the precautions for cash accumulation in Chapter 8, "A Survey of Private Investments." And don't forget my precautions about home safekeeping in Chapter 8.

✓ *Purchase an electrical generator for use during periods when outside power is not available.* If you live in a sunny area of the country, you might even consider purchasing a photovoltaic (solar powered) electrical backup system. Solar water heating is also viable in some areas, and is usually considerably less expensive to purchase and install than a photovoltaic system.

✓ *Purchase a good short-wave radio.* Once an emergency is imposed, you'll want to avoid transmitting (if such transmission is banned), but you'll at least be able to listen in on what is occurring in other parts of the nation and the world. President Roosevelt banned ownership of short-wave radios in World War II, but the law was not widely enforced. A prohibition today would be easy to enforce in cities, but not in rural areas.

A good choice for a short-wave antenna that is easy to disguise is the Ventenna VT-155. This antenna slips over your attic vent pipe on your roof. It looks like a vent pipe, not an antenna. Many radio hobby suppliers either stock or can obtain this antenna.

✓ *Purchase items that you could barter in an emergency.* After World War II, Germany existed on a barter economy with cigarettes being the most common medium of exchange. Alcoholic beverages are another item that can also be bartered or provided as a gift to influential individuals. Other barterable items include those that might be rationed. The potential list is almost endless: batteries, tires, kerosene, toilet paper, coffee, sugar, etc.

✓ *Learn to repair the major life-sustaining appliances in your own home.* At least obtain manuals and spare parts. This would include, at minimum, your furnace, refrigerator, stove, hot water heater, and water pump (if you have a well on your property.)

✓ *Talk to people who have lived under emergency controls to see how they adapted.* Any American that lived through World War II has first-hand experience of government by emergency. So does any immigrant from the Soviet Union, Eastern Europe, or Communist China. Or go to a library and look for issues of local newspapers that date back to the World War II era. You'll find first-hand evidence of how people cope under emergency controls.

Two good sources of information for preparing for government by emergency are Dr. Gary North's *Government by Emergency,* which I mentioned previously, and John Pugsley's *The Alpha Strategy.*[166]

The AIDS Epidemic

By the turn of the century, AIDS will have made the Black Plague look like a Sunday School picnic

--Jonathan Mann, director of the World Health Organization Global AIDS program

AIDS is rapidly becoming the most important disease since the Black Plague. Our government estimates that an absolute minimum of 1 million Americans now carry the AIDS virus, although many experts estimate the true number to be much higher. Dr. Taki Anagnoston, author of *Surviving the AIDS Plague,* estimates that there are nearly *20 million* AIDS-infected Americans. Whatever the number of people who carry the virus may be, only about one in 50 are actually AIDS-sick. Most of the remainder don't even realize they are infected.[167]

Even if somehow *no new infections* were to occur in the United States, *every person* who has been exposed to AIDS, so far as scientists know, will eventually come down with the disease. Can you imagine an epidemic where nearly 20 million Americans die? This will be the legacy of AIDS in the United States. In other parts of the world, the legacy will be far worse. In Africa, perhaps 25 percent or more of the population will perish from AIDS, according to the latest estimates.

What does AIDS have to do with privacy? Plenty. Epidemics don't have rights. The privacy implications of fighting the spread of this (as far as we know) always-fatal affliction are staggering.

√ *As the AIDS epidemic worsens, an AIDS test will become a routine part of application for employment, insurance, etc.* A positive test will make it virtually impossible for the victim to work or obtain medical or life insurance.

√ *AIDS test results will become public knowledge.* Test results will be made available to public health officials and by extension, to insurance companies and credit bureaus. Eventually, the results of your AIDS test will be added to the microchip contained in your national ID card.

√ *Members of groups known to be susceptible to AIDS will suffer increased discrimination.* For instance, male homosexuals have so far bore the brunt of the AIDS epidemic in the United States. Insurance companies are already denying coverage to persons who are admitted or suspected homosexuals. Some insurance companies have even denied coverage to individuals living in zip codes where large numbers of homosexuals are suspected to reside, or who work in particular occupations. For instance, the Hartford Life Insurance Co. and New England Life both list "entertainment groups" as ineligible for many types of coverage.

---

[166]John Pugsley, *The Alpha Strategy* (New York: Harper & Row, 1981)

[167]Taki N. Anagnoston, *Surviving the AIDS Plague* (America West Publishers, P.O. Box 986, Tehachapi, Calif. 93581; 1988, [1991])

✓ *Mass quarantines of AIDS victims will begin.* AIDS hospices (critics called them "concentration camps"), which have already been the subject of an unsuccessful California ballot initiative, may be built. AIDS victims (and perhaps even those merely testing positive for the AIDS virus) shipped there to die.

✓ *The public health and insurance systems will collapse.* AIDS is extraordinarily expensive to treat. Medically treating an AIDS-sick patient costs anywhere from $50,000 to $200,000 every year. Medically treating 10 million victims will cost, at minimum, $500 billion annually. The money will come from the usual sources--higher taxes, more infringements on our privacy, and even larger government deficits. Or it may not be spent at all, which means that AIDS deaths will occur much more quickly.

These measures may sound unlikely given the recent efforts to give AIDS victims civil rights, prohibit discrimination against AIDS-infected employees, and indeed, force employers to hire AIDS-infected job candidates. Such measures will only make the eventual backlash against AIDS victims stronger when the true proportions of the epidemic become apparent.

Just wait a few years until the annual number of AIDS deaths in the United States numbers in the hundreds of thousands. There is no cure for AIDS and there are so many varieties of the virus that a vaccine is highly unlikely. AIDS will spark a worldwide panic. Privacy will be the last concern of those who must deal with this deadly plague.

Biological Privacy

The discovery of the genetic code in 1953 speared development of a entirely new technology in the last 35 years. Techniques now being tested can actually repair genetic flaws--and more importantly from the standpoint of privacy, to detect them with greater and greater precision.

Do you think that an insurance company or employer would be interested if a genetic screening found that you had a predisposition to alcoholism or to heart disease? Such technology is not yet in wide use. But it is now possible for insurance companies, employers and the government to deny employment or insurance (or end it!) subject to the results of a mandatory test of your blood or urine.[168]

The completion of the "Human Genome Project" promises to provide researchers with a genetic map of the entire human body. This map will prove invaluable in the decades to come in both preventing and treating genetic disorders. According to Philip Reilly, head of Boston's Shriver Medical Center for Mental Retardation, discrimination based on genetic testing "could be a big problem 10 years from now, when we might have 100 tests for genetic diseases."

Such tests could put millions of people into high-risk disease categories, branding them for insurance and employment purposes in much the same way those diagnosed with AIDS are already marked. A 1991 survey of America's largest companies showed 12 of the Fortune 500 already use genetic monitoring or screening.

Tests are already available that detect inherited susceptibility to several genetic conditions in the fetus of a pregnant mother, including cystic fibrosis, sickle cell anemia, Huntington's Disease, hemophilia, and muscular dystrophy. Experimental techniques now being developed would detect susceptibility to hypertension, dyslexia, Alzheimer's Disease, and cancer.

---

[168]A fascinating report from the U.S. Office of Technology Assessment covers this subject in detail. It is entitled *Biology, Medicine and the Bill of Rights*. (Washington, D.C.: U.S. Government Printing Office, Stock No. 052-003-01133-6, 1989)

Since there is no legislation in place to protect medical records from disclosure (see "Privacy and Your Medical Records," Chapter 4), this information is routinely released to insurance companies and employers.

This has already led to "genetic discrimination" against individuals with less desirable genetic profiles. Those unfortunate enough to carry genes predisposing them toward any future condition that could affect their health are becoming uninsurable.

Sometimes, the results of the tests lead insurance companies to recommend abortions. One insurance company asked a pregnant mother to abort her fetus when tests showed the baby would almost certainly be born with spinal bifida, a severe and often fatal birth defect. In another case, a physician at a health maintenance organization diagnosed a pregnant mother as carrying a fetus with cystic fibrosis, and told her that the HMO would not pay for the delivery or care of the baby once it was born. He advised her to obtain an abortion.

A new computer system developed by scientists at George Washington University permits physicians and families of severely ill patients calculate the patient's chances of dying. In the not-distant future, medical insurance companies may refuse to reimburse procedures on patients that the computer tells them are going to "die anyway," particularly if the victims have a "genetic defect" making them more susceptible to certain conditions.

Unfortunately, there is no way of knowing how severely a genetic predisposition will manifest itself. A positive test provides no prediction of the course of the disease and the costs it might entail. The age of onset and the severity of gene-associated diseases vary widely due to differing lifestyles, courses of treatment and how the genes are "expressed." Much research remains to determine how these factors influence the severity of a given condition.

Health and life insurance companies typically require access to the medical records of people seeking coverage and ask about pre-existing medical conditions. If you don't disclose these conditions, you could lose your insurance.

Several insurance companies already define a "pre-existing medical conditions" (for which coverage usually isn't available) as including a genetic susceptibility to a condition that hasn't yet developed. Make sure you are adequately insured, and gainfully employed, *before* these tests come into wider use.

The precision of such screening also means that it will increasingly be used to construct "fingerprints;" unique personal identifiers based on your genetic code. Actually, the genetic profiles are far less precise than fingerprints; there is about a one-in-a-million chance that two people will share the same genetic profile.

But such uncertainty has not stopped various governmental entities from setting up a national database of DNA information. U.S. armed forces now plan to compile genetic files of DNA "dogtags" for each soldier, sailor, or airman. And in May 1992, the Supreme Court allowed a state court to force a woman to have her blood drawn to determine if another woman is related--and thus entitled to part of the family estate.

Twenty states are in various stages of setting up computerized systems of genetic information. Virginia, for instance, now requires DNA samples from state felons so their "fingerprint" can be recorded in a computerized database. The FBI is funding much of the expense for the systems, and hopes to have a national genetic database in place by the late 1990s.

Privacy and the U.S. Census

Prior to the 1990 census, the U.S. Bureau of the Census organized a massive media campaign to publicize it. Among other topics, the Bureau advertised that information related in census forms is confidential and that "the census is safe."

The Census Bureau claims that it goes to great lengths to keep census returns secret. But the immense task of compiling the census requires computerization. Moreover, once the data is computer-compiled, it is released in the form of "statistical abstracts" and made available to marketing and government organizations.

While your identity is protected in such abstracts, as I described in Chapter 4, it is possible to generate a remarkably accurate profile of your income and social status by matching census data on the neighborhood you live in with your Social Security number.

Is the census, in fact, safe? Don't ask that question of a Japanese-American. In the early years of World War II, 112,000 U.S. citizens of Japanese ancestry were rounded up and interned for the duration of the war in concentration camps. In the 1970s, it was finally revealed how the Army had found where these individuals lived: through data released by the Census Bureau. And in World War I, the Census Bureau provided law enforcement officials with the names and addresses of young men to the Justice Department who had refused to register for the draft. And of course, as I mentioned in Chapter 7, census data is shared with FinCEN.[169]

The 1990 census resulted in the lowest voluntary completion rate (65 percent) in history. Were Americans sending a protest vote over this invasion of their privacy to Washington? Are we finally learning that information we provide the government can come back to haunt us?

When you complete the census form in the year 2000, my advice is not to break the law by inserting false data into the census form. But government forms are difficult. You may not be able to understand everything, particularly questions that inquire as to your racial background or income. You should then write, "I don't know" or "I don't understand," or "N/A" as answers to these questions.

The Future of Government Surveillance

Modern technology, and a greatly expanded view of government's rightful societal role, have dealt a body blow to the Bill of Rights. But there is still much more to come, unless we wake up to the threat. The following material from my special report *Counter-Surveillance*, describes what we may have to look forward to:

> ✓ *Personal and financial dossiers*. In the not-distant future, buyer profiles will give way to computer-generated dossiers that will contain details of your life from cradle to grave. They will include everything from your kindergarten teacher's observations of your "aggressive tendencies" to an identification of your "body profile" in a store selling firearms. FinCEN is the prototype [for this] system. Eventually, it may be expanded to include medical records, educational transcripts, etc. to create master dossiers on every American.

---

[169]This episode is described in David Burnham, *The Rise of the Computer State* (New York: Random House, 1980)

Dossiers will not by themselves incriminate anyone, any more than credit records alone can. But when matched against other computerized records and screened against various measures of "suspicious" or "anti-social" behavior, they could be highly incriminating. For instance, your purchase of a firearm, when noted in your dossier, would not in itself be a remarkable event. Nor would your first-grade teacher's notation of your anti-social behavior.

But suppose a government research report suggests that 3 percent of firearms buyers who demonstrated anti-social behavior in their youth eventually commit violent crimes? Using this evidence, an investigator could build a case for "further investigation" of anyone with this combination of positive findings in their dossier.

√ *No practical limitation on police searches.* In the last decade, the Supreme Court has progressively narrowed the Fourth Amendment definition of an unreasonable search. These more restrictive definitions, combined with breathtaking advances in computer and electronic technology, may by the 21st century make the Fourth Amendment irrelevant.

In 1984, the Supreme Court ruled that a "no trespassing" sign on a person's property did not protect the owner's privacy. The owner had no "reasonable expectation" that the signs would keep intruders, *including police,* off the property.

In 1986, the Court ruled that law enforcement agencies did not need a warrant in order for agents in airplanes to use evidence obtained in random flyovers for civil or criminal prosecution. In 1988, it ruled that no warrant is needed in order for a law enforcement agency to search your garbage. In 1989 the Court added helicopter searches to the types of flyover surveillance that could be made without probable cause.

Similarly, in 1991, the court declared that police do not need warrants to search packages found in cars. It also ruled that police can randomly board and search buses and trains.

What then constitutes an "unreasonable" search? Certainly not a satellite search. Since surveillance from a helicopter or airplane is not illegal, the government should be entitled to use satellites for this purpose as well. It is now possible for a satellite (or an aircraft equipped with sophisticated camera equipment) to read a letter over your shoulder. Judging by its previous decisions, the Supreme Court is likely to rule that such surveillance is perfectly legal.

Nor are these measures unpopular. For instance, during 1992, citizens living in Maine and California counties targeted by low-flying helicopters seeking out marijuana cultivation held town meetings to debate the issue. Almost everywhere, citizens voted overwhelmingly in favor of continued helicopter surveillance. The votes, while non-binding, are a powerful reminder that not only do we not oppose surveillance, but that we demand more of it!

Our demand for ever-increasing surveillance will be met by technologies now being introduced to law enforcement. New audio and video surveillance devices are already in use that can hear and record conversations, body shape, and motion through solid walls. Westinghouse Electric Corp. now offers police agencies a portable radar system that can "see" through brick walls. Such equipment recently was employed to dismantle a drug and money laundering ring operating in California. Officers used it to find an underground vault in a barn. Of course, there is no assurance that police use of the technology, formerly available only to the military, will be limited to drug or money laundering cases.

In a few years, the video and imaging techniques will be sufficiently advanced so that you can be positively identified by reconstructing your "body profile." If your body profile is found at the scene of a crime, this evidence would presumably be admissible in court.

Similarly, wouldn't a law enforcement agency be entitled to scan the walls of your home or office to determine if your body profile matches one found at a crime scene? Why couldn't such scanning be performed at random by officials seeking out "suspicious activity?"

Wouldn't the Constitution require probable cause for such seizures to take place? Not at all; the NSA and many other agencies already conduct electronic scans from vans, helicopters, airplanes, and satellites without probable cause. Similarly, the government requires no probable cause to conduct computer matches from data provided by credit bureaus and marketing companies. What better place to look for potential criminal behavior than through the walls of your own home? Ultimately, the computer dossiers compiled from birth will be continuously scanned to determine new subjects for investigation.

Police in the 21st century may even scan the thoughts of potential criminals. Today, suspected sex offenders may be hooked into a "plythismograph," a device used to measure sexual arousal. The offenders are then shown pornographic movies, and their level of sexual arousal (or lack of it) helps determine their sentence. (Currently, results from a plythismograph cannot be used as evidence at trial.)

Research is underway that enables computers to read the thoughts of the handicapped to help them move paralyzed limbs. A team from Austria's Graz University recently developed such a "brain-computer interface." Future uses of this technology (which undoubtedly will provide revolutionary advances for the handicapped) may include telepathic scanning, with skilled operators monitoring the thought waves of anyone suspected of criminal potential.

The most efficient way to conduct a search is to continuously monitor a person's location. To accomplish this goal, why not surgically implant tracking devices in convicted criminals? Pets already receive such implants, and their use has already helped worried owners find lost animals. And while we're at it, why stop at convicted criminals? Anyone might commit a crime at some point in their lives! Eventually, laws may require every baby in the United States to have a homing device implanted at birth; a national ID implant. Wherever you travel, your location could be pinpointed using this transmitter. The device might be equipped with a unique identifier; perhaps your Social Security number.

✓ *No practical limit on property seizures.* In the last two decades, Congress has enacted laws that greatly expand the power of the law enforcement authorities to seize property. The police need not prove that a crime was committed to seize property; they must merely show probable cause. This now includes a dog "alerting" to the scent of cash, or a paid informant telling authorities of his suspicions.

Electronic body profiling technology, mind-reading technology, etc. are likely to be expensive to develop. But since new forfeiture laws dictate that the proceeds of seizures be reinvested in law enforcement, police agencies are assured of an ever-growing flow of seized property to purchase state-of-the-art surveillance equipment.

Today, there are more than 100 offenses for which federal, state, or local governments can seize your property. How might these laws be used in the future? One clue is the Bush Administration's 1992 anti-crime bill, which would have expand the list of forfeitable offenses to include computer and credit-card fraud, mail fraud, and military procurement fraud. Presumably, if you exceed the credit limit on a credit card, the government could seize your home for credit-card fraud. (The proposal didn't pass, but similar legislation was introduced in the 1993 Congressional session.)

✓ *Further erosion of the right not to incriminate yourself.* The Fifth Amendment states that if you are accused of a crime, you are not obliged to assist authorities in proving your guilt. The government must prove its case without your help.

[But] technological innovation is rapidly making the Fifth Amendment obsolete. Body profiling technology could conceivably incriminate you in the privacy of your own home. Another new technology that promises to greatly assist law enforcement is "DNA profiling." One danger of DNA profiling is the potential for false accusation. In an earlier era, a clever criminal might have obtained your fingerprints so that you would take the blame for his crime. For instance, he could offer you a drink of water--and then place the water glass at the scene of his crime. This is no longer necessary. All he needs is a single hair, a flake of skin, or a drop of blood. If any of these items are planted at the scene of a crime, and match your DNA profile, you may be accused of committing it.

Ultimately, your DNA profile may be added to the information on your national ID card. But through the process of "surveillance creep," the practice may spread to those convicted of any crime, not just violent ones. A strong case could be made for everyone to have a genetic profile electronically stored for access when needed, much the way fingerprints are used today.

✓ *New types of preventive detention and mind control.* As government builds personal dossiers on us all, the public will demand preventive measures using this data. For instance, it might demand that the movements of an individual whose dossier indicates potential anti-social behavior be restricted.

Electronic monitoring of convicted criminals already exists. To avoid imprisonment, the criminal agrees to wear a bracelet around the ankle or wrist that always pinpoints his location. But why wait for a criminal conviction? Recent bail-reform laws permit "dangerous criminals" to be jailed without bail, before any trial takes place. Presumably, you could also be electronically monitored without trial as well.

Would *habeas corpus*--the right to challenge the legality of a criminal conviction--override society's interest in knowing potentially dangerous criminals are being monitored? The Constitution states that habeas corpus may be suspended in wartime. Certainly, the President could declare a "national drug emergency" and declare that it is the equivalent of a war. This constitutional right is unlikely to stand in the way of society's "right to safety" or "right to public order."

Another form of monitoring combines punishment and surveillance simultaneously, and promises to be useful (and much less expensive) than imprisonment, even for relatively serious offenders. A convicted (or suspected) criminal might be placed under permanent house arrest by attaching electrodes to the monitor. He would be shocked if he ventured more than a certain distance from his assigned territory.

National ID microchips could also be implanted in every baby at birth. This would permit cradle-to-grave monitoring will exist for the entire population. Perhaps all national ID implants would include electrodes, ready for instant activation by law enforcement officials, "just in case."

Another feature that might be added to your national ID implant would be a *subliminal implant.* Upon activation, perhaps after you broke a law, the implant would constantly repeat a message to obey the law, respect authority, etc. But why wait until you break the law? Why not have the government examine our computerized dossiers and force anyone with an "anti-social profile" to have their subliminal implant activated? Come to think of it, why not have everyone's subliminal implants activated, all the time? Don't we all need to respect authority?

What Should Be Done?

I've presented information in this book that should frighten, even terrify you. Is there any way to roll back the tide of Big Government and return to our nation's constitutional principles of due process, property rights, and limited government?

Yes, but it will take major--gigantic--changes in our mindsets.

1. *Defang the IRS.* The IRS invades our privacy in untold ways, and supports an army of attorneys and accountants whose efforts would be mostly unnecessary if the IRS were abolished or

dramatically reduced in size. Simplify the income tax and eliminate the Tax Court, where defendants are guilty until proven innocent. Or replace the income tax with a national sales tax collected at the point-of-sale. According to Citizens for an Alternative Tax System, a national sales tax of 16 percent would be sufficient to end the income tax, not to mention eliminating the IRS.

2. *End the War on Drugs.* In 1992, the Senate Judiciary Committee concluded that the 10-year War on Drugs had been a colossal failure--one that had needless cost taxpayers more than $30 billion. Ninety-nine percent of the deaths from the use of drugs come from the overuse of legal drugs--alcohol and tobacco. Ending the War on Drugs will hugely reduce the scope of organized crime in America, because it will end the biggest source of its profits. It will also make it possible to eliminate virtually all money laundering and forfeiture statutes.

Ending the War on Drugs is not the same as endorsing drug use. It is simply an acknowledge-ment that drug prohibition, as alcohol prohibition in the 1920s, simply doesn't work. We can't keep drugs out of maximum security prisons. How then can we purge them from our society without turning our nation into the equivalent of an open-air prison camp?

The money now spent for drug enforcement efforts could then be shifted into treatment efforts for those who wish to overcome their addiction. We don't imprison the five million or so men and women addicted to addicted to alcohol or the 30 million or so addicted to tobacco. We treat them. We allow them to work for a living. Certainly those addicted to illegal drugs, although far fewer in number (perhaps 3 million at most), deserve no less.

3. *Give people a property stake in personal information.* Information has value, and therefore should be treated as property. Personal information should not be released without the consent (and the compensation) of the individual concerned. Following this simple precept would go a long way toward curbing the abuses of credit bureaus and other information resellers I described in Chapter 4.

4. *End the War on Cash.* With the War on Drugs ended and the income tax abolished, the underground economy will shrink dramatically. There will no longer be a need for cash controls. The government can print counterfeit-proof money (ideally backed by gold), but without secret elements that make it possible to register each bill to an individual owner.

5. *End "lightning bolt" law by abolishing civil forfeiture.* Asset forfeiture laws that permit your property to be seized regardless without due process, and with no proof of your individual guilt or innocence are barbaric. The principal of property rights is the backbone of any free country. But property rights mean nothing in a nation that permits the government to seize property without due process.

6. *Pass a constitutional sovereignty amendment.* The amendment should state that Congress does not have the power to override the Constitution by consenting to the President's signature on a treaty.

7. *End government by emergency.* It's time to abolish FEMA, FinCEN, Rex 84, MJTF, and similar efforts, and begin dismantling the more than 12,000 emergency regulations under which the Constitution could be subverted.

8. *Adopt the English, "loser pays" civil litigation system.* If the instigator of a civil lawsuit had to pay all legal expenses of the winner, frivolous lawsuits would become a thing of the past.

9. *Privatize Social Security.* What person in their right mind would look forward to a life of 37.5 percent Social Security tax, 31 percent (or higher) federal income tax, plus state and local income taxes? This is the legacy Social Security leaves to our children. By abolishing income taxes and

privatizing Social Security, citizens could fund their own retirement. This would also be a huge incentive for saving and investment, and result in an unprecedented economic boom.

10. *Cut government spending and government regulation by 50 percent.* Abolish the Department of Education, the EPA, the Agency for International Development, the Bureau of Justice Assistance, and all the other Washington bureaucracies that bloat our budget, pick our pockets, and smother us in red tape. At minimum, freeze federal spending and employment and put a permanent moratorium on the issuance of new government regulations.

Aren't these recommendations controversial? You bet. But it's time we began talking about the issues. Can you imagine Rush Limbaugh waxing indignant about forfeiture? Or Paul Harvey demanding that Congress abolish FEMA? Or Dan Rather calling for an end to the War on Drugs?

I make two critical assumptions in making these recommendations. The first assumption is that it's worth maintaining the United States as the "home of the free and the land of the brave." The second is that any act that Congress, the President, government bureaucracies, or the judiciary takes that lessens our liberty must meet our vigorous resistance.

Our battle is not liberal against conservative, or authoritarian against anarchist. It is "We the people"--all of us--against the unabated power of Big Government and the financiers that profit from it; those that Carroll Quigley wrote so admiringly of in *Tragedy and Hope*.

Let us hope we prevail. The stakes are as high as they can get: the nation that our children will inherit.

A Collision Course[170]
by Dr. Gary North

Picture this scene. Two freight trains are hurtling down the tracks in opposite directions, headed for each other at high speed. A collision appears inescapable. And then, wonder of wonders, someone signals the engineer of one train, gets him to slow down, and then switches the track, so that the train is shuttled off to the side. Then he switches the track back where it had been, just in time for the other train to roll by harmlessly. The train stops, backs up, hooks up to the cars of the sidetracked train, and then resumes its trip down the tracks.

Call one train socialism and the other train the free market, and you've got the picture . . . if things go well.

I have written for several years about a new political movement: *privatization*. National governments can reduce economic losses and increase tax revenues by selling off inefficient government-owned businesses to the private sector. (Shuttling them aside, in other words.) This would reverse the Fabian socialist experiment of the post-World War II era.

It used to be thought by Fabian socialists that once the voters allowed the government to nationalize anything, it would stay nationalized. They were correct for about 35 years. But the visible failure of socialist ownership and management can no longer be ignored. The fiscal crisis that every national government is experiencing is bleeding the systems dry. They are desperate to find new revenue sources and to reduce expenditures. Voters all over the Western world are refusing to pay any more money into socialist sink holes. So, wonder of wonders, they are selling off government-owned,

---

[170]Extracted from *Remnant Review,* Feb. 18, 1988.

red-ink-producing assets to private investors. This is the *de-capitalization of the State* and the *re-capitalization of the market*. The State will immediately spend all the money it gets from a sale; the market will keep the physical assets and licenses and put them to more productive use.

What we are seeing is a looming collision between freedom and socialism. Not that a large number of socialists are voluntarily abandoning socialism; it is being abandoned for them by the politicians and the income-bled voters. The voters are unconcerned about ideology and labels. All they know is that they are tired of paying for government projects that don't work. So, we see a conflict between entrenched bureaucrats and the politicians. In those cases that government-owned services are clearly run incompetently, and for which there are market alternatives close at hand, with investors ready to buy the assets, free market politicians have an opportunity to reverse the direction of the society. Their formerly Keynesian political associates will vote with them, just to stop the red ink.

The socialist programs that do seem permanent are the system of direct money transfers known as welfare. In the United States, these include aid to dependent children, old age pensions, food stamps, and Medicare. Similar programs exist elsewhere. Once addicted to their welfare checks, the interest groups just cannot turn loose. The justification for the maintenance of these payments is ethical: people need help; therefore, we owe it to them to pay. Even better, some group with fewer votes owes it to them. So the system's expenditures ratchet upward; the payments escalate.

But revenues don't.

This is why the IRS and the Social Security Administration are desperate to get every child's name, age, and address into their databases. They have to make sure that the coming generation is on file. They have to finance the crumbling welfare system. The next generation will not be able to become net beneficiaries of the wealth-transfer process.

This is the end of the line. And if the bureaucrats don't have the names and addresses of the next generation, the latter may not toe the line. Here, in my view, is the inescapable collision. It will be a political collision, one in which both sides will be unwilling to compromise. Both sides will be far more intractable than the old socialist-capitalist debate over the government ownership of the means of economic production. The capitalists can at least offer to buy back the means of production. Who will "buy back" the promise to support whole classes of people?

What we are seeing is the classic "zero-sum game." Reduced taxes and reduced welfare expenditures immediately benefit one group -- taxpayers who have lost hope in ever being paid off in the future by the welfare system -- but immediately harm other groups: those who are too old or too sick to work, who have no hope in re-entering the market as producers. Unless families and voluntary charities are willing and financially able to pick up the slack, there is no way to reconcile this political conflict.

Privatization of an economic asset is far easier to sell to voters or politicians than the privatization of the welfare system. But if the latter idea isn't sold, then the economies of the industrial world will go bankrupt. Demographics assures this: too many old people, too few births. Only mass immigration of younger foreign workers could delay this, and most voters resist the legalization of mass immigration.

The fact is, the collision between freedom and control is not a single collision to be avoided, but a series of them. If you are in a position to take advantage of a particular freedom, do so. Don't count on its continuing availability.

It doesn't hurt to take a few low-cost steps to protect ourselves against those threats that do seem to be high on some bureaucrat's list or recommended policies. I do recommend that you take steps to reduce the likelihood that any one government decision can separate you from your capital and your future. A foreign bank account is legal. Owning property abroad is legal. Owning property in the name of a Caribbean-registered or Isle of Man-registered trust or corporation is legal. It is still legal to create paperwork barriers between you and the authorities. In the future, it may not be legal or comparably inexpensive to take such steps; it can be done today. An ounce of prevention in advance is worth a pound of cure later on.

What we need to buy is time. If the time that this civilization receives is frittered away over the next twenty years the way it has been for the last twenty, then we will probably have dark days ahead. But if we can buy time--and better private charities, private schools, monogamous marriages, and reduced government intervention in the economy--then we can wait for a reversal of the march into socialism. I think we have begun to see the first stages of this reversal.

I am not a gold bug. I am a freedom bug. Gold is simply a tool. I want most of my assets invested in my business. But I want reserves. My preferred reserves today are liquid currencies (foreign), short-term money market funds, gold and silver coins, non-pyramid real estate, and debt freedom. If you can get these, you are in good shape.

CONCLUSION

If you are convinced, as I am, that the threat to your personal and financial privacy is real, and that it is worth taking at least a few preliminary steps to increase the expense to others of invading it, then this report can get you started. The first steps are that: first steps. Here are few of them, for those of you who are looking for a brief review.

✓ Secure the doors and windows of your home against uninvited intrusion

✓ Send sensitive correspondence without a return address

✓ Rent a post office box, ideally from a private mail forwarding service, and use it for all but routine correspondence

✓ Put this box number on your checks, if you have any address at all on your checks

✓ Use an assumed name in private correspondence

✓ Obtain a copy of your credit report and correct any inaccuracies

✓ Obtain an unlisted phone number or a listed phone number under an assumed name

✓ Use pay telephones for calls that you wish to keep private

✓ Establish trusts and limited partnerships to protect yourself from lawsuits and asset seizures

✓ Open a non-interest-paying bank account and maintain your safety deposit box in that bank. Or rent a safety deposit box at a private vault

✓ Pay cash for purchases that you want to keep private. But be careful not to break any money laundering laws when you use cash or cash equivalents

✓ Ask your accountant and attorney to return any non-routine documents in their possession relating to you

✓ Sell any vehicles that flaunt your wealth or success

✓ Get out of debt

✓ Refrain from discussing private matters with casual acquaintances

✓ Open a foreign bank account, or even better, two foreign bank accounts in two foreign countries. Once again, be careful not to break any money laundering laws when you use cash or cash equivalents.

LIST OF SUPPLIERS

Security consultants and suppliers

Paul Nelson
c/o Nelson Associates
9850 Sandalfoot Blvd., Suite 114
Boca Raton, Fla. 33428

(security consultant, security awareness training)

Ross Engineering, Inc.
44880 Falcon Place #198
Sterling, Va. 22170
Phone: 703/318-8600

(electronic security consulting)

Private redialing services and equipment

Private Lines, Inc
400 S. Beverly Dr., Suite 214
Beverly Hills, Calif. 90212

All-American Associates
12 Galloway Ave., Suite 3A
Hunt Valley, Md. 21030
Phone: 410/628-9300

Credit bureaus

To obtain a copy of your credit report, contact the local office of any of the credit bureaus listed below, or contact:

CBI/Equifax
P.O. Box 4081
Atlanta, Ga. 30302
Phone: 800/685-1111 or 404/252-2268

Trans Union
P.O.Box 7000
North Olmstead, Ohio 44070

TRW
P.O. Box 749029
Dallas, Tex. 75374
Phone: 214/235-1200, ext. 251

TRW Credentials Service
P.O. Box 14008
Orange, Calif. 92613-1408
Phone: 800/262-7432

Mail Preference Services

Equifax Consumer Direct Division
Suite 350, Market Square
801 Pennsylvania Ave., NW
Washington, D.C. 20004

Junk Mail Busters
Suite 5038, Four Embarcadero Center
San Francisco, Calif. 94111

Direct Marketing Association Mail Preference List
11 W. 42nd St.
P.O. Box 3861
New York, N.Y. 10163-3861

Mailing List Brokers

MetroMail Corp.
901 West Bond
Lincoln, Neb. 68521

R. L. Polk & Co.
List Services Division
6400 Monroe Blvd.
Taylor, Mich. 48180

Donnelley Marketing
1235 N Ave.
Nevada, Iowa 50201

Write these companies to get off mailing lists

Telephone marketing service providers

Haines & Co., Inc.
Criss-Cross Directory
2383 Walnut Ave. E.
Fullerton, Calif. 92631

R. L. Polk & Co.
List Service Division
6400 Monroe Blvd.
Taylor, Mich. 48180

Direct Marketing Association
Telephone Preference Service
11 W. 42nd St.
P.O. Box 3861
New York, N.Y. 10163

Write these companies to have your name removed from telephone solicitation and cross-matching directories.

Private Citizen, Inc.
Box 233
Naperville, Ill. 60566

Join this organization to be taken off telemarketer call lists.

U.S. Vendors of Precious Metals

Mocatta Metals
Four World Trade Center, Suite 5200
New York City, N.Y. 10048
Phone: 800/662-2882

Ron Paul & Assoc. Precious Metals
P.O. Box 4231
Burlingame, Calif. 94011
Phone: 800/982-7070 or 415/348-3000

Investment Rarities
7850 Metro Parkway, Suite 121
Minneapolis, Minn. 55425
Phone: 800/328-1860

International Financial Consultants, Inc.
1700 Rockville Pike #400
Rockville, Md. 20852
Phone: 800/831-0007 or 301/881-8600

C & M Clearing Corp.
3155 Roswell Rd., Suite 310
Atlanta, Ga. 30305
Phone: 404/261-6566

International Collectors' Associates
166 Turner Drive
Durango, Colo. 81301
Phone: 800/525-9556 or 303/259-4100

Private Security Vaults

Arlington Security Vault, Inc.
2499 N. Harrison St.
Arlington, Va. 22207
Phone 703/237-1133

This is probably the most secure private vault in the United States.

National Association of Private Security Vaults
716 E. Washington St.
Syracuse, N.Y. 13210
Phone 315/475-7743

Write for the location of the private security vault nearest you.

Nevada and/or Wyoming Incorporation

Corporate Service Center, Inc.
1280 Terminal Way, Suite 15
Reno, Nev. 89502
Phone: 800/638-2320 or 702/329-7716

Jack Clark
Nevada-International Business Center
1401 Trolley Way
Carson City, Nev. 89701
Phone: 702/883-5550

Corporations in Other States

The Company Corporation
Three Christina Center
201 N. Walnut St
Wilmington, Del. 19801
Phone: 800/542-2677

Asset Protection Plans

Peter Double
c/o Robertson, Double & Boase
6917 Kings Harbour Dr.
Rancho Palos Verdes, Calf. 90274
Phone: 310/544-9521; fax: 310/377-4469

William and Scott Comer
P.O. Box 268--9260 Colonville Rd.
Clare, Mich. 48617
Phone: 517/386-7729; fax: 517/386-4466

Engel & Rudman
5105 DTC Parkway, Suite 450
Englewood, Colo. 80111
Phone: 303/741-1111; fax: 303/694-4028

Robert V. Beaudry
Resources Planning Group
2001 Wilshire Blvd. #505
Santa Monica, Calif. 90403
Phone: 800/952-7955; fax: 310/829-2202

The 10 Strongest U.S. Banks

According to *Banking Safety Digest* newsletter, the following institutions are the ten largest banks that have been in banking watchdog Veribanc's "Blue Ribbon" category for at least the last eight consecutive quarters. Blue-Ribbon banks have at least a 7.5 percent equity-to-assets ratio and a liquidity ratio above 45 percent.

The equity-to-assets measurement is important because equity provides a capital cushion that a bank can fall back upon in case of losses from bad investments or loans--before it turns to the federal government. Liquidity is important in that it allows the bank to return depositors' money from either cash or easily-liquidated investments.

The 10 top Blue Ribbon banks are:

Manhattan Savings Bank
415 Madison Ave.
New York, N.Y. 10017
Phone: 212/688-3000

Farmers & Merchants Bank of Long Beach
302 Pine Ave., Box 1370
Long Beach, Calif. 90802
Phone: 213/437-0011

National Bank of Alaska
301 W. Northern Lights Blvd.
Box 100600
Anchorage, Alaska 99510
Phone: 907/276-1132

First National Bank of Ohio
106 S. Main St.
Akron, Ohio 44308
Phone: 216/384-8000

Trust Company Bank
25 Park Place, NE/P.O. Box 4418
Atlanta, Ga. 30302
Phone: 404/588-7711

United Counties Trust Company
Four Commerce Drive
Cranford, N.J. 07016
Phone: 908/931-6600

Fleet Bank of New York
69 State St.
Albany, N.Y. 12201
Phone: 518/447-4115

Sun Bank/South Florida, N.A.
500 E. Las Olas Blvd.
Fort Lauderdale, Fla. 33301
Phone: 305/467-5000

Dauphin Deposit Bank & Trust Co.
213 Market St.
P.O. Box 2961
Harrisburg, Pa. 17105
Phone: 717/255-2121

Jefferson National Bank
123 E. Main St.
Charlottesville, Va. 22902
Phone: 516/621-6000

I do not recommend keeping a large portion of your portfolio in the U.S. banking system. However, no Blue Ribbon bank has ever failed. In the event of an economic crisis, they are likely to be relatively safe depositories for your wealth. For more information on Blue Ribbon banks in your area, contact:

Veribanc
P.O. Box 461
Wakefield, Mass. 01880
Phone: 800/442-2657 or 617/245-8370

Barter Associations

International Reciprocal Trade Association
9513 Beach Mill Rd.
Great Falls, Va. 22066

National Commodity and Barter Association
8000 E. Girard Ave. #215
Denver, Colo. 80231
Phone: 303/337-9617

Offshore Banks and Brokers

Switzerland

Ankerbank
P.O. Box 159
1001 Lausanne, Switzerland

Cambio + Valorenbank
Utoquai 55
8021 Zurich, Switzerland

Swiss Volksbank
P.O. Box 8021
8021 Zurich, Switzerland

Camafin Trust AG
P.O. Box 93C
8802 Kilchberg-Zurich, Switzerland

Austria

Creditanstalt
Schottengasse 6-8
1010 Vienna, Austria

Royal Trust Bank (Austria)
Rathausstrasse 20
P.O. Box 306
A-1011 Vienna, Austria

Raiffeisen Zentralbank
Herrengasse 1
1010 Vienna, Austria

Girozentrale
Schubertring 5
1010 Vienna, Austria

Laenderbank
Am Hof 2
1010 Vienna, Austria

Liechtenstein

Liechtensteinische Landesbank
Stadlte 44, P.O. Box 384
Vaduz, Liechtenstein

Landesbank of Liechtenstein
Postfach 85
SL 9490 Vaduz, Liechtenstein

Great Britain

Standard Chartered Bank (London)
Bishop Gate
Four Crosby Square
London, England EC3A 6SB

Channel Islands

TSB Channel Islands Ltd. (Overseas)
P.O. Box 597
8 David Place
St. Helier, Jersey, Channel Islands, UK

Isle of Man

Standard Chartered Bank, Ltd.
Athol Street
Douglas, Isle of Man

Isle of Man Bank, Ltd. (Overseas)
2 Athol Street
Douglas, Isle of Man

Canada

Canadian Imperial Bank of Commerce
Commerce Court
Toronto, Ontario M5L 1A2 Canada

Bank of British Columbia
Division of Hong Kong Bank
885 W. Georgia
Vancouver, B.C. V6C 3G1 Canada

Bahamas

Gotthard Bank International (Nassau)
P.O. Box N-6312
Nassau, the Bahamas

Corrmar Bank & Trust, Ltd.
P.O. Box N-4232
Nassau, the Bahamas

Bermuda

The Bank of Bermuda, Ltd.
P.O. Box HM1020
Hamilton HMDX, Bermuda

The Bank of N. T. Butterfield
P.O. Box 195
Hamilton, Bermuda

Cayman Islands

Swiss Bank and Trust Co., Ltd.
Swiss Bank Building
Fort Street/P.O. Box 852
Georgetown, Grand Cayman, BWI

Midland Bank & Trust Corp. (Cayman), Ltd.
Midland Bank & Trust Building
P.O. Box 1109
Georgetown, Grand Cayman, BWI

Hong Kong

Hong Kong & Shanghai Bank
1 Queen's Road Central
Hong Kong

Offshore Companies and Trusts

Keyte & Co., Ltd.
17 Rodney Road
Cheltenham, Glos GL50 1HX, England

Freeport Services, Ltd.
4 Athol St.
Douglas, Isle of Man

Island Resources, Ltd.
Ballacurrie House
Summerhill, Onchan, Isle of Man

Bilaudit Treauhand und Kontrolsellen, AG
Herrengasse 12/P.O. Box 85
Vaduz, Liechtenstein

Foreign Real Estate

Ted Thomas
c/o Genesis International
185 Front St., Suite 207
Danville, Calif. 94526

Revac, S.A.
52 rue de Montbrillant
1202 Geneva, Switzerland

Swiss Annuities

BEFI Consulting, AG
Rothbachweg 11, P.O. Box 101
4950 Huttwil, Switzerland

Isle of Man Insurance

Isle of Man Assurance, Ltd.
P.O. Box 179
IOMA House, Prospect Hill
Douglas, Isle of Man

Alternative Travel Documents

Scope International, Ltd.
62 Murray Rd., Waterlooville
Hants PO8 9JL
Great Britain

(complete information on alternative legal travel documents from foreign countries)

International Company Services (Gibraltar), Ltd.
Suite 2B, Mansion House
143 Main St.
Gibraltar

(complete information on alternative legal travel documents from foreign countries)

Publishers of Privacy-Related Books and Related Materials

LPP, Ltd.
1280 Terminal Way, Suite 15
Reno, Nev. 89502
Phone: 800/528-0559 or 702/885-2509

(books and newsletters)

Eden Press
P.O. Box 8410
Fountain Valley, Calif. 92728

(books, videos, tapes)

Paladin Press
P.O. Box 1307
Boulder, Colo. 80306

(books, videos, tapes)

Loompanics Unlimited
P.O. Box 1197
Port Townsend, Wash. 98368

(books, videos, tapes)

U.S. Mail Forwarding Services (Contact either company to find their nearest facilities.)

Pak-Mail Centers of America
3033 S. Parker Road, Suite 1200
Aurora, Colo. 80014
Phone: 303/752-3500

Mail Boxes, Etc. USA
5555 Oberlin Drive
San Diego, Calif. 92121
Phone: 619/452-1553

Canadian Mail Forwarding Service

Wayne Budd, Inc.
RR1, Box 63
Eldorado, Ontario, Canada K0K 1Y0
Phone: 613/473-4838

Miscellaneous

Nitro-Pak
13309 Rosecrans Ave.
Santa Fe Springs, Calif. 90670
Phone: 213/802-0099

(survival and related equipment and information)

Arrowhead Mills
110 South Lawton
P.O. Box 2059
Hereford, Tex. 79045

(survival foods)

Medical Information Bureau
P.O. Box 105
Essex Station, Mass. 02112

(medical records custodian for insurance companies)

American Arbitration Association of America
140 W. 51st St.
New York, N.Y. 10020-1203
Phone: 212/484-4000

(provides forum for mediation of disputes outside of court)

U.S. General Accounting Office
Washington, D.C. 20548

(source for "GAO" reports mentioned in text)

Superintendent of Documents
U.S. Government Printing Office
Washington, D.C. 20402

(source for information on government periodicals and subscription services)

House Document Room
Phone: 202/225-3456

Senate Document Room
Hart Building
Washington, D.C. 20510-7106

(contact to obtain copies of pending legislation before Congress)

313

Appendix A:
Government Reporting and Other Information Forms

CUSTOMER: Complete Items 1, 3-7, 15 and 19 | (Item 2 for P.O. Use ONLY)

| 1. Name to which box number(s) is(are) assigned | 2. Box/Caller Nos. _____ Thru _____ |

3. Name of person making application *(If representing an organization, show title and name)*

4. Will this box be used for soliciting or doing business with the public? *(Check one)*
 a. ☐ YES b. ☐ NO

5. Address *(No., Street, City, State and ZIP Code. Record address change on reverse and line out address below.)* | 6. Telephone No. *(If any)*

APPLICANT PLEASE NOTE: Execution of this application signifies your agreement to comply with all postal rules relative to Post Office boxes or caller service.

7. Signature of applicant *(Same as Item 3)* | 8. Date of application

ITEMS 8-15: TO BE COMPLETED BY POST OFFICE

9. Type of identification *(Driver's license military identification, other; show identification no.)* | 10. Eligibility for carrier-delivery ☐ CITY ☐ RURAL ☐ NONE | 11. Box size needed

12. Dates of Service		13. Service Assigned	14. Information Verified by
a. Started	b. Ended	a. ☐ Post Office Box b. ☐ Caller	a. *(Initials)*
		c. ☐ Reserve Number	

PS Form **1093**, Dec. 1986   (PART I) APPLICATION FOR POST OFFICE BOX OR CALLER SERVICE

Use separate card for each number or inclusive group of numbers, and type of service. File Part I alphabetically by Customer's Name.

CUSTOMER: Complete Items 15 and 19.

| SPECIAL ORDERS | ITEMS 16-18: TO BE COMPLETED BY POST OFFICE |

15. Postmaster:

The following named persons, or authorized representatives of the organizations listed are authorized to accept mail addressed to this(these) post office box or caller number(s). Continue on reverse if necessary.

☐ Check if reverse is used.

a. Applicant *(Same as Item 3)*

b. Name in which box rented *(Same as Item 1)*

c. Other

d. Other

CUSTOMER NOTE: Possession of post office box Key or combination may be considered by the Postal Service to be valid evidence that possessor is authorized to remove mail from boxes.

16. Post Office Box/Caller number for which this card is applicable
_____ through _____

17. ☐ Check if box is to be used for Express Mail reshipment.

18.

Post Office

Date Stamp

19. I have read instructions and will comply

Signature of Applicant *(Same as Item 3)*

PS Form **1093**, Dec. 1986   (PART II) APPLICATION FOR POST OFFICE BOX OR CALLER SERVICE

Use separate card for each number or inclusive group of numbers, and type of service. File Part II by box or caller number.

INSTRUCTIONS FOR WORKING COMBINATION BOX

1. Clear dial by three revolutions to the right, stop on _____
2. Turn dial to the left and stop the second time around on _____
3. Turn right and stop at _____
4. Turn latch key LEFT to open.

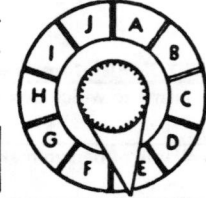

Your ZIP + 4 is: [ ][ ][ ][ ][ ] — [ ][ ][ ][ ]

Rules for use of Post Office Box and Caller Service

IMPORTANT: Post Office Box and Caller Service are Subject to the following and the regulations in Parts 951 and 952 *DMM.*

I. Mail, which is properly addressed to a post office box or caller service number, will be delivered through that post office box or caller service for

> Individual boxholders or callers, or anyone residing in their household.

> A firm, corporation, association, or public or private, institution, or any one associated with the organization. . . . . .

II. Customers should promptly notify correspondents of their current box or caller number address.

III. Post Office Box or caller service fees are to be paid in advance for one or two semiannual periods. A notice of fees due will be placed in a box or included with caller mail 20 days before the due date. If a boxholder is out of town and has submitted a temporary forwarding order, the notice will be mailed to the temporary address. It is the responsibility of the boxholder to assure that payment is made on time. If payment is sent by mail, it must be received by the postmaster by the due date. Payment may be by cash or by check payable to the postmaster. Do not send cash by mail. If a check is returned by the bank, the box will be closed until that check is made good.

IV. If fee is not paid on time, the post office box will be secured so that mail cannot be removed through the door. If box rent or caller fees are not paid after 10 days, mail will be removed and treated as undeliverable, unless forwarded on a change of address order. Closed post office boxes will be immediately available to new customers.

V. Post office boxes or caller service may not be used for any purpose prohibited by Postal Regulations. (See Parts 951 and 952 *Domestic Mail Manual. (DMM).*

VI. Boxes and caller numbers may not be used for the sole purpose of having the Postal Service forward or transfer mail to another address free of charge.

VII. Boxholders shall promptly remove mail, or have it removed, from their boxes. Advance arrangements must be specifically made with the postmaster if mail is to be accumulated for more than 30 days and an overflow condition is probable.

VIII. Keys for key-type post office boxes will be issued upon payment of $1 for each key, including those initially issued for each post office box. When a box is surrendered, the Postal Service will repurchase a maximum of two keys. Keys for post office box may be obtained only from the Postal Service.

IX. Customers who use post office box or caller service, are required to maintain a current Form 1093. *Application for Post Office Box or Caller Service,* on file with the Postal Service. Any information on the application, which changes or becomes obsolete, must be corrected by promptly updating the Form 1093 on file with the postmaster at the office where the post office box or caller service is used.

X. A box may be closed or caller service terminated as provided in Parts 951 and 952 *DMM.*

The customer may appeal a closure in writing to higher authority by following the detailed procedures in Sections 951.84 and 952.44 *DMM.*

XI. Concerning information required for the completion of this form:
  A. The collection of this information is authorized by 39 U.S.C. 403,404.
  B. This information will be used to provide the applicant with post office box or caller service.
  C. This information may be routinely disclosed:
   1. To persons authorized by law to serve judicial process for the purpose of serving such process.
   2. To a government agency, when necessary for the performance of its duties.
   3. To anyone, when the box is being used for the purpose of doing or soliciting business with the public.
   4. To a Congressional Office, at the request of the boxholder.
   5. In response to a subpoena or court order.
   6. Where pertinent to a legal proceeding in which the Postal Service is a party.
  D. Completion of this form is voluntary; however, if this information is not provided, the applicant will be unable to use a box or receive caller service.

XII. Customers are referred to Parts 951 and 952 *DMM* for a more detailed explanation of these regulations.

PS Form **1093,** Dec. 1986 **(PART III)**

☆ U.S. GPO: 1987—202-395/72997

U.S. POSTAL SERVICE

APPLICATION FOR DELIVERY OF MAIL THROUGH AGENT

1. Date

In consideration of delivery of my or our mail to the agent named below, the addressee and agent agree that: (1) the Postal Service will not forward my or our mail on a change of address order upon termination of this agency relationship; (2) the forwarding or return of my or our mail is the responsibility of the agent; and (3) all mail, including letters and other first class mail, delivered to the agent under this authorization must be prepaid with new postage when redeposited in the mails.

NOTE: This publication must be executed in duplicate by applicant in the presence of the agent, his authorized employee or a notary public. A signed copy will be kept on file by the agent in such manner that it is at all times available for examination by postal representatives.

TO: Postmaster

PRIVACY ACT: The collection of this information is authorized by 39 USC' 403, 404. It serves as the written authority for the delivery of mail other than as addressed. As a routine use, this information may be disclosed to an appropriate law enforcement agency for investigative or prosecution proceedings, to a congressional office at your request, to a labor organization as required by the NLRA, and where pertinent, in a legal proceeding to which the Postal Service is a party. Completion of this form is voluntary, however, if this information is not provided the mail will be withheld from delivery to the agent and delivered to the addressee, or, if the address of the addressee is that of the agent, returned to the sender.

2. Mail addressed to (*Name, address and ZIP Code*)	3. Deliver to and in care of (*Name, address and ZIP code of agent*)
4. Name of applicant (*Print or type*)	4a. Home address (*Number, street and ZIP code*)
5. Name of firm or corporation	5a. Business address (*Name, street and ZIP code*)
6. Kind of business	
7. *If address is a FIRM, name each member whose mail is to be delivered*	8. *If a CORPORATION, give names and addresses of its officers*
9. Reference (*Name, address and ZIP code*)	10. Reference (*Name, address and ZIP code*)
11. If business name of the address (*Corporation or Trade Name*) has been registered, give name of county and state, and date of registration.	
12. Signature of agent	13. Signature of applicant (*If firm or corporation, application must be signed by officer. Show title.*)

PS Form **1583**, Nov. 1982

★ U.S.G P.O.: 1987 – 181-700/55537

WELCOME TO THE UNITED STATES

DEPARTMENT OF THE TREASURY
UNITED STATES CUSTOMS SERVICE

FORM APPROVED
OMB NO. 1515-0041

CUSTOMS DECLARATION

19 CFR 122.27, 148.12, 148.13, 148.110, 148.111

Each arriving traveler or head of family must provide the following information (only **ONE** written declaration per family is required):

1. Name: _____
   Last   First   Middle Initial

2. Date of Birth: _____/_____/_____ 3. Airline/Flight _____
            Day   Month   Year

4. Number of family members traveling with you _____

5. U.S. Address: _____

   City: _____ State: _____

6. I am a U.S. Citizen   YES ☐   NO ☐
   If No,
   Country: _____

7. I reside permanently in the U.S.   YES ☐   NO ☐
   If No,
   Expected Length of Stay: _____

8. The purpose of my trip is or was ☐ BUSINESS   ☐ PLEASURE

9. I am/we are bringing fruits, plants, meats, food,   YES ☐   NO ☐
   soil, birds, snails, other live animals, farm
   products, or I/we have been on a farm or ranch
   outside the U.S.

10. I am/we are carrying currency or monetary   YES ☐   NO ☐
    instruments over $10,000 U.S. or foreign
    equivalent.

11. The total value of all goods I/we purchased or
    acquired abroad and am/are bringing to the U.S.
    is (see instructions under Merchandise on reverse
    side): $ _____
                                         US Dollars

► **MOST MAJOR CREDIT CARDS ACCEPTED.**

SIGN ON REVERSE SIDE AFTER YOU READ WARNING.

(Do not write below this line.)

INSPECTOR'S NAME	STAMP AREA
BADGE NO.	

Paperwork Reduction Act Notice: The Paperwork Reduction Act of 1980 says we must tell you why we are collecting this information, how we will use it and whether you have to give it to us. We ask for this information to carry out the Customs, Agriculture, and Currency laws of the United States. We need it to ensure that travelers are complying with these laws and to allow us to figure and collect the right amount of duties and taxes. Your response is mandatory.

Statement required by 5 CFR 1320.21: The estimated average burden associated with this collection of information is 3 minutes per respondent or recordkeeper depending on individual circumstances. Comments concerning the accuracy of this burden estimate and suggestions for reducing this burden should be directed to U.S. Customs Service, Paperwork Management Branch, Washington, DC 20229, and to the Office of Management and Budget, Paperwork Reduction Project (1515-0041), Washington, DC 20503.

Customs Form 6059B (092089)

DEPARTMENT OF THE TREASURY
UNITED STATES CUSTOMS SERVICE

REPORT OF INTERNATIONAL TRANSPORTATION OF CURRENCY OR MONETARY INSTRUMENTS

Form Approved
OMB No. 1515-0079

This form is to be filed with the United States Customs Service

Privacy Act Notification
on reverse

PART I — FOR INDIVIDUAL DEPARTING FROM OR ENTERING THE UNITED STATES

1. NAME (Last or family, first and middle)	2. IDENTIFYING NO. (See instructions)	3. DATE OF BIRTH (Mo./Day/Yr.)

4. PERMANENT ADDRESS IN UNITED STATES OR ABROAD	5. OF WHAT COUNTRY ARE YOU A CITIZEN/SUBJECT?

6. ADDRESS WHILE IN THE UNITED STATES	7. PASSPORT NO. & COUNTRY

8. U.S. VISA DATE	9. PLACE UNITED STATES VISA WAS ISSUED	10. IMMIGRATION ALIEN NO. (If any)

11. CURRENCY OR MONETARY INSTRUMENT WAS: (Complete 11A or 11B)

A. EXPORTED		B. IMPORTED	
Departed From: (City in U.S.)	Arrived At: (Foreign City/Country)	From: (Foreign City/Country)	At: (City in U.S.)

PART II — FOR PERSON SHIPPING, MAILING OR RECEIVING CURRENCY OR MONETARY INSTRUMENTS

12. NAME (Last or family, first and middle)	13. IDENTIFYING NO. (See instructions)	14. DATE OF BIRTH (Mo./Da./Yr.)

15. PERMANENT ADDRESS IN UNITED STATES OR ABROAD	16. OF WHAT COUNTRY ARE YOU A CITIZEN/SUBJECT?

17. ADDRESS WHILE IN THE UNITED STATES	18. PASSPORT NO. & COUNTRY

19. U.S. VISA DATE	20. PLACE UNITED STATES VISA WAS ISSUED	21. IMMIGRATION ALIEN NO. (If any)

22. CURRENCY OR MONETARY INSTRUMENTS DATE SHIPPED / DATE RECEIVED	23. CURRENCY OR MONETARY INSTRUMENTS ☐ Shipped To ☐ Received From	NAME AND ADDRESS	24. IF THE CURRENCY OR MONETARY INSTRUMENT WAS MAILED, SHIPPED, OR TRANSPORTED COMPLETE BLOCKS A AND B. A. Method of Shipment (Auto, U.S. Mail, Public Carrier, etc.) B. Name of Transporter/Carrier

PART III — CURRENCY AND MONETARY INSTRUMENT INFORMATION (SEE INSTRUCTIONS ON REVERSE) (To be completed by everyone)

25. TYPE AND AMOUNT OF CURRENCY/MONETARY INSTRUMENTS		Value in U.S. Dollars	26. IF OTHER THAN U.S. CURRENCY IS INVOLVED, PLEASE COMPLETE BLOCKS A AND B. (SEE SPECIAL INSTRUCTIONS)
Coins	☐ A. ▶ $		A. Currency Name
Currency	☐ B. ▶		
Other Instruments (Specify Type)	☐ C. ▶		B. Country
(Add lines A, B and C) .... TOTAL AMOUNT ▶ $			

PART IV — GENERAL - TO BE COMPLETED BY ALL TRAVELERS, SHIPPERS AND RECIPIENTS

27. WERE YOU ACTING AS AN AGENT, ATTORNEY OR IN CAPACITY FOR ANYONE IN THIS CURRENCY OR MONETARY INSTRUMENT ACTIVITY? (If "Yes" complete A, B and C) ☐ Yes ☐ No

PERSON IN WHOSE BEHALF YOU ARE ACTING ▶	A. Name	B. Address	C. Business activity occupation or profession

Under penalties of perjury, I declare that I have examined this report, and to the best of my knowledge and belief it is true, correct and complete.

28. NAME AND TITLE	29. SIGNATURE	30. DATE

GENERAL INSTRUCTIONS

This report is required by Treasury Department regulations (31 Code of Federal Regulations 103).

Who Must File. — Each person who physically transports, mails, or ships, or causes to be physically transported, mailed, shipped or received currency or other monetary instruments in an aggregate amount exceeding $10,000 on any one occasion from the United States to any place outside the United States, or into the United States from any place outside the United States.

A TRANSFER OF FUNDS THROUGH NORMAL BANKING PROCEDURES WHICH DOES NOT INVOLVE THE PHYSICAL TRANSPORTATION OF CURRENCY OR MONETARY INSTRUMENTS IS NOT REQUIRED TO BE REPORTED.

Exceptions. — The following persons are not required to file reports: (1) a Federal reserve bank, (2) a bank, a foreign bank, or a broker or dealer in securities in respect to currency or other monetary instruments mailed or shipped through the postal service or by common carrier, (3) a commercial bank or trust company organized under the laws of any State or of the United States with respect to overland shipments of currency or monetary instruments shipped to or received from an established customer maintaining a deposit relationship with the bank, in amounts which the bank may reasonably conclude do not exceed amounts commensurate with the customary conduct of the business, industry or profession of the customer concerned, (4) a person who is not a citizen or resident of the United States in respect to currency or other monetary instruments mailed or shipped from abroad to a bank or broker or dealer in securities through the postal service or by common carrier, (5) a common carrier of passengers in respect to currency or other monetary instruments in the possession of its passengers, (6) a common carrier of goods in respect to shipments of currency or monetary instruments not declared to be such by the shipper, (7) a travelers' check issuer or its agent in respect to the transportation of travelers' checks prior to their delivery to selling agents for eventual sale to the public, nor by (8) a person engaged as a business in the transportation of currency, monetary instruments and other commercial papers with respect to the transportation of currency or other monetary instruments overland between established offices of banks or brokers or dealers in securities and foreign persons.

WHEN AND WHERE TO FILE:

A. Recipients. — Each person who receives currency or other monetary instruments shall file Form 4790, within 30 days after receipt, with the Customs officer in charge at any port of entry or departure or by mail with the Commissioner of Customs, Attention: Currency Transportation Reports, Washington, D.C. 20229.

B. Shippers or Mailers. — If the currency or other monetary instrument does not accompany the person entering or departing the United States, Form 4790 may be filed by mail on or before the date of entry, departure, mailing, or shipping with the Commissioner of Customs, Attention: Currency Transportation Reports, Washington, D.C. 20229.

C. Travelers. — Travelers carrying currency or other monetary instruments with them shall file Form 4790 at the time of entry into the United States or the time of departure from the United States with the Customs officer in charge at any Customs port of entry or departure.

An additional report of a particular transportation, mailing, or shipping of currency or the monetary instruments, is not required if a complete and truthful report has already been filed. However, no person otherwise required to file a report shall be excused from liability for failure to do so if, in fact, a complete and truthful report has not been filed. Forms may be obtained from any United States Customs Service office.

PENALTIES. — Civil and criminal penalties, including under certain circumstances a fine of not more than $500,000 and imprisonment of not more than five years, are provided for failure to file a report, supply information, and for filing a false or fraudulent report. In addition, the currency or monetary instrument may be subject to seizure and forfeiture. See sections 103.47, 103.48 and 103.49 of the regulations.

DEFINITIONS:

Bank. — Each agent, agency, branch or office within the United States of a foreign bank and each agency, branch or office within the United States of any person doing business in one or more of the capacities listed: (1) a commercial bank or trust company organized under the laws of any state or of the United States; (2) a private bank; (3) a savings and loan association or a building and loan association organized under the laws of any state or of the United States; (4) an insured institution as defined in section 401 of the National Housing Act; (5) a savings bank, industrial bank or other thrift institution; (6) a credit union organized under the laws of any state or of the United States; and (7) any other organization chartered under the banking laws of any state and subject to the supervision of the bank supervisory authorities of a state.

Foreign Bank. — A bank organized under foreign law, or an agency, branch or office located outside the United States of a bank. The term does not include an agent, agency, branch or office within the United States of a bank organized under foreign law.

Broker or Dealer in Securities. — A broker or dealer in securities, registered or required to be registered with the Securities and Exchange Commission under the Securities Exchange Act of 1934.

INDENTIFYING NUMBER. — Individuals must enter their social security number, if any. However, aliens who do not have a social security number should enter passport or alien registration number. All others should enter their employer identification number.

Investment Security. — An instrument which : (1) is issued in bearer or registered form; (2) is of a type commonly dealt in upon securities exchanges or markets or commonly recognized in any area in which it is issued or dealt in as a medium for investment; (3) is either one of a class or series or by its terms is divisible into a class or series of instruments; and (4) evidences a share, participation or other interest in property or in an enterprise or evidences an obligation of the issuer.

Monetary Instruments. — Coin or currency of the United States or of any other country, travelers' checks, money orders, investment securities in bearer form or otherwise in such form that title thereto passes upon delivery, and negotiable instruments (except warehouse receipts or bills of lading) in bearer form or other in such form that title thereto passes upon delivery. The term includes bank checks, travelers' checks and money orders which are signed but on which the name of the payee has been omitted, but does not include bank checks, travelers' checks or money orders made payable to the order of a named person which have not been endorsed or which bear restrictive endorsements.

Person. — An individual, a corporation, a partnership, a trust or estate, a joint stock company, an association, a syndicate, joint venture, or other unincorporated organization or group, and all entities cognizable as legal personalities.

SPECIAL INSTRUCTIONS:

You should complete each line which applies to you. Part II. — Line 22, Enter the exact date you shipped or received currency or the monetary instrument(s). Line 23, Check the applicable box and give the complete name and address of the shipper or recipient. Part III. — Line 26, If currency or monetary instruments of more than one country is involved, attach a schedule showing each kind, country, and amount.

PRIVACY ACT AND PAPERWORK REDUCTION ACT NOTICE

Pursuant to the requirements of Public Law 93-579, (Privacy Act of 1974), notice is hereby given that the authority to collect information on Form 4790 in accordance with 5 U.S.C. 552a(e)(3) is Public Law 91-508; 31 U.S.C. 5316; 5 U.S.C. 301; Reorganization Plan No. 1 of 1950; Treasury Department No. 165, revised, as amended; 31 CFR 103; and 44 U.S.C. 3501.

The principal purpose for collecting the information is to assure maintenance of reports or records where such reports or records have a high degree of usefulness in criminal, tax, or regulatory investigations or proceedings. The information collected may be provided to those officers and employees of the Customs Service and any other constituent unit of the Department of the Treasury who have a need for the records in the performance of their duties. The records may be referred to any other department or agency of the Federal Government upon the request of the head of such department or agency.

Disclosure of this information is mandatory. Failure to provide all or any part of the requested information may subject the currency or monetary instruments to seizure and forfeiture, as well as subject the individual to civil and criminal liabilities.

Disclosure of the social security number is mandatory. The authority to collect this number is 31 CFR 103.25. The social security number will be used as a means to identify the individual who files the record.

The collection of this information is mandatory pursuant to 31 U.S.C. 5316.

Department of the Treasury TD F 90-22.1 (4-90) **SUPERSEDES ALL PREVIOUS EDITIONS**	**REPORT OF FOREIGN BANK AND FINANCIAL ACCOUNTS** For the calendar year 19 **Do not file this form with your Federal Tax Return**	Form Approved: OMB No. 1505-0021 Expiration Date: 2/93

This form should be used to report financial interest in or signature authority or other authority over one or more bank accounts, securities accounts, or other financial accounts in foreign countries as required by Department of the Treasury Regulations (31 CFR 103). You are not required to file a report if the aggregate value of the accounts did not exceed $10,000. Check all appropriate boxes. SEE INSTRUCTIONS ON BACK FOR DEFINITIONS. File this form with Dept. of the Treasury, P.O. Box 32621 Detroit, MI 48232.

1. Name (Last, First, Middle)

2. Social security number or employer identification number if other than individual

3. Name in item 1 refers to
☐ Individual
☐ Partnership
☐ Corporation
☐ Fiduciary

4. Address (Street, City, State, Country, ZIP)

5. ☐ I had signature authority or other authority over one or more foreign accounts, but I had no "financial interest" in such accounts (see instruction J). Indicate for these accounts:

(a) Name and social security number or taxpayer identification number of each owner _____

(b) Address of each owner _____

(Do not complete item 9 for these accounts)

6. ☐ I had a "financial interest" in one or more foreign accounts owned by a domestic corporation, partnership or trust which is required to file TD F 90-22.1. (See instruction L). Indicate for these accounts:

(a) Name and taxpayer identification number of each such corporation, partnership or trust _____

(b) Address of each such corporation, partnership or trust _____

(Do not complete item 9 for these accounts)

7. ☐ I had a "financial interest" in one or more foreign accounts, but the total maximum value of these accounts (see instruction I) did not exceed $10,000 at any time during the year. (If you checked this box, do not complete item 9).

8. ☐ I had a "financial interest" in 25 or more foreign accounts. (If you checked this box, do not complete item 9.)

9. If you had a "financial interest" in one or more but fewer than 25 foreign accounts which are required to be reported, and the total maximum value of the accounts exceeded $10,000 during the year (see instruction I), write the total number of those accounts in the box below:
Complete items (a) through (f) below for one of the accounts and attach a separate TD F 90-22.1 for each of the others. Items 1, 2, 3, 9, and 10 must be completed for each account.

Check here if this is an attachment. ☐

(a) Name in which account is maintained

(b) Name of bank or other person with whom account is maintained

(c) Number and other account designation, if any

(d) Address of office or branch where account is maintained

(e) Type of account. (If not certain of English name for the type of account, give the foreign language name and describe the nature of the account. Attach additional sheets if necessary.)
☐ Bank Account   ☐ Securities Account   ☐ Other (specify)

(f) Maximum value of account (see instruction I)
☐ Under $10,000   ☐ $10,000 to $50,000   ☐ $50,000 to $100,000   ☐ Over $100,000

10. Signature

11. Title (Not necessary if reporting personal account)

12. Date

PRIVACY ACT NOTIFICATION

Pursuant to the requirements of Public Law 93-579, (Privacy Act of 1974), notice is hereby given that the authority to collect information on TD F 90-22.1 in accordance with 5 U.S.C. 552(e)(3) is Public Law 91-508; 31 U.S.C. 1121; 5 U.S.C. 301, 31 CFR Part 103.

The principal purpose for collecting the information is to assure maintenance of reports or records where such reports or records have a high degree of usefulness in criminal, tax, or regulatory investigations or proceedings. The information collected may be provided to those officers and employees of any constituent unit of the Department of the Treasury who have a need for the records in the performance of their duties. The records may be referred to any other department or agency of the Federal Government upon the request of the head of such department or agency for use in a criminal, tax, or regulatory investigation or proceeding.

Disclosure of this information is mandatory. Civil and criminal penalties, including under certain circumstances a fine of not more than $500,000 and imprisonment of not more than five years, are provided for failure to file a report, supply information, and for filing a false or fraudulent report.

Disclosure of the social security number is mandatory. The authority to collect this number is 31 CFR 103. The social security number will be used as a means to identify the individual who files the report.

INSTRUCTIONS

A. Who Must File a Report—Each United States person who has a financial interest in or signature authority or other authority over bank, securities, or other financial accounts in a foreign country, which exceeds $10,000 in aggregate value at any time during the calendar year, must report that relationship each calendar year by filing TD F 90-22.1 with the Department of the Treasury on or before June 30, of the succeeding year.

An officer or employee of a commercial bank which is subject to the supervision of the Comptroller of the Currency, the Board of Governors of the Federal Reserve System, or the Federal Deposit Insurance Corporation need not report that he has signature or other authority over a foreign bank, securities or other financial account maintained by the bank unless he has a personal financial interest in the account.

In addition, an officer or employee of a domestic corporation whose securities are listed upon national securities exchanges or which has assets exceeding $1 million and 500 or more shareholders of record need not file such a report concerning his signature authority over a foreign financial account of the corporation, if he has no personal financial interest in the account and has been advised in writing by the chief financial officer of the corporation that the corporation has filed a current report which includes that account.

B. United States Person—The term "United States person" means (1) a citizen or resident of the United States, (2) a domestic partnership, (3) a domestic corporation, or (4) a domestic estate or trust.

C. When and Where to File—This report shall be filed on or before June 30 each calendar year with the Department of the Treasury, Post Office Box 32621, Detroit, MI 48232, or it may be hand carried to any local office of the Internal Revenue Service for forwarding to the Department of the Treasury, Detroit, MI.

D. Account in a Foreign Country—A "foreign country" includes all geographical areas located outside the United States, Guam, Puerto Rico, and the Virgin Islands.

Report any account maintained with a bank (except a military banking facility as defined in instruction E) or broker or dealer in securities that is located in a foreign country, even if it is a part of a United States bank or other institution. Do not report any account maintained with a branch, agency, or other office of a foreign bank or other institution that is located in the United States, Guam, Puerto Rico, and the Virgin Islands.

E. Military Banking Facility—Do not consider as an account in a foreign country, an account in an institution known as a "United States military banking facility" (or "United States military finance facility") operated by a United States financial institution designated by the United States Government to serve U.S. Government installations abroad, even if the United States military banking facility is located in a foreign country.

F. Bank, Financial Account—The term "bank account" means a savings, demand, checking, deposit, loan or any other account maintained with a financial institution or other person engaged in the business of banking. It includes certificates of deposit.

The term "securities account" means an account maintained with a financial institution or other person who buys, sells, holds, or trades stock or other securities for the benefit of another.

The term "other financial account" means any other account maintained with a financial institution or other person who accepts deposits, exchanges or transmits funds, or acts as a broker or dealer for future transactions in any commodity on (or subject to the rules of) a commodity exchange or association.

G. Financial Interest—A financial interest in a bank, securities, or other financial account in a foreign country means an interest described in either of the following two paragraphs:

(1) A United States person has a financial interest in each account for which such person is the owner of records or has legal title, whether the account is maintained for his or her own benefit or for the benefit of others including non-United States persons. If an account is maintained in the name of two persons jointly, or if several persons each own a partial interest in an account, each of those United States persons has a financial interest in that account.

(2) A United States person has a financial interest in each bank, securities, or other financial account in a foreign country for which the owner of record or holder of legal title is: (a) a person acting as an agent, nominee, attorney, or in some other capacity on behalf of the U.S. person; (b) a corporation in which the United States person owns directly or indirectly more than 50 percent of the total value of shares of stock; (c) a partnership in which the United States person owns an interest in more than 50 percent of the profits (distributive share of income); or (d) a trust in which the United States person either has a present beneficial interest in more than 50 percent of the assets or from which such person receives more than 50 percent of the current income.

H. Signature or Other Authority Over an Account—

Signature Authority—A person has signature authority over an account if such person can control the disposition of money or other property in it by delivery of a document containing his or here signature (or his or her signature and that of one or more other persons) to the bank or other person with whom the account is maintained.

Other authority exists in a person who can exercise comparable power over an account by direct communication to the bank or other person with whom the account is maintained, either orally or by some other means.

I. Account Valuation—For items 7, 9, and Instruction A, the maximum value of an account is the largest amount of currency and non-monetary assets that appear on any quarterly or more frequent account statement issued for the applicable year. If periodic account statements are not so issued, the maximum account asset value is the largest amount of currency and non-monetary assets in the account at any time during the year. Convert foreign currency by using the official exchange rate at the end of the year. In valuing currency of a country that uses multiple exchange rates, use the rate which would apply if the currency in the account were converted into United States dollars at the close of the calendar year.

The value of stock, other securities or other non-monetary assets in an account reported on TD F 90-22.1 is the fair market value at the end of the calendar year, or if withdrawn from the account, at the time of the withdrawal.

For purposes of items 7, 9, and Instruction A, if you had a financial interest in more than one account, each account is to be

valued separately in accordance with the foregoing two paragraphs.

If you had a financial interest in one or more but fewer than 25 accounts, and you are unable to determine whether the maximum value of these accounts exceeded $10,000 at any time during the year, check item 9 (do not check item 7) and complete Item 9 for each of these accounts.

J. United States Persons with Authority Over but No Interest in an Account—Except as provided in Instruction A and the following paragraph, you must state the name, address, and identifying number of each owner of an account over which you had authority, but if you check item 5 for more than one account of the same owner, you need identify the owner only once.

If you check item 5 for one or more accounts in which no United States person had a financial interest, you may state on the first line of this item, in lieu of supplying information about the owner, "No U.S. person had any financial interest in the foreign accounts." This statement must be based upon the actual belief of the person filing this form after he or she has taken reasonable measures to endure its correctness.

If you check item 5 for accounts owned by a domestic corporation and its domestic and/or foreign subsidiaries, you may treat them as one owner and write in the space provided, the name of the parent corporation, followed by "and related entities," and the identifying number and address of the parent corporation.

K. Consolidated Reporting—A corporation which owns directly or indirectly more than 50 percent interest in one or more other entities will be permitted to file a consolidated report on TD F 90-22.1, on behalf of itself and such other entities provided that a listing of them is made part of the consolidated report. Such reports should be signed by an authorized official of the parent corporation.

If the group of entities covered by a consolidated report has a financial interest in 25 or more foreign financial accounts, the reporting corporation need only note that fact on the form, it will, however, be required to provide detailed information concerning each account when so requested by the Secretary or his delegate.

L. Avoiding Duplicate Reporting—If you had financial interest (as defined in instruction G(2)(b), (c) or (d) in one or more accounts which are owned by a domestic corporation, partnership or trust which is required to file TD F 90-22.1 with respect to these accounts in lieu of completing item 9 for each account you may check item 6 and provide the required information.

M. Providing Additional Information—Any person who does not complete item 9, shall when requested by the Department of the Treasury provide the information called for in item 9.

N. Signature (Item 10)—*This report must be signed* by the person named in Item 1. If the report is being filed on behalf of a partnership, corporation, or fiduciary, it must be signed by an authorized individual.

O. Penalties—For criminal penalties for failure to file a report, supply information, and for filing a false or fraudulent report see 31 U.S.C. 5322(a), 31 U.S.C. 5322(b), and 18 U.S.C. 1001.

The estimated average burden associated with this collection of information is 10 minutes per respondent or recordkeeper depending on individual circumstances. Comments concerning the accuracy of this burden estimate and suggestions for reducing the burden should be directed to the Department of the Treasury, Office of Financial Enforcement, Room 4320 Main Treasury Building, Washington, DC 20220, and to the Office of Management and Budget, Paperwork Reduction Project (1505-0021), Washington, DC 20503.

UNITED STATES DEPARTMENT OF STATE

APPLICATION FOR ☐ PASSPORT ☐ REGISTRATION

SEE INSTRUCTIONS—TYPE OR PRINT IN INK IN WHITE AREAS

1. NAME FIRST NAME　　　　　　　　　　MIDDLE NAME

LAST NAME

2. MAILING ADDRESS

STREET

CITY, STATE, ZIP CODE

COUNTRY　　　　　　　IN CARE OF

☐ 5 Yr.　☐ 10 Yr.　Issue Date _____

R　D　O　DP

End. # _____　Exp. _____

3. SEX　**4. PLACE OF BIRTH** City, State or Province, Country　**5. DATE OF BIRTH** Mo. Day Year　**6. SEE FEDERAL TAX LAW NOTICE ON REVERSE SIDE** SOCIAL SECURITY NUMBER

Male　Female

7. HEIGHT Feet Inches　**8. COLOR OF HAIR**　**9. COLOR OF EYES**　**10. (Area Code) HOME PHONE**　**11. (Area Code) BUSINESS PHONE**

12. PERMANENT ADDRESS (Street, City, State, ZIP Code)　**13. OCCUPATION**

14. FATHER'S NAME	BIRTHPLACE	BIRTH DATE	U.S. CITIZEN ☐ YES ☐ NO	**16. TRAVEL PLANS** *(Not Mandatory)* COUNTRIES	DEPARTURE DATE
15. MOTHER'S MAIDEN NAME	BIRTHPLACE	BIRTH DATE	U.S. CITIZEN ☐ YES ☐ NO		LENGTH OF STAY

17. HAVE YOU EVER BEEN ISSUED A U.S. PASSPORT?　YES ☐　NO ☐　IF YES, SUBMIT PASSPORT IF AVAILABLE.　☐ Submitted

IF UNABLE TO SUBMIT MOST RECENT PASSPORT, STATE ITS DISPOSITION: COMPLETE NEXT LINE

NAME IN WHICH ISSUED　PASSPORT NUMBER　ISSUE DATE (Mo., Day, Yr.)　DISPOSITION

SUBMIT TWO RECENT IDENTICAL PHOTOS

2" × 2"　FROM 1" TO 1-3/8"

18. HAVE YOU EVER BEEN MARRIED? ☐ YES　☐ NO　DATE OF MOST RECENT MARRIAGE　Mo. Day Year

WIDOWED/DIVORCED? ☐ YES　☐ NO　IF YES, GIVE DATE　Mo. Day Year

SPOUSE'S FULL BIRTH NAME　SPOUSE'S BIRTHPLACE

19. IN CASE OF EMERGENCY, NOTIFY *(Person Not Traveling With You)*　RELATIONSHIP

(Not Mandatory)

FULL NAME

ADDRESS　(Area Code) PHONE NUMBER

20. TO BE COMPLETED BY AN APPLICANT WHO BECAME A CITIZEN THROUGH NATURALIZATION

I IMMIGRATED TO THE U.S. (Month, Year)　I RESIDED CONTINUOUSLY IN THE U.S. From (Mo., Yr.) To (Mo., Yr.)　DATE NATURALIZED (Mo., Day, Yr.)

PLACE

21. DO NOT SIGN APPLICATION UNTIL REQUESTED TO DO SO BY PERSON ADMINISTERING OATH

I have not, since acquiring United States citizenship, performed any of the acts listed under "Acts or Conditions" on the reverse of this application form (unless explanatory statement is attached). I solemnly swear (or affirm) that the statements made on this application are true and the photograph attached is a true likeness of me.

Subscribed and sworn to (affirmed) before me

Month　Day　Year

(SEAL)　X

☐ Clerk of Court or
☐ PASSPORT Agent
☐ Postal Employee
☐ (Vice) Consul USA At _____

(Sign in presence of person authorized to accept application)

(Signature of person authorized to accept application)

22. APPLICANT'S IDENTIFYING DOCUMENTS　☐ PASSPORT　☐ DRIVER'S LICENSE　☐ OTHER (Specify)　No.

ISSUE DATE Month Day Year　EXPIRATION DATE Month Day Year　PLACE OF ISSUE　ISSUED IN THE NAME OF

23. FOR ISSUING OFFICE USE ONLY (Applicant's evidence of citizenship)

☐ Birth Cert.　SR　CR　City　Filed/Issued:
☐ Passport　Bearer's Name:
☐ Report of Birth
☐ Naturalization/Citizenship Cert.　No.:
☐ Other:
☐ Seen & Returned
☐ Attached

APPLICATION APPROVAL

_____
Examiner Name

_____
Office, Date

24.

FEE _____　EXEC. _____　POST _____

FORM DSP-11 (12-87)　(SEE INSTRUCTIONS ON REVERSE)　Form Approved OMB No. 1405-0004 (Exp. 8/1/89)

FOLD

FOLD

PASSPORT APPLICATION

FEDERAL TAX LAW:

Section 6039E of the Internal Revenue Code of 1986 requires a passport applicant to provide his/her name (#1), mailing address (#2), date of birth (#5), and social security number (#6). If you have not been issued a social security number, enter zeroes in box #6. Passport Services will provide this information to the Internal Revenue Service routinely. Any applicant who fails to provide the required information is subject to a $500 penalty enforced by the IRS. All questions on this matter should be referred to the nearest IRS office.

ACTS OR CONDITIONS

(If any of the below-mentioned acts or conditions has been performed by or applies to the applicant, the portion which applies should be lined out, and a supplementary explanatory statement under oath (or affirmation) by the applicant should be attached and made a part of this application.)

I have not, since acquiring United States citizenship, been naturalized as a citizen of a foreign state; taken an oath or made an affirmation or other formal declaration of allegiance to a foreign state; entered or served in the armed forces of a foreign state; accepted or performed the duties of any office, post, or employment under the government of a foreign state or political subdivision thereof; made a formal renunciation of nationality either in the United States or before a diplomatic or consular officer of the United States in a foreign state; or been convicted by a court or court martial of competent jurisdiction of committing any act of treason against, or attempting by force to overthrow, or bearing arms against, the United States, or conspiring to overthrow, put down, or to destroy by force, the Government of the United States; or having been naturalized, within one year after such naturalization, returned to the country of my birth or any other foreign country to take up a permanent residence.

WARNING: False statements made knowingly and willfully in passport applications or in affidavits or other supporting documents submitted therewith are punishable by fine and/or imprisonment under provisions of 18 USC 1001 and/or 18 USC 1542. Alteration or mutilation of a passport issued pursuant to this application is punishable by fine and/or imprisonment under the provisions of 18 USC 1543. The use of a passport in violation of the restrictions contained therein or of the passport regulations is punishable by fine and/or imprisonment under 18 USC 1544. All statements and documents submitted are subject to verification.

PRIVACY ACT STATEMENT:

The information solicited on this form is authorized by, but not limited to, those statutes codified in Titles 8, 18, and 22, United States Code, and all predecessor statutes whether or not codified, and all regulations issued pursuant to Executive Order 11295 of August 5, 1966. The primary purpose for soliciting the information is to establish citizenship, identity, and entitlement to issuance of a United States Passport or related facility, and to properly administer and enforce the laws pertaining thereto.

The information is made available as a routine use on a need-to-know basis to personnel of the Department of State and other government agencies having statutory or other lawful authority to maintain such information in the performance of their official duties; pursuant to a court order; and, as set forth in Part 171, Title 22, Code of Federal Regulations (see *Federal Register,* Volume 42, pages 49791 through 49795).

Failure to provide the information requested on this form may result in the denial of a United States Passport, related document, or service to the individual seeking such passport, document, or service.

HOW TO APPLY FOR A U.S. PASSPORT. U.S. passports are issued only to U.S. citizens or nationals. Each person must obtain his or her own passport.

IF YOU ARE A FIRST-TIME APPLICANT, please complete and submit this application in person. (Applicants under 13 years of age usually need not appear in person unless requested. A parent or guardian may execute the application on the child's behalf.) Each application must be accompanied by (1) PROOF OF U.S. CITIZENSHIP, (2) PROOF OF IDENTITY, (3) TWO PHOTOGRAPHS, (4) FEES (as explained below) to one of the following acceptance agents: a clerk of any Federal or State court of record or a judge or clerk of any probate court accepting applications; a designated postal employee at a selected post office; or an agent at a Passport Agency in Boston, Chicago, Honolulu, Houston, Los Angeles, Miami, New Orleans, New York, Philadelphia, San Francisco, Seattle, Stamford, or Washington, D.C.; or a U.S. consular official.

IF YOU HAVE HAD A PREVIOUS PASSPORT, inquire about eligibility to use Form DSP-82 (mail-in application).

Address requests for passport amendment, extension of validity, or additional visa pages to a Passport Agency or a U.S. Consulate or Embassy abroad. Check visa requirements with consular officials of countries to be visited well in advance of your departure.

(1) PROOF OF U.S. CITIZENSHIP.

(a) APPLICANTS BORN IN THE UNITED STATES. Submit previous U.S. passport or **certified** birth certificate. A birth certificate must include your given name and surname, date and place of birth, the date the birth record was filed, and seal or other certification of the official custodian of such records. A record filed more than 1 year after the birth is acceptable if it is supported by evidence described in the next paragraph.

IF NO BIRTH RECORD EXISTS, submit registrar's notice to that effect. Also submit an early baptismal or circumcision certificate, hospital birth record, early census, school, or family Bible records, newspaper or insurance files, or notarized affidavits of persons having knowledge of your birth (preferably with at least one record listed above). Evidence should include your given name and surname, date and place of birth, and seal or other certification of office (if customary) and signature of issuing official.

(b) APPLICANTS BORN OUTSIDE THE UNITED STATES. Submit previous U.S. passport or Certificate of Naturalization, or Certificate of Citizenship, or a Report of Birth Abroad, or evidence described below.

IF YOU CLAIM CITIZENSHIP THROUGH NATURALIZATION OF PARENT(S), submit the Certificate(s) of Naturalization of your parent(s), your foreign birth certificate, and proof of your admission to the United States for permanent residence.

IF YOU CLAIM CITIZENSHIP THROUGH BIRTH ABROAD TO U.S. CITIZEN PARENT(S), submit a Consular Report of Birth (Form FS-240) or Certification of Birth (Form DS-1350 or FS-545), or your foreign birth certificate, parents' marriage certificate, proof of citizenship of your parent(s), and affidavit of U.S. citizen parent(s) showing all periods and places of residence/physical presence in the United States and abroad before your birth.

(2) PROOF OF IDENTITY. If you are not personally known to the acceptance agent, you must establish your identity to the agent's satisfaction. You may submit items such as the following containing your signature AND physical description or photograph that is a good likeness of you: previous U.S. passport; Certificate of Naturalization or of Citizenship; driver's license (not temporary or learner's license); or government (Federal, State, municipal) identification card or pass. Temporary or altered documents are not acceptable.

IF YOU CANNOT PROVE YOUR IDENTITY as stated above, you must appear with an IDENTIFYING WITNESS who is a U.S. citizen or permanent resident alien who has known you for at least 2 years. Your witness must prove his or her identity and complete and sign an Affidavit of Identifying Witness (Form DSP-71) before the acceptance agent. You must also submit some identification of your own.

(3) TWO PHOTOGRAPHS. Submit two identical photographs of you alone, sufficiently recent to be a good likeness (normally taken within the last 6 months), 2 × 2 inches in size, with an image size from bottom of chin to top of head (including hair) of between 1 and 1-3/8 inches. Photographs must be clear, front view, full face, taken in normal street attire without a hat or dark glasses, and printed on thin paper with a plain light (white or off-white) background. They may be black and white or color. They must be capable of withstanding a mounting temperature of 225° Fahrenheit (107° Celsius). Photographs retouched so that your appearance is changed are unacceptable. Snapshots, most vending machine prints, and magazine or full-length photographs are unacceptable.

(4) FEES. Submit $42 if you are 18 years of age or older. The passport fee is $35. In addition, a fee of $7 is charged for the execution of the application. Your passport will be valid for 10 years from the date of issue except where limited by the Secretary of State to a shorter period. Submit $27 if you are under 18 years of age. The passport fee is $20 and the execution fee is $7. Your passport will be valid for 5 years from the date of issue, except where limited as above.

Pay the passport and execution fees in one of the following forms: checks—personal, certified, traveler's; bank draft or cashier's check; money order, U.S. Postal, international, currency exchange; or if abroad, the foreign currency equivalent, or a check drawn on a U.S. bank.

Make passport and execution fees payable to Passport Services (except if applying at a State court, pay execution fee as the State court requires) or the appropriate Embassy or Consulate, if abroad. No fee is charged to applicants with U.S. Government or military authorization for no-fee passports (except State courts may collect the execution fee). Pay special postage if applicable.

Form **W-9**

(October 1983)

Department of the Treasury
Internal Revenue Service

Payer's Request for Taxpayer Identification Number

Please print or type

| Name as shown on account (if joint account, also give joint owner's name) |
| Address |
| City, State, and ZIP code |

List account number(s) here (See Instructions) ▶ ....

PART I.—Taxpayer Identification Number

Enter the taxpayer identification number in the appropriate box. For most individual taxpayers, this is the social security number.

Note: If the account is in more than one name, see the chart on page 2 for guidelines on which number to give the payer.

Social security number

OR

Employer identification number

PART II.—Backup Withholding On Accounts Opened After 12/31/83

Check the box if you are NOT subject to backup withholding under the provisions of section 3406(a)(1)(C) of the Internal Revenue Code . . . . ▶ ☐

(See **Highlight** below.)

Certification.—Under the penalties of perjury, I certify that the information provided on this form is true, correct, and complete.

Signature ▶   Date ▶

Instructions (Section references are to the Internal Revenue Code.)

Highlight for Interest or Dividend Accounts Opened After 12/31/83—Backup Withholding

You may be notified that you are subject to backup withholding under section 3406(a)(1)(C) because you have underreported interest or dividends or you were required to but failed to file a return which would have included a reportable interest or dividend payment. If you have NOT been so notified, check the box in PART II. **Note:** Backup withholding may apply to existing accounts as well as accounts opened after December 31, 1983.

Caution: There are other situations where you may be subject to backup withholding. Please read the instructions below carefully.

Purpose of Form

Use this form to report the taxpayer identification number (TIN) of the record owner of the account to the payer (or broker).

Beginning January 1, 1984, payers must generally withhold 20% of taxable interest, dividend, and certain other payments if you fail to furnish payers with the correct taxpayer identification number (this is referred to as backup withholding). For most individual taxpayers, the taxpayer identification number is the social security number.

To prevent backup withholding on these payments, be sure to notify payers of the correct taxpayer identification number and, for accounts you open after December 31, 1983, properly certify that you are not subject to backup withholding under section 3406(a)(1)(C).

You may use this form to certify that the taxpayer identification number you are giving the payer is correct and, for accounts opened after December 31, 1983, that you are not subject to backup withholding.

If the payer provides a different form than Form W-9 to request the taxpayer identification number, please use it.

Backup Withholding

You are subject to backup withholding if:

(1) You fail to furnish your taxpayer identification number to the payer, OR

(2) The Internal Revenue Service notifies the payer that you furnished an incorrect taxpayer identification number, OR

(3) You are notified that you are subject to backup withholding (under section 3406(a)(1)(C)), OR

(4) For an interest or dividend account opened after December 31, 1983, you fail to certify to the payer that you are **not** subject to backup withholding under (3) above, or fail to certify your taxpayer identification number.

For payments other than interest or dividends, you are subject to backup withholding only if (1) or (2) above applies.

(See the section on the back titled "Payees Exempt from Backup Withholding.")

Payments of Interest, Dividends, and Patronage Dividends

Accounts Opened Before January 1, 1984

To certify that the taxpayer identification number is correct for accounts opened before January 1, 1984, fill out your name and address, enter your account number(s) (if applicable), complete Part I, sign and date the form and return it to the payer.

Accounts Opened After December 31, 1983

To certify that the taxpayer identification number is correct and that you are not subject to backup withholding under section 3406(a)(1)(C) for accounts opened after December 31, 1983, fill out your name and address, enter your account number(s) (if applicable), complete Parts I and II, sign and date the form and return it to the payer.

If you are subject to backup withholding and are merely providing your correct taxpayer identification number to the payer, fill out your name, address, enter your account number(s) (if applicable), and complete Part I.

Other Payments

If you are merely providing your correct taxpayer identification number to the payer for payments other than interest, dividends, and patronage dividends, you need not sign this form. Fill out your name and address, enter your account number(s) (if applicable), complete Part I and return the form to the payer.

Account Numbers

If you have more than one account with the same payer (for example, a savings account and a certificate of deposit at the same bank), the payer may request a separate Form W-9 for each account depending on how the payer's records are kept.

What Number to Give the Payer

Give the payer the social security number or employer identification number of the record owner of the account. If the account belongs to you as an individual, give your social security number. If the account is in more than one name or is not in the name of the actual owner, see the chart on page 2 for guidelines on which number to report.

Obtaining a Number

If you don't have a taxpayer identification number or you don't know your number, obtain **Form SS-5**, Application for a Social Security Number Card, or **Form SS-4**, Application for Employer Identification Number, at the local office of the Social Security Administration or the Internal Revenue Service and apply for a number. Write "applied for" in Part I in place of your number. When you get a number, submit a new Form W-9 to the payer.

(Give this form to the payer, not to the Internal Revenue Service)

Form **W-9** (10-83)

Penalties

(1) Penalty for Failure to Furnish Taxpayer Identification Number.—If you fail to furnish your taxpayer identification number to a payer, you are subject to a penalty of $50 for each such failure unless your failure is due to reasonable cause and not to willful neglect.

(2) Failure to Report Certain Dividend and Interest Payments.—If you fail to include any portion of an includible payment for interest, dividends, or patronage dividends in gross income, such failure will be treated as being due to negligence and will be subject to a penalty of 5% on any portion of an underpayment attributable to that failure unless there is clear and convincing evidence to the contrary.

(3) Civil Penalty for False Information With Respect to Withholding.—If you make a false statement with no reasonable basis which results in no imposition of backup withholding, you are subject to a penalty of $500.

(4) Criminal Penalty for Falsifying Information.—Falsifying certifications or affirmations may subject you to criminal penalties including fines and/or imprisonment.

Payees Exempt from Backup Withholding

Payees specifically exempted from backup withholding on **ALL** payments include the following:

- A corporation.
- A financial institution.
- An organization exempt from tax under section 501(a), or an individual retirement plan.
- The United States or any agency or instrumentality thereof.
- A State, the District of Columbia, a possession of the United States, or any subdivision or instrumentality thereof.
- A foreign government, a political subdivision of a foreign government, or any agency or instrumentality thereof.
- An international organization or any agency or instrumentality thereof.
- A registered dealer in securities or commodities registered in the U.S. or a possession of the U.S.
- A real estate investment trust.
- A common trust fund operated by a bank under section 584(a).
- An exempt charitable remainder trust, or a non-exempt trust described in section 4947(a)(1).
- An entity registered at all times under the Investment Company Act of 1940.
- A foreign central bank of issue.

Payments of **dividends** and **patronage dividends** not generally subject to backup withholding include the following:

- Payments to nonresident aliens subject to withholding under section 1441.
- Payments to partnerships not engaged in a trade or business in the U.S. and which have at least one nonresident partner.
- Payments of patronage dividends where the amount received is not paid in money.
- Payments made by certain foreign organizations.

Payments of **Interest** not generally subject to backup withholding include the following:

- Payments of interest on obligations issued by individuals. **Note:** *You may be subject to backup withholding if this interest is $600 or more and is paid in the course of the payer's trade or business and you have not provided your correct taxpayer identification number to the payer.*
- Payments of tax-exempt interest (including exempt-interest dividends under section 852).
- Payments described in section 6049(b)(5) to nonresident aliens.
- Payments on tax-free covenant bonds under section 1451.
- Payments made by certain foreign organizations.

Exempt payees described above should file Form W-9 to **avoid** possible **erroneous** backup withholding. Because certain payments exempt from backup withholding are nevertheless subject to information reporting, if you file this form with the payer, furnish your taxpayer identification number, write "exempt" on the face of the form, and return it to the payer. If the payments are interest, dividends, or patronage dividends, also sign and date the form.

Certain payments other than interest, dividends, and patronage dividends that are not subject to information reporting are also not subject to backup withholding. For details, see the regulations under sections 6041, 6041A(a), 6045, and 6050A.

Privacy Act Notice.— Section 6109 requires most recipients of dividend, interest, or other payments to give taxpayer identification numbers to payers who must report the payments to IRS. IRS uses the numbers for identification purposes. Payers must be given the numbers whether or not recipients are required to file tax returns. Beginning January 1, 1984, payers must generally withhold 20% of taxable interest, dividend, and certain other payments to a payee who does not furnish a taxpayer identification number to a payer. Certain penalties may also apply.

Guidelines for Determining the Proper Identification Number to Give the Payer.— Social security numbers have nine digits separated by two hyphens: i.e., 000-00-0000. Employer identification numbers have nine digits separated by only one hyphen: i.e., 00-0000000. The table below will help you determine the number to give the payer.

For this type of account:	Give the SOCIAL SECURITY number of—
1. An individual's account	The individual
2. Two or more individuals (joint account)	The actual owner of the account or, if combined funds, any one of the individuals[1]
3. Husband and wife (joint account)	The actual owner of the account or, if joint funds, either person[1]
4. Custodian account of a minor (Uniform Gift to Minors Act)	The minor[2]
5. Adult and minor (joint account)	The adult or, if the minor is the only contributor, the minor[1]
6. Account in the name of guardian or committee for a designated ward, minor, or incompetent person	The ward, minor, or incompetent person[3]
7. a. The usual revocable savings trust account (grantor is also trustee)	The grantor-trustee[1]
b. So-called trust account that is not a legal or valid trust under State law	The actual owner[1]
8. Sole proprietorship account	The owner[4]

For this type of account:	Give the EMPLOYER IDENTIFICATION number of—
9. A valid trust, estate, or pension trust	Legal entity (Do not furnish the identifying number of the personal representative or trustee unless the legal entity itself is not designated in the account title.)[5]
10. Corporate account	The corporation
11. Religious, charitable, or educational organization account	The organization
12. Partnership account held in the name of the business	The partnership
13. Association, club, or other tax-exempt organization	The organization
14. A broker or registered nominee	The broker or nominee
15. Account with the Department of Agriculture in the name of a public entity (such as a State or local government, school district, or prison) that receives agricultural program payments	The public entity

[1] List first and circle the name of the person whose number you furnish.
[2] Circle the minor's name and furnish the minor's social security number.
[3] Circle the ward's, minor's, or incompetent person's name and furnish such person's social security number.
[4] Show the name of the owner.
[5] List first and circle the name of the legal trust, estate, or pension trust.

Note: If no name is circled when there is more than one name, the number will be considered to be that of the first name listed.

Form **4789**
(Rev. January 1989)

Department of the Treasury
Internal Revenue Service

Currency Transaction Report

▶ File a separate report for each transaction.   ▶ Please type or print.
▶ For Paperwork Reduction Act Notice, see page 3.
(Complete all applicable parts—See instructions)

OMB No. 1545–0183
Expires: 12-31-89

If amended report, see instructions and check here . . . . ▶ ☐

Part I Identity of individual who conducted this transaction with the financial institution

1 If multiple individuals involved, see instructions and check here . . . . ▶ ☐

2 Last name	3 First name	4 Middle initial	5 Social security number

6 Address (number and street)	7 Occupation, profession, or business

8 City	9 State	10 ZIP code	11 Country (if not U.S.)

12 Method used to verify identity: a Describe ▶ ....
  b Issued by ▶   c Number ▶

13 Reason items 2–12 are not completed: a ☐ Armored car service (enter name) ▶ ....
  b ☐ Mail deposit/shipment   c ☐ Night deposit or ATM transaction   d ☐ Multiple transactions (see instructions)

Part II Individual or organization for whom this transaction was completed

14 If multiple individuals or organizations are involved, see instructions and check here . . . . ▶ ☐

15 Individual's last name	16 First name	17 Middle initial	18 Social security number

19 a Name of organization	b Check if: (1) ☐ broker/dealer in securities, or (2) ☐ financial institution (see instructions)	20 Employer identification number

21 Address (number and street)	22 Occupation, profession, or business

23 City	24 State	25 ZIP code	26 Country (if not U.S.)

Part III Customer's account number(s) affected by transaction

27 **S** ☐ Savings ▶ ....   **T** ☐ Securities ▶ ....   **H** ☐ CD/Money market ▶ ....
  C ☐ Checking ▶   **L** ☐ Loan ▶   **O** ☐ Other (specify) ▶

Part IV Type of transaction. Check applicable boxes to describe transactions

28 ☐ Currency exchange (currency for currency)

29 CASH IN: **F** ☐ CD/Money market purchased   30 CASH OUT: **R** ☐ CD/Money market redeemed
  D ☐ Deposit   **H** ☐ For wire transfer   **C** ☐ Check cashed   **U** ☐ From wire transfer
  G ☐ Security purchased   **A** ☐ Receipt from abroad   **T** ☐ Security redeemed   **B** ☐ Shipment abroad
  P ☐ Check purchased   **K** ☐ Other cash in (specify) ▶ ....   **W** ☐ Withdrawal   **Y** ☐ Other cash out (specify) ▶ ....

31 Total amount of currency transaction (in U.S. dollars). ▶ $	32 Amount in Item 31 in $100 bills or higher $	33 Date of transaction (month, day, and year)

34 If other than U.S. currency is involved, please furnish the following information: a Exchange made ☐ for or ☐ from U.S. currency

b Currency name	c Country	d Total amount of each foreign currency (in U.S. dollars) . . ▶ $

35 If a check or wire transfer was involved in this transaction, please furnish the following information (see instructions):   ▶ ☐
  a If more than one check or wire transfer is involved, see instructions and check here . . . .

b Date of check or wire transfer	c Amount of check or wire transfer (in U.S. dollars) $	d Payee

e Drawer of check	f Drawee bank and MICR number

Part V Financial institution where currency transaction took place

36 Check applicable box to indicate type of financial institution   a ☐ Bank (enter code number from instructions here) ▶ ....
  b ☐ Savings and loan association   c ☐ Credit union   d ☐ Security broker/dealer   e ☐ Other

37 Name of financial institution	38 Employer identification number

39 Address (number and street)	40 Social security number

41 City	42 State	43 ZIP code	44 MICR number

Sign Here ▶

45 Signature (preparer)	46 Title	47 Date
48 Type or print preparer's name	49 Approving official (signature)	50 Date

Multiple Transactions
(Complete applicable parts below if box 1, 14, or 35a on page 1 is checked)

Part I   Continued—Complete if box 1 on page 1 is checked

2 Last name	**3** First name	**4** Middle initial	**5** Social security number

6 Address (number and street)	**7** Occupation, profession, or business

8 City	**9** State	**10** ZIP code	**11** Country (if not U.S.)

12 Method used to verify identity: **a** Describe ▶

b Issued by ▶   **c** Number ▶

---

2 Last name	**3** First name	**4** Middle initial	**5** Social security number

6 Address (number and street)	**7** Occupation, profession, or business

8 City	**9** State	**10** ZIP code	**11** Country (if not U.S.)

12 Method used to verify identity: **a** Describe ▶

b Issued by ▶   **c** Number ▶

Part II   Continued—Complete if box 14 on page 1 is checked

15 Individual's last name	**16** First name	**17** Middle initial	**18** Social security number

19 a Name of organization	**b** Check if: **(1)** ☐ broker/dealer in securities, or **(2)** ☐ financial institution (see instructions)	**20** Employer identification number

21 Address (number and street)	**22** Occupation, profession, or business

23 City	**24** State	**25** ZIP code	**26** Country (if not U.S.)

---

15 Individual's last name	**16** First name	**17** Middle initial	**18** Social security number

19 a Name of organization	**b** Check if: **(1)** ☐ broker/dealer in securities, or **(2)** ☐ financial institution (see instructions)	**20** Employer identification number

21 Address (number and street)	**22** Occupation, profession, or business

23 City	**24** State	**25** ZIP code	**26** Country (if not U.S.)

Part IV   Continued—Complete if box 35a on page 1 is checked

35 b Date of check or wire transfer	**c** Amount of check or wire transfer (in U.S. dollars) $	**d** Payee

e Drawer of check	**f** Drawee bank and MICR number

---

35 b Date of check or wire transfer	**c** Amount of check or wire transfer (in U.S. dollars) $	**d** Payee

e Drawer of check	**f** Drawee bank and MICR number

General Instructions

Paperwork Reduction Act Notice.—The Paperwork Reduction Act of 1980 says we must tell taxpayers why we are collecting this information, how we will use it, and whether you have to give it to us.

The requested information is useful in criminal, tax, and regulatory investigations. In addition to directing the Federal Government's attention to unusual or questionable transactions, the reporting requirement discourages the use of currency in illegal transactions. Financial institutions are required to provide the information under 31 CFR 103.22, 103.26, and 103.27.

The estimated average time needed to complete this form, depending on individual circumstances, is 41 minutes. If you have comments concerning the accuracy of this time estimate or suggestions for making this form more simple, we would be happy to hear from you. You can write to the **Internal Revenue Service,** Washington, DC 20224, Attention: IRS Reports Clearance Officer TR:FP; or the **Office of Management and Budget,** Paperwork Reduction Project, Washington, DC 20503.

Who Must File.—Each financial institution other than a casino must file a Form 4789 for each deposit, withdrawal, exchange of currency, or other payment or transfer, by, through, or to the financial institution, which involves a transaction in currency of more than $10,000. Multiple transactions by or for any person which in any one day total more than $10,000 should be treated as a single transaction, if the financial institution is aware of them.

Exemptions.—See 31 CFR 103.22(b) for exemptions from the filing requirements by banks on certain customers.

When and Where to File.—File this form by the 15th day after the date of the transaction with the Internal Revenue Service Detroit Computing Center, P.O. Box 32621, Detroit, MI 48232 ATTN: CTR, or hand carry it to your local IRS office. Keep a copy of each Form 4789 for 5 years from the date you file it.

Penalties.—Civil and criminal penalties (up to $500,000) are provided for failure to file a report or to supply information, and for filing a false or fraudulent report. See 31 CFR, sections 103.47 and 103.49.

Definitions

Bank.—See 31 CFR 103.11 for the definition of a bank.

Currency.—The coin and currency of the United States or of any other country, which circulate in and are customarily used and accepted as money in the country in which issued. It includes United States silver certificates, United States notes, and Federal Reserve notes, but does not include bank checks or other negotiable instruments not customarily accepted as money.

Financial Institution.—Each agency, branch, or office in the United States of any person doing business in one or more of the capacities following:

(1) a bank;
(2) a broker or dealer in securities, registered or required to be registered with SEC under the Securities Exchange Act of 1934;

(3) a person who engages as a business in dealing in or exchanging currency (for example, a dealer in foreign exchange or a person engaged primarily in the cashing of checks);

(4) a person who engages as a business in issuing, selling, or redeeming traveler's checks, money orders, or similar instruments, except one who does so as a selling agent exclusively, or as an incidental part of another business;

(5) a licensed transmitter of funds, or other person engaged in the business of transmitting funds abroad for others.

Person.—An individual, corporation, partnership, trust or estate, joint stock company, association, syndicate, joint venture, or other unincorporated organization or group, and all entities treated as legal personalities.

Transaction in Currency.—A transaction involving the physical transfer of currency from one person to another. A transaction in currency does not include a transfer of funds by means of bank check, bank draft, wire transfer, or other written order that does not include the physical transfer of currency.

Specific Instructions

Amended report.—If this amends a previously filed report, check the box in the upper right corner. Staple a copy of the previously filed report to this amended report and complete only those entries which you are correcting on the amended report.

Part I—Identity of individual who conducted the transaction.—This part must always be completed. If the individual conducts the transaction for another person, be sure to complete Part II also.

Box 1—Multiple individuals.—If two or more individuals conduct a transaction, check Box 1. All individuals must be positively identified. Enter information in Part I for one of the individuals. Complete the entry spaces on the back of the form for the other individuals. For example, a check made out to John Doe and Thomas Smith may be presented for payment at a financial institution. Both of the joint payees are present. Complete Part I on the front of the form for John Doe, and complete Part I on the back for Thomas Smith.

Items 2, 3, and 4—Name of person conducting transaction.—Enter the last name in Item 2, the first name in Item 3, and the middle initial in Item 4.

Item 5—Social security number.—A social security number must be provided if an individual is conducting the transaction for himself or herself. If the individual is conducting a transaction for another person or is a nonresident alien who does not have a social security number, write NONE in the space and complete Item 12.

Items 6, 8, 9, 10, and 11—Address.—Enter the permanent address, including ZIP code, of the individual who entered the financial institution to conduct the transaction. A P.O. Box number is not a street address.

Item 7—Occupation, profession, or business.—Fully identify the occupation, profession or business of the individual conducting the transaction; for example, secretary, carpenter, attorney, etc. Do not use nondescriptive terms such as merchant, self-employed, businessman, etc.

Item 12—Method used to verify identity.—All individuals (except employees of armored car services) conducting a currency transaction for themselves or for another person must be positively identified. For individuals who are established customers, identifying information previously obtained from the customer and in the financial institution's records may be provided. Statements such as "known customer" are not sufficient as identifying information. For U.S. citizens, ask to see and inspect a driver's permit or any other written identification document acceptable to the financial institution in normal check cashing operations. For an alien, ask to see and inspect his or her passport, alien ID card, or other official document showing nationality or residence. Enter the type of document in Item a, such as driver's license, signature card, charge card, passport, etc. Enter in Item b, the name of the state issuing the driver's permit, the name of the bank or store issuing the charge card, etc. Enter the number of the license, account, card, etc., in Item c.

Item 13—Reason items 2-12 not completed; armored car service, mail, night deposit, or ATM transaction.— Check Box a if the transaction was a delivery by an armored car service licensed by a state or local government. Enter the name of the armored car service in the space provided.

Check Box b if the currency was received or shipped through the U.S. Postal Service.

Check Box c if the transaction was a night deposit or an ATM (automated teller machine) transaction.

Check Box d if this report involves multiple transactions that when totalled became a reportable transaction and the individual(s) who conducted the transactions cannot be identified.

If you check Box a, b, c, or d, you do not have to complete any other entries in Part I. However, be sure to complete Parts II, III, IV, and V.

Part II—Individual or organization for whom transaction was completed.—If the individual in Part I is conducting the transaction for himself or herself, do not complete Part II. In all other cases, including armored car service, mail, night deposit, or ATM transactions, complete Part II.

Box 14—Multiple individuals or organizations.—If this transaction is being conducted for more than one individual or organization, check Box 14, and complete the applicable entries on the back of the form. Do this also if the individual in Part I conducts a transaction that involves both himself or herself and another individual or organization.

Items 15, 16, and 17—Name of Individual.—Enter the last name in Item 15, first name in Item 16, and middle initial in Item 17, of the individual for whom the transaction was completed.

Item 18—Social security number.—Enter the social security number of the individual for whom the transaction was completed. You will have this in your records. If the individual is a nonresident alien and does not have a social security number, write NONE in the space for the number.

Items 19 and 20—Organization's name and EIN.—If the transaction involves a business, show the business name in Item 19a, and the employer identification number (EIN) in Item 20. This is a 9-digit number shown as 00-0000000. If the organization does not have an EIN, write NONE in Item 20.

Check Box 19b(1) if the individual or organization is a broker or dealer in securities. Check Box 19b(2) if the individual or organization is a financial institution described in item (3), (4), or (5) under the *Definitions* of a *Financial Institution* on page 3.

Items 21, 23, 24, 25, and 26—Address.—Enter the permanent address including the ZIP code of the individual or organization for whom the transaction is completed in the appropriate boxes. If the address is outside the U.S., be sure to show the country in Item 26. A P.O. Box number is not a street address.

Item 22—Occupation, profession, or business.—Fully identify the occupation, profession, or business of the individual or organization for whom the transaction was completed. Use descriptive terms, such as securities broker, attorney, auto dealer, etc. Do not use nondescriptive terms, such as self-employed, merchant, businessman, etc.

Part III—Customer's account number affected by the transaction.

Box 27—Type of account and account number.—Check the boxes and enter the account numbers of the accounts affected by the transaction. If a deposit or withdrawal is made from a savings, checking, share, or other account, check the appropriate box and enter the account number. Other accounts would include all accounts with broker-dealers. If the transaction does not affect any account, make no entry in Part III. For example, a cashiers check purchased with cash may not affect any account and does not require any entry in this part. Please note that the code letters before the boxes are for IRS processing purposes.

Part IV—Type of transaction.—Check the boxes that describe the transaction. For international transactions with foreign financial agencies (banks, currency exchange dealers, securities dealers, etc.) involving receipts of currency for deposit, purchases of currency, withdrawal, shipments of currency for deposit, or sales

of currency, check the appropriate box "Receipts from abroad" or "Shipments abroad" in Item 29 or 30.

Box 28—Currency exchange.—Check this box if currency was exchanged for currency. This includes exchanging U.S. currency for foreign currency (be sure to complete Item 34) and vice versa. It also includes exchanging small denomination bills of U.S. currency for large denomination bills of U.S. currency, or vice versa.

Box 29—Cash In.—Check the appropriate box(es) when currency is received by the financial institution as part of a transaction.

Box 30—Cash out.—Check the appropriate box(es) when the financial institution pays out currency as part of a transaction.

Item 31—Total amount of currency.—Enter the total amount of currency in the transaction. If a transaction involves both currency and checks, such as a deposit transaction, enter only the amount of the currency.

Item 32—Amount In $100 bills or higher.—Enter the amount of the total currency transaction reported in Item 31 that is in denominations of U.S. currency of $100 or higher. For example, if the total currency transaction is $100,000 and $50,000 is in U.S. currency of $100 or higher denominations, enter $100,000 in Item 31 and $50,000 in Item 32.

Item 33—Date.—Enter the month, day, and year of the currency transaction. Use the actual calendar date, not the banking day date.

Item 34—Foreign currency.—If the currency transaction involves a foreign currency, enter the information in the appropriate spaces. Enter the name of the currency in Item b, the country in Item c, and the total amount of the foreign currency in U.S. dollars in Item d. Check the appropriate box in Item a, if foreign currency was exchanged for U.S. currency or U.S. currency was exchanged for foreign currency. For example, a currency transaction involving Italian lira being deposited would have lira entered in Item b, Italy entered in Item c, and the amount, converted into U.S. dollars, entered in Item d. Since currency was not exchanged, no entry is made in Item a. If currency of two or more foreign countries is involved in the transaction, attach a separate sheet of paper that clearly identifies the individual or organization for whom the transaction was completed (Items 15 through 20) and report the information for each foreign currency required by Item 34.

Item 35—Check or wire transfer.—If multiple checks or wire transfers are involved in the transaction, check Box a and furnish the information for one of the instruments on the front of the form and for the other instruments on the back of the form in the spaces provided. If you have to report more instruments than there are entry spaces, attach a sheet of paper that

clearly identifies the individual or organization for whom the transaction is completed (Items 15 through 20) and furnish the information for Items b through f for each check or wire transfer.

Date.—Enter the date shown on the check or the wire transfer of funds in Item b.

Amount.—Enter the amount of the check or wire transfer in Item c. Show the amount in U.S. dollars only.

Payee.—Enter the name of the individual or organization to whom the check or wire transfer of funds is made payable in Item d.

Drawer.—Enter the name of the individual or organization that wrote the check or who wire transferred funds in Item e.

Drawee bank and MICR number.—Enter the name of the bank and MICR number on which the check or wire transfer of funds is drawn in Item f.

Part V.—Financial Institution where transaction took place.

Box 36—Type of financial Institution.—Check the box that describes the type of financial institution you are.

Box 36a—Banks.—Enter the appropriate code number for the Federal agency that performs examinations for compliance with the Bank Secrecy Act regulations:

Code 1—Comptroller of the Currency

Code 2—FDIC

Code 3—Federal Reserve System

Code 4—None of the above

Items 37, 39, 41, 42, 43, and 44—Name, address, and MICR number.—Enter the full legal name, street address, city, State, ZIP code, and MICR number of the financial institution where the transaction occurred. *If the transaction occurred at a branch office, enter the complete street address and MICR number of the branch, not the headquarters' address and MICR number.* A P.O. Box number is not a street address. Enter the MICR number in Item 44.

Item 38—EIN.—Enter the financial institution's employer identification number (EIN) .

Item 40—SSN.—If the financial institution does not have an EIN, enter the financial institution owner's social security number.

Items 45, 46, 47, and 48—Preparer's signature, title, and date.—Form 4789 must be signed in Item 45 by an individual authorized or designated by the financial institution to sign it. His or her title should be shown in Item 46 and the date of signature entered in Item 47. This signer's name should be typed or printed legibly in Item 48.

Items 49 and 50—Approving official's signature and date.—The official who reviews and approves the information on the form must sign in Item 49 and enter the date of signing in Item 50.

Form **8300**	**Report of Cash Payments Over $10,000 Received in a Trade or Business**	OMB No. 1545-0892
(Rev. February 1992) Department of the Treasury Internal Revenue Service	Failure to file this form or filing a false form may result in imprisonment. ▶ See instructions. Please type or print.	Expires 09-30-94

1 Check appropriate boxes if: **a** ☐ amends prior report; **b** ☐ suspicious transaction.

Part I   Identity of Individual From Whom the Cash Was Received

2 If more than one individual is involved, see instructions and check here . . . . ▶ ☐

3 Last name	**4** First name	**5** Middle initial	**6** Social security number

7 Address (number, street, and apt. or suite no.)	**8** Occupation, profession, or business

9 City	**10** State	**11** ZIP code	**12** Country (if not U.S.)	**13** Date of birth (see instructions)

14 Method used to verify identity: **a** Describe identification ▶ _____

b Issued by _____   **c** Number _____

Part II   Person (See Definitions) on Whose Behalf This Transaction Was Conducted

15 If this transaction was conducted on behalf of more than one person, see instructions and check here. . . . . . ▶ ☐

16 This person is an: ☐ individual or ☐ organization   **17** If funded by another party, see instructions and check here . ▶ ☐

18 Individual's last name or Organization's name	**19** First name	**20** Middle initial	**21** Social security number

22 Doing business as (DBA) name (see instructions)	Employer identification number

23 Alien identification: **a** Describe identification ▶ _____

b Issued by _____   **c** Number _____

24 Address (number, street, and apt. or suite no.)	**25** Occupation, profession, or business

26 City	**27** State	**28** ZIP code	**29** Country (if not U.S.)	**30** Date of birth (see instructions)

Part III   Description of Transaction and Method of Payment

31a ☐ personal property purchased   **d** ☐ business services provided   **g** ☐ exchange of cash
b ☐ real property purchased   **e** ☐ intangible property purchased   **h** ☐ escrow or trust funds
c ☐ personal services provided   **f** ☐ debt obligations paid   **i** ☐ other (specify) ▶

32 Specific description of property or service purchased. Give serial or registration number of car, boat, airplane, etc., address of real estate, etc.

33 Total price $ .00	**34** Amount of U.S. currency received $ .00	**35** Amount in $100 bills or larger $ .00

36a Amount of cash received in other than U.S. currency (see instructions) . . . . $ .00

b Specific description of cash received in other than U.S. currency _____

37 If part of an installment sale, give information below and check box . . . . ▶ ☐

a Number of payments _____   **b** Amount of each payment $ _____ .00

c Frequency: ☐ monthly ☐ other (describe)

38 Date of transaction _____

d Balloon payment (amount) $ _____ .00

Part IV   Business Reporting This Transaction

39 Name of reporting business	**40** Employer identification number

41 Street address (number and street) where transaction occurred	Social security number

42 City	**43** State	**44** ZIP code	**45** Nature of your business

46 Under penalties of perjury, I declare that to the best of my knowledge the information I have furnished above is true, correct, and complete.

Sign Here

_____ (Authorized signature–See instructions) (Type or print signer's name below)   _____ (Title)   _____ (Date signed)   ( ) _____ (Telephone number of business)

Cat. No. 62133S   Form **8300** (Rev. 2-92)

Multiple Parties
(Complete applicable parts below if box 2 or 15 on page 1 is checked)

Part I   Continued—Complete if box 2 on page 1 is checked

3 Last name	4 First name	5 Middle initial	6 Social security number

7 Address (number, street, and apt. or suite no.)	8 Occupation, profession, or business

9 City	10 State	11 ZIP code	12 Country (if not U.S.)	13 Date of birth (see instructions)

14 Method used to verify identity: **a** Describe identification ▶ ....
   b Issued by   **c** Number

3 Last name	4 First name	5 Middle initial	6 Social security number

7 Address (number, street, and apt. or suite no.)	8 Occupation, profession, or business

9 City	10 State	11 ZIP code	12 Country (if not U.S.)	13 Date of birth (see instructions)

14 Method used to verify identity: **a** Describe identification ▶ ....
   b Issued by   **c** Number

Part II   Continued—Complete if box 15 on page 1 is checked

16 This person is an:☐ individual or ☐ organization **17** If funded by another party, see instructions and check here · ▶ ☐

18 Individual's last name or Organization's name	19 First name	20 Middle initial	21 Social security number

22 Doing business as (DBA) name (see instructions)	
	Employer identification number

23 Alien identification: **a** Describe identification ▶ ....
   b Issued by   **c** Number

24 Address (number, street, and apt. or suite no.)	25 Occupation, profession, or business

26 City	27 State	28 ZIP code	29 Country (if not U.S.)	30 Date of birth (see instructions)

16 This person is an:☐ individual or ☐ organization **17** If funded by another party, see instructions and check here · ▶ ☐

18 Individual's last name or Organization's name	19 First name	20 Middle initial	21 Social security number

22 Doing business as (DBA) name (see instructions)	
	Employer identification number

23 Alien identification: **a** Describe identification ▶ ....
   b Issued by   **c** Number

24 Address (number, street, and apt. or suite no.)	25 Occupation, profession, or business

26 City	27 State	28 ZIP code	29 Country (if not U.S.)	30 Date of birth (see instructions)

Paperwork Reduction Act Notice.—The requested information is useful in criminal, tax, and regulatory investigations, for instance by directing the Federal Government's attention to unusual or questionable transactions. Trades or businesses are required to provide the information under 26 U.S.C. 6050I.

The time needed to complete this form will vary depending on individual circumstances. The estimated average time is 27 minutes. If you have comments concerning the accuracy of this time estimate or suggestions for making this form more simple, you can write to both the **Internal Revenue Service,** Washington, DC 20224, Attention: IRS Reports Clearance Officer T:FP, and the **Office of Management and Budget,** Paperwork Reduction Project (1545-0892), Washington, DC 20503. DO NOT send this form to either of these offices. Instead, see **When and Where To File** below.

Changes You Should Note

Section 6050I of the Internal Revenue Code was revised by the Revenue Act of 1990 to provide that, to the extent provided by the regulations, the term "cash" includes any monetary instrument, whether or not in bearer form, with a face amount of not more than $10,000 (other than certain checks). The regulatory change in the definition of cash is effective for cash amounts received on or after 02/03/92. See the **Definitions** section of these instructions and Regulations section 1.6050I-1 for more details.

General Instructions

Who Must File.—Each person engaged in a trade or business who, during that trade or business, receives more than $10,000 in cash in one transaction or two or more related transactions, must file Form 8300. Any transactions conducted between a payer (or its agent) and the recipient in a 24-hour period are related transactions. Transactions are considered related even if they occur over a period of more than 24 hours if the recipient knows, or has reason to know, that each transaction is one of a series of connected transactions. This form may be filed voluntarily for any suspicious transaction (see **Definitions**), even if it does not exceed $10,000.

Multiple Payments.—How and when you must report receipt of cash deposits, cash installment payments, or other similar payments or prepayments depend on the dollar amounts of the initial and subsequent payments.

If the initial payment exceeds $10,000, it must be reported within 15 days. If the initial payment does not exceed $10,000, the recipient must add the initial payment and subsequent payments made within 1 year. When the total exceeds $10,000, you must file Form 8300 within 15 days. If subsequent payments, alone or combined, received within any 1-year period exceed $10,000, they must be reported separately within 15 days of the date they exceed $10,000 if they have not been previously reported. (If more than one report is required to be filed within a 15-day period, a single, combined report may be filed

instead. The combined report must be filed no later than the due date for filing the first report.) If subsequent payments, alone or combined, received within 1 year do not exceed $10,000, they need not be reported.

Exceptions.—Regulations section 1.6050I-1 provides for exceptions to the reporting requirements, including:

(1) Financial institutions required to file **Form 4789,** Currency Transaction Report, are exempt from filing Form 8300 for the same transaction.

(2) Casinos required to file (or exempt from filing) **Form 8362,** Currency Transaction Report by Casinos, are exempt from filing Form 8300 for the same transaction. However, nongaming businesses (such as shops, restaurants, and hotels) at the casinos must report on Form 8300 receipt of cash in excess of $10,000.

(3) Cash received by a person other than in the person's trade or business is not reportable.

(4) Cash transactions that occur entirely outside the United States are generally exempt from the reporting requirements. The United States includes the 50 states and the District of Columbia. However, if any part of the transaction occurs in Puerto Rico, or a possession or territory of the United States, and the recipient is subject to the general jurisdiction of the IRS under the Internal Revenue Code, the transaction must be reported by the recipient.

(5) An agent who: (a) receives cash from a principal, (b) uses all of the cash within 15 days in a cash transaction that is reportable on Form 8300 or 4789, and (c) discloses all the information necessary to complete Part II of Form 8300 to the recipient of the cash in the second transaction, does not have to file Form 8300 for the initial receipt of the cash.

When and Where To File.—File this form by the 15th day after the date of the transaction with the **Internal Revenue Service,** Detroit Computing Center, P.O. Box 32621, Detroit, MI 48232, or hand carry it to your local IRS office. Keep a copy of each Form 8300 for 5 years from the date you file it.

Penalties.—Civil and criminal penalties, including up to 5 years imprisonment, are provided for failure (or causing the failure) to file a report, for filing (or causing the filing) of a false or fraudulent report, and for structuring a transaction.

Statement To Be Provided.—You must provide a written statement to each person named in Form 8300 on or before January 31 of the year following the calendar year in which the cash is received. The statement must show the name and address of the business, the total amount of reportable cash received, and that the information was furnished to the IRS. Keep a copy for your records.

Definitions

Person.—The term person means an individual, corporation, partnership, trust or estate, joint stock company, association, syndicate, joint venture, or other unincorporated organization or group,

and all entities treated as legal personalities, including organizations that are exempt from tax.

Recipient.—The term recipient generally means the person receiving the cash. Each store, division, branch, department, headquarters, or office ("branch") (regardless of the physical location) comprising a portion of a person's trade or business shall be a separate recipient. However, a branch will not be considered a separate recipient if the branch (or a central unit linking such branch with other branches) would in the ordinary course of business have reason to know the identity of payers making cash payments to other branches of such person's trade or business.

Transaction.—The term transaction includes (but is not limited to) the purchase of goods, services, personal or real property, and intangible property by a customer; a debt obligation paid for with cash; the receipt and conversion of cash to a negotiable instrument (e.g., a receipt of cash from a person in exchange for a check); and the receipt of cash to be held in escrow or trust.

Cash—Amounts received before 02/03/92.—The term cash means the coin and currency of the United States or of any other country, which circulate in and are customarily used and accepted as money in the country in which issued.

Cash—Amounts received on or after 02/03/92.—The term cash means, in addition to the above definition, a cashier's check, bank draft, traveler's check, or money order having a face amount of not more than $10,000 received in a Designated Reporting Transaction as defined below, or received in any transaction in which the recipient knows that such instrument is being used in an attempt to avoid the reporting of the transaction under section 6050I.

Designated Reporting Transaction.—A designated reporting transaction is a retail sale (or the receipt of funds by a broker or other intermediary in connection with a retail sale) of:

● *A consumer durable,* which is an item of tangible personal property of a type suitable under ordinary usage for personal consumption or use that can reasonably be expected to be useful for at least 1 year under ordinary usage, and that has a sales price of more than $10,000.

● *A collectible,* which is any work of art, rug, antique, metal, gem, stamp, or coin as described in section 408(m)(2)(A) through (D) without regard to section 408(m)(3).

● *A travel or entertainment activity,* which is an item of travel or entertainment that pertains to a single trip or event if the combined sales price of the item and all other items relating to the same trip or event that are sold in the same transaction (or related transactions) exceeds $10,000.

Retail Sale.—The term retail sale means any sale (whether or not the sale is for resale or for any other purpose) made in the course of a trade or business if that trade or business principally consists of making sales to ultimate consumers.

Exceptions.—Unless the recipient knows that it is being used in an attempt to avoid the reporting of the transaction, a cashier's check, bank draft, traveler's check, or money order received in a designated reporting transaction is not treated as cash if—

● The instrument constitutes the proceeds of a loan from a bank (as defined in 31 CFR 103). The recipient may rely on a copy of the loan document, a written statement from the bank, or similar documentation (such as a written lien instruction from the issuer of the instrument) to substantiate that the instrument constitutes loan proceeds.

● The instrument is received in payment on a promissory note or an installment sales contract (including a lease that is considered a sale for Federal income tax purposes). However, the exception only applies if the notes or contracts with the same or substantially similar terms are used in the ordinary course of your trade or business in connection with sales to the ultimate consumers and the total amount of payments on the note or contract that are received on or before the 60th day after the date of the sale does not exceed 50% of the purchase price.

● The instrument is received under payment plans requiring one or more down payments and the payment of the balance of the purchase price by the time of the sale (in the case of an item of travel or entertainment, the earliest date that any item of travel or entertainment pertaining to the same trip or event is furnished). However, this only applies if you use plans with the same or substantially similar terms in the ordinary course of your trade or business in connection with sales to ultimate consumers; and the instrument is received more than 60 days before the date of sale (in the case of an item of travel or entertainment, the date the final payment is due).

Suspicious Transaction.—The term suspicious transaction means a transaction in which it appears that a person is attempting to cause Form 8300 not to be filed, or a false or incomplete form to be filed, or where there is an indication of possible illegal activity.

Specific Instructions

Complete all parts. Skip Part II if the individual in Part I is conducting the transaction on his or her behalf only.

Item 1.—If you are reporting a suspicious transaction (see **Definitions**), check box 1b. For a suspicious transaction, you are also encouraged to telephone the local Internal Revenue Service Criminal Investigation Division. If you do not know the number, please call toll-free 1-800-800-2877.

Part I

Item 2.—If two or more individuals conducted the transaction you are reporting, check the box and complete Part I on any one of the individuals. Provide the same information on the other individual(s) on the back of the form. If more than three individuals are involved, provide the same information on additional sheets of paper and attach them to this form.

Item 6.—Enter the social security number of the individual named. If the individual has no number, enter "None."

Item 8.—Use fully descriptive terms such as plumber or attorney, and not nondescriptive terms such as merchant, businessman, or self-employed.

Item 13.—Enter six numerals for the date of birth of the individual named. For example, if the individual's birth date was July 6, 1960, enter 07 06 60.

Item 14.—You must verify the name and address of the individual identified. Verification must be made by examination of a document normally acceptable as a means of identification when cashing checks (for example, a driver's license, passport, or other official document). In item 14a, enter the type of document used to verify the identification. In item 14b, identify the issuer of that document. In item 14c, enter the document's number. For example, if the individual has a Utah driver's license, enter "driver's license" in item 14a, "Utah" in item 14b, and its number in item 14c.

Part II

Item 15.—If the transaction is being conducted on behalf of more than one person (for example, if the individual in Part I is buying a vehicle on behalf of two persons), check the box and complete Part II on any one of the persons. Provide the same information requested in Part II on the other person(s) on the back of the form. If more than three persons are involved, provide the same information on additional sheets of paper and attach them to this form.

Item 16.—If the person named is an individual, check the "individual" box. For any person other than an individual, check the "organization" box. Check both boxes if the transaction is on behalf of both an individual and an organization.

Item 17.—Check the box if any of the cash received is from a party or parties not identified in Part I or II. Provide the same information on that party or parties on additional sheets of paper and attach them to this form.

Items 18 through 21.—If the person on whose behalf the transaction was conducted is an individual, complete items 18, 19, and 20. Enter his or her social security number (SSN) in item 21 (enter "None" if the person does not have one). If the individual is a sole proprietor and has an employer identification number (EIN), enter both the SSN and EIN in item 21. If the person is an organization, put its name in item 18 and its EIN in item 21. If it does not have an EIN, enter "None" in item 21.

Item 22.—If a sole proprietor or other organization named in items 18–20 is doing business as (DBA) under a name other than that entered in items 18–20, enter the DBA name here.

Item 23.—If the person is an alien without an SSN, complete this item. Enter a general description of the type of official document issued to that person in item 23a (e.g., "passport"), the country that

issued the document in item 23b, and the document's number in item 23c.

Item 30.—See item 13 instructions.

Part III

Item 31.—Check the appropriate box(es) that describe the transaction. If the transaction is not specified in boxes a–h, check box i and briefly describe it (e.g., car lease).

Items 33 through 36b.—Provide the total price of the goods purchased, services provided, amount of cash exchanged, etc. (e.g., the total cost of a vehicle purchased, cost of catering service, exchange of currency) in item 33. Enter the total amount of U.S. currency received reportable on this return (see **Multiple Payments** for reporting requirements) in item 34 and the amount of $100 (and larger) bills in item 35. Show only nearest dollar amounts. Round 50 cents or more to the next whole dollar.

Enter in item 36a the amount of all cashier's check(s), bank draft(s), traveler's check(s), and/or money order(s) each having a face amount of not more than $10,000 and any currency and/or coin of another country received. See the definitions of **Cash**. Provide a specific description of these items in 36b. This should include the name of the issuer, date issued, amount and number of each cashier's check, bank draft, traveler's check, and/or money order plus the country of issuance and amount (in U.S. dollar equivalent) of any currency and/or coin of another country. If more space is required enter the information required by item 36b on additional sheets of paper and attach them to this form.

Item 37.—If the transaction is part of an installment sale, check the box. In item 37a, enter the number of payments agreed upon; in item 37b, enter the amount of each installment payment; in item 37c, check the "monthly" box if the payments are to be made monthly, or the "other" box if the payments are made at any other intervals and describe the intervals (e.g., weekly or semi-annually). If the installments are for different amounts, attach a schedule.

Item 38.—If the combined amount of cash received in two or more installment payments exceeds $10,000, enter the payment date that causes the combined amount to exceed $10,000. Also, see **Multiple Payments.**

Part IV

Item 40.—Enter the EIN of the reporting business. Enter your SSN only if your business has no EIN.

Item 45.—Describe the nature of the business filing the report. Use descriptive terms (auto dealer, jewelry dealer) rather than nondescriptive terms (business, store).

Item 46.—This report must be signed by an authorized individual. Also type or print the name of the signer below the signature and enter the telephone number of the business filing the report.

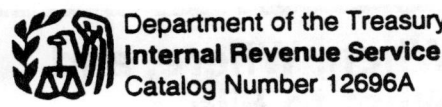

Department of the Treasury
Internal Revenue Service
Catalog Number 12696A

Publication 1544
(Rev. Nov. 91)

Reporting Cash Payments of Over $10,000
(Received in a Trade or Business)

Declaration of Independence

When in the Course of human events it becomes necessary for one people to dissolve the political bands which have connected them with another, and to assume among the powers of the earth, the separate and equal station to which the Laws of Nature and of

Introduction

If, in one year, you receive more than $10,000 in cash from one buyer as a result of a transaction in your trade or business, you must report it to the Internal Revenue Service (IRS) on Form 8300, *Report of Cash Payments Over $10,000 Received in a Trade or Business.*

This publication explains why, when, and where to report these cash payments. It also discusses the substantial penalties for not reporting them.

Some organizations do not have to file Form 8300, including financial institutions who must file Form 4789, *Currency Transaction Report*, and casinos who must file Form 8362, *Currency Transaction Report by Casinos.* They are not discussed in this publication.

This publication explains key issues and terms related to Form 8300. However, you should also read the instructions attached to the form. They explain what to enter on each line.

Why Report These Payments?

Congress passed the Tax Reform Act of 1984 and the Anti-Drug Abuse Act of 1988. These Acts require you to report certain cash payments of over $10,000.

Often smugglers and drug dealers use large cash payments to "launder" money from illegal activities. Laundering means converting "dirty" or illegally-gained money to "clean" money.

The government can often trace this laundered money through the payments you report. Your compliance with the law provides valuable information that can stop those who evade taxes and those who profit from the drug trade and other criminal activities.

To help the government trace laundered money, Congress has expanded the definition of cash. See *What Is Cash?* later in this publication.

Who Must File Form 8300?

Generally, any person in a trade or business who receives more than $10,000 in cash in a single transaction or in related transactions must file Form 8300.

For example, you may be required to file Form 8300 if you are a dealer in jewelry, furniture, boats, aircraft, or automobiles; a pawnbroker; an attorney; a real estate broker; an insurance company; or a travel agency.

However, you do not have to file Form 8300 if the transaction is not related to your trade or business. For example, if you own a jewelry store and sell your personal automobile for more than $10,000 in cash, you would not submit a Form 8300 for that transaction.

Transaction defined. A "transaction" occurs when:

Goods, services, or property are sold

Property is rented

Cash is exchanged for other cash

A contribution is made to a trust or escrow account

A loan is made or repaid

Cash is converted to a negotiable instrument, such as a check or a bond

Person defined. A "person" includes an individual, a company, a corporation, a partnership, an association, a trust, or an estate.

What Payments Must Be Reported?

You must file Form 8300 to report cash paid to you if it is:

1) Over $10,000,
2) Received in either:
   a) One lump sum of over $10,000, or
   b) Installment payments that cause the total cash received within one year of the initial payment to total more than $10,000,
3) Received in the course of your trade or business,
4) Received from the same buyer (or agent), and
5) Received in a single transaction or in related transactions (defined later).

What Is Cash?

Cash is:

1) The coins and currency of the United States (and any other country), and
2) Certain cashier's checks, bank drafts, traveler's checks, and money orders you receive on or after *February 3, 1992*, if they have a face amount of *$10,000 or less* and they are received in:
   a) A designated reporting transaction (defined later), or
   b) Any transaction in which you know the payer is trying to avoid the reporting of the transaction on Form 8300.

Cash may include a cashier's check even if it is called a "treasurer's check" or "bank check."

Cash does not include a check drawn on an individual's personal account.

A cashier's check, bank draft, traveler's check, or money order with a face amount of *more than $10,000* is not treated as cash. (These items are not defined as cash and you do not have to file Form 8300 when you receive them because, if they were bought with currency, the bank or other financial institution that issued them must file a report on Form 4789.)

Example 1. You are a coin dealer. Bob Green buys gold coins from you for $13,200 on February 3, 1992. He pays for them with $6,200 in U.S. currency and a cashier's check having a face amount of $7,000. The cashier's check is treated as cash. You have received more than $10,000 cash and must file Form 8300 for this transaction.

Example 2. You are a retail jeweler. Mary North buys an item of jewelry from you for $12,000 on May 20, 1992. She pays for it with a personal check payable to you in the amount of $9,600 and traveler's checks totaling $2,400. Because the personal check is not treated as cash, you have not received more than $10,000 cash in the transaction. You are not required to file Form 8300.

Example 3. You are a boat dealer. Emily Jones buys a boat from you for $16,500 on July 6, 1992. She pays for it with a cashier's check payable to you in the amount of $16,500. The cashier's check is not treated as cash because its face amount is more than $10,000. You are not required to file Form 8300 for this transaction.

Designated Reporting Transaction

A designated reporting transaction is the retail sale of any of the following:

1) A consumer durable, such as an automobile or boat. A consumer durable is property, other than land or buildings, that:
   a) Is suitable for personal use,

b) Can reasonably be expected to last at least one year under ordinary use,

c) Has a sales price of more than $10,000, and

d) Can be seen or touched.

For example, a $20,000 car is a consumer durable, but a $20,000 dump truck or factory machine is not. The car is a consumer durable even if you sell it to a buyer who will use it in a business.

2) A collectible (a work of art, rug, antique, metal, gem, stamp, or coin).

3) Travel or entertainment, if the total sales price of all items sold for the same trip or entertainment event in one transaction (or related transactions) is more than $10,000.

To figure the total sales price of all items sold for a trip or entertainment event, you include the sales price of items such as airfare, hotel rooms, and admission tickets.

Example. You are a travel agent. On December 1, 1992, Ed Johnson asks you to charter a passenger airplane to take a group to a sports event in another city. He also asks you to book hotel rooms and admission tickets for the group. In payment, he gives you two money orders, each for $6,000. You have received more than $10,000 cash in this designated reporting transaction. You must file Form 8300.

Retail sale. The term "retail sale" means any sale made in the course of a trade or business that consists mainly of making sales to ultimate consumers.

Thus, if your business consists mainly of making sales to ultimate consumers, all sales you make in the course of that business are retail sales, including any sales of items that will be resold.

Broker or intermediary. A designated reporting transaction includes the retail sale of items (1), (2), or (3) listed above, even if the funds are received by a broker or other intermediary, rather than directly by the seller.

Exceptions to definition of cash. A cashier's check, bank draft, traveler's check, or money order you received in a designated reporting transaction is not treated as cash if one of the following exceptions applies.

Exception for certain bank loans. A cashier's check, bank draft, traveler's check, or money order is not treated as cash if it is the proceeds from a bank loan. As proof that it is from a bank loan, you may rely on a copy of the loan document, a written statement or lien instruction from the bank, or similar proof.

Example. You are a car dealer. Mandy White buys a new car from you for $11,500 on September 15, 1992. She pays you with $2,000 of U.S. currency and a cashier's check for $9,500 payable to you and her. You can tell that the cashier's check is the proceeds of a bank loan because it includes instructions to you to have a lien put on the car as security for the loan. For this reason, the cashier's check is not treated as cash. You do not have to file Form 8300 for the transaction.

Exception for certain installment sales. A cashier's check, bank draft, traveler's check, or money order is not treated as cash if it is received in payment on a promissory note or an installment sales contract (including a lease that is considered a sale for federal tax purposes). However, this exception applies only if:

1) You use similar notes or contracts in other sales to ultimate consumers in the ordinary course of your trade or business, and

2) The total payments for the sale that you receive on or before the 60th day after the sale are 50 percent or less of the purchase price.

Exception for certain down payment plans. A cashier's check, bank draft, traveler's check, or money order is not treated as cash if you received it in payment for a consumer durable or collectible, and all three of the following statements are true.

1) You receive it under a payment plan requiring:
   a) One or more down payments, and
   b) Payment of the rest of the purchase price by the date of sale.

2) You receive it more than 60 days before the date of sale.

3) You use payment plans with the same or substantially similar terms when selling to ultimate consumers in the ordinary course of your trade or business.

A cashier's check, bank draft, traveler's check, or money order received for travel or entertainment is not treated as cash under this exception if all three of the following statements are true.

1) You receive it under a payment plan requiring:
   a) One or more down payments, and
   b) Payment of the rest of the purchase price by the earliest date that any travel or entertainment item (such as airfare) is furnished for the trip or entertainment event.

2) You receive it more than 60 days before the date on which the final payment is due.

3) You use payment plans with the same or substantially similar terms when selling to ultimate consumers in the ordinary course of your trade or business.

What Is A Related Transaction?

Any transactions between a buyer (or an agent of the buyer) and a seller that occur within a 24-hour period are related transactions. If you receive over $10,000 in cash during two or more transactions with one buyer in a 24-hour period, you must treat the transactions as one transaction and report the payments on Form 8300.

For example, if you sell two products for $6,000 each to the same customer in one day and the customer pays you in cash, these are related transactions. Because they total $12,000 (more than $10,000), you must file Form 8300.

More than 24 hours between transactions. Transactions are related even if they are more than 24 hours apart if you know, or have reason to know, that each is one of a series of connected transactions.

For example, you are a travel agent. A client pays you $8,000 in cash for a trip. Two days later, the same client pays you $3,000 more in cash to include another person on the trip. These are related transactions, and you must file Form 8300 to report them.

What About Suspicious Transactions?

If you receive $10,000 or less in cash, you may voluntarily file Form 8300 if the transaction appears to be suspicious.

A transaction is suspicious if it appears that a person is trying to cause you not to file Form 8300 or is trying to cause you to file a false or incomplete Form 8300, or if there is a sign of possible illegal activity.

If you are suspicious, you are encouraged to call the local IRS Criminal Investigation Division as soon as possible. Or, you can call toll free 1-800-800-2877.

When, Where, and What to File

The amount you receive and when you receive it determine when you must file. Generally, you must file Form 8300 within 15 days of receiving a payment.

More than one payment. In some transactions, the buyer may arrange to pay you in cash installment payments. If the first payment is more than $10,000, you must file Form 8300 within 15 days. If the first payment is not more than $10,000, you must add the first payment and any later payments made within one year of the first payment. When the total cash payments are more than $10,000, you must file Form 8300 within 15 days.

After you file Form 8300, you must start a new count of cash payments received from that buyer. If you receive more than $10,000 in additional cash payments from that buyer within a one-year period, you must file another Form 8300. You must file the form within 15 days of the payment that causes the additional payments to total more than $10,000.

If you are already required to file Form 8300 and you receive additional payments within the 15 days before you must file, you can report all the payments on one form.

Where to file. You can mail the form to the address given in the Form 8300 instructions, or you can hand carry it to your local IRS office.

Required statement to buyer. You must give a written statement to each person named on any Form 8300 you file. The statement must show the name and address of your business and the total amount of reportable cash you received from the person during the year. It must state that you are also reporting this information to the IRS.

You must send this statement to the buyer by January 31 of the year after the year in which you received the cash that caused you to file the form.

Recordkeeping. You must keep a copy of every Form 8300 you file for 5 years.

Filing late. You may have received cash payments after 1984 (when the law went into effect) that meet Form 8300 filing requirements. If you realize that you did not file Form 8300 when you should have, you should file a form as soon as possible.

Examples

Example 1. Pat Brown is the sales manager for Small Town Cars. On June 1, 1992, Jane Smith purchases a new car from Pat and pays $18,000 in cash. Pat requests identification from Jane to get the necessary information to complete Form 8300. A filled-in form is shown in this publication.

Pat must mail the form to the address shown in the form's instructions by June 16, 1992. He must also send a statement to Jane by February 1, 1993.

Example 2. Using the same facts given in Example 1, suppose Jane had arranged to make cash payments of $6,000 each on June 1, July 1, and August 1. Pat would be required to file a Form 8300 by July 16 because he would have received two cash payments within one year (June and July) that total over $10,000. Pat would not have to report the remaining $6,000 cash payment because it is less than $10,000. However, he could report it if he felt it was a suspicious transaction.

Penalties

There are *civil penalties* for failure to:

- File a correct Form 8300 by the date it is due, or
- Provide the required statement to those named in the Form 8300.

If you intentionally disregard the requirement to file a correct Form 8300 by the date it is due, the penalty is the larger of:

1) $25,000, or
2) The amount of cash you received and were required to report (up to $100,000).

There are *criminal penalties* for:

- Willful failure to file Form 8300,
- Willfully filing a false or fraudulent Form 8300,
- Stopping or trying to stop Form 8300 from being filed, and
- Setting up, helping to set up, or trying to set up a transaction in a way that would make it seem unnecessary to file Form 8300.

If you willfully fail to file Form 8300, you can be fined up to $250,000 ($500,000 for corporations) or sentenced to up to 5 years in prison, or both. These dollar amounts are based on Section 3571 of Title 18 of the U.S. Code.

The penalties for failure to file also apply to any buyer who attempts to interfere with or prevent the seller from filing a correct Form 8300. This includes any attempt by the buyer to set up the transaction in a way that would make it seem unnecessary to file Form 8300.

How to Get Form 8300

If you need copies of Form 8300, call the IRS toll free at 1–800–TAX–FORM (1–800–829–3676).

Form 8300

(Rev. February 1992)

Department of the Treasury
Internal Revenue Service

Report of Cash Payments Over $10,000 Received in a Trade or Business

Failure to file this form or filing a false form may result in imprisonment.

▶ See instructions.
Please type or print.

OMB No. 1545-0892

Expires 09-30-94

1 Check appropriate boxes if: **a** ☐ amends prior report; **b** ☐ suspicious transaction.

Part I Identity of Individual From Whom the Cash Was Received

2 If more than one individual is involved, see instructions and check here . . . . ▶ ☐

3 Last name Smith	**4** First name Jane	**5** Middle initial A.	**6** Social security number 333 00 3333

7 Address (number, street, and apt. or suite no.) 100 Main Avenue	**8** Occupation, profession, or business cosmetics distributor

9 City Hometown	**10** State PA	**11** ZIP code 10101	**12** Country (if not U.S.)	**13** Date of birth (see instructions) 10 06 59

14 Method used to verify identity: **a** Describe identification ▶ driver's license
b Issued by PA   **c** Number 333-00-3333

Part II Person (See Definitions) on Whose Behalf This Transaction Was Conducted

15 If this transaction was conducted on behalf of more than one person, see instructions and check here. . . . . ▶ ☐

16 This person is an: ☐ individual or ☐ organization **17** If funded by another party, see instructions and check here . ▶ ☐

18 Individual's last name or Organization's name	**19** First name	**20** Middle initial	**21** Social security number

22 Doing business as (DBA) name (see instructions)	
	Employer identification number

23 Alien identification: **a** Describe identification ▶
b Issued by   **c** Number

24 Address (number, street, and apt. or suite no.)	**25** Occupation, profession, or business

26 City	**27** State	**28** ZIP code	**29** Country (if not U.S.)	**30** Date of birth (see instructions)

Part III Description of Transaction and Method of Payment

31a ☒ personal property purchased **d** ☐ business services provided **g** ☐ exchange of cash
b ☐ real property purchased **e** ☐ intangible property purchased **h** ☐ escrow or trust funds
c ☐ personal services provided **f** ☐ debt obligations paid **i** ☐ other (specify) ▶

32 Specific description of property or service purchased. Give serial or registration number of car, boat, airplane, etc., address of real estate, etc.
GoFast 4-door sedan   Serial No. XX-ABCDEFG123456789

33 Total price $ 18,000 .00 **34** Amount of U.S. currency received $ 18,000 .00 **35** Amount in $100 bills or larger $ 18,000 .00

36a Amount of cash received in other than U.S. currency (see instructions) . . . . $ .00
b Specific description of cash received in other than U.S. currency

37 If part of an installment sale, give information below and check box . . . . . ▶ ☐   **38** Date of transaction 06 01 92
a Number of payments _____ **b** Amount of each payment $ _____ .00
c Frequency: ☐ monthly ☐ other (describe) _____ **d** Balloon payment (amount) $ _____ .00

Part IV Business Reporting This Transaction

39 Name of reporting business Small Town Cars	**40** Employer identification number 10 1234567
41 Street address (number and street) where transaction occurred 5000 Industrial Avenue	Social security number

42 City Hometown	**43** State PA	**44** ZIP code 10101	**45** Nature of your business car dealership

46 Under penalties of perjury, I declare that to the best of my knowledge the information I have furnished above is true, correct, and complete.

Sign Here _Pat Brown_   sales manager 6/4/92 (111)222-3344

(Authorized signature–See instructions) (Title) (Date signed) (Telephone number of business)

(Type or print signer's name below)
Pat Brown

National Taxpayers Union Foundation

Analyzing How The General Interest May Best Be Represented

Detailed Explanation
of the
Taxpayers' Bill of Rights
as passed in
The Miscellaneous Revenue Act of 1988

1. Disclosure of rights of taxpayers.

When the IRS contacts a taxpayer concerning the determination or collection of any tax, the IRS must provide a written statement of the rights of the taxpayer and the obligations of the IRS during the audit, appeals, refund, and collection processes. The IRS must also work to ensure that taxpayers are not sent multiple statements as a result of a single audit, proposed deficiency, or collection action.

The IRS must prepare the written statement of rights of the taxpayer and obligations of the IRS not later than 180 days after the date of enactment.

2. Taxpayer interview safeguards.

<u>Reasonable time and place</u>. The IRS must publish, within one year, regulations for determining whether the selection of a time and place for interviewing a taxpayer is reasonable. Congress has indicated that it is generally unreasonable for the IRS to require a taxpayer to attend an examination at an IRS office which is not the one located closest to the taxpayer's home. Similarly, it is generally not reasonable for the IRS to audit a taxpayer at his or her place of business if the business is so small that doing so requires the taxpayer to close the business. This does not preclude the IRS from going to the taxpayer's place of business to establish facts that can only be established by a direct visit, such as inventory and asset verifications. In determining the reasonableness of the time and place of an interview, the regulations are to take into account the possibility of physical danger to an IRS agent.

<u>Recordings</u>. A taxpayer is permitted, upon advance notice to the IRS, to make an audio recording of an in-person interview at the taxpayer's own expense. IRS employees also are authorized to record taxpayer interviews, provided the taxpayer receives prior notice of such recording and is supplied a copy or a transcript of the recording upon request and payment of reproduction or printing costs.

<u>IRS explanation of rights</u>. Prior to initial in-person audit interviews, the IRS must explain to taxpayers the audit process and taxpayers' rights under that process. In addition, prior to initial in-person collection interviews, the IRS must explain the collection process and taxpayers' rights under that process. For this purpose, routine telephone conversations initiated by either the taxpayer or the IRS are not considered initial interviews. A written statement

handed to the taxpayer at an audit or collection interview or within a short time before the interview is sufficient. The explanation (whether written or oral) must provide that the taxpayer has the right to suspend the interview to consult with a qualified representative.

Taxpayer representatives. The bill provides that a taxpayer may be represented during a taxpayer interview by any attorney, certified public accountant, enrolled agent, enrolled actuary, or any other person permitted to represent a taxpayer before the IRS, who is not disbarred or suspended from practice before the IRS and who has a properly executed power of attorney from the taxpayer.

If a taxpayer clearly states during an interview with the IRS (other than an interview pursuant to an administrative summons) that he wishes to consult with that representative, the interview must be suspended to afford the taxpayer a reasonable opportunity to consult with the representative. Absent an administrative summons, a taxpayer cannot be required to accompany the representative to an interview. The IRS may continue to request that taxpayers voluntarily attend interviews.

The suspension procedure is to be available to facilitate taxpayers' access to their representatives and not to delay needlessly the interview process. Congress intended that in instances of abuse of this process (such as repeated suspensions of interviews to contact different representatives) the IRS may issue an administrative summons.

The IRS may directly notify a taxpayer that the taxpayer's representative is responsible for unreasonable delay or hindrance, request that the taxpayer appear for an interview, and inform the taxpayer that an administrative summons requiring the taxpayer's attendance at an interview may be issued.

In cases where the IRS notifies a taxpayer that the taxpayer's representative is responsible for unreasonable delay or hindrance, the IRS may continue to utilize current IRS Manual procedures relating to bypassing a taxpayer's representative.

The provisions relating to taxpayer interviews do not apply to criminal investigations or investigations relating to the integrity of any officer or employee of the IRS.

The provisions relating to taxpayer interviews apply to interviews conducted on or after the date that is 90 days after the date of enactment.

3. **Taxpayers may rely on written advice of the Internal Revenue Service.**

The IRS is required to abate any portion of any penalty or addition to tax that is attributable to erroneous written advice furnished by the IRS to a taxpayer, where such advice was specifically requested in writing by the taxpayer and reasonably relied upon, unless the taxpayer failed to provide adequate or accurate information when requesting the advice. It is intended that this provision not be construed to require the IRS to provide written advice to taxpayers.

The IRS must issue regulations within 180 days to implement this provision. The provision is effective for advice requested on or after January 1, 1989.

4. Taxpayer assistance orders.

The Taxpayer Ombudsman (or any designee of the Ombudsman) is provided statutory authority to issue a taxpayer assistance order if the taxpayer is suffering or about to suffer a significant hardship as a result of the manner in which the IRS is administering the tax laws. The Ombudsman may take action whether or not a taxpayer has filed an application requesting relief. An authorized taxpayer's representative may file an application on behalf of a taxpayer with the Ombudsman for a taxpayer assistance order. A taxpayer assistance order may require remedial actions, such as release from levy of property of the taxpayer. A taxpayer assistance order is binding on the IRS unless modified or rescinded by the Ombudsman, a district director, any superior of a district director, a service center director, compliance center director, regional director of appeals, or a superior of such directors.

Any applicable statute of limitations is suspended starting on the date that the taxpayer files an application for a taxpayer assistance order with the Ombudsman and ending on the date that the Ombudsman makes a decision on the taxpayer's application (or a later date if the Ombudsman's order resulting from a taxpayer's application provides for continued suspension of the statute of limitations). The statute of limitations is not suspended in cases where the Ombudsman issues an order in the absence of an application for relief by the taxpayer.

The IRS must issue regulations within 90 days of the date of enactment to implement this provision. This provision is effective on January 1, 1989.

5. Basis for evaluation of IRS employees.

The IRS is prohibited from using records of tax enforcement results to evaluate IRS employees directly involved in collection activities and their immediate supervisors or to impose or suggest production quotas or goals. Each district director must certify quarterly that enforcement results are not being used in a prohibited manner.

This provision is effective for evaluations conducted on or after January 1, 1989.

6. Procedures relating to IRS regulations.

The IRS is required to solicit or allow comments from the Small

Business Administration (SBA) after the publication of proposed regulations or before the promulgation of final regulations. The SBA is allowed four weeks after the receipt of the regulations to provide its comments on the impact of the regulations on small businesses.

In addition, each time the IRS issues temporary regulations, the IRS must simultaneously issue those regulations in proposed form. The IRS may continue its present practice of issuing proposed regulations by cross-reference at the time temporary regulations are issued. Temporary regulations are permitted to remain in effect for no more than three years after the date of their issuance. The expiration of temporary regulations at the end of this three-year period is not to affect the validity of those regulations during the three-year period.

This provision is effective for regulations issued after the 10th day after the date of enactment.

7. The IRS must improve the content of tax due and deficiency notices.

Notices proposing taxes due or deficiency notices must contain both a description of the basis for, and an identification of the amounts of tax due, interest, additions to tax, and penalties. An inadequate description in a notice of deficiency or tax due will not invalidate the notice.

This information should be included in the original notice sent by IRS; later copies of a particular notice sent to the same taxpayer need not contain this information if the IRS determines that including it would be confusing to taxpayers.

Although the provision is limited to the specified notices, the Congress expects the IRS to make every effort to improve the clarity of all notices and explanations that are sent to taxpayers. The Congress believes that all correspondence should be sufficiently clear to enable a taxpayer to understand an IRS question about a tax return as well as any adjustments or penalties applied to a tax return.

The provision applies to mailings made on or after January 1, 1990.

8. Installment payment of tax liability.

The IRS is granted statutory authority to enter into a written installment payment agreement if the IRS determines that an agreement will facilitate collection of the tax owed. The agreement is to remain in effect for the term of the agreement unless (1) the taxpayer provided inaccurate or incomplete information, (2) the taxpayer fails to pay an installment when due, (3) the taxpayer fails to pay any other tax liability when due, (4) the taxpayer fails to respond to any reasonable request by the IRS to supply updated financial information, or (5) the IRS determines that the collection of any tax to which an agreement relates is in jeopardy.

In addition, the IRS may alter, modify or terminate an installment payment agreement if the IRS determines that the financial condition of the taxpayer has significantly changed. This action may be taken only if the IRS notifies the taxpayer of the determination at least 30 days prior to the date of the action and provides the reason for such determination in the notification.

This provision is effective for installment agreements entered into after the date of enactment.

9. Assistant Commissioner for Taxpayer Services.

The provision establishes statutorily an Assistant Commissioner for Taxpayer Services who shall be responsible for taxpayer services as designated by the Commissioner, such as telephone, walk-in, and taxpayer educational services, and the design and production of tax and informational forms. The Assistant Commissioner for Taxpayer Services, jointly with the Taxpayer Ombudsman, must annually report to the Congress concerning the quality of taxpayer services provided by the IRS.

This provision is effective on the 180th day after the date of enactment.

10. Levy safeguards.

Notice. The law increases the waiting period for seizures of property from 10 days to 30 days after notice. As under present law, the notice and waiting period requirements do not apply if the IRS finds that collection of the tax is in jeopardy. The notice preceding levy is required contain a simple and nontechnical description of administrative procedures and appeals applicable to specific aspects of collection, as well as a description of the alternatives available to taxpayers that may prevent levy on taxpayers' property.

Property subject to levy. The type of property exempt from levy is significantly expanded. The $1,500 exemption from levy for fuel, provisions, furniture, and personal household effects is raised to $1,550 in 1989 and $1,650 in 1990 and later years. The $1,000 exemption from levy for books, tools, machinery, or equipment that are necessary for the trade, business, or profession of the taxpayer is raised to $1,050 in 1989 and $1,100 in 1990 and later years. The provision exempts from levy a taxpayer's principal residence unless an IRS district director or assistant director personally approves the levy in writing or the collection of the tax is found to be in jeopardy.

In cases where tangible personal property essential to a taxpayer's trade or business is levied upon by the IRS, an accelerated appeals process must be provided by the IRS in order to determine whether the levy should be released due to any statutory grounds (e.g., the IRS determines that release of such levy will facilitate the collection of tax, the IRS determines that such levy is creating an economic hardship on the taxpayer or the fair market value of the property exceeds such liability and release of the levy on a part of such property could be made without hindering the collection of the tax). For this purpose, property is essential business property only if the business of the taxpayer cannot continue without it.

No levy may be made on property if the estimated expenses of levy and sale exceed the fair market value of the property.

Certain AFDC, SSI, State and local welfare, and JTPA benefits are also now exempt from levy.

The IRS is prohibited from levying on the property of any person on any day which he is required to appear in response to a summons issued by the IRS, unless the IRS determines that the collection of tax is in jeopardy.

Banks and other financial institutions are required to hold accounts garnished by the IRS for 21 days after receiving the IRS notice of levy, in order to provide taxpayers an opportunity to notify the IRS of errors with respect to garnished accounts. Any interest accruing on the accounts during the 21-day period is to be surrendered to the IRS at the end of the 21-day period. The levy on any account may be released before the expiration of the 21-day period with the permission of the IRS.

Levy on wages. The amount of wages exempt from levy for each week is increased to an amount equal to the taxpayer's standard deduction and personal exemptions allowable for the taxable year in which the levy occurs, divided by 52. Under the previous law, the exemption was $75 per week plus $25 for each dependant. For a family of four, that gives an exemption of $254 per week in 1989, compared to $150 per week under the previous law.

Release of levy. The IRS must release a levy on property if (1) the liability for which the levy was made is satisfied, (2) the IRS determines that release will facilitate the collection of the liability, (3) an installment payment agreement has been executed with respect to such liability, (4) the IRS has determined that the levy is creating an economic hardship due to the taxpayer's financial condition, or (5) the fair market value of the property exceeds the liability and partial release would not hinder collection of the tax and related costs owed to the IRS. The release of a levy under this provision is not to prevent a subsequent levy on the same property. The taxpayer may request that the IRS sell levied property.

These provisions are generally effective for levies issued after July 1, 1989.

11. Administrative appeal of liens.

The IRS is required to write regulations within 180 days after enactment that provide taxpayers with an administrative procedure to obtain review of the filing of a notice of lien in the public record and an opportunity to petition for the release of such lien. This administrative procedure is intended to be used to correct erroneous filings and not to challenge the underlying deficiency leading to the imposition of a lien.

If the IRS determines that filing of a notice of lien was erroneous (i.e., the tax liability that gave rise to the lien had been satisfied or the liability had been assessed in violation of the tax law's restrictions on assessment), the IRS is required to issue a certificate of release of lien expeditiously (and, to the extent practicable, within 14 days) after determining that the filing of the notice of lien was erroneous and must include in the certificate a statement that the filing of the lien was erroneous. This ensures that the public record contains a statement that the filing of the notice of the lien was not attributable to the taxpayer's fault, which will help repair of the taxpayer's credit and other financial records. This certificate of release of an erroneous lien must be issued whether or not the lien was challenged in an administrative review procedure.

The provision is effective 60 days after the issuance of the mandated regulations.

12. Taxpayers may recover damages sustained due to failure to release a lien.

Taxpayers are provided with the right to sue the Federal Government in Federal district court if any IRS employee knowingly or negligently fails to release a lien on the taxpayer's property as required under the Tax Code. Taxpayers may recover the costs of the action and damages equal to the actual direct economic damages sustained by the taxpayer which otherwise would not have been sustained, as well as the costs of the action itself. The Treasury Department must issue regulations that prescribe reasonable procedures for a taxpayer to notify the IRS of the failure to release a lien. A taxpayer's claim under this provision is barred unless the action is commenced within two years after the date the right of action accrues. The law deletes the Senate's proposal to grant the IRS authority to settle administratively claims under this provision. However, it is the intent of the Congress that the general settlement authority of the IRS provided under Tax Code section 7122 be utilized, where appropriate, to settle actions brought under this provision.

The conference agreement applies to taxpayer notices provided and damages arising after December 31, 1988.

13. Taxpayers may recover damages sustained due to unauthorized actions by IRS.

Taxpayers are granted the right to sue the Federal Government in Federal district court for damages up to $100,000 if in connection with the collection of any Federal tax, an IRS employee recklessly or intentionally disregards any provision of the federal tax law or regulations. The taxpayer may recover the costs of the action plus actual direct economic damages sustained by the taxpayer as a proximate result of the unlawful actions or inaction of the IRS employee.

The amount of damages awarded under the provision will be reduced by the amount of such damages which could have reasonably been mitigated by the taxpayer.

The IRS may settle administratively claims under this provision. A judgment for damages under this provision may not be awarded by a court unless the taxpayer has exhausted administrative remedies. A taxpayer's claim under this provision is barred unless the action is commenced within two years after the discovery by the taxpayer of the improper IRS action. If the district court determines that the taxpayer's lawsuit is frivolous or groundless, the court may impose a penalty on the taxpayer of up to $10,000.

The provision applies to actions of IRS employees that occur after the date of enactment.

14. Assessable penalty for improper disclosure or use of information by preparers of returns.

The law provides that if a tax return preparer discloses any information furnished to him or her in connection with the preparation of an income tax return, or uses such information for any purpose other than to prepare the return, then the preparer shall be subject to a civil penalty of $250 for each such disclosure or use, up to a maximum of $10,000 per calendar year. The penalty shall not be imposed if disclosure or use of return information was made pursuant to a court order or one of the present-law provisions of the Internal Revenue Code that permit disclosure under specified circumstances. In addition, the present-law criminal penalty imposed upon return preparers who improperly disclose or use information furnished to them in connection with the preparation of an income tax return is changed so that the criminal penalty applies only where the return preparer knowingly or recklessly disclosed or used such information.

The provision applies to disclosures or uses after December 31, 1988.

15. Review of jeopardy levy and assessment procedures.

Assessment of a tax is the final act by the IRS that establishes the liability of a taxpayer for a tax. After assessment, the IRS will attempt to collect the tax. The Code authorizes the IRS to make a jeopardy assessment (i.e., to immediately assess and demand payment of a tax and any penalties and interest) where collection would be endangered if regular procedures are followed. Furthermore, if the IRS determines that collection of tax would be jeopardized by waiting the regular 30-day period after notice and demand for payment have been provided to the taxpayer, the IRS can collect the tax by jeopardy levy (i.e., immediately sieze certain of the taxpayer's property). The Code provides special rules relating to administrative review and judicial review (by Federal district courts) of jeopardy assessments.

The existing rules relating to the review of jeopardy assessments are extended to the review of jeopardy levies. The Tax Court is provided jurisdiction concurrent with Federal district courts with respect to challenges to a jeopardy assessment or jeopardy levy if the taxpayer has filed a petition with the Tax Court prior to the making of the assessment or levy with respect to any deficiency covered by the jeopardy assessment or jeopardy levy notice. In all other cases, the appropriate district court continues to have exclusive jurisdiction over such an action.

The provision applies to jeopardy levies issued and jeopardy assessments made after July 1, 1989.

16. Awarding of costs and certain fees in administrative and civil actions.

Under the previous law, a taxpayer who is a "prevailing party" in a tax case in any Federal court may be awarded reasonable litigation costs if the position of the United States was not substantially justified. Costs incurred during the IRS administrative process generally were not recoverable.

To be awarded reasonable litigation costs, the taxpayer must establish that the position of the United States in the case was not substantially justified. In addition, the person must substantially prevail with respect to the amount in controversy or the most significant issue(s) in the case.

In determining whether the position of the United States was substantially justified, the position of the United States is determined beginning with the position in the civil proceeding, or, if applicable, the position taken by the IRS district counsel administratively. This generally does not include positions taken in the audit or appeals processes.

The new law says the position of the United States is determined as of the earlier of (1) the date of the receipt by the taxpayer of the notice of the decision of the IRS Office of Appeals, or (2) the date of the notice of deficiency. If neither is applicable, the position of the United States is that taken in the litigation.

The new law also allows recovery of reasonable administrative costs after the position of the United States is determined.

The new law gives the IRS the authority to settle claims for administrative costs and litigation costs. A decision by the IRS granting or denying an award of costs is appealable to the Tax Court under the small case procedures.

The provision applies to actions commenced after the date of enactment.

17. Expanded Jurisdiction of the Tax Court.

Under the previous law, a taxpayer was often forced to fight the IRS in both the Tax Court and federal District Court on similar issues. For example, if a taxpayer was fighting a tax case in the Tax Court and was faced with a premature IRS assessment of tax, the taxpayer was forced to challenge that assessment in a District Court, not the Tax Court.

The bill expands the jurisdiction of the Tax Court, without restricting the jurisdiction of other federal courts, in certain types of cases.

Tax court jurisdiction is now expanded to include:

* Restraining the assessment and collection of any tax by the IRS if the tax is the subject of a timely filed petition pending before the Tax Court.

* Ordering the refund of the overpayment plus interest if the IRS fails to refund to a taxpayer an over- payment determined by the Tax Court.

* Reviewing the IRS's determination to sell seized property under one of the law's exceptions to the stay of a sale (such as the property is liable to perish or become greatly reduced in value by keeping or cannot be stored without great expense).

* Redetermining the interest due by the taxpayer on a deficiency determined by the Tax Court.

DK15:11

NOTES

FREE CATALOG OFFER!

For a free catalog of publications available from LPP, Ltd., please write to: LPP, Ltd., 1280 Terminal Way, Suite 15, Department P5, Reno, Nev. 89502; phone: 800/528-0559 or 702/885-2509. Or simply mail the coupon on the bottom of this page to the above address.

Publications authored by Mark Nestmann include:

How to Achieve Personal and Financial Privacy in a Public Age (5th ed.)

Counter-Surveillance: Who's Watching You, and What to Do About It (2nd ed.)

How to Open a Foreign Bank Account Close to Home (3rd ed.)

Corporate Security: How to Stop Thieves, Saboteurs, and Spies from Bankrupting Your Business (with Paul Nelson)

How to Write Your Own Will and Avoid Probate

The Credit Con Game

104 Ways to Protect Your Privacy

Nestmann is also editor of *Low Profile* newsletter, "your monthly guide to privacy and asset protection."

Publications available from LPP, Ltd. by other authors include:

Tax Havens of the World (4th ed., by Thomas Azzara)

Freedom, Asset Protection, and You (by Bill Comer)

The Nevada Corporation Handbook (from Corporate Service Center, Inc.)

LPP, Ltd.   1280 Terminal Way, Suite 15   Department P5   Reno, Nev. 89502

YES!!! Please rush me your **FREE** catalog of privacy and asset protection publications. I understand this information is provided for informational purposes only and that I am under absolutely no obligation to purchase anything.

NAME _____

ADDRESS _____

CITY/STATE/ZIP _____